Main Problems in
American
History

Advisory Editor
in
History

R. Jackson Wilson
Smith College

VOLUME TWO

Main Problems in American History

Edited by

Howard H. Quint
Late of the University of Massachusetts, Amherst
Milton Cantor
University of Massachusetts, Amherst
Dean Albertson
University of Massachusetts, Amherst

1987 FIFTH EDITION

The Dorsey Press
Chicago, Illinois 60604

© THE DORSEY PRESS, 1964, 1968, 1972, 1978, and 1988

Acquisitions editor: David Follmer
Project editor: Jane Lightell
Production manager: Stephen K. Emry
Designer: Paula Lang
Compositor: Arcata Graphics/Kingsport
Typeface: 10/12 Times Roman
Printer: Arcata Graphics/Kingsport

ISBN 0-256-06022-3

Library of Congress Catalog Card No. 87–71668

Printed in the United States of America

1 2 3 4 5 6 7 8 9 0 K 5 4 3 2 1 0 9 8

To the memory of our friend and colleague
Howard H. Quint

Preface

We have designed this two-volume work, the collaborative effort of thirty-seven scholars, primarily for college survey courses in American history. It does not replace textbooks customarily used to impart basic information to the student. Nor does it serve as a substitute for the reading of historical literature. Its function is to acquaint students with historical problems that are directly related to the general context of a survey course—yet highly significant in themselves.

These problems, we believe, are particularly well adapted for use in small discussion sections of large lecture courses, inasmuch as they offer both a focus and a direction to such class meetings. As instructors and students know, such sessions are frequently a chore for the former and a bore to the latter. The reasons are not hard to discover: either the law of diminishing returns is defied by a review of the week's work, or a brave but futile effort is made to discuss documentary readings—assigned with little or no relationship to an understood frame of reference. In recent years, efforts have been made for students to read articles giving conflicting interpretations of historical events in the hope that they will see the exciting clashes of issues that make history the fascinating discipline that it is. But often such articles, appearing in scholarly journals and written for specialists, have a strong historiographical emphasis. They may confuse—more than enlighten—freshmen and sophomores.

We have attempted to write each in his own way, an interpretive essay that will serve as a point of departure for a challenging class discussion. We do not claim the final word on any subject; we have sought only to open up problems for further probing. Many instructors and students will take issue with our analyses or interpretations; their independent reactions should generate the intellectual interplay that must be at the heart of any satisfactory class discussion. We have made no effort to shape the essays to any particular pattern, to prevent the various writers from stepping on each other's scholarly toes, or at times from traversing the same historical ground, although we have sought to avoid repetition of the same factual details as much as possible.

Appended to each essay is a small number of documents that have a direct relationship to points raised in the essays. In this way, documents that alone might be dull and insignificant become alive and meaningful. This method of presentation helps students understand how historians use primary source materials in arriving at conclusions and in writing history. Whenever possible, the contributors have selected documents that have not been overworked in source books; consequently, they are reasonably fresh for students and instructors alike.

In this fifth edition of *Main Problems in American History* we have totally eliminated seven of the problems appearing in the last edition, replaced ten existing ones, markedly revised others, and added new contributions on the women's movement and recent social and political history. Nearly all remaining problems have been revised in response to suggestions by individuals who previously have taught from these volumes.

February 1987

Howard H. Quint
Milton Cantor
Dean Albertson

Contents

chapter

Reconstruction: The Nation's Unfinished Business

Henry F. Bedford
Albuquerque Academy

Reconstruction, Abraham Lincoln remarked, as he received the news of Appomattox, ''is fraught with great difficulty.'' The President soberly emphasized the uncertain future, rather than the Union's triumph, for he did not expect military victory alone to restore sectional peace. He knew that the nation had no agreed terms for reunion to offer the defeated states, and no formula for new racial relationships to replace slavery.

Statesmen of the time discussed these issues in legal and constitutional terms. Were southern states entitled to constitutional rights as if they had never rebelled? Or were they, as Thaddeus Stevens claimed, ''conquered provinces,'' subject to the unlimited power of Congress over federal territories? Was Reconstruction the President's prerogative, for his power to pardon was certainly relevant; or was it, instead, the responsibility of Congress, which must consent before the South would again be represented in the national legislature? Could Congress demand the ratification of a constitutional amendment as a condition for readmission? Could a state that was unqualified to participate in Congress legally ratify any amendment?

The Constitution held no final answers to these questions, as those who posed them knew.

The legalistic debate simply masked a basic disagreement over policy. Defenders of the South claimed the protection of continuous statehood in order to preserve what remained of the old way of life. Advocates of racial justice, by contrast, argued that the seceded states had abandoned the protection of the Constitution when they abandoned the Union.

Lincoln dismissed the prolonged argument about the legality of secession as ''a merely pernicious abstraction.'' He believed Reconstruction could be accomplished ''without deciding or even considering'' whether the Confederacy had been outside the Union. Lincoln stressed agreement, not dispute: ''We all agree that the seceded States, so called, are out of their proper practical relation with the Union; and that the sole object of the government . . . is to again get them into that proper practical relation.''

Some Republicans thought the President's political conception of Reconstruction was too narrow. These critics, imprecisely called Radicals, did not at first agree on the severity of punishment the South must endure or on the measure of equality that Blacks must be conceded. Some Radicals—both in Washington and elsewhere—unquestionably used

1

Reconstruction to serve their own careers and purses. Others meant to safeguard the civil rights of Blacks, their citizenship, and equality before the law. Still others advocated Negro suffrage, often on the condition that prospective voters satisfied a property qualification or passed a literacy test. And a few—very few—Radicals hoped that Reconstruction might ultimately result in real racial equality.

Thaddeus Stevens, the Pennsylvania congressman who was the sternest Radical of all, proposed to confiscate all southern land except individual holdings of less than 200 acres. He suggested that some of this land be granted to Negroes to assure their economic independence. The rest, Stevens said, should be sold to reduce the national debt, to establish a fund for Union soldiers or their widows and children, and to replace northern property destroyed during the war. For if the South paid no reparation, northern taxpayers would, in effect, subsidize the defeated enemy by bearing the war's indirect costs. That situation, Stevens charged, was absurd.

Tough, unyielding Thaddeus Stevens may have been right. Without economic security, Black freedom was not firmly based; peonage and slavery have much in common. Yet for all Stevens' egalitarian conviction, even his motives were probably mixed. His interest in compensating northern propertyholders for wartime losses surely derived in part from the fact that Confederate forces had destroyed his iron mines. And he admitted forthrightly his concern that emancipation might endanger Republican political supremacy and the program of economic nationalism the party had enacted. The fortuitous secession of the South had permitted passage of protective tariffs (which, like other ironmasters, Stevens believed were essential), the national banking system, the Homestead Act, and federal aid to transcontinental railroads. When Stevens and other Republicans protested that the Republic could not be entrusted to "whitewashed rebels," they had this program, as well as the freedmen, in mind.

They had reason for concern. The Thirteenth Amendment, as Stevens pointed out, abolished the former practice of counting a slave as three-fifths of a person; as a result, the South once readmitted would be entitled to more Congressmen than had represented the section before the war. More Congressmen meant more electoral votes, thus endangering Republican control of the White House, for Democrats could fuse their northern minority with the South to create a national majority. Besides endangering economic legislation already adopted, such a coalition might accept the notion that national bonds should be redeemed in the inflated greenbacks with which they had often been purchased—instead of in gold as the bond promised. Northern businessmen, whose opinions weighed heavily with Republican politicians, preferred fiscal orthodoxy. The North glimpsed the promise of industrial plenty; it seemed no time for economic experimentation.

The South was equally unready for social and political experimentation in the form of Radical Reconstruction, and perhaps Abraham Lincoln agreed. A deadlock between Congress and the President seemed possible when Lincoln pocket vetoed the Wade-Davis bill, the first Radical attempt to punish and reshape the South. Once a staunch Whig, Lincoln may have hoped to gain support for gradual change from the same coalition of moderates in both sections that had sustained his old party. Some Radicals so mistrusted the President that they welcomed Johnson's succession. For Andrew Johnson seemed to have nothing in common with those substantial Southerners whom Lincoln hoped might become the pillars of a southern Republican Party. But to the surprised dismay of the Radicals, the self-made man from Tennessee, who had never acted like a Southerner during the war, appeared ready to join the Confederacy after Appomattox.

For in 1865, Johnson used his power to pardon almost without limit. While Radicals fumed because Congress was in impotent recess, Johnson encouraged amnestied Southerners to establish new constitutions, hold elections, and complete Reconstruction before Congress resumed in December. He insisted that the South ratify the Thirteenth Amendment, repudiate the Confederate debt, and repeal ordinances of secession. White Southerners hastened to adopt Johnson's terms, which were surely among the most generous ever imposed on a defeated foe. Although the President withheld political rights from a few prominent former Confederates, voters all over the South chose many of the men who had led them out of the Union to lead them back in. Mississippi and South Carolina elected Confederate generals as governors; Georgia chose the Confederacy's vice president, Alexander Stephens, for the Senate of the United States. Southern whites demonstrably did not understand that defeat had changed the rules and that, for the moment, their elections had to satisfy a northern constituency as well as record the verdict of local voters.

Returns in 1865 heightened northern suspicion that a costly victory was given away cheaply. Negroes and others who had added equality to such war aims as abolition and union, denounced Johnson's program. For example, a group of black Virginians pointed out that Johnson's plan permitted former Confederates, who were organizing and dominating the state government, to suppress both black and white supporters of the Union. The President had left them, these freedmen complained, ''entirely at the mercy of . . . unconverted rebels,'' and they appealed for ''an *equal chance* with the white *traitors*'' whom the President had pardoned. Without the protection of the ballot and federal arms to enforce equal rights, the blacks expected that their former masters would make freedom ''more intolerable'' than slavery.

Those whom Johnson pardoned did indeed try to preserve as much of the prewar social order as possible. Most white Southerners believed slavery was essential to the region's civilization; they still believed that legal freedom

could never make their former slaves the equal of any white man. So the black codes that southern legislatures adopted to replace slave codes fell well short of racial equality.

The black codes allowed freedmen to form families. They permitted one black to marry another and made black parents legally responsible for their children. Most statutes also defined the legal rights of freedmen, and they often made blacks the legal equals of whites in the courtroom, although in some states blacks could not testify against whites.

Equality ceased with these provisions. Apprenticeship regulations bounded the economic and social freedom of young blacks; courts ordered the apprenticeship of unemployed young freedmen and gave preference to their former masters, an arrangement that often differed little from slavery. Vagrancy regulations and laws forbidding disorderly conduct gave enforcement officers wide discretion and similarly restricted the social and economic life of black adults. Any Mississippi Negro who could not pay the poll tax or who lacked regular employment was guilty of vagrancy. Those convicted could be leased to employers who would pay fines and costs; former masters again had preference, and again the result might be only technically distinguishable from bondage. Even if a freedman avoided these statutes, other laws kept him out of the white community. For instance, the only black passengers permitted in first-class railroad cars in Mississippi were maids, who were allowed to wait on their white mistresses.

But the South's version of Reconstruction was incomplete without the approval of Congress, where reaction to the black codes was prompt and hostile. Even Republican moderates were unconvinced that the governments Johnson had approved represented loyal, reformed, and contrite Southerners. Radicals denounced Johnson's work as a sham and urged Congress to undertake genuine Reconstruction. Rebels had proudly reestablished '' 'the white man's Government,' '' Thaddeus Stevens reported, and Congress ought to prove resolutely that such governments were entirely unacceptable components of the federal Republic. Demagogues, including "some high in authority," he continued with a barbed reference to the President, had appealed to the "lowest prejudices of the ignorant" to maintain the dominance of southern whites. Stevens held that the white race had "no exclusive right forever to rule this nation," nor did he shrink from the conclusion: This nation, he said, must not be " 'the white man's Government,' " but rather "the Government of all men alike. . . ."

Stevens was still ahead of his party. Most northern states did not yet permit blacks to vote, and most Republicans were not yet ready to demand equal political rights for the freedmen. But northern Republicans did insist on more change than Johnson had secured. Congress sent the southern legislators home in December 1865 and established congressional terms for reunion in two bills and a proposed constitutional amendment. The President vetoed both bills and joined those who opposed the amendment. His intransigence blighted any hope for a compromise program. For moderate Republicans, forced to choose between Stevens' radicalism and the unreconstructed governments Johnson had endorsed, chose radicalism. Andrew Johnson's political ineptitude and the adamant refusal of white Southerners to concede blacks more than technical emancipation drove the Republican Party to Thaddeus Stevens and military reconstruction.

Moderates began with a bill to prolong the life of the Freedmen's Bureau and to give it a quasi-judicial authority over disputes arising from discrimination or denial of civil rights. The bill deprived state courts of jurisdiction in such cases and specifically contradicted southern black codes by making punishable the discrimination that they permitted. Though the bill's sponsors thought they had secured the President's approval, Johnson vetoed the measure. The bureau, he held, had grown out of the war's emergency and was based on the constitutional grant of power for war, which Congress could not legitimately invoke in peace. Once ordinary institutions, including civil courts, were reestablished, the bureau should disband.

Congress could not immediately override Johnson's veto, and moderates again tried to resolve the impasse with the Civil Rights bill of 1866. This measure specifically made blacks American citizens, thus overturning the *Dred Scott* decision, and guaranteed "the full and equal benefit of all laws . . . for the security of person or property" to all citizens. Federal courts had jurisdiction in cases where citizens were deprived of equal rights. The bill received the support of every House Republican and all but three Republican senators. And Andrew Johnson vetoed it because it infringed on the reserved powers of the states.

Congress overrode that veto, and, for good measure, salvaged the Freedmen's Bureau bill, which also passed over Johnson's veto. To preserve its handiwork, Congress then framed what became the fourteenth amendment. Johnson could not prevent the submission of the amendment to the states, but his hostility encouraged southern states to block ratification temporarily. Tennessee, the President's own state, ratified the amendment and was rewarded by full restoration to the Union. Other Southerners rejected the amendment and waited.

They waited too long, for the price of readmission went up. Andrew Johnson took his cause to the country in the congressional election of 1866. His performance on the stump struck the public as undignified, and his tour was as inept as his performance in the White House. Voters sent to Washington a new Congress with enough Radical votes to overwhelm the President.

Radicals lost no time. Congress took the initiative on Reconstruction and asserted its control over the rest of the government as well.

The presidential authority to command the army was abridged by a requirement that all orders be issued through the Army Chief of Staff, Ulysses S. Grant, who could not be removed or reassigned without the Senate's consent. The Tenure of Office Act required the Senate's approval for removal of any official for whom senatorial confirmation was necessary; Radicals hoped thereby to protect members of Johnson's Cabinet, particularly Secretary of War Edwin Stanton, who opposed the President's program. Control of the Army was crucial to the Radicals because they expected to develop a plan of military reconstruction. Congress took steps to eliminate involuntary congressional recesses and limited the power of the Supreme Court to decide cases that might invalidate congressional programs.

Andrew Johnson was not intimidated. He vetoed the Reconstruction Act and those supplemental measures Congress later added to make the program comprehensive. Since Congress promptly overrode them, his vetoes were futile. By these acts, Congress combined ten states into five military districts and subordinated state governments to military commanders. The governments and constitutions Johnson had approved in 1865 were discarded, and new constitutions granting Negro suffrage and guaranteeing racial equality were required. This legislation unquestionably mocked the traditional rights of states, as both Johnson and the South claimed. Radicals, however, had minimal interest in the constitutional pretenses of the defeated section and counted the doctrine of states' rights an unmourned casualty of the Civil War.

They set out to make the Presidency an unmourned casualty of Reconstruction. Although the resolution of the House impeached Andrew Johnson, the target at which many Radicals aimed was the office itself. The charge against Johnson specified eleven offenses, most of which arose from the President's attempt to remove Stanton from the Cabinet. But, Thaddeus Stevens confessed, he, for one, did not impeach the President for any particular offense, or even for all of them together. Stevens wanted to remove Johnson for his political mistakes, not for his moral or legal lapses. Impeachment, Stevens believed, was simply the only available method of ridding the nation of the President's wretched judgment.

The House debated all of Andrew Johnson's alleged crimes: his partiality toward the South, his public disrespect of Congress and its leadership, his undignified inauguration as Vice President, his baselessly rumored complicity in Lincoln's assassination, and his deliberate violations of the Tenure of Office Act. The President was acquitted partly because the Senate found the bill of particulars too flimsy a basis for so unprecedented a step. He was also acquitted because a few senators chose to support the independence of the executive branch rather than establish a precedent that might lead to a ministry responsible to the legislature, as is a parliamentary cabinet. The margin of the Senate was slim; Johnson survived by one vote. Thirty-five Republicans voted to convict; twelve Democrats and seven Republicans found for the President. With the roll calls in the Senate, Washington ceased to be the main forum for debate over Reconstruction. The President was isolated; Congress had done its part. At last, Reconstruction was to occur in the South.

Americans since the 1870s have harshly judged the process. Black Reconstruction was an undignified, corrupt, expensive, and regrettable social experiment from which enlightened white conservatives freed the South in 1877. The freedmen, their often venal northern allies the carpetbaggers, and a few unprincipled southern white scalawags looted southern treasuries, discredited themselves, and demonstrated the political incapacity of the black population. Return to white control, according to this view, preserved the section from bankruptcy and barbarism.

The belief, like most stereotypes, had a factual basis. Reconstruction did bring unprecedented taxes to the southern states; not all the money was honestly spent. Negroes did not universally resist financial temptation, nor were they always dignified and wise in their legislative deliberations. Illustrative statistics abound. Florida spent more for printing in 1869 than the entire state government had cost in 1860. Sometimes, bookkeeping was so casual that even a state legislature could not calculate the state debt. According to one estimate, the South Carolina debt tripled in three years, while another figure indicated that it had increased nearly six times. South Carolina also maintained at public expense a luxurious restaurant and bar that impartially dispensed imported delicacies to legislators of both races.

But the term Black Reconstruction is misleading, and the usual view of the process that the phrase describes is inaccurate. Only in South Carolina did blacks ever control the legislature—and only in one house at that. They held high office elsewhere in the South—Mississippi sent two blacks to the Senate of the United States—but they were by no means so dominant as the term Black Reconstruction implied. White politicians, to be sure, had to have black support to succeed, but the simplistic picture of black rule is incorrect.

Nor is the image of corrupt extravagance entirely justified. Rebuilding after a war is always expensive, and taxpayers always resent the bill. Further, Reconstruction governments not only had to restore public buildings and services; they also had to furnish new facilities and services that had been inadequate in most of the South. In many southern states, for example, public education for either race dates from these legislatures. Often, for the first time, states also accepted limited responsibility for the welfare of the indigent and the sick.

The notorious corruption of Reconstruction frequently came from ambitious schemes to bring new life to the southern economy and to break the region's dependence on agriculture by introducing railroads and industry. Only the state commanded enough credit to entice the railroads that seemed to be the indispensable foundation of prosperity. Southern states issued bonds to finance railroad construction, but the proceeds sometimes vanished before the track was laid. Fraud in the development of the American rail network, however, was not peculiar to the South; as had happened elsewhere, public funds were converted to private use, and politicians pocketed fees that might more candidly have been called bribes. Nor were corrupted legislatures confined to the South in the post-Civil War era. The peculation of southern legislators was trifling by comparison with the simultaneous scandals of the Grant administration.

And not all corrupt southerners were black. Some blacks were bribed and some misused public funds, though no individual stole so much as the white treasurer of Mississippi embezzled immediately after the state was supposedly saved from irresponsible blacks. And for every purchased politician, there must have been a buyer. The fast-buck promoters of railroads and industry were whites, not blacks, few of whom were enriched by the plunder they were said to have secured from public treasuries.

Few blacks, indeed, were able to find even a legitimate source of wealth. Their lack of property reinforced provisions in the black codes that limited mobility. Any freedman who could not prove steady employment had to have a license authorizing some other arrangement. The contract that proved employment often specified annual wage payments, a practice that forced employees into debt for what was consumed while earning the first year's wage. And if a black left his employer before the contract expired, he forfeited wages earned earlier in the year.

Wages were ordinarily paid with a portion of the crop, for the war-shattered southern economy lacked local capital to renew agricultural production. Forced to rebuild their farms on credit, impoverished landowners hired impoverished farmers to work the land, and both looked to a big harvest to pay bills and interest already charged at the local store. If a profit resulted, it was probably too small to carry either owner or laborer through the subsequent season, and so the cycle continued.

When the laborer was black, as he often was, contract and credit effectively replaced the restrictions of slavery. For without economic independence, blacks lacked the means to sustain constitutional equality. Usually, a threat to turn him off the land or stop his credit at the store was enough to make a sharecropper docile. Often, an unfulfilled contract or an unpaid debt legally required him to remain on a plot of land that had already proved unprofitable. When he resisted economic leverage and legal restraint, the Ku Klux Klan and its imitators perfected direct and brutal means of reminding him of his inferiority. So credit, statute, and terror evolved as new ways to return the freed black as nearly as possible to his old bondage. Constitutional amendments were unenforced in some areas, even before federal troops retired. As blacks were intimidated, whites passed laws to keep their former slaves from the polls and from the company of their former masters. Formal segregation and constitutional disfranchisement were natural sequels in another generation.

Black Reconstruction depended on a benevolent national administration that would keep troops in the South until whites could be won to toleration or blacks could secure their own equality. Bayonets are perhaps an unlikely method of securing equality; in any case, the northern voter and, hence, the national government, tired of the task too soon. The use of military means for democratic ends is only one of the ambiguities that plague those who would understand and evaluate Reconstruction, for the period is replete with dilemmas of ends

and means. White Southerners wanted to preserve what they could of their customary way of life: in the process, some were deceitful; some were cruel; most were unyielding on the central issue of white supremacy. Blacks wanted to become free Americans, and in the attempt, some were foolish and some were corrupt, but most were humbly patient. Radicals wanted to reconstruct the South: most of them expected to assure continued Republican hegemony; some expected to get rich; others intended to secure racial justice.

The tragedy of Reconstruction is that so little was permanently accomplished. White Southerners took refuge in a sentimentalized past. Blacks displayed more patience and more humility and in the end were the principal victims of the tragedy. Radicals died, and their party found laissez faire a more congenial ideology than racial equality.

SUGGESTED READINGS

Benedict, Michael L. *A Compromise of Principle.* New York: W. W. Norton, 1975.

————. *The Impeachment and Trial of Andrew Johnson.* New York: W. W. Norton, 1973.

Berlin, Ira, et al. *Freedom: A Documentary History of Emancipation.* Cambridge: Cambridge University Press, 1985.

Brodie, Fawn M. *Thaddeus Stevens: Scourge of the South.* New York: W. W. Norton, 1959.

Carter, Dan T. *When the War Was Over.* Baton Rouge: Louisiana State University Press, 1985.

Donald, David. *Charles Sumner and the Rights of Man.* New York: Alfred A. Knopf, 1970.

————. *The Politics of Reconstruction, 1863–1867.* Baton Rouge: Louisiana State University Press, 1965.

DuBois, W. E. Burghardt. *Black Reconstruction.* New York: Russell & Russell, 1935.

Fleming, Walter L., ed., *Documentary History of Reconstruction.* Gloucester, Mass.: Peter Smith, 1960.

Franklin, John Hope. *Reconstruction.* Chicago: University of Chicago Press, 1962.

Gutman, Herbert G. *The Black Family in Slavery and Freedom*. New York: Pantheon, 1976.

Hyman, Harold M. *A More Perfect Union*. New York: Alfred A. Knopf, 1973.

Litwack, Leon F. *Been in the Storm So Long*. New York: Alfred A. Knopf, 1979.

McKitrick, Eric. *Andrew Johnson and Reconstruction*. Chicago: University of Chicago Press, 1960.

McPherson, James M. *The Struggle for Equality*. Princeton: Princeton University Press, 1964.

Painter, Nell I. *The Exodusters*. Lawrence, Kansas: University Press of Kansas, 1977.

Richardson, Joe M. *Christian Reconstruction*. Athens: University of Georgia Press, 1986.

Rose, Willie Lee. *Rehearsal for Reconstruction*. Indianapolis: Bobbs-Merrill, 1964.

Stampp, Kenneth M. *The Era of Reconstruction, 1865–1877*. New York: Alfred A. Knopf, 1965.

Williamson, Joel. *After Slavery: The Negro in South Carolina during Reconstruction*. Chapel Hill: University of North Carolina Press, 1965.

Woodward, C. Vann. *Reunion and Reaction*. Boston: Little, Brown, 1951.

DOCUMENT 16.1
The Constitutional Basis for Reconstruction

THE AMENDMENTS

The Thirteenth [proposed 1 Feb. 1865; declared ratified 18 Dec. 1865]:

Section 1. Neither slavery nor involuntary servitude, except as a punishment for crime whereof the party shall have been duly convicted, shall exist within the United States, or any place subject to their jurisdiction.

The Fourteenth (proposed 16 June 1866; declared ratified 28 July 1868]:

Section 1. All persons born or naturalized in the United States, and subject to the jurisdiction thereof, are citizens of the United States and of the State wherein they reside. No State shall make or enforce any law which shall abridge the privileges or immunities of citizens of the United States; nor shall any State deprive any person of life, liberty, or property, without due process of law; nor deny to any person within its jurisdiction the equal protection of the laws.

Section 2. Representatives shall be apportioned among the several States according to their respective numbers, counting the whole number of persons in each State, excluding Indians not taxed. But when the right to vote at any election for the choice of electors for President and Vice President of the United States, Representatives in Congress, the Executive and Judicial officers of a State, or the members of the Legislature thereof, is denied to any of the male inhabitants of such State, being twenty-one years of age, and citizens of the United States, or in any way abridged, except for participation in rebellion, or other crime, the basis of representation therein shall be reduced in the proportion which the number of such male citizens shall bear to the whole number of male citizens twenty-one years of age in such States.

Section 3. No person shall be a Senator or Representative in Congress, or elector of President and Vice President, or hold any office, civil or military, under the United States, or under any State, who, having previously taken an oath, as a member of Congress, or as an officer of the United States, or as a member of any State legislature, or as an executive or judicial officer of any State, to support the Constitution of the United States, shall have engaged in insurrection or rebellion against the same, or given aid and comfort to the enemies thereof. But Congress may by a vote of two-thirds of each House, remove such disability.

Section 4. The validity of the public debt of the United States authorized by law, including debts incurred for payment of pensions and bounties for services in suppressing insurrection or rebellion, shall not be questioned. But neither the United States nor any state shall assume or pay any debt or obligation incurred in aid of insurrection or rebellion against the United States, or any claim for the loss or emancipation of any slave; but all such debts, obligations, and claims shall be held illegal and void.

Section 5. The Congress shall have power to enforce, by appropriate legislation, the provisions of this article.

The Fifteenth [proposed 27 Feb. 1869; declared ratified 30 Mar. 1870]:

Section 1. The right of citizens of the United States to vote shall not be denied or abridged by the United States or by any State on account of race, color, or previous condition of servitude.

Section 2. The Congress shall have power to enforce this article by appropriate legislation.

DOCUMENT 16.2
Black Codes

After Appomattox, the southern states conceded military defeat and acknowledged legal emancipation. But the black codes that were enacted throughout much of the Confederacy in the year following Lee's surrender derived from the statutes and customs of slavery—as the police regulations of a Louisiana parish demonstrate.

Whereas it was formerly made the duty of the police jury to make suitable regulations for the police of slaves within the limits of the parish; and whereas slaves have become emancipated by the action of the ruling powers; and whereas it is necessary for public order, as well as for the comfort and correct deportment of said freedmen, that suitable regulations should be established for their government in their changed condition, the following ordinances are adopted with the approval of the

Source: W. L. Fleming, ed., *Documentary History of Reconstruction* (Cleveland: Arthur H. Clark, 1906), vol. 1, pp. 279–81.

United States military authorities commanding in said parish, viz:

Sec. 1. *Be it ordained by the police jury of the parish of St. Landry,* That no negro shall be allowed to pass within the limits of said parish without special permit in writing from his employer. Whoever shall violate this provision shall pay a fine of two dollars and fifty cents, or in default thereof shall be forced to work four days on the public road, or suffer corporeal punishment as provided hereinafter.

Sec. 2. . . . Every negro who shall be found absent from the residence of his employer after ten o'clock at night, without a written permit from his employer, shall pay a fine of five dollars, or in default thereof, shall be compelled to work five days on the public road, or suffer corporeal punishment as hereinafter provided.

Sec. 3. . . . No negro shall be permitted to rent or keep a house within said parish. Any negro violating this provision shall be immediately ejected and compelled to find an employer; and any person who shall rent, or give the use of any house to any negro, in violation of this section, shall pay a fine of five dollars for each offence.

Sec. 4. . . . Every negro is required to be in the regular service of some white person, or former owner, who shall be held responsible for the conduct of said negro. But said employer or former owner may permit said negro to hire his own time by special permission in writing, which permission shall not extend over seven days at any one time. . . .

Sec. 5. . . . No public meetings or congregations of negroes shall be allowed within said parish after sunset, but such public meetings and congregations may be held between the hours of sunrise and sunset, by the special permission in writing of the captain of patrol, within whose beat such meetings shall take place. This prohibition, however, is not to prevent negroes from attending the usual church services, conducted by white ministers and priests. . . .

Sec. 6. . . . No negro shall be permitted

to preach, exhort, or otherwise declaim to congregations of colored people, without a special permission in writing from the president of the police jury. . . .

Sec. 7. . . . No negro who is not in the military service shall be allowed to carry firearms, or any kind of weapons, within the parish, without the special written permission of his employers, approved and indorsed by the nearest and most convenient chief of patrol. Any one violating the provisions of this section shall forfeit his weapons and pay a fine of five dollars, or in default of the payment of said fine, shall be forced to work five days on the public road, or suffer corporeal punishment as hereinafter provided.

Sec. 8. . . . No negro shall sell, barter, or exchange any articles of merchandise or traffic within said parish without the special written permission of his employer, specifying the article of sale, barter or traffic. . . .

Sec. 9. . . . Any negro found drunk, within the said parish shall pay a fine of five dollars, or in default thereof work five days on the public road, or suffer corporeal punishment as hereinafter provided. . . .

Sec. 14. . . . The corporeal punishment provided for in the foregoing sections shall consist in confining the body of the offender within a barrel placed over his or her shoulders, in the manner practiced in the army, such confinement not to continue longer than twelve hours, and for such time within the aforesaid limit as shall be fixed by the captain or chief of patrol who inflicts the penalty.

DOCUMENT 16.3
The Vision of One Radical

Whatever his motives, and regardless of Presidents and lesser obstacles, Thaddeus Stevens meant to punish the South for its war and to force white society to begin immediate restitution for the ancient wrong of bondage.

THE FREEDMEN MUST VOTE (1867)

Unless the rebel States, before admission, should be made republican in spirit, and placed under the guardianship of loyal men, all our blood and treasure will have been spent in vain. I waive now the question of punishment which, if we are wise, will still be inflicted by moderate confiscations. . . . Impartial suffrage, both in electing the delegates and ratifying their proceedings, is now the fixed rule. There is more reason why colored voters should be admitted in the rebel States than in the Territories. In the States they form the great mass of the loyal men. Possibly with their aid loyal governments may be established in most of those States. Without it all are sure to be ruled by traitors; and loyal men, black and white, will be oppressed, exiled, or murdered. There are several good reasons for the passage of this bill. In the first place, it is just. I am now confining my argument to negro suffrage in the rebel States. Have not loyal blacks quite as good a right to choose rulers and make laws as rebel whites? In the second place, it is a necessity in order to protect the loyal white men in the seceded States. The white Union men are in a great minority in each of those States. With them the blacks would act in a body; and it is believed that in each of said States, except one, the two united would form a majority, control the States, and protect themselves. Now they are the victims of daily murder. . . .

Another good reason is, it would insure the ascendency of the Union party. . . . I believe . . . that on the continued ascendency of that party depends the safety of this great nation. If impartial suffrage is excluded in the rebel States, then every one of them is sure to send a solid rebel representative delegation to Congress, and cast a solid rebel electoral vote. They, with their kindred Copperheads of the

Source: *Congressional Globe,* January 3, 1867, p. 252.

North, would always elect the President and control Congress. While slavery sat upon her defiant throne, and insulted and intimidated the trembling North, the South frequently divided on questions of policy between Whigs and Democrats, and gave victory alternately to the sections. Now, you must divide them between loyalists, without regard to color, and disloyalists, or you will be the perpetual vassals of the free-trade, irritated, revengeful South. . . . I am for negro suffrage in every rebel State. If it be just, it should not be denied; if it be necessary, it should be adopted; if it be a punishment to traitors, they deserve it.

THE SOUTH MUST PAY (1867)

Whereas it is due to justice, as an example to future times, that some proper punishment should be inflicted on the people who constituted the "confederate States of America," both because they, declaring an unjust war against the United States for the purpose of destroying republican liberty and permanently establishing slavery, as well as for the cruel and barbarous manner in which they conducted said war, in violation of all the laws of civilized warfare, and also to compel them to make some compensation for the damages and expenditures caused by said war: Therefore,

Be it enacted . . . That all the public lands belonging to the ten States that formed the government of the so-called "confederate States of America" shall be forfeited by said States and become forthwith vested in the United States.

Sec. 2. . . . The President shall forthwith proceed to cause the seizure of such of the property belonging to the belligerent enemy as is deemed forfeited by the act of July 17, A. D. 1862, and hold and appropriate the same as enemy's property, and to proceed to condemnation with that already seized. . . .

Source: *Congressional Globe,* March 19, 1867, p. 203.

Sec. 4. . . . Out of the lands thus seized and confiscated the slaves who have been liberated by the operations of the war and the amendment to the Constitution or otherwise, who resided in said "confederate States" on the 4th day of March, A. D. 1861, or since, shall have distributed to them as follows, namely: to each male person who is the head of a family, forty acres; to each adult male, whether the head of a family or not, forty acres; to each widow who is the head of a family, forty acres—to be held by them in fee simple, but to be inalienable for the next ten years after they become seized thereof. . . . At the end of ten years the absolute title to said homesteads shall be conveyed to said owners or to the heirs of such as are then dead.

Sec. 5. . . . Out of the balance of the property thus seized and confiscated there shall be raised, in the manner hereinafter provided, a sum equal to fifty dollars, for each homestead, to be applied by the trustees hereinafter mentioned toward the erection of buildings on the said homesteads for the use of said slaves; and the further sum of $500,000,000, which shall be appropriated as follows, to-wit: $200,-000,000 shall be invested in United States six per cent, securities; and the interest thereof shall be semi-annually added to the pensions allowed by law to the pensioners who have become so by reason of the late war; $300,-000,000, or so much thereof as may be needed, shall be appropriated to pay damages done to loyal citizens by the civil or military operations of the government lately called the "confederate States of America."

Sec. 6. . . . In order that just discrimination may be made, the property of no one shall be seized whose whole estate on the 4th day of March, A. D. 1865, was not worth more than $5,000, to be valued by the said commission, unless he shall have voluntarily become an officer or employee in the military or civil service of "the Confederate States of America," or in the civil or military service of some one of said States, and in enforcing all confiscations the sum or value of $5,000 in real or personal property shall be left or assigned to the delinquent. . . .

DOCUMENT 16.4
Terror

The Ku Klux Klan and its imitators intimidated blacks to keep them from demanding the rights allowed by law. The narrative below is that of Elias Hill, a crippled black preacher from South Carolina.

On the night of the 5th of last May, after I had heard a great deal of what they had done in that neighborhood, they came. It was between 12 and 1 o'clock at night when I was awakened and heard the dogs barking, and something walking, very much like horses. As I had often laid awake listening for such persons, for they had been all through the neighborhood, and disturbed all men and many women, I supposed that it was them. They came in a very rapid manner, and I could hardly tell whether it was the sound of horses or men. At last they came to my brother's door, which is in the same yard, and broke open the door and attacked his wife, and I heard her screaming and mourning. I could not understand what they said, for they were talking in an outlandish and unnatural tone, which I had heard they generally used at a negro's house. I heard them knocking around in her house. I was lying in my little cabin in the yard. At last I heard them have her in the yard. She was crying, and the Ku-Klux were whipping her to make her tell where I lived. I heard her say, "Yon is his house." She has told me since that they first asked who had taken me out of her house. They said, "Where's Elias?" She said, "He

Source: *Report of the Joint Select Committee to Inquire into the Condition of Affairs in the Late Insurrectionary States* (Washington, D. C., 1872), vol. 1, pp. 44–46.

doesn't stay here; yon is his house." They were then in the yard, and I had heard them strike her five or six licks when I heard her say this. Some one then hit my door. It flew open. One ran in the house, and stopping about the middle of the house, which is a small cabin, he turned around, as it seemed to me as I lay there awake, and said, "Who's here?" Then I knew they would take me, and I answered, "I am here." He shouted for joy, as it seemed, "Here he is! Here he is! We have found him!" and he threw the bed-clothes off of me and caught me by one arm, while another man took me by the other and they carried me into the yard between the houses, my brother's and mine, and put me on the ground beside a boy. The first thing they asked me was, "Who did that burning? Who burned our houses?"—gin-houses, dwelling-houses and such. Some had been burned in the neighborhood. I told them it was not me; I could not burn houses; it was unreasonable to ask me. Then they hit me with their fists, and said I did it, I ordered it. They went on asking me didn't I tell the black men to ravish all the white women. No, I answered them. They struck me again with their fists on my breast. . . . Two of them went into the house. My sister says that as quick as they went into the house they struck the clock at the foot of the bed. I heard it shatter. One of the four around me called out, "Don't break any private property, gentlemen, if you please; we have got him we came for, and that's all we want." I did not hear them break anything else. They staid in there a good while hunting about and then came out and asked me for a lamp. I told them there was a lamp somewhere. They said "Where?" I was so confused I said I could not tell exactly. They caught my leg—you see what it is—and pulled me over the yard, and then left me there knowing I could not walk nor crawl, and all six went into the house. I was chilled with the cold lying in the yard at that time of night, for it was near 1 o'clock, and they had talked and beat me and so on until half an hour had passed since they first approached. After they had staid in the house for a considerable time, they came back to where I lay and asked if I wasn't afraid at all. They pointed pistols at me all around my head once or twice, as if they were going to shoot me, telling me they were going to kill me; wasn't I ready to die, and willing to die? Didn't I preach? That they came to kill me—all the time pointing pistols at me. This second time they came out of the house, after plundering the house, searching for letters, they came at me with these pistols, and asked if I was ready to die. I told them that I was not exactly ready; that I would rather live; that I hoped they would not kill me that time. They said they would; I had better prepare. One caught me by the leg and hurt me, for my leg for forty years has been drawn each year, more and more year by year, and I made moan when it hurt so. One said "G—d d—n it, hush!" He had a horsewhip, and he told me to pull up my shirt, and he hit me. He told me at every lick, "Hold up your shirt." I made a moan every time he cut with the horsewhip. I reckon he struck me eight cuts right on the hip bone; it was almost the only place he could hit my body, my legs are so short—all my limbs drawn up and withered away with pain. I saw one of them standing over me or by me motion to them to quit. They all had disguises on. I then thought they would not kill me. One of them then took a strap, and buckled it around my neck and said, "Let's take him to the river and drown him." "What course is the river?" they asked me. I told them east. Then one of them went feeling about, as if he was looking for something, and said, "I don't see no east! Where is the d—d thing?" as if he did not understand what I meant. After pulling the strap around my neck, he took it off and gave me a lick on my hip where he had struck me with the horsewhip. . . . He said I would now have to die. I was somewhat afraid, but one said not to kill me. They said,

"Look here! Will you put a card in the paper next week like June Moore and Sol Hill?" They had been prevailed on to put a card in the paper to renounce all republicanism and never vote. I said, "If I had the money to pay the expense, I could." They said I could borrow, and gave me another lick. They asked me, "Will you quit preaching?" I told them I did not know. I said that to save my life. They said I must stop that republican paper that was coming to Clay Hill. It has been only a few weeks since it stopped. The republican weekly paper was then coming to me from Charleston. It came to my name. They said I must stop it, quit preaching, and put a card in the newspaper renouncing republicanism, and they would not kill me; but if I did not they would come back the next week and kill me. With that one of them went into the house where my brother and my sister-in-law lived, and brought her to pick me up. As she stooped down to pick me up one of them struck her, and as she was carrying me into the house another struck her with a strap. She carried me into the house and laid me on the bed. Then they gathered around and told me to pray for them. I tried to pray. They said, "Don't you pray against Ku-Klux, but pray that God may forgive Ku-Klux. Don't pray against us. Pray that God may bless and save us." I was so chilled with cold lying out of doors so long and in such pain I could not speak to pray, but I tried to, and they said that would do very well, and all went out of the house. . . .

DOCUMENT 16.5
The Return of White Supremacy

Even before federal troops left the region, southern whites began to substitute political organization for overt terror in their attempt

Source: W. L. Fleming, ed., *Documentary History of Reconstruction* (Cleveland: Arthur H. Clark, 1906), vol. 2, pp. 387–88; 394–95.

to end Reconstruction. The excerpts from newspapers below come from Mississippi and Georgia; the political resolutions were adopted by most county Democratic organizations in Alabama. Together the readings reflect the region's determination to maintain white supremacy.

A MISSISSIPPI EDITORIAL (1875)

The republican journals of the North made a great mistake in regarding the present campaign in Mississippi in the light of a political contest. It is something more earnest and holy than that—it is, so far as the white people and land-owners are concerned, a battle for the control of their own domestic affairs; a struggle to regain a mastery that has been ruthlessly torn from them by selfish white schemers and adventurers, through the instrumentality of an ignorant horde of another race which has been as putty in their hands, molded to our detriment and ruin.

The present contest is rather a revolution than a political campaign—it is the rebellion, if you see fit to apply that term, of a downtrodden people against an absolutism imposed by their own hirelings, and by the grace of God we will cast it off next November, or cast off the willfully and maliciously ignorant tools who eat our bread, live in our houses, attend the schools that we support, come to us for aid and succor in their hour of need, and yet are deaf to our appeals when we entreat them to assist us in throwing off a galling yoke that has been borne until further endurance is but the basest of cowardice. . . .

We favor a continuance of the canvass upon the broad and liberal basis that has heretofore characterized it, that is, we favor appealing to the negro by everything good and holy to forsake his idols and unite with us in ridding the State of a way that we despise; but at the same time that we extend the olive-branch and plead for alliance and amity, we should not hesitate to use the great and all-powerful weapon that is in our control; we should not falter in the pledge to ourselves and our neighbors to discharge from our employ and our friendship forever, every laborer who persists in the diabolical war that has been waged against the white man and his interests ever since the negro has been a voter.

A GEORGIA EDITOR ASKS FOR "BRUTE FORCE" (1874)

Let there be White Leagues formed in every town, village and hamlet of the South, and let us organize for the great struggle which seems inevitable. The radicalism of the republican party must be met by the radicalism of white men. We have no war to make against the United States Government, but against the republican party our hate must be unquenchable, our war interminable and merciless. Fast fleeting away is the day of wordy protests and idle appeals to the magnanimity of the republican party. By brute force they are endeavoring to force us into acquiescence to their hideous programme. We have submitted long enough to indignities, and it is time to meet brute-force with brute-force. . . . It will not do to wait till radicalism has fettered us to the car of social equality before we make an effort to resist it. The signing of the [Civil Rights] bill will be a declaration of war against the southern whites. It is our duty to ourselves, it is our duty to our children, it is our duty to the white race whose prowess subdued the wilderness of this continent, whose civilization filled it with cities and towns and villages, whose mind gave it power and grandeur, and whose labor imparted to it prosperity, and whose love made peace and happiness dwell within its homes, to take the gage of battle the moment it is thrown down. If the white democrats of the North are men, they will not stand idly by and see us borne down by northern radicals and half-barbarous negroes. But no matter what they may do, it is time for us to organize. We have been temporizing long enough. Let northern radicals understand that military supervision of southern elections and the civil-rights bill mean war, that war means bloodshed, and that we are terribly in earnest, and even they, fanatical as they are, may retrace their steps before it is too late.

RESOLUTION OF ALABAMADEMOCRATS (1874)

Resolved, That we, the people. . . . for the protection of our dearest and most sacred interests, our homes, our honor, the purity and integrity of our race, and to conserve the peace and tranquility of the country, accept the issue of race thus defiantly tendered and forced upon us, notwithstanding our determination and repeated efforts to avoid it; and further

Resolved, That nothing is left to the white man's party but social ostracism of all those who act, sympathize or side with the negro party, or who support or advocate the odious, unjust, and unreasonable measure known as the civil rights bill; and that from henceforth we will hold all such persons as enemies of our race, and we will not in the future have intercourse with them in any of the social relations of life.

chapter

The Impact of Industrialization on American Society

Sigmund Diamond
Columbia University

In the early summer of 1853 the yacht *North Star,* bearing on board the most renowned American businessman of the day, Commodore Cornelius Vanderbilt, steamed into the port of London during the course of a world cruise. The reputation of the Commodore, less towering than it was to become, was already something to conjure with; and the London press, even as it greeted him, attempted to extract from the story of his life something of value for its readers. Why did Vanderbilt have such high prestige in the United States, the *London Daily News* pondered, and produced the answer to its own query:

> America . . . is the great arena in which the individual energies of man, uncramped by oppressive social institutions, or absurd social traditions, have full play, and arrive at gigantic development. . . .
>
> It is the tendency of American institutions to foster the general welfare, and to permit the unchecked powers of the highly gifted to occupy a place in the general framework of society which they can obtain nowhere else. The great feature to be noted in America is that all its citizens have full permission to run the race in which Mr. Vanderbilt has gained such immense prizes. In other countries, on the contrary, they are trammelled by a thousand restrictions. . . .
>
> Your men of rank here—your makers of millions for themselves and tens of millions for the country—too often spend their time, their intellect, their labor, in order that they may be able to take rank among a class of men who occupy their present position in virtue of what was done for them by some broad-shouldered adventurer, who, fortunately for them, lived eight hundred years ago in Normandy. . . . Here is the great difference between the two countries. In England a man is too apt to be ashamed of having made his own fortune, unless he has done so in one of the few roads which the aristocracy condescend to travel—the bar, the church, or the army.
>
> It is time that the *millionaire* should cease to be ashamed of having made his own fortune. It is time that *parvenu* should be looked on as a word of honor. It is time that the middle classes should take the place which is their own, in the world which they have made. The middle classes have made the modern world. The Montmorencis, the Percys, the Howards, made the past world—and they had their reward. Let them give place to better men.

We do not have to accept the correctness of the newspaper's diagnosis to be convinced of the validity of the condition it was describing—that even so titanic a businessman as Vanderbilt was not regarded in the same way by people throughout the world, that the special characteristics of the cultural traditions and social structure of each country affect the degree to which it is possible for a country to produce a Vanderbilt and the way in which he will be esteemed.

But, of course, not even participation in the same cultural tradition or membership in the same society is enough to guarantee uniformity of outlook. So it was that even to his own countrymen Cornelius Vanderbilt was the object of assessments so diverse as to suggest that their authors could not have been speaking of the same person. To the boards of directors of the railroads with which he had been associated, Vanderbilt had "stood as the nation's foremost representative of public enterprise and material progress." A "true man, a sincere friend, a devoted husband and father, a liberal employer, an extraordinary genius of affairs, and a citizen of high public spirit," his career had been a dazzling success.

> Beginning in an humble position, with apparently little scope of action and small promise of opportunity, he rose, by his genius, his indomitable energy, and his clear forecast, to the control of vast enterprises. . . . In a period of crafty devices for sinister ends, he taught the way of success through legitimate means. . . . As a citizen, he was true to the honor and welfare of his country. . . . If his patriotism was thus substantial, his philanthropy was equally generous and effective.

But to the editor of the *Nation,* E. L. Godkin—certainly no enemy of the social order—the same Vanderbilt was

> a man who never served the country at large, nor the State, nor the city, in any public office; nor ever spent the time which is money in advancing the cause of any charity; nor in promoting education, which the self-made man may despise; nor in fostering the arts, which can always wait.

He was, in short, the

> lineal successor of the medieval baron that we read about, who may have been illiterate indeed; and who was not humanitarian; and not finished in his morals; and not, for his manners, the delight of the refined society of his neighborhood; nor yet beloved by his dependents; but who knew how to take advantage of lines of travel, who had a keen eye for roads, and had the heart and hand to levy contributions on all who passed his way.

The correctness of the perception of the *London Daily News*—that the absence of feudal-aristocratic traditions in the United States as compared with England accounts for the higher prestige of the parvenu in the former country—must not blind us to the fact that even within the United States the career of the businessman was susceptible of diametrically different verdicts. The same Vanderbilt who to his associates—and to many others—was a man of "high public spirit," was to Godkin—and to many others—an authentic robber baron, though in the wrong time and in the wrong place, swooping down from his mountain fastness to levy tribute on unprotected travelers.

Clearly, then, the status of the businessman in American society, high though it was in comparison with other societies, was not exactly unchallenged. And even among those who accorded the businessman their highest praise, there was a discernible—and in the years to come a momentous—disagreement as to what in fact was responsible for the high status he had achieved in his society. For Vanderbilt's corporate associates, his "glittering success" was not "due to any early adventitious advantages. He was essentially the creator, not the creature, of the circumstances which he molded to his purposes." But only twenty years later, Vanderbilt's longtime friend and colleague,

U.S. Senator Chauncey M. Depew, speaking at the unveiling of a statue of his associate at Vanderbilt University, was somewhat less certain about the sources of Vanderbilt's success. True, he "neither asked nor gave quarter. . . . He was not the creation of luck nor chance nor circumstances." But was he entirely the architect of his own fortunes? Was there not something in his surroundings that contributed to his success? Senator Depew thought that there was.

> The American Commonwealth is built upon the individual. It recognizes neither classes nor masses. . . . We have thus become a nation of self-made men. We live under just and equal laws and all avenues for a career are open. . . . Freedom of opportunity and preservation of the results of forecast, industry, thrift and honesty have made the United States the most prosperous and wealthy country in the world. Commodore Vanderbilt is a conspicuous example of the products and possibilities of our free and elastic conditions. . . . The same country, the same laws, the same open avenues, the same opportunities which he had before him are equally before every man.

What was the real object of the orator's praise—the qualities of the man which lifted him above his surroundings, or the "free and elastic conditons" of American society which placed no obstacles in the way of Vanderbilt's—or anyone's—rise to success? And did he neglect to point out that a large percentage of the self-made men had indeed risen not from the bottom but rather from the middle and top rungs of the economic ladder as a result of their happy accident of birth?

Illustrated in even this mere handful of quotations is a series of significant questions. What assurance has the great American man of business had that the community would elevate him to the position of distinction to which he aspired? What changes have taken place in the status of the businessman in American society,

and what changes have occurred in the explanations that have been offered to account for his status? What inferences about American social thought—and about American society—may be drawn from the fact that the career of the successful businessman, which at one time is pointed to as a testimonial to the good qualities a man must have in order to overcome obstacles, is at another time pointed to as a testimonial to the good qualities of a society which puts no obstacles in the way of achieving business success? What are the functions and practices that the community associates with the status of the businessman, and how have these been evaluated differently over time and by different groups at the same point of time?

Such questions would be of importance in understanding a society at any time and at any place, but certain developments in the history of the United States in the decades following the Civil War conspired to make them of crucial importance. For it was in those decades that a new society—an industrial society—was being formed; and in its formation—which involved the uprooting of millions of people, the learning of new ideas and habits and routines, the lifting of new groups to power and the suppression of the once powerful—the businessman stepped out into the limelight as the most powerful of the movers and shakers of his age.

In the changes that transformed American society, nothing was left untouched—the relation of citizens to their government and of groups of people to each other, the churches and the schools, the family; but behind these changes, emphasizing the crucial importance of the role of the businessman, lay a new method of production and distribution, based on factory and machine, with an increasingly refined technology that made use of ever-larger supplies of capital and specialized labor and of new modes of organizing and disciplining human energies. Land and people alike were being remade, as industrialization and urbanization changed the face of the landscape and forced millions of migrants from rural America and rural Europe to learn the techniques and disciplines of an industrial society.

In 1900 the United States, the world's largest producer of food and raw materials, had become as well the world's leading manufacturer. But even a detailed recitation of the statistics of economic growth cannot fully summarize all the changes involved in the processes of industrialization. For untold millions, industrialization meant to be ripped loose from the places and from the ideas that earlier had been counted on to provide social stability. Between 1870 and 1900, total population in the United States, stimulated by both a high birth-rate and massive immigration, nearly doubled—from forty million to seventy-six million—but the increase was not evenly distributed throughout the country or throughout the economy; some regions and some occupations grew far more rapidly than others. Not quite 60 percent of the American labor force worked on farms in 1860, but only 37 percent did so in 1900; only 26 percent worked in transportation and industry in 1860, but 46 percent did so in 1900. The farm, the small New England town, the middle western river entrepôt were everywhere being shoved aside by the populaton centers more characteristic of the new stage of economic development that had been reached—the mill town, the coal town, the steel town, and, above all, the great metropolitan city.

For it was the great city, that most characteristic product of industrial society, that ·grew most spectacularly in the years following the close of the Civil War. In 1860, only one-sixth of the American people lived in urban areas; in 1900, one third. During that same forty-year period the population of the nation's great cities grew more than twice as fast as that of the nation as a whole. New York, Chicago, and Philadelphia were, by the end of the century, true metropolises, each with well over a million people and each already showing

that striking combination of wonder and squalor that was to become the hallmark of the twentieth-century city. As early as 1890, four out of every five persons in Massachusetts were living in towns; rural Massachusetts, having largely disappeared from the census returns, continued to live on mainly in the realms of nostalgia and the poetic imagination.

In the midst of such movement and change, nothing remained settled, not even the moral and intellectual standards that for so long had provided the criteria for measuring the value of institutions and ideas. The sturdy yeoman was now a hayseed; the independent artisan was now a factory hand; David Harum had become a captain of industry; the center of affairs had shifted from the small-town countinghouse to the polished boardroom of a bank in New York or Chicago. To swim with the wave of economic change meant choosing a different career and living in a different place; it meant beng reeducated, learning new skills and new ideas; it meant rejecting much of what one had been taught to regard as standard and value. And even those who fought to preserve the old had to come to grips with the forces that were making their world obsolete. To swim with the tide or against the tide of economic change seemed to make little difference. Economic change was providing the environment in which, increasingly, most men lived out their lives; and in the creation of that new environment the decisions of businessmen—affecting the lives of millions of their countrymen—bulked ever larger.

Driving this change forward was a revolution that began in transportation and communication and then spread quickly to production and distribution. Between 1870 and 1900, railroad mileage increased from 30,000 to 193,000; as early as 1887, nearly 33,000 towns in the United States were being served by the railroad network. Merchants in Boston, Baltimore, New York, Philadelphia, and dozens of inland towns—eager to tap the distant markets brought within their reach by the development of cheap transportation—were stimulated to mobilize the capital and organize the skills needed to lay down the railroad network. Sometimes their hopes proved illusory, sometimes realistic, but in any case their decision to move ahead with the development of the railroad was the major economic stimulus of the post-Civil War period.

For one thing, railroad construction itself provided a direct and powerful stimulus to industrial production. As early as the 1880s, the railroads employed a labor force of more than 200,000; they provided, therefore, an enormous market for the products of stone quarries, lumber mills, and iron factories and for the excess capital of both foreign and domestic investors. Most important, of course, was the stimulus the railroad gave to the growth of the iron and steel industry. By linking the sections of the country more closely, the railroad made it possible to bring together more efficiently and cheaply the elements of industrial production. The railroad first created the demand for locomotives, rolling stock, bridges, and rails, and then provided the means for satisfying that demand—a fast, cheap, sure way of bringing iron ore to coal. Indeed, so insatiable was the demand of the railroad for steel that the steel industry transformed itself technologically to meet that demand. Rolling mills and blast furnaces using coke could out-produce the old charcoal-fueled ovens at the rate of 10 to 1. No longer were scarce supplies of expensive charcoal permitted to set limits on the size of furnaces and, therefore, on the amount they could produce; fed on unlimited supplies of cheap coal from western Pennsylvania, the size of the furnaces—stimulated by the voracious appetite of the railroad—increased steadily. Blast furnaces which shortly before the Civil War were producing at an average rate of 40 tons per day were producing at a daily average rate of 400 tons as the century drew to a close. Steel production—140,000 tons in 1873 and 500,000 tons in 1878—

reached 2.5 million tons in 1886. By the end of the century the Carnegie Steel Company alone was producing about four-fifths as much steel as the entire British steel industry.

But the railroad stimulated the economy in still another way—by creating the great national market that made mass production possible. Local businessmen who dominated regional markets now faced serious competition from products manufactured in distant factories and hauled to every market cheaply by the railroad. Businessmen, encouraged now by the greater size of their markets, increased their production in order to take advantage of lower costs and experimented with the development of lower-cost production methods. Stimulated to reduce costs to lower and lower levels so as to capture wider and wider markets, the steel industry brought down the price of rails from $160 per ton to $17 per ton between 1875 and 1898. Other industries felt the same stimulating effects of the growing market made possible by cheap transportation. Well before the assembly line, bringing down production costs, had been introduced in the automobile industry by Henry Ford, it was being widely used in the textile industry, in meat packing, in canning, and in flour milling.

Changes in technology—as in the case of mass production—were of great importance indeed, but by themselves they would not have succeeded in boosting the level of production to the point that it in fact reached. Changes in organization were also required.

First, of course, came changes in the organization of work in the factory. Standardization of parts, which long had been practiced in the Connecticut gun industry, spread to other industries—sewing machines and clocks, for example—and eventually into the standardization of the final assembly of all sorts of products. Nor was the drive for "rationalization" restricted to the workshop. Accounting and auditing departments, the sales division, and the head office were closely scrutinized and subjected to increasingly rigorous methods of supervision in an attempt to cut costs by providing standardized methods of procedure. Organization—the social structure of the firm—was seen to be a variable that, like land, labor, and capital, influenced the level of costs and productivity; and fundamental changes were made in traditional methods of assigning tasks in shop and office, supervising the activities of the labor force, determining the proper relation between supervisory and production personnel, and fixing the locus of authority for the performance of particular functions within the firm.

The factory was rationalized and organized, the office was rationalized and organized—and so was industry itself. To compete successfully for markets required the utilization of the latest techniques of science and technology to reduce costs to competitive levels. The very costs of modernization, however, were so great that only when factories operated at or near capacity could economies of production be achieved. But to operate at such levels would cause prices to fall. Every glimmer of hope for potential new markets—the establishment of a new railroad line, a new wave of immigration, the growth of a city, the opening of new territory, the enactment of a new tariff—was desperately grasped and was followed by a frenzy of expansion, only to be followed in turn by idle plant and equipment when the new markets had been saturated. Like the ruthless competition between industrial rivals, the ability of industry to achieve economies of production only when operating at capacity tended to drive down prices and, therefore, to threaten the security of even the most efficient producers. To escape from this cruel dilemma became an overriding concern of American businessmen toward the turn of the century, and led them into a search for "order," the most important outcome of which was the discovery of the importance of organization of the market.

First came efforts to organize the market by introducing changes within the structure of a single firm. Andrew Carnegie, for example, was already the dominant producer in the basic iron and steel industry when, in the 1880s, he began to reach out into all branches of the industry—into coalfields, railroads, and coking plants, into the Michigan and Mesabi iron ranges, into ore ships on the Great Lakes and ports to handle them. Even so, he could not free himself from the threat of combinations in the steel-consuming industries that were strong enough to affect his prices. In 1900, he announced plans that would carry combination a long step forward—his own entry into the manufacture of steel wire, tubes, and similar products—and was dissuaded from attempting to realize them by the offer of J. P. Morgan to buy him out for $450 million. Ultimately, it was Morgan himself who attempted to bring order into the industry in the way forecast by Carnegie—through the organization of the United States Steel Corporation, the world's first billion-dollar company.

Organizational efforts to curtail competition and create stability could not, however, in the very nature of the case, be confined to the level of the single firm. In the effort to create intercompany agreements, it was the railroad that pioneered, primarily because it had been the railroad that first felt the effects of unbridled competition. Direct mergers carried out under the auspices of the banking houses that financed the consolidations were attempted, and so were "traffic associations," formed to fix rates and share traffic among competing lines. But railroads were more vulnerable than other industries to some measure of government regulation, and railroad entrepreneurs were not given a free hand to solve their competitive problems in the way in which they would have preferred. Eventually, government regulation was required; but even so, by 1900 the vast national railroad network had been so shaken down that only six large systems controlled 95 percent of the mileage. Where the railroads led, other industries were quick to follow.

As early as the 1870s, "pools" were formed to divide territorial markets, fix production quotas, and set prices; but these "gentlemen's agreements"—generally formed during the despair that prevailed at the bottom of a business depression—could not withstand the tendency of their own members to cheat or to defect during the optimism that prevailed when the business cycle turned upward, when there was promise of new killings to be made. John D. Rockefeller's Standard Oil Company was the first spectacular example of an even more effective form of business organization—the trust. The shareholders of a number of competing firms turned over their voting stock to "trustees" in return for nonvoting, interest-bearing certificates; the small group of trustees could then fix pricing and marketing policies for all of the once-competing companies within the trust. But this, too, proved only an interim form of organization. Held to be in violation of the law, it was soon replaced, with the help of agreeable state legislatures which provided the necessary enabling legislation, by the holding company, a single firm which controlled the operations of several subordinate units by holding a controlling interest in them.

In the center of the apparatus whose decisions produced a far-flung network of relationships from which virtually no one was excluded, which affected the lives and the livelihoods of all, was the businessman. The making of those decisions involved the late nineteenth-century businessman in activities that would have been utterly foreign 'to his forebears. At an earlier time the successful businessman had had to concern himself only with costs and prices; other factors could be taken for granted. At an earlier time, but no longer— for now even costs and prices depended upon such variables as the programs of political parties, the temper of the legislature, the attitude of labor and its degree of organization, the state of public opinion—all of them variables over which the businessman did not have full

and complete control. Yet, if he was to operate in the climate of security which he found necessary for the successful prosecution of his affairs, more and more of his environment had to be brought within his purview and made susceptible to his influence. The businessman was, then, increasingly powerful; but he was also, by virtue of the way in which every area of the social environment impinged upon him, increasingly vulnerable as well.

Were his flamboyance and his self-consciousness the result of his own awareness of his power and vulnerability? Whether they were or not, the fact is that the businessman of the late nineteenth century stepped out front and center with an éclat that his forebears had never exhibited. For one thing, the great man of business had become far more numerous than ever before. When Moses Yale Beach, owner of the *New York Sun,* had compiled a list of the richest merchants of New York City in 1845, he found only twenty-one millionaires. In 1892 the *New York Tribune* counted more than 4,000 in the United States. The businessman-millionaire had, moreover, become far more visible to his fellow citizens; the great scale of his business activities, his forays into politics, his heroic appetites in the fields of entertainment and culture made of him a figure rarely if ever out of sight in the comings and goings of his time and place. As the light fell upon him, it was seen that he sat at the center of the web of influence that penetrated into every section of the country. His decisions helped shape the environment in which all Americans had to live; and, increasingly, that environment began to rub harder and more irritatingly against large numbers of people. Small wonder, then, that the businessman became a subject of analysis and discussion, an object for emulation or for scorn.

With the passage of time the businessman tended increasingly to become, for both defenders and critics, a symbol of an entire social order. His critics came to interpret his misdeeds less as the expression of his idiosyncratic nature than as the inevitable consequences of a society gone wrong; his defenders, therefore, of necessity had to become defenders of the social order as well. In the first quarter of the nineteenth century, when the social order needed no defense, and when all that needed to be explained was why each person held the position that he did within that society, the success of the great businessman was expressed as a tribute to him who had the stuff to get ahead. In the last quarter of the nineteenth century, when the social order stood very much in need of defense, the success of the businessman—by now accepted by both friend and foe as a symbol of that order—was expressed as a tribute to a social order which showered its blessings equally upon all. But 1899 was the year of the death of Horatio Alger, Jr., and 1900 was the year of the birth of the United States Steel Corporation; and the cult of success—if it ever was an accurate description of American social reality—was certainly no longer that. In a society made up increasingly of overlapping organizations, the idea of individual success as the victory of character over circumstances continued to live on, but it was less the reflection of a living reality than it was a technique by which the millions who made up the labor force could be motivated to accept the discipline of a capitalist industrial society.

SUGGESTED READINGS

Cawelti, John G. *Apostles of the Self-Made Man.* Chicago: University of Chicago Press, 1965.

Chandler, Alfred D. *Strategy and Structure: Chapters in the History of the Industrial Enterprise.* Cambridge, Mass.: MIT Press, 1962.

———. *The Visible Hand; The Managerial Revolution in American Business.* Cambridge, Mass.: Harvard University Press, 1977.

Cochran, Thomas C. *Business in American Life: A History.* New York: McGraw-Hill, 1972.

———. *Two Hundred Years of American Business.* New York: Basic Books, 1977.

Diamond, Sigmund. *The Reputation of the American Businessman.* New York: Harper & Row, Colophon Books, 1966.

———, ed. *The Nation Transformed.* New York: George Braziller, 1963.

Hayes, Samuel P. *The Response to Industrialism.* Chicago: University of Chicago Press, 1957.

Hurst, James Willard. *The Legitimacy of the Business Corporation in the Law of the United States, 1870–1970.* Charlottesville, Va.: University of Virginia Press, 1970.

Josephson, Matthew. *The Robber Barons.* New York: Harcourt Brace Jovanovich, 1934.

Kirkland, Edward Chase. *Dream and Thought in the Business Community, 1860–1900.* Ithaca, N.Y.: Cornell University Press, 1956.

———. *Industry Comes of Age.* New York: Holt, Rinehart & Winston, 1961.

Rischin, Moses, ed. *The American Gospel of Success.* Chicago: Quadrangle Books, 1965.

Robertson, James Oliver. *America's Business.* New York: Hill & Wang, 1985.

Sutton, Francis X., et al. *The American Business Creed.* Cambridge, Mass.: Harvard University Press, 1956.

Weibe, Robert. *Business and Reform: A Study of the Progressive Movement.* Cambridge, Mass.: Harvard University Press, 1962.

Weiss, Richard. *The American Myth of Success.* New York: Basic Books, 1969.

Wyllie, Irvin G. *The Self-Made Man in America: The Myth of Rags to Riches.* New Brunswick, N.J.: Rutgers University Press, 1954.

DOCUMENT 17.1
What the Social Classes Owe to Each Other

Tough-minded William Graham Sumner, who left the ministry of the Episcopal church to become an academic sociologist, strongly

Source: William Graham Sumner, *What the Social Classes Owe to Each Other* (New York: Harper & Bros., 1883), pp. 43–57.

opposed resort to political action as a means of achieving social and economic amelioration. Contrariwise, he provided moral and intellectual justification for the possessors of wealth.

Is it wicked to be rich? Is it mean to be a capitalist? If the question is one of degree only, and it is right to be rich up to a certain point and wrong to be richer, how shall we find the point? . . .

There is an old ecclesiastical prejudice in favor of the poor and against the rich. In days when men acted by ecclesiastical rules these prejudices produced waste of capital, and helped mightily to replunge Europe into barbarism. The prejudices are not yet dead, but they survive in our society as ludicrous contradictions and inconsistencies. One thing must be granted to the rich: they are good-natured. Perhaps they do not recognize themselves, for a rich man is even harder to define than a poor one. It is not uncommon to hear a clergyman utter from the pulpit all the old prejudice in favor of the poor and against the rich, while asking the rich to do something for the poor; and the rich comply, without apparently having their feelings hurt at all by the invidious comparison. We all agree that he is a good member of society who works his way up from poverty to wealth, but as soon as he has worked his way up we begin to regard him with suspicion, as a dangerous member of society. A newspaper starts the silly fallacy that "the rich are rich because the poor are industrious," and it is copied from one end of the country to the other as if it were a brilliant apothegm. "Capital" is denounced by writers and speakers who have never taken the trouble to find out what capital is, and who use the word in two or three different senses in as many pages. Labor organizations are formed, not to employ combined effort for a common object, but to indulge in declamation and denunciation, and especially to furnish an easy living to some officers who do not want to work. People who have rejected dog-

matic religion, and retained only a residuum of religious sentimentalism, find a special field in the discussion of the rights of the poor and the duties of the rich. We have denunciations of banks, corporations, and monopolies, which denunciations encourage only helpless rage and animosity, because they are not controlled by any definitions or limitations, or by any distinctions between what is indispensably necessary and what is abuse, between what is established in the order of nature and what is legislative error. Think, for instance, of a journal which makes it its special business to denounce monopolies, yet favors a protective tariff, and has not a word to say against trades-unions or patents! Think of public teachers who say that the farmer is ruined by the cost of transportation, when they mean that he cannot make any profits because his farm is too far from the market, and who denounce the railroad because it does not correct for the farmer, at the expense of its stockholders, the disadvantage which lies in the physical situation of the farm! Think of that construction of this situation which attributes all the trouble to the greed of "moneyed corporations"! Think of the piles of rubbish that one has read about corners, and watering stocks, and selling futures!

Undoubtedly, there are, in connection with each of these things, cases of fraud, swindling, and other financial crimes; that is to say, the greed and selfishness of men are perpetual. They put on new phases, they adjust themselves to new forms of business, and constantly devise new methods of fraud and robbery, just as burglars devise new artifices to circumvent every new precaution of the lock-makers. The criminal law needs to be improved to meet new forms of crime, but to denounce financial devices which are useful and legitimate because use is made of them for fraud, is ridiculous and unworthy of the age in which we live. Fifty years ago good old English Tories used to denounce all joint-stock companies in the same way, and for similar reasons.

All the denunciations and declamations

which have been referred to are made in the interest of "the poor man." His name never ceases to echo in the halls of legislation, and he is the excuse and reason for all the acts which are passed. He is never forgotten in poetry, sermon, or essay. His interest is invoked to defend every doubtful procedure and every questionable institution. Yet where is he? Who is he? Who ever saw him? When did he ever get the benefit of any of the numberless efforts in his behalf? When, rather, was his name and interest ever invoked, when, upon examination, it did not plainly appear that somebody else was to win—somebody who was far too "smart" ever to be poor, far too lazy ever to be rich by industry and economy?

*   *   *   *   *

The great gains of a great capitalist in a modern state must be put under the head of wages of superintendence. Any one who believes that any great enterprise of an industrial character can be started without labor must have little experience of life. Let any one try to get a railroad built, or to start a factory and win reputation for its products, or to start a school and win a reputation for it, or to found a newspaper and make it a success, or to start any other enterprise, and he will find what obstacles must be overcome, what risks must be taken, what perseverance and courage are required, what foresight and sagacity are necessary. Especially in a new country, where many tasks are waiting, where resources are strained to the utmost all the time, the judgment, courage, and perseverance required to organize new enterprises and carry them to success are sometimes heroic. Persons who possess the necessary qualifications obtain great rewards. They ought to do so. It is foolish to rail at them. Then, again, the ability to organize and conduct industrial, commercial, or financial enterprises is rare; the great captains of industry are as rare as great generals. The great weakness of all co-operative enterprises is in the matter of supervision. Men of routine or men who can

do what they are told are not hard to find; but men who can think and plan and tell the routine men what to do are very rare. They are paid in proportion to the supply and demand of them. . . .

The aggregation of large fortunes is not at all a thing to be regretted. On the contrary, it is a necessary condition of many forms of social advance. If we should set a limit to the accumulation of wealth, we should say to our most valuable producers, "We do not want you to do us the services which you best understand how to perform, beyond a certain point." It would be like killing off our generals in war. A great deal is said, in the cant of a certain school, about "ethical views of wealth," and we are told that some day men will be found of such public spirit that, after they have accumulated a few millions, they will be willing to go on and labor simply for the pleasure of paying the taxes of their fellow-citizens. Possibly this is true. It is a prophecy. It is as impossible to deny it as it is silly to affirm it. For if a time ever comes when there are men of this kind, the men of that age will arrange their affairs accordingly. There are no such men now, and those of us who live now cannot arrange our affairs by what men will be a hundred generations hence.

There is every indication that we are to see new developments of the power of aggregated capital to serve civilization, and that the new developments will be made right here in America. Joint-stock companies are yet in their infancy, and incorporated capital, instead of being a thing which can be overturned, is a thing which is becoming more and more indispensable. I shall have something to say [subsequently]. . . . about the necessary checks and guarantees, in a political point of view, which must be established. Economically speaking, aggregated capital will be more and more essential to the performance of our social tasks. Furthermore, it seems to me certain that all aggregated capital will fall more and more under personal control. Each great company will be known as controlled by one master mind. The reason for this lies in the great superiority of personal management over management by boards and committees. This tendency is in the public interest, for it is in the direction of more satisfactory responsibility. The great hinderance to the development of this continent has lain in the lack of capital. The capital which we have had has been wasted by division and dissipation, and by injudicious applications. The waste of capital, in proportion of the total capital, in this country between 1800 and 1850, in the attempts which were made to establish means of communication and transportation, was enormous. The waste was chiefly due to ignorance and bad management, especially to State control of public works. We are to see the development of the country pushed forward at an unprecedented rate by an aggregation of capital, and a systematic application of it under the direction of competent men. This development will be for the benefit of all, and it will enable each one of us, in his measure and way, to increase his wealth. We may each of us go ahead to do so, and we have every reason to rejoice in each other's prosperity. There ought to be no laws to guarantee property against the folly of its possessors. In the absence of such laws, capital inherited by a spendthrift will be squandered and reaccumulated in the hands of men who are fit and competent to hold it. So it should be, and under such a state of things there is no reason to desire to limit the property which any man may acquire.

DOCUMENT 17.2
A Call to Action

James Baird Weaver (1833–1912), emerged from the Civil War as brigadier general, and in the decades that followed became a principal

Source: James Baird Weaver, *A Call to Action* (Des Moines: Iowa Printing Co., 1892), pp. 362–78.

spokesman for those middle westerners who demanded currency reform and government control of corporate monopolies, especially the railroads. Weaver, a Greenbacker, was the presidential candidate of the Peoples party in 1892. His descriptions of the excesses of the wealthy and the plight of the poor were typical of the social criticism of American reformers at the turn of the century.

If the master builders of our civilization one hundred years ago had been told that at the end of a single century, American society would present such melancholy contrasts of wealth and poverty, of individual happiness and widespread infelicity as are to be found to-day throughout the Republic, the person making the unwelcome prediction whould [*sic*] have been looked upon as a misanthropist, and his loyalty to Democratic institutions would have been seriously called in question. Our federal machine, with its delicate inter-lace work of National, State and municipal supervision, each intended to secure perfect individual equality, was expected to captivate the world by its operation and insure domestic contentment and personal security to a degree never before realized by mankind.

But there is a vast difference between the generation which made the heroic struggle for Self-government in colonial days, and the third generation which is now engaged in a mad rush for wealth. The first took its stand upon the inalienable rights of man and made a fight which shook the world. But the leading spirits of the latter are entrenched behind class laws and revel in special privileges. It will require another revolution to overthrow them. That revolution is upon us even now. . . .

SOCIAL EXTRAVAGANCE

In the year 1884, as we are told by Ward McAllister, in his book entitled "Society as I Found It," a wealthy gentleman gave a banquet at

Delmonico's at which the moderate number of seventy-two guests, ladies and gentlemen, were entertained. The gentleman giving the banquet had unexpectedly received from the Treasury of the United States a rebate of $10,000 for duties which had been exacted from him through some alleged misconception of the law. He resolved to spend the entire sum in giving a single dinner which should excel any private entertainment ever given in New York. He consulted Charles Delmonico, who engaged to carry out his wishes. The table was constructed with a miniature lake in the center thirty feet in length, enclosed by a network of golden wire which reached to the ceiling, forming a great cage. Four immense swans were secured from one of the parks and placed in this lake. High banks of flowers of every hue surrounded the lake and covered the entire table, leaving barely enough room for the plates and wine glasses. The room was festooned with flowers in every direction. Miniature mountains and valleys with carpets of flowers made vocal with sparkling rivulets, met the eye on every hand. Golden cages filled with sweet singing birds hung from the ceiling and added their enchantment to the gorgeous spectacle. Soft, sweet music swept in from adjoining rooms, and all that art, wealth and imagination could do was done to make the scene one of unexampled beauty. And then the feast! All the dishes which ingenuity could invent or the history of past extravagance suggest, were spread before the guests. The oldest and costliest wines known to the trade flowed like the water that leaped down the cascades in the banqueting hall. The guests were wild with exultation and delight and tarried far into the night. But in a few brief hours the romanticism had passed, the carousel was broken, and the revelers were face to face with the responsibilities which none of us can evade. The fool and his money had parted.

* * * * *

PRINCE ASTOR'S WEDDING

In the year 1890, young Astor, a scion of the celebrated family which has so long been prominent in New York financial circles, was married. Both the groom and the bride represented millions of wealth and the wedding was an imposing and gorgeous affair. Twenty-five thousand dollars were expended on the day's ceremony. The presents were valued at $2,000,000, and the couple and their attendants and a number of friends, immediately departed on an expensive yachting cruise which was to cost them $10,000 a month to maintain. In speaking of these nuptials the *Christian Union* said: "When we read this we are reminded of Thackeray's description of the extravagance of the Prince Regent during the Napoleonic wars. 'If he had been a manufacturing town, or a populous rural district, or an army of 5,000 men, he would not have cost more. The nation gave him more money, and more and more. The sum is past counting.' "

Looked at soberly, the sums lavished upon our American commoners are as disgraceful to our institutions as were the squanderings of the Prince Regent to those of England. If the scandal is less it is because the disastrous concentration of hereditary wealth has as yet awakened less serious thought among us than the disastrous concentration of hereditary power had awakened in England. In the case of the Astors, quite as much as of the Prince Regent, the enormous sums expended are the gift of the Nation, obtained without compensating service on the part of the recipients. The burden upon the labor of the country is as great.

A SPORTSMAN'S DINNER

Early in the present year, 1891, a well-known New York State Senator gave a notable banquet in honor of two distinguished citizens of that State, both of whom are prominently mentioned in connection with the nomination for the

Presidency of the United States. The following description of the table and decorations appeared in the daily press at the time:

> The library is upon the second floor of the club house, known for years to residents of this city as the Stewart Mansion. It is a large room, grandly furnished, and just the place for a dinner of this limited proportion. The table has been especially constructed for the occasion, and it is said that for two days a landscape gardener and a florist were employed in decorating it. A glance at it made this appreciable. Most of those present were ardent sportsmen, and to this instinct the table appealed in the strongest measure. It looked like an immense marsh, just the place for fowl, and up from the waters of the small lakes which dotted the view, four live diamond-backed terrapins shot up their heads every now and again and winked slyly at the guests. Cattail, ferns, grass and wild flowers hid the banks of the lakes, and amid this greenery stuffed wild waterfowl hidden, as if in the attempt to escape the guns of the sportsman. In the center of the pool lay the gnarled stump of an immense oak, and imbedded in this was a nest containing an egg for each of the guests.

THE BANKER'S BANQUET

The following editorial appeared in the Kansas City *Times,* August 30, 1889:

> The contract for serving the banquet for the convention of the American Banker's Association was yesterday awarded to C. M. Hill, of the Midland Hotel. There were sixty competitors. The price is such as to insure one of the finest banquets ever served in this country. No expense will be spared to make the affair a grand success, even aside from the *menu*. The banquet will be given in the Priests of Pallas' Temple, at Seventh and Lydia. It will be necessary to build and furnish an annex, where the cooking can be done for 1,500 covers. The preparations seem to take into contemplation a great flow of wine, as there will be six thousand wine glasses and about forty wine servers. There will be in all nearly three hundred waiters. It is estimated that the entire cost of the banquet will be from $15,000 to $20,000. Mr. Hill anticipates some difficulty in securing efficient waiters, and with this particular object in view, will make a trip to New York and Chicago.

This impious feast which took place in the very heart of the mortgage-ridden and debt-cursed West, was the most shocking and brazen exhibition of wanton extravagance and bad morals combined, which the laboring millions of America were ever called upon to behold. What a travesty upon common sense and the ordinary instinct of self-preservation to intrust the finances of a great Nation and the welfare of labor to the hands of such men. . . .

AT THE RICH MAN'S GATE

About the time these princely entertainments were given, and in the same year with some of them, one of the metropolitan journals caused a careful canvass to be made of the unemployed of that city. The number was found to be *one hundred and fifty thousand persons who were daily unsuccessfully seeking work within the city limits of New York.* Another one hundred and fifty thousand earn less than sixty cents per day. Thousands of these are poor girls who work from eleven to sixteen hours per day.

In the year 1890, over 23,000 families, numbering about 100,000 people, were forcibly evicted in New York City owing to their inability to pay rent, and one-tenth of all who died in that city during the year were buried in the Potters Field.

In the *Arena* for June, 1891, will be found a description of tenement house horrors, by Mr. B. O. Flower. He has done a valuable service to humanity by laying before the world the result of his investigations. After describing a family whose head was unable to find work, Mr. Flower says:

. . . This poor woman supports her husband, her two children and herself, by making pants at twelve cents a pair. No rest, no surcease, a perpetual grind from early dawn, often till far into the night; and what is more appalling, outraged nature has rebelled; the long months of semi-starvation and lack of sleep have brought on rheumatism, which has settled in the joints of her fingers, so that every stitch means a throb of pain. The afternoon we called she was completing an enormous pair of custom-made pants of very fine blue cloth, for one of the largest clothing houses in the city. The suit would probably bring sixty or sixty-five dollars, yet her employer graciously informed his poor white slave that as the garment was so large he would give her an *extra cent*. Thirteen cents for fine custom-made pants, manufactured for a wealthy firm, which repeatedly asserts that its clothing is not made in tenement houses! Thus with one of the most painful diseases enthroned in that part of the body which must move incessantly from dawn till midnight, with two small dependent children and a husband powerless to help her, this poor woman struggles bravely, confronted ever by a nameless dread of impending misfortune. Eviction, sickness, starvation—such are the ever present spectres, while every year marks the steady encroachment of disease and the lowering of the register of vitality. Moreover, from the window of her soul falls the light of no star athwart the pathway of life. . . .

The making at home of clothing, cigars, etc., in New York and Brooklyn is paid at prices on which no women could live were there not other workers in the family. Some of their occupations involved great risks to girls, such as the loss of joints, of fingers, of the hand, or sometimes of the whole arm.

One of the official statisticians says upon this subject: "The tenement house system of work and the large influx of foreign immigration in New York City affected women workers more than any other class of laborers. The moral condition of the working women is influenced for evil by the tenement house home in a way too vast for discussion here. One noteworthy cause of immorality is the taking of men as lodgers for the sake of extra income. Another is the long distance girls are compelled to traverse after dark, especially on leaving stores which remain open till ten or eleven o'clock on Saturday night. Another is the working of friendless young women in the metropolis, where they live without home restraint, suffering every conceivable discomfort, subject to long periods of idleness, which they often enter upon with an empty purse. And yet, the truest heroism of life and conduct may be found here beneath rags and dirt. As far as ventilation is concerned, a regulated work-shop is the exception. The average room is either stuffy and close, or hot and close, and even where windows abound they are seldom opened. Toilet facilities are generally scant and inadequate, a hundred workers being dependent sometimes on a closet or sink, and that, too, often out of order."

There are many factories in the rooms of which from one hundred to two hundred women and men are packed like sardines in a box, with little or no ventilation, troubled by the inconveniences of steam, smoke, darkness, and all sorts of stenches intensified by heat. In many cases no provisions exist for escaping the danger of fire and other disasters. There are industries in which the rooms are constantly filled with dust, causing dangerous diseases of the organs of respiration. Rheumatism is caused by dampness in laundries, dyeing and meat packing establishments, canneries, etc. Rattling machinery has caused many women to become hard of hearing; excessive heat affects their entire system, and in food factories salt and spices give them asthma and bronchitis. Thousands of women who run sewing machines or are compelled to stand all day die of consumption and other diseases. The moral conditions of the shops vary with the nature of the occupation, the character of the foremen or forewomen, and the interest the proprietor takes in his employes. Wherever the sexes work together indiscriminately great laxity obtains, and in many an instance the employers openly declare that so long as their work is done they do not inquire or care how bad the girls may be.

Considering the cost of living, wages are little, if any, higher in New York than in other cities.

In some shops week workers are locked out for the half day if late, or docked for every minute of time lost, an extra fine being often added. Fining for bad work is general. The shop rules are stringent in most cases, and in certain industries wages are reduced by charges for machine rent, cotton, repairs, etc., to an extent not obtaining elsewhere. The seamstresses constitute the poorest class and a regular system of fraud is practiced upon these defenceless creatures. For instance: A standing advertisement is kept in the papers asking for girls to do tailor sewing. When one applies she is told that it will take her several weeks to learn, but that good wages will afterwards be paid. The girl accepts and goes to work, and after four or five weeks demands pay. Then she is told she is not satisfactory and cannot be employed. Thus many hundreds of poor girls not only give their labor for nothing but supply their own machines to the fraudulent factory, thereby saving the bosses a considerable outlay.

The boarding houses where working women are compelled to live have for the most part bare and filthy floors, broken or blackened window panes and rickety furniture. Meager meals of ill-selected and ill-cooked food, the sights, sounds and smells of the filthy surroundings—these constitute the home comforts provided by these cheap boarding and lodging houses. Two girls are sometimes crowded into a little hall chamber, carpetless and fireless; three, and even four share a larger room without comfort or convenience. The dining room is often the family kitchen, living room and laundry. The sleeping rooms are so cold in winter that failing utterly to keep warm until the hour for retiring, the girls are allured by the warmth and brightness of the dance houses and saloons, where they must of necessity, meet undesirable and unsafe acquaintances.

*   *   *   *   *

AT CHICAGO

In the latter part of the year 1891, a committee from a Chicago Trade and Labor Assembly, at the request of a body of striking cloakmakers, made an investigation of the condition of that class of workers in the city. They were accompanied by an officer of the City Health Department, the City Attorney and artists and reporters of the local press. They found that thirteen thousand persons were engaged in the manufacture of clothing in Chicago, over one-half of whom were females. In order to reduce the cost of production the firms engaged in the manufacture of clothing have adopted the European Sweating System, which is in brief, as follows: The material for garments is cut to size and shape and delivered by the large firms to individual contractors known as sweaters, who relieve the firm of all other care or expense, taking the goods to what are known as sweating dens, usually located in the poorest neighborhoods of the great city. These sweaters are employed by the most opulent firms. The committee visited a large number of these dens, nearly all of which were dwelling houses which served as living and sleeping rooms for the sweater's family and the employes. In one room ten feet by forty, they found thirty-nine young girls, twelve children between ten and twelve years of age, eleven men and the sweater and his wife. The room and all the surroundings were filthy in the extreme. The rates of wages were of course very low, and yet the fear of discharge rendered it impossible to obtain satisfactory information. The committee found two thousand one hundred children at work in these dismal places who were under age and employed in violation of existing laws against child labor. Sanitary laws were also overriden in all of these miserable abodes. We take the following from the report of the committee:

> The condition of the places visited was horrible. Overcrowding, long hours and low pay were the rule. Girls ten years old were found to be working ten and twelve hours a day for 80 cents per week. Ten girls were found, none over ten years old, who worked sixteen hours a day for from 75 cents to $1.20 per week. In a De Koven street den were found a half dozen men working eighteen hours a day for from $4 to $9 per week. At 168 Maxwell street were found ten men that worked sixteen hours a day each and received $6.50 to $9 per week. In the same place were six girls working from two to fourteen hours a day whose weekly pay averaged $3. One child was found in a house that worked for 75 cents per week. At 455 South Canal street a girl was found who declined to tell what she received fearing she would be discharged, and discharge meant starvation. At 69 Judd street the wages of the men were found to be from $5 to $9 per week, and one child there received $1 per week. The women worked fourteen hours a day. The product of this shop was sold to Marshall Field & Co. At 151 Peoria street, is a cloak-finishing establishment. Here the women receive one and one-half cents each for finishing cloaks. One woman was found on the street with a bundle of cloaks she had finished. She said that by hard work she finished twenty cloaks a day and earned thirty cents. This supported herself and two babies. The place 258 Division street was by far the worst visited. Eleven men worked

twelve hours a day and received $5 to $9.50 per week. Twelve children here worked twelve hours for 75 cents per week. The place was terribly crowded, there being no water or light.

And yet in the face of these glaring conditions, which are common in all of our populous cities, empty headed political charlatans still vex the public with their puerile rant about protection for American labor.

*   *   *   *   *

DIVES IN HIS PALACE

At the close of the year of our Lord 1891, while the Christian world was celebrating the lowly birth in the manger at Bethlehem, and while the wretched sweaters of Chicago were bending their aching backs in their dismal prisons, a wealthy merchant of the city moved into his resplendent mansion which had just been finished for his reception. He celebrated the event with a week of festivity. One of the local papers gave the following description of this palace:

> It is located on Michigan boulevard and Thirty-fourth street, and has been in the course of construction for nearly two years. Among its principal features is an immense ball-room, which includes a completely fitted stage, a complete barber shop, a music room, which is divided by Mexican onyx columns from a conservatory, and one of the finest private libraries in the country. On the floor of the drawing room is a large aubixon rug, woven in one piece, the cost of which alone was upwards of ten thousand dollars. The floor of the large reception room is of Italian marble mosaic, and one of its attractive features is an old moorish fireplace. The dining room walls are finished in old tapestry of almost fabulous value. The bath rooms are white marble and onyx, the main one having an onyx wainscoting five feet in height, and above this a frescoing of pond lily design.

There are study rooms for the youthful members of the family, while the apartments that have been reserved for guests would almost compare with the descriptions that have been handed down of portions of the interior of Solomon's temple.

* * * * *

AND HAS IT COME TO US SO SOON

About the close of the recent Jackson Park World's Fair strike, we clipped from the columns of one of the Chicago dailies the following local editorial. Speaking of the poor strikers the paper said:

The outlook discouraged them. None had any great supply of money and few had places to sleep. The outlook was altogether discouraging, and was made even more so by the action of the police, who broke up the picket lines as fast as they were formed, and even refused to allow them to congregate in any numbers.

About 9 o'clock in the morning a hundred or so weary strikers were stretched in the sun on the prairie near Parkside endeavoring to get some sleep, when word was passed for a meeting at Sixty-seventh street and Stony Island avenue. By 9:30 o'clock two hundred men had congregated there and Dr. Willoughby, the owner of the lot, objected. He notified the police that he did not want any trespassing on his premises, and Lieut. Rehm and a squad of ten officers were dispatched to the scene. He ordered the strikers to disperse, but they failed to obey with alacrity, and the police had to drive them off. There was some slight resistance, and several heads suffered in consequence from contact with policemen's batons.

We trust the brief pages of this chapter may suffice to call the attention of the reader to the ghastly condition of American society and to remind him of the imperative call which is made upon him as an individual to do all in his power to arrest the alarming tendencies of our times. In the opinion of the writer, unless the people of America shall immediately take political matters into their own hands, the contrasts suggested in this chapter portend a tragic future. The millionaire and the pauper cannot, in this country, long dwell together in peace, and it is idle to attempt to patch up a truce between them. Enlightened self respect and a quickened sense of justice are impelling the multitude to demand an interpretation of the anomalous spectacle, constantly presented before their eyes, of a world filled with plenty and yet multitudes of people suffering for all that goes to make life desirable. They are calling to know why idleness should dwell in luxury and those who toil in want; and they are inquiring why one-half of God's children should be deprived of homes upon a planet which is large enough for all. The world will find a solution for these insufferable afflictions in the glorious era but just ahead. Even now the twilight discloses the outlines of a generous inheritance for all and we hear the chirping of sweet birds making ready to welcome with melody and gladness the advent of the full orbed day.

DOCUMENT 17.3
The Road to Business Success

Andrew Carnegie (1835–1919) was not only the nation's most articulate spokesman of the cult of success and the ideas of which it was composed; he was himself the very epitome of that cult. In innumerable articles, and in such books as Triumphant Democracy *and* The Gospel of Wealth, *he held up the image of the self-made man and set forth the social*

Source: Andrew Carnegie, "The Road to Business Success," an address to the students of Curry Commercial College, Pittsburgh, June 23, 1885, in *The Empire of Business* (New York: Doubleday, Page & Co., 1902), pp. 3–18.

philosophy of a society built upon competition and emulation.

It is well that young men should begin at the beginning and occupy the most subordinate positions. Many of the leading businessmen of Pittsburgh had a serious responsibility thrust upon them at the very threshold of their career. They were introduced to the broom, and spent the first hours of their business lives sweeping out the office. I notice we have janitors and janitresses now in offices, and our young men unfortunately miss that salutary branch of a business education. But if by chance the professional sweeper is absent any morning, the boy who has the genius of the future partner in him will not hesitate to try his hand at the broom. The other day a fond fashionable mother in Michigan asked a young man whether he had ever seen a young lady sweep in a room so grandly as her Priscilla. He said no, he never had, and the mother was gratified beyond measure, but then said he, after a pause, "What I should like to see her do is sweep out a room." It does not hurt the newest comer to sweep out the office if necessary. I was one of those sweepers myself, and who do you suppose were my fellow sweepers? David McCargo, now superintendent of the Alleghany Valley Railroad; Robert Pitcairn, superintendent of the Pennsylvania Railroad, and Mr. Moreland, City Attorney. We all took turns, two each morning did the sweeping; and now I remember Davie was so proud of his clean white shirt bosom that he used to spread over it an old silk bandana hankerchief which he kept for the purpose, and we other boys thought he was putting on airs. So he was. None of us had a silk handkerchief.

Assuming that you have all obtained employment and are fairly started, my advice to you is "aim high." I would not give a fig for the young man who does not already see himself the partner or the head of an important firm. Do not rest content for a moment in your thoughts as head clerk, or foreman, or general manager in any concern, no matter how extensive. Say to yourself, "My place is at the top." *Be king in your dreams. . . .*

And here is the prime condition of success, the great secret: concentrate your energy, thought, and capital exclusively upon the business in which you are engaged. Having begun in one line, resolve to fight it out on that line, to lead in it, adopt every improvement, have the best machinery, and know the most about it.

The concerns which fail are those which have scattered their capital, which means that they have scattered their brains also. They have investments in this, or that, or the other, here, there, and everywhere. "Don't put all your eggs in one basket" is all wrong. I tell you "put all your eggs in one basket, and then watch that basket." Look around you and take notice; men who do that do not often fail. It is easy to watch and carry the one basket. It is trying to carry too many baskets that breaks most eggs in this country. He who carries three baskets must put one on his head, which is apt to tumble and trip him up. One fault of the American business man is lack of concentration.

To summarize what I have said: Aim for the highest; never enter a barroom; do not touch liquor, or if at all only at meals; never speculate; never indorse beyond your surplus cash fund; make the firm's interest yours; break orders always to save owners; concentrate; put all your eggs in one basket, and watch that basket; expenditure always within revenue; lastly, be not impatient, for, as Emerson says, "no one can cheat you out of ultimate success but yourselves."

I congratulate poor young men upon being born to that ancient and honourable degree which renders it necessary that they should devote themselves to hard work. A basketful of bonds is the heaviest basket a young man ever had to carry. He generally gets to staggering under it. We have in this city creditable instances of such young men, who have pressed to the front rank of our best and most useful citizens. These deserve great credit. But the vast majority of the sons of rich men are unable to resist the temptations to which wealth subjects them, and sink to unworthy lives. I would almost as soon leave a young man a curse, as burden him with the almighty dollar. It is not from this class you have rivalry to fear. The partner's sons will not trouble you much, but look out that some boys poorer, much poorer than yourselves, whose parents cannot afford to give them the advantages of a course in this institute, advantages which should give you a decided lead in the race—look out that such boys do not challenge you at the post and pass you at the grand stand. Look out for the boy who has to plunge into work direct from the common school and who begins by sweeping out the office. He is the probable dark horse that you had better watch.

DOCUMENT 17.4
Poor Little Stephen Girard

The young men who listened to Carnegie and believed him did not all become presidents of their companies as a result, but no doubt most of them were encouraged to work harder. But what would have been the effect on behavior, especially on labor discipline, of those who listened to the cynical Mark Twain?

The man lived in Philadelphia who, when young and poor, entered a bank, and says he: "Please, sir, don't you want a boy?" And the stately personage said: "No, little boy, I don't want a little boy." The little boy, whose

---

Source: Mark Twain, "Poor Little Stephen Girard," in Anna Randall-Diehl, ed., *Carleton's Popular Readings* (New York, 1879), pp. 183–84.

heart was too full for utterance, chewing a piece of licorice stick he had bought with a cent stolen from his good and pious aunt, with sobs plainly audible, and with great globules of water rolling down his cheeks, glided silently down the marble steps of the bank. Bending his noble form, the bank man dodged behind a door, for he thought the little boy was going to shy a stone at him. But the little boy picked up something, and stuck it in his poor but ragged jacket. "Come here, little boy," and the little boy did come here; and the bank man said: "Lo, what pickest thou up?" And he answered and replied: "A pin." And the bank man said: "Little boy, are you good?" and he said he was. And the bank man said: "How do you vote?—excuse me, do you go to Sunday school?" and he said he did. Then the bank man took down a pen made of pure gold, and flowing with pure ink, and he wrote on a piece of paper, "St. Peter"; and he asked the little boy what it stood for, and he said "Salt Peter." Then the bankman said it meant "Saint Peter." The little boy said: "Oh!"

Then the bank man took the little boy to his bosom, and the little boy said, "Oh!" again, for he squeezed him. Then the bank man took the little boy into partnership, and gave him half the profits and all the capital, and he married the bank man's daughter, and now all he has is all his, and all his own too.

My uncle told me this story, and I spent six weeks in picking up pins in front of a bank. I expected the bank man would call me in and say: "Little boy, are you good?" and I was going to say "Yes"; and when he asked me what "St. John" stood for, I was going to say "Salt John." But the bank man wasn't anxious to have a partner, and I guess the daughter was a son, for one day says he to me: "Little boy, what's that you're picking up?" Says I, awful meekly, "Pins." Says he: "Let's see 'em." And he took 'em, and I took off my cap, all ready to go in the bank, and become a partner, and marry his daughter. But

I didn't get an invitation. He said: "Those pins belong to the bank, and if I catch you hanging around here any more I'll set the dog on you!" Then I left, and the mean old fellow kept the pins. Such is life as I find it.

DOCUMENT 17.5
The Science of Railways: Organization and Forces

An important element in the kind of social discipline sought by American owners and managers at the end of the nineteenth century was the cultivation of the "proper" attitude toward corporate executives. Here one of their spokesmen discusses how to maintain efficiency and order within the railroad, and sets forth one of the roles of the executive.

Subordination is a cardinal principle of organized labor—subordination to the employer, subordination to each other according to rank and natural precedence. It is based upon a just conception of the rights of men in their relation to property. All men, however, are entitled to justice and humane treatment.

The discipline of corporate forces is as absolute as that of a man of war. Obedience to superior authority is unqualified. It is, however, the privilege and duty of every subordinate in emergencies, when an order is given, to make such suggestions as the circumstances of the case demand. Here his responsibility ends, except in criminal cases.

An order once given, must be obeyed. Absolutism such as this involves grave responsibilities. It presupposes skill, accurate knowledge and appreciation.

In the administrative department of carriers

lack of discipline breeds insubordination, idleness and extravagance. It engenders kindred evils in the operating department, with the added element of danger.

It is necessary that the forces of a railroad should possess *esprit de corps,* coupled with interest, intelligence and courage that no event can deaden or divert.

While the discipline of corporate life is as absolute as that of an army, there is this difference between them: army life destroys the individuality of all below the rank of officer; corporate life intensifies the personality of subordinates by recognition and promotion. Everyone knows that promotion will follow intelligence, faithfulness and industry. The officers of railroads are drawn from the ranks. It is therefore for the interests of such corporations to build up the intelligence and morale of subordinates; to strengthen the force by careful selection and cultivation. Individuals should be taught to think and act for themselves in all cases where discretion can safely be allowed. They will thus be taught self reliance, and the exercise of prudence and good judgment. . . .

In general, that form of organization is best for corporate property that enforces the most minute responsibility and offers the greatest encouragement to those who work for it; that enables a company to know the measure of faithfulness and capacity of its servants; that rewards the trustworthy and takes cognizance of the derelict. . . .

It is probable that many labor associations have, at the bottom, a belief that the employer does not properly regard the interests of his employe. This belief is false. But in order to dispel it and in doing so break up such combinations as are subversive of the employe's interest, railways must actively interest themselves in the concerns of those who work for them. Their interests are jeopardized, not because they have been disregardful but because their employes believed they have. This erroneous

Source: Marshall M. Kirkman, *The Science of Railways: Organization and Forces* (5th ed.; New York and Chicago: World Railway Publishing Co., 1896), vol. 1, pp. 69–70, 170–75.

impression the owner must correct if he would not have foreign and unfriendly agents meddling in his affairs. There are two ways in which corporations may and do manifest their interest in those who work for them. In America it is done by kindly treatment, the payment of high wages, continued service, promotion, and by making the employe self reliant and independent. In many countries wages are unavoidably low, and so corporations eke out their efforts by small annuities and distress funds, and by special interest in the sicknesses, discomforts and forebodings of those who work for them.

The vicissitudes of corporate service require a paternal form of government. The owner must be the father. Failure to recognize this will aggravate the growth of unfriendly labor associations. . . .

In general, employes are safer in the hands of the employer than in those of anyone else. His interest is permanent, material and fatherly.

The conception of the employer by those who work for him must be broad and charitable.

Nothing is attainable without this. Employes must not be quick to believe they are treated unjustly, are overlooked or forgotten. They must be governed by reason. They must accept the conditions of life as they are. They must go ahead sturdily and cheerfully, believing that if they comprehend their business and are active in the discharge of it, their services will be recognized. They must also appreciate this truth, that those who are preferred are, on the whole, worthy of it. That while there are exceptions to the rule, they are unworthy of regard. Disappointed men, instead of repining, must seek by renewed zeal and attachment the recognition they desire. They must not seek, in such emergencies, through combinations, or otherwise, to force what they cannot peaceably attain. . . .

Unflagging industry and continual study is the only road to preferment. All others are makeshift, temporary and incomplete. When men do not progress as fast as they think they should, let them work and study the harder; do more and better work. There is no other road to preferment. . . .

chapter

Labor's Response to Modern Industrialism

Herbert G. Gutman
The Graduate Center, City University of New York

The United States industrialized between 1840 and 1900. Although the process was slow and uneven, industrialism, once started, proved irrevocable and appeared irresistible. All aspects of human experience felt its consequences: where people worked, the tools they used, how they traveled, what they ate and wore, their leisure habits, their thoughts about themselves and the world in which they lived, and the pace of life itself. In many ways the industrialization of a modern nation is the most significant set of social and economic changes affecting a people—and perhaps the most difficult to analyze. Compare the problem of evaluating the impact of industrialization upon a people with, let us say, the successes of John Adams as a diplomat or Andrew Jackson's motives in attacking the second Bank of the United States, or, better still, the causes of the Mexican War. Once done, the relative difficulty of appraising the effect of industrial development and the responses to it become self-evident. The *process* of industrialization extends over a greater length of time and has many more indirect consequences than the influence of a single great leader or of particular events surrounding a momentary political and diplomatic crisis. For this reason, among others, analysis

of the industrial process and the responses to it is important. Our own United States, after all, has as its central quality the fact that it is an industrial nation.

Industrialization meant many things to nineteenth century Americans: the process by which investment capital poured into the building of new railroads and factories as well as into the development of mines; the widespread application of new sources of nonanimal power to the productive process; the application of new machinery to agriculture in an effort to increase productivity; the introduction of new systems of mechanized production. And it meant more, too. Industrialization also accelerated the movement of people from farm to city. Centers of trade, manufacturing, and commerce grew rapidly, as did a laboring population dependent on others for work and income.

Part of the industrial process is revealed in the simple reporting of elementary statistical trends and the wondrous fashion in which contemporaries viewed such data. A few examples suffice. The number of Cincinnati workers engaged in manufacturing increased from 9,040 in 1840 to 58,508 in 1872. In the latter year, 350,000 wage earners lived in New York City, and more than 200,000 crowded into Philadel-

37

phia. Pittsburgh, center of the iron and steel industry, impressed one contemporary as a city "like 'hell with the lid taken off.' The entire landscape seems ablaze. . . . The factories are so continuous on the various streets that if placed in a . . . row they would reach thirty-five miles." Steam-propelled machinery became increasingly important. In 1870, 2,346,142 horsepower was used in manufacturing; thirty years later the figure stood at 11,300,081. Coal production soared from 14,610,042 tons in 1860 to 513,525,477 tons in 1914. "One horse power," a prominent Philadelphia manufacturer declared in 1872, "equals the labor-power of ten able-bodied men. . . . This is wealth—embodied wealth in its most advanced form. . . . Human labor is economized; the ingenuity of man has devised labor-saving machinery by which vast economies are affected, and none need labor sixteen hours a day. . . ." Industrial production rose spectacularly, and four industries led the way: iron and steel and allied manufactures, food and kindred processed goods, textiles, and lumber and its finished products. In 1890, for the first time, the value of manufactured products exceeded that of agricultural goods; ten years later, it had doubled. No less a personage than Horace Greeley paid glowing tribute to this industrial progress. Together with Albert Brisbane and others, he penned a 1,300-page paean in 1872 entitled *The Great Industries of the United States*. Characterizing leading inventors and manufacturers as men who led the people "out of the plodding ways which the feudal age . . . imposed upon the race," Greeley and his associates cheerfully concluded: "Though prompted in the main by the spirit of self-aggrandizement, these men have proved themselves the chief philanthropists of the time and have borne the standard of progress. . . ."

Yet the industrial process cannot be measured simply by statistics indicating economic growth. Industrialism also meant a new way

of life for whole sectors of the population. In 1859 the nation counted 1,311,346 wage earners. By 1914, more than seven million persons depended on wages for income. In these years, and even earlier, the skilled craftsmen declined in importance, and the factory worker replaced him as the symbol of the new industrial order. The commissioners of the Massachusetts Bureau of Labor Statistics admitted the importance of economic growth in the early postbellum years; but significantly, they asked if it was "logical to reason" that the building of a railroad, itself a sign of unquestioned progress, meant that "the laborers who excavate . . . the grade . . . , dig the ore . . . , and cast the rails" automatically were "prosperous and growing rich."

A critical aspect of the industrial process is its effect on the standard of comfort. But even more is involved, for much of the history of industrialization between 1840 and 1900 is the story of the painful process by which an old way of life gave over to a new one. And in this context the central issue was the rejection or modification of traditional sets of "rules" and "commands" that no longer fit the more modern industrial context. What did it mean to work in a factory for the first time after one was used to the routine of a small shop or, better still, of agricultural life? How could an employer, himself uneasy in his new position of power, impose discipline on persons unaccustomed to the demands of factory labor? What did unemployment mean to persons entirely dependent for the first time on others for income with which to purchase necessities? Although he spoke in language peculiar to nineteenth-century America, Carroll D. Wright, the first commissioner of labor for the United States, put it well in 1878:

> The divine economy takes neither the old machine nor the discarded operator of it into account, but puts in the place of one a more perfect piece of mechanism, and in the place of the other an intellect of a much higher

order, and contemplates the general results to humanity, and not the loss to the individual. . . . An examination, carried in any direction, demonstrates the proposition that all progress, every step in advance, is over apparent destruction, and, like every pioneer who has startled the world by his discoveries, and by them benefited his kind, is over the graves of men.

Stripped to its essence, Wright's words capsuled a central dilemma inherent in the industrial process: The new social order, serviced by steam and coal and rails, and centering around the factory and the mine, exacted a heavy price from those who surrendered an earlier and less complex way of life. The craftsman's pride in his work lost its meaning as he was overwhelmed by specialization and the machine. The New York Wood Carvers' Union, for example, complained that "unlimited competition" meant lower prices and forced the manufacturer to seek cheaper productive methods. "Ingenious machinery has then to be used to such a degree that skilled workingmen . . . become superfluous. All mechanics become *factory workmen* and [all] production *machine work*. There is no escape from that." Similarly, a cigar maker complained of the revolutionary effects of the cigar mold on his craft: "The mode by which most segars . . . are produced to-day is so divided that skilled labor is no longer required. The inventive genius has superseeded [*sic*] skill. . . ."

The growing importance of unskilled and semiskilled labor also altered the status of women and children. Always useful on the farm, they proved equally valuable in the factory. New England's early cotton mills illustrated this development. But it was intensified by the ethos of the entire period—by the emphasis placed on investment capital and cheap production. The Massachusetts Bureau of Labor Statistics found that factory labor proved that a woman could operate machinery and perform manual labor out of her home. Not surprisingly,

one of every three factory workers in Philadelphia in 1870 was a woman. Child labor also increased in these years. Horace Greeley and his associates insisted that "the pride of the nation is in its children, and in none so much as in those who pre-eminently distinguish themselves in the arts of peace—domestic manufacturing. . . ." A New York daily advised its readers that "a bright twelve year old girl" easily could be "taught to make a cap in four weeks." And so it went. In addition to a new status for skilled craftsmen in the bustling factories, there was a new kind of labor for women and children who worked to supplement the meager wages of unskilled fathers.

New conditions of work and life tell much about the impact of the industrial order upon the wage earner, but his response to these conditions is an equally important part of the story. At times the wage earner was passive. Was his silence the result of satisfaction? Or was protest made difficult by the very conditions of the new industrial order? At other times the wage earner protested. Bitter strikes and lockouts—most usually caused by the demand for labor organization or for better wages, hours, and working conditions—characterized innumerable industrial disputes. The violence that accompanied the great railroad strikes in 1877 and the bitterness on all sides during the Homestead strike and the Pullman boycott in the 1890s were outstanding illustrations, but there were countless unrecorded and lesser disputes between workers and employers between 1840 and 1900. What explained the bitterness of industrial conflict at that time? Were skilled workers more discontented than unskilled? Were immigrant workers more satisfied than native-born laborers? Did the violence in the United States during its prime years of industrialization, as some historians argue, far exceed that of any European nation? How does one account for such bitterness and violence?

One clue to the answer of these questions about the social behavior of wage earners rests in understanding just *who* the workers were, *what* they did *before* they entered the factory, and the values and attitudes they carried with them into the new industrial order and used to interpret it. In general, four kinds of persons became wage earners in the United States between 1840 and 1900. Two of them already were accustomed to urban experience but knew little of factory life. One consisted of the urban skilled craftsmen, who surrendered independence and skill to the factory and the machine. Unskilled urban day laborers, so numerous in preindustrial cities, made up the other. Rural Americans, most often sons and daughters of farmers—familiar at best with the small town—were a third important element drawn to the industrial city by the dynamism of shop and factory. The fourth group—the foreign-born—came mostly from Europe and, to a much lesser extent, from the Orient. Immigrants, largely from Ireland, Germany, Great Britain, and the Scandinavian countries, totaled about one third of all the workers in the mining, mechanical, and manufacturing industries in the late nineteenth century. Furthermore, an increasing number of newcomers were pouring in from Southern and Eastern Europe. British immigrants excepted, few of the foreign-born brought industrial experience with them to the United States.

How did each of these groups react to the industrial order in America? Persons sensitive to the process *and* the problems of social change most often view the former in one of two ways. They compare the present with the past and judge what is becoming by what has been. Or they criticize the present by comparing it to a utopian order that lies in the future. Several problems of analysis emerge. Did those workers who questioned the direction of the industrial order use the past or the future as their point of reference? If they judged primarily by past experience, did they tend to romanticize it? If the future served as the point of reference,

what ideal of social reconstruction most appealed to what group: cooperatives, socialism, abolition of the "wages system," or simple trade unions that sought through organization to improve living conditions without changing the structure of the new order?

Whatever their point of reference or particular criticism, wage earners who questioned the industrial order often shared a general revulsion against the quality of *dependence* that characterized the new way of life. Each element had its own reasons for resenting dependence. With high expectations, the immigrant came in search of opportunity, which he viewed as the fulfillment of the dream of independent ownership and self-sufficiency. The urban skilled worker, on the other hand, witnessed a genuine decline in his status and self-image. Native-born persons who entered the labor force experienced a *new* quality of dependence for the first time. What did the factory mean to the son of a farmer who moved from a western New York farm to work in a Cleveland iron mill or oil refinery? How did a person accustomed to the rigors and simplicity of a small New England or Pennsylvania town react to the regimen imposed by a Fall River textile mill or a Pittsburgh coal mine? And how did the native-born worker, a citizen *before* he became a worker and in this sense unique in the nineteenth-century world, react to his new dependent status?

Before the coming of industrialism, the American dream (or ideal) had abjured a dependent status. In the early years of the Republic, Thomas Jefferson warned: "Dependence begets subservience and venality, suffocates the germ of virtue, and prepares fit tools for the designs of ambition." Years later, Abraham Lincoln, shortly before winning the nomination as candidate for the presidency on the Republican ticket, asserted the ideal in positive terms. During a strike of shoe workers, Lincoln spoke in New Haven, Connecticut:

. . . What is the true condition of the laborer? I take it that it is best for all to leave each man free to acquire property as fast as he can. Some will get wealth. I don't believe in a law to prevent a man from getting rich; it would do more harm than good. So while we do not propose any war upon capital, we do wish to allow the humblest man an equal chance to get rich with everybody else. When one starts poor, as most do in the race of life, free society is such that he knows he can better his condition; he knows that there is no fixed condition of labor, for his whole life. . . . I want every man to have a chance . . . in which he *can* better his condition—when he may look forward and hope to be a hired laborer this year and the next, work for himself afterward, and finally hire men to work for him! That is the true system. . . .

Here, then, was the dream—independence, self-sufficiency, and upward mobility based largely on merit and personal talent.

The industrial way of life tested this ideal in many ways. It is instructive to compare Lincoln's statement with that of Terence V. Powderly less than three decades later. In his memoir, *Thirty Years of Labor,* this head of the Knights of Labor eloquently lamented the passing of the old order. He described the new obstacles to the old ideal and revealed a characteristic response to dependent status:

. . . With the introduction of machinery, large manufacturing establishments were erected in the cities and towns. . . . The village blacksmith shop was abandoned, the road-side shoe shop was deserted, the tailor left his bench, and all together these mechanics turned away from their country homes and wended their way to the cities wherein the large factories had been erected. . . . They no longer carried the keys of the workshop, for workshop, tools, and keys belonged not to them, but to their master. . . . Competition between man and man is healthy to both, but competition between man and the machine is injurious to the former. He who offered to sell his labor after the introduction of machinery, could not hope to compete with a fellowman in the work he proposed to do; he was forced to compete with a machine, or a whole row of machines, being managed by boys or girls who worked for inadequate wages. . . . Beneath the shadow of machinery, merit went for naught so far as man's natural ability to perform labor was concerned.

In this light, can one argue that the individualist and "entrepreneurial" tradition, which encouraged rapid capital accumulation and, at times, a ruthless insensitivity to others, also shaped the embittered response of workers to the condition of dependence?

Response to dependence took many forms. Often, it was little more than a lament. In other instances it was sheer anger and frustration. At times it revealed a deep sense of betrayal. Some workers sought only a means of escape from city and factory. Others were aggrieved that an ostensibly democratic government should support only one group, the new industrial capitalists, or merely stand by and watch the "natural laws" of social development unfold. Still others questioned the morality and ethics of the new era. And finally, some argued that dependence best could be overcome by self-organization among the wage earners. Here, too, many problems for analysis arise. In these years, unions collapsed almost as quickly as they came into being. E. L. Godkin, editor of the *Nation,* insisted in 1868 that "the trades-unions . . . have, in reality, put the laborer and the capitalist for the first time on equal terms, economically considered." Unions, Godkin explained, "have rendered, and are rendering, to the working classes, one essential service—by enabling them, for the first time in their history, to contract with masters as free agents and on equal terms." Was it the rapid growth of the economy? Was it the changing composition of the labor force? Was it the attitude of employers and their power, supported by a sympathetic government? Or was it the very dream itself of independent proprietorship?

SUGGESTED READINGS

Bruce, Robert V. *1877: Year of Violence.* Indianapolis: Bobbs-Merrill, 1959.

Commons, John R., and Associates. *History of Labour in the United States.* 4 vols. New York: Macmillan, 1918–35.

Cooper, Patricia. *Men, Women, and Work Culture in American Cigar Factories, 1900–1919.* Urbana: University of Illinois Press, 1987.

Cumbler, John. *Working Class Community in Industrial America.* Westport, Conn.: Greenwood Press, 1979.

David, Henry. *The History of the Haymarket Affair.* New York: Russell & Russell, 1958.

Dawley, Alan. *Class and Community.* Cambridge, Mass.: Harvard University Press, 1976.

Faler, Paul. *Mechanics and Manufacturers in the Early Industrial Revolution.* Albany, N.Y.: State University of New York Press, 1981.

Foner, Philip S. *History of the Labor Movement in the United States.* 2 vols. New York: International Publishers, Inc., 1947–55.

Grob, Gerald N. *Workers and Utopia: A Study of Ideological Conflict in the American Labor Movement, 1865–1900.* Evanston, Ill.: Northwestern University Press, 1961.

Gutman, Herbert G. *Work, Culture and Society.* New York: Alfred A. Knopf, 1976.

Hirsch, Susan E. *Roots of the American Workingclass.* Philadelphia: University of Pennsylvania Press, 1978.

Laslett, John P. *Labor and the Left: A Study of Socialist and Radical Influences in the American Labor Movement, 1881–1924.* New York: Basic Books, 1970.

Montgomery, David. *Beyond Equality. Labor and the Radical Republicans, 1862–1872.* New York: Alfred A. Knopf, 1967.

Taft, Philip. *The A. F. of L. in the Time of Gompers.* New York: Harper & Row, 1957.

Thernstrom, Stephan. *Poverty and Progress: Social Mobility in a Nineteenth Century City.* Cambridge, Mass.: Harvard University Press, 1964.

Van Tine, Warren, *The Making of the American Labor Bureaucrat.* Amherst: University of Massachusetts Press, 1973.

Walkowitz, Daniel. *Worker City, Company Town.* Urbana: University of Illinois Press, 1978.

Ware, Norman J. *The Industrial Worker, 1840–1860.* Gloucester, Mass.: Peter Smith, 1958.

DOCUMENT 18.1
The Passing of the Old Order and the Recognition of Dependence

Soon after the Civil War ended, the Massachusetts Bureau of Labor Statistics compiled data and drew conclusions about the transition from a craft-oriented to a factory-dominated economy.

THE MACHINE

Skill, once the strong defence of the artisan, is now trembling in the balance, today of value, to-morrow of none, rapidly retiring, with its apprenticed pupils before the advance of machinery. In fact, it is about conquered. Men of skill in trades which it was never supposed invention would reach, have been compelled to enlist into the service of machinery, or turned adrift to learn new trades, or gone to swell the ranks of unskilled laborers—nothing save the increased demand for articles manufactured, coming in to their rescue. . . . As the machine is the embodiment of skill, there is small need of skill on the part of the machine-tender. He is transformed from an adept to

---

Source: Massachusetts Bureau of Labor Statistics, *Annual Report, 1872* (Boston, 1873), pp. 341–42.

be the servant of automatic apparatus, and the subdivision of labor renders this service simple and easily acquired. But few trades remain, in all departments of which a man can become an adept, and wherein he has opportunity to exercise his constructive faculties, for he knows that the machinery he tends will adjust its work with the needed precision. He needs neither to calculate nor to make allowance; his principal function is "to feed the thing he tends," and if properly fed, the machine works up its food and digests it to the expected result, with unfailing certainty.

Charles Litchman's father manufactured shoes. For six years Litchman worked as a salesman for his father. Between 1870 and 1874, he owned his own shoe factory. He then studied law, worked "at the bench" in a shoe factory, and became Grand Servitor of the Knights of St. Crispin, a labor union of shoe workers. In November 1879 he testified before a congressional committee investigating labor conditions.

SPECIALIZATION

Mr. Litchman: . . . The first effect of the introduction of labor-saving machinery is the degradation of the labor.

The Chairman: How so?

Mr. Litchman: By the sub-division of labor a man now is no longer a tradesman. He is part of a tradesman. In my own trade of shoemaking, twenty years ago the work was done almost entirely by hand, and the man had to learn how to make a shoe. Now with the use

Source: "Testimony of Charles H. Litchman," *Causes of the General Depression in Labor and Business*, Investigated by a Select Committee of the House of Representatives, 46th Cong., 2d sess., Misc. House Doc. No. 5 (Washington, D.C.: U.S. Government Printing Office, 1879), pp. 422–33.

of machines of almost superhuman ingenuity, a man is no longer a shoemaker, but only the sixty-fourth part of a shoemaker, because there are sixty-four sub-divisions in making shoes; and a man may work forty years at our trade and at the end of forty years he will know no more about making a whole shoe than when he commenced business.

The Chairman: He would only know how to make a peg or a waxed end?

Mr. Litchman: Yes; or he would be a laster, or a beveler, or heeler, or nailer, or he would be running and using a machine, or a peg-measure, or attending to any one of the sixty-four sub-divisions into which the trade is parceled out. . . . You cannot turn back the hands upon the dial of human progress and say that all machinery must be banished. You would not take up the rails, destroy the locomotive, and break up the railroad cars, and go back to stage-coaches and horses. . . . Yet all these improvements, while in the abstract they benefit mankind, have as their first result the degradation of labor by the sub-division of labor. Under our present wage-labor system, capital gets the whole advantage of the introduction of [the] human brain into human labor.

*   *   *   *   *

The Chairman: How many of [the] 48,000 [Massachusetts] shoemakers can make a shoe?

Mr. Litchman: I have no means of knowing, but I would venture to assert that not one-tenth of them can make a shoe, and the shoe that they could make would be the old kind of a turned shoe. I cannot make a machine shoe. My sixty-fourth part of making shoes is standing at the bench and cutting the uppers.

*   *   *   *   *

The Chairman: Does this rule which you have applied to the manufacturing of shoes apply to all other branches of manufacturing industry?

Mr. Litchman: It does substantially. I have no hesitation in saying that. It applies to every trade, not even excepting stone cutting. . . .

DOCUMENT 18.2
The Condition of Dependence: Unemployment

Unemployment at different times resulted from technological change, seasonal patterns of work, and cyclical fluctuations.

SEASONAL WORK[1]

. . . Since the old system of working in little shops was abandoned for that of large manufactories, there has been a steady diminution in the length of the working season per year. Before the time of factories, there would be a steady run of employment for from seven to ten years, only interrupted by commercial depressions or revulsions. The working hours would be from twelve to fifteen. The season for lighting up was from September 20 to May 20. Since that time, there has never been a year of steady work. At first a month only would be lost; now it has got so that we lose over four months' time every year. The system is worse here than elsewhere because machinery has been thoroughly introduced.

In January 1874, the Federal Council of the International Workingmen's Association urged Congressman Benjamin Butler to support a bill that would "provide for all citizens who desire to settle on the public lands with transportation for themselves and families, and also lumber,

seed, tools, food and all other necessaries for their establishment as farmers on the public lands for the term of one year, cost of same . . . to be a mortgage on their farm." When this petition appeared in the New York Sun, *Emanuel Richards supported it.*

CYCLICAL UNEMPLOYMENT[2]

Sir: The petition . . . to the Government to settle the poor on public lands . . . [is] what I have long desired and hoped for. I am a good mechanic with a family of seven children. I have no work and no hope of anything better for myself than a life of dependence, crime, or hard hand-to-mouth labor. I would like to take my children out of the city. I can till the ground. I hope you will be in this . . . the friend of the people, and help us to an independent, useful life on the great prairies of the West.

DOCUMENT 18.3
The Condition of Dependence: Work Contracts

Located in Johnstown, Pennsylvania, the Cambria Iron Works, according to The New York Times, *included four modern blast furnaces, forty-two double-turn puddling furnaces, and more than 5,000 workers. In April 1874, after a bitter dispute with its coal miners, the Cambria managers introduced a new contract, and the trade journal* Iron Age *admonished "every employer in the country . . . [to] adopt the same policy as that adopted by the Cambria Company" and end "this whole wretched business of trade union tyranny."*

---

[1] Source: Massachusetts Bureau of Labor Statistics, "Testimony of Unidentified Worker," *Annual Report, 1870–1871* (Boston, 1871), pp. 242–43.

---

[2] Source: Emanuel Richards to the editor, *New York Sun,* January 15, 1874.

RULES ADOPTED BY THE CAMBRIA IRON WORKS, APRIL 6, 1874

* * * * *

9. Any person or persons known to belong to any secret association or open combination whose aim is to control wages or stop the works, or any part thereof, shall be promptly and finally discharged. Persons not satisfied with their work or their wages can leave honorably by giving the required notice; and persons quitting work, or inducing, or attempting to induce others to quit work other than in the manner prescribed in these rules and regulations, shall forfeit whatever may be due or owing to such person or persons absolutely.

10. Any person going to work intoxicated, or absenting himself from work, without having previously given notice and obtained leave, will be discharged or fined, at the option of the company. Any person failing to do his work in a proper manner, or failing to do a satisfactory amount, may expect to be dismissed whenever it may suit the convenience of the company.

11. Quarreling or rioting about the works, or on the company's premises, shall be punished by a fine of not less than $5 nor more than $10, or the discharge of the offender, who may also be prosecuted for violation of the law.

12. All money collected as fines and penalties will be set apart and reserved for those workers injured by accident.

* * * * *

14. Persons detected in stealing coal will be charged the price of a load of coal for every lump stolen . . . and for a repetition of the offense will be discharged.

15. Persons living in the company's houses will be charged for all damages done to the houses beyond the ordinary wear and tear, and will be compelled to leave at once upon ceasing to be employed by the company. In renting the houses, preference will always be given to those whose business requires them to live near the works.

* * * * *

19. In hiring, promoting, and discharging workmen, superintendents and foremen must regard only the interest of the company and the merits of employees.

P. Lorillard & Company, the largest tobacco manufacturer in the country, had its works in Jersey City, New Jersey, and employed nearly 4,000 men, women, and children, including large numbers of recent immigrants, in the manufacture of smoking tobacco, chewing tobacco, and snuff. In 1880, it offered these workers a new contract.

A TOBACCO FACTORY, 1880

I, the undersigned, in consideration of employment being furnished to me and wages agreed to be paid me, by the firm of P. Lorrilard & Co., do hereby agree and covenant with the said firm, its survivors, successors and assigns, to allow the said firm, or its proper agent or agents for the purpose appointed, to search and examine my person, clothing or other personal effects and property, at any and all times while I am upon the premises of said firm, or while leaving the said premises; and also to allow the said firm, or its proper agents, to enter and search my house or place of abode, without suit, let, hinderance, or molestation, with a view to detect and ascertain whether I have taken or secreted any of the goods, wares, tools or any other property of the said firm; and law, custom, or enactment to the contrary

Source: "Rules Adopted by the Cambria Iron Works, April 6, 1874," printed in *Iron Age*, December 31, 1874.

Source: Contract enclosed in Dick ——— to the editor, n.d., *Fall River Labor Standard*, June 5, 1880.

notwithstanding. And I do further, for the consideration above named, agree that all injury to life, limb, body, or health, by reason of my employment by said firm shall be at my own risk, and I . . . will not use or prosecute said firm for damage by reason of any such injury that may occur to me, in or upon the premises of the said firm or when about the business of the said firm. And I hereby covenant that I will faithfully observe and keep the rules of said firm, for the government of employees, which said rules are hereby made a part of this agreement; and will promptly obey the orders of my foreman, and other superiors in said employment. Witness my hand this _____day of _____ 18_____.

DOCUMENT 18.4
The Condition of Dependence: Health and the Factory System

Five hundred cigar workers and their supporters met in Germania Hall, New York City, in September 1874 to protest against tenement-house cigar manufacturing and to start a long campaign for legislation to abolish work of this kind in the home. The following resolution was passed.

TENEMENT-HOUSE MANUFACTURING

. . . It has become the custom of many cigar manufacturers in this city to rent tenement houses, fill them with families of cigar makers, and carry on the trade of cigar making therein. These houses are used to serve as a workshop, a packing, sleeping, and dwelling room without an opportunity to purify the locality from the odor of moist tobacco. It has been proven by physicians and a committee of investigation that small pox and other contagious diseases have infected some of these tenement houses.

Source: *New York Sun,* September 28, 1874.

The neighborhood and the city are threatened by disease, and are in constant danger thereof . . . [because] these poison-breeding shops are permitted to exist. The consumers of these articles, when made by workmen so affected, are likewise threatened with infection, and their health endangered in an alarming way. It is the sacred and bounden duty of the Board of Health to remove all shops of this kind because the Board has been created solely to protect the inhabitants of the city in their health. . . .

Constant contact with the cotton factory workers in Fall River led Dr. John B. Whitaker to write the Massachusetts Bureau of Labor Statistics in 1871.

A MEDICAL REPORT

. . . 1. Accidents and casualties are very numerous, partly owing to the exposed machinery and partly owing to carelessness. . . . It is really painful to go round among the operatives and find the hands and fingers mutilated, in consequence of accidents. 2. Unnatural or monotonous working positions . . . in some cases [make the worker] round-shouldered, in other cases producing curvature of the spine and bowlegs. 3. Exhaustion from overwork. In consequence of the long hours of labor, the great speed the machinery is run at, the large number of looms the weavers tend, and the general over-tasking, so much exhaustion is produced, in most cases, that immediately after taking supper, the tired operatives drop to sleep in their chairs. . . . 4. Work by artificial light. It is very injurious to the eyes. The affections consist principally in conjunctiviti, opacity of cornea, granulations of the lids, &c. 5. The inhalation of foreign articles. . . . I have been called to cases where I suspected this to be

Source: Dr. John B. Whitaker, Fall River, 1871, to the gentlemen of the Massachusetts Bureau of Labor Statistics, printed in Massachusetts Bureau of Labor Statistics, *Annual Report, 1870–1871,* pp. 504–6.

the cause of trouble in the stomach. After giving an emetic, they have in some cases vomited little balls of cotton. . . . 10. Predisposition to pelvic diseases . . . among the female factory operatives produces difficulty in parturition. The necessity for instrumental delivery has very much increased within a few years, owing to the females working in the mills while they are pregnant and in consequence of deformed pelvis. . . . 11. . . . Predisposition to sexual abuse. There is no doubt that this is very much increased, the passions being excited by contact and loose conversation. . . . They are, also, as a general thing, ignorant—at least to the extent that they do not know how to control their passions nor to realize the consequences. . . . 12. Predisposition to depression of spirits. . . . Factory life predisposes very much to depression of spirits. Hence you see the careworn haggard look, the dull expression of the eye. . . . Hypochondria and hysteria are quite common amongst the females. . . . 15. Connection between continuous factory labor and premature old age. . . . Very few live to be old that work in a factory. . . . With regard to provision on the part of the operative, for sickness there is none, they having about as much as they can do to live while they are able to work. When sickness comes, they have either to assume debts they will never be able to pay, or call upon the city or State to take care of them. . . .

DOCUMENT 18.5
The Condition of Dependence: Child Labor

A Fall River textile worker criticized the use of children in factories before a special

Source: "Testimony of John Wild," *Massachusetts Report of Special Committee on the Hours of Labor and the Condition and Prospects of the Industrial Classes,* Mass. House Doc. No. 98 (Boston, n.d.), p. 6.

investigating committee appointed by the Massachusetts legislature in the 1860s.

A SEVEN-YEAR-OLD

Question: How old are the children? *Answer:* Seven and eight.

Question: Have you a child of seven working in the mills? *Answer:* Yes I have. . . .

Question: Does he get any schooling now? *Answer:* When he gets done in the mill, he is ready to go to bed. He has to be in the mill ten minutes before we start up, to wind spindles. Then he starts about his own work and keeps on till dinner time. Then he goes home, starts again at one and works till seven. When he's done he's tired enough to go to bed. Some days he has to clean and help scour during dinner hour. . . . Some days he has to clean spindles. Saturdays he's in all day.

The overseer who gave this testimony had seventeen years' experience in the Massachusetts cotton mills.

A KINDLY OVERSEER

. . . Six years ago I ran night work from 6:45 P.M. to 6 A.M. with 45 minutes for meals, eating in the room. The children were drowsy and sleepy. [I] have known them to fall asleep standing up at their work. I have had to sprinkle water in their faces to arouse them after having spoken to them till hoarse; this was done gently and without any intention of hurting them.

Otis G. Lynch, superintendent of the Enterprise Manufacturing Company, which employed 100 children between the ages of 10 and 15 years among its 485 workers in an Augusta, Georgia cotton mill, explained his attitude toward child labor to a U.S. Senate committee in 1883.

Source: Massachusetts Bureau of Labor Statistics, *Annual Report, 1870–1871*, p. 126.

A SOUTHERN FACTORY

Question: Is it a good thing according to your experience that children of from ten to fifteen years of age should work in the factories? *Answer:* I think it would be better for them if they were not compelled to work at all, but,—

Question: (Interposing). You would want them to work a part of the time in order to learn a business for life, would you not? *Answer:* Yes, sir. Circumstances now force them into the mill. They come in with their mothers.

* * * * *

Question: You think, I suppose, that it would be better for the children to have a chance to be outdoors? *Answer:* Yes, sir.

Question: But the testimony is that many of those children seem to enjoy their work in the factory. *Answer:* Oh, yes. It is not laborious work, and it is not continuous; there is more or less rest as they go along.

Question: Not much play, I suppose? *Answer:* Some little; not much. Of course, we have discipline in the mill, but the labor is not continuous or excessive.

Question: Do the children remain in the mill during the whole eleven hours as the older operatives do? *Answer:* Yes.

* * * * *

Question: . . . If you lost your present supply of white labor you think that you would be compelled to substitute foreign white labor rather than negro labor? *Answer:* Yes.

Question: For some reason or other the negro is not well adapted to cotton manufacturing, I take it? *Answer:* He is not adapted to the management of intricate machinery.

Source: "Testimony of Otis G. Lynch, Augusta, Georgia," *Report of the Committee of the Senate upon the Relations between Labor and Capital* (Washington, D.C.: U.S. Government Printing Office, 1885), vol. 4, 748–58.

Question: But this intricate machinery is not so troublesome but what ten-year-old white people can take care of it and run much of it? *Answer:* Oh, the colored people can be used in factories if circumstances should make it necessary.

DOCUMENT 18.6
The Condition of Dependence: Life outside the Mill or Mine

In 1877 the Ohio commissioner of labor asked for detailed descriptions from coal and iron ore miners about the prevalence and the character of store pay, scrip money, and company stores in the coal and iron ore regions. The responses printed below are by a coal miner in Athens County and an ore digger in Lucas County.

Lucas County. Store pay is our ruin. . . . The store keeps no meat, no potatoes, no lard, and the most of the time this summer no flour, no butter, no eggs; but we can get hominy at 5 cents per pound, crackers at 10 cents per pound, and rice at 10 cents per pound. Now, it must be evident, that if I work for store-pay, and the store has no meat, I must go without it; and if they have no flour, I must buy crackers. If we were paid in cash, we could go to Toledo, and save, at least, 40 per cent. . . . How can a man be a moral, liberty-loving citizen, when he can not send his children to school for want of clothes, or take his wife to church in decent attire?

Athens County. . . . When a man's work is done, it is money that is due him, yet he must take just what he can get, or do without. If he sues for it a stay is taken, and his family can starve. There should be no stay on the

Source: Ohio Bureau of Labor Statistics, "The Payment of Wages," *Annual Report, 1877* (Columbus, 1878), pp. 156–92.

wages of labor, and the man or company should be compelled under penalty to pay wages every two weeks, in currency. . . . We cannot exchange . . . [the store money] with farmers or others. A farmer comes to my door. He has produce, just what I need. He sells for thirty cents. He also wants something out of the store, and would willingly give me the produce and take the ''check'' on the store, but the store will not receive the check from him, so he is obliged to sell his produce to the store, and I am forced to pay the store forty cents for the article I could have bought for thirty cents. . . .

DOCUMENT 18.7
The Reaffirmation of Individual Responsibility in an Industrial Society

Employers vigorously defended their prerogatives and criticized efforts by trade unions and city or state governments to interfere with their freedom of action. They often drew support from eminent social theorists. Henry V. Rothschild manufactured wholesale clothing in New York City, and J. H. Walker owned a shoe factory in Worcester, Massachusetts. William Graham Sumner was professor of political and social science at Yale College. All three testified before a congressional committee in 1878.

HENRY V. ROTHSCHILD

Question: Your remedy is, for the moral improvement of the working classes, to keep them

Source: *Investigation by a Select Committee of the House of Representatives Relative to the Causes of the General Depression in Labor and Business,* 45th Cong., 3d sess., Misc. House Doc. No. 29 (Washington, D.C.: U.S. Government Printing Office, 1879), pp. 131–36, 108–208, 310–21.

so busy that they cannot indulge in dissipation? *Answer:* That is a most significant point, and it is the only form in which the workingman can be improved. . . . I say the legislature has no right to encroach upon me as to whether I shall employ men eight hours, or ten, or fifteen hours. It is a matter of mutual agreement, and the legislature has no right, according to the principles of the Declaration of Independence, to impose upon me what hours of labor I shall have between myself and my employes. . . . Political economy teaches us that the laborers and the capitalists are two different forms of society. . . . The laborer should do as good as he can for himself, and the capitalist should do as good as he can for himself; it is a matter between laborer and the capitalist.

Question: You think the community have no interest in that question at all? *Answer:* They have an interest so far as if an unprincipled employer tyrannizes in some way over the laborer; that is a different thing.

Question: How would you interfere in that case—by legislation or not? *Answer:* If a tyranny arises, from which we are not amply protected at the present day, the legislature can always interfere, without a doubt. But this is no tyranny, if the contract arises between a laborer and the employer. The horse-car drivers of New York are employing their hands 14 and 16 hours a day. They are all willing to work; they are not bound to accept the labor; it is a matter between themselves and their employers.

Question: But do they want to work that length of time? *Answer:* All labor is irksome.

J. H. WALKER

Question: The most important fact before this committee is that we have in this country a large amount of unemployed labor. *Answer:* A man might just as well hang himself because he has a boil, as to talk about changing our laws or institutions because the country has a local ache just now.

Question: What remedy are we to take for this surplus population? *Answer:* Leave them alone; that is the remedy.

Question: You think they will take care of themselves? *Answer:* Let them alone. "The man who will not work shall not eat."

* * * * *

Question: Are we to have these panics in the future as we have had them? Can they be avoided? *Answer:* Nothing will prevent "panics" until human nature is radically changed. Their comparative severity will increase with advancing civilization, unless the disposition to protect themselves . . . by saving a portion of their earnings is more universal among the people than it now is. . . . The laws and institutions of the country can no more be adjusted to them than they can be to the condition of yellow fever. . . .

WILLIAM GRAHAM SUMNER

Question: What is the effect of machinery on those laborers whom for the time being it turns out of employment? *Answer:* For the time being they suffer, of course, a loss of income and a loss of comfort. . . .

Question: Is there any way to help it? *Answer:* Not at all. There is no way on earth to help it. The only way is to meet it bravely, go ahead, make the best of circumstances; and if you cannot go on in the way you were going, try another way, and still another until you work yourself out as an individual. . . .

Question: Do you admit that there is what you call distress among the laboring classes of this country? *Answer:* No sir; I do not admit any such thing. I cannot get evidence of it. . . . I do not know of anything that the government can do that is at all specific to assist labor—to assist non-capitalists. The only things that the government can do are generally things such as are in the province of a government. The general things that a government can do to assist the non-capitalist in the accumulation of capital (for that is what he wants) are two things. The first thing is to give him the greatest possible liberty in the directing of his own energies for his own development, and the second is to give him the greatest possible security in the possession and use of the products of his own industry. I do not see any more than that that a government can do. . . . Society does not owe any man a living. In all cases that I have ever known of young men who claimed that society owed them a living, it has turned out that society paid—in the State prison. I do not see any other result. . . . The fact that a man is here is no demand upon other people that they shall keep him alive and sustain him. He has got to fight the battle with nature as every other man has; and if he fights it with the same energy and enterprise and skill and industry as any other man, I cannot imagine his failing—that is, misfortune apart. . . .

DOCUMENT 18.8
The Response to Dependence: The Railroad Strikes of 1877

The railroad strikes of 1877 affected the entire nation and for the first time made the labor question a national one. The destruction of life and property in several cities brought home to many the impact of the industrial order on the wage-earning classes. Responses varied. Henry Ward Beecher, the prominent Protestant minister, addressed his followers in Brooklyn's Plymouth Church. A. C. Buell was special correspondent in New York City for the New Orleans Daily Democrat.

Source: *The New York Times,* July 30, 1877.

THE REVEREND HENRY WARD BEECHER

. . . It is true that $1 a day is not enough to support a man and five children, if the man insists on smoking and drinking beer. Is not a dollar a day enough to buy bread? Water costs nothing. Men cannot live by bread, it is true; but the man who cannot live on bread and water is not fit to live. When a man is educated away from the power of self-denial, he is falsely educated. A family may live on good bread and water in the morning, water and bread at midday, and good water and bread at night. Such may be called the bread of affliction, but it is fit that man should eat the bread of affliction. . . . The great laws of political economy cannot be set at defiance.

A. C. BUELL

. . . The most striking fact developed by this movement is the terrible antipathy which has grown up among the poor and laboring classes against those who possess great wealth. . . . John Jones and William Smith, laborers, regard William H. Vanderbilt, Jay Gould, and Tom Scott, capitalists, as their natural enemies, whose welfare means their loss and whose downfall would redound to their gain. . . . Today, Tom Scott could not get through Pittsburgh, or Vanderbilt through Buffalo, alive! . . . You may call it whatsoever name you please—Communism, Agrarianism, Socialism, or anything else— . . . in the estimation of the vast majority of the American people the millionaire has come to be looked upon as a public enemy! . . . We have just now had a foretaste of real Civil War; of that conflict of classes, which is the most terrible of all species of war. . . . The inadequacy of the present governmental system to combat servile insurrections has been forced home upon the capitalistic classes as a fact that can no longer be evaded. . . . The average citizen may forget the danger as soon as it is past, but not the man of millions. He has seen the ghost of the Commune, and it will stalk his dreams every night until he can feel with his prototype of the old world the security of mercenary bayonets enough to garrison every considerable town. . . .

DOCUMENT 18.9
Opposition to Dependence

Martin A. Foran, president of the Coopers' International Union in the early 1870s and later an Ohio congressman, disputed the popular contention that the government could not interfere in relations between employers and their workers. He spoke in Indianapolis in December 1873, a few months after the start of a severe depression.

MARTIN A. FORAN

. . . We hear a great deal about the presumptuous absurdity of asking the government to interpose its protecting arm in behalf of the people in emergencies and crises of the nature through which we are now passing. We are told that doing so is a strange and unusual proceeding in free America, . . . that to do so would recognize a principle at variance with the spirit and genius of our institutions. . . . What, permit me to ask, is the object of government? Why do we form governments? Is it not for the purpose of having each citizen pro-

Source: A. C. Buell, special correspondent, New York, July 30, 1877, *New Orleans Daily Democrat,* August 4, 1877.

Source: Speech by Martin A. Foran printed in *Coopers' New Monthly* (January 1874), vol. 1, pp. 5–6.

tected in all his social rights and privileges? Why give up, surrender a portion of our natural rights, those rights which God has given in *ventre sa mere,* unless it be for the purpose of having the balance of them more securely and safely protected? Certainly, the object of a true Democratic government is not to confer exclusive privileges and artificial rights upon a very small portion of the people. . . . It is the conferring of such exclusive rights, powers, and privileges upon corporate monopolies, national banks, especially, that has brought upon us the present panic. . . . Should we not demand, are we not justified in demanding from the sovereign power a revocation of the laws that have entailed upon us these evils? If not, then, it were better we had no government at all. . . .

Craft workers often argued that the principle of scarcity *would work to their advantage and maintain or improve their status and condition. At times, such arguments meant the exclusion of ethnically different groups. The following circular was distributed by Atlanta workers in 1875. Similar documents urged the exclusion of immigrants, especially Chinese workers. The principle of scarcity was put forth in all parts of the country.*

ATLANTA WORKERS

We, the undersigned mechanics and working men, appreciating the difficulties that beset us on every hand, and which, through the cupidity of certain proprietors, contractors, and capitalists, whose greed of gain would force us into hopeless poverty, and thus virtually enslave us and our children forever, hereby, individually and collectively, pledge our sacred honor that from and after this date—

1. We will not deal in a business way, or

support for public office, any man or men (whether grocer, dry goods, provision or other dealer) who oppresses us by employing negro instead of skilled white labor.

2. We will not trade with any retail dealer who purchases his supplies from a man or men who employ negro instead of skilled white labor.

3. We will not rent a house or houses owned by persons who employ negro to the exclusion of skilled white labor in their construction or repairs.

In 1883, Adolph Strasser and Samuel Gompers, leaders of the cigar workers, offered broader justifications for trade unions to a committee of the U.S. Senate.

ADOLPH STRASSER[1]

. . . We have no ultimate ends. We are going on from day to day. We are fighting only for immediate objects—objects that can be realized in a few years. . . . We want to dress better and to live better, and become better off and better citizens generally. . . . No well-organized trade [union] can be riotous. New organizations having no funds to back them may become desperate and may do damage to property, but when a trade is well organized you will find that no violence will be committed under such conditions. . . .

SAMUEL GOMPERS[2]

. . . If you wish to improve the condition of the people, you must improve their habits and customs. The reduction of the hours of labor reaches the very root of society. It gives the workingmen better conditions and better oppor-

---

Source: Petition printed in *Iron Age,* July 22, 1875, p. 14.

[1] Source: *Report of the Committee of the Senate upon the Relations between Labor and Capital, 1883,* vol. 1. pp. 294–95, 373–75.

[2] Source: Ibid., p. 460.

tunities, and makes of him what has been too long neglected—a consumer instead of a mere producer. . . . A man who goes to his work before the dawn of the day requires no clean shirt to go to work in, but is content to go in an old overall or anything that will cover his members; but a man who goes to work at 8 o'clock in the morning wants a clean shirt; he is afraid his friends will see him, so he does not want to be dirty. He also requires a newspaper; while a man who goes to work early in the morning and stays at it late at night does not need a newspaper, for he has no time to read, requiring all the time he has to recuperate his strength sufficiently to get ready for his next day's work. . . . . The general reduction of the hours per day . . . would create a greater spirit in the working man; it would make him a better citizen, a better father, a better husband, a better man in general. . . . The trades unions are not what too many men

have been led to believe they are, importations from Europe. . . . Modern industry evolves these organizations out of the existing conditions where there are two classes in society, one incessantly striving to obtain the labor of the other class for as little as possible . . . ; and the members of the other class being, as individuals, utterly helpless in a contest with their employers, naturally resort to combinations to improve their condition, and, in fact, they are forced by the conditions which surround them to organize for self-protection. Hence trade unions. . . . Wherever trades unions have organized and are most firmly organized, there are the rights of the people respected. . . . I believe that the existence of the trades-union movement, more especially where the unionists are better organized, has evoked a spirit and a demand for reform, but has held in check the more radical elements in society. . . .

chapter

Populism

Lawrence Goodwyn
Duke University

For a movement that appeared only briefly on the American political horizon in the 1890s before disappearing forever from view, Populism has proved remarkably enduring. Generation after generation of historians—in the Progressive Era before World War I, during the great depression of the 1930s, and in the turbulent 1960s—have found parallels in their own time that seemed to recall the world of the Populists. So again and again scholars have returned to the 1890s, using new research techniques and uncovering new sources in an effort to make sense of the agrarian revolt and thus place it properly in the framework of the ongoing American experience.

This seems a surprising historical fate for the Populists, especially considering the fact that their movement not only failed to come within close range of national power, but never gained full legislative and executive authority in a single American state. Why should modern Americans, a predominantly urban people, care about the long-ago protests of western and southern farmers? What is there about Populism that made it a fixture of the American historical landscape and enabled it to draw the sustained attention of contemporary observers of the American scene?

The most obvious reason turns on the conjunction of two circumstances: the visible con-

tinuing influence of large corporations on the American economy and on political life and the fact that Populism represented a large-scale popular protest against corporate influence. Unresolved questions of corporate politics versus popular democracy ensure that the Populist precedent will always interest students of American life.

In the 1880s and 1890s, agrarian reformers warned that "concentrated capital" had begun to alter the shape of American politics in ways that seemed fundamentally to undercut the democratic hopes of such founding fathers as Thomas Jefferson. They warned that corporate money could not only hire lobbyists to influence legislation, but that this folkway could function with such efficiency as to undercut the democratic process itself. Populists were not at all persuaded that the nation's press could adequately protect the society from such incursions by business, because the press itself was a business that largely reflected business attitudes. Under such constraints, the laws passed by business-dominated legislatures increasingly worked to insulate the society from popular governance. The end result, the reformers argued, was a corporate state rather than a democratic one. The Populist conclusion: the very rules of the game were being changed and American society was becoming increasingly corporate and hierarchical. The average citizen, whether a farmer, a worker, or the proprietor of a small business, was being subjected to patterns of exploitation that were inherently unfair.

The questions raised by the agrarian reformers thus went beyond the particular controversies of their own day to encompass issues of freedom and equity that concern every generation of Americans. The fact that the Populist indictment was so broad constitutes the essential reason their movement has proved so interesting to succeeding generations. The agrarian critique seemed to address the very shape of American culture itself, raising troubling and enduring questions about the impact of industrialization upon inherited democratic forms. Is industrial society necessarily so highly organized, so stratified, and so intricately influenced by powerful economic forces that commonly held ideas about fairness and equity no longer can find effective political expression? Is the engine of the two-party system truly oiled by corporate money? Are politicians unresponsive to the general welfare not so much because they are individually "corrupt" or "greedy" but simply because they need to be careful not to alienate the corporate funders who finance their reelection campaigns? Has politics, in its broadest outlines, become essentially a matter of money, with the area for individual thought and compromise restricted to very narrow options within an overall pro-corporate framework? Have the very concepts of a citizen democracy, of popular government, and of an American commonweal been rendered obsolete by the ceaseless march of industrialization? In their own time, the Populists answered these questions with a yes and a no. "Yes," the hour was late. But "no," time had not run out on the idea of a popular movement to rebuild the nation's democratic underpinnings.

Before sketching some of the details of the Populist effort, it seems prudent to emphasize that their basic presumption as to what consti-

tuted "serious politics" was different in one fundamental respect from the presumptions most modern Americans bring to their political activities. As the Populists assessed the raw evidence coming from their state legislatures and from the national Congress in Washington, it seemed clear that most elected officeholders, whether they called themselves Republicans or Democrats, voted "for the people" when they could. But—as Populists never tired of pointing out—most issues divided citizen needs from business needs so that politicians had to make a choice between popular aspiration and corporate aspiration. As Populists dissected the parliamentary evidence from every decade since the Civil War, the choice made by most of the functionaries of both major parties was unmistakably corporate. From a popular perspective, the very art of running for office consisted of finding a way to make a public speech that sounded pro-people while keeping one's voting record pro-corporate. Such "shams" and "deceptions" had become the standard fare of American political life, the rhetorical engine that ran the ship of state. Moreover, the structure of legislative and congressional committees, grounded in encrusted patterns of seniority and political patronage of all kinds, ensured that the two parties would remain synchronized with the corporate managers who provided the campaign funds, journalistic support, and cultural credibility conducive to long-term electoral success. In a word, the parties had ceased to be expressions of popular intent. Populists therefore did not believe serious political reform was possible if one worked through either of the two major parties. If the two business-oriented parties constituted the essence of the political system, there was not much point in working through "the system." Trying to achieve reform through unreformed institutions was a fruitless enterprise. All who didn't understand this fundamental fact of American political life were fated to waste their time going through motions of political reform that could produce no real result. The only possible remedy was for the citizenry itself to create a new party—a People's party. To the Populists, then, realpolitik consisted of public actions leading to the creation of this new party. Any other kind of politics was pointless.

Whether in the 1890s or today, most Americans don't think about politics in quite this fashion. True, there is a general presumption in the popular culture that a certain bias toward the wealthy exists in the American political system. It is implicit in the popular saying: "The rich get richer and the poor get poorer." Similarly, there is the widespread supposition that powerful forces manipulate public decisions in a way that leaves the average person little room for maneuver: in the popular refrain, "You can't fight city hall." But such views constitute parlor wisdom, or, more often, barroom wisdom. As such, they represent a private intuition rather than a guide to public conduct. At an operative level, the phrase "You can't fight city hall" is a statement of resignation: things may not be ideal, but there is nothing to be done about it. This is a core belief of contemporary culture and because it is, Populism as a historical event is hard for modern Americans to grasp. This is so for the simple reason that Populism was grounded in the unresigned belief that something could, in fact, be done. The People's party was a public assertion rather than a barroom anecdote. Whether one characterizes such a belief as "romantic" or "provincial," or sees it as a straightforward manifestation of autonomous activity, the belief itself is transparently an essential starting point for democratic politics. That is to say, not much is possible in terms of democratic self-activity in the absence of such intention.

Populism surfaced in the generation after the Civil War when the clear outlines of an industrial society first became broadly visible. It was an era of freewheeling commercial buccaneers, such as John D. Rockefeller, Andrew Carnegie, and Jay Gould—a period dubbed by late historians as the era of the Robber Barons who built giant industrial "trusts" that drove out competition and established effective oligopolies and monopolies in all the nation's basic industries. From the Populist perspective, the claims of the industrial and financial tycoons that their efforts represented the essence of "progress" for America was nothing more than hollow and self-serving propaganda. Rather, said the agrarian reformers, the untrammeled power of the robber barons, far from being "progressive," resulted in gouged customers, underpaid workers, and the corruption of the political process itself. In short, where others saw growth and expansion, Populists saw the narrowing of individual possibility. Where others hailed technological change as undifferentiated proof of "modernization," the Populists detected new forces of social control that warred against diversity and opportunity. In raising warning after warning about the long-term implications of business concentration of economic life and business control over the political process, the Populists saw themselves as defenders of what they called "the plain people of the republic."

It was the sweep of the Populist analysis and the audacity of their proposed remedies that so startled their fellow countrymen of the 1890s and have fascinated historians ever since. Indeed, if one were to begin by describing the Populists' culminating political creed— their famous "Omaha Platform" of 1892—the sheer scope of its intention, not to mention the vigorous and sometimes purple prose of its lengthy preamble, would land the modern student in the midst of so many complex economic, social, and political issues that it would be quite easy to lose sight of the Populists themselves.

In an era when U.S. senators were elected by state legislatures rather than by popular vote, the evidence of business lobbying was sufficiently transparent and persuasive as to provide immediate relevance to basic components of the Populist critique. So much so, in fact, that after the turn of the century, other American reformers succeeded in achieving direct election of senators in the hope of containing at least the most visible of corporate lobbying tactics. Indeed, such successful reform proposals as the direct election of senators and the introduction of the Australian or secret ballot led some casual observers to conclude that though Populism itself was defeated, the essence of the Populist program eventually was enacted. In this reading, the Populist "sin" was not that Populists were wrong, but rather that they were just a bit ahead of their time.

Such a conclusion would not have made much sense to the original Populists. Their interest in electoral reform was not perceived as an end in itself but as a means to a more democratic structuring of the economy. It was the economic reform of "concentrated capital" to which they devoted their central attention. The organic problem historically afflicting agriculturalists the world over was both stark and simple: lack of capital to live on. No one would think of asking salaried employees to finance their own food and shelter for six months before getting a paycheck; they wouldn't have been able to, had they been so asked. But farmers had to find a way to live while their crops grew. Farm families planted in the spring, harvested in the fall, and had to eat in the meantime. Through the ages, whether in societies that functioned under feudalism, early mercantilism, or capitalism, people who worked the land borrowed the money or money equivalent necessary to sustain them. Their only equity was their crop which, under whatever system, they, in effect, mortgaged. The price they paid was unsurious whether rendered to the lord of the feudal manor, to rural moneylenders who provided supplies, or to post–Civil War mortgage companies of various kinds. Indeed, in this basic exchange relationship reposed what can be called an organic law of city-building and, indeed, of "civilization" itself. The way

societies acquire "capital" to build "capitols" is universal: it involves a measure of more or less orderly exploitation of the agricultural class by an urban class. This process of creating capital has been characterized as "primitive accumulation." In the Populist phrase, the process can euphemistically be described as "farming the farmers." In both cases, the effect is to siphon the profit from agricultural production out of the countryside to the city. Throughout history, most so-called "peasant uprisings" and "agrarian revolts" have had their origin in this simple and enduring dynamic: farmers paid usurious rates of interest for the credit they needed to buy food and supplies during the growing season. In mortgaging their crops to acquire needed credit, they routinely lost control over the sale of their produce. The people who benefited economically from agricultural production were not those who worked the land but rather those who provided credit. It was the latter who ended up owning the land; the actual farmers were merely temporary residents upon the land: tenants.

The great promise of America, and the cornerstone of American democracy, was the presence of free land which worked against the formation of a landed gentry and a titled nobility along European lines. A subsistence or barter economy facilitated the maintenance of a "yeoman democracy" and the Jeffersonian ideals that provided such a social vision with political substance.

But the coming of industrialization in the second half of the nineteenth century brought into being a market economy to replace the subsistence economy. In the post–Civil War American South, farmers increasingly found themselves enmeshed in what came to be known as "the crop-lien system." They acquired food, seed, and fertilizer from rural suppliers who "furnished" these essentials in exchange for a mortgage or lien on the crop. These "furnishing merchants" charged such exorbitant rates of interest that at the end of the harvest time the farmers' income from his crop rarely equaled his accumulated debt. Having failed to "pay out," the yeoman faced the coming winter without funds. The furnishing merchant thereupon agreed to "carry him" through until the next harvest, taking a new crop lien as security. Through the 1870s and 1880s, the lien system was polished in practice and codified into laws until it came to define the economic relationships of millions of Southerners. Farmers discoverd that the interest they were paying on everything they consumed limited their lives in a new and terrible way; the rates imposed were frequently in excess of 100 percent annually, sometimes over 200 percent. The crop-lien system had subtle ramifications that made this mountain of interest possible. At the heart of the process was a simple two-price system for all items—one price for cash customers and a second and much higher price for credit customers. Interest of 25 to 50 percent would then be charged on this inflated base. An item carrying a "cash price" of ten cents would be sold on credit for fourteen cents and at the end of the year would bring the merchant, after the addition of, say, 33 percent interest, a total of nineteen cents—almost double the standard purchasing price. Once a farmer had signed his first crop lien he was in bondage to his merchant as long as he failed to pay out. The farmer rarely was even aware of the disparity between cash and credit prices for he usually had no basis for comparison. As a contemporary explained, "many of the merchants did a credit business so exclusively they set no cash prices." The furnishing merchant and his ledger of debt became the farmers' sole significant contact with the outside world. Across the South, he was known as "the furnishing man," or "the advancing man." To black farmers he became, simply "the Man."

Virtually the only way to escape the lien system was to pull up stakes and head west to the new lands in Texas. But there, too, the furnishing merchant awaited. Doubly frus-

trated, some new migrants in Texas bound together in 1877 to form an "alliance" of farmers. After some years of experimentation in various forms of cooperative marketing, the alliancemen devised some adventurous schemes in an effort to circumvent the credit monopoly of the supply merchants. They formed trade stores where they could purchase supplies collectively and various "bulking" arrangements in which they pooled their cotton in their own Alliance warehouses where they could attract faraway buyers who might pay more than the local supply merchants. By 1885, the Texas Alliance had achieved some marginal successes and the word went out that the new organization meant what it said about helping "the dirt farmer." Alliance spokesmen, such as S. O. Daws and William Lamb, became skilled at isolating and describing the commercial foes of farmer cooperatives—town merchants and cotton buyers. Eventually, they focused on the national banking system which encouraged a contracted currency that kept money scarce and interest rates high. Efforts at economic cooperation had led the growing movement to new political insights into how an industrializing economy exploited farmers. Linked in suballiances of thirty or so farmers (as many as 2,000 suballiances in a single county) and joined by a chain of county "lecturers" into a vast statewide organization, the Texas cooperative movement enrolled 250,000 members by 1887. Alliance lecturers had acquired a story to tell and, in that year, they set out across the South and West to tell it.

The message to farmers was simple, direct, and powerful as a recruiting mechanism: join the cooperative, work together to build your own warehouses, create your own pooling arrangements, your own trade stores, and in so doing, free yourselves of the peonage of the crop-lien system. By the thousands, and then by the hundreds of thousands, farmers heard the message and joined. By 1891, the cooperative movement, formally calling itself the National Farmers Alliance and Industrial Union, had reached into forty-three states and territories and recruited almost two million members.

Lurking beneath these statistics, impressive though they are, were more subtle political and cultural realities that need to be specified in order to make clear the democratic impulses animating Populism. Tactically, the rise of the Alliance was traceable to the recruiting power of the cooperative movement. But in a deeper psychological and political sense, the Alliance was experimenting in a new kind of popular autonomy. As such, it was engaged in a cultural struggle to redefine the form and meaning of social life and politics in America. Out of the individual sense of self of spokesmen such as S. O. Daws and William Lamb, the Alliance had begun to develop a collective sense of purpose symbolized by the ambitious strivings of increasing thousands of farmers who were anxious to show the world why they intended to "stand united." Inexorably, the mutually supportive dynamics inherent in these individual and collective modes of a behavior began to produce something new among the huge population that Alliancemen called "the plain people." This consisted of a new way of interpreting society, a way of thinking that represented a shaking off of inherited forms of deference.

The achievement was not an easy one; if it were, history would record far more democratic movements than it has. It is proper to take a moment to specify the agrarian organizing achievement. Alliance farmers had spent much of their lives in circumstances of insecurity and, even, humiliation. Political resignation was the normal result. What the Alliance offered was a way to counterbalance resignation with hope. The lessons of the cooperative experience opened farmers' eyes to the working of the commercial world. It helped explain— and thus to "demystify"—such arcane subjects as the national banking system. It offered, in short, a new way of looking at things that engendered in heretofore deferential people a tan-

gible political purpose. This, at root, was what Populism meant to its individual participants; it increased one's scale of thought by offering the prospect of changing one's basic situation in society.

Unobtrusively, in ways city people had difficulty perceiving, a new folkway appeared across the South and West in the late 1880s— self-help farmer cooperatives. There were all kinds, loosely grouped in two forms as marketing co-ops and purchasing co-ops. The co-ops also materialized in different sizes, local, state, and regional. The largest, geographically, was in the Midwest where a multistate livestock marketing co-op was constructed under the leadership of the Kansas State Alliance. The largest in terms of members was the Texas Alliance Exchange which attempted in 1888 to market the entire cotton crop of the 250,000 member Texas Alliance. There were also different kinds of local trade stores, some owned by Alliance members, and others in which local suballiances signed an agreement with one merchant to purchase supplies at discount prices.

These economic endeavors constituted the functioning heart of the agrarian movement. Though the co-ops were diverse in structure, all had the same essential purpose: to achieve, collectively, what farmers acting individually could not achieve—access to equitable rates of credit. While southern farmers labored to escape the furnishing merchant and the crop-lien system, western farmers attempted to escape high-interest chattel mortgages as well as the monopolistic pricing margins levied by grain elevator terminals and high freight rates charged by railroads.

The midwestern livestock cooperative succeeded for one year in marketing part of the region's livestock in an effective manner that sharply reduced the profits of middlemen. Unfortunately, the same middlemen had great power. The Chicago Livestock Commission delivered a fatal blow by refusing the farmers access to the commission's trading center. The merchant traders of the Windy City blandly explained that the farmer cooperative, in distributing profits to its members, violated the ''anti-rebate'' rule of the commission. In such ways did the commercial institutions of the society combat the ''business methods'' of the Alliance. Possessing firm control of railroad links necessary for the transporting of crops, of the grain elevator terminals and, above all, of the sources of bank credit, commercial America was well placed to block the Alliance effort. The huge cotton marketing effort in Texas in 1888 was thwarted when regional financial banks refused to offer credit to farmers seeking to use collective ''joint notes'' as collateral. Credit, the problem of individual farmers, was also the collective problem of the Alliance.

In the aggregate, large-scale credit cooperatives constituted an adventurous and even ingenious system for agricultural production in a rapidly industrializing society. If an orderly and systematic flow of credit could be obtained, the cooperative plans of the Alliance were eminently workable. But the potential sources of such credit—the nation's commercial institutions—were precisely the one's engaged in the practice of ''farming the farmers.'' The stark reality was a simple one: the agrarian cooperatives were attempting fundamentally to alter the power relationships between farmers on the one hand, and merchants, bankers, traders, and railroads on the other. The latter saw no need to participate in new credit arrangements that fundamentally undercut the profits to be made in marketing the nation's agricultural production.

The Alliance movement's leading exponent of large-scale cooperatives was Charles Macune. As president of the Texas Alliance, he had devised the 1888 ''joint note'' plan for collateral that banks had refused to honor. Brooding over this impasse, Macune devised in 1889 an organic structural solution: necessary credit would come from the federal govern-

ment. Macune's ''Sub-Treasury Land and Loan System'' was the culminating economic innovation of the agrarian movement. His plan called for government warehouses to be erected in every county in the nation that annually yielded over $500,0000 worth of agricultural produce. Through these ''sub-treasuries,'' farmers could store their crops to await higher prices before selling. They were to be permitted to borrow up to 80 percent of the local market price upon storage, and could sell their sub-treasury ''certificates of deposit'' at the prevailing market price at any time of the year. Farmers were to pay interest at the rate of 2 percent per annum. Wheat, corn, oats, barley, rice, rye, tobacco, cotton, wool, and sugar were included in the marketing program.

The Sub-Treasury plan carried far-reaching ramifications for the farmer, the nation's monetary system, the government, and the citizenry as a whole. It shattered the existing system of agricultural credit and permitted farmers to avoid the rock-bottom prices prevailing at harvest. It also gave the farmers desperately needed flexibility in the selling of their certificates. Above all it ended the practice of siphoning off the farmer's basic profit through excessive interest charges. In effect, Macune's system replaced the high-interest crop lien and chattel mortgage with a plan that mortgaged the crop to the federal government at low interest. It placed a permanent floor underneath the cooperatives, thus providing the nation's farmers, once and for all, with a means of regaining a measure of real control over their own economic lives.

The political fate of the Sub-Treasury proposal provided the final ''educational'' lesson that turned Alliancemen into Populists. When the movement's national spokesmen went before Congress in 1890 with their proposal, they got a cold reaction from lawmakers in both parties. Congressmen, it turned out, had received forceful ''briefings'' on the Sub-Treasury Plan from their most influential constitutents—bankers, and lobbyists for railroads, mortgage companies, grain traders, and the like. The Sub-Treasury was denounced as "impractical" and "unworkable" by business spokesmen. *The New York Times* pronounced the new monetary system "one of the wildest and most fantastic projects ever seriously proposed by sober man."

It was, as a matter of fact, nothing of the sort. As a monetary system, the Macune plan has passed muster with disinterested modern economists who have analyzed it. It abruptly ended the long contraction of the currency that had confined the society—both its commercial and its agricultural sectors—since the end of the Civil War. In providing a flexible currency in which the volume of money in circulation would rise with population growth and with the increasing productivity of the nation, the sub-treasury system would have facilitated economic growth in a manner markedly superior to the narrow, gold-based system then in effect. Above all, the sub-treasury system structurally provided a much more democratic monetary system. In boosting agricultural income without adding to consumer costs, it redistributed income from creditors to debtors in a way that would have vastly stimulated consumer purchasing power. The practical results would have been very good for business as well as for farmers.

This was not understood at the time. The "gold standard" was more than a political belief. It was an article of faith—a central economic dogma fervently believed in by the banking community and supported by "sound" (i.e., orthodox) economists in the nation's universities. As nineteenth-century conventional wisdom had it, the gold standard meant a "sound dollar" while the "fiat" dollars injected into the economy through the government sub-treasuries were "funny money." At bottom, the nation's bankers argued that the sub-treasury system was "immoral."

In 1890, the agrarian movement reached its crossroads. The cooperative mobilization had attracted the farmers of the nation's granary and the nation's cotton belt. They had built a vast structure of self-help that counted over 40,000 suballiances from coast to coast. Every suballiance had its "business agent" for cooperation and each had its "lecturer" who not only helped spread the good news of the movement but who also helped interpret the reasons behind the political opposition to it.

But the Alliance movement became more than an idea; it became something of a culture as well. Alliance summer encampments brought thousands to huge festivals of cooperation. The Fourth of July was designated as "Alliance Day" and twilight meals were served to huge throngs who heard platoons of agrarian orators denounce the "money barons" and the "railroad monopolies" who pursued self-interested policies that kept the nation's producers in peonage.

Through such dynamics, a cooperative economic movement became a full-scale political revolt. The politicians of both "old parties" were pilloried for being in league with business lobbyists. The sequence of cause and effect led inexorably from economic innovation to political insurgency: although the cooperatives were the hope of the future, the lack of credit seemed to doom them; the Sub-Treasury Plan offered a way out, but both major parties opposed it; the Alliance, then, had to organize the American people into a new party. Its name was obvious: it would be called the "People's Party."

The Kansas Alliance led the way in 1890. An "Alliance ticket" was put into the field against both the Democrats and Republicans. The vast internal machinery of the cooperative movement was mobilized for political insurgency. The lecturers of cooperation simply became political lecturers. Indeed, the most renowned lecturers headed the Alliance ticket as candidates for statewide office and for the national Congress. To the familiar forms of speechmaking and rallies, the Alliance added a new ingredient—a wagon parade of itself. Wagon trains from suballiances combined with those from other suballiances, county wagon trains combined with those from other counties and the resulting spectacle was literally miles long. Some industrious soul counted, or said he counted, 7,886 persons and 1,500 vehicles in one six-mile long procession through the city of Wichita. Public life in Kansas became a "pentecost of politics."

Alliance politics on "the living issues" was countered by old-time sectional politics that dated from the Civil War. When the 1890 Alliance national president, L. L. Polk of North Carolina, came to Kansas, Republican newspapers "waved the bloody shirt" and denounced the Alliance movement as a plot by "ex-Confederates." Polk was wildly (and erroneously) described as an "ultra-secession Democrat" who had shot down federal prisoners in cold blood at Gettysburg and had practiced barbarous cruelties on Union soldiers while commandant of Salisbury prison—a post, it might be noted in passing, he never held. The *Wichita Capital,* a Republican newspaper, circulated the story that "the old soldiers of Wichita" were threatening to tar and feather "The Escaped Prison-Hell Keeper." Other vintage artillery was also unlimbered to repel the reform cannonading on the monetary system. Jerry Simpson, an Alliance congressional candidate, was variously described as "unpatriotic" and a "swindler." For the religious-minded, he was "an infidel" and an "atheist." As a politician, he was an "anarchist," and as a human being, he had "simian" characteristics. Worst of all, he had "hellish influence."

In normal political times—periods without a popular movement—such tactics might have persuaded rank-and-file voters. But the farmers of the Alliance had their own interior lines of communication in their far-flung lecturing system, and they had reform newspapers all over Kansas. On election day, a political earthquake hit Kansas. The Alliance candidate for governor

was narrowly defeated, but hardly any other reform candidate lost. Of 125 state representatives in the Kansas legislature, 96 would be Alliancemen. Additionally, five Alliancemen were elected to Congress. In Washington, Republican President Harrison described the result as "our election disaster." "If the Alliance can pull one-half of our Republican voters," he said, "our future is not cheerful."

Through the months of 1891–92, the Alliance movement across the South and West slowly endeavored to mobilize itself for the new People's Party. In many places, the cultural wrenching was difficult, especially in the South. There, the Democratic party was more than just the ancient party of Jefferson and Jackson; it was the party of "The Lost Cause," the party of "the fathers." It was also the party of white supremacy. A vote against the Democratic party was perceived as a fundamental act of cultural subversion. Down South, one had to turn one's back on a number of inherited loyalties to become a Populist.

To counter this kind of cultural politics, the Alliance unleashed its lecturing system to educate the nation on the new Sub-Treasury system. Schools were set up on the issue and scores of lecturers briefed on the intricacies of the new democratic monetary system. The word went down from the state alliances, to congressional districts, to the counties, to the suballiances. The Alliance, in effect, was treating itself to a new kind of politics in America— a vast popular plebiscite on the nation's economic relationships.

In the summer of 1892, delegates gathered in Omaha to formally consolidate the new third party, write a platform, and nominate a presidential ticket. The platform was a formal codification of previous Alliance pronouncements, formulated first in Texas in 1886 and 1888, and polished in National Alliance Conventions in St. Louis in 1889, at Ocala, Florida, in 1890, and at Indianapolis in 1891. The "Omaha Platform" of Populism simply tracked these documents. The national banking system was to be replaced; the railroads were to be government owned; U.S. senators were to be elected by popular vote rather than by lobby-controlled state legislatures. The People's party intended, its spokesmen declared, to bring a democratic "new day" to America.

In a transparent effort to combat sectional politics (Democratic advocates of "The Lost Cause" in the South and Republican wavers of "the bloody shirt" in the North), the Populists selected Union and Confederate generals to head their national ticket. The presidential nominee was James Baird Weaver of Iowa. The vice presidential candidate was James G. Field of Virginia. Both set forth to talk about economic democracy and political reform, rather than about the war.

Populism's maiden voyage in 1892 was impressive for a new political institution. The third party gathered over a million votes and Weaver received twenty-two electoral votes for president. The agrarian insurgency reorganized regional constituencies in unpredictable ways. One result was the Democrat Grover Cleveland replaced the Republican Harrison. Another result was that both major parties, somewhat shaken by Populism, began paying more attention to economic issues in an effort to refurbish their public image.

The need for such altered tactics became demonstrable after 1893 when the severely contracted currency precipitated a financial panic that culminated in a nationwide depression. With the ranks of the unemployed swelling, the Populist appeal took on added relevance.

The People's party made dramatic gains in the South in the 1894 elections, despite Democratic party claims that defections to Populism would split the white vote and lead to "Negro domination." In frantic efforts to divert popular attention from economic matters, the race issue was uniformly employed against the new party throughout Dixie, sometimes with visible effect. Nevertheless, substantial Populist inroads upon old Democratic constituencies, particularly in Georgia, Alabama, Texas, and North

Carolina, convinced many Democrats that their party, too, had to address the "financial question." A new faction of "Silver Democrats" developed in the party. They called for more silver coinage to increase currency volume. Such a palliative could not provide the structural undergirding of the cooperatives that the Sub-Treasury system offered, but it gave the Democrats a much more attractive appearance before the electorate. To a lesser extent, Republicans began to have their silver advocates, too. In such ways, Populism altered the national political dialogue, even in urban areas where the reform party had sunk few roots before 1892.

The Populists failed, organizationally, to achieve their ultimate dream—which was to create a North-South, urban-rural, black-white, coalition of farmers and workers. Sectionalism was a problem, race was a problem, and so was religion. The last divided urban Catholic workers from rural Protestant farmers. Above all, the reform movement never developed in the cities a recruiting appeal that remotely matched the impact of the cooperative movement on agricultural districts. Populists learned a basic rule of politics: one had to gain access to potential new recruits before they could be "talked to" and converted. The co-ops had attracted Democratic farmers in the South and Republican farmers in the North and the subsequent experiences inside the co-ops had altered the economic and political perspectives of all concerned. But the process had taken years. In America's urban centers, the new party had to start from scratch. It possessed the rhetorical appeal of the Omaha Platform, but little else. Movement-building, Populists learned, was a very complicated process. And unless a movement was built in each locale, rank-and-file citizens made political choices on the basis of inherited sectional, religious, and racial loyalties.

Populism effectively came to an end in the 1896 election. The Democrats, badly shaken by Populist gains in 1894, nominated William

Jennings Bryan on a platform of "free silver." Bryan's emotionally effective "Cross of Gold" speech denounced the existing monetary system in ways that made him almost seem a Populist.

The third party, meeting after Bryan's nomination, faced a dilemma. As the depression deepened, it seemed that almost everybody in America had begun to talk about "the financial question." Unfortunately for the reformers, few knew enough about monetary systems to employ the "greenback" theoretical sweep that was organic to Populist analysis. Worried that the silver issue would attract a sufficient number of impoverished but relatively uninformed citizens, the Populists faced the prospect of a divided reform constituency. Many decided the best way out was for the Populists to nominate Bryan so as to provide a united front against orthodox "goldbug" Republicans. This view prevailed, to the consternation of Populism's hardcore of cooperators and lecturers who had originally organized the movement. The latter, schooled for years on greenback monetary analysis, denounced Bryan as a demagogue. But to no avail. In a stormy, divided convention, Bryan received the Populist nomination.

The resulting contest between Bryan and William McKinley was something of a landmark in American politics. It certainly was regarded so at the time. The 1896 campaign was called "The Battle of the Standards" as McKinley upheld the gold standard against Bryan's advocacy of silver coinage. The deeper issues of Populist economic reform got lost in the din. The loss of the third party's identity through "fusion" with the Democrats robbed the reform movement of its momentum and demoralized its most dedicated activists. The election day triumph of McKinley over Bryan was a culminating blow.

For a time, it seemed the agrarian movement might alter the nation's political landscape, but in the end, inherited patterns of major party politics prevailed. Without structural reform of the monetary system, large-scale agricultural

credit cooperatives could not survive. And without the co-ops, the agrarian movement had no organizational base. Suballiances lost their members and lecturers fell silent. Without a co-op, there was no prospect of a "new day" to lecture about.

For generations thereafter, the "financial question" disappeared as an issue in American politics. Although agricultural specialists repeatedly demonstrated that the American family farm was a uniquely efficient unit of production, the small farmer virtually vanished as consolidation of landownership became a permanent trend in the economy. The general explanation for this development was that corporate farmers were more efficient. Only specialists understood that "economies of scale" in agriculture are very low and that the ascendancy of "agribusiness" was more a product of special interest tax and farm subsidy policies than a product of size.

In recent years, the enormous rise in Third World debt has focused the attention of increasing numbers of scholars on ominous parallels between the economic and political crisis of the 1890s in America and what may well become the global financial and political crisis of the 1990s. Third World countries, relying heavily on agricultural sales for foreign earnings, have found themselves trapped in a cycle of high-interest debt and low commodity prices. Such countries, in short, face a debt crunch remarkably similar to the one that gave rise to American Populism. Unfortunately, the financial relationships between wealthy lender-nations and agrarian sectors of developing nations are scarcely any better understood today than when the Populist case was placed before the nation a century ago. As a result of such self-insulation, the popular aspirations of the peoples of the Third World have easily become as threatening to many modern Americans as the revolt of our own farmers was to goldbug bankers in the late nineteenth century. Though American foreign policy and American weapons have defended anachronistic feudal and military hierarchies in South America, Africa, and Asia, such actions being justified at home as necessary to the ''defense of democracy,'' neither the policy nor the justification has proved notably persuasive to the non-Americans who are the mass victims of such hierarchies. The resulting unpopularity of America puzzles Americans. Since the passing of Populism, the subtleties of monetary systems and commodity exchange remain outside the normal range of political discussion. Under such constraints, the ultimate political price that Americans may be forced to pay for their narrowed cultural range in the twentieth century has emerged as a question of sobering dimension. Populism, in short, was not merely an interesting political movement in the American past. The issues of Populism remain singularly relevant to the America future.

SUGGESTED READINGS

Clanton, O. Gene. *Kansas Populism: Men and Ideas.* Lawrence: University of Kansas Press, 1969.

Goodwin, Lawrence C. *Democratic Promise: The Populist Movement in America.* New York: Oxford University Press, 1976.

———. *The Populist Movement: A Short History of the Agrarian Revolt.* New York: Oxford University Press, 1978.

Hahn, Stephen. *The Roots of Southern Populism: Yeoman Farmers and the Transformation of the Georgia Upcountry, 1850–1890.* New York: Oxford University Press, 1983.

Hair, William I. *Bourbonism and Agrarian Protest: Louisiana Politics, 1877–1900.* Baton Rouge: Louisiana State University Press, 1969.

Nugent, Walter T. K. *The Tolerant Populists: Kansas Populism and Nativism.* Chicago: University of Chicago Press, 1963.

Pollack, Norman. *The Populist Response to Industrial America.* Cambridge, Mass.: Harvard University Press, 1963.

———. *The Populist Mind.* Indianapolis: Bobbs-Merrill, 1967.

Rogers, William Warren. *The One-Gallused Rebellion: Agrarianism in Alabama, 1865–1896.* Baton Rouge: Louisiana State University Press, 1970.

Saloutos, Theodore. *Farmer Movements in the South, 1865–1933.* Berkeley and Los Angeles: University of California Press, 1960.

Sharkey, Robert P. *Money, Class, and Party: An Economic Study of Civil War and Reconstruction.* Baltimore: The Johns Hopkins University Press, 1959.

Tindall, George B., ed. *A Populist Reader.* New York: Harper & Row (Torchbooks), 1966.

Woodward, C. Vann. *Tom Watson: Agrarian Rebel.* New York: Macmillan, 1938.

DOCUMENT 19.1
Farm Grievances and Aspirations

A central component of populism was the National Reform Press Association which numbered over 1,000 rural weeklies throughout the nation. The tone and spirit of these journals is reflected in the prose of one of the principal officers of the Press Association, W. Scott Morgan of Arkansas. Morgan's passionate account of the movement, designed to win additional converts, is appropriately entitled History of the Wheel and the Alliance and the Impending Revolution. *The excerpts below convey typical agrarian views on the spread of monopolies and the need for careful planning to make farmer cooperatives successful.*

No apology is necessary for the publication of a work of this character. The wide-spread discontent among the laboring masses throughout the country, with a growing desire to know

---

Source: W. Scott Morgan, *History of the Wheel and the Alliance and the Impending Revolution* (Fort Scott, Kansas: J. H. Rice & Sons, 1889).

more of the causes which have led to the present depressed condition of the productive interests, has induced the author to give to the public a work which, it is to be hoped, will at least throw some light on questions concerning the interests of the producers. . . . While we have endeavored to point out existing evils and false systems, and the connection of either of the political parties therewith, we have done so in the hope that these evils and systems should no longer be condoned, but that the farmers should assert their independence and manhood by demanding the abolition of those evils which oppress the productive classes, with an emphasis which cannot be misunderstood. . . .

> Thou hast taken usury and increase and thou hast greedily gained of thy neighbor by extortion, and hast forgotten me, saith the Lord God. Behold, therefore, I have smitten my hand at thy dishonest gain which thou hast made, and at thy blood which has been in the midst of thee. [Ezek. 22:12, 13]

As far back as we have any history of the human family, there has been a constant struggle between those who tilled mother earth, and those who sought to live and thrive by manipulating the products of the soil. In the early history of the nations of the old world, it was the common belief that a certain portion of the people possessed the right to collect taxes and tithes, and impose burdens upon the producing classes. . . . Among the oligarchies of the old world this sentiment still prevails to a great extent. This gave rise to a large, idle and extravagant class of nobility that, in time, became so numerous, so profligate in their expenditures, immoral in their social relations and corrupt in the administration of justice, that the people rose up against those abuses, and, in many instances, deposed the king, slew the nobility, and undertook to found a government whose principles were established on popular rights. But for many years, ignorance of the masses and conflicting ele-

ments, led by selfish and ambitious partisans, frustrated the objects of the larger class of people who worshipped at the shrine of liberty. History, however, furnishes a few instances of short duration where such attempts were successful. It was not until the art of printing was discovered, and education of the masses had gained considerable headway, that a general desire for more freedom of speech, thought and action began to make itself felt among the potentates of the old and new worlds. The great reforms that have been accomplished within the last two centuries, and the errors that have been eradicated from our religious, social and political systems, are the natural outgrowth of popular education.

. . . As the press, the moulder of public opinion, ushered into the world a new civilization, it has been seized and its power is now directed to the enslavement of the people. The power of the press is not realized by the great body of the people. It can sow seeds of error that generations may not eradicate. It can soothe the passions or arouse the prejudices. Its power over the public mind is as potent as the wand of the famous magicians of the East. The press is controlled and has been for years, by the money power of the nation. The agricultural masses, the most numerous and important of any class of people forming the great body of the republic, and whose interests are identical, are kept divided upon the great issues which affect their welfare. They are robbed by an infamous system of finance; they are plundered by transportation companies; they are imposed upon by an unjust system of tariff laws; they are deprived of their lands and other property by an iniquitous system of usury; they are fleeced by the exorbitant exactions of numerous trusts; they are preyed upon by the merchants, imposed upon by the lawyers, misled by the politician and seem to be regarded as the legitimate prey of all other classes. Monopoly names the price of what they have to sell, and charges them what it pleases for what they are compelled to buy. The farmer may hold his crop in vain, for when he does put it on the market he finds that the same manipulators govern and fix the price of his products. Individual effort is fruitless. The natural law of labor is, that the laborer is entitled to all the fruits of his toil. There is no variation to this rule. It is fixed upon the universal law of nature, and any infringement upon it is not only repugnant to the laborer but is dangerous to the welfare of the State. There is, however, a difficulty arising in the application of the rule where labor becomes mixed with other forms of capital, such as material, machinery, etc. To properly and equitably eliminate it and fix a just reward for the laborer, is a problem that should commend itself to all who would reach the bottom of the "labor question."

The true principle, and one that would forever settle strikes, riots and all differences between labor and capital, is, that the laborer should be rewarded according to that that he does, and not according to what the employer can get the labor performed for. We are aware of the fact that when we make this remark we are treading on debatable ground, but if it is necessary, in order to sustain our position, we can fall back upon that universal natural law, "The laborer is entitled to all the fruits of his toil." A universal violation of this rule would culminate in the adoption of the barbaric one that "might makes right," and the weak would be compelled to succumb to the strong. The great railroad monopolies, vast and powerful corporations, have established a series of abuses which have gradually and almost effectually undermined the solid basis upon which our internal commerce was supposed to rest. . . . The railroads have to a considerable extent ceased to figure on rates at which they can afford to carry freight, but have made a calculation of what a thing can be produced at and a bare subsistence obtained by the producers, and they take the difference between this figure and the market price of the article at the point

of delivery, for freight charges. Nor is the great railway corporations the only means of oppression with which the farmer has to contend. . . . Another serious drawback and heavy tax upon the farmer is the exorbitant prices he is compelled to pay for supplies while raising his crop, and this is more especially true if he buys on a credit, as most farmers do, especially in the Southern States. We do not mean to say that the town or country merchant is making too much money; it is the system that is at fault more than the men.

Said an Iowa farmer recently: "The railroads of this State discriminate unjustly against the farmers in the transportation of crops; that is, give other men advantages which they deny to farmers. Let me explain: here is a wheat or corn buyer who makes a living by purchasing grain of the farmers and shipping it to Chicago. Of course he makes a profit on it—grows rich in fact. Now the farmers think that if they ship their own grain directly to Chicago they might save the profit that this middle-man makes. They engage a lot of cars, load them, and send them forward, but they find when they have paid the freight and the other expenses which the middle-man must necessarily also incur, they don't have as much left for their grain as he offered them. Now how is that explained? The railroad company gives the grain trader a drawback on the grain he ships, which it refuses to the farmers; and in some instances, at least, these traders are in partnership with railway officials. I thought when the idea of co-operative shipments was first proposed, that these favors were given solely on account of the amount of business that these men brought to the railroads. I supposed that the deductions were simply those that would be naturally made to wholesale trade, and in speeches to farmers I told them so. But we have learned differently, for when our farmers have combined and offered freight in large quantities to the railroad companies, they have refused to give us the advantages which they give the favorites. The terms of these contracts are secret. . . .

In the development of any great movement or social tendency, a natural law produces four distinct stages; first, the birth of the idea; second, its propagation by missionary work; third, its embodiment in practical forms; and, finally, the growth of these forms into permanent institutions. In regard to co-operation in this country, only the second stage has, in reality, been reached. For although distributive societies exist in various places, they are more the result of individual energy and thought than any common social impulse. But the thought—the idea—is in the world, and it has come to stay. And there is this to be remembered for encouragement to those seeking to develop co-operative industry in the United States; fifty years ago, co-operation, in the sense in which the word is now used, was almost an unknown term—now it is on the lips and in the thoughts of millions.

One among the more important branches of co-operation which farmers' and laborers' organizations are adopting is that of establishing co-operative stores. Many of these have been organized of late years with a degree of success entirely commensurate with the plan adopted, and the earnestness with which they were supported. It would seem from a careful survey of the past experience of co-operative stores, that the failures and only partial successes were, mostly, if not altogether, attributable to a lack of proper education among the people upon this question. There has been too much dependence on the business manager to make it a success. He would be a shrewd man indeed who could make a success of a co-operative business, when the people for whose benefit the business was organized would not, or could not, see the importance of co-operating with him, at least to the extent of giving him their patronage. There are some things which the people must see, and, seeing, must carry into effect, if we would be successful in our

efforts to emancipate ourselves from the iron grasp of those who manipulate our trade. The great trouble is that we do not teach far enough. We explain to a member how, by the co-operative system, he will be enabled to buy his goods cheaper, and obtain better prices for his products. He grasps the idea readily enough. But his conception of co-operation does not extend beyond the locality nor into the future. By not being more comprehensive we lay the foundation for failure. We leave a gap down for our enemies to enter. The store is established on this principle. We have fierce competition to meet. Other competitive stores will put the price down on articles to a point, perhaps, under cost. We cannot afford to meet their prices. Here is where the trouble comes. We have started out on the narrow and single plank that ''it is best to buy where you can buy the cheapest and sell where you can get the most.'' We have made co-operation a side issue. We have failed to impress the patrons with the idea that this is ''our store,'' and that it is the means to loosen the shackles which bind us to a false system of trade. The men whom we have taught to ''buy where they can buy the cheapest,'' and on whom we depended for our patronage, go elsewhere to buy, never pausing to think of the difference in the objects of the two concerns. The object of the co-operative store is to do a legitimate business; to furnish goods at living profits. The object of the other stores is to break down the co-operative plan and re-establish high prices. The very fact that they offer to sell goods at, or below, ''cost,'' is evidence of a sinister design, and the member that ''bites'' at such a transparent ''bait'' ''sells his birth-right for a mess of pottage.'' We must start out on a broader basis. We must instruct our members that we are bound hand and foot by a system of trade over which we have no control, and no chance of control, except by being true to ourselves, and through united action and individual effort. Each individual forms a link in the chain of effort to throw off this yoke. When he fails of his duty the force of the effort is broken, and failure is likely to ensue.

Co-operation is the distinctive feature of the Farmers' Alliance. . . . It can not afford to turn back. It is in the fight. Its position is exposed. The enemy's guns are trained upon every vulnerable point. It will not do to stand still. Nothing but an aggressive warfare will win. Monopoly and privileged classes are intrenched behind fortifications which the farmers have builded for them. The fight on the one side is waged to retain the privilege to rob and plunder. On the other hand it is made to regain constitutional rights. The fight on the part of the farmer is being made, not only for himself but for generations yet unborn. It is a fight for liberty, equality and a just reward for his labor. To lose is to be dependent, poor and miserable. To win is to be free, comfortable and happy. To banish monopoly of every description is to give new vitality to every industry, and strengthen the foundations of government. To fail, is to drift into centralization, where money and aristocracy will rule and land monopoly be the prevailing system.

DOCUMENT 19.2
Farm Demands and Declarations

A revealing insight into the dynamics of popular movements is available in the following three documents written in 1890, 1891, and 1892 as the National Farmers' Alliance transformed itself from a cooperative economic movement into an insurgent political party. The first document, formulated at the National Alliance convention at Ocala, Florida, in 1890,

Source: *The Proceedings of the Supreme Council of the National Farmers' Alliance and the Industrial Union,* at the National Alliance Convention, Ocala, Florida, 1890, pp. 32–33.

restates, in near final form, the farmer's economic "demands" as they evolved from 1886 to 1890 in platforms promulgated at Cleburne, Texas; Dallas, Texas; Shreveport, Louisiana; Meridian, Mississippi; and St. Louis, Missouri. The second document, issued as the Cincinnati Platform of 1891, incorporates these agrarian issues into a conscious political statement by a still-to-be-organized People's party. The third document, issued when the new party formally created itself in 1892, incorporates a passionate and flowery preamble into the core statement of populism—the Omaha Platform of the People's party. Considered together, the three statements indicate how thoroughly the basic financial and currency concerns of the Farmers' Alliance dominated the People's party also.

THE OCALA DEMANDS, DECEMBER 1890

1. a. We demand the abolition of national banks.

b. We demand that the government shall establish sub-treasuries or depositories in the several states, which shall loan money direct to the people at a low rate of interest, not to exceed two per cent per annum, on non-perishable farm products, and also upon real estate, with proper limitations upon the quantity of land and amount of money.

c. We demand that the amount of the circulating medium be speedily increased to not less than $50 per capita.

2. We demand that Congress shall pass such laws as will effectually prevent the dealing in futures of all agricultural and mechanical productions; providing a stringent system of procedure in trials that will secure the prompt conviction, and imposing such penalties as shall secure the most perfect compliance with the law.

3. We condemn the silver bill recently passed by Congress, and demand in lieu thereof the free and unlimited coinage of silver.

4. We demand the passage of laws prohibiting alien ownership of land, and that Congress take prompt action to devise some plan to obtain all lands now owned by aliens and foreign syndicates; and that all lands now held by railroads and other corporations in excess of such as is actually used and needed by them be reclaimed by the government and held for actual settlers only.

5. Believing in the doctrine of equal rights to all and special privileges to none, we demand—

a. That our national legislation shall be so framed in the future as not to build up one industry at the expense of another.

b. We further demand a removal of the existing heavy tariff tax from the necessities of life, that the poor of our land must have.

c. We further demand a just and equitable system of graduated tax on incomes.

d. We believe that the money of the county should be kept as much as possible in the hands of the people, and hence we demand that all national and state revenues shall be limited to the necessary expenses of the government economically and honestly administered.

6. We demand the most rigid, honest and just state and national government control and supervision of the means of public communication and transportation, and if this control and supervision does not remove the abuse now existing, we demand the government ownership of such means of communication and transportation.

7. We demand that the Congress of the United States submit an amendment to the Constitution providing for the election of United States Senators by direct vote of the people of each state.

*   *   *   *   *

CINCINNATI PLATFORM, MAY 1891

1. That in view of the great social, industrial and economical revolution now dawning on the civilized world and the new and living issues confronting the American people, we believe that the time has arrived for a crystalization of the political reform forces of our country and the formation of what should be known as the People's party of the United States of America.

2. That we most heartily endorse the demands of the platforms as adopted at St. Louis, Missouri, in 1889; Ocala, Florida, in 1890, and Omaha, Nebraska, in 1891, by industrial organizations there represented, summarized as follows:

a. The right to make and issue money is a sovereign power to be maintained by the people for the common benefit. Hence we demand the abolition of national banks as banks of issue, and as a substitute for national bank notes we demand that legal tender Treasury notes be issued in sufficient volume to transact the business of the country on a cash basis without damage or especial advantage to any class or calling, such notes to be legal tender in payment of all debts, public and private, and such notes, when demanded by the people, shall be loaned to them at not more than 2 per cent per annum upon non-perishable products, as indicated in the sub-treasury plan, and also upon real estate, with proper limitation upon the quantity of land and amount of money.

b. We demand the free and unlimited coinage of silver.

c. We demand the passage of laws prohibiting alien ownership of land, and that Congress take prompt action to devise some plan to obtain all lands now owned by alien and foreign syndicates, and that all land held by railroads and other corporations in excess of such as is actually used and needed by them be reclaimed

Source: *The National Economist*, May 30, 1891.

by the government, and held for actual settlers only.

d. Believing the doctrine of equal rights for all and special privileges to none, we demand that taxation, national, state, or municipal, shall not be used to build up one interest or class at the expense of another.

e. We demand that all revenue—national, state, or county—shall be limited to the necessary expenses of the government, economically and honestly administered.

f. We demand a just and equitable system of graduated tax on income.

g. We demand the most rigid, honest, and just national control and supervision of the means of public communication and transportation, and if this control and supervision does not remove the abuses now existing we demand the government ownership of such means of communication and transportation.

h. We demand the election of President, vice-President and United States Senators by a direct vote of the people.

3. That we urge the united action of all progressive organizations in attending the conference called for February 22, 1892, by six of the leading reform organizations.

4. That a national central committee be appointed by this conference to be composed of a chairman, to be elected by this body, and of three members from each state represented, to be named by each state delegation.

5. That this central committee shall represent this body, attend the national conference on February 22, 1892, and, if possible, unite with that and all other reform organizations there assembled. If no satisfactory arrangement can be effected, this committee shall call a national convention not later than June 1, 1892, for the purpose of nominating candidates for President and vice-President.

6. That the members of the central committee for each state where there is no independent political organization, conduct an active system of political agitation in their respective states.

Resolved, That the question of universal suffrage be recommended to the favorable consideration of the various states and territories.

Resolved, That while the party in power in 1879 pledged the faith of the nation to pay a debt in coin that had been contracted on a depreciated currency, thus adding nearly $1,000,000,000 to the burdens of the people, which meant gold for the bondholders and depreciated currency for the soldier, and holding that the men who imperiled their lives to save the life of a nation should have been paid in money as good as that paid to the bondholders—we demand the issue of legal tender and treasury notes in sufficient amount to make the pay of the soldiers equal to par with coin, or such other legislation as shall do equal and exact justice to the Union soldiers of this country.

Resolved, That as eight hours constitute a legal day's work for government employees in mechanical departments, we believe this principle should be further extended so as to apply to all corporations employing labor in the different states of the Union.

Resolved, That this conference condemns in unmeasured terms the action of the directors of the World's Columbian Exposition on May 19, in refusing the minimum rate of wages asked for by the labor organizations of Chicago.

Resolved, That the Attorney General of the United States should make immediate provision to submit the act of March 2, 1889, providing for the opening of Oklahoma to homestead settlement, to the United States Supreme Court, so that the expensive and dilatory litigation now pending there be ended.

* * * * *

OMAHA PLATFORM, JULY 1892

Assembled upon the 116th anniversary of the Declaration of Independence, the People's

Source: *The National Economist,* July 9, 1892.

Party of America, in their first national convention, invoking upon their action the blessing of Almighty God, puts forth, in the name and on behalf of the people of this country, the following preamble and declaration of principles:—

The conditions which surround us best justify our cooperation: we meet in the midst of a nation brought to the verge of moral, political, and material ruin. Corruption dominates the ballot-box, the legislatures, the Congress, and touches even the ermine of the bench. The people are demoralized; most of the States have been compelled to isolate the voters at the polling-places to prevent universal intimidation or bribery. The newspapers are largely subsidized or muzzled; public opinion silenced; business prostrated; our homes covered with mortgages; labor impoverished; and the land concentrating in the hands of the capitalists. The urban workmen are denied the right of organization for self-protection; imported pauperized labor beats down their wages; a hireling standing army, unrecognized by our laws, is established to shoot them down, and they are rapidly degenerating into European conditions. The fruits of the toil of millions are boldly stolen to build up colossal fortunes for a few, unprecedented in the history of mankind; and the possessors of these, in turn, despise the republic and endanger liberty. From the same prolific womb of governmental injustice we breed the two great classes—tramps and millionaires.

The national power to create money is appropriated to enrich bondholders; a vast public debt, payable in legal tender currency, has been funded into gold-bearing bonds, thereby adding millions to the burdens of the people. Silver, which has been accepted as coin since the dawn of history, has been demonetized to add to the purchasing power of gold by decreasing the value of all forms of property as well as human labor; and the supply of currency is purposely abridged to fatten usurers, bankrupt enterprise, and enslave industry. A vast conspiracy against mankind has been organized on two continents, and it is rapidly taking possession of the world. If not met and overthrown at once, it forebodes terrible social convulsions, the destruction of civilization, or the establishment of an absolute despotism.

We have witnessed for more than a quarter of a century the struggles of the two great political parties for power and plunder, while grievous wrongs have been inflicted upon the suffering people. We charge that the controlling influences dominating both these parties have permitted the existing dreadful conditions to develop without serious effort to prevent or restrain them. Neither do they now promise us any substantial reform. They have agreed together to ignore in the coming campaign every issue but one. They propose to drown the outcries of a plundered people with the uproar of a sham battle over the tariff, so that capitalists, corporations, national banks, rings, trusts, watered stock, the demonetization of silver, and the oppressions of the usurers may all be lost sight of. They propose to sacrifice our homes, lives and children on the altar of mammon; to destroy the multitude in order to secure corruption funds from the millionaires.

Assembled on the anniversary of the birthday of the nation, and filled with the spirit of the grand general and chieftain who established our independence, we seek to restore the government of the Republic to the hands of "the plain people," with whose class it originated. We assert our purposes to be identical with the purposes of the National Constitution, "to form a more perfect union and establish justice, insure domestic tranquillity, provide for the common defence, promote the general welfare, and secure the blessings of liberty for ourselves and our posterity." We declare that this republic can only endure as a free government while built upon the love of the whole people for each other and for the nation; that it cannot be pinned together by bayonets; that the civil war is over, and that every passion and resentment which grew out of it must die with it; and that we must be in fact, as we are in name, one united brotherhood of freemen.

Our country finds itself confronted by conditions for which there is no precedent in the history of the world; our annual agricultural productions amount to billions of dollars in value, which must, within a few weeks or months, be exchanged for billions of dollars of commodities consumed in their production; the existing currency supply is wholly inadequate to make this exchange; the results are falling prices, the formation of combines and rings, the impoverishment of the producing class. We pledge ourselves, if given power, we will labor to correct these evils by wise and reasonable legislation, in accordance with the terms of our platform. We believe that the powers of government—in other words, of the people—should be expanded (as in the case of the postal service) as rapidly and as far as the good sense of an intelligent people and the teachings of experience shall justify, to the end that oppression, injustice, and poverty shall eventually cease in the land.

While our sympathies as a party of reform are naturally upon the side of every proposition which will tend to make men intelligent, virtuous, and temperate, we nevertheless regard these questions—important as they are—as secondary to the great issues now pressing for solution, and upon which not only our individual prosperity but the very existence of free institutions depends; and we ask all men to first help us to determine whether we are to have a republic to administer before we differ as to the conditions upon which it is to be administered; believing that the forces of reform this day organized will never cease to move forward until every wrong is remedied, and equal rights and equal privileges securely established for all the men and women of this country.

We declare, therefore,—

First. That the union of the labor forces of the United States this day consummated shall be permanent and perpetual; may its spirit enter all hearts for the salvation of the republic and the uplifting of mankind!

Second. Wealth belongs to him who creates it, and every dollar taken from industry without an equivalent is robbery. ''If any will not work, neither shall he eat.'' The interests of rural and civic labor are the same; their enemies are identical.

Third. We believe that the time has come when the railroad corporations will either own the people or the people must own the railroads; and, should the government enter upon the work of owning and managing all railroads, we should favor an amendment to the Constitution by which all persons engaged in the government service shall be placed under a civil service regulation of the most rigid character, so as to prevent the increase of the power of the national administration by the use of such additional government employees.

First, *Money.* We demand a national currency, safe, sound, and flexible, issued by the general government only, a full legal tender for all debts, public and private, and that, without the use of banking corporations, a just, equitable, and efficient means of distribution direct to the people, at a tax not to exceed two percent per annum, to be provided as set forth in the sub-treasury plan of the Farmers' Alliance, or a better system; also, by payments in discharge of its obligations for public improvements.

(a) We demand free and unlimited coinage of silver and gold at the present legal ratio of sixteen to one.

(b) We demand that the amount of circulating medium be speedily increased to not less than fifty dollars per capita.

(c) We demand a graduated income tax.

(d) We believe that the money of the country should be kept as much as possible in the hands of the people, and hence we demand that all state and national revenues shall be limited to the necessary expenses of the government economically and honestly administered.

(e) We demand that postal savings banks be established by the government for the safe deposit of the earnings of the people and to facilitate exchange.

Second, *Transportation.* Transportation being a means of exchange and a public necessity, the government should own and operate the railroads in the interest of the people.

(a) The telegraph and telephone, like the post-office system, being a necessity for the transmission of news, should be owned and operated by the government in the interest of the people.

Third, *Land.* The land, including all the natural sources of wealth, is the heritage of the people, and should not be monopolized for speculative purposes, and alien ownership of land should be prohibited. All land now held by railroads and other corporations in excess of their actual needs, and all lands now owned by aliens, should be reclaimed by the government and held for actual settlers only.

Resolutions

Whereas, Other questions have been presented for our consideration, we hereby submit the following, not as a part of the platform of the People's party, but as resolutions expressive of the sentiment of this convention.

1. *Resolved,* That we demand a free ballot and a fair count in all elections, and pledge ourselves to secure it to every legal voter without federal intervention, through the adoption by the States of the unperverted Australian or secret ballot system.

2. *Resolved,* That the revenue derived from a graduated income tax should be applied to the reduction of the burden of taxation now resting upon the domestic industries of this country.

DOCUMENT 19.3
"To Redeem Woman from Her Enslaved Condition"

The excerpt below, drawn from an 1891 tract, describes the conditions under which farm women lived and labored. It reflects on the sensitivities of the Farmers' Alliance toward women and describes efforts to improve the quality of their lives.

In the past, woman has been secondary as a factor in society. She has been placed in this position because the people have been educated to believe that she is mentally inferior to the sterner sex. Only of late has the discussion of her social and political rights been brought prominently before the country. The male portion of our population, through a false gallantry, have assumed that they are the protectors of the "weaker sex": women have been led to believe that they had no political or social rights to be respected, and a very large majority of them have bowed in quiet submission.

History proves that the more crude and savage society is, the lower women are placed in the social scale. The men of savage races compel their women to do all the work; in fact, to be their slaves. When this social question is investigated from a scientific standpoint, the wonder is that man has ever been able to emerge from his original condition, while the situation of the mothers of the race has been such as to naturally impede intellectual progress. Only the plain manifestation of the laws of nature and the human mind has enabled man to raise himself above the crude forms of barbarism, and establish what is now termed civilized society.

Source: Bettie Gay, "The Influence of Women in the Alliance," in *The Farmers Alliance History and Agricultural Digest,* ed. N.A. Dunning (Washington, D.C., The Alliance Publishing Company, 1891).

Education concerning the effects of social conditions is demonstrating that most of the moral evils which afflict society are produced by the unnatural conditions which are imposed upon women. Nature has endowed her with brains; why should she not think? If she thinks, why not allow her to act? If she is allowed to act, what privilege should men enjoy of which she should be deprived? These are pertinent questions which society should begin to consider.

Go into the rural districts, and look at the position occupied by the wives and daughters of the farmers. They have, until of late, occupied a social position which tended only to discourage intellectual effort. In most of the churches women have been allowed no voice; and the very moment some brainy woman in a community would rise above her surroundings and take an interest in public questions, the men, as well as the women, would begin to discourage her efforts. She would be told by her father, brother, or husband, that such questions are not the concern of women. But the Alliance has come to redeem woman from her enslaved condition, and place her in her proper sphere. She is admitted into the organization as the equal of her brother, and the ostracism which has impeded her intellectual progress in the past is not met with, and men have begun to recognize the fact that, when the women are educated, the battle for human rights will have been fought and won.

Her position in the Alliance is the same as it is in the family—the companion and helpmeet of man. In it she is given the opportunity to develop her faculties. She is made to feel that she is the equal of man, and that she can make herself useful in every department of human affairs; that her mission in the world is more than merely to be called wife or mother (both of which are honorable), but her work is one of sympathy and affection, and her help is as much needed in the great work of reform.

Only in late years have women been considered a necessary factor in reform movements. This has been brought about by advanced thinkers, who have studied sociology and the science of intellectual and moral development. Society seems never to have thought of the fact that there is no progress without opportunity, and that depriving women of their social and political rights has taken from them the inducement to become educated upon great questions. The Alliance contemplates the opening of every avenue of intelligence, which will induce women to become educated, and capable of taking care of themselves in the struggle for existence, and the establishment of a social system which will guarantee to every human being the results of his labor. The condition of the wives and daughters of the farmers is but little better than that of the women who work in factories. In probably a majority of instances, in the South and Southwest, the women assist in cultivating and gathering the crops. Such a condition of industrial serfdom the Alliance, with other reform organizations, expects to overthrow.

In the effort for reform, none can be more interested than women, as they are the chief sufferers whenever poverty or misfortune overtakes the family. They are the ones to look after the welfare of the children of the family. They, more readily than the fathers, see what is necessary to make the family happy and comfortable. But, having been educated to believe that bad conditions are caused by Divine Providence, or are the result of mismanagement, many of them have borne the social evils in silence, and trusted for happiness after they shall have crossed "the silent river."

Through the educational influence of the Alliance, the prejudice against woman's progress is being removed, and within the last five years much has been accomplished in that direction. Women are now recognized as a prominent factor in all social and political movements. In the meetings of the Alliance she comes in contact with educated reformers, whose sympathies she always has. Her presence has a tendency to control the strong tempers of many of the members, and places a premium upon politeness and gentility. She goads the stupid and ignorant to a study of the principles of reform, and adds an element to the organization, without which it would be a failure. Being placed upon an equality with men, and her usefulness being recognized by the organization in all of its work, she is proud of her womanhood, and is better prepared to face the stern realities of life. She is better prepared to raise and educate her offspring, by teaching the responsibility of citizenship and their duty to society.

The meetings give recreation to the mind, and the physical being is for a time relieved from incessant toil. The entire being is invigorated, and the mind is prepared for the reception of such truths as fit her to be companion, mother, and citizen. As stated above, woman . . . comes prominently to the front in the Alliance, and demands that she be allowed to render service in the great battle for human rights, better conditions, happier homes, and a higher civilization generally. In fact, she has come to the conclusion that she has some grievances for which remedies should be found, and that she owes it as a duty to herself and society to help work out the social and political salvation of the people.

I believe that there are remedies for most of the evils which afflict society; that poverty and want are the chief causes of crime; and the reason why so many people are found occupying unnatural conditions, is because of the violation of the principles of justice and right, by the government allowing the few to monopolize the land, money, and transportation, which deprives a large portion of the people of their natural right to apply their labor to the gifts of nature. Under such conditions, the people become dependent, hopeless slaves—a condition which drives the last spark of manhood

and womanhood from their bosom—and they become outcasts and criminals, and fill our jails and penitentiaries and other places of shame.

. . . The faces and forms of many of the farmers' wives bear marks of premature age. Their sensibilities are deadened with the cares and toils of life. They have enjoyed but few of the benefits of modern civilization, and but few of the luxuries of life which they have helped to create. They have plodded along, while conscienceless greed has fattened upon their labor. . . .

But this is a new era in human progress, when woman demands an equal opportunity in every department of life. She is no longer to be considered a tool, a mere plaything, but a human being, with a soul to save and a body to protect. Her mind must be cultivated, that she may be made more useful in the reform movement and the development of the race. . . .

Through a system of education, in the Alliance and kindred organizations, we are slowly but surely eradicating the false doctrines of the Dark Ages, and the traditions of the pagans, handed down to us through false teaching. To remove these evils is the grandest work of the age, and the woman who holds herself aloof from reform organizations, either through false pride or a lack of moral courage, is an object of pity, and falls far short of the duty she owes to herself, society, and posterity.

* * * * *

The education of the masses is the hope of the world, and a healthy public sentiment must be created in the interest of labor. Poverty must be abolished, and the natural rights of the people must be respected. It is unnecessary for me to pay any tribute to, or heap any abuse upon, woman. She is precisely what her opportunities have made her, whether she is found in a palace or a hovel. She is flesh and blood, and whatever virtues or vices she may possess, can only be attributed to environment and opportunity.

What we need, above all things else, is a better womanhood—a womanhood with the courage of conviction, armed with intelligence and the greatest virtues of her sex, acknowledging no master and accepting no compromise. When her enemies shall have laid down their arms, and her proper position in society is recognized, she will be prepared to take upon herself the responsibilities of life, and civilization will be advanced to that point where intellect instead of brute force will rule the world. . . .

DOCUMENT 19.4
"Cannot White and Black Tenants Act Together?"

Tom Watson, a Georgia congressman, was a new Jeffersonian at odds with his state's Democratic bourbon leadership. In his successful campaign for Congress on the Farmers' Alliance program in 1890, he denounced the ''vampires'' of Wall Street, proclaimed his Populist views, and was elected by the votes of both blacks and whites. Later in his career, after the turn of the century, Watson gave up his advocacy of Negro rights and became an archetypal southern demagogue.

The key to the new political movement called the People's Party has been that the Democratic farmer was as ready to leave the Democratic ranks as the Republican farmer was to leave the Republican ranks. In exact proportion as the West received the assurance that the South was ready for a new party, it has moved. In exact proportion to the proof we could bring that the West had broken Republican ties, the

Source: Thomas E. Watson, "The Negro Question in the South," *Arena* 6 (1892), pp. 545–50.

South has moved. *Without* a decided break in both sections, neither would move. *With* that decided break, both moved.

The very same principle governs the race question in the South. The two races can never act together permanently, harmoniously, beneficially, till each race demonstrates to the other a readiness to leave old party affiliations and to form new ones, based upon the profound conviction that, in acting together, both races are seeking new laws which will benefit both. On no other basis under heaven can the "Negro Question" be solved.

Now, suppose that the colored man were educated upon these questions just as the whites have been; suppose he were shown that his poverty and distress came from the same sources as ours; suppose we should convince him that our platform principles assure him an escape from the ills he now suffers, and guarantee him the fair measure of prosperity his labor entitles him to receive,—would he not act just as the white Democrat who joined us did? Would he not abandon a party which ignores him as a farmer and laborer; which offers him no benefits of an equal and just financial system: which promises him no relief from oppressive taxation; which assures him of no legislation which will enable him to obtain a fair price for his produce?

Granting to him the same selfishness common to us all; granting him the intelligence to know what is best for him and the desire to attain it, why would he not act from that motive just as the white farmer has done?

That he would do so, is as certain as any future event can be made. Gratitude may fail; so may sympathy and friendship and generosity and patriotism; but in the long run, self-interest *always* controls. Let it once appear plainly that it is to the interest of a colored man to vote with the white man, and he will do it. Let it plainly appear that it is to the interest of the white man that the vote of the Negro should supplement his own, and the question of having that ballot freely cast and fairly counted, becomes vital to the *white man*. He will see that it is done.

Now let us illustrate: Suppose two tenants on my farm; one of them white, the other black. They cultivate their crops under precisely the same conditions. Their labors, discouragements, burdens, grievances, are the same.

The white tenant is driven by cruel necessity to examine into the causes of his continued destitution. He reaches certain conclusions which are not complimentary to either of the old parties. He leaves the Democracy in angry disgust. He joins the People's Party. Why? Simply because its platform recognizes that he is badly treated and proposes to fight his battle. Necessity drives him from the old party, and hope leads him into the new. In plain English, he joins the organization whose declaration of principles is in accord with his conception of what he needs and justly deserves.

Now go back to the colored tenant. His surroundings being the same and his interests the same, why is it impossible for him to reach the same conclusions? Why is it unnatural for him to go into the new party at the same time and with the same motives?

Cannot these two men act together in peace when the ballot of the one is a vital benefit to the other? Will not political friendship be born of the necessity and the hope which is common to both? Will not race bitterness disappear before this common suffering and this mutual desire to escape it? Will not each of these citizens feel more kindly for the other when the vote of each defends the home of both? If the white man becomes convinced that the Democratic Party has played upon his prejudices, and has used his quiescence to the benefit of interests adverse to his own, will he not despise the leaders who seek to perpetuate the system?

The People's Party will settle the race question. First, by enacting the Australian ballot system. Second, by offering to white and black a rallying point which is free from the odium of former discords and strifes. Third, by presenting a platform immensely beneficial to both races and injurious to neither. Fourth, by making it to the *interest* of both races to act together for the success of the platform. Fifth, by making it to the *interest* of the colored man to have the same patriotic zeal for the welfare of the South that the whites possess.

Now to illustrate. Take two planks of the People's Party platform: that pledging a free ballot under the Australian system and that which demands a distribution of currency to the people upon pledges of land, cotton, etc.

The guaranty as to the vote will suit the black man better than the Republican platform, because the latter contemplates Federal interference, which will lead to collisions and bloodshed. The Democratic platform contains no comfort to the Negro, because, while it denounces the Republican programme, as usual, it promises nothing which can be specified. It is a generality which does not even possess the virtue of being "glittering."

The People's Party, however, not only condemns Federal interference with elections, but also distinctly commits itself to the method by which every citizen shall have his constitutional right to the free exercise of his electoral choice. We pledge ourselves to isolate the voter from all coercive influences and give him the free and fair exercise of his franchise under state laws.

Now couple this with the financial plank which promises equality in the distribution of the national currency, at low rates of interest.

The white tenant lives adjoining the colored tenant. Their houses are almost equally destitute of comforts. Their living is confined to bare necessities. They are equally burdened with heavy taxes. They pay the same high rent for gullied and impoverished land.

They pay the same enormous prices for farm supplies. Christmas finds them both without any satisfactory return for a year's toil. Dull and heavy and unhappy, they both start the plows again when "New Year's" passes.

Now the People's Party says to these two men, "You are kept apart that you may be separately fleeced of your earnings. You are made to hate each other because upon that hatred is rested the keystone of the arch of financial despotism which enslaves you both. You are deceived and blinded that you may not see how this race antagonism perpetuates a monetary system which beggars both."

This is so obviously true it is no wonder both these unhappy laborers stop to listen. No wonder they begin to realize that no change of law can benefit the white tenant which does not benefit the black one likewise; that no system which now does injustice to one of them can fail to injure both. Their every material interest is identical. The moment this becomes a conviction, mere selfishness, the mere desire to better their conditions, escape onerous taxes, avoid usurious charges, lighten their rents, or change their precarious tenements into smiling, happy homes, will drive these two men together, just as their mutually inflamed prejudices now drive them apart.

Suppose these two men now to have become fully imbued with the idea that their material welfare depends upon the reforms we demand. Then they act together to secure them. Every white reformer finds it to the vital interest of his home, his family, his fortune, to see to it that the vote of the colored reformer is freely cast and fairly counted.

Then what? Every colored voter will be thereafter a subject of industrial education and political teaching.

Concede that in the final event, a colored man will vote where his material interests of farmers, croppers, and laborers; concede that under full and fair discussion the people can be depended upon to ascertain where their interests lie—and we reach the conclusion that the Southern race question can be solved by the People's Party on the simple proposition that

each race will be led by self-interest to support that which benefits it, when so presented that neither is hindered by the bitter party antagonisms of the past.

Let the colored laborer realize that our platform gives him a better guaranty for political independence; for a fair return for his work; a better chance to buy a home and keep it; a better chance to educate his children and see them profitably employed; a better chance to have public life freed from race collisions; a better chance for every citizen to be considered as a *citizen* regardless of color in the making and enforcing of laws,—let all this be fully realized, and the race question at the South will have settled itself through the evolution of a political movement in which both whites and blacks recognize their surest way out of wretchedness into comfort and independence.

The illustration could be made quite as clearly from other planks in the People's Party platform. On questions of land, transportation and finance, especially, the welfare of the two races so clearly depends upon that which benefits either, that intelligent discussion would necessarily lead to just conclusions.

Why should the colored man always be taught that the white man of his neighborhood hates him, while a Northern man, who taxes every rag on his back, loves him? Why should not my tenant come to regard me as his friend rather than the manufacturer who plunders us both? Why should we perpetuate a policy which drives the black man into the arms of the Northern politician?

Why should we always allow Northern and Eastern Democrats to enslave us forever by threats of the Force Bill?

Let us draw the supposed teeth of this fabled dragon by founding our new policy upon justice—upon the simple but profound truth that, if the voice of passion can be hushed, the self-interest of both races will drive them to act in concert. There never was a day during the last twenty years when the South could not have flung the money power into the dust by patiently teaching the Negro that we could not be wretched under any system which would not afflict him likewise; that we could not prosper under any law which would not also bring its blessings to him.

To the emasculated individual who cries "Negro supremacy!" there is little to be said. His cowardice shows him to be a degeneration from the race which has never yet feared any other race. Existing under such conditions as they now do in this country, there is no earthly chance for Negro domination, unless we are ready to admit that the colored man is our superior in will power, courage, and intellect.

Not being prepared to make any such admission in favor of any race the sun ever shone on, I have no words which can portray my contempt for the white men, Anglo-Saxons, who can knock their knees together, and through their chattering teeth and pale lips admit that they are afraid the Negroes will "dominate us."

The question of social equality does not enter into the calculation at all. That is a thing each citizen decides for himself. No statute ever yet drew the latch of the humblest home—or ever will. Each citizen regulates his own visiting list—and always will.

The conclusion, then, seems to me to be this: the crushing burdens which now oppress both races in the South will cause each to make an effort to cast them off. They will see a similarity of cause and a similarity of remedy. They will recognize that each should help the other in the work of repealing bad laws and enacting good ones. They will become political allies, and neither can injure the other without weakening both. It will be to the interest of both that each should have justice. And on these broad lines of mutual interest, mutual forbearance, and mutual support the present will be made the stepping-stone to future peace and prosperity.

DOCUMENT 19.5
A Religious Revival

Farming was one of the loneliest occupations on earth. The Populist revolt provided the serious but happy opportunity for thousands of farm families to hitch up their wagons and journey to distant towns to hear Alliance speakers. Movement encampments were massive gatherings of people who knew and trusted each other, for their common politics forms bonds of cohesion just as effective as any other kind of religious revival. Populist encampments had much the same flavor and tone as the union organizing meetings and the great anti-Vietnam demonstrations of the next century.

But while indignation and sometimes bristling anger was a part of the message of reform, there was another and far more elusive ingredient at work in Kansas in 1890. It has been called a "pentecost of politics," a "religious revival," a "crusade," and it was surely all of those things. But it was also long parades of hundreds of farm wagons and floats decorated with evergreen to symbolize "the living issues" of the Alliance that contrasted with dead tariffs and bloody shirts of the old parties. It offered brass bands and crowds "so large that much of the time it was necessary to have four orators in operation at one time in order for all to hear." It was 2,000 bushels of wheat being donated by hard-pressed farmers to help finance their political movement. And it was parades composed simply of the Alliance itself. Some industrious soul counted, or said he counted, 7,886 persons and 1,500 vehicles in one six-mile-long procession through the city of Wichita. One wonders how the townsfolk of Wichita regarded this vast tide of people. Were they intrigued? attracted? frightened?

Source: Lawrence Goodwyn, *The Populist Movement* (New York: Oxford University Press, 1978), pp 135–36.

With parades, speeches, schoolhouse debates, brass bands, Alliance picnics, the politics of Populism took form in Kansas in the months of 1890. If Texans had led the farmers to the Alliance, Kansans led the Alliance to the People's Party.

Yet, in its deepest meaning, Populism was much more than the tactical contributions of Kansans or Texans. It was, first and most centrally, a movement that imparted a sense of self-worth to individuals and provided them with the instruments of self-education about the world they lived in. The movement taught them to believe that they could perform specific political acts of self-determination. The Alliance demands seemed bold to many other Americans who had been intimidated as to their proper status in the society, and the same demands sounded downright presumptuous to the cultural elites engaged in the process of intimidation. But to the men and women of the agrarian movement, encouraged by the sheer drama and power of their massive parades, their huge summer encampments, their far-flung lecturing system, their suballiance rituals, their trade committees and warehouses, their dreams of the new day of the cooperative commonwealth, it was all possible because America was a democratic society and people in a democracy had a right to do whatever they had the ethical courage and self-respect to try to do. Unveiled in Kansas in 1890, then, was the new democratic culture, one created by the cooperative movement of the Alliance.

DOCUMENT 19.6
The "Cross of Gold" Speech

Perhaps the most enduring single document of the landmark presidential campaign of 1896 is the famous "Cross of Gold" speech by

Source: William Jennings Bryan, *The First Battle: A Story of the Campaign of 1896* (Chicago: W. B. Conkey, 1896), pp. 199–206.

William Jennings Bryan. Its expansive rhetoric so transported the delegates to the Democratic National Convention that it is credited by many historians with ensuring his nomination. Though the speech effectively gave expression to much of the emotional fervor of a sizable body of American popular opinion in the depression-ridden 1890s, its emphasis upon "free silver" to the exclusion of more structural approaches to reform of the American financial system deeply troubled the Populist strategists who had played the central role in bringing the agrarian revolt to the attention of the nation. The "Cross of Gold" speech, then, is more representative of "Bryanism" than of the Omaha Platform of the Peoples' party. It nevertheless stands as a singular example of presidential campaign rhetoric in American history.

I would be presumptuous, indeed, to present myself against the distinguished gentlemen to whom you have listened if this were a mere measuring of abilities; but this is not a contest between persons. The humblest citizen in all the land, when clad in the armor of a righteous cause, is stronger than all the hosts of error. I came to speak to you in defense of a cause as holy as the cause of liberty—the cause of humanity.

When this debate is concluded, a motion will be made to lay upon the table the resolution offered in commendation of the administration, and also the resolution offered in condemnation of the administration. We object to bringing this question down to the level of persons. The individual is but an atom; he is born, he acts, he dies; but principles are eternal; and this has been a contest over a principle.

Never before in the history of this country has there been witnessed such a contest as that through which we have just passed. Never before, in the history of American politics has a great issue been fought out as this issue has been by the voters of a great party. On the fourth of March, 1895, a few Democrats, most of them members of Congress, issued an address to the Democrats of the nation, asserting that the money question was the paramount issue of the hour; declaring that a majority of the Democratic party had the right to control the action of the party on this paramount issue; and concluding with the request that the believers in the free coinage of silver in the Democratic party should organize, take charge of, and control the policy of the Democratic party. Three months later, at Memphis, an organization was perfected, and the silver Democrats went forth openly and courageously proclaiming their belief, and declaring that, if successful, they would crystallize into a platform the declaration which they had made. Then began the conflict. With a zeal approaching the zeal which inspired the Crusaders who followed Peter the Hermit, our silver Democrats went forth from victory unto victory until they are now assembled, not to discuss, not to debate, but to enter up the judgement already rendered by the plain people of this country. In this contest brother has been arrayed against brother, father against son. The warmest ties of love, acquaintance and association have been disregarded; old leaders have been cast aside when they have refused to give expression to the sentiments of those whom they would lead, and new leaders have sprung up to give direction to this cause of truth. Thus has the contest been waged, and we have assembled here under as binding and solemn instructions as were ever imposed upon representatives of the people.

We do not come as individuals. As individuals we might have been glad to compliment the gentleman from New York [Senator Hill], but we know that the people for whom we speak would never be willing to put him in a position where he could thwart the will of the Democratic party. I say it was not a question of persons; it was a question of principle, and it is not with gladness, my friends, that we find ourselves brought into conflict with those who are now arrayed on the other side.

The gentleman who preceded me [ex-Governor Russell] spoke of the State of Massachusetts; let me assure him that not one present in all this convention entertains the least hostility to the people of the State of Massachusetts, but we stand here representing the people who are the equals, before the law, of the greatest citizens in the State of Massachusetts. When you [turning to the gold delegates] come before us and tell us that we are about to disturb your business interests, we reply that you have disturbed our business interests by your course.

We say to you that you have made the definition of a business man too limited in its application. The man who is employed for wages is as much a business man as his employer, the attorney in a country town is as much a business man as the corporation counsel in a great metropolis; the merchant at the crossroads store is as much a business man as the merchant of New York; the farmer who goes forth in the morning and toils all day—who begins in the spring and toils all summer—and who by the application of brain and muscle to the natural resources of the country creates wealth, is as much a business man as the man who goes upon the board of trade and bets upon the price of grain; the miners who go down a thousand feet into the earth, or climb two thousand feet upon the cliffs, and bring forth from their hiding places the precious metals to be poured into the channels of trade are as much business men as the few financial magnates who, in a back room, corner the money of the world. We come to speak for this broader class of business men.

Ah, my friends, we say not one word against those who live upon the Atlantic coast, but the hardy pioneers who have braved all the dangers of the wilderness, who have made the desert to blossom as the rose—the pioneers away out there [pointing to the West], who rear their children near to Nature's heart, where they can mingle their voices with the voices of the birds—out there where they have erected school houses for the education of their young, churches where they praise their Creator, and cemeteries where rest the ashes of their dead—these people, we say, are as deserving of the consideration of our party as any people in this country. It is for these that we speak. We do not come as aggressors. Our war is not a war of conquest; we are fighting in the defense of our homes, our families, and posterity. We have petitioned, and our petitions have been scorned; we have entreated, and our entreaties have been disregarded; we have begged, and they have mocked when our calamity came. We beg no longer; we petition no more. We defy them.

The gentleman from Wisconsin has said that he fears a Robespierre. My friends, in this land of the free you need not fear that a tyrant will spring up from among the people. What we need is an Andrew Jackson to stand, as Jackson stood, against the encroachments of organized wealth.

They tell us that this platform was made to catch votes. We reply to them that changing conditions make new issues; that the principles on which Democracy rests are as everlasting as the hills, but that they must be applied to new conditions as they arise. Conditions have arisen, and we are here to meet those conditions. They tell us that the income tax ought not be brought in here; that it is a new idea. They criticize us for our criticism of the Supreme Court of the United States. My friends, we have not criticized; we have simply called attention to what you already know. If you want criticisms, read the dissenting opinions of the court. There you will find criticisms. They say that we passed an unconstitutional law; we deny it. The income tax law was not unconstitutional when it was passed; it was not unconstitutional when it went before the Supreme Court for the first time; it did not become unconstitutional until one of the judges changed his mind, and we cannot be expected to know when a judge will change his mind. The income tax is just. It simply intends to put the burdens of government upon the backs

of the people. I am in favor of an income tax. When I find a man who is not willing to bear his share of the burdens of the government which protects him, I find a man who is unworthy to enjoy the blessings of a government like ours.

They say that we are opposing national bank currency; it is true. If you will read what Thomas Benton said, you will find he said that, in searching history, he could find but one parallel to Andrew Jackson; that was Cicero, who destroyed the conspiracy of Cataline and saved Rome. Benton said that Cicero only did for Rome that Jackson did for us when he destroyed the bank conspiracy and saved America. We say in our platform that we believe that the right to coin and issue money is a function of government. We believe it. We believe that it is a part of sovereignty, and can no more with safety be delegated to private individuals than we could afford to delegate to private individuals the power to make penal statutes or levy taxes. Mr. Jefferson, who was once regarded as good Democratic authority, seems to have differed in opinion from the gentleman who has addrest us on the part of the minority. Those who are opposed to this proposition tell us, that the issue of paper money is a function of the bank, and that the Government ought to go out of the banking business. I stand with Jefferson rather than with them, and tell them, as he did, that the issue of money is a function of government, and that banks ought to go out of the governing business. . . .

And now, my friends, let me come to the paramount issue. If they ask us why it is that we say more on the money question than we say upon the tariff question, I reply that, if protection has slain its thousands, the gold standard has slain its tens of thousands. If they ask us why we do not embody in our platform all the things that we believe in, we reply that when we have restored the money of the Constitution all other necessary reforms will be possible; but that until this is done there is no other reform that can be accomplished.

Why is it that within three months such a change has come over the country? Three months ago, when it was confidently asserted that those who believe in the gold standard would frame our platform and nominate our candidates, even the advocates of the gold standard did not think that we could elect a President. And they had good reason for their doubt, because there is scarcely a State here today asking for the gold standard which is not in the absolute control of the Republican party. But note the change. Mr. McKinley was nominated at St. Louis upon a platform which declared for the maintenance of the gold standard until it can be changed into bimetalism by international agreement. Mr. McKinley was the most popular man among the Republicans, and three months ago everybody in the Republican party prophesied his election. How is it to-day? Why, the man who was once pleased to think that he looked like Napoleon—that man shudders to-day when he remembers that he was nominated on the anniversay of the battle of Waterloo. Not only that, but as he listens he can hear with ever-increasing distinctness the sounds of the waves as they beat upon the lonely shores of St. Helena.

Why this change? Ah, my friends, is not the reason for the change evident to any one who will look at the matter? No private character, however pure, no personal popularity, however great, can protect from the avenging wrath of an indignant people a man who will declare that he is in favor of fastening the gold standard upon this country, or who is willing to surrender the right of self-government and place the legislative control of our affairs in the hands of foreign potentates and powers.

We go forth confident that we shall win. Why? Because upon the paramount issue of this campaign there is not a spot of ground upon which the enemy will dare to challenge battle. If they tell us that the gold standard is a good thing, we shall point to their platform and tell them that their platform pledges the party to get rid of the gold standard and substitute bimetalism. If the gold standard is a good thing, why try to get rid of it? I call your attention to the fact that some of the very people who are in this convention today and who tell us that we ought to declare in favor of international bimetalism—thereby declaring that the gold standard is wrong and that the principle of bimetalism is better—these very people four months ago were open and avowed advocates of the gold standard, and were then telling us that we could not legislate two metals together, even with the aid of all the world. If the gold standard is a good thing, we ought to declare in favor of its retention and not in favor of abandoning it; and if the gold standard is a bad thing, why should we wait until other nations are willing to help us to let go? Here is the line of battle, and we care not upon which issue they force the fight; we are prepared to meet them on either issue or on both. If they tell us that the gold standard is the standard of civilization, we reply to them that this, the most enlightened of all the nations of the earth, has never declared for a gold standard and that both the great parties this year are declaring against it. If the gold standard is the standard of civilization, why, my friends, should we not have it? If they come to meet us on that issue we can present the history of our nation. More than that; we can tell them that they will search the pages of history in vain to find a single instance where the common people have ever declared themselves in favor of the gold standard. They can find where the holders of fixt investments have declared for a gold standard, but not where the masses have.

Mr. Carlisle said in 1878 that this was a struggle between "the idle holders of idle capital" and "the struggling masses, who produce the wealth and pay the taxes of the country"; and, my friends, the question we are to decide is: Upon which side will the Democratic party fight; upon the side of "the struggling masses"?

That is the question which the party must answer first, and then it must be answered by each individual hereafter. The sympathies of the Democratic party, as shown by the platform, are on the side of the struggling masses who have ever been the foundation of the Democratic party. There are two ideas of government. There are those who believe that, if you will only legislate to make the well-to-do prosperous, their prosperity will leak through on those below. The Democratic idea, however, has been that if your legislate to make the masses prosperous, their prosperity will find its way up through every class which rests upon them.

You come to us and tell us that the great cities are in favor of the gold standard; we reply that the great cities rest upon our broad and fertile prairies. Burn down your cities and leave our farms, and your cities will spring up again as if by magic, but destroy our farms and the grass will grow in the streets of every city in the country.

My friends, we declared that this nation is able to legislate for its own people on every question, without waiting for the aid or consent of any other nation on earth; and upon that issue we expect to carry every State in the Union. I shall not slander the inhabitants of the fair State of Massachusetts nor the inhabitants of the State of New York by saying that, when they are confronted with the proposition, they will declare that this nation is not able to attend to its own business. It is the issue of 1776 over again. Our ancestors, when but three millions in number, had the courage to declare their political independence of every other nation; shall we, their descendants, when we have grown to seventy millions, declare that we are less independent than our forefathers? No, my friends, that will never be the verdict of our people. Therefore we care not upon what lines the battle is fought. If they say bimetalism is good, but that we cannot have it until the other nations help us, we reply that, instead of having gold standard because England has, we will restore bimetalism, and then let England have bimetalism because the United States has it. If they dare to come out in the open field and defend the gold standard as a good thing, we will fight them to the uttermost. Having behind us the producing masses of this nation and the world, supported by the commercial interests, the laboring interests, and the toilers everywhere, we will answer their demand for a gold standard by saying to them: You shall not press down upon the brow of labor this crown of thorns, you shall not crucify mankind upon a cross of gold.

chapter 20

American Imperialism

Norman A. Graebner
University of Virginia

Contemporaries sensed—and historians have since agreed—that 1898 was a turning point in the history of the American Republic. The events of that year, culminating in Commodore George Dewey's victory at Manila, ushered the United States onto the international stage as a world power. Yet neither the concept of world power nor that of national expansion represented anything new or unique in the nation's history. Significant changes in a country's power position never occur overnight. For a century the United States had been important enough to influence the decisions of the great states of Europe. During the nineteenth century, especially after the American Civil War, Europe's leaders recognized increasingly that the United States had become the equal of the traditional powers in its ability to sustain a war.

To be sure, acquisition of the Philippine Islands was a clear departure from established national precedent. If expansion had been a recurrent concern of the American people, it had been limited to regions contiguous to the United States. The only exception had been Alaska. With the annexation of the Philippines the nation abandoned for the first time its strategy of hemispheric isolation in favor of a major strategic commitment in the western Pacific. Also, for the first time, the United States estab-lished its sovereignty over territories that were never intended for self-government under the aegis of the U.S. Constitution. Instead, the Philippine population, ethnically and culturally remote from American society, was destined from the beginning for the imposition of minority Caucasian rule.

What mattered in the events of 1898 was not that the United States had become a world power or an imperialistic nation but that, in acquiring the Philippines, it had deserted those principles of statecraft which had determined important decisions throughout the previous century. Essentially the defiance of diplomatic tradition lay in the determination of American officials to anchor the country's imperialistic behavior to abstract moral principles rather than to the political wisdom of the past. Neither the war against Spain nor acquisition of the Philippine Islands resulted from any recognizable or clearly enunciated national interest. They emanated, rather, from a sense of moral obligation. The critical decisions of 1898 were scarcely compatible with assumptions and methods upon which earlier generations of Americans had attempted to defend the national interest abroad. In this respect they inaugurated a new age for the United States in world affairs.

Most historians—but certainly not all—agree that the United States had no legitimate cause for declaring war against Spain in April 1898. The Spanish government had recognized its failure in Cuba and was doing all within its power, short of granting independence, to relieve conditions on the island. Conscious of their complete incapacity to wage a successful war, Spanish officials sought to avoid open conflict with the United States; they moved as rapidly as Spanish opinion would permit to meet American demands. But the "yellow press" of the United States, pointing to Spanish atrocities in Cuba, clamored for war, especially after the destruction of the *Maine* in Havana harbor. The conviction of most Republican editors and politicians that Cuban liberty was a popular and just cause—which would demand little of the American people—mobilized both the GOP majority in Congress and the McKinley administration behind the clamor for action. Two days after President William McKinley learned of the Spanish government's extensive concessions to his demands, he nonetheless permitted the Congress to decide the whole question, knowing full well that it would vote for war.

Few Americans justified the Spanish-American War in terms of the security and well-being of the United States. Theodore Roosevelt observed in his *Autobiography:* "Our own interests [in Cuba] were great. . . . But even greater were our interests from the standpoint of humanity. Cuba was at our very doors. It was a dreadful thing for us to sit supinely and watch her death agony." Walter Hines Page termed the war "a necessary act of surgery for the health of civilization." To Senator John T. Morgan, the United States had been drawn into the war by a sense of humanity and the "duty we owe to Christian civilization." That the United States achieved its initial goal of freeing Cuba and thus fulfilled its great moral purpose at little national expense merely confirmed the growing conviction that policy anchored primarily to national interest, without regard to humanity, was no longer legitimate for a nation so fortunate in its institutions and so militarily and economically powerful.

Traditional political considerations played no greater role in the decision to acquire the Philippines than in the declaration of war itself. If the solemnly declared purpose of the war did not transcend the simple liberation of Cuba, even this limited objective necessitated some degree of military victory over Spain. To destroy Spanish sea power in the Pacific and thereby protect American commerce, the administration ordered Commodore Dewey to Manila Bay. On May 1, 1898, he destroyed the Spanish squadron anchored there with the loss of but one American life. Soon McKinley dispatched an expeditionary force to establish U.S. authority in the islands. Most Americans thought the problems of order and security in the Philippines sufficient to demand the occupation of Manila, completed in August; for them this action was no prelude to annexation of the islands.

But the sudden deployment of U.S. naval power in the distant Pacific and the possibilities it held for empire building were not lost on a powerful minority of American expansionists. The dramatic events of 1898 followed a logic of their own. They could not be divorced, at least in the expansionist mind, from the increasing American involvement in the Pacific. The force behind this concern was largely commercial. On foundations generously constructed in wartime, American business after 1865 quickly pushed the nation's industrial capacity beyond domestic demands. Indeed, the optimism in railroad and industrial construction led to such perennial overbuilding that it tumbled the national economy into periodic depressions, the worst two blanketing the years 1873–78 and 1893–97. Each depression stimulated further business consolidation, but it also demonstrated the need for foreign markets if the economy was ever to perform at full capacity again.

In developing their overseas strategy,

American leaders were careful to direct official policy toward the quest for markets and not the acquisition of islands. Still, the actual penetration of the Pacific by American merchants, sea captains, and naval officers had long confronted Washington with a variety of specific policy challenges, some political as well as economic. The administration of Benjamin Harrison after 1889 concerned itself with Samoa and Hawaii; it succeeded in annexing neither. During the depressed nineties, spokesmen of the conservative Cleveland administration perpetuated the distinction between the country's need for enlarged markets and the dangers involved in the acquisition of insular possessions. Secretary of State Walter Q. Gresham opposed the annexation of Pacific islands, but he suggested, along with others, that the United States negotiate for coaling stations which would give it commercial advantages without involving it in dangerous political and military responsibilities. In practice trade expansion received little encouragement from the actual policies the government pursued; the pressure for markets at best had a generalized, not a specific, influence on American territorial expansion into the Pacific.

Unlike Samoa and Hawaii, the Spanish Philippines had of necessity remained off limits to imperialist ambitions. Against the immediate background of the country's varied and growing interests in the Pacific, however, the reduction of Spanish power in the Islands confronted the United States with an unanticipated dilemma. What was to be the disposition of the Philippines, now partially in American hands? Doubts and confusion within the administration were profound, for prior to Dewey's naval victory no organized sentiment for the acquisition of any portion of the Philippine archipelago existed at all. Finley Peter Dunne's Mr. Dooley remarked that the American people "did not know whether the Philippines were islands or canned goods." But during the summer months of 1898 imperialist sentiment rolled across the

nation, assuring at last the congressional vote for Hawaiian annexation and capturing support of newspaper editors and businessmen who wanted nothing less than the retention of Manila.

Slowly a national policy emerged. At the end of July President McKinley, responding to expansionist pressure, announced that any truce with Spain must stipulate that the United States continue to occupy Manila until the conclusion of a treaty. Then, on September 16, the president clarified his intentions more precisely in his instructions to the peace commissioners. The president wrote:

> Without any original thought of complete or even partial acquisition, the presence and success of our arms at Manila imposes upon us obligations which we cannot disregard. The march of events rules and over-rules human action. . . . We cannot be unmindful that without any desire or design on our part the war has brought us new duties and responsibilities which we must meet and discharge as becomes a great nation on whose growth and career from the beginning the Ruler of Nations had plainly written the high command and pledge of civilization.

Except for this suggestion that American responsibility and interests might require a cession of the island of Luzon, the president assigned to the American commissioners in Paris the task of determining the actual terms of the treaty with Spain. In Paris the commissioners faced narrowing choices. Strategically it appeared inescapable that the United States acquire either the entire Philippine archipelago or no portion of it. Senator George Gray, the lone Democratic member of the commission, opposed any acquisitions in the Philippines, but the majority favored the retention of all the Islands, as well as Puerto Rico and Guam. With this decision McKinley concurred.

That the United States acquired the Philippines with some reluctance does not mean it lacked freedom of choice. But that freedom hardly survived the initial decision to destroy Spanish authority in the Islands. Thereafter, their restoration to Spain would have defied the will of the vast majority of Filipinos; to cast the Islands adrift seemed nothing less than a total negation of responsibility. Like the Spanish-American War itself, the ultimate decision to annex the Philippines was rationalized in terms of humanitarianism. There was no alternative, President McKinley later explained to a group of visiting clergymen, ''but to take them all, and to educate the Filipinos, and uplift and Christianize them, and by God's grace do the very best we could by them, as our fellowmen, for whom Christ also died. . . .''

Opponents of expansion—and they were legion—placed powerful intellectual obstacles in the path of the imperialists. Any acquisition of territory in the Philippine archipelago, they warned, would defy the spirit of both the Declaration of Independence and the Constitution. Neither of these documents, they said, provided for the government of peoples not designated for statehood. Even more sobering was the observation that the Philippine Islands were so distant, exposed, and defenseless that they would constitute a hostage which other world powers could employ in bargaining with the United States. Senator Alexander Clay of Georgia put his colleagues on notice of the price which might be exacted of the nation for its new involvement in the Far East:

> We want no complications or war with England, France, Germany, Russia, China, Japan, or any other foreign power. We want no territory or population liable and likely to involve us in complications which may lead to war with any of these powers. The danger of frequent and almost constant wars between foreign nations in the Far East . . . should be a warning against the acquisition of this foreign territory and population. . . . The United States has heretofore been solid, compact, contiguous, and impregnable. . . . When we go out into the seas beyond the Western Hemisphere and acquire other countries, we increase our responsibilities, weaken our defenses, and enormously increase the expenses of our Army and Navy. We must not come to the conclusion because we destroyed the Spanish fleets, that we could so easily cope with the navies of the European powers.

For most Americans and even members of Congress such warnings passed unnoticed. So remote were the burdens of empire that many assumed that the acquisition of the Philippines actually strengthened the nation. Yet, unless the Islands themselves possessed sources of power which equaled or exceeded that required for their defense, they would become a strategic liability. As the British *Saturday Review* saw it, the new American commitment in the Far East was so extensive that the reliance of the United States on British naval power was greater than ever before. The suddenness and completeness of the changes wrought by the events and opportunities of 1898 measured the extent to which illusions emanating from easy success had supplanted analysis in the conduct of the nation's external affairs.

Still the final acquisition of the Philippines was not cost free. Throughout the months of decision American officials ignored the fact that Filipino insurgents under Emilio Aguinaldo had freed much of the island of Luzon, leaving the Spaniards in control of Manila, their remaining stronghold. Momentarily in exile on the Asian mainland, Aguinaldo agreed to support the American effort in the Philippines in exchange for Philippine independence. With that promise Aguinaldo returned to the Islands on one of Commodore Dewey's vessels. Following his easy victory over the Spanish fleet, Dewey refused to recognize the Filipino rebels gathering outside Manila. When American forces accepted the surrender of Manila, they barred the insurgents from entering the city. With his ultimate failure to free the Islands, Aguinaldo prepared for war. Fighting broke out in February 1899. It quickly assumed the form of a guerrilla struggle that, in time, raised a full spectrum of moral issues. Disposing of the Philippine guerrillas proved to be far more troublesome and costly than defeating the Spaniards. The American forces suffered some 7,000 casualties, dead and wounded; enemy combat casualties approached 20,000, with untold thousands of civilians dying from war, disease, and crop destruction. Anti-imperialists wondered why the United States would suppress an independence movement. Condemning what they termed ''the President's war,'' they compelled the Senate to investigate the atrocities committed by American forces. The hearings, which began early in 1902, were partisan and bitter. With Aguinaldo's capture the Philippine-American War finally ended on July 4, 1902.

The continuing assumption that American will was unlimited, at least in the Far East, underlay the promulgation of the Open Door policy toward China in the summer of 1899. Behind this burgeoning concern for China was a series of successful British, French, German, and Russian efforts, in 1897 and 1898, to gain leaseholds and spheres of influence along the China coast. The McKinley administration's intention to oppose any European moves to restrict permanently the commerce of China and endanger that country's territorial integrity appeared feasible enough. And the magnificent undertaking of saving China from dismemberment—through mere circulation of the famous Open Door Notes to which all interested European powers gave their equivocal approval—merely intensified the illusion that great achievements abroad required little but proper motivation. Ignoring the skepticism of other countries, the American press hailed the Open Door policy as one of the most brilliant diplomatic achievements in the nation's history. For the Republican leadership, facing an election year, it was highly welcome. The bold stroke for China satisfied the demand for protection of American commercial interests. By guaranteeing Chinese rights against foreign encroachment, the policy appeared to support the cause of freedom.

American policy toward China, like that toward the Philippines, overlooked the enormity of the resulting commitment. In the Boxer Rebellion crisis of 1900, China was saved less by the second round of Open Door Notes than by the rivalries of the European forces. Despite momentary U.S. success in sustaining the Manchu empire, it was soon clear to Secretary of State John Hay, with whom the Open Door was identified, that the United States was not prepared to defend Chinese political and territorial integrity with force. In the wake of the Boxer Rebellion, Hay was troubled by a series of Russian maneuvers in Manchuria that clearly defied the Open Door principle. The secretary now recognized the fallacy of building policy on high-minded declarations alone. ''The talk of the papers about our 'pre-eminent moral position giving us the authority to dictate to the world,' '' he observed, ''is mere flapdoodle.'' Yet, for Hay, there was no avenue of retreat. To the popular mind his concept of the Open Door appeared so laudable in objective and so sound in precept that no later administration dared retract it. The United States had entered an age of permanent overcommitment in the Far East.

During subsequent years the American commitment to the Open Door principle in China became more pervading—this despite the greater military strength and more extensive interests of other powers in the western Pacific. Theodore Roosevelt, as president after 1901, attempted to limit the principle of equal opportunity in China to trade, not investment, especially in Manchuria then coming under Russian dominance. Roosevelt viewed the American commitment to China's territorial and administrative integrity an overcommitment which the United States should scrap at the first opportunity. For Roosevelt the dangers of overcommitment became more acute when Japan met the Russian challenge in Manchuria directly, defeating Russia in the Russo-Japanese War of 1904–05 and thereafter assuming control of both South Manchuria and Korea. Roosevelt hoped that the new balance of power in the Far East would check the ambitions of both Russia and Japan. To him it appeared essential, moreover, that the United States, if it continued to hold Hawaii and the Philippines, maintain adequate naval power in the Pacific.

Not all American officials and journalists shared Roosevelt's moderate attitude toward Japan. Behind the growing demand for a more determined American effort to curtail Japanese expansion was the fear that Tokyo would ultimately deprive the United States of its share of the Chinese market, especially the commercial and investment opportunities in Manchuria. Willard Straight, the young American consul general at Mukden (now Shenyang), South Manchuria, assumed command of the anti-Japanese crusade. He insisted that the United States had the right, under the Open Door principle, to employ its superior financial resources to eliminate Japan from South Manchuria entirely. During 1907 he planned a railroad, to be built with foreign capital, from Hsinmintum to Fakumen (Hsinmin to Fak'u), then continue on to Tsitsihar (Ch'ich'ihaerh) in North Manchuria. Straight explained the purpose of the proposed line to Francis M. Huntington Wilson of the State Department in January 1908: "The Hsinmintum-Fakumen line . . . will very seriously compete with the South Manchurian Railway, will not only tap a rich and rapidly developing country, part of the produce of which is now carried over the Japanese road, but will almost certainly attract all the through European traffic as well as secure all the mails." Tokyo met the challenge by revealing the secret protocols attached to a Sino-Japanese treaty of 1905 wherein China agreed that no foreign investors could construct a parallel line in the vicinity of the Japanese-controlled South Manchurian

Railway. Elihu Root, the new secretary of state, had no desire to challenge the primacy of Japan's interests in South Manchuria; like Hay, he accepted the argument that not every Japanese infraction of equal opportunity in South Manchuria defied the principle of the Open Door.

Root balked, however, when Russia, early in 1908, established administrative control of Harbin (Haerhpin) in North Manchuria to the complete exclusion of Chinese authority. If Japan followed this example the demise of the Open Door principle in all Manchuria would be complete. The secretary exerted enormous pressure on both the Russian and Japanese governments to refrain from erasing Chinese administrative and political authority in their areas of influence. Still he wanted no trouble over Manchuria and sought to smooth over months of accumulating United States-Japanese tension by signing the so-called Root-Takahira Agreement of November 1908. This statement declared it the common policy of the United States and Japan to support both the status quo in the western Pacific as well as the territorial integrity of China.

With the presidency of William Howard Taft (1909–13) China assumed a new importance. Taft, Huntington Wilson, and Philander C. Knox, the new secretary of state, believed that China, strengthened by administrative reforms, would develop its resources, inprove its living conditions, resist external aggression, and enforce the Open Door to guarantee equal opportunity for all countries. Straight left his post in the American consular service to become the agent of a newly formed American banking group seeking investments in China. These investments, in turn, would enhance the authority of the Chinese government. Turning the attention of the investors toward Manchuria, Straight proposed the construction of a Chinchow-Aigun Railway, another line designed to compete directly with the South Manchurian. Taft and Knox supported Straight's new plan to ease the Japanese out of South Manchuria through investments alone. Under Knox's guidance the program eventually took the form of a neutralization scheme whereby the Chinese government, aided by foreign loans, would gain control of all Manchurian railways. If the Japanese refused to cooperate, British and American investors would jointly underwrite the Chinchow-Aigun project. Upon learning of this new American effort to weaken the Japanese position in South Manchuria, Roosevelt warned Taft in December 1910:

> Our vital interest is to keep the Japanese out of our country, and at the same time preserve the good will of Japan. The vital interest of the Japanese, on the other hand, is in Manchuria and Korea. It is therefore peculiarly our interest not to take any steps as regards Manchuria which will give the Japanese cause to feel, with or without reason, that we are hostile to them, or a menace—in however slight a degree—to their interests. . . . I do not believe in our taking any position anywhere unless we can make good; and as regards Manchuria, if the Japanese choose to follow a course of conduct to which we are adverse, we cannot stop it unless we are prepared to go to war. . . . [A]s has been proved by the whole history of Manchuria, alike under Russia and under Japan, the ''open-door'' policy, as a matter of fact, completely disappears as soon as a powerful nation determines to disregard it, and is willing to run the risk of war rather than forego its intentions.

Knox's policies, based on the alleged power of investments, expected too much for too little. The British government refused to support any program detrimental to Japanese interests in the Far East. The neutralization scheme had the eventual effect of pushing Tokyo and St. Petersburg into an agreement whereby they underwrote each other's sphere of influence in Manchuria. Even in its failure to determine Manchuria's future, the Taft administration managed to place the United States and Japan on a collision course. In their determination to protect the Open Door for investment in Manchuria, Taft and Knox either detected pervading American interests there or were simply unmindful of the dangers inherent in their anti-Japanese pursuits. Already it was apparent to the skeptics that the United States faced the ultimate choice of modifying drastically its commitments to China or assuming the risk of war with Japan. That the country's interests in China, when contrasted to their potential costs, might prove to be negligible troubled only the most astute analysts; the defense of those interests, officials could surmise, would always demand little of the American people.

American intervention in the Caribbean began with the destruction of Spanish power in Cuba; thereafter it was continuous. In large measure the motives of responsible Washington officials remained humanitarian. That sentiment which had encouraged the intervention in Cuba sought, after 1900, to assure that country permanent peace and stability. Both Cuban and American interests demanded in Havana a government capable of maintaining order, of organizing an adequate system of public finance, and of sustaining profitable relations with the United States. Few concerned with Cuba's future would have quarreled with President McKinley's declared purpose of establishing a government in Cuba ''capable of maintaining order and observing its international obligations, insuring peace and tranquility and the security of its citizens as well as our own.'' To strengthen American control over Cuban affairs, Congress, in 1901, imposed the Platt Amendment which placed the island's external relations in American hands. Meanwhile Washington made grants of financial aid and maintained a temporary military occupation in Cuba under General Leonard Wood. Altogether these policies served Cuba well, achieving reasonably good government, better transportation, new industries and schools, and some control of famine and disease.

Roosevelt's interventionism which resulted in the acquisition of the Panama Canal Zone again served the country's economic and security interests. That Roosevelt, in this episode, damaged the reputation of the United States in Latin America resulted, in part, from behavior within the Colombian government which the president regarded dishonorable. The Isthmian canal issue itself emerged with renewed insistence from the Spanish-American War. The ninety-eight-day voyage of the battleship *Oregon* from Juan de Fuca Strait to Cuba demonstrated the need of a shorter passage between the Atlantic and Pacific for American merchant and naval vessels. In the Hay-Pauncefote Treaty of 1901 the United States secured from Britain, a country which had long shared American interests in Central America, the right to build, control, and fortify its own canal. Eventually the United States selected the Panama route over a passage through Nicaragua as the more feasible and less expensive.

Roosevelt soon faced difficulty in his attempt to negotiate the rights to a canal across the Isthmus of Panama with the revolution-torn government of Colombia. Colombian officials and much of the Colombian press resented the American decision to pay the French-dominated New Panama Canal Company $40 million for its exclusive rights, obtained earlier from Colombia, to build a canal across Panama. Beset by political agitation, the Colombian government refused to ratify the United States-Colombian treaty. Roosevelt, conscious of the perennial discontent of the Panamanians toward the Bogotá government, saw immediately that the establishment of an independent Panama would resolve the American dilemma.

Where Roosevelt could not act, others did. Philip Bunau-Varilla, a French citizen and director of the French canal company, and his New York lawyer, William Nelson Cromwell, saw the $40 million drifting away. In this crisis they invited Dr. Amador, leader of the Panamanian independence movement, to New York

City; there they arranged the Panama revolution. Dr. Amador returned to Panama and there, on November 3, 1903, staged a bloodless revolution. Three days later the United States extended de facto recognition to the new government of Panama. On November 13 Roosevelt formally accepted Bunau-Varilla's credentials as Panama's first minister to the United States; this act granted de jure recognition to Panama. Five days later the Hay-Bunau-Varilla Treaty, signed in Washington, granted the United States a canal zone with the right to build a canal across the isthmus. The Panama Constitution permitted the United States to intervene in Panamanian affairs to maintain peace and order.

One critical question remained: Could the United States protect the Caribbean from European encroachment? It had occurred to some American. that the Monroe Doctrine was not a self-enforcing barrier against possible German ambitions in the Western Hemisphere. Washington limited its strategic concerns to the Caribbean, not because Europe confined its interests to that region but because a number of Caribbean states displayed a special measure of political and financial irresponsibility toward foreign investors. During 1902 Venezuela's notorious government defaulted on its foreign debts. In early December an Anglo-German-Italian squadron blockaded the Venezuelan coast with considerable damage to Venezuelan property. On December 12 the United States transmitted Venezuela's offer of arbitration to the blockading powers; within one week both Britain and Germany accepted the arrangement. Thereafter London lost interest in the venture, preferring that the United States take responsibility for Venezuela's debts. The lingering hostility aroused by the blockade now centered on Germany. The crisis intensified in January 1903 when German warships fired on two Venezuelan forts. Finally in February Berlin yielded to an American proposal and lifted the blockade. Later Roosevelt revealed, with apparent accuracy, that he had warned the German government privately to limit its demands on Venezuela or he would order the American Caribbean fleet to Venezuelan waters.

Roosevelt's interventionism in the Caribbean to counter that of Europe reached its ultimate formulation in his Corollary to the Monroe Doctrine. The president saw clearly that the United States would either witness further interference by European creditor nations in Latin-American affairs or would assume the role of policeman to control disputes which emanated from the reckless financial policies of the Caribbean republics. He believed correctly that it was far easier to fix the bounds of loose financial practices than to counter foreign interventions which such practices invited. For Roosevelt it appeared equally essential that the United States maintain a measure of law and order in the Americas whether political disorder challenged the security of the United States or not. To that end he warned the Latin American governments in December 1904: "Chronic wrongdoing, or an impotence which results in a general loosening of the ties of civilized society, may in America, as elsewhere, ultimately require intervention by some civilized nation, and in the Western Hemisphere the adherence of the United States to the Monroe Doctrine may force the United States, however reluctantly, in flagrant cases of such wrongdoing or impotence, to the exercise of an international police power."

The Roosevelt Corollary reinforced the notion that the Caribbean was an exclusive American preserve. It defied normal diplomatic practice in two essential respects. First, it established a right to intervene where neither self-defense nor treaty obligations were at issue. Second, it assumed that the European powers had fewer rights in the Western Hemisphere than did the United States—an assumption which European governments persistently denied. If Europeans accepted American exclusiveness in the Caribbean, they did so not be-

cause the United States possessed special rights in the Western Hemisphere, but because it possessed superior interests and power.

American interventionism under the Roosevelt Corollary did not lack humanitarian intent. Even as Roosevelt prepared to establish U.S. control of the customs administration of Santo Domingo in 1905, he explained to Congress: "Santo Domingo grievously needs the aid of a powerful and friendly nation. This aid we are able . . . to bestow. She has asked for this aid, and the expressions of friendship, repeatedly sanctioned by the people and Government of the United States, warrant her in believing that it will not be withheld. . . ." Beginning in 1906, American officials promoted hemispheric cordiality with a continuous display of goodwill. That year Secretary Root made an unprecedented tour of Latin America and attended the Third International Conference of American States at Rio de Janeiro. There the secretary expressed U.S. concern for the economic development of Latin America. Only by helping friendly states to achieve prosperity and growth, he said, could the United States hope to enlarge its own prosperity, commerce, and wealth.

Dollar diplomacy, as it evolved during the Roosevelt and Taft administrations, was more than a national effort to ease the path of American investment abroad. It was, more accurately, an effort to urge reluctant investors to place U.S. capital where it would serve the American interest in hemispheric stability. Eventually, perhaps, such investments would create markets for U.S. products. "If the American dollar," wrote Secretary Knox, "can aid suffering humanity and lift the burden of financial difficulty from states with which we live on terms of intimate intercourse and earnest friendship, all I can say is that it would be hard to find better employment." Through economic progress and sound governmental finance alone, believed Knox, could Caribbean nations achieve political stability.

Unfortunately, in practice, the United States sought political stability in the Caribbean, not democracy or humanitarian progress. To maintain stable regimes that would underwrite its economic and strategic interests, the United States placed troops in Panama in 1903, Cuba in 1906, Nicaragua in 1909 and 1912, Honduras in 1912, Mexico in 1914, Haiti in 1915, and the Dominican Republic in 1916. American policies of intervention, which often overthrew unwanted governments with surprising ease, bound the United States to the elites of the Caribbean states, not to those without economic or political power. It was not strange that the perennial involvement of the United States in Central American affairs did little to mitigate the exploitative nature of the Caribbean economies or ameliorate the condition of the poor. Concentrated wealth and power, resting on a foundation of mass poverty, remained the norm. Against that reality U.S. policy could never bring permanent stability to the countries of Central America. If American expansionism in East Asia raised the issue of war with Japan, that in the Caribbean posed questions of judgment and morality. So predominant was U.S. power in the Caribbean that no level of interventionism seemed capable of endangering the region's general peace.

SUGGESTED READINGS

Beisner, Robert L. *Twelve against Empire: The Anti-Imperialists, 1898–1900.* New York: McGraw-Hill, 1968.

Challener, Richard D. *Admirals, Generals, and American Foreign Policy, 1898–1914.* Princeton, N.J.: Princeton University Press, 1973.

Dulles, Foster Rhea. *The Imperial Years.* New York: Thomas Y. Crowell, 1956.

Griswold, A. Whitney. *The Far Eastern Policy of the United States.* New York: Harcourt Brace Jovanovich, 1938.

Healy, David F. *The United States in Cuba, 1898–1902: Generals, Politicians, and the Search for Policy.* Madison: University of Wisconsin Press, 1963.

Kennan, George F. *American Diplomacy, 1900–1950.* Chicago: University of Chicago Press, 1951.

LaFeber, Walter. *The New Empire: An Interpretation of American Expansion, 1860–1898.* Ithaca, N.Y.: Cornell University Press, 1963.

May, Ernest R. *Imperial Democracy.* New York: Harcourt Brace Jovanovich, 1961.

Millis, Walter. *The Martial Spirit.* Boston: Houghton Mifflin, 1931.

Neu, Charles E. *The Troubled Encounter: The United States and Japan.* New York: John Wiley & Sons, 1975.

Pratt, Julius W. *The Expansionists of 1898.* Baltimore: The Johns Hopkins Press, 1936.

Rystad, Goran. *Ambiguous Imperialism: American Foreign Policy and Domestic Politics at the Turn of the Century.* Lund, Sweden: Esselte Studium, 1975.

Scholes, Walter V., and Marie V. Scholes. *The Foreign Policies of the Taft Administration.* Columbia: University of Missouri Press, 1970.

Varg, Paul A. *Open Door Diplomat: The Life of W. W. Rockhill.* Urbana: University of Illinois Press, 1952.

Wisan, J. E. *The Cuban Crisis as Reflected in the New York Press, 1895–1898.* New York: Columbia University Press, 1934.

DOCUMENT 20.1
The Anglo-Saxon and the World's Future

Josiah Strong, a gifted young Congregational minister, was secretary of his denomination's Home Missionary Society. A leading religious journalist, he also was a pioneer in the social gospel movement. The selection below is characteristic of his belief in the future destiny and God-given "mission" of the United States.

Source: Josiah Strong, *Our Country* (New York: Baker and Taylor, 1885), pp. 159, 161, 165, 174–76.

Every race which has deeply impressed itself on the human family has been the representative of some great idea—one or more—which has given direction to the nation's life and form to its civilization. . . . The Anglo-Saxon is the representative of two great ideas, which are closely related. One of them is that of civil liberty. . . . The noblest races have always been lovers of liberty. That love ran strong in early German blood, and has profoundly influenced the institutions of all the branches of the great German family; but it was left for the Anglo-Saxon branch fully to recognize the right of the individual to himself, and formally to declare it the foundation stone of government.

The other great idea of which the Anglo-Saxon is the exponent is that of a pure *spiritual* Christianity. . . .

It is not necessary to argue to those for whom I write that the two great needs of mankind, that all men may be lifted up into the light of the highest Christian civilization, are, first, a pure, spiritual Christianity, and, second, civil liberty. Without controversy, these are the forces which, in the past, have contributed most to the elevation of the human race, and they must continue to be, in the future, the most efficient ministers to its progress. It follows, then, that the Anglo-Saxon, as the great representative of these two ideas, the depositary of these two greatest blessings, sustains peculiar relations to the world's future, is divinely commissioned to be, in a peculiar sense, his brother's keeper. Add to this the fact of his rapidly increasing strength in modern times, and we have well nigh a demonstration of his destiny. . . .

It is not unlikely that, before the close of the next century, this race will outnumber all the other civilized races of the world. Does it not look as if God were not only preparing in our Anglo-Saxon civilization the die with which to stamp the peoples of the earth, but as if he were also massing behind that die the mighty

power with which to press it? My confidence that this race is eventually to give its civilization to mankind is not based on mere numbers—China forbid! I look forward to what the world has never yet seen united in the same race; viz., the greatest numbers, *and* the highest civilization.

There can be no reasonable doubt that North America is to be the great home of the Anglo-Saxon, the principal seat of his power, the center of his life and influence. . . .

. . . It seems to me that God, with infinite wisdom and skill, is training the Anglo-Saxon race for an hour sure to come in the world's future. Heretofore there has always been in the history of the world a comparatively unoccupied land westward, into which the crowded countries of the East have poured their surplus populations. But the widening waves of migration, which millenniums ago rolled east and west from the valley of the Euphrates, meet to-day on our Pacific coast. There are no more new worlds. The unoccupied arable lands of the earth are limited, and will soon be taken. The time is coming when the pressure of population on the means of subsistence will be felt here as it is now felt in Europe and Asia. Then will the world enter upon a new stage of its history—*the final competition of races, for which the Anglo-Saxon is being schooled.* Long before the thousand millions are here, the mighty *centrifugal* tendency, inherent in this stock and strengthened in the United States, will assert itself. Then this race of unequaled energy, with all the majesty of numbers and the might of wealth behind it—the representative, let us hope, of the largest liberty, the purest Christianity, the highest civilization—having developed peculiarly aggressive traits calculated to impress its institutions upon mankind, will spread itself over the earth. If I read not amiss, this powerful race will move down upon Mexico, down upon Central and South America, out upon the islands of the sea, over upon Africa and beyond. And can any one doubt that the result of this competition of races will be the "survival of the fittest"? . . .

. . . "At the present day," says Mr. Darwin, "civilized nations are everywhere supplanting barbarous nations, excepting where the climate opposes a deadly barrier; and they succeed mainly, though not exclusively, through their arts, which are the products of the intellect." Thus the Finns were supplanted by the Aryan races in Europe and Asia, the Tartars by the Russians, and thus the aborigines of North America, Australia and New Zealand are now disappearing before the all-conquering Anglo-Saxons. It would seem as if these inferior tribes were only precursors of a superior race, voices in the wilderness crying: "Prepare ye the way of the Lord!" . . .

DOCUMENT 20.2
The Advantages of Naval and Territorial Expansion

Alfred Thayer Mahan was an Annapolis graduate who served in the U.S. Navy during the Civil War, was appointed to the Naval War Board in the Spanish-American War, and subsequently advanced to the rank of rear admiral. A "big-navy" man and a leading exponent of expansionism, he was admired by the entire bloc of imperialist spokesmen, Theodore Roosevelt in particular. Mahan argued that the national security demanded a growing naval force, an Isthmian canal, and Caribbean and Pacific island possessions. He presented his message within the social Darwinian framework, his central thesis being that international competition was a naked struggle for power—with control of the sea being an indispensable factor.

Indications are not wanting of an approaching change in the thoughts and policy of Americans

Source: Alfred Thayer Mahan, "The United States Looking Outward," in *The Interest of America in Sea Power* (New York: Harper & Bros., 1897), pp. 3–27.

as to their relations with the world outside their own borders. For the past quarter of a century, the predominant idea, which has asserted itself successfully at the polls and shaped the course of the government, has been to preserve the home market for the home industries. . . .

. . . Within, the home market is secured; but outside, beyond the broad seas, there are the markets of the world, that can be entered and controlled only by a vigorous contest, to which the habit of trusting to protection by statute does not conduce. . . .

. . . The interesting and significant feature of this changing attitude is the turning of the eyes outward, instead of inward only, to seek the welfare of the country. To affirm the importance of distant markets, and the relation to them of our own immense powers of production, implies logically the recognition of the link that joins the products and the markets,— that is, the carrying trade; the three together constituting that chain of maritime power to which Great Britain owes her wealth and greatness. Further, is it too much to say that, as two of these links, the shipping and the markets, are exterior to our own borders, the acknowledgment of them carries with it a view of the relations of the United States to the world radically distinct from the simple idea of self-sufficingness? We shall not follow far this line of thought before there will dawn the realization of America's unique position, facing the older worlds of the East and West, her shores washed by the oceans which touch the one or the other, but which are common to her alone.

Coincident with these signs of change in our own policy there is restlessness in the world at large which is deeply significant, if not ominous. It is beside our purpose to dwell upon the internal state of Europe, whence, if disturbances arise, the effect upon us may be but partial and indirect. But the great seaboard powers there do not stand on guard against their continental rivals only; they cherish also aspirations for commercial extension, for colonies, and for influence in distant regions, which may bring, and, even under our present contracted policy, already have brought them into collision with ourselves. The incident of the Samoa Islands, trivial apparently, was nevertheless eminently suggestive of European ambitions. America then roused from sleep as to interests closely concerning her future. At this moment internal troubles are imminent in the Sandwich Islands, where it should be our fixed determination to allow no foreign influence to equal our own. All over the world German commercial and colonial push is coming into collision with other nations. . . .

. . . In a general way, it is evident enough that this canal [through the Central American Isthmus], by modifying the direction of trade routes, will induce a great increase of commercial activity and carrying trade throughout the Caribbean Sea; and that this now comparatively deserted nook of the ocean will become, like the Red Sea, a great thoroughfare of shipping, and will attract, as never before in our day, the interest and ambition of maritime nations. Every position in that sea will have enhanced commercial and military value, and the canal itself will become a strategic centre of the most vital importance. Like the Canadian Pacific Railroad, it will be a link between the two oceans; but, unlike it, the use, unless most carefully guarded by treaties, will belong wholly to the belligerent which controls the sea by its naval power. In case of war, the United States will unquestionably command the Canadian Railroad, despite the deterrent force of operations by the hostile navy upon our seaboard; but no less unquestionably will she be impotent, as against any of the great maritime powers, to control the Central American canal. Militarily speaking, and having reference to European complications only, the piercing of the Isthmus is nothing but a disaster to the United States, in the present state of her military and naval preparation. It is espe-

cially dangerous to the Pacific coast; but the increased exposure of one part of our seaboard reacts unfavorably upon the whole military situation.

Despite a certain great original superiority conferred by our geographical nearness and immense resources,—due, in other words, to our natural advantages, and not to our intelligent preparations,—the United States is woefully unready, not only in fact but in purpose to assert in the Caribbean and Central America a weight of influence proportioned to the extent of her interests. We have not the navy, and, what is worse, we are not willing to have the navy, that will weigh seriously in any disputes with those nations whose interests will conflict there with our own. We have not, and we are not anxious to provide, the defence of the seaboard which will leave the navy free for its work at sea. We have not, but many other powers have, positions, either within or on the borders of the Caribbean which not only possess great natural advantages for the control of that sea, but have received and are receiving that artificial strength of fortification and armament which will make them practically inexpugnable. On the contrary, we have not on the Gulf of Mexico even the beginning of a navy yard which could serve as the base of our operations. . . .

. . . Though distant, our shores can be reached; being defenceless, they can detain but a short time a force sent against them. . . .

Yet, were our sea frontier as strong as it now is weak, passive self-defence, whether in trade or war, would be but a poor policy, so long as the world continues to be one of struggle and vicissitude. All around us now is strife; "the struggle of life," "the race of life," are phrases so familiar that we do not feel their significance till we stop to think about them. Everywhere nation is arrayed against nation; our own no less than others. What is our protective system but an organized warfare? . . .

DOCUMENT 20.3
Anti-Imperialism: The Argument against Expansionism

Among the many arguments leveled at American expansion into the western Pacific at the turn of the century, one—presented by Andrew Carnegie—appeared especially significant. It challenged the popular notion that the new acquisitions would require no special military expenditures and that the new commitments would not unduly expose the United States to embarrassment or attack.

Let another phase of the question be carefully weighed. Europe is today an armed camp, not chiefly because the home territories of its various nations are threatened, but because of fear of aggressive action upon the part of other nations touching outlying "possessions." France resents British control of Egypt and is fearful of its West African possessions; Russia seeks Chinese territory, with a view to expansion in the Pacific; Germany also seeks distant possessions; Britain, who has acquired so many dependencies, is so fearful of an attack upon them that this year she is spending nearly eighty millions of dollars upon additional warships, and Russia, Germany and France follow suit. Japan is a new element of anxiety; and by the end of the year it is computed she will have 67 formidable ships of war. The naval powers of Europe, and Japan also, are apparently determined to be prepared for a terrific struggle for possessions in the Far East, close to the Philippines—and why not for these islands themselves? Into this vortex the Republic is cordially invited to enter by those powers who expect her policy to be of benefit to them, but her action is jealously watched by those

Source: Andrew Carnegie, "Distant Possessions—The Parting of the Ways," *North American Review* (August 1898), vol. 167, pp. 239–48.

who fear that her power might be used against them.

It has never been considered the part of wisdom to thrust one's hand into the hornet's nest, and it does seem as if the United States must lose all claim to ordinary prudence and good sense if she enter this arena, and become involved in the intrigues and threats of war which make Europe an armed camp.

It is the parting of the ways. We have a continent to populate and develop; there are only 23 persons to the square mile in the United States. England has 370, Belgium 571, and Germany 250. A tithe of the cost of maintaining our sway over the Philippines would improve our internal waterways; deepen our harbors; build the Nicaraguan Canal; construct a waterway to the ocean from the Great Lakes; an inland canal along the Atlantic seaboard; a canal across Florida, saving 800 miles distance between New York and New Orleans; connect Lake Michigan with the Mississippi; deepen all the harbors upon the lakes; build a canal from Lake Erie to the Allegheny River; slackwater through movable dams the entire length of the Ohio River to Cairo; thoroughly improve the Lower and Upper Mississippi, and all our seaboard harbors. All these enterprises would be as nothing in cost in comparison to the sums required for the experiment of possessing the Philippine Islands, 7,000 miles from our shores. If the object be to render our Republic powerful among nations, can there be any doubt as to which policy is the better? To be more powerful at home is the surest way to be more powerful abroad. To-day the Republic stands the friend of all nations, the ally of none; she has no ambitious designs upon the territory of any power upon another continent; she crosses none of their ambitious designs, evokes no jealousy of the bitter sort, inspires no fears; she is not one of them, scrambling for "possessions"; she stands apart, pursuing her own great mission, and teaching all nations by example. Let her become a power annexing foreign territory, and all is changed in a moment.

If we are to compete with other nations for foreign possessions we must have a navy like theirs. It should be superior to any other navy, or we play a second part. It is not enough to have a navy equal to that of Russia or of France, for Russia and France may combine against us just as they may against Britain. We at once enter the field as a rival of Britain, the chief possessor of foreign possessions, and who can guarantee that we shall not even have to measure our power against her?

What it means to enter the list of military and naval powers having foreign possessions may be gathered from the following considerations. First, look at our future navy. If it is only to equal that of France it means 51 battleships; if of Russia, 40 battleships. If we cannot play the game without being at least the equal of any of our rivals, then 80 battleships is the number Britain possesses. We now have only 4, with 5 building. Cruisers, armed and unarmed, swell the number threefold, Britain having 273 ships of the line built or ordered, with 308 torpedo boats in addition; France having 134 ships of the line and 269 torpedo boats. All these nations are adding ships rapidly. Every armor and gun making plant in the world is busy night and day. Ships are indispensable, but recent experience shows that soldiers are equally so. While the immense armies of Europe need not be duplicated, yet we shall certainly be too weak unless our army is at least twenty times what it has been—say 500,000 men. . . .

To-day two great powers in the world are compact, developing themselves in peace throughout vast coterminous territories. When war threatens they have no outlying "possessions" which can never be really "possessed," but which they are called upon to defend. They fight upon the exposed edge only of their own soil in case of attack, and are not only invulnera-

ble, but they could not be more than inconvenienced by the world in arms against them. These powers are Russia and the United States. . . . Britain, France, Germany, Belgium, Spain, are all vulnerable, having departed from the sagacious policy of keeping possessions and power concentrated. Should the United States depart from this policy, she also must be so weakened in consequence as never to be able to play the commanding part in the world, disjointed, that she can play whenever she desires if she remains compact.

Whether the United States maintain its present unique position of safety or forfeit it through acquiring foreign possessions, is to be decided by its action in regard to the Philippines; for, fortunately, the independence of Cuba is assured, for this the Republic has proclaimed to the world that she has drawn the sword. But why should the less than two millions of Cuba receive national existence and the seven and a half millions of the Philippines be denied it? The United States, thus far in their history, have no page reciting self-sacrifice made for others; all their gains have been for themselves. This void is now to be grandly filled. The page which recites the resolve of the Republic to rid her neighbor Cuba from the foreign "possessor" will grow brighter with the passing centuries, which may dim many pages now deemed illustrious. Should the coming American be able to point to Cuba and the Philippines rescued from foreign domination and enjoying independence won for them by his country and given to them without money and without price, he will find no citizen of any other land able to claim for his country services so disinterested and so noble.

We repeat there is no power in the world that could do more than inconvenience the United States by attacking its fringe, which is all that the world combined could do, so long as our country is not compelled to send its forces beyond its own compact shores to defend worthless ''possessions.'' If our country were blockaded by the united powers of the world for years, she would emerge from the embargo richer and stronger, and with her own resources more completely developed. We have little to fear from external attack. No thorough blockade of our enormous seaboard is possible; but even if it were, the few indispensable articles not produced by ourselves (if there were any such) would reach us by way of Mexico or Canada at slightly increased cost. . . .

DOCUMENT 20.4
Anti-Imperialism: The Appeal to Conservative Tradition

A major position taken by antiexpansionists challenged the new American habit of rationalizing national action with appeals to patriotism and democratic ideology. William Graham Sumner, the Yale sociologist, urged his countrymen to remember the true sources of national greatness and idealism.

. . . The war with Spain was precipitated upon us headlong, without reflection or deliberation, and without any due formulation of public opinion. Whenever a voice was raised in behalf of deliberation and the recognized maxims of statesmanship, it was howled down in a storm of vituperation and cant. Everything was done to make us throw away sobriety of thought and calmness of judgment, and to inflate all expressions with sensational epithets and turgid phrases. It cannot be denied that everything in regard to the war has been treated in an exalted strain of sentiment and rhetoric very unfavorable to the truth. At present the whole periodical press of the country seems

Source: William Graham Sumner, ''The Conquest of the United States by Spain,'' *Yale Law Journal* (January 1899), vol. 8, no. 4, pp. 168–93.

to be occupied in tickling the national vanity to the utmost by representations about the war which are extravagant and fantastic. There will be a penalty to be paid for all this. Nervous and sensational newspapers are just as corrupting, especially to young people, as nervous and sensational novels. The habit of expecting that all mental pabulum shall be highly spiced, and the corresponding loathing for whatever is soberly truthful, undermines character as much as any other vice. Patriotism is being prostituted into a nervous intoxication which is fatal to an apprehension of truth. It builds around us a fool's paradise, and it will lead us into errors about our position and relations just like those which we have been ridiculing in the case of Spain. . . .

. . . The laws of nature and of human nature are just as valid for Americans as for anybody else, and if we commit acts, we shall have to take consequences, just like other people. Therefore prudence demands that we look ahead to see what we are about to do, and that we gauge the means at our disposal, if we do not want to bring calamity on ourselves and our children. We see that the peculiarities of our system of government set limitations on us. We cannot do things which a great centralized monarchy could do. The very blessings and special advantages which we enjoy, as compared with others, bring disabilities with them. That is the great fundamental cause of what I have tried to show throughout this lecture, that we cannot govern dependencies consistently with our political system, and that, if we try it, the state which our fathers founded will suffer a reaction which will transform it into another empire just after the fashion of all the old ones. That is what imperialism means. That is what it will be, and the democratic republic, which has been, will stand in history as a mere transition form like the colonial organization of earlier days.

And yet this scheme of a republic which

our fathers formed was a glorious dream which demands more than a word of respect and affection before it passes away. . . . Our fathers would have an economical government, even if grand people called it a parsimonious one, and taxes should be no greater than were absolutely necessary to pay for such a government. . . . No adventurous policies of conquest or ambition, such as, in their belief, kings and nobles had forced, for their own advantage, on European states, would ever be undertaken by a free democratic republic. Therefore the citizen here would never be forced to leave his family, or to give his sons to shed blood for glory and to leave widows and orphans in misery for nothing. Justice and law were to reign in the midst of simplicity, and a government which had little to do was to offer little field for ambition. In a society where industry, frugality and prudence were honored, it was believed that the vices of wealth would never flourish.

We know that these beliefs, hopes and intentions have been only partially fulfilled. We know that, as time has gone on, and we have grown numerous and rich, some of these things have proved impossible ideals, incompatible with a large and flourishing society, but it is by virtue of this conception of a commonwealth that the United States has stood for something unique and grand in the history of mankind, and that its people have been happy. It is by virtue of these ideals that we have been "isolated," isolated in a position which the other nations of the earth have observed in silent envy, and yet there are people who are boasting of their patriotism, because they say that we have taken our place now amongst the nations of the earth by virtue of this war. My patriotism is of the kind which is outraged by the notion that the United States never was a great nation until in a petty three months campaign it knocked to pieces a poor, decrepit bankrupt old state like Spain. To hold such an opinion as that is to abandon all American standards,

to put shame and scorn on all that our ancestors tried to build up here, and to go over to the standards of which Spain is a representative.

DOCUMENT 20.5
The Responsibilities and Dangers of an Expansionist Policy

Herbert Croly was the founder and editor of The New Republic *magazine. He was also the main philosopher-proponent of progressivism. In this selection he points out the perils of Pacific expansionism in relation to a mature domestic policy.*

A genuinely national foreign policy for the American democracy is not exhausted by the Monroe Doctrine. The United States already has certain colonial interests; and these interests may hereafter be extended. I do not propose at the present stage of this discussion to raise the question as to the legitimacy in principle of a colonial policy on the part of a democratic nation. The validity of colonial expansion even for a democracy is a manifest deduction from the foregoing political principles, always assuming that the people whose independence is thereby diminished are incapable of efficient national organization. On the other hand, a democratic nation cannot righteously ignore an unusually high standard of obligation for the welfare of its colonial population. It would be distinctly recreant to its duty, in case it failed to provide for the economic prosperity of such a population, and for their educational discipline and social improvement. It by no means follows, however, that because there is no rigid objection on democratic principles to colonial expansion, there may not be the

Source: Herbert Croly, *The Promise of American Life* (New York: Macmillan, 1909), pp. 308–10.

strongest practical objection on the score of national interest to the acquisition of any particular territory. A remote colony is, under existing international conditions, even more of a responsibility than it is a source of national power and efficiency; and it is always a grave question how far the assumption of any particular responsibility is worth while.

Without entering into any specific discussion, there can, I think, be little doubt that the United States was justified in assuming its existing responsibilities in respect to Cuba and its much more abundant responsibilities in respect to Porto Rico. Neither can it be fairly claimed that hitherto the United States has not dealt disinterestedly and in good faith with the people of these islands. On the other hand, our acquisition of the Philippines raises a series of much more doubtful questions. These islands have been so far merely an expensive obligation, from which little benefit has resulted to this country and a comparatively moderate benefit to the Filipinos. They have already cost an amount of money far beyond any chance of compensation, and an amount of American and Filipino blood, the shedding of which constitutes a grave responsibility. Their future defense against possible attack presents a military and naval problem of the utmost difficulty. In fact, they cannot be defended from Japan except by the maintenance of a fleet in Pacific waters at least as large as the Japanese fleet; and it does not look probable that the United States will be able to afford for another generation any such concentration of naval strength in the Pacific. But even though from the military point of view the Philippines may constitute a source of weakness and danger, their possession will have the political advantage of keeping the American people alive to their interests in the grave problems which will be raised in the Far East by the future development of China and Japan.

The future of China raises questions of American foreign policy second only in impor-

tance to the establishment of a stable American international organization; and in relation to these questions, also, the interests of the United States and Canada tend both to coincide and to diverge (possibly) from those of Great Britain. Just what form the Chinese question will assume, after the industrial and the political awakening of China has resulted in a more effective military organization and in greater powers both of production and consumption, cannot be predicted with any certainty; but at present, it looks as if the maintenance of the traditional American policy with respect to China, viz., the territorial integrity and the free commercial development of that country, might require quite as considerable a concentration of naval strength in the Pacific as is required by the defense of the Philippines. It is easy enough to enunciate such a policy, just as it is easy to proclaim a Monroe Doctrine which no European Power has any sufficient immediate interest to dispute; but it is wholly improbable that China can be protected in its territorial integrity and its political independence without a great deal of diplomacy and more or less fighting. During the life of the coming generation there will be brought home clearly to the American people how much it will cost to assert its own essential interests in China; and the peculiar value of the Philippines as an American colony will consist largely in the fact that they will help American public opinion to realize more quickly than it otherwise would the complications and responsibilities created by Chinese political development and by Japanese ambition.

The existence and the resolute and intelligent facing of such responsibilities are an inevitable and a wholesome aspect of national discipline and experience. The American people have too easily evaded them in the past, but in the future they cannot be evaded; and it is better so. The irresponsible attitude of Americans in respect to their national domestic problems may in part be traced to freedom from equally grave international responsibilities. In truth, the work of internal reconstruction and amelioration, so far from being opposed to that of the vigorous assertion of a valid foreign policy, is really correlative and supplementary thereto; and it is entirely possible that hereafter the United States will be forced into the adoption of a really national domestic policy because of the dangers and duties incurred through her relations with foreign countries.

chapter

"The Nadir": Black Life after Reconstruction, 1877–1910

Thomas C. Holt
The University of Chicago

In 1954 on the eve of the U.S. Supreme Court's *Brown* v. *Board of Education* decision outlawing segregation in education, historian Rayford Logan wrote a history of race relations in the late-nineteenth century in which he characterized that period as the nadir of black life in America. Viewed objectively, Logan's description could be disputed; after all, slavery was surely a worse plight for blacks than any other they have experienced before or since. But from the perspective of the high expectations black Americans had following the abolition of slavery, their conditions of life at the turn of the century were perhaps more bitterly perceived and more difficult to accept. In a nation built on the premise that "all men are created equal," slavery's injustice was palpable and repeatedly intruded into political and social debates. By contrast, protests against the economic, social, and political injustices of black life at the dawn of the twentieth century were barely audible; and when heard, not credited. In many ways, contemporary scholarship still fails to fully account for the nature, the causes, or the consequences of America's version of apartheid.

The decade following Lee's surrender at Appomattox was one of tremendous change and hope for black Americans. For all its flaws the radical Republican effort to reconstruct the South laid the basis for realizing a more democratic society than that region had ever known. Slavery was destroyed by force of arms; and in December 1865, the Thirteenth Amendment to the U.S. Constitution confirmed its destruction. A series of Reconstruction laws granted freed people civil and political rights. Federal agencies and reorganized state governments provided access to education and other public services previously denied southern blacks and many southern whites as well. Attracted by prospects of unprecedented economic and political opportunities, thousands of northern blacks moved South. Former slaves challenged their former masters' authority on the plantations and in public forums. They resisted the planters' efforts to make them work in the manner and under the conditions they had in slavery. They met in state conventions to demand equal rights and economic justice. In cities across the nation they promoted sit-ins and boycotts to protest racial discrimination in public transportation and other accommodations. In 1875 a federal civil rights law was passed barring such discrimination. Even in the face of southern white intimidation and violence blacks voted and held office. They built schools, churches, mutual aid societies, and other community institutions. They reconstructed families. In short, they tried to give substance to the freedom they had won.

But the last two decades of the nineteenth century witnessed an almost complete reversal of these achievements. By the end of the century most black Americans lived impoverished lives on southern plantations, were barred from the ballot box, segregated in most areas of public life, and victimized by lynch mobs in record numbers. In contrast with earlier periods of racial oppression, the nation seemed indifferent to their plight. Indeed many northern observers agreed with white southerners that "the Negro Problem" sprang from faults within the black community. Their poverty was caused by their incapacities in the workplace; their exclusion from the political process was prudent recognition that they would abuse the privilege of voting; their social separation was consonant with the requirements of the Constitution and human nature.

Historians today would agree that the conditions of black life following Reconstruction betrayed the promise of freedom, but they often disagree about the origins or causes of those conditions. Was the sharecropping system within which most blacks labored merely a continuation from slavery of a system of racial domination, or was it a reasonably free labor market? Were segregation laws regulating most areas of public life created in response to new conditions in the 1890s, or a continuation of antebellum patterns? Some argue that these conditions reflect the former slaveholders' continued power over southern society; others that powerful new classes responding to new conditions were responsible. And, finally, how does one evaluate the character and appropriateness of the diverse black responses to these conditions? When does outward accommodation become a shrewd form of resistance? When does uncompromising resistance become counterproductive?

SHARECROPPING, PEONAGE, AND CONVICT LEASE

For half a century after emancipation, the overwhelming majority of blacks continued to live in the South and to work its farms and plantations as sharecroppers or tenants. By 1890 about nine of every ten black American workers were employed on a farm or as a domestic servant; another 7 percent found work as skilled artisans or in manufacturing. Sharecropping and tenancy had evolved during the first decade following the Civil War among both black and white farmworkers. It endured until the mid-twentieth century when economic and political pressures created by New Deal agricultural policies in the 1930s, population changes stimulated by the two world wars, and mechanization of southern agriculture eroded and eventually destroyed it.

Scholars now generally accept the view that sharecropping was a kind of compromise between planters who, having lost their main collateral for credit with their slave property, could not pay wages, and freed people who, disappointed at not receiving land with their freedom, resisted attempts to impose any labor system reminiscent of slavery. Black men often refused to sign labor contracts, and women and children withdrew from field labor. Following experimentation with a variety of labor systems during the Reconstruction decade, share-tenancy systems emerged as the best way to allocate the risks and profits of cotton and tobacco farming. For planters, family sharecropping appeared to be the best way to regain control of the labor force, especially that of black women and children. For blacks, it at least resembled the family farm of their dreams and a measure of autonomy from the planter's control. The planter paid the sharecropper with part of the crop (usually half) at the end of the year. Tenants, who owned their stock and tools, rented the land from the planter, paying him a share of the crop (usually a fourth). Both tenants and croppers were "furnished" food, clothing, and other necessities by the planter or a local merchant until the crop was harvested. In return the planter took a lien on the worker's share of the crop until the loan for his supplies was repaid.

But share arrangements were beneficial only as long as workers had legal status as owners of their share and cotton prices were high. After Republicans lost control of southern state legislatures, new laws were passed denying workers any legal control over the crop. Their share was merely a wage payment, not a sign of joint ownership. Furthermore, the falling world market price for cotton meant that they were more likely to share in a loss than a profit at year's end. Thus, over time, the system became more and more oppressive for blacks as well as for increasing numbers of southern whites who became locked into it. The combination of falling cotton prices and extraordinarily high-interest charges on the furnishing loans made it virtually impossible for the cropper or tenant to pay off his lien. He usually ended the year indebted to the planter or merchant.

Most economists agree that this system contributed to southern poverty and underdevelopment in the late nineteenth and early twentieth centuries. They do not agree, however, about whether it was an optimal system given the circumstances of the postwar South, or in what ways and to what extent it oppressed black workers. Some economic historians argue that the share-tenancy system did not discriminate against or coerce black labor. Racism pervaded the South's political and social institutions, these scholars concede, but its economic system was governed by a free market and was surprisingly fair and progressive, under the circumstances. White farmers were subject to the crop liens just as blacks were. Given the landowners lack of capital and the black workers' lack of education and managerial skill, the system was the best that could have been devised. The high interest rates reflected the genuine risks and true costs of credit. Finally, the true test of a free labor force is whether the worker

can change his employer in search of a better deal; and this black workers did constantly. In sum, the injustice of southern race relations must be sought in its social and political institutions and extralegal violence, not in its labor market.

Other historians look at the same set of facts and argue that the racial canker was imbedded in the economic system itself. In contrast with whites, who were more likely to be tenants or renters, blacks were disproportionately confined to the sharecropper ranks, the lowest rung on the agricultural ladder. Although they worked the richer soils of the black belt plantations, black croppers were assigned a smaller acreage than whites. Most importantly, these scholars argue, the economists' distinction between market and nonmarket forces in society is fallacious. The political system, the law, social repression, and extralegal violence were all instruments for controlling black laborers, denying them options outside plantation agriculture. Black physical mobility was a mirage. The worker could change his employer, but he still had to work on some plantation, if he wanted to eat. During the final two decades of the nineteenth century, as political control was consolidated, the inferior legal status of the sharecropper was more clearly codified in the statutes: he was merely a wage laborer who received his pay in kind rather than in cash. In many areas, labor control became more direct and brutal, with mounted overseers in the fields and bells marking the hours of labor.

To evaluate the potential for geographical or economic mobility among southern black farmers, one must also examine the alternatives outside the plantation sector. Northern as well as southern black craftsmen, who had dominated some trades in several antebellum southern cities, lost their footing in the late nineteenth-century American economy. Customers turned to white craftsmen and service workers; craft unions excluded blacks from apprenticeships, and technological changes eliminated some crafts altogether. Blacks provided the majority of the workers in several southern industries, for example, in iron, steel, and saw mills, and in turpentine and tobacco factories. But they were systematically excluded from the region's major growth industry, cotton mills. This was especially ironic in view of the fact that many of the antebellum cotton mills had been run by black labor exclusively. But boosters of textile expansion in the 1880s solicited potential investors with the promise that the new mills would provide jobs for widows and orphans of Confederate soldiers. Few blacks qualified by those criteria.

A further measure of how unfree the southern labor market was, was the fact that many of its key, economically progressive industries used a partly unfree labor force. Convict laborers were ubiquitous in southern mines, on southern railroads, in turpentine camps, as well as on plantations. Begun as an economy measure during the early postwar years, the practice was continued by Democratic regimes and became profitable to the states involved. By the late 1880s, for example, convict leasing accounted for 10 percent of the local state revenue in Alabama and Tennessee. It was also tremendously profitable for the employers. In 1886 a Mississippi railroad contractor saved $16 per hand each month by replacing free workers with convicts.

Not surprisingly, the South's prison population rose dramatically in the 1880s and 1890s, doubling in Virginia, quadrupling in Mississippi, and rising eightfold in Alabama. Tennessee, Virginia, Alabama, Mississippi, and Georgia had relatively stable white prison populations, but the total number of black inmates in those states shot up sevenfold. Black convicts were jailed mostly for property crimes and received long prison sentences for trivial offenses. The most notorious example was the 1876 Mississippi "pig law" that defined as grand larceny the theft of anything worth $10.

Southern courts became virtual labor recruiters. It was standard practice to deliver to an employer, for "a very small" bond payment, blacks convicted of misdemeanors, such as breaking a fence, fighting, and disorderly conduct. Peonage, wherein a workers' debt to his employer was continued from year to year and used to force his continued labor, was also prevalent. Despite a Supreme Court decision in *Alonzo Bailey* v. *Alabama* (1911), declaring this practice a violation of the Thirteenth Amendment, it persisted well into the twentieth century.

Finally, much of the extralegal violence inflicted on blacks was economically motivated. And even where it was not, the threat of violence served to intimidate any potential complainants. More than 100 blacks fell victim to lynch mobs each year during the 1890s; a thousand more died in this manner between 1900 and 1915. Southern lynchings were such public, well-advertised spectacles that its difficult to argue that they did not have the connivance of legal authorities. Two thousand spectators witnessed the lynching of Sam Hose in Georgia in April 1899. Ten thousand Texans witnessed similar events in the towns of Paris in 1903 and in Waco in 1916. After the victims were stabbed, mutilated, and burned to death, their remains were sold as relics.

DISFRANCHISEMENT AND SEGREGATION

Given the controls imposed on the ways southern blacks could earn a living and the violence they endured, one would think that further oppressive measures would be superfluous. Yet, by the turn of the century blacks found it increasingly difficult, if not impossible, to vote, to get an education, to be served in public places, or to ride trains or streetcars under conditions other than degrading.

Rutherford B. Hayes's understanding of the compromise that had gained him the presidency in 1877, was that the basic civil rights of black southerners would be protected by the new

Democratic regimes. Surely this was, on one level, just a sop to northern consciences disturbed at their betrayal of the black voters who had supported the Republican party so faithfully, often at the risk of their lives. But it probably also represented a genuine belief that the southerners of the better sort would actually protect the rights of the blacks, as long as the blacks did not challenge their power or their right to rule. In either case, the promise was not kept. During the 1880s and 1890s, federal protection of southern blacks' civil rights diminished along with northern concern for their welfare. Under President Chester A. Arthur, the party sought to rebuild its southern branch by mollifying potential white recruits at the expense of their traditional black supporters. Hereafter the ideal southern Republican party would be lily-white.

The Supreme Court complicated and blocked the few efforts that Republicans did make to secure black civil rights. Court decisions during the 1870s and 1880s severely limited the protections blacks enjoyed under the Fourteenth and Fifteenth Amendments. The majority opinions in the *Slaughterhouse* cases (1873) and *U.S.* v. *Cruikshank* (1876) were that the Fourteenth Amendment's equal protection clause applied only to those rights enjoyed as a citizen of the nation rather than as the citizen of a state. In *U.S.* v. *Reese* (1876) the Court insisted that the Fourteenth Amendment only protected citizens against discriminatory acts by a state rather than private individuals. The Court also decided that the Fifteenth Amendment did not confer voting rights in any positive sense, but merely prevented the denial of those rights on explicitly and overtly racial grounds. The effect of these decisions was to invalidate those laws passed during Reconstruction to protect black voters from organized violence.

Over the next decade, election violence increased, as did all manner of election frauds and chicanery. Florida and South Carolina

Democrats loaded the ballot boxes with tissue ballots and extra-small tickets, nicknamed ''little jokers.'' When counters found that the number of ballots exceeded the number of voters, they put all the ballots back in the box and, blindfolded, eliminated the excess by withdrawing and discarding the thicker, larger Republican ballots. Several states set up separate ballot boxes for the various offices, thus indirectly creating a literacy test for the voter who had to deposit his vote in the correct box. Most states with large black populations found creative ways to gerrymander election districts so as to minimize their votes. Voter registration procedures were also administered so as to discourage black voters.

But despite these measures blacks continued to vote and to elect their leaders to federal and state offices throughout the 1880s. Between 1876 and 1895, scores of black state legislators and congressmen served in North Carolina, South Carolina, Louisiana, Virginia, and Mississippi. Black voters remained a potent force in southern politics and often held the balance of power when the white vote was split. And electoral splits among white voters appeared with increasing regularity, especially during the Populist campaigns of the early 1890s.

The last major effort Republicans made to bring fairness to southern elections was the Lodge Election Bill of 1890, requiring federal registrars and supervisors of elections. The bill was defeated in Congress. So once it was clear that the federal government would not intervene, southern Democrats consolidated their control of the election machinery by turning to more regular and legal mechanisms to suppress the black vote. Between 1890 and 1905, all the former Confederate states established legislative or constitutional measures that systematically disfranchised black voters. Poll taxes, literacy tests, and registration requirements created an effective, legal barrier to potential black voters, and to many poor whites as well. Louisiana, Alabama, and North Carolina adopted "grandfather clauses" that allowed persons to vote if they could have voted in 1867, or if they were descendants of 1867 voters. Voter turnout in the South fell to less than half that in northern states. The Republican party was practically eliminated from southern politics; the South became a one-party region.

At the same moment blacks were being pushed out of the voting booth, they were being excluded from or separated in public places. Again Supreme Court decisions confirmed southern racial oppression. In 1883, the Court invalidated the 1875 Civil Rights Act, claiming that the federal government could proscribe discrimination undertaken by states but not by individual citizens. Thirteen years later the Court declared in *Plessy* v. *Ferguson* (1896) that even state-mandated racial discrimination was constitutionally permissible as long as equal facilities were provided to both races. Homer Plessy had complained that Louisiana's law requiring him to sit in a separate railroad car stigmatized him with "the badge of slavery." But the Court majority insisted that this interpretation of the state's intent was unwarranted. Justice John Marshall Harlan, the lone dissenter in this case, labeled such reasoning "a thin disguise" of an obvious injustice. Clearly segregation was not voluntary on the part of blacks but coerced by whites, and thus was inherently a form of stigmatization and degradation. Furthermore, Harlan predicted, the result of the majority's decision would be to legislate and condone racial prejudice, which would spread into all areas of southern life from the cradle to the grave.

Harlan was right. The late 1890s and the early twentieth century witnessed a plethora of segregationist legislation, much of it regulating the pettiest details of social life and personal contact: Jim Crow bibles in Atlanta courtrooms, segregated prostitutes in New Orleans, separate schoolbooks in North Carolina. Segregation became so pervasive that by the 1950s, when the system came under increasingly militant

legal attack, most people assumed that such separation had always existed; that it was an integral part of southern folkways and customs, a venerable "southern way of life."

This contention was challenged by historian C. Vann Woodward. Writing *The Strange Career of Jim Crow* on the eve of the U.S. Supreme Court's Brown decision, Woodward argued that segregation was a creation of the modernizing New South rather than a legacy of immemorial southern traditions. In the political ferment of the 1890s, conservative Democrats and radical Populists had competed for the black vote. Since neither group could be certain of winning this competition, they both made blacks the political scapegoats, agreeing to exclude them from the ballot box and segregate them in public life.

Early critics of the Woodward thesis, Joel Williamson being among the most prominent, argued that he erred in seeing segregation as an entirely new phenomenon in the 1890s. While it may have been codified into law during this period, it was actually a continuation of de facto practices of the postbellum and even antebellum South. Woodward's defenders responded that these earlier precedents notwithstanding, it is very significant that racial separation intensified and was institutionalized in law during the last decade of the century. In *A Rage for Order* (1986), Joel Williamson concedes this point and incorporates it into his new thesis that a qualitative change did occur in the 1890s. Southern society fell under the spell of more virulent racist ideology, practices, and leaders than ever before. He traces these changes to psychological and cultural anxieties among southerners beset by economic distress and fixated with what they perceived to be a growing black menace. Unfortunately, the logical and causal connections between the psychological—mainly sexual—anxieties Williamson describes and the larger societal forces and events remains unclear.

In a comparative study of American and

South African racism, *The Highest Stage of White Supremacy* (1982), African historian John Cell also emphasizes tensions within southern society during this period, but of a different sort and location. Cell argues that segregation was more likely to occur in urbanizing, modernizing areas of the American South, especially in the Piedmont, than in traditional, rural areas. The racial tensions and anxieties stimulated by job competition from and social mobility of blacks encouraged repression in the form of discrimination and segregation. Thus, ironically, it was the progressive, modernizing leaders of the New South who were responsible for this reactionary institution.

In *Race Relations in the Urban South* (1978), Howard Rabinowitz takes an entirely different approach than most other scholars. Much of the debate over the origins of segregation is irrelevant to the situation most blacks found themselves in during the late nineteenth century, he argues. Blacks were actually less concerned about segregation of public facilities than with their complete or partial exclusion from schools, hospitals, and jobs outside agriculture. Given their circumstances, many black leaders welcomed segregated facilities as an improvement over what they had. During this period blacks themselves demanded that white teachers be replaced by blacks in public schools. Southern blacks voluntarily separated themselves in various economic and social institutions, including churches, mutual aid societies, and insurance and banking companies. Segregation was not simply the product of white racism, but of a complex interaction among black and white southerners and northern white leaders.

ACCOMMODATION OR RESISTANCE

Many prominent blacks during this period, especially southern educators and others dependent on white patronage, urged accommodation rather than resistance to segregation and dis-

franchisement. They reasoned that the only hope of restraining the violence of white mobs was the intervention and protection of the southern white elite, which generally prided itself for its paternalistic handling of the race issue. Meanwhile blacks must prove themselves capable and worthy of American citizenship by abandoning political agitation, and becoming an economic asset to the South. They would also accept the emerging social separation of the races in exchange for racial peace.

Booker T. Washington was one of these leaders. Washington was the founder of Alabama's Tuskegee Institute, an institution dedicated to providing industrial education for southern black youth. In 1895 Washington set forth his policy of racial accommodation in a speech at the Atlanta Cotton States' Exposition. From that day, he became America's most prominent black citizen and the most respected spokesman for black aspirations. Washington argued that earning a livelihood was more important than access to public accommodations or voting. He asked white support for industrial education among southern blacks. He urged northern blacks to pursue careers in business, organizing the National Negro Business League in 1900 for that purpose.

He enjoyed some success in these efforts. Wealthy philanthropists like John D. Rockefeller and Andrew Carnegie did give significant grants to Tuskegee and other black colleges. Approximately seventy-five Negro banks were established between 1900 and 1914, most of them concentrated in the South. Despite his public advocacy of accommodation, Washington secretly supported several challenges to Jim Crow legislation and peonage. But his policy had some glaring deficiencies as well. Most black-owned businesses were small "mom and pop" retailers, barbers, real estate agents, or craftsmen. His industrial education program was preparing black youngsters for jobs that new technologies were making obsolete, while exacerbating the problem of integrating the new skilled crafts. Much of the philanthropic aid to black schools was either given for the explicit purpose of supporting segregated education, or had that effect.

Most black leaders of Washington's day would not have disagreed with his advocacy of economic development and industrial education, but many could not abide anything less than militant condemnation of southern terrorism nor restrain their disgust with a policy that, publicly at least, surrendered their basic civil rights. W. E. B. Du Bois was the most prominent opponent of Washington's philosophy. At the time of the Atlanta speech, Du Bois agreed with Washington's emphasis on economic self-help and sent him a congratulatory telegram. But eight years later in *Souls of Black Folk,* he insisted that political rights were necessary to the protection of economic rights, that the industrially educated masses must have an academically trained ''talented tenth'' to lead them, and that manhood could never be sustained by appeasing those who would take it away. He was particularly angered at Washington for the underhanded methods he employed to silence criticism by other black leaders. By that time it was strongly suspected that the so-called Tuskegee Machine employed spies, provocateurs to inform on and disrupt the activities of his critics, and that he bribed newspapers to write favorable copy on Washington. We now know that those suspicions were true.

In 1909 Du Bois and many other Washington critics founded the National Association for the Advancement of Colored Peoples (NAACP), an organization committed to a militant campaign against lynching and all other forms of racial oppression. Although Washington tried to undermine the new organization, it grew in strength, and Du Bois, as editor of its magazine *The Crisis,* soon supplanted Washington as the most respected spokesman for black America.

The struggle between Du Bois and Washington animated and divided the black elite for a generation. In point of fact, the real struggle was more about power and leadership within the black community than accommodation and resistance. Washington's activities embraced both accommodation and protest; Du Bois advocated self-help and integration. There was much that he and Washington could have agreed on. In the end, what they could not compromise was Washington's ''Tuskegee machine'' that sought to control opinion, patronage, and leaders of black America.

For the masses of blacks the intellectual debates were probably irrelevant. They had always displayed a penchant for pragmatic, ideologically eclectic responses to the problems at hand. Following Washington's philosophy, thousands of them purchased land and started businesses. The more important of the businesses—banks and insurance companies—often began as mutual aid societies. Land purchases were often aided by various collective efforts, like rotating credit associations (in which members pooled their savings) and cooperative purchases. Following Du Bois's philosophy, thousands more engaged in militant, broad-based community resistance to the initiation of Jim Crow. There had been successful protests, including sit-ins, street demonstrations against segregated horsecars during Reconstruction in Richmond, New Orleans, Charleston, and Louisville, and a boycott in Savannah, Georgia. Between 1891 and 1906, there were boycotts against Jim Crow car services in at least twenty-eight southern cities. In several cities the blacks formed black-owned alternative public transit systems; this was perhaps a mixture of Du Bois and Washington. Of course, these protests were not successful, but they provided a tradition of resistance that would be revived in Montgomery, Alabama, in 1956 where the modern civil rights movement was launched.

When all else failed, the black masses simply moved away. Following violent and fraudulent elections in 1878 and 1880, thousands left Louisiana, Mississippi, and Alabama in what became known as the Kansas Exodus of 1879. Others took ship for Liberia, Africa, from southern and northern ports. Finally, during World War I, when European immigration was cut off, northern industries recruited southern black labor for the first time. This time hundreds of thousands left southern farms for northern factories, while thousands more left the rural South for the urban South. This Great Migration proved to be one of many mortal blows to the southern racial and economic system that had enthralled black Americans for half a century after emancipation. In some senses, it proved to be the most effective form of resistance of all.

SUGGESTED READINGS

Cell, John W. *The Highest Stage of White Supremacy: The Origins of Segregation in South Africa and the American South.* New York: Cambridge University Press, 1982.

Du Bois, W. E. B. *The Souls of Black Folk.* New York: Crest, 1961 (originally published in 1903), pp. 42–54

Fredrickson, George M. *The Black Image in the White Mind: The Debate on Afro-American Character and Destiny, 1817–1914.* New York: Harper & Row, 1971.

Harlan, Louis R. *Booker T. Washington: The Making of a Black Leader, 1856–1901.* New York: Oxford University Press, 1972.

———. *Booker T. Washington: The Wizard of Tuskegee, 1901–1915.* New York: Oxford University Press, 1983.

Jaynes, Gerald D. *Branches without Roots: Genesis of the Black Working Class in the American South, 1862–1882.* New York: Oxford University Press, 1986.

Kousser, J. Morgan. *The Shaping of Southern Politics: Suffrage Restriction and the Establishment of the One Party South, 1880–1910.* New Haven, Conn.: Yale University Press, 1974.

Logan, Rayford W. *The Betrayal of the Negro: From Rutherford B. Hayes to Woodrow Wilson.* New York: Collier, 1965.

Meier, August. *Negro Thought in America, 1880–1915.* Ann Arbor: University of Michigan, 1963.

Newby, I. A. *Jim Crow's Defense: Anti-Negro Thought in America, 1900–1930.* Baton Rouge: Louisiana State University Press, 1965.

Rabinowitz, Howard N. *Race Relations in the Urban South, 1865–1890.* New York: Oxford University Press, 1978.

Rosengarten, Theodore. *All God's Dangers: The Life of Nate Shaw.* New York: Alfred A. Knopf, 1974.

Washington, Booker T. *Up from Slavery: An Autobiography.* New York: Doubleday, 1901.

Williamson, Joel. *Rage for Order: Black-White Relations in the American South since Emancipation.* New York: Oxford University Press, 1986.

Woodward, C. Vann. *Origins of the New South, 1877–1913.* Baton Rouge: Louisiana State University, 1951.

———. *The Strange Career of Jim Crow.* 3rd rev. ed. New York: Oxford University Press, 1974.

DOCUMENT 21.1

A Shares Contract

This sample contract reflects the typical arrangement between planters and freedmen during the Reconstruction Era. Many of the features protective of the freedmen—such as overtime pay for extra work—ceased to be acknowledged once Democrats regained control of southern state legislatures and courts.

CONTRACT WITH FREEDMEN

This agreement made and entered into this _____day of _____ 186—, by and between *J C Mitchell* of the *County* of *Fort Bend* State of *Texas* of the first part, and the following

Source: "Records of the Assistant Commissioner for the State of Texas," Bureau of Refugees, Freedmen, and Abandoned Lands, Record Group 105, National Archives, Washington, D.C.

named Freedmen of the State of _____ of the second part, Witnesseth: That we do hereby covenant and agree, each for him or herself, with the said *J C Mitchell* his heirs and assigns of the first part, to work honestly and faithfully to the best of our ability on said *J C Mitchell's plantation* located in the *County* of *Fort Bend* State of *Texas* aforesaid, for the term of *one year* time to commence from the date of our arrival at said *plantation*. The said _____ of the first part in consideration of the faithful discharge of the duties assumed by us of the second part, does hereby agree to pay the said Freedmen the following rates of wages, viz: 1st Class men $____ per _____, 2d Class men $____ per _____, 3d Class men $____ per _____; 1st Class women $ ____ per _____, 2d Class women $____ per _____, 3d Class women $____ per _____; Boys over 15 years of age and under 18 years $____ per _____, Girls over 15 and under 18, $____ per _____ payable

---

Said _____ of the first part furthermore agrees to furnish the said Freedmen of the second part with good and sufficient quarters, _____ wholesome food, fuel, and such medical treatment as can be rendered by the person superintending the place. Said *J C Mitchell* of the 1st part in consideration of the faithful discharge of the duties assumed by the parties of the second part, does hereby agree to furnish *the freedmen* the necessary tools and implements for the cultivation of the land, and allow said Freedmen *one third* interest in the crops raised on said *plantation* by their labor. It is also mutually agreed that ten hours shall constitute a day's work, and if any labor in excess of ten hours per day is rendered it shall be paid for as extra labor. Said parties of the second part do furthermore agree to do all necessary work on Sundays or at night when it is for the protection of plantation or crops against destruction by storms, floods, fire or frost, provided always that such service shall be paid

for as extra labor; extra labor to be paid for at the rate of one day's labor and one-half rations extra for each six hours work. Provided, that our employer failing to comply with any part of this agreement, this contract shall be annulled; also provided, that should any of the parties of the second part leave said *plantation* without proper authority, or engage elsewhere, or neglect or refuse to work as herein agreed, they or any part of them so offending shall be liable to be discharged and forfeit all wages due up to that time.

Also Provided, that this Contract shall constitute the first lien upon all crops raised by the labor of said parties of the Second part.

Said J C Mitchell shall have power to make such rules and regulations necessary to the management of the plantation as are not inconsistent with the term of this contract; all lost time to [be] deducted from the one third interest in crop of the freedmen.

DOCUMENT 21.2
Plessy v. *Ferguson:* The Majority Opinion by Justice Henry Billings Brown

Justice Brown, a Massachusetts-bred Yankee, Yale graduate, and Michigan resident, wrote the Supreme Court opinion that gave southern Jim Crow constitutional legitimacy for more than half a century. Brown argued that segregation was a natural consequence of racial differences and that it implied no degradation of black people.

This case turns upon the constitutionality of an act of the General Assembly of the State of Louisiana, passed in 1890, providing for separate railway carriages for the white and colored races. . . .

The constitutionality of this act is attacked

Source: *Plessy* v. *Ferguson,* 163 U.S. 537 (1896).

upon the ground that it conflicts both with the Thirteenth Amendment of the Constitution, abolishing slavery, and the Fourteenth Amendment, which prohibits certain restrictive legislation on the part of the States.

1. That it does not conflict with the Thirteenth Amendment, which abolished slavery and involuntary servitude, except as a punishment for crime, is too clear for argument. . . .

A statute which implies merely a legal distinction between the white and colored races— a distinction which is founded in the color of the two races, and which must always exist so long as white men are distinguished from the other race by color—has no tendency to destroy the legal equality of the two races, or reestablish a state of involuntary servitude. . . .

The object of the [fourteenth] amendment was undoubtedly to enforce the absolute equality of the two races before the law, but in the nature of things it could not have been intended to abolish distinctions based upon color, or to enforce social, as distinguished from political equality, or a commingling of the two races upon terms unsatisfactory to either. Laws permitting, and even requiring, their separation in places where they are liable to be brought into contact do not necessarily imply the inferiority of either race to the other, and have been generally, if not universally, recognized as within the competency of the state legislatures in the exercise of their police power. The most common instance of this is connected with the establishment of separate schools for white and colored children, which has been held to be a valid exercise of the legislative power even by courts of states where the political rights of the colored race have been longest and most earnestly enforced. . . .

So far, then, as a conflict with the Fourteenth Amendment is concerned, the case reduces itself to the question whether the statute of Louisiana is a reasonable regulation, and with respect to this there must necessarily be a large discretion on the part of the legislature. In determining the question of reasonableness it is at liberty to act with reference to the established usages, customs and traditions of the people, and with a view to the promotion of their comfort, and the preservation of the public peace and good order. Gauged by this standard, we cannot say that a law which authorizes or even requires the separation of the two races in public conveyances is unreasonable, or more obnoxious to the Fourteenth Amendment than the acts of Congress requiring separate schools for colored children in the District of Columbia, the constitutionality of which does not seem to have been questioned, or the corresponding acts of state legislatures.

We consider the underlying fallacy of the plaintiff's argument to consist in the assumption that the enforced separation of the two races stamps the colored race with a badge of inferiority. If this be so, it is not by reason of anything found in the act, but solely because the colored race chooses to put that construction upon it. The argument necessarily assumes that if, as has been more than once the case, and is not unlikely to be so again, the colored race should become the dominant power in the state legislature, and should enact a law in precisely similar terms, it would thereby relegate the white race to an inferior position. We imagine that the white race, at least, would not acquiesce in this assumption. The argument also assumes that social prejudices may be overcome by legislation, and that equal rights cannot be secured to the Negro except by an enforced commingling of the two races. We cannot accept this proposition. If the two races are to meet upon terms of social equality, it must be the result of natural affinities, a mutual appreciation of each other's merits and a voluntary consent of individuals. . . . Legislation is powerless to eradicate racial instincts or to abolish distinctions based upon physical differences, and the attempt to do so can only result in accentuating the difficulties of the present situation. If the civil and political rights of both races be equal one cannot be inferior to the other civilly or politically. If one race be inferior to the other socially, the Constitution of the United States cannot put them upon the same plane. . . .

DOCUMENT 21.3
Plessy v. *Ferguson:* Dissenting Opinion by Justice John Marshall Harlan

Justice Harlan, a former slaveholder from Kentucky, was the lone dissenter in the Plessy *case. His insistence that state sanctioned racial separation was inherently discriminatory—a badge of slavery—prefigured the* Brown Decision *of 1954.*

In respect of civil rights, common to all citizens, the Constitution of the United States does not, I think, permit any public authority to know the race of those entitled to be protected in the enjoyment of such rights. Every true man has pride of race, and under appropriate circumstances when the rights of others, his equals before the law, are not to be affected, it is his privilege to express such pride and to take such action based upon it as to him seems proper. But I deny that any legislative body or judicial tribunal may have regard to the race of citizens when the civil rights of those citizens are involved. Indeed, such legislation, as that here in question, is inconsistent not only with that equality of rights which pertains to citizenship, National and State, but with the personal liberty enjoyed by every one within the United States.

The Thirteenth Amendment does not permit the withholding or the deprivation of any right necessarily inhering in freedom. It not only struck down the institution of slavery as previously existing in the United States, but it prevents the imposition of any burdens or disabili-

Source: *Plessy* v. *Ferguson,* 163 U.S. 537 (1896).

ties that constitute badges of slavery or servitude.

*   *   *   *   *

These notable additions to the fundamental law [i.e., the thirteenth, fourteenth, and fifteenth amendments] were welcomed by the friends of liberty throughout the world. They removed the race line from our governmental systems. They had, as this court has said, a common purpose, namely, to secure "to a race recently emancipated, a race that through many generations have been held in slavery, all the civil rights that the superior race enjoy." They declared, in legal effect, this court has further said, "that the law in the States shall be the same for the black as for the white; that all persons, whether colored or white, shall stand equal before the law of the States, and in regard to the colored race, for whose protection the amendment was primarily designed, that no discrimination shall be made against them by law because of their color." We also said: "The words of the amendment, it is true, are prohibitory, but they contain a necessary implication of a positive immunity, or right, most valuable to the colored race—the right to exemption from unfriendly legislation against them distinctively as colored—exemption from legal discriminations, implying inferiority in civil society, lessening the security of their enjoyment of the rights which others enjoy, and discriminations which are steps toward reducing them to the conditions of a subject race."

*   *   *   *   *

It was said in argument that the statute of Louisiana does not discriminate against either race, but prescribes a rule applicable alike to white and colored citizens. But this argument does not meet the difficulty. Every one knows that the statute in question had its origin in the purpose, not so much to exclude white persons from railroad cars occupied by blacks, as to exclude colored people from coaches occupied by or assigned to white persons. Railroad corporations of Louisiana did not make discrimination among whites in the matter of accommodation for travellers. The thing to accomplish was, under the guise of giving equal accommodation for whites and blacks, to compel the latter to keep to themselves while travelling in railroad passenger coaches. No one would be so wanting in candor as to assert the contrary. The fundamental objection, therefore, to the statute is that it interferes with the personal freedom of citizens. . . . If a white man and a black man choose to occupy the same public conveyance on a public highway, it is their right to do so, and no government, proceeding alone on grounds of race, can prevent it without infringing the personal liberty of each.

It is one thing for railroad carriers to furnish, or to be required by law to furnish, equal accommodations for all whom they are under a legal duty to carry. It is quite another thing for government to forbid citizens of the white and black races from travelling in the same public conveyance, and to punish officers of railroad companies for permitting persons of the two races to occupy the same passenger coach.

The white race deems itself to be the dominant race in this country. And so it is, in prestige, in achievements, in education, in wealth and in power. So, I doubt not, it will continue to be for all time, if it remains true to its great heritage and holds fast to the principles of constitutional liberty. But in the view of the Constitution, in the eye of the law, there is in this country no superior, dominant, ruling class of citizens. There is no caste here. Our Constitution is color-blind, and neither knows nor tolerates classes among citizens. In respect of civil rights, all citizens are equal before the law. The humblest is the peer of the most powerful. The law regards man as man, and takes no account of his surroundings or of his color

when his civil rights as guaranteed by the supreme law of the land are involved. It is, therefore, to be regretted that this high tribunal, the final expositor of the fundamental law of the land, has reached the conclusion that it is competent for a State to regulate the enjoyment by citizens of their civil rights solely upon the basis of race.

In my opinion, the judgment this day rendered will, in time, prove to be quite as pernicious as the decision made by this tribunal in the *Dred Scott case*. . . . The present decision, it may well be apprehended, will not only stimulate aggressions, more or less brutal and irritating, upon the admitted rights of colored citizens, but will encourage the belief that it is possible, by means of state enactments, to defeat the beneficent purposes which the people of the United States had in view when they adopted the recent amendments of the Constitution, by one of which the blacks of this country were made citizens of the United States and of the States in which they respectively reside, and whose privileges and immunities, as citizens, the States are forbidden to abridge. . . . The destinies of the two races, in this country, are indissolubly linked together, and the interests of both require that the common government of all shall not permit the seeds of race hate to be planted under the sanction of law. What can more certainly arouse race hate, what more certainly create and perpetuate a feeling of distrust between these races, than state enactments, which, in fact, proceed on the ground that colored citizens are so inferior and degraded that they cannot be allowed to sit in public coaches occupied by white citizens? That, as all will admit, is the real meaning of such legislation as was enacted in Louisiana.

* * * * *

The arbitrary separation citizens, on the basis of race, while they are on a public highway, is a badge of servitude wholly inconsistent with the civil freedom and the equality before the law established by the Constitution. It cannot be justified upon any legal grounds.

If evils will result from the commingling of the two races upon public highways established for the benefit of all, they will be infinitely less than those that will surely come from state legislation regulating the enjoyment of civil rights upon the basis of race. We boast of the freedom enjoyed by our people above all other peoples. But it is difficult to reconcile that boast with a state of the law which, practically, puts the brand of servitude and degradation upon a large class of our fellow citizens, our equals before the law. The thin disguise of "equal" accommodations for passengers in railroad coaches will not mislead any one, nor atone for the wrong this day done. . . .

DOCUMENT 21.4
The Atlanta Compromise

Booker T. Washington's address to the Cotton States Exposition in Atlanta on September 18, 1895, was heralded as a rational basis for racial accommodation. Blacks would withdraw from political activities and social agitation in return for assistance in economic development.

A ship lost at sea for many days suddenly sighted a friendly vessel. From the mast of the unfortunate vessel was seen a signal: "Water, water; we die of thirst!" The answer from the friendly vessel at once came back: "Cast down your bucket where you are. . . ." The captain of the distressed vessel, at last heeding the injunction, cast down his bucket, and it came up full of fresh, sparkling water from the mouth of the Amazon River. To those of my race who depend upon bettering their condi-

Source: Booker T. Washington, *Up from Slavery: An Autobiography* (Cambridge, Mass.: Riverside Press, 1901), pp. 219–24.

tion in a foreign land, or who underestimate the importance of cultivating friendly relations with the Southern white man, who is their next-door neighbor, I would say: "Cast down your bucket where you are"—cast it down in making friends in every manly way of the people of all races by whom we are surrounded.

Cast it down agriculture, mechanics, in commerce, in domestic service, and in the professions. And in this connection it is well to bear in mind that whatever other sins the South may be called to bear, when it comes to business, pure and simple, it is in the South that the Negro is given a man's chance in the commercial world, and in nothing is this Exposition more eloquent than in emphasizing this chance. Our greatest danger is that in the great leap from slavery to freedom we may overlook the fact that the masses of us are to live by the productions of our hands, and fail to keep in mind that we shall prosper in proportion as we learn to dignify and glorify common labor, and put brains and skill into the common occupations of life; shall prosper in proportion as we learn to draw the line between the superficial and the substantial, the ornamental gewgaws of life and the useful. No race can prosper till it learns that there is as much dignity in tilling a field as in writing a poem. It is at the bottom of life we must begin, and not at the top. Nor should we permit our grievances to overshadow our opportunities.

To those of the white race who look to the incoming of those of foreign birth and strange tongue and habits for the prosperity of the South, were I permitted, I would repeat what I say to my own race, "Cast down your bucket where you are." Cast it down among the eight million Negroes whose habits you know, whose fidelity and love you have tested in days when to have proved treacherous meant the ruin of our firesides. Cast down your bucket among these people who have, without strikes and labor wars, tilled your fields, cleared your forests, builded your railroads and cities, brought forth treasures from the bowels of the earth, and helped make possible this magnificent representation of the progress of the South. Casting down your bucket among my people, helping and encouraging them as you are doing on these grounds, and, with education of head, hand, and heart, you will find that they will buy your surplus land, make blossom the waste places in your fields, and run your factories. While doing this, you can be sure in the future, as in the past, that you and your families will be surrounded by the most patient, faithful, law-abiding, and unresentful people that the world has seen. As we have proved our loyalty to you in the past, in nursing your children, watching by the sick bed of your mothers and fathers, and often following them with tear-dimmed eyes to their graves, so in the future, in our humble way, we shall stand by you with a devotion that no foreigner can approach, ready to lay down our lives if need be, in defence of yours, interlacing our industrial, commercial, civil, and religious life with yours in a way that shall make the interests of both races one. In all things that are purely social we can be as separate as the fingers, yet one as the hand in all things essential to mutual progress.

* * * * *

The wisest among my race understand that the agitation of questions of social equality is the extremest folly, and that progress in the enjoyment of all the privileges that will come to us must be the result of severe and constant struggle rather than of artificial forcing. No race that has anything to contribute to the markets of the world is long in any degree ostracized. It is important and right that all privileges of the law be ours, but it is vastly more important that we be prepared for the exercise of those privileges. The opportunity to earn a dollar in a factory just now is worth infinitely more than the opportunity to spend a dollar in an opera house.

DOCUMENT 21.5
Of Mr. Booker T. Washington and Others

With this essay, young W. E. B. Du Bois emerged as Booker T. Washington's most thoughtful and forceful critic. A compromise that conceded political rights and human dignity in exchange for material progress, Du Bois argued, was in danger of losing both.

Easily the most striking thing in the history of the American Negro since 1876 is the ascendancy of Mr. Booker T. Washington. It began at the time when war memories and ideals were rapidly passing; a day of astonishing commercial development was dawning; a sense of doubt and hesitation overtook the freedmen's sons,— then it was that his leading began. Mr. Washington came, with a single definite programme, at the psychological moment when the nation was a little ashamed of having bestowed so much sentiment on Negroes, and was concentrating its energies on Dollars.

* * * * *

Among his own people, . . . Mr. Washington has encountered the strongest and most lasting opposition, amounting at times to bitterness, and even to-day continuing strong and insistent even though largely silenced in outward expression by the public opinion of the nation. . . . There is among educated and thoughtful colored men in all parts of the land a feeling of deep regret, sorrow, and apprehension at the wide currency and ascendancy which

Source: W. E. B. Du Bois, *The Souls of Black Folks: Essays and Sketches,* 3rd ed. (Chicago: A. C. McClurg, 1903), pp. 41–2, 45–6, 49–52, 54–5, 57–8.

some of Mr. Washington's theories have gained. . . . If the best of the American Negroes receive by outer pressure a leader whom they had not recognized before, manifestly there is here a certain palpable gain. Yet there is also irreparable loss,—a loss of that peculiarly valuable education which a group receives when by search and criticism it finds and commissions its own leaders. . . . Nearly all the former ones [Negro leaders] had become leaders by the silent suffrage of their fellows, had sought to lead their own people alone, and were usually, save [Frederick] Douglass, little known outside their race. But Booker T. Washington arose as essentially the leader not of one race but of two,—a compromiser between the South, the North, and the Negro.

*   *   *   *   *

Mr. Washington represents in Negro thought the old attitude of adjustment and submission; but adjustment at such a peculiar time as to make his programme unique. This an age of unusual economic development, and Mr. Washington's programme naturally takes an economic cast, becoming a gospel of Work and Money to such an extent as apparently almost completely to overshadow the higher aims of life. Moreover, this is an age when the more advanced races are coming in closer contact with the less developed races, and the race-feeling is therefore intensified; and Mr. Washington's programme practically accepts the alleged inferiority of the Negro races. Again, in our own land, the reaction from the sentiment of war time has given impetus to race-prejudice against Negroes, and Mr. Washington withdraws many of the high demands of Negroes as men and American citizens. In other periods of intensified prejudice all the Negro's tendency to self-assertion has been called forth; at this period a policy of submission is advocated. In the history of nearly all other races and peoples the doctrine preached at such crises has been that manly self-respect

is worth more than lands and houses, and that a people who voluntarily surrender such respect, or cease striving for it, are not worth civilizing.

In answer to this, it has been claimed that the Negro can survive only through submission. Mr. Washington distinctly asks that black people give up, at least for the present, three things,—

First, political power,
Second, insistence on civil rights,
Third, higher education of Negro youth,—

and concentrate all their energies on industrial education, the accumulation of wealth, and the conciliation of the South. This policy has been courageously and insistently advocated for over fifteen years, and has been triumphant for perhaps ten years. As a result of this tender of the palm branch, what has been the return? In these years there have occurred:

1. The disfranchisement of the Negro.
2. The legal creation of a distinct status of civil inferiority for the Negro.
3. The steady withdrawal of aid from institutions for the higher training of the Negro.

These movements are not, to be sure, direct results of Mr. Washington's teachings; but his propaganda has, without a shadow of doubt, helped their speedier accomplishment. The question then comes: Is it possible, and probable, that nine millions of men can make effective progress in economic lines if they are deprived of political rights, made a servile caste, and allowed only the most meagre chance for developing their exceptional men? If history and reason give any distinct answer to these questions, it is an emphatic *No.* And Mr. Washington thus faces the triple paradox of his career:

1. He is striving nobly to make Negro artisans businessmen and property-owners; but it

is utterly impossible, under modern competitive methods, for workingmen and property-owners to defend their rights and exist without the right of suffrage.

2. He insists on thrift and self-respect, but at the same time counsels a silent submission to civic inferiority such as is bound to sap the manhood of any race in the long run.

3. He advocates common-school and industrial training and depreciated institutions of higher learning; but neither the Negro common-schools, nor Tuskegee itself, could remain open a day were it not for teachers trained in Negro colleges, or trained by their graduates.

* * * * *

[Washington's Negro critics] insist that the way to truth and right lies in straightforward honesty, not in indiscriminate flattery; in praising those of the South who do well and criticising uncompromisingly those who do ill; in taking advantage of the opportunities at hand and urging their fellows to do the same, but at the same time in remembering that only a firm adherence to their higher ideals and aspirations will ever keep those ideals within the realm of possibility. They do not expect that the free right to vote, to enjoy civic rights, and to be educated, will come in a moment; they do not expect to see the bias and prejudice of years disappear at the blast of a trumpet; but they are absolutely certain that the way for a people to gain their reasonable rights is not by voluntarily throwing them away and insisting that they do not want them; that the way for a people to gain respect is not by continually belittling and ridiculing themselves; that, on the contrary, Negroes must insist continually,

in season and out of season, that voting is necessary to modern manhood, that color discrimination is barbarism, and that black boys need education as well as white boys.

* * * * *

. . . [O]n the whole the distinct impression left by Mr. Washington's propaganda is, first, that the South is justified in its present attitude toward the Negro because of the Negro's degradation; secondly, that the prime cause of the Negro's failure to rise more quickly is his wrong education in the past; and thirdly, that his future rise depends primarily on his own efforts. Each of these propositions is a dangerous half-truth. The supplementary truths must never be lost sight of: first, slavery and race-prejudice are potent if not sufficient causes of the Negro's position; second, industrial and common-school training were necessarily slow in planting because they had to await the black teachers trained by higher institutions— . . . and, third, while it is great truth to say that the Negro must strive and strive *mightily* to help himself, it is equally true that unless his striving be not simply seconded, but rather aroused and encouraged, by the initiative of the richer and wiser environing group, he cannot hope for great success.

In his failure to realize and impress this last point, Mr. Washington is especially to be criticised. His doctrine has tended to make the whites, North and South, shift the burden of the Negro problem to the Negro's shoulders and stand aside as critical and rather pessimistic spectators; when in fact the burden belongs to the nation, and the hands of none of us are clean if we bend not our energies to righting these great wrongs. . . .

chapter 22

American Indian Policy: 1865–1987

Howard R. Lamar
Yale University

"The study of government policy at any level is best done by hindsight. Avowed beliefs of politicians and political parties are often subject to the expediencies of the moment and the road to programmatic hell is well paved, a beautiful boulevard of good intentions. Even the most astute of scholars has a difficult time discerning how policies were formulated and put into effect." This statement by Vine Deloria, Jr., a leading Sioux writer, spokesman and lawyer, nicely summarized the many inconsistencies and even reversals in Indian policy pursued by the federal government over the past 120 years. Deloria could have added that in contrast, from the Indian point of view, the history of Indian-white relations from 1865 to the present is, in essence, the story of a determined minority seeking to preserve its native culture and lifestyle in the face of an overwhelming majority determined to "civilize," Christianize, and assimilate it into white society. Unlike the free blacks after 1865, Indians did not seek citizenship or equal civil or property rights within the Union; they wanted simply to be left alone. Thus the federal government alternately treated them either as an enemy or as childlike wards. Moreover, since Indians were not in the American "mainstream," Indian relations have not always conformed to the great turning points in our national history.

The close of the Civil War in 1865, for example, had a profound effect on the lives of most black and white Americans. The very year it ended saw the Oglala Sioux defeat U.S. troops in an expensive Plains war called the Powder River campaign. Indeed, between 1862 and 1886 Indian-white hostilities occurred annually, with the last major and tragic encounter taking place between the Sioux and U.S. soldiers at Wounded Knee on South Dakota's Pine Ridge Reservation, December 29, 1890.

Postbellum Indian policy may be conveniently marked by four overlapping stages or periods: thirty years of military hostilities from 1860 to 1890; a series of idealistic but not always realistic reforms, beginning with the Peace Policy in 1869 and climaxing in a program of assimilation and severalty which lasted from the time of the Dawes Act of 1887 to 1920; a period of white self-doubt lasting from 1920 to 1960, characterized by two radical reversals of policy; a revival of tribalism in 1934, and a decision to terminate the reservations in 1953. This last and most recent phase began in the 1960s with the emergence of a Pan-Indian movement led by Native American spokespersons who demanded a larger voice in making Indian policy. By 1980 a new era of Indian "self-determination" was becoming a reality, a change symbolized by the passage in 1975 of an "Indian Self-determination and Education Assistance Act," which allowed all tribes the opportunity to assume control of governmental programs and services that had once been provided by the Bureau of Indian Affairs (BIA). The new rights included control over housing, community development, and law enforcement. Within ten years the tribes had begun to administer more than 50 percent of all BIA programs. But as we shall see, these more democratic policies came only after a long and often tragic set of confrontations between Indians and whites over the past 125 years.

The thirty years of military conflict were the inevitable result of a rapid, overwhelming invasion of the lands west of the Mississippi by hundreds of thousands of miners, farmers, town builders, and cattle ranchers between 1860 and 1890. Virtually all Indian actions in the West after 1850 were in response to the white population movement. Each of the five transcontinental railroads built in those years cut a swath through Indian lands. After 1865 the white presence was supported by the army, two thirds of which was stationed in the West.

The swiftness of the white takeover is difficult to imagine. In 1860 miners in the Pikes Peak region and in Nevada, and the Mormons in Salt Lake City, were the only white population worthy of note between the borders of Kansas and Nebraska and the California settlements. West Texas was still Indian country, as was most of the vast area between the Rio Grande towns of New Mexico and southern California. Millions of buffalo grazing on the Great Plains supported not a dying Indian lifestyle but a dynamic new Indian culture characterized by nomadic bands mounted on horses. The Sioux, the Cheyenne, and the Comanche were the most formidable of these tribes. Thirty years later the hostile tribes had been defeated; all tribes were confined to reservations, and both the buffalo herds and the Plains culture were gone. The Indians had become, in effect, wards of the nation.

The military phase began in 1862 when the Santee Sioux living in western Minnesota re-

belled against land-grabbing whites and the abuse of crooked agents. Other grievances included the violation of Sioux women and the demoralization of the tribe by whiskey peddlars. The Sioux attacked settlements at New Ulm and elsewhere, killing nearly 800 whites; but by September 1862, some Sioux bands had been defeated and later thirty-eight Indians were hanged at Mankato, Minnesota, for their part in "The War of the Outbreak." But peace did not come to the Minnesota-Dakota frontier until federal troops carried out punitive campaigns against other Sioux tribes in 1864.

To the south in the newly created Territory of Colorado, the Cheyenne saw their hunting grounds disrupted by the flow of miners and settlers along the Platte River route. They began to raid stage coach stations and attack settlers, and at one point Denver itself was cut off from the East and suffered food shortages. The territorial governor, John Evans, ambitious for Colorado to become a state and fearful that Indian troubles would delay that process, authorized formation of a company of 100-day volunteers in 1864, under the command of Colonel John M. Chivington, to chastise Chief Black Kettle's Cheyenne bands. At the same time, the Cheyenne, thinking that they had come to terms with the federal troops stationed at Fort Lyon in southwestern Colorado, and consequently were under their protection, had settled for the winter on Sand Creek, some miles from the fort. In late November 1864, Chivington and the volunteers surprised them in a dawn attack, killing more than 200 men, women, and children. Far from bringing peace to the Central Plains frontier, news of Sand Creek put other Cheyenne tribes on the warpath. Not until the Battle of the Washita in 1868 did prospects for peace brighten. Defeat of the Cheyenne Dog Soldiers at Summit Springs, Colorado, in July 1869 marked an end to Central Plains warfare for the time being.

In the Southwest, General James H. Carleton, Union commander of New Mexico and Arizona, turned his attention to the reduction of the Navajo. For over 200 years Navajo raids had taken their toll on New Mexican, Spanish-American, and Pueblo settlements. Aware that Indians did not fight in the winter months, Carleton ordered the famous mountain man, Colonel Kit Carson, to carry out a series of ruthless winter campaigns, or "scouts," against the Navajo. Resorting to a scorched-earth policy, Carson killed or captured Navajo horses and sheep, destroyed food supplies, and uprooted the Indians' fruit trees. Between 1862 and 1864, he captured over 7,000 Navajo, who were taken from their remote canyon stronghold in the Four Corners area to Fort Sumner on the Pecos River in eastern New Mexico. There for the next three years Carleton sought to teach the Navajo to farm and to become Christians. But a series of droughts ruined the crops at Fort Sumner and reduced the Indians to starvation. The survivors were then allowed to retrace their "Long Walk" to their native canyons. Traumatized by their sojourn at Fort Sumner, they never again fought the United States.

Federal troops had less success against the Oglala Sioux and the Northern Cheyenne in Wyoming and Montana in 1865. They were ordered to open and guard a wagon road to the new gold fields at Bozeman, Montana; and this road as well as the forts they built violated treaty rights. In a brilliant display of war by attrition, Chiefs Red Cloud, Little Wolf, Crazy Horse, and the Indians harassed the troops at every step, killing eighty in one ambush. In the end the forts were abandoned and the troops recalled.

The shock of the Sand Creek massacre and the expensive Powder River war raised such a public outcry that Congress investigated both events. It authorized a peace commission in 1867 to end hostilities with the Plains tribes and to place them on reservations, by peaceful means if possible, or by force if necessary, and to feed them until they had learned to live as whites and as self-sustaining farmers. This earliest "Peace Policy" began when treaties

were signed at Medicine Lodge (Kansas) in 1867. These treaties created reservations for the Southern Plains tribes, while others made at Fort Laramie a year later carved out a large reservation for the northern tribes, among them Red Cloud's Oglala Sioux. The peace commission also recommended that the government abandon the treaty system, and simply enter into contractual agreements requiring congressional approval—and Congress agreed in 1871.

Meanwhile an influential set of eastern reformers, led by Herbert Welsh and Henry Pancoast, persuaded incoming President Ulysses S. Grant to inaugurate a "Quaker Policy" for the Indians in 1869. Under Grant, the Quakers and various Protestant denominations—to the great distress of the Catholic church in America—were to appoint Indian agents to administer the western reservations. The Central Plains superintendency, for example, was under Quaker jurisdiction, while the Sioux tribes along the Missouri found themselves dealing with agents and missionaries appointed by the Episcopal church. The term "Peace Policy" had a doubly ironic meaning for the Indian. He had to live on a reservation in order to avoid being tracked down by the army and, once there, he had to agree to Christian conversion.

The reformers—many of them former abolitionists—rightly felt that a number of Indian outbreaks had been caused by the activities of crooked agents and contractors. In addition to having churches appoint at least ostensibly honest agents, the reformers persuaded Congress to create a Board of Indian Commissioners, comprised of religious leaders and public-spirited citizens, which would oversee the Indian Bureau.

On face, the Peace Policy seemed a humane way to bring Indians into the mainstream of American life. The army would force the Indians onto the reservation where missionary agents would christianize them, teach them the three Rs, and train them to be farmers. In reality, the policy was fraught with practical difficulties and logical inconsistencies. Congress, moreover, seldom appropriated enough funds to implement the program which, if it were to work, required a vast food supply and a rationing system involving the purchase of thousands of cattle as well as the hiring of hundreds of teachers and farmers. Indeed, many of the Indian outbreaks of the 1870s and 1880s were caused by starvation on the reservations.

Perhaps the most fatuous aspect of the Peace Policy was the expectation that Indians who had never farmed could somehow succeed in raising crops on previously uncultivated lands. Church-appointed agents proved to be no more competent and not much more honest than their predecessors, and throughout its long history (1869–1934) the Board of Indian Commissioners never succeeded in keeping down corruption in the Bureau of Indian Affairs. Constant bickering between the Department of the Interior and the War Department as to which had jurisdiction over the Indians at times reduced the policy to chaos.

Failure of the Peace Policy was dramatized by the fact that between 1869 and 1879 the government had to mount twelve costly military campaigns against the Indians, during which 948 officers and men, 460 civilians, and 4,500 Indians lost their lives. In the Arizona Territory the Peace Policy was so unpopular that when the Apache tribes were placed on four reservations, a party of whites and Papago Indians—the latter traditional enemies of the Apache—raided the Camp Grant Reservation in 1870 and killed over 100 Apaches. In the war that followed, General George Crook used Apache scouts to track down other Apaches. His methods of setting Apache against Apache and of creating prisoner-of-war camps were ruthless; but his instincts were in fact humane. He respected the Indians, enlisted loyal Apaches into the army, and later was instrumental in having himself sued by Standing Bear, a Ponca chief,

so that an Indian could gain the status of a legal person in federal courts. By 1873 Crook had brought a semblance of peace to Arizona, though fighting did not end until 1886, when Geronimo, the most notorious renegade chief, was captured and sent as a military prisoner to Fort Sill, Indian Territory.

Kiowa and Comanche raids in the Southern Plains region of western Texas during the early 1870s prompted General William T. Sherman to launch the 1874 Red River campaign, a no-quarter ''search and destroy'' war of attrition that finally brought the tribes to Indian Territory reservations. Actually, their surrender stemmed as much from the fact that most of the buffalo were being killed by professional hunters as it did from military harassment.

In northern California the Modoc Indians, resentful of reservation life and of constant mistreatment by whites, fled the reservation and killed General Edward S. Canby, who had been sent to treat with them. They fought desperately until captured and settled in the Indian Territory, an area seized from the Five Civilized Tribes as punishment for their support of the Confederacy during the Civil War. They then joined more than twenty tribal remnants from many parts of the West who were forced to live there. Other conflicts occurred when exiled tribesmen made futile attempts to return to their native region.

When gold was discovered in the Black Hills, North Dakota, in 1874–75, in a part of the vast Sioux reservation, invading miners disturbed Indian relations to the point that various tribes left the reservation. In a three-pronged military campaign to bring the Indians back, federal troops pursued them into the Wyoming-Montana region. In a series of skirmishes and battles climaxing in the Battle of the Little Big Horn, General Custer, having unwisely divided his command, encountered several thousand Indians. He and half his troopers were surrounded and cut down. Meanwhile, army forces were badly mauled at the Battle of the

Rosebud. Not until 1881 were the western Sioux returned to the reservation.

An all-too-familiar pattern was repeated in the Northwest in 1877, when the small Nez Perce tribe under Chief Joseph, unhappy with their Idaho reservation, sought to return to their Oregon homeland. Terrified settlers, assuming the Indians were hostile, called for military protection. After a battle with army units at White Bird Canyon, Joseph and his starving tribesmen fled over mountainous terrain for a thousand miles before surrendering to an army unit only a few miles south of the Canadian border.

What remained of the Peace Policy received still another jolt in 1879 when Nathan Meeker, a bigoted, strong-willed agent to the Colorado Utes, so enraged his charges by brutally suppressing traditional customs that they quite understandably murdered him. They also defeated local troops before fleeing and, when finally tracked down, were obliged to leave their native Colorado for a reservation in Utah.

Anthony F. C. Wallace has observed, in his classic *Death and Rebirth of the Seneca Nation* that a people under constant physical and psychological stress will seek to end the crises by reforming their lifestyle or by purifying themselves, a process which often takes the form of a religious revival. Throughout the 1870s and the 1880s, Indian shamans led religious movements born of desperation. The most significant of these occurred in Nevada where Wovoka, a Paiute religious figure, combined beliefs taken from tribal traditions, Mormon teachings, and Protestant missionaries to start a millennial movement popularly called the Ghost Dance religion. If the Indians returned to their former ways, he preached, the whites would be destroyed and the old life, existing before the white man came, would be restored. Wovoka's message mingled hope and expectation, but when the South Dakota Sioux took up the Ghost Dance religion, they turned it into a militant movement and claimed

that only a silver bullet from a white soldier's gun could pierce the sacred white shirt of the Indian believer. As the Ghost Dance movement spread, federal agents on the Pine Ridge reservation became so alarmed that they arrested Sitting Bull, the famous Sioux religious leader, as well as other chiefs, in an effort to stop the gathering Indian resistance. In the struggle that followed, Sitting Bull and Big Foot were killed, and the Battle of Wounded Knee—in the bitter December cold—left several hundred Indian men, women, and children dead.

One of the assumptions of the Peace Policy was that the Indians on the reservation would soon become like white Americans in habits, beliefs, and loyalties. But as early as 1874, it was clear that church reforms, rationing, and reservations were not working. The reformers concluded that they had to destroy the authority of the chiefs, whom they saw as the main obstacle to assimilation. They did not understand that the chiefs, especially in the Plains region, controlled only a few bands. Likewise, they utterly failed to realize that certain chiefs, like Spotted Tail of the Sioux or Standing Bear of the Poncas, were able, even brilliant, negotiators. Somehow these tribal leaders kept the peace and simultaneously protected their tribesmen. But other chiefs often were in the pay of the whites, and constantly compromised the lands and rights of their people. These accommodationists were naturally resisted by those leaders, such as Sitting Bull, who wanted to hold the line against assimilation. Still other chiefs were politicians, who allied themselves first with one side and then the other. Therefore, in addition to the overwhelming presence of the whites and the army, the Indians suffered from divided leadership and from extreme factionalism, characteristics that have continued in intratribal relationships to the present day.

Paralleling the policy of curbing the chiefs was a movement to "kill the tribe and save the individual," which helped shape the emerging assimilation policy of the 1870s and 1880s.

Along with Congress's decision to end the treaty system—which reduced the power of the chiefs—the reformers succeeded in bringing tribesmen under federal jurisdiction for certain crimes committed on the reservation beginning in 1885. During the 1870s Indian agents like John P. Clum of the San Carlos Apache reservation began to employ their charges as police to enforce order on the reservation, thereby eliminating the need for federal troops. The idea was tried on the Indian Territory reservations as well. It eventually spread to most of the agencies and peaked in the 1880s and 1890s. For the first time in history, Indians participated in the enforcement of U.S. civil and criminal laws. Indian judges were also appointed in some areas, to hear cases and to administer punishment, the most famous being Quanah Parker, a Comanche chief who dispensed law and order in Indian Territory for many years.

Reformers still were not satisfied: The Indian must become a red, white, and blue American. In the early 1880s, Philadelphians formed the Indian Rights Association, while others organized a Friends of the Indian group, which held annual conferences at Lake Mohonk, New York, to discuss the Indian problem. Reflecting a Jeffersonian faith in the small farm and the values associated with individual property rights, the reformers urged Congress to pass a severalty act granting Indians homesteads. Finally, in 1887, a measure of Senator Henry L. Dawes of Massachusetts, the General Allotment Law, granted 160 acres to an Indian family, 80 acres to single adults and orphans, and 40 acres for others. This land, once acquired, could not be sold for twenty-five years. Essentially, the Dawes Act passed because western congressmen realized that if all Indians—and there were only some 225,000 in 1880—received a homestead, nearly 90 million acres of the 130 million in reservation lands would be thrown open for sale as part of the public domain.

From the start the Dawes Act was a disaster.

Indians often chose their homesteads not for good farmland but because of the availability of wood and water. Those resisting severalty had it forced upon them, because the Dawes Act gave the white agent the right to choose the plot for the Indians. If an Indian died without heirs, his land was sold and the money placed in the tribal trust funds held in Washington. Then, in 1906, Congress passed the Burke Act, another well-meaning reform, which removed the clause preventing a responsible Indian owner from selling his land before twenty-five years had expired. Initially, the government followed a conservative policy of granting unencumbered title; but during the Wilson administration "competency commissions" went out to the reservations, and declared Indians competent if they were of mixed blood descent, free of venereal disease, or attended school for a stated number of months. By 1920 the devastating effects of the Dawes and Burke acts were all too apparent. The Indians had lost two thirds of their lands and a majority of them were pauperized.

Under the Dawes Act, federal support for Indian education increased impressively. Boarding schools were built, where Indian children lived away from the influence of their families. They were taught to speak English, as well as to read and write. So strong was the urge of the reformer to assimilate the Indian child that General Richard H. Pratt, an army officer who had come to respect Indians during his tour of duty in Indian Territory, started an Indian boarding school at Carlisle Barracks, Pennsylvania. There, he hoped the children would not encounter the anti-Indian prejudices of western communities.

Despite the efforts of Carlisle, at Haskell Institute, and at other boarding schools to educate several generations of selected Indian students, cultural assimilation did not take place. The graduates were simply never accepted into American society. Western communities, moreover, fiercely resisted efforts throughout the first half of the twentieth century to place Indian children in regular public schools. Morale was so low and despair and suicide so prevalent on the reservations between 1900 and 1930 that anthropologists and friends of the Indians began a concerted effort to preserve some of the old tribal culture as a way of giving the Indians some pride in the very customs and crafts that the assimilationists had tried so hard to destroy.

James Mooney, an ethnologist, was one of those who realized the importance of native religious beliefs to the Indian. He thought that the Native American church, which had developed from a Plains peyote cult, but which also had many Christian overtones, deserved protection. In 1918 he succeeded in having the church incorporated under the state laws of Oklahoma. As such, it could not be harassed by missionaries or by the state itself. Although the Indian had many friends during the first years of the twentieth century, and while many discerning anthropologists and collectors came to value Indians' crafts, the nation's Native Americans continued to decline in numbers and in morale.

A turning point of sorts came in 1922, when Senator Holm Bursum of New Mexico crassly attempted to get an act through the Congress that would have seized lands traditionally owned by the Pueblo Indians of his state. To the friends of the Indian, and especially to young John Collier, the Bursum bill was not only another cynical land grab in the name of severalty but an attack on the idea of community. Collier, who had been a social worker in New York, believed that industrialization had destroyed a sense of community in the United States, and that one of the few places it still survived was among the Pueblo tribes of the Southwest.

At the same time *Sunset Magazine* and other journals began to expose corruption in the Bureau of Indian Affairs, as well as in frauds practiced on the oil-rich Osage tribes of Oklahoma. The Harding and Coolidge administra-

tions whitewashed the guilty officials, but the reformers were so aroused that the Rockefeller Foundation was persuaded to make inquiries. It asked Dr. Lewis Meriam to prepare an extensive report on the state of Indian education, and on Indian conditions generally. The Meriam report, *The Problem of Indian Administration,* published in 1928, has been called the first intelligent account of Indian affairs in the nation's history. Acting upon its recommendations, Secretary of the Interior Herbert Work appointed Charles J. Rhoads, president of the Indian Rights Association, and Henry Scattergood, a Quaker philanthropist, to clean up the Indian Bureau.

The Meriam report became the basis for the most radical change in Indian policy in over 100 years. When Franklin D. Roosevelt assumed office in 1933, he permitted John Collier, his choice for Indian commissioner, to write his own reform law: the Wheeler-Howard Act or the Indian Reorganization Act of 1934. Echoing the Meriam report and the thinking of a new school of anthropologists, Collier argued that the Indian could only fully realize himself in the tribal organization. The tribe, he asserted, should be restored in the form of a modern business, political, and cultural corporation. His measure also prohibited future allotment of acreage, and provided funds for the purchase of more tribal lands as a means of creating a more adequate base for subsistence. A subsequent law, the Johnson-O'Malley Act, ordered the Bureau of Indian Affairs to farm out its various services to expert agencies—a move that gave Indians access to better health and educational services. In 1935 an arts and crafts act encouraged manufacture of native crafts and sought to enlarge the market for them.

Of the nation's 172 tribes, only 75 or so were incorporated under the terms of the Wheeler-Howard Act; but a spectacular revival of crafts occurred, and a new spirit of hope appeared on the reservations. For the first time in two centuries Indian landholdings grew rather than decreased. Federal health programs lowered the high rate of infant mortality to the point that the Indian population began to grow for the first time since the 1860s. By 1956, it had increased to 450,000. Indian hatred of boarding schools resulted in a shift to Indian day schools. Funds also were provided for Indians to attend regular high schools and colleges. During Collier's long tenure as Indian commissioner (1933–45), the tribes had a defender of the sort they had never known before.

In the perspective of time it now appears that Collier's tribalization, or "grouphood" policies—as he liked to call them—had just gotten under way when the economy-minded Congresses of the late 1930s began to cut program funds; and after the outbreak of World War II, most of the programs were halted and the Indian Service itself was moved to Chicago to make room for wartime agencies in Washington! Although 100,000 Indians left the reservation during the 1940s to work at defense jobs, or to serve in the armed forces, the Indians as a whole were largely ignored. Male adult unemployment on the reservation remained near 50 percent between 1941 and 1945.

After the war, a new generation of Indian experts—anthropologists, and politicians—concluded that it was both cruel and unrealistic to keep the Indian frozen, as it were, in a cultural museum. Some congressmen accused the Indian Service of fostering communism on the reservation by encouraging tribalism. Unlike any other people, said the new reformers, the Indian was being kept from the inevitable process of change. As the years rolled on, it was argued, he would be less prepared than ever to enter the twentieth century. Harry Truman listened sympathetically to these arguments, and his administration set in motion assimilationist programs; among them was one providing $80 million over a ten-year period to bring industry to the Navajo-Hopi reservation.

The major policy change came, however, when the Eisenhower administration advocated that the Indians be taken off the reservations and relocated in the city, where they might better find employment and enter the American mainstream. Congress quickly obliged by repealing the Wheeler-Howard Act by an overwhelming nonpartisan vote. In 1954 Congress began passing a series of termination acts, which called for the breaking up of reservations and the sale of Indian lands and resources. The resulting income was to be divided among the individuals who had lived on the reservation. Fortunately for the Indians, termination acts had to be passed for each individual tribe, and the experience of the Menominee Indians of Wisconsin and of the Klamath tribes of Oregon proved so grim once their lands and timber had been sold that the termination policy was halted.

The fight over termination coincided with the civil rights movements for black Americans taking place in the 1950s and 1960s. A new generation of postwar Indian leaders, some veterans of World War II, others with experience in war industries, and still others educated in the schools provided by the Wheeler-Howard Act, joined the movement to demand justice for the Indians. However, in this instance justice meant keeping reservation lands and "self-determination." The National Congress of the American Indians, representing one third of the tribes, was now joined by other organizations seeking "Red Power." As the demand for Red Power increased, some fifty tribal representatives allied with Washington State Indian groups to protest violation of the latter's traditional fishing rights on the Columbia River. Shooting and violence by white vigilantes marred the "fish in" but Congress eventually restored some of these rights. Such extensive tribal cooperation for a single purpose was both a new experience for the American Indians and a demonstration of the fact that a Pan-Indian movement was developing among

Native Americans who had gone to work and live in the city.

By the 1960s, in fact, over 50 percent of the Indian population was urban with a great number living in Chicago, Denver, Minneapolis-St. Paul, Phoenix, and Los Angeles. Besides having discovered a common bond in their Indianness, the urban Indian also retained an affection for older tribal traditions and for the reservation itself. Paradoxically, the Indian now wanted to live in two worlds rather than one.

The ''New Indians'' had outspoken and aggressive leaders. In 1969, Mel Thom, a Paiute, and Herbert Blatchford, a Navajo, led an occupation of Alcatraz Island in San Francisco Bay, demanding that it be turned into a university and a cultural center for Indians. The effort failed; but in November 1972, representatives of various Indian groups, among them the American Indian Movement (AIM), occupied the offices of the Bureau of Indian Affairs in Washington to advertise their grievances, and to demand the right to set their own Indian policy.

A year later, Russell Means and other AIM leaders occupied a portion of Pine Ridge Reservation—scene of the battle of Wounded Knee in 1890—and demanded among other things that the reservation be recognized as a sovereign state. This effort also failed but Wounded Knee II demonstrated that the Indian spirit was far from broken and that problems of assimilation had not been solved.

Indians, whether radical or conservative, urban or rural, all joined in the fight against termination. Beginning in 1972, and culminating in the 1975 Indian Self-Determination and Educational Assistance Act, first the Nixon and then the Ford administration adopted the policy of ''self-determination without termination,'' which in practical terms meant that the Indians themselves would assume control of the Indian Service, handle educational programs, and receive encouragement to develop business both on and off the reservation.

Postwar termination policies had some surprising results, but none more so than those of the Indian Claims Commission Act of 1946. Anticipating that the reservations might be closed, Congress set up a special commission to settle outstanding Indian claims against the government. A Court of Claims was also created to review the commission's decisions. The act allowed tribes to seek redress for injustices dating back to the founding of the nation. Fraudulent land sales, unjust treaties, unpaid annuities—all came up for review. Claim after claim was settled in favor of the tribes, and in a famous case Congress restored the Blue Lake area to the Pueblo Indians of Taos. Similarly, the Indian tribes of Maine, who claimed that vast areas of the state of Maine had been taken from them illegally, won a generous settlement. In 1971 the U.S. government in the Alaska Native Claims Settlement Act, conveyed $965.5 million and 44 million acres to the Native Americans of Alaska (Aleut, Eskimo, and Indian) in part to clear title so that oil development could go forward in that state.

Generally speaking, up to 1934 American Indian policy reflected the changing passions and values of succeeding generations of white public officials and reformers. Since 1934, however, Indians have had an increasing voice in decision making about Indian matters. Today Native American spokesmen, many of them teachers, lawyers, writers, public health experts, and government officials communicate with a large and responsive national audience. Indian-American lawyers now press their cases in court; several Indians have been elected to Congress, and more sit in the legislatures of at least six western states. Schools on reservations are now run by Indian personnel, and the old Indian Service is almost a thing of the past.

Still, the very practical problems of prejudice, injustice, massive unemployment, and substandard living conditions remain. And a sometimes debilitating debate between pro-development and traditional factions on the reservations continues to occur. Significantly, it has not been a better policy, but the emergence of a tolerance for cultural pluralism in the United States, plus the Indian insistence on a separate identity and self-determination, that has brought about healthy changes not dreamed of by the assimilationists of the 1880s.

SUGGESTED READINGS

Berger, Thomas R. *Village Journey: The Report of the Alaska Native Review Commission.* New York: Hill & Wang, 1985.

Brown, Dee. *Bury My Heart at Wounded Knee: An Indian History of the American West.* New York: Bantam Books, 1973.

Deloria, Vine, Jr. *Custer Died for Your Sins: An Indian Manifesto.* New York: Macmillan, 1969.

————, ed. *American Indian Policy in the Twentieth Century.* Norman: University of Oklahoma Press, 1985.

————, and Lytle, Clifford. *The Nations Within: The Past and Future of American Indian Sovereignty.* New York: Pantheon Books, 1984.

Ellis, Richard N., ed. *Western American Indians: Case Studies in Tribal History.* Lincoln: University of Nebraska Press, 1972.

Fixico, Donald L. *Termination and Relocation: Federal Indian Policy, 1945–1960.* Albuquerque: University of New Mexico Press, 1986.

Fritz, Henry E. *Movement for Indian Assimilation, 1860–1890.* Philadelphia: University of Pennsylvania Press, 1963.

Hagan, William T. *Indian Police and Judges: Experiments in Acculturation and Control.* New Haven, Conn.: Yale University Press, 1966.

Mardock, Robert W. *Reformers and the American Indian.* Columbia: University of Missouri Press, 1971.

Moses, L. G., and Wilson, Raymond, eds. *Indian Lives: Essays on Nineteenth- and Twentieth-Century Native American Leaders.* Albuquerque: University of New Mexico Press, 1985.

Neihardt, John G. *Black Elk Speaks.* Lincoln: University of Nebraska Press, 1961.

Philp, Kenneth R., ed. *Indian Self-Rule: First-Hand Accounts of Indian-White Relations from Roosevelt to Reagan.* Salt Lake City and Chicago: Howe Brothers, 1986.

Szasz, Margaret. *Education and the American Indian: The Road to Self-Determination, 1928–1973.* Albuquerque: University of New Mexico Press, 1974.

Utley, Robert M. *The Indian Frontier of the American West, 1846–1890.* Albuquerque: University of New Mexico Press, 1984.

Washburn, Wilcomb E. *The Indian in America.* New York: Harper & Row, 1975.

DOCUMENT 22.1
The Peace Policy

After the Sand Creek massacre in 1864 and the expensive Powder River war in 1865, both the reformers and the public demanded a policy of peace toward the Indian as an alternative to extinction by war. The "Peace Policy" officially began when President Ulysses S. Grant assumed office in 1869 and turned certain reservations over to Quaker groups to administer. Grant described his Peace Policy in his first annual message to Congress. This policy, it should be noted, was based upon the assumption that the Indian would be assimilated into American society.

From the foundation of the Government to the present the management of the original inhabitants of this continent—the Indians—has been a subject of embarrassment and expense, and has been attended with continuous robberies, murders, and wars. From my own experience upon the frontiers and in Indian countries, I do not hold either legislation or the conduct of the whites who come most in contact with the Indian blameless for these hostilities. The

Source: James R. Richardson, comp., *A Compilation of the Messages and Papers of the Presidents* (New York, n.d.), vol. 9, pp. 3992–93.

past, however, can not be undone, and the question must be met as we now find it. I have attempted a new policy toward these wards of the nation (they can not be regarded in any other light than as wards), with fair results so far as tried, and which I hope will be attended ultimately with great success. The Society of Friends is well known as having succeeded in living in peace with the Indians in the early settlement of Pennsylvania, while their white neighbors of other sects in other sections were constantly embroiled. They are also known for their opposition to all strife, violence, and war, and are generally noted for their strict integrity and fair dealings. These considerations induced me to give the management of a few reservations of Indians to them and to throw the burden of the selection of agents upon the society itself. . . . The result has proven most satisfactory. For superintendents and Indian agents not on the reservations, officers of the Army were selected. The reasons for this are numerous. Where Indian agents are sent, there, or near there, troops must be sent also. The agent and the commander of troops are independent of each other, and are subject to orders from different Departments of the Government. The army officer holds a position for life; the agent, one at the will of the President. The former is personally interested in living in harmony with the Indian and in establishing a permanent peace, to the end that some portion of his life may be spent within the limits of civilized society; the latter has no such personal interest. Another reason is an economic one; and still another, the hold which the Government has upon a life officer to secure a faithful discharge of duties in carrying out a given policy.

The building of railroads, and the access thereby given to all the agricultural and mineral regions of the country, is rapidly bringing civilized settlements into contact with all the tribes of Indians. No matter what ought to be the relations between such settlements and the aborigines, the fact is they do not harmonize well,

and one or the other has to give way in the end. A system which looks to the extinction of a race is too horrible for a nation to adopt without entailing upon itself the wrath of all Christendom and engendering in the citizen a disregard for human life and the rights of others, dangerous to society. I see no substitute for such a system, except in placing all the Indians on large reservations, as rapidly as it can be done, and giving them absolute protection there. As soon as they are fitted for it they should be induced to take their lands in severalty and to set up Territorial governments for their own protection. . . .

DOCUMENT 22.2
Implementing the Peace Policy

The three documents cited below spell out unmistakably the ambitious goals of the Peace Policy advocates. The first document is from the annual report of 1869 of Ely S. Parker, Grant's Indian commissioner. Many of Parker's ideas were borrowed from recommendations made by the newly created Board of Indian Commissioners (Document 2), which spoke feelingly of white injustice to the Indian in ways that resemble statements made by Indian leaders today; but they were notably lacking in sympathy for any aspect of Indian culture. Both Parker and the commissioners agreed that Congress should end the treaty system and that a work ethic be developed among the Indians. Note that the Commissioners are already urging that Indians be given individual farms—a policy that was adopted with the passage of the Dawes Act of 1887.

Besides concentrating the tribes on reservations and turning them into farmers,

Source: *Report of the Commissioner of Indian Affairs for the Year 1869* (Washington: U.S. Government Printing Office, 1870), pp. 4–9, 45–50, passim; 119–21, passim; 342.

the paramount concern of the Peace Policy supporters was to christianize the tribes and educate the children—two processes that were indistinguishable in their own minds. One of the more successful efforts to educate Indian children occurred at the Santee Sioux Agency in Nebraska, which was the site of an Episcopal mission school. The report of Reverend Samuel D. Hinman (Document 3) is revealing, not only for his examples of progress in education but for the goals he attributes to the Indians.

1

REPORT OF THE COMMISSIONER OF INDIAN AFFAIRS

". . . What shall be done for the amelioration and civilization of the race?" For a long period in the past, great and commendable efforts were made by the government and the philanthropist, and large sums of money expended to accomplish these desirable ends, but the success never was commensurate with the means employed. Of late years a change of policy was seen to be required, as the cause of failure, the difficulties to be encountered, and the best means of overcoming them, became better understood. The measures to which we are indebted for an improved condition of affairs are, the concentration of the Indians upon suitable reservations, and the supplying them with means for engaging in agricultural and mechanical pursuits, and for their education and moral training. As a result, the clouds of ignorance and superstition in which many of these people were so long enveloped have disappeared, and the light of a Christian civilization seems to have dawned upon their moral darkness, and opened up a brighter future. Much, however, remains to be done for the multitude yet in their savage state, and I can but earnestly invite the serious consideration of those whose duty it is to legislate in their behalf, to the justice and importance

of promptly fulfilling all treaty obligations, and the wisdom of placing at the disposal of the department adequate funds for the purpose. . . .

Under an act of Congress approved April 10, 1868, two millions of dollars were appropriated to enable the President to maintain peace among and with various tribes, bands, and parties of Indians; to promote their civilization; bring them, when practicable, upon reservations, and to relieve their necessities, and encourage their efforts at self-support. The Executive is also authorized to organize a board of commissioners, to consist of not more than ten persons, selected from among men eminent for their intelligence and philanthropy, to serve without pecuniary compensation, and who, under his direction, shall exercise joint control with the Secretary of the Interior over the disbursement of this large fund. . . .

With a view to more efficiency in the management of affairs of the respective superintendencies and agencies, the Executive has inaugurated a change of policy whereby a different class of men from those heretofore selected have been appointed to duty as superintendents and agents. There was doubtless just ground for it, as great and frequent complaints have been made for years past, of either the dishonesty or inefficiency of many of these officers. Members of the Society of Friends, recommended by the society, now hold these positions in the Northern Superintendency, embracing all Indians in Nebraska; and in the Central, embracing tribes residing in Kansas, together with the Kiowas, Comanches, and other tribes in the Indian country. The other superintendencies and agencies, excepting that of Oregon and two agencies there, are filled by army officers detailed for such duty. The experiment has not been sufficiently tested to enable me to say definitely that it is a success, for but a short time has elapsed since these Friends and officers entered upon duty; but so far as I can learn the plan works advantageously, and will probably prove a positive benefit to the service, and the indications are that the interests of the government and the Indians will be subserved by an honest and faithful discharge of duty, fully answering the expectations entertained by those who regard the measure as wise and proper. . . .

Arrangements now, as heretofore, will doubtless be required with tribes desiring to be settled upon reservations for the relinquishment of their rights to the lands claimed by them and for assistance in sustaining themselves in a new position, but I am of the opinion that *they should not be of a treaty nature*. It has become a matter of serious import whether the treaty system in use ought longer to be continued. In my judgment it should not. A treaty involves the idea of a compact between two or more sovereign powers, each possessing sufficient authority and force to compel a compliance with the obligations incurred. The Indian tribes of the United States are not sovereign nations, capable of making treaties, as none of them have an organized government of such inherent strength as would secure a faithful obedience of its people in the observance of compacts of this character. They are held to be the wards of the government, and the only title the law concedes to them to the lands they occupy or claim is a mere possessory one. But, because treaties have been made with them, generally for the extinguishment of their supposed absolute title to land inhabited by them, or over which they roam, they have become falsely impressed with the notion of national independence. It is time that this idea should be dispelled, and the government cease the cruel farce of thus dealing with its helpless and ignorant wards. Many good men, looking at this matter only from a Christian point of view, will perhaps say that the poor Indian has been greatly wronged and ill treated; that this whole country was once his, of which he has been despoiled, and that he has been driven from place to place until he has hardly left to

him a spot where to lay his head. This indeed may be philanthropic and humane, but the stern letter of the law admits of no such conclusion, and great injury has been done by the government in deluding this people into the belief of their being independent sovereignties, while they were at the same time recognized only as its dependents and wards.

Hostilities to some extent, though not to that of war by tribes, have unfortunately existed more or less during the past year. In May and June last some of the Cheyennes and Arapahoes attacked citizens of Kansas settled upon the Republican, Smoky Hill, and Saline Rivers, killing a number of men, women, and children, capturing others, and destroying or carrying off considerable property. The love of plunder and the spirit of revenge seem not to have been subdued in many of the Indians of these tribes by the chastisement they received heretofore, nor by the magnanimity of the government in promising to provide for and treat them as friendly if they would go upon their reservations. Active and severe measures by the military against them have resulted in the destruction of many, and compelled others either to surrender or come in and ask to be located upon a reservation with those of their people who are peaceably disposed. The discontented of the various bands of Sioux have also shown a determined spirit of antagonism to the government, in acts of occasional murder and depredations in Dakota and Wyoming Territories, but the main body of the Sioux who, under General Harney, were located on the great reservation provided for them by treaty stipulations, are comparatively quiet, and it is thought can be kept so, as well as induced to change their mode of life. In Montana a part of the Piegans have been on the warpath, and apprehensions have been entertained of serious troubles; murders of citizens have been committed by other Indians, and citizens have retaliated, but the danger of a serious outbreak, it is believed, is past. With the wild and intractable Apaches, in Arizona, there seems to be a continual state of warfare and outrage which the military arm in use there is unable to wholly suppress, and this will be the case always, until these Indians can be induced to leave their almost inaccessible retreats and settle upon a reservation. Members of the Kiowas and Comanches have been renewing their attacks upon citizens of Texas and their property, but no extensive raiding by the tribes, as in former years, has occurred during the past year, nor have other tribes had as much cause for complaint against these bands as heretofore. The Apaches and Navajoes have also been charged with outrages against citizens of New Mexico, and so troublesome have they been that the governor of the Territory deemed it his duty to issue a proclamation declaring the Navajoes outlaws, and authorizing the people to defend their persons and property against their attacks. . . .

2

Pittsburg, November 23, 1869

Sir: The commission of citizens appointed by the President under the act of Congress of April 10, 1869, to co-operate with the administration in the management of Indian affairs, respectfully report:

*   *   *   *   *

The history of the government connections with the Indians is a shameful record of broken treaties and unfulfilled promises.

The history of the border white man's connection with the Indians is a sickening record of murder, outrage, robbery, and wrongs committed by the former as the rule, and occasional savage outbreaks and unspeakably barbarous deeds of retaliation by the latter as the exception.

The class of hardy men on the frontier who represent the highest type of the energy and enterprise of the American people, and are just and honorable in their sense of moral obligation and their appreciations of the rights of others, have been powerless to prevent these wrongs, and have been too often the innocent sufferers from the Indian's revenge. That there are many good men on the border is a subject of congratulation, and the files of the Indian Bureau attest that among them are found some of the most earnest remonstrants against the evils we are compelled so strongly to condemn.

The testimony of some of the highest military officers of the United States is on record to the effect that, in our Indian wars, almost without exception, the first aggressions have been made by the white man, and the assertion is supported by every civilian of reputation who has studied the subject. In addition to the class of robbers and outlaws who find impunity in their nefarious pursuits upon the frontiers, there is a large class of professedly reputable men who use every means in their power to bring on Indian wars, for the sake of the profit to be realized from the presence of troops and the expenditure of government funds in their midst. They proclaim death to the Indians at all times, in words and publications, making no distinction between the innocent and the guilty. They incite the lowest class of men to the perpetration of the darkest deeds against their victims, and, as judges and jurymen, shield them from the justice due to their crimes. Every crime committed by a white man against an Indian is concealed or palliated; every offense committed by one Indian against a white man is borne on the wings of the post or the telegraph to the remotest corner of the land, clothed with all the horrors which the reality or imagination can throw around it. Against such influences as these the people of the United States need to be warned. The murders, robberies, drunken riots and outrages perpetrated by Indians in time of peace—taking into consideration the relative population of the races on the frontier—do not amount to a tithe of the number of like crimes committed by white men in the border settlements and towns. Against the inhuman idea that the Indian is only fit to be exterminated, and the influence of the men who propagate it, the military arm of the government cannot be too strongly guarded. It is hardly to be wondered at that inexperienced officers, ambitious for distinction, when surrounded by such influences, have been incited to attack Indian bands without adequate cause, and involve the nation in an unjust war. It should, at least, be understood that in the future such blunders should cost the officer his commission, and that such destruction is infamy.

Paradoxical as it may seem, the white man has been the chief obstacle in the way of Indian civilization. The benevolent measures attempted by the government for their advancement have been almost uniformly thwarted by the agencies employed to carry them out. The soldiers, sent for their protection, too often carried demoralization and disease into their midst. The agent, appointed to be their friend and counsellor, business manager, and the almoner of the government bounties, frequently went among them only to enrich himself in the shortest possible time, at the cost of the Indians, and spend the largest available sum of the government money with the least ostensible beneficial result. The general interest of the trader was opposed to their enlightenment as tending to lessen his profits. Any increase of intelligence would render them less liable to his impositions; and, if occupied in agricultural pursuits, their product of furs would be proportionally decreased. The contractor's and transporter's interests were opposed to it, for the reason that the production of agricultural products on the spot would measurably cut off their profits in furnishing army supplies. The interpreter knew that if they were taught, his occupation would be gone. The more submissive and patient the tribe, the greater the number of outlaws infesting their vicinity; and all these were the missionaries teaching them the most degrading vices of which humanity is capable. If in spite of these obstacles a tribe made some

progress in agriculture, or their lands became valuable from any cause, the process of civilization was summarily ended by driving them away from their homes with fire and sword, to undergo similar experiences in some new locality.

Whatever may have been the original character of the aborigines, many of them are now precisely what the course of treatment received from the whites must necessarily have made them—suspicious, revengeful, and cruel in their retaliation. In war they know no distinction between the innocent and the guilty. In his most savage vices the worst Indian is but the imitator of bad white men on the border. To assume that all of them, or even a majority of them, may be so characterized with any degree of truthfulness, would be no more just than to assume the same of all the white people upon the frontier. Some of the tribes, as a whole, are peaceful and industrious to the extent of their knowledge, needing only protection, and a reasonable amount of aid and Christian instruction, to insure the rapid attainment of habits of industry, and a satisfactory advance toward civilization. Even among the wildest of the nomadic tribes there are larger bands, and many individuals in other bands, who are anxious to remain quietly upon their reservation, and are patiently awaiting the fulfillment of the government promise that they and their children shall be taught to "live like the white man."

To assert that "the Indian will not work" is as true as it would be to say that the white man will not work. In all countries there are non-working classes. The chiefs and warriors are the Indian aristocracy. They need only to be given incentives to induce them to work. Why should the Indian be expected to plant corn, fence lands, build houses, or do anything but get food from day to day, when experience has taught him that the product of his labor will be seized by the white man to-morrow? The most industrious white man would become a drone under similar circumstances. Nevertheless, many of the Indians are already at work, and furnish ample refutation of the assertion that "the Indian will not work." There is no escape from the inexorable logic of facts. . . .

The policy of collecting the Indian tribes upon small reservations contiguous to each other, and within the limits of a large reservation, eventually to become a State of the Union, and of which the small reservations will probably be the counties, seems to be the best that can be devised. Many tribes may thus be collected in the present Indian territory. The larger the number that can be thus concentrated the better for the success of the plan; care being taken to separate hereditary enemies from each other. When upon the reservation they should be taught as soon as possible the advantage of individual ownership of property; and should be given land in severalty as soon as it is desired by any of them, and the tribal relations should be discouraged. To facilitate the future allotment of the land the agricultural portions of the reservations should be surveyed as soon as it can be done without too much exciting their apprehensions. The titles should be inalienable from the family of the holder for at least two or three generations. The civilized tribes now in the Indian territory should be taxed, and made citizens of the United States as soon as possible.

The treaty system should be abandoned, and as soon as any just method can be devised to accomplish it, existing treaties should be abrogated.

The legal status of the uncivilized Indians should be that of wards of the government; the duty of the latter being to protect them, to educate them in industry, the arts of civilization, and the principles of Christianity; elevate them to the rights of citizenship, and to sustain and clothe them until they can support themselves.

The payment of money annuities to the Indians should be abandoned, for the reason that such payments encourage idleness and vice, to the injury of those whom it is intended to benefit. Schools should be established, and teachers employed by the government to introduce the English language in every tribe. It is believed that many of the difficulties with Indians occur from misunderstandings as to the meaning and intention of either party. The teachers employed should be nominated by some religious body having a mission nearest to the location of the school. The establishment of Christian missions should be encouraged, and their schools fostered. The pupils should at least receive the rations and clothing they would get if remaining with their families. The religion of our blessed Saviour is believed to be the most effective agent for the civilization of any people.

3

Santee Agency, Nebraska
September 10, 1869

Sir: I have the honor herewith to report for the schools of the Episcopal Mission for the past year.

The mission buildings, begun in the autumn of 1867, have been completed, and for the first time since our location here we have been enabled to have regular sessions of the school. We have three terms of 13 weeks each, occupying the whole winter and early summer, and leaving the hot months of July and August for the long vacation. Besides this we give only a few days for recreation at Christmas and Easter time.

The number of pupils enrolled has been over 200, about equally divided between boys and girls. The attendance has been for the two winter terms, 175, and for the summer, 90.

I have employed five teachers, and English only has been taught. Mrs. H. has also taught singing, having the whole school as learners.

Three of my teachers have been Indians, one young man and two young women. They have had charge of the younger classes, and have succeeded remarkably well.

In the afternoon one of my teachers has taught knitting, and many of the young girls have become quite proficient, and are now able to knit their own stockings. Sewing they already know, and excel most white persons in the neatness of their work. We hope soon to teach breadmaking and other household arts.

Their progress in learning English must necessarily be slow; but under favorable influences the next generation will very generally be in language and habit like the whites.

The great hinderance to our whole work here has been the unsettled state of the Indians. They have wished their lands surveyed, and have expected that they would be allowed to them in severalty. They have waited long, and are now wellnigh discouraged; many of them have already gone to take lands for themselves, and many more are about going.

*   *   *   *   *

Samuel D. Hinman
Pastor of the Mission
Asa M. Janney,
U.S. Indian Agent for Santee Sioux

DOCUMENT 22.3
The Indian View: 1870–1890

By the 1870s certain Indian leaders, especially those of the Plains tribes, had captured the public's imagination. It was a first step in the transition of the white mind from an abstract image of the Indian to that of recognizing, even admiring, Indian personalities. The process was aided by the fact that dozens of chiefs and warriors visited Washington and toured the East to voice grievances and to ask for help. Indian oratory, though sometimes embellished by an overzealous interpreter or journalist, was nevertheless powerful and had

Source: *New York Times*, June 16, 1870.

its impact upon white audiences, army officers, and government officials. The four Indian spokesmen quoted below suggest a very different perspective from that of the missionary-reformer.

CHIEF RED CLOUD, OGLALA SIOUX— NEW YORK, 1870

My Brothers and my Friends who are before me today: God Almighty has made us all, and He is here to hear what I have to say to you today. The Great Spirit made us both. He gave me lands and He gave you lands. You came here and we received you as brother. When the Almighty made you, He made you all white and clothed you. When He made us He made us with red skins and poor. When you first came we were very many and you were few. Now you are many and we are few. You do not know who appears before you to speak. He is a representative of the original American race, and first people of this continent. We are good, and not bad. The reports which you get about us are all on one side. You hear of us only as murderers and thieves. We are not so. If we had more lands to give to you we would give them, but we have no more. We are driven into a very little island, and we want you, our dear friends, to help us with the Government of the United States. The Great Spirits made us poor and ignorant. He made you rich and wise and skillful in things which we know nothing about. The good Father made you to eat tame game and us to eat wild game. Ask any one who has gone through to California. They will tell you we have treated them well. You have children. We, too, have children, and we wish to bring them up well. We ask you to help us do it. At the mouth of Horse Creek, in 1852, the Great Father made a treaty with us. We agreed to let him pass though our territory unharmed for fifty-five years. We kept our word. We committed no murders, no depredations, until the troops came there. When the troops were sent there trouble and disturbance arose. Since that time there have been various goods sent from time to time to us, but only once did they reach us, and soon the Great Father took away the only good man he had sent us, Col. Fitzpatrick. The Great Father said we must go to farming, and some of our men went to farming near Fort Laramie, and were treated very badly indeed. We came to Washington to see our Great Father that peace might be continued. The Great Father that made us both wishes peace to be kept; we want to keep peace. Will you help us? In 1868 men came out and brought papers. We could not read them, and they did not tell us truly what was in them. We thought the treaty was to remove the forts and that we should then cease from fighting. But they wanted to send us traders on the Missouri. We did not want to go on the Missouri, but wanted traders where we were. When I reached Washington the Great Father explained to me what the treaty was, and showed me that the interpreters had deceived me. All I want is right and justice. I have tried to get from the Great Father what is right and just. I have not altogether succeeded. I want you to help me to get what is right and just. I represent the whole Sioux nation, and they will be bound by what I say. I am no Spotted Tail, to say one thing one day and be bought for a pin the next. Look at me. I am poor and naked, but I am the Chief of the nation. We do not want riches, but we want to train our children right. Riches would do us no good. We could not take them with us to the other world. We do not want riches, we want peace and love.

CHIEF SITTING BULL—HUNKPAPA SIOUX

What treaty that the whites have kept has the red man broken? Not one. What treaty that the whites ever made with us red men have they kept? Not one. When I was a boy the Sioux owned the world. The sun rose and set in their lands. They sent 10,000 horsemen to battle. Where are the warriors to-day? Who slew them? Where are our lands? Who owns them? What white man can say I ever stole his lands or a penny of his money? Yet they say I am a thief. What white woman, however lonely, was ever when a captive insulted by me? Yet they say I am a bad Indian. What white man has ever seen me drunk? Who has ever come to me hungry and gone unfed? Who has ever seen me beat my wives or abuse my children? What law have I broken? Is it wrong for me to love my own? Is it wicked in me because my skin is red; because I am a Sioux; because I was born where my fathers lived; because I would die for my people and my country?

CHIEF TEN BEARS, COMANCHE— KANSAS, 1876

. . . You said that you wanted to put us upon a reservation, to build our houses and make us medicine lodges. I do not want them. I was born upon the prairie where the wind blew free and there was nothing to break the light of the sun.

I was born where there were no inclosures and where everything drew a free breath. I want to die there and not within walls. I know every stream and every wood between the Rio Grande and the Arkansas, I have hunted and lived over that country. I lived like my fathers before me, and, like them, I lived happily.

When I was at Washington the Great Father told me that all the Comanches' land was ours and that no one should hinder us in living upon it. So why do you ask us to leave the rivers and the sun and the wind and live in houses?

Source: W. Fletcher Johnson, ''Life of Sitting Bull'' (1891), p. 201, as reprinted in *Great Documents in American History,* ed. Wayne Moquin and Charles Van Doren (New York: Praeger Publishers, 1973), pp. 208–10.

Source: ''The American Indian,'' February 1930, as reprinted in *Great Documents in American History,* ed. Wayne Moquin and Charles Van Doren (New York: Praeger Publishers, 1973), pp. 208–10.

Do not ask us to give up the buffalo for the sheep. The young men have heard talk of this, and it has made them sad and angry. Do not speak of it more. I love to carry out the talk I get from the Great Father. When I get goods and presents I and my people feel glad, since it shows that he holds us in the eye.

If Texans had kept out of my country there might have been peace. But that which you now say we must live on is too small. The Texans have taken away the places where the grass grew the thickest and the timber the best. Had we kept that, we might have done the things you ask. But it is too late. The white man has the country which we loved, and we only wish to wander on the prairies until we die. Any good thing you say to me shall not be forgotten. I shall carry it as near to my heart as my children, and it shall be as often on my tongue as the name of the Great Father. I want no blood upon my land to stain the grass. I want it all clear and pure, and I wish it so that all who go through among my people may find peace when they come in and leave it when they go out. . . .

CHIEF JOSEPH, NEZ PERCE—1877

Tell General Howard I know his heart. What he told me before, I have it in my heart. I am tired of fighting. Our chiefs are killed. Looking Glass is dead. Toohoolhoolzote is dead. The old men are all dead. It is the young men who say, "Yes" or "No." He who led the young men is dead. It is cold, and we have no blankets. The little children are freezing to death. My people, some of them, have run away to the hills, and have no blankets, no food. No one knows where they are—perhaps freezing to death. I want to have time to look for my children, and see how many of them I can find. Maybe I shall find them among the dead. Hear me, my chiefs! I am

Source: *Harper's Weekly*, November 17, 1877.

tired. My heart is sick and sad. From where the sun now stands I will fight no more forever.

DOCUMENT 22.4
Life on the Reservation

Proponents of small reservations for the Indian appear to have been unaware that treating Indians as wards gave the Indian Service and especially the local Indian agent extraordinary powers. Often the reservation became an outdoor prison in which the inmates were told to be self-sufficient but were not allowed to go on hunts or provide for themselves in traditional ways. Charles A. Eastman, an educated Sioux who became a physician and practiced on the Pine Ridge Agency, recorded his own impressions of reservation life in his book, The Indian Today *(1915).*

The Indian of the Northwest came into reservation life reluctantly, very much like a man who has dissipated his large inheritance and is driven out by foreclosure. One morning he awoke to the fact that he must give up his freedom and resign his vast possessions to live in a squalid cabin in the backyard of civilization. For the first time his rovings were checked by well-defined boundaries, and he could not hunt or visit neighboring tribes without a passport. He was practically a prisoner, to be fed and treated as such; and what resources were left him must be controlled by the Indian Bureau through its resident agent.

Who is this Indian agent, or superintendent, as he is now called? He is the supreme ruler on the reservation, responsible directly to the Commissioner of Indian Affairs; and all requests or complaints must pass through his office. The agency doctor, clerks, farmers, superintendents of agency schools, and all other local

Source: Charles A. Eastman, *The Indian Today* (Boston, 1915), pp. 41–45.

employees report to him and are subject to his orders. Too often he has been nothing more than a ward politician of the commonest stamp, whose main purpose is to get all that is coming to him. His salary is small, but there are endless opportunities for graft.

If any appeal from the agent's decisions, they are "kickers" and "insubordinate." If they are Indians, he can easily deprive them of privileges, or even imprison them on trumped-up charges; if employees, he will force them to resign or apply for transfers; and even the missionaries may be compelled, directly or indirectly, to leave the reservation for protesting too openly against official wrongdoing. The inspector sent from Washington to investigate finds it easy to "get in with" the agent and very difficult to see or hear anything that the agent does not wish him to hear or see. Many Indians now believe sincerely in Christ's teachings as explained to them by their missionaries, but they find it impossible to believe that this Government is Christian, or the average official an honest man.

Any untutored people, however, are apt imitators, and so these much-exploited natives become politicians in spite of themselves. The most worthless of the tribe are used as the agent's spies and henchmen; a state of affairs demoralizing on the face of it. As long as the Indian Bureau is run in the interest of the politicians, and Indian civilization is merely an incident, the excellent and humanitarian policies approved by the American people will not be fully carried into effect. . . .

The Indian is no fool; on the other hand, he is a keen observer and an apt student. Although an idealist by nature, many of the race have proved themselves good business men. But under the reservation system they have developed traits that are absolutely opposed to the racial type. They become time-serving, beggarly, and apathetic. Some of their finest characters, such as Chief Joseph, have really died of a broken heart. These are men who

could not submit to be degraded; the politicians call them "incorrigible savages."

The distribution of rations to the Plains Indians was, as I have explained, originally a peace measure, and apparently a necessity in place of their buffalo which the white man had exterminated. For many years Texas beef was issued monthly "on the hoof"; that is, the cattle were driven out one by one upon the plain, and there surrounded and shot down by representatives of the groups to which they belonged. Bacon, flour, sugar, and coffee were doled out to the women, usually as often as once in two weeks, thus requiring those who lived at a considerable distance from the agency to spend several days of each month on the road, neglecting their homes and gardens, if they had any. Once a year there was a distribution of cheap blankets and shoddy clothing. The self-respect of the people was almost fatally injured by these methods. This demoralizing ration-giving had been gradually done away with as the Indians progressed toward self-support, but is still found necessary in many cases.

Not all features of reservation life are bad; for while many good things are shut out and some evils flourish, others are excluded. Liquor traffic among Indians has been forbidden by law since the colonial period; and the law is fairly well enforced by a number of special officers; yet in a few tribes there has been in recent years much demoralization through liquor. It is generally admitted that there is more crime and rowdyism on the reservation than in civilized communities of equal size. In 1878 a force of native police was authorized to keep order, eject intruders, act as truant officers, and perform other duties under the direction of the agent. Though paid only ten or twelve dollars a month, these men have been faithful and efficient in the performance of duties involving considerable hardship and sometimes danger. Their loyalty and patriotism are deserving of special praise. In making arrests and bringing in desperate prisoners, as in the case of Pretty Elk the Brule Sioux murderer, and of the chief, Sitting Bull, the faithful police have sometimes lost their lives.

DOCUMENT 22.5
The Crisis in Indian Education and the Meriam Report of 1928

When the Dawes Act was passed in 1887 Congress also provided increased funds for Indian education, for Dawes's faith that individual land ownership would Americanize the Indian was matched by his belief that boarding schools for Indian youth, in which the students lived away from the influence of their parents, would soon create a fully assimilated generation of future Indian leaders. Since the stress was on agriculture, practical skills, and domestic work, the schools were more often than not workhouses, in which the students worked for a living or were sent out to live on white farms, where they served as laborers.

Dr. Lewis Meriam's famous report, The Problem of Indian Administration, *published in 1928, was a massive indictment of the entire Indian Service. Since it was the basis for the most radical change in Indian policy in the twentieth century, portions of his general recommendations are cited below.*

Formal Education of Indian Children. For several years the general policy of the Indian Service has been directed away from the boarding school for Indian children and toward the public schools and Indian day schools. More Indian children are now in public schools maintained by the state or local governments than in special Indian schools maintained by the nation. It is, however, still the fact that the boarding school, either reservation or non-

reservation, is the dominant characteristic of the school system maintained by the national government for its Indian wards.

The survey staff finds itself obliged to say frankly and unequivocally that the provisions for the care of the Indian children in boarding schools are grossly inadequate.

The outstanding deficiency is in the diet furnished the Indian children, many of whom are below normal health. The diet is deficient in quantity, quality, and variety. The effort has been made to feed the children on a per capita of eleven cents a day, plus what can be produced on the schoolfarm, including the dairy. At a few, very few, schools, the farm and the dairy are sufficiently productive to be a highly important factor in raising the standard of the diet, but even at the best schools these sources do not fully meet the requirements for the health and development of the children. At the worst schools, the situation is serious in the extreme. The major diseases of the Indians are tuberculosis and trachoma. Tuberculosis unquestionably can best be combated by a preventive, curative diet and proper living conditions, and a considerable amount of evidence suggests that the same may prove true of trachoma. The great protective foods are milk and fruit and vegetables, particularly fresh green vegetables. The diet of the Indian children in boarding schools is generally notably lacking in these preventive foods. Although the Indian Service has established a quart of milk a day per pupil as the standard, it has been able to achieve this standard in very few schools. . . .

Next to dietary deficiencies comes overcrowding in dormitories. The boarding schools are crowded materially beyond their capacities. A device frequently resorted to in an effort to increase dormitory capacity without great expense, is the addition of large sleeping porches. They are in themselves reasonably satisfactory, but they shut off light and air from the inside rooms, which are still filled with beds beyond their capacity. The toilet facilities have in many

Source: Lewis Meriam et al., *The Problem of Indian Administration* (Baltimore: The Johns Hopkins Press, 1928).

cases not been increased proportionately to the increase in pupils, and they are fairly frequently not properly maintained or conveniently located. The supply of soap and towels has been inadequate.

The medical service rendered the boarding school children is not up to a reasonable standard. Physical examinations are often superficial and enough provision is not made for the correction of remediable defects.

The boarding schools are frankly supported in part by the labor of the students. Those above the fourth grade ordinarily work for half a day and go to school for half a day. A distinction in theory is drawn between industrial work undertaken primarily for the education of the child and production work done primarily for the support of the institution. However, teachers of industrial work undertaken ostensibly for education say that much of it is as a matter of fact production work for the maintenance of the school. The question may very properly be raised as to whether much of the work of Indian children in boarding schools would not be prohibited in many states by the child labor laws, notably the work in the machine laundries. At several schools the laundry equipment is antiquated and not properly safeguarded. To operate on a half-work, half-study plan makes the day very long, and the child has almost no free time and little opportunity for recreation. Not enough consideration has been given the question of whether the health of the Indian children warrants the nation in supporting the Indian boarding schools in part through the labor of these children.

* * * * *

Although the problem of the returned Indian student has been much discussed, and it is recognized that in many instances the child returns to his home poorly adjusted to conditions that confront him, the Indian Service has lacked the funds to attempt to aid the children when they leave school either to find employment away from the reservation or to return to their homes and work out their salvation there. Having done almost no work of this kind, it has not subjected its schools to the test of having to show how far they have actually fitted the Indian children for life. Such a test would undoubtedly have resulted in a radical revision of the industrial training offered in the schools. Several of the industries taught may be called vanishing trades and others are taught in such a way that the Indian students cannot apply what they have learned in their own home and they are not far enough advanced to follow their trade in a white community in competition with white workers without a period of apprenticeship. No adequate arrangements have been made to secure for them the opportunity of apprenticeship.

* * * * *

Family and Community Development. The Indian Service has not appreciated the fundamental importance of family life and community activities in the social and economic development of a people. The tendency has been rather toward weakening Indian family life and community activities than toward strengthening them. The long continued policy of removing Indian children from the home and placing them for years in boarding school largely disintegrates the family and interferes with developing normal family life. The belief has apparently been that the shortest road to civilization is to take children away from their parents and insofar as possible to stamp out the old Indian life. The Indian community activities particularly have often been opposed if not suppressed. The fact has been appreciated that both the family life and the community activities have many objectionable features, but the action taken has often been the radical one of attempting to destroy rather than the educational process of gradual modification and development.

* * * * *

Both the government and the missionaries have often failed to study, understand, and take a sympathetic attitude toward Indian ways, Indian ethics, and Indian religion. The exceptional government worker and the exceptional missionary have demonstrated what can be done by building on what is sound and good in the Indian's own life.

Legal Protection and Advancement. Much of the best work done by the Indian Service has been in the protection and conservation of Indian property, yet this program has emphasized the property rather than the Indian. Several legal situations exist which are serious impediments to the social and economic development of the race.

Most notable is the confusion that exists as to legal jurisdiction over the restricted Indians in such important matters as crimes and misdemeanors and domestic relations. . . .

In some jurisdictions, Courts of Indian Offenses have been established, presided over by Indian judges, whose small salaries are specifically appropriated by Congress, thus giving congressional sanction to the system. The judges are administratively appointed. They operate under very general regulations propounded by the Indian Service. In a large measure they determine both law and fact. Their decisions are subject to administrative but not judicial review.

The Indian Service has been bitterly assailed for maintaining these courts. The survey staff, however, believes that they are well adapted to the needs of primitive Indians remote from organized white communities, and that on the whole they work well. They are more open to criticism for lenity than for severity. The penalties they impose are generally slight and are very humanely administered.

*   *   *   *   *

Although the Indian Service has rendered much valuable service in conserving Indian property, it has not gone far enough in protecting the individual Indian from exploitation. . . .

The exploitation of Indians in Oklahoma has been notorious, but this exploitation has taken place under the state courts and the guardians appointed by them. Recent legislation, largely restoring the old authority of the national government over the property of restricted Osage Indians, has wonderfully improved the situation in that jurisdiction, and the work of the Indian Service for the protection of the property of these Indians is an outstanding achievement worthy of high commendation, although much remains to be done for the social advancement and adjustment of the Osages. The condition among the Five Civilized Tribes leaves much to be desired. . . .

*   *   *   *   *

Failure to Develop Cooperative Relationships. The Indian Service has not gone far enough in developing cooperative relationships with other organizations, public and private, which can be of material aid to it in educational development work for the Indians.

The present administration has given one outstanding illustration of what can be achieved through the cooperation with other federal agencies by its action in bringing in the Public Health Service to aid in the reorganization of the medical work. The Secretary of the Interior, too, has secured aid from the Department of Agriculture for his much needed committee to determine the facts regarding Indian irrigation projects. Here and there in the field are found other instances of cooperation with the Department of Agriculture. Even if every single instance were listed, the surprising fact would be how little cooperative effort there is. In the same department with the Indian Office is the United States Bureau of Education, with its staff of specialists and its experience in caring for the Indians of Alaska, but apparently it has never been invited to cooperate in any large way or to make a survey of the Indian Service schools, although it is frequently invited to make surveys of state and municipal school systems. The Children's Bureau, the Bureau of Labor Statistics, and the United States Employment Service of the Department of Labor, have staffs of specialists who could be of great aid to the Indian Service if they were called in, and far greater use than at present could be made of the Department of Agriculture, especially the Bureau of Home Economics, and even of the Public Health Service. . . .

* * * * *

Recommendations. The fundamental requirement is that the task of the Indian Service be recognized as primarily educational, in the broadest sense of that word, and that it be made an efficient educational agency, devoting its main energies to the social and economic advancement of the Indians, so that they may be absorbed into the prevailing civilization or be fitted to live in the presence of that civilization at least in accordance with a minimum standard of health and decency.

To achieve this end the Service must have a comprehensive, well-rounded educational program, adequately supported, which will place it at the forefront of organizations devoted to the advancement of a people. This program must provide for the promotion of health, the advancement of productive efficiency, the acquisition of reasonable ability in the utilization of income and property, guarding against exploitation, and the maintenance of reasonably high standards of family and community life. It must extend to adults as well as to children and must place special emphasis on the family and the community. Since the great majority of the Indians are ultimately to merge into the general population, it should cover the transitional period and should endeavor to instruct Indians in the utilization of the services provided by public and quasi public agencies for the people at large in exercising the privileges of citizenship and in making their contribution in service and in taxes for the maintenance of the government. It should also be directed toward preparing the white communities to re-

ceive the Indian. By improving the health of the Indian, increasing his productive efficiency, raising his standard of living, and teaching him the necessity for paying taxes, it will remove the main objections now advanced against permitting Indians to receive the full benefit of sevices rendered by progressive states and local governments for their populations. By actively seeking cooperation with state and local governments and by making a fair contribution in payment for services rendered by them to untaxed Indians, the national government can expedite the transition and hasten the day when there will no longer be a distinctive Indian problem and when the necessary governmental services are rendered alike to whites and Indians by the same organization without discrimination.

In the execution of this program scrupulous care must be exercised to respect the rights of the Indian. This phrase ''rights of the Indian'' is often used solely to apply to his property rights. Here it is used in a much broader sense to cover his rights as a human being living in a free country. Indians are entitled to unfailing courtesy and consideration from all government employees. They should not be subjected to arbitrary action. Recognition of the educational nature of the whole task of dealing with them will result in taking the time to discuss with them in detail their own affairs and to lead rather than force them to sound conclusions. The effort to substitute educational leadership for the more dictatorial methods now used in some places will necessitate more understanding of and sympathy for the Indian point of view. Leadership will recognize the good in the economic and social life of the Indians in their religion and ethics, and will seek to develop it and build on it rather than to crush out all that is Indian. The Indians have much to contribute to the dominant civilization, and the effort should be made to secure this contribution, in part because of the good it will do the Indians in stimulating a proper race pride and self-respect.

DOCUMENT 22.6
Indian Responses to Recent and Contemporary Government Policies

Three contemporary Indian responses to the many changes in Indian policy since 1934 suggests that while Indian self-determination has been partly achieved, an age-old debate between Indian and white values and goals continues. In the first, Oren Lyons, an Onondaga artist and tribal council member, expresses ongoing Indian beliefs as well as a firm commitment to self-determination. In the second, the careers of two Navajo tribal chairmen, Peter MacDonald and Peterson Zah, demonstrate the tension between modernization and traditionalism among the members of the largest tribe (150,000) in the United States. The third represents a sampling of Native American responses to the Alaska Native Claims Settlement Act (ANCSA) of 1971. That act conveyed to Aleuts, Eskimo, and Indian people of Alaska, $962.5 million in money and 44 million acres of land, but required the groups to create villages and regional business corporations to handle the funds and the lands. It further stipulated that in 1991 these resources would no longer be protected and could be sold outright by their Native American owners. Here Indians voice a growing fear that the land grabs that deprived them of their holdings under the Dawes Act of 1887, may well be repeated on a massive scale in Alaska.

1

OREN LYONS (ONONDAGA)

What I have to say will be a reflection of my nation's point of view and should not be con-

Source: Oren Lyons quoted in Kenneth R. Philp, ed. *Indian Self-Rule: First-Hand Accounts of Indian-White Relations from Roosevelt to Reagan.* Salt Lake City and Chicago: Howe Brothers, 1986.

strued as speaking for other nations or people. We were one of those nations that did not accept the IRA. We rejected the IRA in a formal vote. It was one of the few times that our people voted in an alien process. One of the chiefs of the longhouse went from house to house. He said, "I know you do not like to vote. I know you are against voting, but if you vote once in your life, this is the time." The IRA was defeated by very few votes.

I am a faith keeper and a subchief of the Onondaga nation. I represent the Turtle Clan in the council. The Onondaga nation is the fire keeper for the Six Nations of Iroquois. Our position is that we are sovereign and independent nations. We have the right to continue our life as it was given to all of our people.

Today we have IRA governments, BIA governments, and traditional governments. The processes of Indian governments are flexible. We have had to adapt to our white brothers and sisters or else disappear. We have always faced the problem of being separate and independent and trying to survive in a very dominating society that has interests and directions of its own.

We have recognized the equal status of non-Indians because they are a manifestation of the creation and demand respect. But that was not a perspective that came from the other side. Whites felt that they were superior and that we were uncivilized "tribes."

The basis of all the Indian nations, as I know them, is the family. At the center of the family is the woman. She is the central fire—the power of life. For thousands of years, Indian people developed methods of continuing a vibrant family life, but these methods were smashed and eradicated in a very short time. In their place institutions such as the IRA were substituted to restructure Indian society.

At one time, a beautiful cultural and social fabric, with tremendous varieties of design, was woven on this continent. Then, our brothers and sisters from overseas came over here and took apart that fabric strand by strand and restructured it. They have taken something beautiful and destroyed it.

You can tell the health and welfare of a nation by looking at its children and elders. If children are in despair, running about without control, and alienated from their families, then society is in great strife. If elders are separated from their families, not enjoying their last years, then you have a very sick society. If Indians accept this kind of society for their people they must bear the consequences.

Indian people should hold on to what they have. I cannot accept the Department of the Interior as an ultimate authority that oversees every decision we make. Self-determination under the federal government is a very limited self-determination. It is defined by what outsiders perceive to be good for you.

2

POLITICS IN THE NAVAJO NATION, 1970–1986

The 1970s were years of intense activity throughout the Navajo Reservation. At the beginning of the decade, Navajos turned back Raymond Nakai's bid for a third term as tribal chairman and elected instead the articulate, well-educated Peter MacDonald. By the end of the decade, MacDonald's name would be synonymous with modern Indian leadership. His twelve-year tenure in the chairman's office was characterized by programs designed to achieve the elusive goals of Navajo self-determination and self-sufficiency. To reduce the tribe's dependence on outside sources, his administration fostered programs to stimulate em-

Source: George M. Lubick, "Peterson Zah: A Progressive Outlook and a Traditional Style," in *Indian Lives: Essays on Nineteenth- and Twentieth-Century Native American Leaders,* ed. L. G. Moses and Raymond Wilson (Albuquerque: University of New Mexico Press, 1985), pp. 190–193, 203, 210.

ployment, to develop tribal enterprises, and to teach Navajos new skills. Keenly interested in the preservation of the tribe's cultural heritage, MacDonald sought to extend control over education through the creation of a Navajo Division of Education, an agency that began operating early in his first term.

Development of the tribe's mineral resources received MacDonald's special attention; and under his leadership, the tribe negotiated leases with such corporate giants as El Paso Natural Gas and Exxon, in a concerted effort to obtain equitable royalties from the exploitation of Navajo uranium and coal and to provide employment for Navajos. In 1975, MacDonald was among the founders of the Council of Energy Resource Tribes. Funded by corporate and federal grants, CERT used its expertise to help Native Americans develop their mineral resources for their own benefit.

MacDonald's development policies were, of necessity, long-range programs, but, in the meantime, tribal government could count on federal money to finance a variety of social services on the reservation. Particularly during MacDonald's first administration, Washington provided the Navajo reservation with generous funding.

MacDonald's energy policies generated opposition in some quarters, and critics of his administration openly protested during his second term as chairman. But his adversaries remained ineffectual, and MacDonald won reelection to a third term in 1978 by a comparatively wide margin. His goals did not change perceptibly over the years, and in his third inaugural address in January 1979, he returned to the themes enunciated eight years earlier. "We must claim what is ours—actively and aggressively," he told the inauguration audience. Further, he emphasized the need to strengthen tribal unity and then exhorted Navajos to "dream great dreams" and dare to put them into action.

By the early 1980s MacDonald had reached the peak of his power and influence. His reputation extended well beyond the reservation boundaries, and he was recognized as one of the country's most powerful Indian leaders. At the same time, the Navajo Nation was enjoying an unaccustomed degree of economic success. Despite high unemployment on the reservation and drastic cuts in federal programs by Ronald Reagan's administration, the tribe recorded "probably the best financial year in its history" in 1981. Revenues exceeded expenditures by more than 27 million dollars—the result of the deregulation of petroleum which led eventually to increased royalties for the tribe. . . .

In less than two years, however, MacDonald's seemingly unassailable political hold on the reservation had been breached. In his 1982 campaign for a fourth term as chairman, he encountered the soft-spoken head of DNA—Peoples' Legal Services, Peterson Zah, an opponent fully as articulate as the incumbent and equally charismatic. DNA *(Dinébeiina Nahiilna Be Agaditahe),* the federally funded legal services organization on the reservation, had been immensely popular since its inception in 1967, and as head of the program since 1972 Zah had developed an extensive constituency among rural and traditionalist Navajos. Equally important, he proved to be a forceful, energetic campaigner, . . . but few people anticipated the extent of his victory on November 2, 1982. As late returns trickled in from remote chapter houses, they confirmed that Zah had defeated "the most powerful Indian leader in America" by nearly five thousand votes.

Zah, then forty-five years old, represented a unique blend of the traditional and progressive in modern Navajo culture. Journalists who covered the 1982 campaign typically noticed only the obvious, modern side of Zah and focused on his university education, his successful administration of the legal services program, and his promises to reform and reorganize Navajo government. Yet Zah's ideas and goal were shaped by the much more subtle forces of Na-

vajo tradition—the beliefs and values that grew out of his background in the remote, traditional community of Low Mountain in the central part of the reservation.

During Zah's boyhood and youth, Low Mountain had little contact with the outside world and was sometimes neglected by the Navajo tribal government as well. The area had been the center of opposition to government programs, and during the stock reduction programs of the 1930s it was considered antagonistic, if not hostile, toward non-Indians. Its residents practiced some dry farming but were primarily stock raisers. Zah's father had not completed his education, and his mother received no schooling. She was an accomplished weaver, however, and her blankets were sometimes the only source of income for the family. The family's home was located in the Navajo-Hopi Joint-Use Area, where Zah's family had lived amicably with the neighboring Hopis, occasionally trading a sheep for Hopi grain and other produce. . . .

During the campaign Zah . . . relied on his reputation as a reformer and argued force fully for reorganization of tribal government. MacDonald, Zah maintained, had lost sight of the basic needs of Navajos in his pursuit of "power and politics." In contrast Zah pledged to return authority to the tribal council and to local communities. He also attacked MacDonald's lack of concern for education, and proposed a uniform system of education on the reservation. Navajos, he maintained, needed to decide the direction of their children's education, and he advocated a tribal education agency to oversee the instruction of youngsters "in what is best to the Navajo people—Navajo culture and language" in a well-rounded curriculum.

Like MacDonald, Zah was a proponent of Navajo self-sufficiency and viewed taxation of energy companies as a means to foster economic independence. But Zah was keenly aware of the concerns of local residents living near mining sites on the reservation. DNA had defended them over the years and had amassed an extensive stock of information about the impact of mineral exploitation on local communities. Therefore, Zah proposed that in the future, mining companies must first confer with local landowners, "grass roots, hogan-level Navajos," before taking their proposals to the tribal government at Window Rock. . . .

He shared with his predecessor, Peter Mac-Donald, an intense pride in the Navajo heritage and a willingness to foster programs to stimulate both nationalism and self-sufficiency. But his style separated him dramatically from Mac-Donald. Soft-spoken and articulate, he preferred to visit chapter houses and agencies, drawing ideas from all parts of the reservation. He was equally determined to attract young Navajos into service to the Navajo Nation, convinced that young Navajo professionals "possess the intellectual ability and the dedication necessary to administer the entirety of tribal governmental affairs."

3

NATIVE AMERICAN RESPONSES TO THE ALASKA NATIVE CLAIMS SETTLEMENT ACT

[*Janie Leask,* president of Alaska Federation of Natives, Inc.] What has fallen on Native people and their institutions during the past thirteen years is a legal and administrative burden so overwhelming that in many ways implementing ANCSA has become an end in itself. . . .

The entire effort has drawn off tens of millions of dollars which more properly could have been put into business investments, human-resource development, communication between

---

Source: Thomas R. Berger, *Village Journey: The Report of the Alaska Native Review Commission* (New York: Hill and Wang, 1985), pp. 30, 51, 61, 63.

stockholders and corporate leaders, and training and technical assistance for village corporation personnel.

If the implementation costs were heavy for the region, it was worse for the villages, especially for the small ones, because they had so little cash from the Alaska Native Fund to begin with. We now have villages which are almost broke from going through the steps of incorporation, corporate elections, enrollments, stock issuances, land selections, land conveyances, CPA audits, meetings, decisions, public reporting, etc., etc., etc. They haven't made much money or really engaged in much economic development activity. *But they have implemented ANCSA.* And many of them have now come to a point where they may have to sell some of their land in order to keep going.

[*Franklin James, Jr.,* Ketchikan] Us Natives, we should have the right to live our own culture, something that cannot die . . . to take away our culture would be to take away our lives, everything we knew, everything our parents knew, everything our children should know. . . . What is that billion dollars? I'd rather have my fishing and hunting rights.

[*Christine Smith,* Fairbanks] This land is part of . . . our identity. The land is very important. It is part of the religion, it's part of the heritage, and to put a dollar value on it would be something that would come from Congress or from England or Switzerland or something. . . .

[*Bobby Wells,* Kotzbue] I am speaking because I am affected, and where I am affected is from the village. I remember our fathers, our forefathers, how they survived in this world, in strong winds, in cold temperatures. Many of them died during the season but they survived through thousands of years because they knew how to survive. They were taught to share, they were taught to help each other for thousands of years. Today, we are in the same situation, but this time we are not surviving against nature . . . surviving from the land. This time, we are in a time where we are searching, we are fighting to survive among different people, among different races in this Western civilization. What does this Western civilization have to offer? Business.

[*Mary Miller,* Nome] When you look through the corporate eye, our relationship to the land is altered. We draw our identity as a people from our relationship to the land and to the sea and to the resources. This is a spiritual relationship, a sacred relationship. It is in danger because, from a corporate standpoint, if we are to pursue profit and growth, and this is why profit organizations exist, we would have to assume a position of control over the land and the resources and exploit these resources to achieve economic gain. This is in conflict with our traditional relationship to the land, we were stewards, we were caretakers and where we had respect for the resources that sustained us.

chapter 23

Progressivism: Coping with Social Change

James T. Patterson
Brown University

A seemingly endless variety of Americans thought of themselves as "progressive" at the start of the twentieth century. William Jennings Bryan was one. He wanted to curb the "interests," to unseat the "Old Guard," to make government more responsive to the "people." He was at once an ardent prohibitionist and an anti-imperialist. Throughout his life—not just at the Scopes "monkey trial" in 1925—he adhered to fundamentalist religious beliefs.

Bryan's adversary at the Scopes trial, Clarence Darrow, was also a "progressive." After defending Eugene Debs in the *Pullman* case of 1894, the "people's lawyer" fought a string of battles against Big Business and Reaction. Like Bryan, he spent a lifetime opposing monopolistic enterprise; unlike him, he was a militant freethinker on religious questions.

E. A. Ross, one of America's foremost sociologists, also earned the label "progressive." Stanford University's board of trustees, however, considered him a radical; it fired him in 1900. Ross's book, *Sin and Society* (1907), lambasted corporate and political bosses and demanded a range of reforms for social justice. Worried about the "racial" characteristics of aliens from southern and eastern Europe, Ross

also advocated restriction of immigration. Neither he nor many of his progressive contemporaries found nativism incompatible with social reform.

Jane Addams of Hull House—"Saint Joan" to her many admirers—shared Ross's hostility to the "interests." In particular, she was anxious to improve the lot of the urban poor, and to assist women and children workers. Like Bryan, she opposed imperialism; her pacifism amid the superpatriotic hysteria of World War I, which she wished America to avoid, cost her much of her following. Unlike Ross, she appreciated immigrant cultures.

In the 1912 presidential campaign Jane Addams and many other settlement house workers backed Theodore Roosevelt, who ran for president on the Progressive party ticket. Like other settlement house leaders, she welcomed his support of social legislation and his endorsement (belated though it was) of women's suffrage. But Roosevelt could hardly satisfy all those who called themselves "progressive" by 1912. Democrats like Bryan opposed him not only for partisan reasons but also because the former president seemed to welcome big business, provided that it behaved itself. Moreover, Roosevelt enthusiastically supported

151

imperialism and military strength. The champion of "big stick" foreign policy had no trouble reconciling "progressivism" at home and imperialism abroad.

These sketchy portraits of turn-of-the-century Americans only begin to suggest the variety of people who were "progressives" between the 1890s and 1917, the dates which most historians use to periodize the "progressive era." Some favored trust busting; others, while deploring the excesses of monopoly, accepted economic centralization as a fact of life. Some focused on moral reforms, such as the outlawing of alcoholic beverages or of prostitution—reforms that others considered nativist and puritanical. Some were pacifists; others avid imperialists. Many were single-interest reformers—for lower tariffs, regulation of railroads, conservation of natural reserves, or whatever. The range of reforms and the divisions among their advocates make it very difficult to speak of an organized, largely united progressive "movement."

It is equally hazardous to describe progressivism as a static constellation of reforms. Rather, most reformers—and, it appeared, voters—tended to broaden their concerns between the mid-1890s and 1917. Many began by denouncing waste and corruption. Warming to the task of reform, they then demanded an end to "special privilege," the institution of progressive taxation, and the passage of political reforms—the initiative, referenda, and recall of public officials, the direct primary, the popular election of U.S. senators. Others, beginning with muted demands for local budgetary economy, gradually called for state-sponsored social legislation, and then for federal action, including national regulation of corporations. The platforms of all major political parties in 1912 were much broader than people could have anticipated ten or even four years earlier.

"Progressive" reforms also varied according to region, state, and city. Massachusetts seemed "conservative" after 1900 in part be-

cause its reformers had already tackled issues which agitated legislatures in other less industrialized states. In Virginia, so-called progressives were nostalgic agrarians seeking to preserve that state's Jeffersonian traditions. Progressivism in California began as a coalition of antirailroad ranchers and landowners, only to develop by 1912 into a cause led by urbanites, labor union leaders, and ethnic groups. In many urban states, including New York, leaders of ethnic political organizations joined in promoting reforms benefiting working people; elsewhere, middle-class spokespersons led "progressive" movements that were nativist and antilabor. The great variety of progressive campaigns frustrated all attempts at easy categorization.

Appreciating this diversity makes it possible to understand why historians cannot agree on the sources of progressive reform. Contemporaries, like the Kansas journalist William Allen White, thought progressivism was an urban manifestation of Populism. The progressives, he said, "caught the Populists in swimming, and stole all their clothing except the frayed underdrawers of free silver." Most later historians have agreed that progressives endorsed many Populist causes—notably regulation of monopoly and political reform. But these historians have emphasized the urban cast of the progressive era. Indeed, Richard Hofstadter portrayed progressives as middle-class gentry anxious to curb the plutocrats above them and the masses below. Many Progressives, he argued, were WASPs worried about losing social status.

Other historians, notably Samuel Hays and Robert Wiebe, have agreed that progressivism represented a middle class "search for order." They have focused not on the gentry but on "new" professional, business, and academic elites seeking to stabilize a society transformed by urbanization, immigration, and industrialization. Still other historians have concurred that progressivism had an urban base but have emphasized the role of ethnic and working-class spokesmen. And finally, a few historians like Howard Quint have seen more than a casual connection between the social and economic criticism of the active Socialist movement of the period and progressive reforms.

Some of these arguments, such as White's and Hofstadter's, no longer attract much of a following. Many progressive leaders, including Theodore Roosevelt, Robert La Follette, and the insurgent George Norris of Nebraska, actively opposed populism in the 1890s. Many others, like Jane Addams, were urban figures for whom populism had had little appeal. Populists and progressives—generally—were different people. Hofstadter's argument neglects to ask why the gentry did not rise up earlier, or why such people became "reformers" instead of revolutionaries, or apolitical drones. It rests also on questionable empirical grounds, for Hofstadter failed to show significant differences in the class backgrounds of progressives and conservatives.

If there is a consensus among historians today, it is that large numbers of Americans began as early as the 1870s to worry deeply about the great social changes wrought by urbanization, immigration, and industrialization. They feared the social disorder caused by urban crowding, the dangers to representative government stemming from the incredible power wielded by the corporations, from foreign influx, and from the mass unrest associated with rapid industrial growth. At first many tried to sustain antebellum ideals of a "natural" order, in which people, not institutions, imposed order through individual self-restraint. And until the 1880s they were slow to demand social reforms. But the depression of the 1890s hit not only populistic farmers but also urban dwellers. It wiped out many small businesses and brought about a wave of corporate mergers; the specter of monopolistic power loomed ominously. Hard times, indeed, helped to activate disaffected groups that previously had divided along

ethnic, class, or regional lines. The depression also made people self-conscious as "exploited" consumers and drove them toward more radical measures, such as progressive taxation, recall of public officials, and public ownership of railroads and utilities.

By 1900, when better times had returned, many of these temporary alliances broke down. But inflation thereafter created insecurity among the middle and lower classes, and "muckraking" journalists bombarded the reading public with reminders of the greed of corporations and public officials. The "new" middle classes—sometimes allied with lower-class groups, with Socialist intellectuals, or with the more progressive gentry—took the lead in calling for a more rational, "scientific," and stable organization of human society. For them, as for many who came to call themselves progressives, reform ideas evolved under the pressure of changing historical conditions, and aimed in the end at preserving a measure of social stability amid bewildering economic change.

Even at its peak between 1910 and 1914, however, this reform activity was hardly radical in the sense of aiming at the overthrow of capitalism. Few progressives sought to redistribute wealth or to strengthen organized labor. Though deeply humanitarian, many reformers wanted desperately to avoid socialism, class conflict, and social turmoil. Only a relatively small number wished to provide a welfare state, or even to advocate the social reforms then being developed in England. Moreover, with improved economic conditions, Americans came to define themselves less as exploited consumers than as members of job-oriented groups. Busy making a living, they were ready to support organized lobbies that promoted their interests. So though the organizations of the 1880s and 1890s continued to proliferate, most of them struggled primarily for their own particular goals. Thus it was that reform activity, which at times threatened to stir a mass base of "exploited" consumers, evolved into shifting alliances of organized interest groups, the most powerful of which had much to lose from major changes in the capitalist order. Far from inaugurating a welfare state, the progressive era witnessed the rise of what the political scientist Theodore Lowi has called Interest Group Liberation—a political order dominated by producer-oriented pressure groups anxious for public protection.

This essentially functionalist definition of progressive reforms again merely suggests the obvious: The motives and causes of the leaders differed substantially. To understand the period it is best to see what these various groups actually did.

One group of reformers espoused, at least in part, egalitarian and humanitarian concerns. Prominent among them were the settlement-house workers who carried their work into most American cities between the late 1880s and 1914. Most of the leaders were deeply religious, college-educated young people. Appalled by the squalor of the city, they established a variety of institutions—day nurseries, dispensaries, and arts and crafts for the urban poor. The settlement houses, indeed, offered communal living of a sort, especially for the women and children of immigrant neighborhoods.

Seen from the perspective of the 1980s, the settlement houses had little long-range impact. Owing in part to the cutoff of large-scale immigration after 1914, they declined in importance after World War I. Even in their heyday, they rarely affected immigrant men, who were absorbed in trying to make a living. Others were naive and nostalgic in thinking that neighborhood action could remedy deep-seated social problems. The depression of the 1930s revealed that economic stress had to be attacked on a more nearly national basis.

Still, the settlement-house workers did not labor entirely in vain. Exposure to the slums led many of them to recognize the need for a variety of social reforms: minimum wage and

maximum hours laws to protect women workers, factory inspection legislation, regulation of child labor, and juvenile courts. Thanks to their efforts, many states passed measures protecting women and children. Though the social justice workers had to struggle against powerful opposition from employers and from the courts (which declared minimum wage laws unconstitutional until 1937), they did much to expose social conditions. They pioneered, for instance, in developing model legislation, and in popularizing the idea that environmental, not personal problems, lead to social disorder. New Dealers in the 1930s relied heavily on this diagnosis. Any investigation of progressivism which ignores the humanitarian-egalitarian motivation of the social justice movement must be crude and one-sided.

Agitation for women's rights also reflected the egalitarian strain of reform ideology in the period. Not surprisingly, spokespersons for the cause varied widely. A very few, such as Emma Goldman, a Russian-Jewish immigrant, campaigned for anarchism and free love. Much too radical for most Americans, she was regularly harassed, and in 1919 was deported. Less radical, but almost as controversial, was Margaret Sanger, a pioneer for birth control. Despite concerted opposition from religious and conservative spokespersons, birth control became increasingly practiced—if not officially sanctioned—by the 1920s. A third activist, Charlotte Perkins Gilman, challenged what Betty Friedan would later call the "feminine mystique"—the notion that women are born to be housewives and mothers. In *Women and Economics* (1898) she insisted that women, like men, found satisfaction through meaningful work and creative effort. Though her ideas commanded limited attention at the time, they reflected an important trend of twentieth-century industrial society: the movement of women in larger numbers into the work force, and the demands for equal rights which accompanied this movement.

Compared to the drives for sexual freedom,

birth control, and female equality, the cause of women's suffrage became almost a mass movement in the progressive era. As late as 1910, Washington became only the fifth state to approve women's suffrage. Four other states followed in the next two years, and in 1916, when the highly organized Carrie Chapman Catt assumed control of the nationwide effort, the movement surged ahead. During the war, she pragmatically kept her distance from more radical suffragettes, and stressed the patriotic contributions of women selling war bonds and working in factories. Confronted with a highly organized pressure group, the Senate in 1919 sent the proposed Nineteenth Amendment to the states, which ratified it in 1920. The right to vote did little or nothing to improve the socioeconomic status of women or to purify politics. Indeed, by absorbing so much feminist energy, and by predicting utopian consequences, which failed to occur, suffragism set back the drive for women's rights. But women's suffrage was nonetheless a long overdue reform in the direction of political equality for all.

Like the feminists, advocates of racial justice searched in the progressive era for what many contemporaries regarded as radical solutions. Chief among such advocates was W. E. B. Du Bois, a black, middle-class northerner who received his Ph.D at Harvard in 1895. With other founders of the National Association for the Advancement of Colored People (1909), Du Bois denounced the pervasive segregation, political disfranchisement, and racial violence of the age. The so-called progressive era, indeed, was for whites only. Du Bois criticized especially the accommodationist strategy of Booker T. Washington, who advised blacks patiently to acquire occupational skills and counselled against public agitation for social equality.

Du Bois did not impress his white contemporaries. President Woodrow Wilson instituted Jim Crow in federal departments, and racial violence flared in American cities. Du Bois was also less than charitable to Washington, who had to deal—as Du Bois did not—with the institutionalized racism of the South, and whose focus on black self-help appealed to later advocates of civil rights and black nationalism. Still, the rise of militants, such as Du Bois, and of pressure groups, such as the NAACP and the Urban League (1910), suggested that the egalitarian ideal remained alive during the period.

These causes—humanitarian social reform, women's rights, racial justice—especially revealed the egalitarian thrust of progressive ideology. Similar concerns helped sustain other contemporary movements as well: the crusade against monopoly, the drive for equal taxation, the cries against "special interests," and the quest for direct primaries and popular election of senators. Though it is naive to depict such reformers as wholly altruistic, it is cynical to dismiss the egalitarianism of their thinking. For if the progressive era exposed the rise of a functionalist political order, it witnessed also the emergence of a more ideological politics. Issues—ideals of equality and justice—energized many contemporary reformers.

Unfortunately for the subsequent reputation of progressive reformers, humanitarian-egalitarian motives did not always dominate. Many progressives worried less about the rights of the underprivileged than about social disorder. It was no mere coincidence that movements for prohibition, immigration restriction, and anti-unionism expanded greatly at the time.

The crusade for temperance was, of course, nothing new to Americans around 1900. But the forces of immigration, industrialization, and urbanization gave new life to an old movement. Many who once had called for temperance—voluntary self-restraint—now called for prohibition of the manufacture and sale of alcoholic beverages—a coercive measure. Prohibition was strongest in anti-urban, Protestant areas of America—the heart of the Bible belt. It also attracted manufacturers, who yearned for a sober, industrious work force, and conservative traditionalists, who recoiled in aesthetic disgust at public drunkenness. Many prohibitionists observed that support for ethnic political machines flourished in the corner saloon.

But the prohibition movement did not depend only on conservative Protestants, reactionary employers, and nativists. It reflected a repressive, moralistic side of progressivism generally. Bryan, as noted, championed the cause. So did the muckraking socialist, Upton Sinclair. Frances Willard, head of the Women's Christian Temperance Union, campaigned ardently for social justice as well as for prohibition. Many other progressives joined the cause because they feared the power of the liquor lobby in politics—another "special interest"—and because they earnestly deplored the moral and physical effects of excessive drink. Joining the WCTU or the powerful Anti-Saloon League, they pushed through prohibition laws in 27 states before America entered World War I. The war, which generated a spirit of sacrifice, merely completed a process of pressure-group agitation already well under way. America's "Great Experiment" was not an aberrant crusade but a reform that developed wide support in the progressive era.

Immigration restriction, like the campaign against alcohol, predated the progressive era. Congress excluded Chinese as early as 1882. Moreover, the massive influx of immigrants between 1880 and 1914 profoundly upset Americans who wished no part of progressivism. Patrician conservatives, like Senator Henry Cabot Lodge of Massachusetts, led a movement for literacy tests, which discriminated against the uneducated masses of southern and eastern Europe. Woodrow Wilson, as a politically conservative university president in 1902, commented that southern and eastern Europeans were "men out of the ranks where there was neither skill nor energy nor any initiative of quick intelligence." Racists, anti-Catho-

lics, and anti-Semites erected scientific arguments to "prove" the biological inferiority of national groups. Still other conservatives, seeking to isolate themselves from the new ethnics, established exclusive institutions ranging from private schools like Groton to the Daughters of the American Revolution.

As immigration mounted, many reformers joined in making these demands for restriction. Progressive economists, echoing the American Federation of Labor, argued that mass immigration created a surplus of labor which dragged down wages and working conditions. Other progressives feared that the "new" migrants from "undemocratic" southern and eastern Europe would undermine American political institutions. This broad coalition of nativists, patricians, labor leaders, progressive academics, and their followers grew strong enough to overrule a presidential veto of a literacy test in 1917. In the early 1920s it pushed through quota laws discriminating against southern and eastern Europeans, and it excluded Japanese. Like the prohibitionists, the restrictionists succeeded because they organized a genuinely popular movement aimed at sustaining the existing social and political order. If progressivism was at times humanitarian and egalitarian, it was at other times repressive in its effort to preserve an older, simpler America.

Many progressive reforms cannot be described easily as either humanitarian-egalitarian or repressive-nostalgic. Rather, they equated self-interest with the public good. In the process, they stressed the desirability of "scientific," efficient administration.

The campaign for reform of city government was a case in point. Some leaders, such as mayors Samuel ("Golden Rule") Jones of Toledo (1897–1904) and Tom Johnson of Cleveland (1901–1909), joined humanitarians in calling for social justice. Other municipal reformers, however, yearned to cleanse the city of political corruption and mismanagement —that is, to reduce the power of the ethnic machines. Such "structural reformers," as one historian has called them, began demanding literacy tests for voting, stringent voter registration laws (to exclude mobile immigrants), and citywide districts for elections (to cut down the power of ethnic wards). In place of the ward-based ethnic machines, they hoped to establish nonpartisan commissions, to appoint trained city managers, and to put in power educated elites who would supposedly represent the city as a whole. Such efforts, while successful in places for short periods, rarely endured—primarily because they depended on a narrow base of business people and professionals. Whether successful or not, the efforts revealed the growing assertiveness of the rising business and professional classes in American life.

The drive for reform of political institutions suggested similar complexities. Insurgents, such as Wisconsin's Robert La Follette, clearly loathed corporate—Old Guard political elites. By championing such measures as the popular election of senators and the direct primary, he succeeded in depriving the Old Guard of power, and in enacting laws regulating railroads and other public utilities. Wisconsin pioneered in devising progressive income taxation on the state level. But La Follette was in fact an ambitious and a combative politician. A Republican regular in the 1880s, he grew increasingly angry in the 1890s at the refusal of the Wisconsin G.O.P. conservatives to aid his political ambitions. When he finally overcame his opponents, he erected a potent political machine of his own, one which controlled state politics for decades.

La Follette's brand of politics was undeniably honest and popular. Elsewhere, the impact of political reforms was more ambiguous. The direct primary often served to aid the "outs" at the expense of the "ins," or to assist demagogues who in the past had been screened out by state political conventions. Reforms such as the initiative and referendum often assisted

well-financed groups which could secure the required numbers of signatures for petitions. Many of these reforms tended to weaken the political parties, rendering them incapable of developing clear programs of action, and leaving private interest groups in control. Sensing the limitations of state government, many reformers turned to the national level. Others, more profoundly alienated (or effectively disfranchised by racist or nativist "reforms"), despired of the political process. Ironically, as historians have noted, an age of supposedly great political controversy was also characterized by rapidly decreasing voter turnout.

Nothing exposes the ambiguities of progressive solutions better than the effort to control the trusts. There was no denying the power of the egalitarian rhetoric that accompanied this movement, or the sincerity of politicians who introduced state legislation regulating railroads and utilities. Though historians argue over the matter, it is probable that regulatory commissions, such as the Interstate Commerce Commission, kept railroad rates a little lower than they might otherwise have been, and that federal legislation outlawing rebates to preferred corporate customers was in the public interest. Other federal laws checked a few abuses in the packaging and sale of food and drugs. Such agencies as the Federal Trade Commission and Federal Reserve system attempted limited control over vital matters previously reserved to private interests.

But was the regulatory movement really aimed at helping ordinary consumers? Did it change the locus of economic power? Hardly. Much of the push behind railroad legislation came from organized shippers protecting themselves against arbitrary railroad practices. Powerful backing for food and drug laws stemmed from large packers angry at unscrupulous dealings of competitors. Many leading business people demanded an agency, such as the FTC, in order to sidestep the inconsistencies of state laws and the unpredictability of the courts.

Regulatory agencies often became dominated by the very groups they were supposed to regulate, or got bogged down in bureaucratic procedures. Private interests proved more than a match for those ill-equipped, underfinanced public authorities.

The regulatory movement also revealed the limitations of "scientific," "nonpolitical" administration. Like the structural municipal reformers, proponents of regulation usually argued that commissions staffed by experts could arrive at some such goal. But what was a "just" railroad rate, or "fair competition," or "monopoly"? Regulatory commissioners rarely had the power to examine corporate books. Accordingly, they made decisions in semidarkness. When they did have access to such information, they often found it impossible to discover the "public interest." For setting rates or defining "fair competition" meant determining economic priorities; and someone—shipper, carrier, consumer—inevitably got hurt. In this sense the commissions took the struggles among competing economic interests away from democratically elected legislators (who were ill equipped to handle such complex matters) and placed them before appointed elites answerable only indirectly to the public. Such was the nature of one of the "democratic" reforms of the progressive era.

It is tempting to pass judgment on the progressives. Those who praise them point to the settlement houses and the juvenile courts, to such reforms as women's suffrage, the direct election of senators, and the progressive income tax, to social legislation benefiting women and children, and to organizations like the NAACP. They stress the development of environmentalist thinking about social problems and of the growth of purposeful government. Scoffers reply that the progressives supported prohibition, immigration restriction, elitist commissions, and white middle-class municipal governance. They emphasize the nativist, racist, and nostalgic side of progressive thought. They argue that all the sound and fury of the era did little more than soften the rough edges of capitalism, thus preserving its inequities while undermining socialism.

Such judgments are not out of place; there is no good reason why historians should hide their political biases. But it may be more helpful to reiterate that many progressives were responding to the dominant social forces of their own time: industrialization, urbanization, and immigration. They sought, in short, both to protect themselves and to promote a more stable society. These were not contradictory objectives. Above all, they organized, along primarily functional lines, and they sought more rational, scientific answers. If their organizations were often narrow-based, and their solutions timid, it was because they were struggling against dimly understood social forces that engulfed much of the Western world in the nineteenth and twentieth centuries. As the first generation of Americans to cope seriously with these forces, the progressives acted with a perhaps predictable mixture of altruism and self-seeking, of common sense and fear.

SUGGESTED READINGS

Blum, John M. *The Republican Roosevelt*. Cambridge, Mass.: Harvard University Press, 1976.

Bremner, Robert. *From the Depths: The Discovery of Poverty in the United States*. New York: New York University Press, 1956.

Buenker, John. *Urban Liberalism and Progressive Reform*. New York: W. W. Norton, 1973.

Davis, Allen F. *Spearheads for Reform: The Social Settlements and the Progressive Movement, 1890–1914*. New York: Oxford University Press, 1967.

Hays, Samuel P. *The Response to Industrialism, 1885–1914*. Chicago: University of Chicago Press, 1957.

Hofstadter, Richard. *The Age of Reform: From Bryan to F.D.R.* New York: Alfred A. Knopf, 1955.

Kolko, Gabriel. *The Triumph of Conservatism: A Reinterpretation of American History, 1900–1916.* New York: Free Press, 1963.

Lubove, Roy. *Progressives and the Slums: Tenement House Reform in New York City, 1890–1917.* Pittsburgh: University of Pittsburgh Press, 1962.

McCraw, Thomas. *Prophets of Regulation.* Cambridge, Mass.: Harvard University Press, 1984.

Steffens, Lincoln. *The Shame of the Cities.* New York: McClure, Phillips, & Co., 1904.

Thelen, David P. *The New Citizenship: The Origins of Progressivism in Wisconsin, 1885–1900.* Columbia: University of Missouri Press, 1972.

Timberlake, James H. *Prohibition and the Progressive Movement, 1900–1920.* Cambridge, Mass.: Harvard University Press, 1963.

Weinstein, James. *The Corporate Ideal in the Liberal State, 1900–1918.* Boston: Beacon Press, 1968.

Wiebe, Robert H. *The Search for Order, 1877–1920.* New York: Hill & Wang, 1967.

DOCUMENT 23.1
Trusts: The Main Enemy

Nothing worried Americans more than the giant corporations, or trusts, especially during the great merger movement of 1897–1901. In response to such mergers, the Civic Federation of Chicago called a meeting in September 1899. The views of Detroit's reform mayor, Hazen Pingree, suggest the power of Jacksonian ideology aimed at preserving equal opportunity and entrepreneurial activity. (Other political figures, such as Theodore Roosevelt, assumed large corporations were here to stay and favored regulation, not radical trust-busting.)

In all that has been said about trusts, scarcely a word has been written or spoken from the standpoint of their effect on society.

* * * * *

Source: Chicago Conference on Trusts (Chicago: Civic Federation of Chicago 1900), pp. 263–67.

I think that this is the most important consideration of all.

Everybody has been asking whether more money can be made by trusts than by small corporations and individuals—whether cost of production will be increased or decreased—whether investors will be benefited or injured—whether the financial system of the country will be endangered—whether we can better compete for the world's trade with large combinations or trusts—whether prices will be raised or lowered—whether men will be thrown out of employment—whether wages will be higher or lower—whether stricter economy can be enforced, and so on.

In other words, the only idea nowadays seems to be to find out how business or commerce will be affected by trusts. The "Almighty Dollar" is the sole consideration.

I believe that all these things are minor considerations. I think that it is of far greater importance to inquire whether the control of the world's trade, or any of the other commercial advantages claimed for the trust, are worth the price we pay for them.

Will it pay us either as individuals or as a nation to encourage trusts?

In this republic of ours we are fond of saying that there are no classes. In fact, we boast of it. We say that classes belong to monarchies, not to republics. Nevertheless, none of us can dispute the fact that our society is divided into classes, and well defined ones, too. They are not distinguished by differences of social standing. That is, we have no aristocratic titles, no nobility. The distinction with us is based upon wealth. The man is rated by the property he owns. Our social and political leaders and speakers deny this. In doing so, however, they ignore actual conditions. They discuss what ought to be under our form of government—not what is.

The strength of our republic has always been in what is called our middle class. This is made up of manufacturers, jobbers, middle men, retail and wholesale merchants, commercial travelers and business men generally. It would be little short of calamity to encourage any industrial development that would affect unfavorably this important class of our citizens.

Close to them as a strong element of our people are the skilled mechanics and artisans. They are the sinew and strength of the nation. While the business of the country has been conducted by persons and firms, the skilled employee has held close and sympathetic relations with his employer. He has been something more than a mere machine. He has felt the stimulus and ambition which goes with equality of opportunity. These have contributed to make him a good citizen. Take away that stimulus and ambition, and we lower the standard of our citizenship. Without good citizenship our national life is in danger.

It seems to me, therefore, that the vital consideration connected with this problem of the trust is its effect upon our middle class—the independent, individual business man and the skilled artisan and mechanic.

How does the trust affect them? It is admitted by the apologist for the trust that it makes it impossible for the individual or firm to do business on a small scale. It tends to concentrate the ownership and management of all lines of business activity into the hands of a very few. No one denies this. This being so, it follows that the independent, individual business man, must enter the employment of the trust. Self-preservation compels it. Duty to his family forces him to it. He becomes an employee instead of an employer. His trusted foremen and his employees must follow him. They have been in close and daily association with him. The new order of things compels them to separate. They are both to become a part of a vast industrial army with no hopes and no aspirations—a daily task to perform and no personal interest and perhaps no pride in the success of their work. Their personal identity is lost. They become cogs and little wheels in a great

complicated machine. There is no real advance for them. They may perhaps become larger cogs or larger wheels, but they can never look forward to a life of business freedom.

* * * * *

The trust is therefore the forerunner, or rather the creator of industrial slavery.

The master is the trust manager or director. It is his duty to serve the soulless and nameless being called the stockholder. To the latter the dividend is more important than the happiness or prosperity of any one. The slave is the former merchant and business man, and the artisan and mechanic, who once cherished the hope that they might sometime reach the happy position of independent ownership of a business. Commercial feudalism is the logical outcome of the trust. The trust manager is the feudal baron.

These may perhaps be harsh characterizations, but who can deny their truth? Honesty to ourselves and loyalty to our country and its free institutions compel us to face and recognize the situation. . . .

I favor complete and prompt annihilation of the trust,—with due regard for property rights, of course.

DOCUMENT 23.2
The Poverty Problem

Though advocates of social justice publicized the evils of poverty in the 1880s and 1890s, it was left to Robert Hunter, a settlement-house worker, to write the most thorough study of the subject. His book, simply titled Poverty *(1904), remains the most reliable source of information on poverty in a supposedly prosperous age. After publishing the book, Hunter became a Socialist. Note the distinction*

Source: Robert Hunter, *Poverty* (New York: Grosset and Dunlap, 1904), pp. 76–83, 96–97.

that Hunter makes between ''pauperism'' and poverty, and the characteristics he imputes to each group.

Any one going carefully through the figures which have been given will agree that poverty is widespread in this country. While it is possible that New York State has more poverty than other states, it is doubtful if its poverty is much greater proportionately than that of most of the industrial states. Twelve years ago I made what was practically a personal canvass of the poor in a small town of Indiana. There were no tenements, but the river banks were lined with small cabins and shanties, inhabited by the poorest and most miserable people I have almost ever seen. About the mills and factories were other wretched little communities of working people. All together the distress extended to but slightly less than 14 percent of the population, and the poverty extended to not less than 20 percent of the people. I cannot say how typical this town is of other Indiana towns, but I have always been under the impression that conditions were rather better there than in other towns of the same size. In Chicago the conditions of poverty are certainly worse, if anything, than in the smaller towns, and that is also true of the poverty of New York City. On the whole, it seems to me that the most conservative estimate that can fairly be made of the distress existing in the industrial states is 14 percent of the total population; while in all probability no less than 20 percent of the people in these states, in ordinarily prosperous years, are in poverty. This brings us to the conclusion that one-fifth, or 6,600,000 persons in the states of New York, Massachusetts, Connecticut, New Jersey, Pennsylvania, Ohio, Illinois, Indiana, and Michigan are in poverty. Taking half of this percentage and applying it to the other states, many of which have important industrial communities, as, for instance, Wisconsin, Colorado, California, Rhode Island, etc., the conclusion is that not

less than 10,000,000 persons in the United States are in poverty. This includes, of course, the 4,000,000 persons who are estimated to be dependent upon some form of public relief. . . .

These figures of poverty have the weakness of all estimates. But . . . poverty is already wide-spread in this new country, and . . . it seems the height of folly that the nation should disregard so absolutely this enormous problem of misery that not even an inquiry is made as to its extent or as to the causes which add to its volume. Many people give as a reason for this apathy of the fortunate classes that poverty is irremedial. Did not the Lord say, ''The poor always ye have with you''? But those who say this fail to distinguish between the poor, who are poor because of their own folly and vice, and the poor who are poor as a result of social wrongs. The sins of men should bring their own punishment, and the poverty which punishes the vicious and the sinful is good and necessary. Social or industrial institutions that save men from the painful consequences of vice or folly are not productive of the greatest good. There is unquestionably a poverty which men deserve, and by such poverty men are perhaps taught needful lessons. . . .

But . . . there are also the poor which we must not have always with us. The poor of this latter class are, it seems to me, the mass of the poor; they are bred of miserable and unjust social conditions, which punish the good and the pure, the faithful and industrious, the slothful and vicious, all alike. We may not, by going into the homes of the poor, be able to determine which ones are in poverty because of individual causes, or which are in poverty because of social wrongs; but we can see, by looking about us, that men are brought into misery by the action of social and economic forces. And the wrongful action of such social and economic forces is a preventable thing. For instance, to mention but a few, the factories, the mines, the workshops, and the railroads must be forced to cease killing the father or the boy or the girl whose wages alone suffice to keep the family from poverty; or, if the workers must be injured and killed, then the family must at least be fairly compensated, in so far as that be possible. Tenements may be made sanitary by the action of the community, and thereby much of this breeding of wretched souls and ruined bodies stopped. A broader education may be provided for the masses, so that the street child may be saved from idleness, crime, and vagrancy, and the working child saved from ruinous labor. Immigration may be regulated constructively rather than negatively, if not, for a time, restricted to narrower limits. Employment may be made less irregular and fairer wages assured. These are, of course, but a few of the many things which can be done to make less unjust and miserable the conditions in which about 10 million of our people live.

Among the many inexplicable things in life there is probably nothing more out of reason than our disregard for preventive measures and our apparent willingness to provide almshouses, prisons, asylums, hospitals, homes, etc., for the victims of our neglect. Poverty is a culture bed for criminals, paupers, vagrants, and for such diseases as inebriety, insanity, and imbecility; and yet we endlessly go on in our unconcern, or in our blindness, heedless of its sources, believing all the time that we are merciful in administering to its unfortunate results. Those in poverty are fighting a losing struggle, because of unnecessary burdens which we might lift from their shoulders; but not until they go to pieces and become drunken, vagrant, criminal, diseased, and suppliant, do we consider mercy necessary. But in that day reclamation is almost impossible, the degeneracy of the adults infects the children, and the foulest of our social miseries is thus perpetuated from generation to generation. From the millions struggling with poverty come the millions who have lost all self-respect and ambition, who hardly, if ever, work, who are aimless and drifting, who like drink, who have no thought for their children, and who live contentedly on rubbish and alms. But a short time before many of them were of that great, splendid mass of producers upon which the material welfare of the nation rests. They were in poverty, but there were self-respecting; they were hard-pressed, but they were ambitious, determined, and hard-working. They were also underfed, underclothed, and miserably housed—the fear and dread of want possessed them, they worked sore, but gained nothing, they were isolated, heart-worn, and weary. . . .

DOCUMENT 23.3
Muckraking: The Evil United States Senate

One of the most sensational muckraking exposes appeared in Cosmopolitan Magazine *in 1906. It was ''The Treason of the Senate,'' by David Graham Phillips, a 39-year-old novelist. Phillips' portrait of Senator Nelson W. Aldrich of Rhode Island, the most powerful conservative Republican in the Senate, offers an excellent example of colorful muckraking, and of the corrosive distrust of elites and the ''interests'' which animated many reformers.*

He was born in 1841, is only 64 years old, good for another fifteen years, at least, in his present rugged health, before ''the interests'' will have to select another for his safe seat and treacherous task. He began as a grocery boy, got the beginning of one kind of education in the public schools and in an academy at East Greenwich, Rhode Island. He became clerk in a fish store in Providence, then clerk in a grocery, then bookkeeper, partner, and is still a wholesale grocer. He was elected to the legislature, applied himself so diligently

Source: David Graham Phillips, ''Aldrich, the Head of It All,'' *Cosmopolitan Magazine*, April 1906.

to the work of getting his real education that he soon won the confidence of the boss, then Senator Anthony, and was sent to Congress, where he was Anthony's successor as boss and chief agent of the Rhode Island interests. He entered the United States Senate in 1881.

In 1901 his daughter married the only son and destined successor of John D. Rockefeller. Thus, the chief exploiter of the American people is closely allied by marriage with the chief schemer in the service of their exploiters. This fact no American should ever lose sight of. It is a political fact; it is an economic fact. It places the final and strongest seal upon the bonds uniting Aldrich and "the interests."

When Aldrich entered the Senate, twenty-five years ago, at the splendid full age of forty, the world was just beginning to feel the effects of the principles of concentration and combination, which were inexorably and permanently established with the discoveries in steam and electricity that make the whole human race more and more like one community of interdependent neighbors. It was a moment of opportunity, an unprecedented chance for Congress, especially its deliberate and supposedly sagacious senators, to "promote the general welfare" by giving those principles free and just play in securing the benefits of expanding prosperity to all, by seeing that the profits from the cooperation of all the people went to the people. Aldrich and the traitor Senate saw the opportunity. But they saw in it only a chance to enable a class to despoil the masses.

Before he reached the Senate, Aldrich had had fifteen years of training in how to legislate the proceeds of the labor of the many into the pockets of the few. He entered it as the representative of local interests engaged in robbing by means of slyly worded tariff schedules that changed protection against the foreigner into plunder of the native. His demonstrated excellent talents for sly, slippery work in legislative chambers and committee rooms and his security in his seat against popular revulsions and outbursts together marked him for the posi-

tion of chief agent of the predatory band which was rapidly forming to take care of the prosperity of the American people. . . .

The sole source of Aldrich's power over the senators is "the interests"—the sole source, but quite sufficient to make him permanent and undisputed boss. Many of the senators, as we shall in due time and in detail note, are, like Depew and Platt, the direct agents of the various state or sectional subdivisions of "the interests," and these senators constitute about two thirds of the entire Senate. Of the remainder several know that if they should oppose "the interests" they would lose their seats; several others are silent because they feel that to speak out would be useless; a few do speak out, but are careful not to infringe upon the rigid rule of "senatorial courtesy," which thus effectually protects the unblushing corruptionists, the obsequious servants of corruption, and likewise the many traitors to party as well as the people, from having disagreeable truths dinned into their ears. . . .

The greatest single hold of "the interests" is the fact that they are the "campaign contributors"—the men who supply the money for "keeping the party together," and for "getting out the vote." Did you ever think where the millions for watchers, spellbinders, halls, processions, posters, pamphlets, that are spent in national, state, and local campaigns come from? Who pays the big election expenses of your congressman, of the men you send to the legislature to elect senators? Do you imagine those who foot those huge bills are fools? Don't you know that they make sure of getting their money back, with interest, compound upon compound? Your candidates get most of the money for their campaigns from the party committees; and the central party committee is the national committee with which congressional and state and local committees are affiliated. The bulk of the money for the "political trust" comes from "the interests." "The interests," will give only to the "political trust." And that means Aldrich and his Democratic (!)

lieutenant, Gorman of Maryland, leader of the minority in the Senate. Aldrich, then, is the head of the "political trust" and Gorman is his right-hand man. . . .

How does Aldrich work? Obviously, not much steering is necessary, when the time comes to vote. "The interests" have a majority and to spare. The only questions are such as permitting a senator to vote and at times to speak against "the interests" when the particular measure is mortally offensive to the people of his particular state or section. Those daily sham battles in the Senate! Those paradings of sham virtue! Is it not strange that the other senators, instead of merely busying themselves at writing letters or combing their whiskers, do not break into shouts of laughter?

Aldrich's real work—getting the wishes of his principals, directly or through their lawyers, and putting these wishes into proper form if they are orders for legislation or into the proper channels if they are orders to kill or emasculate legislation—this work is all done, of course, behind the scenes. When Aldrich is getting orders, there is of course never any witness. The second part of his task—execution—is in part a matter of whispering with his chief lieutenants, in part a matter of consultation in the secure secrecy of the Senate committee rooms. Aldrich is in person chairman of the chief Senate committee—finance. There he labors, assisted by Gorman, his right bower, who takes his place as chairman when the Democrats are in power; by Spooner, his left bower and public mouthpiece; by Allison, that Nestor of craft; by the Pennsylvania Railroad's Penrose; by Tom Platt of New York, corruptionist and life-long agent of corruptionists; by Joe Bailey of Texas, and several other sympathetic or silent spirits. Together they concoct and sugar-coat the bitter doses for the people—the loot measures and suffocating of the measures in restraint of loot. In the unofficial but powerful steering committee—which receives from him the will of "the interests" and translates it into "party policy"—he works through Allison

as chairman—but Allison's position is recognized as purely honorary. . . .

Such is Aldrich, the senator. At the second session of the last Congress his main achievements, so far as the surface shows, were smothering all inquiry into the tariff and the freight-rate robberies, helping Elkins and the group of traitors in the service of the thieves who control the railway corporations to emasculate railway legislation, helping Allison and Bailey to smother the bill against the food poisoners for dividends. During the past winter he has been concentrating on the "defense of the railways"—which means not the railways nor yet the railway corporations, but simply the Rockefeller–Morgan looting of the people by means of their control of the corporations that own the railways.

Has Aldrich intellect? Perhaps. But he does not show it. He has never in his twenty-five years of service in the Senate introduced or advocated a measure that shows any conception of life above what might be expected in a Hungry Joe. No, intellect is not the characteristic of Aldrich—or of any of these traitors, or of the men they serve. A scurvy lot they are, are they not, with their smirking and cringing and voluble palaver about God and patriotism and their eager offerings of endowments for hospitals and colleges whenever the Amercian people so much as look hard in their direction!

Aldrich is rich and powerful. Treachery has brought him wealth and rank, if not honor, of a certain sort. He must laugh at us, grown-up fools, permitting a handful to bind the might of our eighty millions and to set us all to work for them.

DOCUMENT 23.4
Roosevelt Responds to Muckraking

Phillips' articles evoked a quick response from President Theodore Roosevelt, who forthwith

Source: *New York Tribune,* April 15, 1906.

popularized the use of the term ''muckraker.'' Theodore Roosevelt's piece reveals also his attempt to strike a balance between maintaining existing institutions and reforming the more flagrant abuses of society.

In Bunyan's *Pilgrim's Progress* you may recall the description of the Man with the Muck-rake, the man who could look no way but downward, with the muck-rake in his hands; who was offered a celestial crown for his muck-rake, but who would neither look up nor regard the crown he was offered, but continued to rake to himself the filth of the floor.

In *Pilgrim's Progress* the Man with the Muck-rake is set forth as the example of him whose vision is fixed on carnal instead of on spiritual things. Yet he also typifies the man who in this life consistently refuses to see aught that is lofty, and fixes his eyes with solemn intentness only on that which is vile and debasing. Now, it is very necessary that we should not flinch from seeing what is vile and debasing. There is filth on the floor, and it must be scraped up with the muck-rake; and there are times and places where this service is the most needed of all the services that can be performed. But the man who never does anything else, who never thinks or speaks or writes save of his feats with the muck-rake, speedily becomes, not a help to society, not an incitement to good but one of the most potent forces of evil.

There are in the body politic, economic and social, many and grave evils, and there is urgent necessity for the sternest war upon them. There should be relentless exposure of and attack upon every evil man, whether politician or businessman, every evil practice, whether in politics, in business or in social life. I hail as a benefactor every writer or speaker, every man who, on the platform or in book, magazine or newspaper, with merciless severity makes such attack, provided always that he in his turn remembers that the attack is of use only if it is absolutely truthful. The liar is no whit better than the thief, and if his mendacity takes the form of

slander he may be worse than most thieves. It puts a premium upon knavery untruthfully to attack an honest man, or even with hysterical exaggeration to assail a bad man with untruth. An epidemic of indiscriminate assault upon character does not good but very great harm. The soul of every scoundrel is gladdened whenever an honest man is assailed, or even when a scoundrel is untruthfully assailed.

Now it is easy to twist out of shape what I have just said, easy to affect to misunderstand it, and, if it is slurred over in repetition, not difficult really to misunderstand it. Some persons are sincerely incapable of understanding that to denounce mudslinging does not mean the indorsement of whitewashing; and both the interested individuals who need whitewashing and those others who practise mudslinging like to encourage such confusion of ideas. One of the chief counts against those who make indiscriminate assault upon men in business or men in public life is that they invite a reaction which is sure to tell powerfully in favor of the unscrupulous scoundrel who really ought to be attacked, who ought to be exposed, who ought, if possible, to be put in the penitentiary. If Aristides is praised overmuch as just, people get tired of hearing it; and overcensure of the unjust finally and from similar reasons results in their favor.

Any excess is almost sure to invite a reaction; and, unfortunately, the reaction, instead of taking the form of punishment of those guilty of the excess, is very apt to take the form either of punishment of the unoffending or of giving immunity, and even strength, to offenders. The effort to make financial or political profit out of the destruction of character can only result in public calamity. Gross and reckless assaults on character—whether on the stump or in newspaper, magazine or book—create a morbid and vicious public sentiment, and at the same time act as a profound deterrent to able men of normal sensitiveness and tend to prevent them from entering the public service at any price. As an instance in point, I may mention that one serious difficulty encountered in getting the right type of men to dig the Panama Canal is the certainty that they will be exposed, both without, and, I am sorry to say, sometimes within, Congress, to utterly reckless assaults on their character and capacity. . . .

To assail the great and admitted evils of our political and industrial life with such crude and sweeping generalizations as to include decent men in the general condemnation means the searing of the public conscience. There results a general attitude either of cynical belief in and indifference to public corruption or else of a distrustful inability to discriminate between the good and the bad. Either attitude is fraught with untold damage to the country as a whole. The fool who has not sense to discriminate between what is good and what is bad is well-nigh as dangerous as the man who does discriminate and yet chooses the bad. There is nothing more distressing to every good patriot, to every good American, than the hard, scoffing spirit which treats the allegation of dishonesty in a public man as a cause for laughter. Such laughter is worse than the crackling of thorns under a pot, for it denotes not merely the vacant mind, but the heart in which high emotions have been choked before they could grow to fruition.

There is any amount of good in the world, and there never was a time when loftier and more disinterested work for the betterment of mankind was being done than now. The forces that tend for evil are great and terrible, but the forces of truth and love and courage and honesty and generosity and sympathy are also stronger than ever before. It is a foolish and timid no less than a wicked thing to blink the fact that the forces of evil are strong, but it is even worse to fail to take into account the strength of the forces that tell for good. Hysterical sensationalism is the very poorest weapon wherewith to fight for lasting righteousness. The men who with stern sobriety and truth assail the many evils of our time, whether in the public press, or in magazines, or in books, are the leaders and allies of all engaged in the work for social and political betterment. But if they give good reason for distrust of what they say, if they chill the ardor of those who demand truth as a primary virtue, they thereby betray the good cause and play into the hands of the very men against whom they are nominally at war.

DOCUMENT 23.5
The Progressive Platform of 1912

Six years after denouncing muckraking, Theodore Roosevelt, anxious to return to the White House, ran on the Progressive ticket. By then, he had moved well to the left of his positions in 1906. Indeed, the party platform is an excellent statement of advanced progressive thinking at flood tide of reform strength. Compare his view of the trusts with that of Pingree (Doc. 23.1). Note also what the platform does not recommend, in such areas as public welfare.

The conscience of the people, in a time of grave national problems, has called into being a new party, born of the nation's sense of justice. We of the Progressive party here dedicate ourselves to the fulfillment of the duty laid upon us by our fathers to maintain the government of the people, by the people and for the people whose foundations they laid. . . .

THE OLD PARTIES

Political parties exist to secure responsible government and to execute the will of the people.

From these great tasks both of the old parties have turned aside. Instead of instruments to promote the general welfare, they have become the tools of corrupt interests which use them

Source: Printed in Kirk H. Porter and Donald Bruce Johnson, *National Party Platforms, 1840–1956* (Urbana, 1956), pp. 175–82.

impartially to serve their selfish purposes. Behind the ostensible government sits enthroned an invisible government owing no allegiance and acknowledging no responsibility to the people.

To destroy this invisible government, to dissolve the unholy alliance between corrupt business and corrupt politics is the first task of the statesmanship of the day.

The deliberate betrayal of its trust by the Republican party, the fatal incapacity of the Democratic party to deal with the new issues of the new time, have compelled the people to forge a new instrument of government through which to give effect to their will in laws and institutions.

Unhampered by tradition, uncorrupted by power, undismayed by the magnitude of the task, the new party offers itself as the instrument of the people to sweep away old abuses, to build a new and nobler commonwealth. . . .

THE RULE OF THE PEOPLE

. . . In particular, the party declares for direct primaries for the nomination of State and National officers; for nationwide preferential primaries for candidates for the presidency; for the direct election of United States Senators by the people; and we urge on the States the policy of the short ballot, with responsibility to the people secured by the initiative, referendum and recall. . . .

EQUAL SUFFRAGE

The Progressive party, believing that no people can justly claim to be a true democracy which denies political rights on account of sex, pledges itself to the task of securing equal suffrage to men and women alike.

CORRUPT PRACTICES

We pledge our party to legislation that will compel strict limitation of all campaign contri-

butions and expenditures, and detailed publicity of both before as well as after primaries and elections.

PUBLICITY AND PUBLIC SERVICE

We pledge our party to legislation compelling the registration of lobbyists; publicity of committee hearings except on foreign affairs, and recording of all votes in committee; and forbidding federal appointees from holding office in State or National political organizations, or taking part as officers or delegates in political conventions for the nomination of elective State or National officials.

THE COURTS

The Progressive party demands such restriction of the power of the courts as shall leave to the people the ultimate authority to determine fundamental questions of social welfare and public policy. To secure this end, it pledges itself to provide:

1. That when an Act, passed under the police power of the State, is held unconstitutional under the State Constitution, by the courts, the people, after an ample interval for deliberation, shall have an opportunity to vote on the question whether they desire the Act to become law, notwithstanding such decision.

2. That every decision of the highest appellate court of a State declaring an Act of the Legislature unconstitutional on the ground of its violation of the Federal Constitution shall be subject to the same review by the Supreme Court of the United States as is now accorded to decisions sustaining such legislation.

ADMINISTRATION OF JUSTICE

. . . We believe that the issuance of injunctions in cases arising out of labor disputes should be prohibited when such injunctions would not apply when no labor disputes existed.

We believe also that a person cited for

contempt in labor disputes, except when such contempt was committed in the actual presence of the court or so near thereto as to interfere with the proper administration of justice, should have a right to trial by jury.

SOCIAL AND INDUSTRIAL JUSTICE

The supreme duty of the Nation is the conservation of human resources through an enlightened measure of social and industrial justice. We pledge ourselves to work unceasingly in State and Nation for:

1. Effective legislation looking to the prevention of industrial accidents, occupational diseases, overwork, involuntary unemployment, and other injurious effects incident to modern industry;
2. The fixing of minimum safety and health standards for the various occupations, and the exercise of the public authority of State and Nation, including the Federal Control over interstate commerce, and the taxing power, to maintain such standards;
3. The prohibition of child labor;
4. Minimum wage standards for working women to provide a ''living wage'' in all industrial occupations;
5. The general prohibition of night work for women and the establishment of an 8-hour day for women and young persons;
6. One day's rest in seven for all wage workers;
7. The 8-hour day in continuous 24-hour industries;
8. The abolition of the convict contract labor system; substituting a system of prison production for governmental consumption only; and the application of prisoners' earnings to the support of their dependent families;
9. Publicity as to wages, hours, and conditions of labor; full reports upon industrial accidents and diseases; and the opening to public inspection of all tallies, weights, measures, and check systems on labor products;
10. Standards of compensation for death by industrial accident and injury and trade disease which will transfer the burden of lost earnings from the families of working people to the industry, and thus to the community;
11. The protection of home life against the hazards of sickness, irregular employment, and old age through the adoption of a system of social insurance adapted to American use;
12. The development of the creative labor power of America by lifting the last load of illiteracy from American youth and establishing continuation schools for industrial education under public control and encouraging agricultural education and demonstration in rural schools. . . .

We favor the organization of the workers, men and women, as a means of protecting their interests and of promoting their progress. . . .

BUSINESS

We demand that the test of true prosperity shall be the benefits conferred thereby on all the citizens, not confined to individuals or classes. . . .

We therefore demand a strong National regulation of inter-State corporations. The corporation is an essential part of modern business. The concentration of modern business, in some degree, is both inevitable and necessary for national and international business efficiency. But the existing concentration of vast wealth under a corporate system, unguarded and uncontrolled by the Nation, has placed in the hands of a few men enormous, secret, irresponsible power over the daily life of the citizen—a power insufferable in a free government and certain of abuse. . . .

We urge the establishment of a strong Federal administrative commission of high standing, which shall maintain permanent and active supervision over industrial corporations engaged in inter-State commerce or such of them as are of public importance. . . .

Such a commission must enforce the complete publicity of those corporate transactions which are of public interest; must attack unfair competition, false capitalization and special privilege. . . .

We favor strengthening the Sherman Law by prohibiting agreement to divide territory or limit output; refusing to sell to customers who buy from business rivals; to sell below cost in certain areas while maintaining higher prices in other places; using the power of transportation to aid or injure special business concerns; and other unfair trade practices.

DOCUMENT 23.6
A Critique of Progressivism

In the third year of the Great Depression, the journalist John Chamberlain assessed progressivism from a leftist perspective. To Chamberlain, La Follette was something of a hero, Theodore Roosevelt a villain. Many critical historians in subsequent years have echoed his complaints about Theodore Roosevelt and progressivism.

The Progressive movement, in the years before 1912, came to be symbolized in a national way by three leaders: Bryan, Roosevelt and La Follette. Bryan, however, showed repeatedly that he couldn't win through to office;

Source: John Chamberlain, *Farewell to Reform: The Rise, Life, and Decay of the Progressive Mind in America* (New York: John Day Co., 1932), pp. 235–39, 272, 307–9, 311.

he could only run, stir up a fuss and fall back. His value was that of ambassador of the rural crowd. Roosevelt and La Follette, on the other hand, had genius for politics as well as agitation; they were elected to office on the basis of their expressed ideas.

Each man had his own type of courage; each had a magnificent will. Their backgrounds, however, were as different as homespun is from silk. La Follette was a born democrat; Roosevelt came closer to the English ideal of the disinterested gentleman in politics—which implies disinterestedness within a class orbit, of course. It was no aberration that dictated Roosevelt's genuine detestation of Thomas Jefferson. And if Roosevelt never referred to the people as a "great beast" in public, he was not one to suffer fools in denim shirts gladly. La Follette, in contrast, had a mystical faith in "the people"; he believed that, provided there was plenty of light, the common man would find his own way. The superior population of Wisconsin was excuse enough for his credo. . . .

Indeed, if one makes a thorough scansion of Roosevelt's career, the exhortation to strenuous living, the eternal harping upon activity, the crashing words and writing visage, all seem a little pathological. Action becomes a drug; Roosevelt just an American version of the Rimbaud myth. "The great game [of life] in which we are all engaged" comes down to a childish pirouetting over a void—and Roosevelt was always afraid to look into the void. This is the very negation of spiritual courage.

How different it is with La Follette! It was never "get action" with him, never "take a place and be somebody." It was "put through a specific railroad or income-tax law, and you will find action enough on your hands." "Create a railway rate and valuation board, and you won't have any time to fritter away." "Don't mind whether they call you insane or not if you are certain you are not compromising your principles." "Refuse to take a place unless it is for some specific end." "Create a progressive movement within the Republican Party and you will find you are somebody."

La Follette was words and deeds in close tandem; Roosevelt was words—and an occasional deed for the sake of the record, or to save face. La Follette was a man who sought to make strict economic analysis the basis of his laws; he never talked without facts, the best available facts, and the University of Wisconsin faculty came, characteristically enough, to replace the lobby in his home State. But Roosevelt was, confessedly, "rather an agnostic in matters of economics"; the tariff bored him. With all his interest in cultural and scientific matters, he never understood the spirit of the laboratory—which was the one hope of the Progressive, or Liberal, movement. . . .

Opinions differ on Roosevelt. But even his firmest friends admit a certain weakness in fundamentals; they see his primary value as the sort of person who "sits on the bulge," curbing excesses on the part of labor, on the one hand, and capital, on the other. Roosevelt dramatized the antithesis of "predatory wealth" and "predatory poverty"; he couldn't see, this man who administered "antiscorbutics to socialism," that predaciousness cannot be eliminated until the simpler antithesis of wealth and poverty has been reduced to a synthesis. Gilson Gardner, one of the wisest of tired radicals, sums up the Roosevelt tightrope act in a pithy paragraph. "More honesty," he offers as the Roosevelt credo; "By George, they mustn't do it. The rich must be fair and the poor must be contented—or, if not contented, at least they must be orderly. I will tell them both. No restraining of trade by the great corporations and no rioting by the toiler. Give me the power and I will make them behave." The ideal may be laudable. But just what class of people is there left to delegate the power? A middle class? Yes, for a while, but a middle class cannot

exist permanently in a dynamic society that is creating "great corporations" that need restraining. The "great corporations" must be blotted out or made one corporation beyond the pale of manipulation for private profit. This, Roosevelt never could bring himself to realize. He had too many nice friends who were part of the corporation system.

Opinions differ, too, on La Follette. He was a man who was strong on analysis, and weak, as it turned out, on prognosis. But scratch a man who slights his caliber of character, such a man as Mark Sullivan or Roosevelt himself, and you will find a born compromiser. Roosevelt couldn't understand LaFollette because he couldn't understand patience and devotion to an idea. In his book on *Pre-War America* Sullivan speaks slightingly of La Follette's "anti-railroad bias," his "almost perverse bent toward visualizing himself in the role of martyr." But just a few pages away from the criticism of La Follette, Sullivan himself admits everything that La Follette ever said against the railroad practices of the eighties, nineties and early nineteen-hundreds. And any one who has read the La Follette autobiography will know that the anti-railroad "bias" was only part of a cogent, dynamic economic philosophy, and that it can no more be called bias—in the sense that bias implies an element of unreason—than a mathematician can be called pig-headed for insisting that two and two are irrevocably four in every world but Lewis Carroll's. Certain conclusions flow from certain premises; La Follette's premises may have been proved without twentieth-century social grounding, but his railroad conclusions flow inevitably from his primitive capitalistic postulates. Sullivan, in his skimming way, lets the case against the postulates go; the word "bias" saves him from thinking through to his own position. . . .

As for Progressive government, the results of the three decades of stife antecedent to 1919 are, perhaps, minimal. . . .

The pet political solutions of the Progressives, designed to make government more responsible to the will of the electorate, have notoriously been weak reeds. The initiative and the referendum have produced nothing. Women suffrage has only added, in direct proportion, to Republican and Democratic totals. Direct primaries have proved not even a palliative; they have worked against strong labor and independent party organization, which is the only hope of labor and the consumer in the political field. As Paul Douglas says, where parties are closed organizations, as in England, nominations are made by local nuclei of party workers who know what they want. If a group dislikes the candidates of existing party machines, the only recourse is to put a candidate of its own in the field. The direct primary seemingly weakens the necessity for this; it creates the illusion that an inert "people," spasmodically led, can be aroused to holding the machine politician in line by the threat that they may turn on him at the primary polls. The result is . . . the machine politician promises much, does little . . . and the people are let down. During a two, or four, or six, year period of office-holding, there is much time for an electorate to forget.

The popular election of Senators, instituted in 1913, has made very little actual difference. The real difference between the type of Senator that flourished in the days of the McKinley plutocracy and the type of the present is one of demagoguery; the modern Senator, representing the same interests as his legislature-elected predecessor, is compelled to be a master of the art of obfuscation. Senator Nelson Aldrich, in the 1890 dispensation, could afford to leave the obfuscation to his local manipulator, General Brayton, who kept the legislature in line while his master attended to more important business.

The real human gain of Woodrow Wilson's Administration was the domestication of the eight-hour day in many areas of industry, made possible by the Adamson Law rendering it com-

pulsory on the railroads. The Federal Reserve system is, beyond doubt, better than the previous banking system. It is flexible, it is an instrument which, through its control of the rediscount rate, can take up the slack between productive activity, and speculation at any time if it is properly run. But, in setting down these gains, we have about exhausted the really important positive legislation of thirty years. The business cycle remains; until that is done away with, all legislation looking to the welfare of the common man must appear in the light of small, temporary oscillations along the course of a major graph. . . .

The curbing of the "money power," the abolition of "privilege," the opening up of opportunity by the Single Tax, the redemption of the promises of the New Freedom, all of these have been made the basis for a "return" demand—a demand for the evocation and reestablishment of a vanished, and somehow more "moral" and "honest" *status quo.* And all economic reforms that have been undertaken in the spirit of Bryan, of La Follette, of Wilson, have worked in a way precisely against the grain of Progressive or neo-democratic hopes; instead of "freeing" the common man within the capitalistic system, these reforms have made the system, as a long-run proposition, more difficult of operation; and this, in turn, has reacted upon the common man as employee, as small bondholder, as savings-account depositor, as insurance-policy owner. The value of reforms, as I see it, is that they fail to achieve what they are sanguinely intended to achieve; and in so failing they help make the system which they are intended to patch up only the more unpatchable. In other words, every vote for reform, entered upon intelligently, is a Jesuitical vote for revolution. Conservatives like Nicholas Murray Butler know this; that is why they fear the growth of a bureaucracy intended to administer a "return"; that is why they fear the retention of the anti-trust acts.

chapter

Women's Work, Women's Politics: The Emergence of the "New Woman," 1870–1920

Nancy Schrom Dye
University of Kentucky

Late in December 1873, seventy-five women in the small town of Hillsboro, Ohio, marched down Main Street, entered each of the town's thirteen saloons, knelt in noisy prayer on the sawdust floors, and refused to leave until barkeepers promised to forsake the liquor business forever. In the days that followed, one after another unnerved saloon owner signed the temperance pledge and stood by as middle-class matrons, to the accompaniment of hymns and cheers, rolled kegs of liquor into the street and smashed them with axes. Throughout the winter of 1873–74, small armies of women in more than thirty states and territories followed the example of the Hillsboro band, laying siege to thousands of saloons with hymns, prayers, and, occasionally, hatchets. American women seemed bent on waging war against whiskey, animated by the conviction that alcohol was responsible for a host of social ills. Liquor, they believed, destroyed marriages and family life, and forced many women to endure lives of poverty and abuse.

The "women's crusade," as this spontaneous outburst of temperance militance came to

be called, took place at the beginning of a half century of dramatic change in the lives of American women. The tens of thousands of women who took part in the crusade had grown up in an America of small towns and farms. They had married and borne children in a society that offered women virtually no alternatives to domesticity, maternity, and economic dependence. And they lived in a culture that drew clear, largely unquestioned distinctions between male and female nature, role, and place: women belonged at home, nurturing children. They could not vote, sit on juries, hold office, or, if married, make a binding legal contract. Men, on the other hand, belonged in the public realm of business and politics. Mid-nineteenth-century Americans glorified female domesticity, believing that women, enshrined in the home, were naturally more moral, pure, and pious than men.

The women who took to the streets in the 1870s to abolish the liquor trade accepted this domestic ideal. So fervent was their belief in the sanctity of the home and women's obligation to protect it, however, that they left the private world of the household to destroy what they perceived to be the greatest threat to domestic happiness and stability: the quintessentially male institution of the saloon. In the temperance crusaders' willingness to leave the domestic sphere, we can see the most important way that women's lives were beginning to change in Gilded Age America: the history of modern American women is in large part the history of breaking down rigid barriers between an exclusively private female household and a public male realm of the marketplace and politics.

The daughters of the temperance crusaders—women born between the 1860s and the early 1880s—came of age in an America vastly transformed from the largely agrarian nation their mothers had known. From the end of the Civil War through the first years of the twentieth century, the railroad, the corporation, and the rapid growth of sprawling industrial cities permanently disrupted traditional rural ways of life, and pulled even the smallest of American communities into the nexus of industrial capitalism. These decades of economic transformation witnessed important changes in women's lives, as fertility rates declined, opportunities for education expanded, possibilities for labor force participation multiplied, and a growing women's movement agitated for the legal and political rights previous generations of women had been denied. Then, too, through the establishment of women's clubs, civic leagues, municipal reform organizations, and the like, women expanded their participation in American politics and worked to legitimize their place in public life.

The fifty years between 1870 and 1920, then, mark a critical period in women's history, years that witnessed the creation of what nineteenth-century Americans themselves called a "new woman." In large part, the history of women during these years is the story of women's entrance into the public sphere through work and politics. It is, in short, a story of change. But the story of women in modern America contains important elements of continuity as well. The most powerful of these has been the persistence of the ideal of female domesticity. The belief that women belong at home has continued to influence the ways Americans define women's place. The interplay between these elements of continuity and change—the blurring of distinctions between male and female spheres on the one hand and the persistence of the ideal of female domesticity on the other—constitute the central tension in modern American women's history.

What social and economic factors were responsible for the rise of the "new woman"? How were the distinctions between public and private realms broken down? In good part, the answers to these questions lie in the ways massive industrialization and urbanization affected women's lives. To be sure, the impact of industrial development and urban growth was far from monolithic: race and class as well as gender mediated the effects of economic and social change. We know, however, that industrialization gradually transformed women's work, both inside and outside the home. And we know that women were not passive in the face of major social change: it was largely in response to late nineteenth-century living and working conditions that women entered politics. Through women's entry into the work force and participation in politics, then, the distinctions between an exclusively female private sphere and an exclusively male public sphere gradually broke down.

*   *   *   *   *

In the decades after 1870, ever-increasing numbers of women entered the work force. In and of itself, women's work outside the home was not new: before the Civil War many women had toiled for at least a few years as domestic servants or teachers, and had made up much of the labor force in textiles, America's first major industry. Virtually all black women had labored as slaves in southern fields and households. Between 1870 and 1910, however, the size of the female work force more than tripled. Young, single women, most of them immigrants or the daughters of immigrants, flooded into the expanding industrial labor market to fill the new unskilled jobs created by mechanization and the subdivision of work processes. Women continued to make up much of the textile labor force in the Northeast and provided the major source of labor for the new textile industry in the South. They could be found in garment shops, canneries, and packing houses, printing shops and bookbinderies, commercial laundries, and cigar and tobacco factories. By 1900 there were four times as many women in industry as there had been in 1870.

Massive industrialization spawned other kinds of jobs for women as well. As production increased, businesses experienced a corresponding need for a vastly expanded clerical labor force. At the same time, the introduction of the telephone and the typewriter revolutionized the nature of office work. The introduction of new technology and the creation of new clerical jobs contributed to the *feminization* of office employment. In 1870 women made up only 3 percent of the clerical work force. By 1890 they constituted 17 percent of all office workers. By 1920 women stenographers, typists, and telephone operators dominated clerical work. During the same years, women moved into the growing numbers of retail sales positions in shops and department stores. In short, women were very much a part of the "white-collar revolution" in the years around the turn of the century.

By 1900 one out of every five American women were gainfully employed, and women made up nearly 20 percent of the labor force. Americans expressed considerable ambivalence about the growth of a female working class. Social conservatives decried women's work outside the home, arguing that it would undermine traditional marriage and family life.

Feminists, on the other hand, applauded the trend, and saw work as the road to genuine female autonomy. In point of fact, both conservatives and feminists were off the mark. Very few working women were economically independent. Women's earnings were simply too low, and their economic opportunities too limited. Typically, women labored sixty hours a week in ill-ventilated, unsanitary factories for wages that were less than half of what men of comparable skill earned in the same trades.

Why didn't wage work lead to the kind of economic independence feminists envisioned? In part, the answer to this question lies in the fact that the female labor force was constantly changing: few women spent longer than four or five years at work. Then, too, women could rarely turn to a union for help in bettering wages and conditions. Only one major nineteenth-century labor organization—the Knights of Labor—made serious efforts to unionize women. But the Knights' inclusive unionism that welcomed all workers regardless of skill level, race, or gender gave way by the 1890s to the exclusive craft unionism of the American Federation of Labor. The unions of skilled craftsmen that made up the AFL had little interest in organizing unskilled workers of either sex, and many were frankly hostile to female workers. Women, they believed, were cheap competitors who enabled industrialists to lower wage scales and undermine the integrity of traditional crafts. Then, too, most unionists, like Americans generally, held traditional ideas about women's place, and believed that women belonged at home rather than in the factory or the union hall.

Most important to an understanding of women's disadvantageous position in the work force is the phenomenon known as occupational segregation. Put simply, women and men have always held different jobs and occupied different sectors of the labor force. Around the turn of the century, men dominated heavy industry, mining, and transportation; women clustered in light industry and in service employment. Patterns of occupational segregation held firm within individual industries as well: men held the central, skilled positions, while women toiled at unskilled jobs. Throughout the period, workplaces were segregated by race, too. Blacks were usually excluded from industrial employment in the North and the South. Of the more than one million black women workers in the late nineteenth century, less than 3 percent found industrial jobs. Most continued to toil as agricultural laborers in the rural South, or as domestic servants or laundresses. In the few industries such as tobacco in which black women did find work, blacks and whites worked at different occupations in segregated workrooms. The demand for "equal pay for equal work" that labor reformers, unionists, and feminists rallied around at the turn of the century was, in fact, an empty slogan: women and men did not do equal work because they never had access to the same jobs.

Women's status in the work force also stemmed from two deeply rooted cultural assumptions. First, most Americans believed that few women needed to work outside the home. Employers faced few critics when they justified paying their female employees much less than men because women were young, usually lived at home, and did not have to support themselves or their families. The second assumption most Americans shared was that women's real responsibilities remained in the home, and that women were not suited physically or psychologically for the rigors of the workplace. Both assumptions figured prominently in the successful efforts social reformers launched early in the twentieth century to protect women by legislating their working conditions and wages. Upon the urging of women's organizations such as the National Consumers' League and the Women's Trade Union League, state after state passed laws that limited the number of hours women could work, prohibited night work, and established women's minimum wage boards. In 1907 the U.S. Supreme Court, in *Muller*

v. *Oregon,* upheld the constitutionality of much of this legislation by arguing that as "mothers of the race" women needed the protection of the state.

Then, too, the cultural assumptions that women belonged at home and had no need to earn their livelihoods distorted Americans' perceptions of women's status in the developing industrial economy. A significant number of single women were self-supporting. Because wages were predicated on the assumption that women were supplementary rather than primary breadwinners, self-supporting women were forced to eke out a precarious existence on the very margin of subsistence. Americans also refused to confront the fact that after 1900 much of the increase in the female work force was comprised of married women. The problems of black women, who often worked after they were married and who were more likely than white women to be heads of households, were virtually invisible to the society at large.

Wage work, then, was a powerful force in breaking down the boundaries between public and private spheres. But in unionists' protestations that women belonged at home, in reformers' zeal to protect women, and in pay scales based on the assumption that women need not nor should not be self-sufficient we can trace the persistence of the domestic ideal.

Middle-class women rarely entered the labor force in the late nineteenth or early twentieth centuries, but their lives also changed dramatically. They were the first to benefit from the changes industrialization and the growth of the city brought to household labor. Urban middle-class homes were equipped with gas, running water, and electricity by the turn of the century—amenities that were not to come to much of rural America until the 1930s. Products traditionally made at home—clothing and canned goods, for example—could be purchased in retail stores by the 1880s. Then, too, American families were shrinking in size. At the beginning of the nineteenth century, American women bore an average of seven children; their counterparts in 1900 bore fewer than four. Middle-class women were hardly leisured—housework still involved considerable manual labor and middle-class mothers assumed virtually total responsibility for child care. Nevertheless, the availability of consumer goods and the smaller size of families meant that they were no longer tied to the virtually ceaseless round of pregnancy, childbearing, and household labor that women in earlier generations experienced.

Middle-class women also stood to benefit from new opportunities for education. The nineteenth century was a time of extraordinary educational gain. In 1800 only 50 percent of white American women were literate. By century's end, however, girls were more likely than boys to attend and graduate from high school. What was more, increasing numbers of young women went on to college. In 1890 some 56,000 women were enrolled in a college or university; by 1910 that number had swelled to 140,000—nearly 40 percent of all college students.

The most striking aspect of middle-class women's history in the years between 1870 and 1920 was the proliferation of women's organizations. Millions of women throughout the United States joined temperance societies, women's clubs, civic and municipal leagues, and suffrage organizations. Such groups made up a multifaceted women's movement that provided avenues for women's participation in municipal, state, and national politics, questioned women's status and role in American society, and was instrumental in breaking down the distinctions between private female and public male spheres.

A wide range of issues engaged the attention of women's organizations. The first compelling cause for women in this period, as we have seen, was temperance. The Women's Christian Temperance Union, established in 1873, counted more than 200,000 members by the early 1880s. Under the leadership of Frances Willard, an astute organizer and social reformer, the WCTU campaigned not only against alcohol, but also for better industrial working conditions, educational and labor reform, and woman suffrage. During the same years, the women's club movement gained ground. Local clubs banded together in statewide federations and, in 1892, organized nationally into the General Federation of Women's Clubs. By 1912 more than two million women belonged to organizations affiliated with the federation. Established originally as social and literary societies, many women's clubs transformed themselves into reform organizations by the 1890s, and took on such issues as municipal corruption, public health, sanitation, maternal and child welfare, housing reform, conservation, pure food and milk, and industrial pollution. Women investigated and attempted to improve virtually every aspect of turn-of-the-century urban life. Indeed, through their clubs, municipal leagues, health protective associations, and civic reform groups, women entered formal politics and played a central role in the progressive reform movement.

College-educated women were especially important to women's reform efforts. Once a young woman graduated from college, she faced a personal dilemma, for there was no clearly defined place in American society for highly educated women. Social reformer Jane Addams, for example, drifted through several years of depression after she graduated from Rockford College in the 1870s. In good part, her decision to establish the Chicago settlement house, Hull House, grew out of her search for meaningful work in a society that provided educated women with few rewarding personal or professional options. ''I have seen young girls suffer and grow sensibly lowered in vitality in the first years after they leave school,'' Addams wrote. The recent college graduate, she went on, ''finds 'life' so different from what she expected it to be. She . . . does not understand this apparent waste of herself, this elaborate preparation, if no work is provided for her.'' College graduates' search for meaningful work led many to devote themselves to social reform, often applying their college study of political economy, social science, and statistics to detailed investigations of urban social and economic conditions. The pioneering surveys of poverty, working conditions, maternal and infant welfare, and standards of living so important to progressive reform were in large part the work of young college-educated women who took on jobs as social investigators. Perhaps most important, college women were primarily responsible for developing the settlement house movement in the United States. Jane Addams's vision of living and working with the immigrant poor was shared by many college women, who saw in the settlement movement a way to help ameliorate the plight of the urban working class and provide meaningful work for themselves.

Settlement houses and the networks of women's organizations gave women an important political base in the progressive era. Despite the fact that the overwhelming majority of American women had no vote in any political contest save in the twenty-six states that allowed them to participate in school elections, they played active and highly visible roles in municipal and state politics in the early twentieth century, and gained considerable political clout. Women claimed credit for a broad variety of progressive victories: electing women to local school boards and winning appointments for women as sanitation, health, and factory inspectors, marshaling votes for new city charters and for bond issues to find municipal improvements such as new water systems, helping to oust corrupt city officials, and organizing to win the passage of housing, corrections, occupational safety, child labor, and health legislation. Women's political power rested on their ability to mobilize large numbers of women around reform issues. When Albion Fellows Bacon, an Indiana housing reformer, wanted to secure state housing legislation, for example, she not only lobbied the legislature as an individual, but she turned to the well-organized state federation of women's clubs. When Julia Lathrop, long-time resident of Hull House and first chief of the U.S. Department of Labor Children's Bureau—a federal agency created in 1912 at the behest of women reformers—wanted information about child mortality she, too, turned to women's clubs throughout the nation.

In women's grassroots protests over such issues as clean food and pure milk, inadequate and highly politicized school systems, and high infant mortality was an important critique of American social values. Women reformers reiterated time and again that American political institutions were indifferent to the needs of women and children, and that government at all levels existed to encourage economic growth rather than to respond to human needs. ''It is a serious matter that the federal government is willing to spend time and money to establish departments to see to the breeding and to the raising and to the distribution and to the exportation of various animals,'' Jane Addams declared in 1907, ''but that as yet the federal government . . . has done nothing to see to it that the children are properly protected.'' Women reformers, then, criticized government's identification with the values of the marketplace, and pushed for an expanded conception of the state that would include responsibility for social welfare. In these respects, women reformers were central to articulating and implementing the goals of progressivism.

The entry of women into politics, in and of itself, hastened the demise of the traditional doctrine of spheres. But women's reform activism helped blur the distinctions between public and private realms in another way as well. Women reformers were convinced that in modern industrial society, the home and the community, the private sphere and the public, were enmeshed. They pointed out that whereas in an earlier generation households may have been self-sufficient, the home in the modern city was heavily dependent upon political decisions and institutions over which individual women had no control. No mother, regardless of social class, could guarantee her children's well-being if a corrupt city council refused to erect barriers at trolley crossings or if an urban department of health neglected careful bacteriological inspection of its milk and water supplies. In other words, what had once been private concerns of the household and family were now public issues, and the province of American politics generally.

Women's reform activities were also closely intertwined with American feminism. Most feminists in the early twentieth century linked their concern for the role and status of women with the general well-being of the community. Women should be freed from the confines of domesticity, they argued, in order to work for the betterment of society as a whole. Feminism in the early twentieth century, then, concentrated on the right of women to be public people. Then, too, turn-of-the-century activists believed strongly in the sisterhood of all women, regardless of social class: hence, reformers' efforts to unionize women workers through the Women's Trade Union League and improve women's wages and working conditions through organizations such as consumers' leagues. Many today find this variety of feminism naive in its downplaying of class differences and limited in that it did not directly challenge women's role within marriage or as mothers, but it is undeniable that its vision of sisterhood enabled women to forge a powerful social movement and legitimize a place for themselves in public life. Indeed, we cannot find women in American history since the early twentieth century who have commanded the political influence that women such as Jane Addams, Julia Lathrop, Lillian Wald (founder of New York's Henry Street Nurses' Settlement), or Florence Kelley (head of the National Consumers' League) exercised.

Arguments for woman suffrage illustrate feminists' linkages between the improvement of woman's status in American society on the one hand and the betterment of society as a whole on the other. Suffragists believed that women would bring special qualities to politics and claimed that women, once franchised, could create a uniquely female political agenda.

Women won the right to vote in 1920, after more than seventy years of agitation. Ironically, the ratification of the Nineteenth Amendment served as a culmination rather than as a new beginning for women's political culture. The twenties were years of frustration and disappointment for female activists. The vitality of women's politics and the impressive political networks that women had established in the progressive era eroded in the 1920s. In good part, the decline of women's political activism was due to the conservatism of the decade: nativism, antiradicalism, and a pervasive fear of social change characterized American society in the years following World War I. Not surprisingly, both progressive reform and feminism fell into decline. Then, too, women won the vote just as voting and party identification were becoming less important to Americans. By the time the suffrage amendment was ratified, voter turnout had been declining for more than a decade. Acrimonious disagreements among feminists about protective labor legislation for women and the newly introduced equal rights amendment also contributed to feminist difficulties. Then, too, women's actual political behavior defied suffragists' predictions: once franchised, women did not coalesce around women's issues or vote together as a group. Finally, young women in the twenties put little stock in the female solidarity that had provided the impetus for women's political activity earlier in the century, and redefined feminism to reflect their new concern with individual self-fulfillment rather than with social change.

Although the nature of women's political culture changed radically in the 1920s, trends in their work force participation, the other major factor in redefining women's role, continued throughout the 1920s and the 1930s.

More women continued to enter the work force, although not at as accelerated a pace as in the years around the turn of the century. What was more, the number of married women continued to increase throughout both decades. By 1930 they made up 29 percent of the female work force. By 1940 married women made up 35 percent of all women workers, despite the intense public hostility to married women workers during the Great Depression. Although the percentage of all married women who worked was still quite small—only about 15 percent—a trend toward combining marriage and work was clearly taking shape.

Although women continued to enter the work force in increasing numbers, patterns of occupational segregation remained tenacious. Neither World War I nor the Great Depression altered the divisions between male and female employment. To be sure, during World War I women found jobs as railroad workers, streetcar conductors, and in other previously all-male occupations. These positions, however, ended with mass layoffs in 1918–19. Throughout the 1920s, women continued to cluster in female occupations, most notably clerical work, service employment, and the women's professions of teaching, nursing, and social work.

Women's experiences in the work force throughout the 1920s and 1930s continued to reflect the strength of the domestic ideal. Early in the Great Depression, for example, both the federal government and many state governments regulated the employment of married women as government workers, and prohibited both husband and wife from holding government jobs. What was more, some New Deal legislation discriminated against women. Many of the National Recovery Administration codes, for example, sanctioned paying women far less than men. And the work relief programs of the New Deal made far fewer jobs for women than for men. As historian Susan Ware states, "unless reminded, policymakers simply forgot that women, too, were hurt by the Depression."

By 1920 the emergence of the "new woman" was essentially complete. Participation in the labor force and involvement in politics had weakened the rigid nineteenth-century dichotomy between a private, exclusively female household and an exclusively male public life. But we can see in issues that confront us today—the fact that women, on average, still earn not much more than half of what men are paid, the fact that our society finds it difficult to reconcile the conflicting demands of home and work, the fact that many Americans are profoundly suspicious of an equal rights amendment—the persistence of a traditional ideal of female domesticity.

SUGGESTED READINGS

Blair, Karen. *From Clubwoman to Feminist.* New York: Holmes & Meier Publishing, 1980.

Bordin, Ruth. *Women and Temperance: The Quest for Power and Liberty.* Philadelphia: Temple University Press, 1980.

Davis, Allen. *American Heroine: The Life and Legend of Jane Addams.* New York: Oxford University Press, 1975.

Degler, Carl. *At Odds; Women and the Family in America from the Revolution to the Present.* New York: Oxford University Press, 1980.

Epstein, Barbara. *The Politics of Domesticity.* Middleton, Conn.: Wesleyan University Press, 1981.

Gordon, Linda. *Woman's Body, Woman's Right.* New York: Grossman, 1976.

Greenwald, Maurine. *Women, War, and Work.* Westport, Conn.: Greenwood Press, 1980.

Jones, Jacqueline. *Labor of Love, Labor of Sorrow; Black Women, Work, and the Family from Slavery to the Present.* New York: Basic Books, 1985.

Kessler-Harris, Alice. *Out to Work.* New York: Oxford University Press, 1982.

Milkman, Ruth. ed. *Women, Work, and Protest: A Century of U.S. Women's Labor History.* Boston: Routledge & Kegan Paul, 1985.

Smith-Rosenberg, Carroll. *Disorderly Conduct.* New York: Alfred A. Knopf, 1985.

Ware, Susan. *Holding Their Own: American Women in the 1930s.* Boston: Twayne Publishers, 1982.

DOCUMENT 24.1

The Crusade for Temperance, 1873–1874

Women in Gilded Age America made temperance one of the most powerful social issues of the day. In small towns throughout the United States, they took to the streets to close saloons and abolish the liquor industry. The following is a description of the Women's Crusade in the town of South Charleston, Ohio, in early 1874, taken from Eliza Daniel Stewart's Memories of the Crusade: A Thrilling Account of the Great Uprising of the Women in Ohio in 1873, against the Liquor Crime.

She says:

The women of to-day have, through a baptism of suffering, developed a new phase in the history of their sex. Men for ages have been worshiping, not God, but a hideous serpent, whose mammoth proportions have enabled it to swallow relentlessly myriads of votaries, who have offered themselves living sacrifices to its insatiable demands.

The mother or wife readily recognizes in this creature Strong Drink, and in its victims, father, husband, sons. In the fear of the Lord, and praying for his guidance and protection, taking the sword of the Spirit, and the shield

of faith with the helmet of salvation, and the banner of our Savior's love over us, we marched straight into the presence of our enemy. He raised his head, shot out his forked tongue and thought to frighten us.

But we said in the name of the Lord Jesus and suffering humanity we come. And as the mouths of the lions of old were stopped, so was the power of this beast to harm restrained, and the semblance of death fell upon him for about the space of four months. But, alas, even in this seeming death he deceived the too confident, who were thereby thrown off their watchtower. Nevertheless the nation has been aroused as never before, and though we did not succeed in entirely conquering our enemy, we did awaken the public sentiment, and the work goes on, and will till we do gain the victory.

Fancy the strangeness of the work; we, who had never in all our lives entered one of the dens, where the beast made his lair, were brought face to face with him day and night, till his hated visage became familiar. We did also make the discovery that some rum-sellers at least were susceptible of better impulses than their business engendered or fostered. Though we watched their bars incessantly to prevent the traffic, they treated us with uniform courtesy with but few exceptions. One instance I think of, on a bitter cold morning, when our patrols were almost perishing with cold, two ladies entered one of the most dreaded saloons. The keeper professed great solicitude for their comfort, and proceeded to close all ventilation, and with bar-room stove at white-heat, and about a dozen stalwart tobacco chewers spitting all over it, the situation was fearful. They came near fainting, but they did not yield their post till, fortunately, a couple of their sisters hearing of their situation, came and called them away to another point. The wife of this man assisted him in the sale of liquor, and vindicated the female character even in wickedness, for while the men were usually polite she was abusive.

But the charity that endureth all things, hopeth all things, sustained this consecrated

Source: Mother [Eliza Daniel] Stewart, *Memories of the Crusade: A Thrilling Account of the Great Uprising of the Women of Ohio in 1873, against the Liquor Crime,* 2nd ed. (Columbus, Ohio: William G. Hubbard, 1889), pp. 217–20.

band of women through all trials, whether of patience, faith or physical endurance.

Our Crusade lasted eight weeks, in the months of February and March, in the midst of the most inclement weather. Day after day we marched the streets, watching inside and out of saloons, never allowing a moment in which an unobserved sale could be made. We met alternately at the two churches for prayer and business meetings in the morning, and again in the afternoon, in order to form our line of march to the saloons, at each of which we formed our positions into two lines, one on each side of the pavement. Then we sang those precious hymns that will always be remembered as the rallying cry of the army that expect yet to take the citadel of this archenemy of mankind. And then such petitions would ascend as have seldom touched the great heart of the Father, because they were carried straight to the throne on the strong pinions of faith in His beloved Son, and direct answers came as a benediction to all hearts.

We were armed with the various pledges for saloon-keepers, property-holders, druggists and drinkers, and constantly presented them through committees appointed for the purpose. We sought in all our intercourse with those engaged in the business to have our hearts controlled by the charity that suffereth long and is kind, that it not easily provoked. And we relied firmly upon our Savior's promise, "My grace is sufficient for you," and we were not confounded. Our male citizens did all they could under the circumstances for our comfort and the advancement of our cause. In one instance they achieved almost a miracle. We held two mass-meetings each week in the Town Hall, which were the largest and most enthusiastic meetings ever held in our place. It was at one of these, after the work had been progressing some time, and the weather bitterly inclement, that a large-hearted gentleman proposed to raise funds for the building of a church right in the enemy's stronghold, there being a vacant lot just suited for the purpose. This

occurred on Friday night. The money was raised, and all the carpenters and men gave an herculean lift to the wheel, and the next day—Saturday—at 2 o'clock, our church was regularly dedicated to the service of God, and stood there before us a monument of faith and works, with floor, roof, windows, seats and glowing stove, all complete.

How thankful we felt for this special providence in our favor. Our church overlooked the whole rum traffic in our place. From it the saloon-keepers could hear the voices of prayer and supplication ascending in their behalf, and in its erection they saw a determination of purpose that thoroughly awed them. It was not long till they began signing our pledge, one at a time, till every saloon was emptied, swept and garnished—scrubbed out, I should say, and groceries put in.

DOCUMENT 24.2
Selection from United States Supreme Court *Muller* v. *Oregon* Decision, February 24, 1908.

In the first years of the twentieth century, the U.S. Supreme Court held that legislating men's working hours was unconstitutional because such regulation violated an individual's right to contract. The Court did hold that state regulation of women's hours, however, was a constitutional exercise of the state's police power. In this selection from the Court's 1908 Muller v. Oregon *decision, Justice Brewer explains the judicial rationale for protective legislation. The* Muller *decision paved the way for much women's protective labor legislation in the United States.*

It thus appears that, putting to one side the elective franchise, in the matter of personal and contractual rights they stand on the same plane as the other sex. Their rights in these respects can no more be infringed than the equal rights of their brothers. We held in *Lochner* v. *New York,* 198 U.S. 45, that a law providing that no laborer shall be required or permitted to work in bakeries more than sixty hours in a week or ten hours in a day was not as to men a legitimate exercise of the police power of the State, but an unreasonable, unnecessary, and arbitrary interference with the right and liberty of the individual to contract in relation to his labor, and as such was in conflict with, and void under, the Federal Constitution. That decision is invoked by plaintiff in error as decisive of the question before us. But this assumes that the difference between the sexes does not justify a different rule respecting a restriction of the hours of labor. . . .

It is undoubtedly true, as more than once declared by this court, that the general right to contract in relation to one's business is part of the liberty of the individual, protected by the Fourteenth Amendment to the Federal Constitution; yet it is equally well settled that this liberty is not absolute and extending to all contracts, and that a State may, without conflicting with the provisions of the Fourteenth Amendment, restrict in many respects the individual's power of contract. Without stopping to discuss at length the extent to which a State may act in this respect, we refer to the following cases in which the question has been considered: *Allgeyer* v. *Louisiana,* 165 U.S. 578; *Holden* v. *Hardy,* 169 U.S. 366; *Muller* v. *Oregon,* 208 US 412; *Lochner* v. *New York, supra.*

That woman's physical structure and the performance of maternal functions place her at a disadvantage in the struggle for subsistence is obvious. This is especially true when the burdens of motherhood are upon her. Even when they are not, by abundant testimony of the medical fraternity continuance for a long time on her feet at work, repeating this from day to day, tends to injurious effects upon the body, and as healthy mothers are essential to vigorous offspring, the physical well-being of woman becomes an object of public interest and care

in order to preserve the strength and vigor of the race.

Still again, history discloses the fact that woman has always been dependent upon man. He established his control at the outset by superior physical strength, and this control in various forms, with diminishing intensity, has continued to the present. As minors, though not to the same extent, she has been looked upon in the courts as needing especial care that her rights may be preserved. Education was long denied her, and while now the doors of the school-room are opened and her opportunities for acquiring knowledge are great, yet even with that and the consequent increase of capacity for business affairs it is still true that in the struggle for subsistence she is not an equal competitor with her brother. Though limitations upon personal and contractual rights may be removed by legislation, there is that in her disposition and habits of life which will operate against a full assertion of those rights. She will still be where some legislation to protect her seems necessary to secure a real equality of right. Doubtless there are individual exceptions, and there are many respects in which she has an advantage over him; but looking at it from the viewpoint of the effort to maintain an independent position in life, she is not upon an equality. Differentiated by these matters from the other sex, she is properly placed in a class by herself, and legislation designed for her protection may be sustained, even when like legislation is not necessary for men and could not be sustained. It is impossible to close one's eyes to the fact that she still looks to her brother and depends upon him. Even though all restrictions on political, personal, and contractual rights were taken away, and she stood, so far as statutes are concerned, upon an absolutely equal plane with him, it would still be true that she is so constituted that she will rest upon and look to him for protection; that her physical structure and a proper discharge of her maternal functions—having in view not merely her own health, but the well-being of the race—justify legislation to protect her from the greed as well as the passion of man. The limitations which this statute places upon her contractual powers, upon her right to agree with her employer as to the time she shall labor, are not imposed solely for her benefit, but also largely for the benefit of all. Many words cannot make this plainer. The two sexes differ in structure of body, in the functions to be performed by each, in the amount of physical strength, in the capacity for long-continued labor, particularly when done standing, the influence of vigorous health upon the future well-being of the race, the self-reliance which enables one to assert full rights, and in the capacity to maintain the struggle for subsistence. This difference justifies a difference in legislation and upholds that which is designed to compensate for some of the burdens which rest upon her.

We have not referred in this discussion to the denial of the elective franchise in the State of Oregon, for while that may disclose a lack of political equality in all things with her brother, that is not of itself decisive. The reason runs deeper, and rests in the inherent difference between the two sexes, and in the different functions in life which they perform.

DOCUMENT 24.3
Selection from Frances Elizabeth Willard, Home Protection Manual

The Women's Christian Temperance Union, founded in 1874, grew directly out of the women's crusade. By the late 1870s, the women's temperance movement had moved from the strategy of direct action to close

Source: Frances E. Willard, *Home Protection Manual: Containing An Argument for the Temperance Ballot for Woman, and How to Obtain It, As a Means of Home Protection; Also Constitution and Plan of Work for State and Local W.C.T. Unions* (New York: ''The Independent'' Office, 1879).

saloons to legislative action. In this selection from the Home Protection Manual *WCTU president Frances Willard puts forth what was to become the Women's Christian Temperance Union's justification for woman suffrage.*

''Home Protection'' is the general name given to a movement already endorsed by the W.C.T. Unions of eight states, the object of which is to secure for all women above the age of twenty-one years the ballot as one means for the protection of their homes from the devastation caused by the legalized traffic in strong drink.

In Illinois and Massachusetts the ballot on the single question of license is all that has been asked; but Indiana, Iowa, and Minnesota ask for the ballot in general; while Ohio desires it ''on all temperance questions.'' Maine and Rhode Island have both endorsed the Illinois phase of the movement, though the women of Maine (where prohibitory law is in full force) did this rather as a token of sympathy than with a view to active work. Several other states have signified their purpose to take up the new method ere long. It will be seen that, while the reason for seeking this added weapon in women's hands is in each case *that it may be used against the rum power, in defense of Home,* there is much latitude in the methods by which it is sought, as also in the extent to which the idea is carried out and in the progress which different states have made. . . .

. . . Surely, that is a short-sighted view which says: ''It was womanly to plead with saloon-keepers not to sell; but it is unwomanly to plead with law-makers not to legalize the sale and to give us power to prevent it.'' No wonder the Ohio Crusaders, who have spent hours in the stifling atmosphere of the saloons, do not deem it indelicate to enter airy council-rooms and stately legislative halls; and they, like the W.C.T.U. of Illinois, have enlisted for a seven years' campaign, or one of fourteen years, if need be, not expecting immediate success, but going forth, in the crusade spirit of dependence upon God and consecration to his service. . . .

. . . Out on the Illinois prairies we have resolved to expend on voters the work at first bestowed upon saloon-keepers. We have transferred the scene of our crusade from the dramshop to the council-room of the municipal authorities, whence the dram-shop derives its guaranties and safeguards. Nay, more. The bitter argument of defeat led us to trace the tawny, seething, foaming tide of beer and whisky to its source; and there we found it surging forth from the stately capitol of Illinois, with its proud dome and flag of stripes and stars. So we have made that capitol the center of our operations; and last winter, as one among the many branches of our work, we gathered up 175,000 names of Illinois's best men and women (80,000 being the names of voters), who asked the legislature for a law giving women the ballot on the temperance question. In prosecuting our canvass for these names, we sent copies of our "Home Protection Petition" to every minister, editor, and postmaster in the state; also to all leading temperance men and women, and to every society and corporation from which we had anything to hope.

In this way our great state was permeated, and in most of its towns the petition was brought before the people. The religious press was a unit in our favor. The reform clubs of the state, with ribbons blue and red, helped us with their usual heartiness and efficiency. And what shall be thought of the advance in public sentiment, when (as was often done) all the churches join on Sabbath night in a "Union Home Protection Meeting," and ministers of all denominations (Presbyterians included) conduct the opening exercises, after which a woman presents the religious duty of women to seek and men to supply the temperance ballot; and, to crown all, conservative young ladies go up and down the aisles earnestly asking for signatures, and the audience unite in singing

> Stand up, stand up for Jesus,
>   Ye soldiers of the Cross;
> Lift high His royal banner,
>   It must not suffer loss.

Friends, it means something for women of the churches to take this radical position. America has developed no movement more significant for good since the first dawning of the day we celebrate.

DOCUMENT 24.4
Selections from Jane Addams, "Utilization of Women in City Government"

Women reformers and suffragists argued in the early twentieth century that new industrial and urban conditions justified giving women the vote. In her essay, "Utilization of Women in City Government," Jane Addams describes the living conditions of the early twentieth-century city, and justifies women's role in municipal politics.

We are told many times that the industrial city is a new thing upon the face of the earth, and that everywhere its growth has been phenomenal, whether we look at Moscow, Berlin, Paris, New York, or Chicago. With or without the mediaeval foundation, modern cities are merely resultants of the vast crowds of people who have collected at certain points which have become manufacturing and distributing centres.

For all political purposes, however, the industrial origin of the city is entirely ignored, and political life is organized exclusively in relation to its earlier foundations.

As the city itself originated for the common

Source: Jane Addams, *Newer Ideals of Peace* (Chatauqua, N.Y.: The Chatauqua Press, 1907), pp. 180–207.

protection of the people and was built about a suitable centre of defense which formed a citadel, such as the Acropolis at Athens or the Kremlin at Moscow, so we can trace the beginning of the municipal franchise to the time when the problems of municipal government were still largely those of protecting the city against rebellion from within and against invasion from without. A voice in city government, as it was extended from the nobles, who alone bore arms, was naturally given solely to those who were valuable to the military system. . . .

It has been well said that the modern city is a stronghold of industrialism, quite as the feudal city was a stronghold of militarism, but the modern city fears no enemies, and rivals from without and its problems of government are solely internal. Affairs for the most part are going badly in these great new centres in which the quickly congregated population has not yet learned to arrange its affairs satisfactorily, insanitary housing, poisonous sewage, contaminated water, infant mortality, the spread of contagion, adulterated food, impure milk, smoke-laden air, ill-ventilated factories, dangerous occupations, juvenile crime, unwholesome crowding, prostitution, and drunkenness are the enemies which the modern city must face and overcome would it survive. Logically, its electorate should be made up of those who can bear a valiant part in this arduous contest, of those who in the past have at least attempted to care for children, to clean houses, to prepare foods, to isolate the family from moral dangers, of those who have traditionally taken care of that side of life which, as soon as the population is congested, inevitably becomes the subject of municipal consideration and control.

To test the elector's fitness to deal with this situation by his ability to bear arms, is absurd. A city is in many respects a great business corporation, but in other respects it is enlarged housekeeping. If American cities have failed in the first, partly because office holders have carried with them the predatory instinct learned in competitive business, and cannot help ''working a good thing'' when they have an opportunity, may we not say that city housekeeping has failed partly because women, the traditional housekeepers, have not been consulted as to its multiform activities? The men of the city have been carelessly indifferent to much of this civic housekeeping, as they have always been indifferent to the details of the household. They have totally disregarded a candidate's capacity to keep the streets clean, preferring to consider him in relation to the national tariff or to the necessity for increasing the national navy, in a pure spirit of reversion to the traditional type of government which had to do only with enemies and outsiders.

It is difficult to see what military prowess has to do with the multiform duties, which, in a modern city, include the care of parks and libraries, superintendence of markets, sewers, and bridges, the inspection of provisions and boilers, and the proper disposal of garbage. Military prowess has nothing to do with the building department which the city maintains to see to it that the basements be dry, that the bedrooms be large enough to afford the required cubic feet of air, that the plumbing be sanitary, that the gas-pipes do not leak, that the tenement-house court be large enough to afford light and ventilation, and that the stairways be fireproof. The ability to carry arms has nothing to do with the health department maintained by the city, which provides that children be vaccinated, that contagious diseases be isolated and placarded, that the spread of tuberculosis be curbed, and that the water be free from typhoid infection. Certainly the military conception of society is remote from the functions of the school boards, whose concern it is that children be educated, that they be supplied with kindergartens and be given a decent place in which to play. The very multifariousness and complexity of a city government demands the help of minds accustomed to detail and variety of work, to a sense of obligation for the health and welfare of young children, and to a responsibility for the cleanliness and comfort of others.

Because all these things have traditionally been in the hands of women, if they take no part in them now, they are not only missing the education which the natural participation in civic life would bring to them, but they are losing what they have always had. From the beginning of tribal life women have been held responsible for the health of the community, a function which is now represented by the health department; from the days of the cave dwellers, so far as the home was clean and wholesome, it was due to their efforts, which are now represented by the bureau of tenement-house inspection; from the period of the primitive village, the only public sweeping performed was what they undertook in their own dooryards, that which is now represented by the bureau of street cleaning. Most of the departments in a modern city can be traced to women's traditional activity, but in spite of this, so soon as these old affairs were turned over to the care of the city, they slipped from woman's hands, apparently because they then became matters for collective action and implied the use of the franchise. Because the franchise had in the first instance been given to the man who could fight, because in the beginning he alone could vote who could carry a weapon, the franchise was considered an improper thing for a woman to possess.

Is it quite public spirited for women to say, "We will take care of these affairs so long as they stay in our own houses, but if they go outside and concern so many people that they cannot be carried on without the mechanism of the vote, we will drop them. It is true that these activities which women have always had, are not at present being carried on very well by the men in most of the great American cities, but because we do not consider it 'ladylike' to vote shall we ignore their failure''?

Because women consider the government men's affair and something which concerns itself with elections and alarms, they have become so confused in regard to their traditional business in life, the rearing of children, that they hear with complacency a statement made by . . . sanitary reformers, that one-half of the tiny lives which make up the city's death rate each year might be saved by a more thorough application of sanitary science. Because it implies the use of the suffrage, they do not consider it women's business to save these lives. Are we going to lose ourselves in the old circle of convention and add to that sum of wrong-doing which is continually committed in the world because we do not look at things as they really are? Old-fashioned ways which no longer apply to changed conditions are a snare in which the feet of women have always become readily entangled. . . .

Why is it that women do not vote upon the matters which concern them so intimately? Why do they not follow these vital affairs and feel responsible for their proper administration, even though they have become municipalized? What would the result have been could women have regarded the suffrage, not as a right or a privilege, but as a mere piece of governmental machinery without which they could not perform their traditional functions under the changed conditions of city life? Could we view the whole situation as a matter of obligation and of normal development, it would be much simplified. We are at the beginning of a prolonged effort to incorporate a progressive developing life founded upon a response to the needs of all the people, into the requisite legal enactments and civic institutions. To be in any measure successful, this effort will require all the intelligent powers of observation, all the sympathy, all the common sense which may be gained from the whole adult population.

DOCUMENT 24.5
Selection from the National Women's Trade Union League *Handbook*

The National Women's Trade Union League, founded in 1903, was open to both working-class and middle-class women. Members worked to organize women workers into trade unions, lobbied for protective labor legislation, and attempted to educate the public about industrial women's working conditions and wages. The following document is a selection from the National Women's Trade Union League Handbook. *It provides a vivid description of turn-of-the-century working conditions designed to raise the consciousness of middle-class and working-class women alike.*

LAUNDRY WORKERS

Do you know through how many pairs of hands your shirt or shirtwaist must pass, and with how many different twists and turns from the time you take it to the laundry to the time it reaches you again immaculately clean and perfectly laundered? How would you like to iron a shirt a minute? Think of standing at a mangle just above the wash room with the hot steam pouring up through the floor for ten, twelve, fourteen and sometimes seventeen hours a day! Sometimes the floors are made of cement and then it seems as though one were standing on hot coals, and the workers are dripping with perspiration. In some of the non-union factories the girls work for three dollars and three-fifty a week, and the work is so hard and so exhausting that you seldom find a woman who has been able to work long at the trade. Perhaps

Source: National Women's Trade Union League, *Convention Handbook*. Chicago: Allied Printers, 1909.

you have complained about the chemicals used in the washing of your clothes, which cause them to wear out quickly, but what do you suppose is the effect of these chemicals upon the workers? They are standing ten, twelve, fourteen and seventeen hours a day in intense heat, breathing air laden with particles of soda, ammonia and other chemicals! Is it any wonder that these workers become physical wrecks in a very short time, just because you and I never count the cost? The Laundry Workers' Union is the one way out of these difficulties. In one city it has reduced the hours of work from eighteen and twelve to nine hours, and has increased the wages fifty percent, and in another city the union has reduced the hours of work from eighteen and twelve to nine, and increased the wages from $15.00 a month to $9.00 a week, minimum wage, and $15.00 a week average wage.

THE SEWING TRADES

Have you ever seen a needle making 2,200 stitches a minute? And would you like to be sewing a shirt or a petticoat at a machine with a needle stitching 2,200 times a minute? Supposing a thread breaks, or a point of the needle breaks, and you do not discover it in time— your shirt or your petticoat is ruined. And rather than have that happen you watch that needle and that thread and you never lift your eyes from your work. And if you should be sewing in a non-union factory you will be sewing and watching the needle for ten, twelve, fourteen hours, and your eyes will ache with the strain and your back will ache. But we are so proud of our machine that we think and think how we may improve it. And one day we discover that we can make our machine carry two needles and even ten needles at the same time, and we can make it run still faster, so that each needle will make 4,400 stitches a minute. And now, if you are sewing tucks in a waist or petticoat, you are watching ten needles run at 4,400 stitches a minute—watching to see if a thread breaks, or the point of any one of the ten needles snaps. And they dance up and down like flashes of steel or lightning, and your eyes smart with the strain. But we are improving machinery—not eyes! And sometimes you feel as if the machine were running away from you, and your effort to control it makes your whole body ache. Let us go on supposing that you are running this new and wonderful machine. Have your wages increased with the stitches per minute? You are now producing from twice to twenty times as much as with the old machine; you are putting into your sewing many times greater eye ache and nerve strain. Are your wages keeping pace? Why, no! Just the same average wage of $5.00 to $6.00 a week—in a non-union factory. Isn't it strange? Is it right?

But not all sewing is done by these racing machines; some of it can be done by hand, some by the old foot-power machine. And because you and I with all other women know how to use our needles the employer finds us easily. And, if we are mothers he knows he can find us in our homes, as he found our neighbor across the way; and then we are a convenience; for by permitting the employer to use our home for his workshop we save him the cost of rent, the cost of fuel, the cost of light. You and I want our home for the husband and the children, but our neighbor's husband has been ill long; she is pressed hard by poverty and her need is great; she turns her home into her employer's workshop, and he calls her "a home finisher." Under her deft fingers men's coats, pants, vests become finished. If she works till midnight and coaxes her little boy to sew on buttons she can "finish" a dozen pants a day, and for this work, and for the rent and light and fuel saved her employer, she receives 30 cents a day—and another "sweat shop" has been established. . . .

But, in union there is strength! If you stand with your sisters and your brothers you can control the conditions that are bad; you can create conditions that are good. Join the union of your trade. Join the International Ladies' Garment Workers. Join the United Garment Workers of America. The Union has abolished child labor wherever it controls the trade, has established the eight-hour day, and in some cities the forty-four hour week; sanitary conditions are insisted upon; where over-time is demanded time and a half is paid in wages, while the general wage has been increased over fifty percent. Demand the Union Label.

DOCUMENT 24.6
"Feminist—New Style"

Young women in the 1920s felt little sense of sisterhood with the feminists of their mothers' generation. Self-fulfillment and individual liberation eclipsed the social concerns that female activists in the progressive era had focused upon. In this essay, Dorothy Bromley outlines the "new-style" feminist of the 1920s, and analyses the differences she discerns between the feminism of the early twentieth century and the goals of young women in the twenties.

It is not high time that we laid the ghost of the so-called feminist?

"Feminism" has become a term of opprobrium to the modern young woman. For the word suggests either the old school of fighting feminists who wore flat heels and had very little feminine charm, or the current species who antagonize men with their constant clamor about maiden names, equal rights, woman's place in the world, and many another cause

Source: Dorothy Dunbar Bromley, "Feminist—New Style," *Harper's Magazine* 155 (October 1927); pp. 552–560.

. . . ad infinitum. Indeed, if a blundering male assumes that a young woman is a feminist simply because she happens to have a job or a profession of her own, she will be highly—and quite justifiably insulted for the word evokes the antithesis of what she flatters herself to be. Yet she and her kind can hardly be dubbed "old-fashioned" women. What *are* they, then?

The pioneer feminists were hard-hitting individuals, and the modern young woman admires them for their courage—even while she judges them for the zealotry and their inartistic methods. Furthermore, she pays all honor to them, for they fought her battle. But *she* does not want to wear their mantle (indeed, she thinks they should have been buried in it), and she has to smile at those women who wear it today—with the battle-cry still on their lips. The worst of the fight is over, yet this second generation of feminists are still throwing hand grenades. They bear a grudge against men, either secretly or openly; they make an issue of little things as well as big; they exploit their sex for the sake of publicity; they rant about equality when they might better prove their ability. Yet it is these women—the ones who do more talking than acting—on whom the average man focuses his microscope when he sits down to dissect the "new woman." For like his less educated brethren, he labors under the delusion that there are only two types of women, the creature of instinct who is content to be a "home-maker" and the "sterile intellectual" who cares solely about "expressing herself"—home and children be damned.

But what of the constantly increasing group of young women in their twenties and thirties who are the truly modern ones, those who admit that a full life calls for marriage and children as well as a career? These women if they launch upon marriage are keen to make a success of it and an art of child-rearing. But *at the same time* they are moved by an inescapable inner compulsion to be individuals in their own right.

And in this era of simplified housekeeping they see their opportunity, for it is obvious that a woman who plans intelligently can salvage some time for her own pursuits. Furthermore, they are convinced that they will be better wives and mothers for the breadth they gain from functioning outside the home. In short, they are highly conscious creatures who have obliged to plumb their own resources to the very depths, despite the fact that they are under no delusions as to the present inferior status of their sex in most fields of endeavor.

Numbers of these honest, spirited young women have made themselves heard in article and story. But since men must have things pointed out to them in black and white, we beg leave to enunciate the tenets of the modern woman's credo. Let us call her "Feminist—New Style. . . ."

Even though Feminist—New Style may not see her own course so clearly marked out before her, and even if she should happen to have an income, she will make a determined effort to fit her abilities to some kind of work. For she has observed that it is only the rare American of either sex who can resist the mentally demoralizing effect of idleness. She has seen too many women who have let what minds they have go to seed, so that by the time they are forty or forty-five they are profoundly uninteresting to their husbands, their children, and themselves. Occasionally one of these women will wake up when it is too late and grope desperately for any sort of a "job" to fill her time now that her children need her no longer. Her next-door neighbor who has gone in for philanthropies may not be quite so lonely, but the pity is that she has seldom had to sharpen her mind against the wits of people who think any straighter than she does.

Only less pathetic is the younger married woman who came out of college with an active mind excellently trained, but who in five or ten years' time has allowed that mind to grow shallow for lack of cultivation and fresh planting. This type of woman is avid for excitement, even if it depends on nothing more than the innocuous attentions of a man considerably younger than herself. So she goes round and round the vicious circle, grasping for outside stimuli, never once realizing that her satisfaction with life depends upon her inner resources and the active living they make possible.

Yet if a woman can add to her own resources and thereby live a rich and full life without the stimulus of a job she is to be congratulated and admired as a really civilized person. However, if she remains financially dependent upon her husband she may be mortgaging her own future happiness and liberty of action; for as one frank man admitted the other day, there is hardly a man who will never take advantage of his wife's economic dependence upon him or who will never assume that it gives him special prerogatives.

In brief, Feminist—New Style reasons that if she is economically independent, and if she has, to boot, a vital interest in some work of her own she will have given as few hostages to Fate as it is humanly possible to give. Love may die, and children may grow up, but one's work goes on forever.

She will not, however, live for her job alone, for she considers that a woman who talks and thinks only shop has just as narrow a horizon as the housewife who talks and thinks only husband and children—perhaps more so, for the latter may have a deeper understanding of human nature. She will therefore refuse to give up all of her personal interests, year in and year out, for the sake of her work. In this respect she no doubt will fall short of the masculine ideal of commercial success, for the simple reason that she has never felt the economic compulsion which drives men on to build up fortunes for the sake of their growing families.

Yet she is not one of the many women who look upon their jobs as tolerable meal-tickets or as interesting pastimes to be dropped whenever they may wish. On the contrary, she takes

great pride in becoming a vital factor in whatever enterprise she has chosen, and she therefore expects to work long hours when the occasion demands.

But rather than make the mistake that some women do of domesticating their jobs, i.e., burying all of their affections and interests in them, or the mistake that many men make of milking their youth dry for the sake of building up a fortune to be spent in a fatigued middle-age, she will proceed on the principle that a person of intelligence and energy can attain a fair amount of success—perhaps even a high degree of success—by the very virtue of living a well-balanced life, as well as by working with concentration.

Nor has she become hostile to the other sex in the course of her struggle to orient herself. On the contrary, she frankly likes men and is grateful to more than a few for the encouragement and help they have given her.

In the business and professional worlds, for instance, Feminist—New Style has observed that more and more men are coming to accord women as much responsibility as they show themselves able to carry. She and her generation have never found it necessary to bludgeon their way, and she is inclined to think that certain of the pioneers would have got farther if they had relied on their ability rather than on their militant methods. To tell the truth, she enjoys working with men, more than with women, for their methods are more direct and their view larger, and she finds that she can deal with them on a basis of frank comradeship.

When she meets men socially she is not inclined to air her knowledge and argue about women's right to a place in the sun. On the contrary, she either talks with a man because he has ideas that interest her or because she finds it amusing to flirt with him—and she will naturally find it doubly amusing if the flirtation involves the swift interplay of wits. She will not waste many engagements on a dull-witted man, although it must be admitted that she finds fewer men with stagnant minds than she does women.

When all is said and done, most of the men of her world are such a decent likable lot that she is hard put to it to understand the sex antagonism which actuates certain "advanced" women who secretly look upon their husbands—and all men—as their natural enemies from whom they must wrest every privilege and advantage possible. Such tactics are a futile waste of energy; now that men have admitted that women can be valuable partners not only in the home, but also in business and civic life, the best thing for women to do is to prove their value.

Feminist—New Style professes no loyalty to women *en masse,* although she staunchly believes in individual women. Surveying her sex as a whole, she finds their actions petty, their range of interests narrow, their talk trivial and repetitious. As for those who set themselves up as leaders of the sex, they are either strident creatures of so little ability and balance that they have won no chance to "express themselves" (to use their own hackneyed phrase) in a man-made world; or they are brilliant, restless individuals who too often battle for women's rights for the sake of personal glory. . . .

Empty slogans seem to Feminist—New Style just as bad taste as masculine dress and manners. They serve only to prolong the war between the sexes and to prevent women from learning to think straight. Take these, for instance, "Keep your maiden name." "Come out of the kitchen." "Never darn a sock." After all, what's in a name or in a sock? Madame Curie managed to become one of the world's geniuses even though she suffered the terrible handicap of bearing her husband's name, and it is altogether likely that she darned a sock or two of Monsieur Curie's when there was no servant at hand to do it.

"Keep your maiden name," the slogan which the members of the Lucy Stone League

cry from the housetops so lustily, would seem the most inane of all. Will someone kindly tell us why women don't prove their individuality—and their independence of their husbands—by some sort of real achievement? And would it not be more consistent for them to require that every member not only keep her maiden name but *that she support herself*?

But perhaps they aim not to be consistent—only to get publicity. For instance, one of their members recently married and registered with her husband at a highly respectable New York hotel as Miss Jones and Mr. Smith. Naturally the manager objected, with the result that reporters got wind of the incident and wrote it up, thus giving the clever couple columns of free publicity.

The story also is told that a famous British woman lawyer visiting these shores was feted one night by the Lucy Stone League and the New York Women Lawyers' Association. The Lucy Stoners made their speeches on the same old subject of nomenclature, and when one was asked how she managed with the tradespeople, she replied haughtily, "Oh, I am Mrs. to my butcher, but to *no* one else!" When the visitor expressed a desire to hear from the women lawyers on the subject, it developed that most of those who were married bore their husbands' names and did not consider the subject worthy of argument. Naturally, if a woman has made a name for herself in a business or a profession before her marriage—as was the case with the visitor—it would seem expedient for her to keep that name, or if she is not sure how long she is going to remain married. But when all is said and done, Feminist—New Style considers that it is hardly a matter to go to meeting about.

As for sock-darning, our modern young woman dislikes to darn a man's socks as much as she dislikes to darn her own. If possible she will have a servant do both. But if that is impractical, and if her husband is properly appreciative, she will do the darning herself, and will expect him to relieve her of a few tasks in return.

"Come out of the kitchen" is a fair enough slogan if a woman makes sure that she has left someone capable in her stead. Feminist—New Style likes to know how to cook so that she can direct a servant intelligently and economically; and furthermore she occasionally enjoys preparing a meal herself because it is fun to use her own skill. Unlike the old order of feminists, she is not afraid that if she understands the culinary arts she will get stuck in the kitchen for the rest of her life, for she knows that she can earn more than enough to pay a cook's wages. . . .

Finally, Feminist—New Style proclaims that men and children shall no longer circumscribe her world, although they may constitute a large part of it. She is intensely self-conscious whereas the feminists were intensely sex-conscious. Aware of possessing a mind, she takes a keen pleasure in using that mind for some definite purpose; and also in learning to think clearly and cogently against a background of historical and scientific knowledge. She aspires to understand the meaning of the twentieth century as she sees it expressed in the skyscrapers, the rapid pace of city life, the expressionistic drama, the abstract conceptions of art, the new music, the Joycian novel. She is acutely conscious that she is being carried along in the current of these sweeping forces, that she and her sex are in the vanguard of change. She knows that it is her American, her twentieth-century birthright to emerge from a creature of instinct into a full-fledged individual who is capable of molding her own life. And in this respect she holds that she is becoming man's equal.

chapter

War, Revolution, and Wilsonian Diplomacy

N. Gordon Levin, Jr.
Amherst College

Broadly speaking, two approaches toward the great war in Europe interacted within the Wilson administration from the outbreak of the conflict in August 1914 to the moment of America's entry in April 1917. One approach emphasized neutrality, uniqueness and isolation from the horrors of war, and the evils of Old World diplomacy. This neutral orientation was characterized by attempts to use American influence on behalf of a compromise peace and the creation of a new liberal world order based on international law. The other approach eschewed neutrality, and directly supported the Allied side. It firmly opposed German submarine warfare and called for mediation between the warring parties in a manner acceptable to Great Britain. Yet like its neutral opposite, the pro-Allied orientation included a vision of a new international liberal order to emerge from the wreckage of war, one, incidentally, which made no accommodation to the Russian Bolsheviks who would transform world politics through revolutionary socialism.

Some basic questions are posed by a consideration of Woodrow Wilson's foreign policy. Was the president predominantly a realist or an idealist in his conduct of diplomacy? Or did he fuse realism and idealism in a missionary vision of a liberal world order which also served the political and economic interests of the American nation-state? More specifically, did America enter World War I for reasons of idealism or of power politics?

The enormity of the European conflict reinforced traditional isolationist attitudes in the United States. Editors and Congressmen emphasized America's geographic and moral isolation from Old World power politics. American neutrality was taken to be the diplomatic expression of the difference between a liberal and peaceful United States and a Europe cursed by reaction and war. America, it followed, should keep its distance from a conflict in which it had no conceivable moral or strategic interest.

Within the Wilson administration, this neutralist perspective on the war was embodied most fully in the views of Secretary of State William Jennings Bryan. The Commoner cherished a sense of America's unique moral virtue and, while he was not averse to offering the nation's liberal exceptionalism as a model for the Old World to follow, he opposed any suggestion of involvement with the war beyond the most neutral of mediation efforts. Bryan's desire to keep the United States at peace and free from European power politics led to his resignation in the spring of 1915 as an act of protest against President Wilson's hard line on the issue of the sinking of the *Lusitania* in particular and the German submarine question in general.

President Wilson was not immune to this neutralist and isolationist persuasion in the 1914–17 period. Time and again his speeches conveyed a sense that the war was essentially a European phenomenon which did not concern the United States. Relatedly, the president projected a neutralist vision of the United States as best serving the cause of world peace by her own peaceful example and by the use of her moral and economic power. The United States would assist the warring nations in achieving a peace without victory for either side as the foundation for a new American-inspired system of international law and open trade supported by an association of nations. In short, part of President Wilson's response to the war in Europe involved a fusion of neutralism with a messianic search for a liberal order for the postwar world. Yet, this vision of global reform could also come to be linked with a more pro-Allied approach to the war.

In Wilson's case such a transition meant moving from a neutralist, liberal America confronting a war-ridden and reactionary Europe to a pro-Allied, liberal America joining with progressive and democratic European Allies to confront a uniquely reactionary and militaristic Imperial Germany. On the ideological level, a redefinition of the war as a conflict between German autocracy and Allied democracy was furthered by a growing Anglo-American diplomatic and cultural rapprochement. Strong Anglophile sentiments were found especially among cosmopolitan Anglo-Saxon Protestant elites. Led by Theodore Roosevelt and Massachusetts Senator Henry Cabot Lodge, pro-Allied Republicans maintained political pressure on the Wilson administration after 1914, although to some extent this pressure was balanced by the anti-Allied or neutralist views

of Irish and German Americans and radical agrarian neutralists. However, whatever the strength of his neutralist predilections, President Wilson partly shared general American suspicion of Germany and support for England and France. Two of his closest advisers, Colonel Edward M. House and Secretary of State Robert Lansing strongly favored the Allied cause and perceived German autocracy as a moral and strategic threat to the United States and its hopes for a furture liberal world order. Still, tradition and ideology might not have been enough to push Wilson toward the pro-Allied persuasion had important diplomatic factors not added their weight to the balance.

America's war trade with the Allies grew to immense proportions between 1914 and 1917, as the British control of the sea complemented the availability of food, arms, and credits in the United States. The desire of the Wilson administration to bring about a return to economic prosperity in America led it to make decisions favorable to the Allies regardless of their implications for America's neutral status. Economic motives fused with broader political and cultural factors to bring the administraion to acquiesce de facto to British methods of enforcing their maritime system during the early years of the war. But on the contrary, the president took an unyielding stance toward German submarine warfare. The submarine was seen as a direct challenge to America's neutral trading rights as well as human rights generally.

Thus, while maritime conflicts with the British were filed away for future settlement, the United States moved from crisis to crisis with the Germans over the submarine issue until early 1917, when those elements that favored unlimited submarine warfare regardless of American reaction won out in Germany. Wilson had tended to ignore the extent to which the United States provoked Germany by giving de facto support to the Allied cause. And he had made a clear moral distinction between

British and German naval war methods. Consequently, the president's ethical rejection of the submarine went a long way toward bringing him to perceive of Imperial Germany as uniquely reactionary and militaristic and the war as a contest between the forces of European autocracy and democracy.

The efforts of Wilson and Colonel House to mediate the European war in the 1915–16 period also evolved in an implicitly pro-Allied context. By the second year of the war the Kaiser's armies had advanced well into Allied territory on both the eastern and western fronts and Germany possessed a clear advantage on the war map. Under such circumstances Wilson's efforts to achieve a mediated peace without victory based on the status quo antebellum involved the implicit notion of uncompensated German troop withdrawals on both fronts and the end of German annexationist hopes. Moreover, Colonel House's attempts at mediation in the winter of 1915–16 involved a commitment of American support for ambiguous British war aims of an annexationist nature.

The pro-Allied nature of much Wilsonian diplomacy did not go unchallenged in the United States. Conservative anti-German Republicans were balanced by southern and midwestern agrarian progressives who demanded that America avoid participation in what they saw as an imperialist war on both sides. William Jennings Bryan, Senator Robert La Follette, Senator George Norris, and others believed the United States was being dragged into war on behalf of war traders and Anglophile banking elites. They sought to limit the right of travel on armed Allied merchantmen and to balance diplomatic assaults on the German submarine policy with stronger protests against British naval practices. This agrarian radical position later expressed itself in postwar opposition to Wilson's League of Nations.

Wilson rejected criticism of his submarine diplomacy, defended the need for military preparedness, and argued that acquiescence on

the submarine question would cost the United States heavily in moral prestige as well as strike a blow at neutral commercial rights and international law. The president was prepared, however, to attempt a more neutral stance on the mediation issue in a last desperate effort to achieve peace before the United States was finally forced to go to war over the submarine. By late 1916 he had checked the pro-Allied direction of House's attempts at mediation, campaigned successfully for reelection as a peace-oriented progressive, and launched a public effort to mediate the conflict on the basis of a peace without victory. The culmination of this last Wilsonian peace endeavor, which was taken against the opposition of House and Lansing, was the famous "Peace without Victory" address of January 22, 1917. Here Wilson adopted a neutralist perspective on the war and offered U.S. participation in a League of Nations to stabilize a new liberal world order erected on the foundation of a true compromise peace.

Wilson's last attempt at a really neutral settlement was rejected by both sides, which continued to prefer victory to peace. The German government not only declined mediation on Wilson's terms but also decided to launch unlimited submarine warfare. Soon afterward German diplomatic intrigues with Mexico against the United States came to light in the Zimmerman telegram. In early 1917, then, these German policies, combined with the pro-Allied urgings of House and Lansing and the triumph in March of liberal and pro-Allied Russian revolutionaries, led a tortured Wilson finally to abandon his neutralism. By April the president had made his decision for war. His message to Congress blamed Imperial Germany specifically and not Europe in general for the war. Wilson retained his vision of an American-inspired postwar liberal world order, but that vision was no longer attainable through a peace without victory but rather through the triumph of the Allied "democracies" whose ranks suddenly included Russia. For no longer did a tsarist autocracy serve as a political embarrassment in the struggle against reactionary German imperialism.

During the spring and summer of 1917 the United States developed its economic and military capacities and, at the same time, the president's ideological commitment to the defeat of German imperialism deepened. In August, the administration rejected a Vatican appeal for a compromise peace, with Wilson arguing that a secure peace could be established only with a Germany democratized from within and controlled militarily from without. Yet, while maintaining a firm stance against Germany in the early months of America's participation in the war, the president also had to consider the possible threat of Allied imperialism to his projected liberal world order. He discovered that Allied postwar plans were embodied in a series of secret treaties. These treaties envisioned the dismemberment of the Austro-Hungarian Empire, the partition of the Ottoman Empire, and the economic and political isolation of a territorially diminished Germany. Such plans, if realized, could undermine Wilsonian hopes of a war to end war. Wilson was in a dilemma, for how could the United States oppose these secret treaties openly without fatally upsetting Allied unity against a powerful foe whose own war aims were no less imperialistic? The president's natural inclination was to play down the war aims issue, carry through to victory, and rely upon the moral and economic power of the United States to moderate Allied imperialism and reform world politics at the resultant peace conference. But by late 1917 and early 1918, political and diplomatic realities impinged and prevented him from postponing the question of war aims until victory.

One major problem was the decline in morale in the Allied countries due to military reversals and the protracted nature of the brutal conflict. Liberal and radical forces in all these nations, but most especially in Russia, were more and more critical of Entente war aims and called for a compromise peace without annexations or indemnities.

One should read the president's Fourteen Points speech of January 8, 1918, in this general context. Indeed, the Fourteen Points were a skillful political platform. Liberals and socialists in Allied countries could support those points that projected a new postwar liberal world order characterized by open diplomacy, freedom of the seas, respect for international law, and global cooperation in a League of Nations. On the other hand, conservatives could draw solace from those of the Fourteen Points that kept the door open to political and territorial changes at the expense of Gemany, Turkey, and Austria-Hungary. In spite of or perhaps because of their very ambiguity, the Fourteen Points helped to maintain Allied support for the conflict throughout the final difficult year of 1918. In Germany, however, even the moderates rejected them as a prescription for German defeat. Eventually in late 1918 German liberals and socialists would turn to them out of fear of military collapse. And finally, regardless of their success in England, France, and Italy, the Wilsonian war aims appeal met a setback in Russia where the Bolshevik Revolution of November 1917 destroyed the power of Russian liberal-nationalism and took Russia out of both the war and the Entente alliance.

Throughout the summer and early autumn of 1917, the Wilson administration, along with its European Allies, sought to buttress the pro-war Russian provisional government against its radical opponents. After the Bolshevik triumph, many in Washington continued to hope that a declaration of liberalized Allied war aims might move the Bolsheviks away from their revolutionary absolutism toward approving a liberal war for liberal peace. For this reason, the Fourteen Points address was most specifically aimed at the Bolshevik leaders then engaged in separate peace talks with Germany at Brest-Litovsk.

The Fourteen Points did not move Lenin. Having failed to end the war through a universal revolutionary peace, he preferred to gain a breathing space for internal Bolshevik consolidation by means of a separate peace with Germany. Lenin hoped that Germany's imperialistic gains made at Russian expense at Brest-Litovsk would ultimately be wiped out by revolutionary socialist triumphs throughout Europe. Furthermore, not only did Lenin upset Wilson's diplomatic hopes by signing a separate peace, but the Bolshevik dispersal of the Constituent Assembly early in 1918 dashed any lingering hopes for a return to liberal nationalist control in Russian politics. These developments in Russia reinforced the increased influence of anti-Bolshevik elements within the Wilson administration. The president moved steadily during 1918 to accept Secretary of State Lansing's view that any appeasement of Russian bolshevism or Allied radicalism would hurt the war effort and redound to the interests of German imperialism. By the late winter and early spring of 1918, then, the Wilson administration was defending the position of liberal war against the interrelated challenges of revolutionary socialism on the left and German power on the right. In Europe this policy was expressed by an expanding American combat role on the western front; in Russia it led eventually to intervention in Siberia.

During the autumn of 1918 Germany collapsed militarily and politically and, as the Paris Peace Conference approached, President Wilson set his sights on combining peacemaking with the construction of a postwar liberal international order. Wilson envisaged the moral, political, and economic preeminence of the United States. But Allied conservatives, politically ascendant in Britain, France, and Italy posed a threat to his postwar design in that they intended to use the peace conference to reaffirm the terms of the secret treaties. On the left, the president was challenged in the defeated countries by revolutionary socialist elements which sought to activate the potential for revolution latent in sociopolitical dislocation and national humiliation. Consequently, when the Paris Peace Conference opened in early 1919, Wilson faced a Europe where liberals and moderate socialists were on the defensive, whereas radicals and rightists alike were projecting postwar programs hostile to Wilson's new world order.

During the peace conference American policy aimed at containing bolshevism without simultaneously encouraging either Allied militarism or political reaction. In Eastern Europe Wilson and his advisers favored creation of liberal-nationalist successor states to the Dual Monarchy. They were concerned in that area, with the mutually reinforcing challenges posed by French-supported militarism among the victors and by revolutionary socialism among the defeated. The American answer stressed free trade, food relief, and diplomatic pressures designed to maintain peace in the region and to oust the Hungarian Bolshevik regime of Béla Kun in the summer of 1919.

With regard to Russia, the Wilson administration pursued a limited anti-Bolshevik policy during 1919. At Paris, the president opposed plans for massive Allied intervention in Russia and sought unsuccessfully to negotiate the Bolsheviks out of power by means of an all-Russian peace conference. Wilson naively intended any conference with the Bolsheviks to involve their acceptance of the status of one of several political parties in a democratic and pluralistic Russia. Despite the hopes of Lenin and the urgings of such liberals as William C. Bullitt, Wilson never planned to recognize a Bolshevik regime.

When the Paris Peace Conference opened, there was great concern that Germany might go Bolshevik. There was likewise worry among American delegates lest Allied extremism exacerbate the danger of revolution in Germany. The German settlement had to be moderate enough to buttress those German social democrats and liberals who sought Wilson's support against extreme Allied demands in return for combating German Bolshevism. Toward this end, the Americans tried to get food relief into Germany, to lessen the severity of the Allied blockage, and to arrange a more rational reparations settlement.

Yet this American reintegrationist tendency toward Germany was counterbalanced by the president's desire to punish and control the defeated Germans. In other words, Wilson was more moderate toward Germany than Clemenceau and Lloyd George, but his greater moderation was a matter of degree. It was never enough to please those German political elements that had hoped for his support. Indeed, on the issues surrounding the Polish and Czechoslovakian borders with Germany, the president took an even more anti-German position than Lloyd George. While fearing a successful Communist revolution in Germany, the president was also concerned lest conservatives there would retain excessive influence after the Kaiser's fall. Wilson, then, was not entirely averse to controlling Germany from the outside, since he did not completely trust the Germans within.

Wilson's uneasiness united with his fear of revolution in Germany to inhibit him from openly confronting Allied extremism. Anxious to retain Allied unity, the president sought to obtain concessions from the French on the Rhineland and other issues in return for American security guarantees. In this manner, the League of Nations that emerged from Paris was as much a power-political alliance of the victors as it was the nucleus for a new liberal world order. In other words, the League of Nations contained within itself the basic Wilsonian contradiction at Paris between a reintegrationist and a punitive policy toward Germany.

In a broader sense still, the League's colonial mandate system involved an uneasy compromise between a pragmatic Wilsonian acquiescence in the division of the colonial spoils and an idealistic American attempt to reform the political and economic relations between ad-

vanced and backward nations. The president's grudging acceptance of Japanese control of the Chinese province of Shantung, after the Japanese threatened to boycott the League of Nations, reflected this broader Wilsonian tendency to compromise temporarily with Allied imperialism in the hope of eventually moderating and reforming it through the League of Nations.

After his return to the United States in mid-1919, the president had to defend the League concept against opposition from both left and right. On one level, Wilson presented the League as the potential institutional basis for a transformation of world politics. Nations would be pledged to the mutual defense of each other's independence and territorial integrity, even in cases when their own particular interests were not immediately involved in a case of aggression. Yet always fused inextricably with Wilson's missionary idealism was a realistic sense of America's national interests.

The president wished to impress the American people regarding the connection between a League-supported liberal world order and the concrete interests of an expansive American capitalism anxious to move goods and credits into a stable international market. Also, he argued that the Covenant and Article X would provide the necessary deterrent to any possible German efforts to undo the Versailles Treaty. He was especially anxious to protect the new states of eastern Europe from German pressure. Finally, Wilson and League defenders in the Senate spoke of the containment of Bolshevism in the context of the expected achievement of international stability.

Above all, the president as realist stressed the necessity for an American commitment through the League to a permanent role in the maintenance of international peace. Germany was to be controlled, liberalized, and eventually reintegrated into the Western political economy. The Allies and the new states were to join in maintaining world order. Bolshevism was to be spatially contained in European Russia, while liberal reformism elsewhere would, in time, moderate Lenin's regime and draw men everywhere away from revolutionary socialism. Problems left in the treaty, such as Shantung and reparations, were to be remedied over time through the League and its related committees. And all this was to be possible because the United States would fulfill its missionary liberal destiny by remaining committed to securing world peace and stability.

In the Senate, Wilson's vision was criticized by such progressive isolationists as Senators Borah, Johnson, Norris, and La Follette. These men repeatedly attacked the League as a defensive alliance of the major Allied powers designed to preserve by force the imperialistic settlements of the Paris Peace Conference. Thus, while the president was often accused by Senate conservatives of an excess of idealism, he was constantly criticized by the Senate's progressive isolationists as a fellow traveler of Allied imperialism. The progressive isolationists called for America's extrication from a hopelessly flawed world.

In the final analysis, however, the attack by Senate conservatives led by Senator Henry Cabot Lodge, who had an intense personal animosity for Wilson, was even more crucial than the criticism by Senate progressives in the defeat of the Versailles Treaty. Lodge was no isolationist, and ironically he shared with Wilson a number of specific goals in postwar international affairs. Both Lodge and Wilson were concerned with containing Germany within the borders of the treaty framework. And Lodge favored the Anglo-American Treaty of Guarantee for France against future German aggression, which the president had negotiated at Paris. Like Wilson but unlike the progressive isolationists, Lodge hoped to see the expansion of Bolshevism actively checked in postwar Europe. Given such common goals, how can we understand the great distance between Wilson and Lodge over the League?

Beyond personal factors, the key point

would appear to be that Lodge had a greater faith than Wilson in the self-equilibrating potential of a world run along traditional lines by the victorious Allied powers. Wilson feared a world collapse into the chaos of war and revolution if the United States were not involved in future major world political issues. On the other hand, Lodge was confident that Germany could be controlled and Bolshevism successfully contained if Wilson would stop meddling and simply permit the world to be governed on the basis of a spheres-of-influence consortium by the Entente victors. Lodge disapproved of Wilson's efforts to moderate Allied imperialism at Paris in return for American security guarantees through the League. Moreover, in exchange for a largely free hand in Eurasia, Lodge expected that the European Allies and Japan would continue to respect the Monroe Doctrine as an instrument of American security. In short, Lodge looked forward to the United States resuming its growing but still limited role in world politics as one among several peaceful and satisfied imperial powers.

Wilson clearly contemplated a far larger role for the United States in world politics than did Lodge who, along with Theodore Roosevelt, Elihu Root, and former Secretary of State Philander C. Knox, had possessed rather a monopoly on the "large policy" prior to 1917. The president was advocating a real and steady American involvement in world affairs: in mandates, reparations, and territorial guarantees. But, paradoxically, at the very moment that Wilson sought permanently to involve the United States as never before beyond the Western Hemisphere, he argued that the nation was entering world politics not simply to participate but also to transform it through the League.

During the entire League debate the left isolationists were largely beyond Wilson's reach. Wilson could have brought the United States into the League, however, by uniting his supporters with Lodge's followers to accept the League with reservations. In one way or another the president was urged to compromise by Lansing, Taft, Hoover, House, and many others who had come to share much if not all of his vision of America's postwar world role. Reflecting upon the course of world events after 1920, it might have been far better had the president been willing to compromise on the issue of reservations. In his stubbornness over detail Wilson played into the hands of inveterate foes of the League and denied America the possibility of a partial realization of his grander vision.

In conclusion, what can we say about the Wilsonian heritage in American diplomacy? Did Wilsonian values live on in later periods of American history, in the efforts of Henry Stimson, Cordell Hull, Franklin Roosevelt, Harry Truman, and others, to fashion a liberal world order around the principle of collective security? Did Wilsonian antibolshevism preview America's cold war stance? Or, can we say that the superpower rivalry between Russia and the United States which has characterized the cold war world reality since 1945 involves a much stronger power-political and strategic component than Wilson's more ideological rivalry with a weak Soviet Union in the period of World War I?

SUGGESTED READINGS

Buehrig, Edward H. *Woodrow Wilson and the Balance of Power.* Bloomington: Indiana University Press, 1955.

Diamond, William. *The Economic Thought of Woodrow Wilson.* Baltimore: The Johns Hopkins University Press, 1943.

Farnsworth, Beatrice. *William C. Bullitt and the Soviet Union.* Bloomington: Indiana University Press, 1967.

Lasch, Christopher. *The American Liberals and the Russian Revolution.* New York: Columbia University Press, 1962.

Levin, N. Gordon, Jr. *Woodrow Wilson and World Politics.* New York: Oxford University Press, 1968.

Link, Arthur S. *Wilson the Diplomatist.* Baltimore: The Johns Hopkins University Press, 1957.

Martin, Laurence W. *Peace without Victory, Woodrow Wilson and the British Liberals.* New Haven, Conn.: Yale University Press, 1958.

May, Ernest R. *The World War and American Isolation.* Cambridge, Mass.: Harvard University Press, 1959.

Mayer, Arno J. *The Political Origins of the New Diplomacy, 1917–1918.* New Haven, Conn.: Yale University Press, 1959.

———*Politics and Diplomacy of Peacemaking, Containment, and Counter-revolution at Versailles, 1918–1919.* New York: Alfred A. Knopf, 1968.

Smith, Daniel M. *The Great Departure, The United States and World War One, 1914–1920.* New York: John Wiley & Sons, 1965.

Thompson, John M. *Russia, Bolshevism, and the Versailles Peace.* Princeton, N.J.: Princeton University Press, 1966.

Tillman, Seth P. *Anglo-American Relations at the Paris Peace Conference of 1919.* Princeton: Princeton University Press, 1961.

DOCUMENT 25.1
President Wilson Searches for Peace without Victory

On January 22, 1917, the president climaxed his last great personal peace effort with the "Peace without Victory" address before the Senate. Wilson combined a neutralist stance on the issues dividing the European powers with the projection of an American-inspired liberal world order.

. . . Is the present war a struggle for a just and secure peace, or only for a new balance

Source: Ray Stannard Baker and William E. Dodd, eds., *The Public Papers of Woodrow Wilson*, Vol. 4. *The New Democracy* (New York: Harper & Bros., 1927). pp. 410–14. Copyright 1926, 1954 by Edith Boling Wilson.

of power? If it be only a struggle for a new balance of power, who will guarantee, who can guarantee the stable equilibrium of the new arrangement? Only a tranquil Europe can be a stable Europe. There must be, not a balance of power, but a community of power; not organized rivalries, but an organized common peace.

Fortunately we have received very explicit assurances on this point. The statesmen of both of the groups of nations now arrayed against one another have said, in terms that could not be misinterpreted, that it was no part of the purpose they had in mind to crush their antagonists. But the implications of these assurances may not be equally clear to all—may not be the same on both sides of the water. I think it will be serviceable if I attempt to set forth what we understand them to be.

They imply, first of all, that it must be a peace without victory. It is not pleasant to say this. I beg that I may be permitted to put my own interpretation upon it and that it may be understood that no other interpretation was in my thought. I am seeking only to face realities and to face them without soft concealments. Victory would mean peace forced upon the loser, a victor's terms imposed upon the vanquished. It would be accepted in humiliation, under duress, at an intolerable sacrifice, and would leave a sting, a resentment, a bitter memory upon which terms of peace would rest, not permanently, but only as upon quicksand. Only a peace between equals can last. Only a peace the very principle of which is equality and a common participation in a common benefit. The right state of mind, the right feeling between nations, is as necessary for a lasting peace as is the just settlement of vexed questions of territory or of racial and national allegiance. . . .

And there is a deeper thing involved than even equality of right among organized nations. No peace can last, or ought to last, which does not recognize and accept the principle that governments derive all their just powers from the consent of the governed, and that no right anywhere exists to hand peoples about from sovereignty to sovereignty as if they were property. . . .

. . . Any peace which does not recognize and accept this principle will inevitably be upset. It will not rest upon the affections or the convictions of mankind. The ferment of spirit of whole populations will fight subtly and constantly against it, and all the world will sympathize. The world can be at peace only if its life is stable, and there can be no stability where the will is in rebellion, where there is not tranquility of spirit and a sense of justice, of freedom, and of right.

So far as practicable, moreover, every great people now struggling towards a full development of its resources and of it powers should be assured a direct outlet to the great highways of the sea. Where this cannot be done by the cession of territory, it can no doubt be done by the neutralization of direct rights of way under the general guarantee which will assure the peace itself. . . .

And the paths of the sea must alike in law and in fact be free. The freedom of the seas is the *sine qua non* of peace, equality, and co-operation. . . . It need not be difficult either to define or to secure the freedom of the seas if the governments of the world sincerely desire to come to an agreement concerning it.

It is a problem closely connected with the limitation of naval armaments and the co-operation of the navies of the world in keeping the seas at once free and safe. And the question of limiting naval armaments opens the wider and perhaps more difficult question of the limitation of armies and of all programs of military preparation. Difficult and delicate as these questions are, they must be faced with the utmost candor and decided in a spirit of real accommodation if peace is to come with healing in its wings, and come to stay. Peace cannot be had without concession and sacrifice. There can be no sense of safety and equality among the nations if great preponderating armaments are henceforth to continue here and there to be built up and maintained. . . .

I have spoken upon these great matters without reserve and with the utmost explicitness because it has seemed to me to be necessary if the world's yearning desire for peace was anywhere to find free voice and utterance. Perhaps I am the only person in high authority amongst all the peoples of the world who is at liberty to speak and hold nothing back. I am speaking as an individual, and yet I am speaking also, of course, as the responsible head of a great government, and I feel confident that I have said what the people of the United States would wish me to say. May I not add that I hope and believe that I am in effect speaking for liberals and friends of humanity in every nation and of every program of liberty? I would fain believe that I am speaking of the silent mass of mankind everywhere who have as yet had no place or opportunity to speak their real hearts out concerning the death and ruin they see to have come already upon the persons and the homes they hold dear.

And in holding out the expectation that the people and Government of the United States will join the other civilized nations of the world in guaranteeing the permanence of peace upon such terms as I have named I speak with the greater boldness and confidence because it is clear to every man who can think that there is in this promise no breach in either our traditions or our policy as a nation, but a fulfilment, rather, of all that we have professed or striven for.

I am proposing, as it were, that the nations should with one accord adopt the doctrine of President Monroe as the doctrine of the world: that no nation should seek to extend its polity over any other nation or people, but that every people should be left free to determine its own polity, its own way of development, unhindered, unthreatened, unafraid, the little along with the great and powerful.

I am proposing that all nations henceforth avoid entangling alliances which would draw them into competitions of power; catch them in a net of intrigue and selfish rivalry, and disturb their own affairs with influences intruded from without. There is no entangling alliance in a concert of power. When all unite to act in the same sense and with the same purpose all act in the common interest and are free to live their own lives under a common protection. . . .

These are American principles, American policies. We could stand for no others. And they are also the principles and policies of forward looking men and women everywhere, of every modern nation, of every enlightened community. They are the principles of mankind and must prevail.

DOCUMENT 25.2
President Wilson Seeks Peace through Liberal War

Wilson's War Message of April 2, 1917— delivered at a Joint Session of Congress— revealed that he had come to accept the Lansing view of the war as a struggle between Allied democracy and Germany autocracy. It is clear that the Russian Revolution played a role in the president's ideological transition. Yet, a vision of an eventual postwar liberal world order links this address with the earlier one of January 22.

While we do these things, these deeply momentous things, let us be very clear, and make very clear to all the world what our motives and our objects are. My own thought has not been driven from its habitual and normal course by the unhappy events of the last two months,

---

Source: Ray Stannard Baker and William E. Dodd, eds., *The Public Papers of Woodrow Wilson,* Vol. 5. *War and Peace* (New York: Harper & Bros., 1927), pp. 11–16. Copyright 1926, 1954 by Edith Boling Wilson.

and I do not believe that the thought of the Nation has been altered or clouded by them. I have exactly the same things in mind now that I had in mind when I addressed the Senate on the twenty-second of January last, the same that I had in mind when I addressed the Congress on the third of February and on the twenty-sixth of February. Our object now, as then, is to vindicate the principles of peace and justice in the life of the world as against selfish and autocratic power and to set up amongst the really free and self-governed peoples of the world such a concert of purpose and of action as will henceforth insure the observance of those principles. Neutrality is no longer feasible or desirable where the peace of the world is involved and the freedom of its peoples, and the menace to that peace and freedom lies in the existence of autocratic governments backed by organized force which is controlled wholly by their will, not by the will of their people. We have seen the last of neutrality in such circumstances. We are at the beginning of an age in which it will be insisted that the same standards of conduct and of responsibility for wrong done shall be observed among nations and their governments that are observed among the individual citizens of civilized states.

We have no quarrel with the German people. We have no feeling towards them but one of sympathy and friendship. It was not upon their impulse that their government acted in entering this war. It was not with their previous knowledge or approval. It was a war determined upon as wars used to be determined upon in the old, unhappy days when peoples were nowhere consulted by their rulers and wars were provoked and waged in the interest of dynasties or of little groups of ambitious men who were accustomed to use their fellow men as pawns and tools. Self-governed nations do not fill their neighbor states with spies or set the course of intrigue to bring about some critical posture of affairs which will give them an opportunity to strike and make conquest. Such designs can be successfully worked out only under cover

and where no one has the right to ask questions. Cunningly contrived plans of deception or aggression, carried, it may be, from generation to generation, can be worked out and kept from the light only within the privacy of courts or behind the carefully guarded confidences of a narrow and privileged class. They are happily impossible where public opinion commands and insists upon full information concerning all the nation's affairs.

A steadfast concert for peace can never be maintained except by a partnership of democratic nations. No autocratic government could be trusted to keep faith within it or observe its covenants. It must be a league of honor, a partnership of opinion. Intrigue would eat its vitals away; the plottings of inner circles who could plan what they would and render account to no one would be a corruption seated at its very heart. Only free peoples can hold their purpose and their honor steady to a common end and prefer the interests of mankind to any narrow interest of their own.

Does not every American feel that assurance has been added to our hope for the future peace of the world by the wonderful and heartening things that have been happening within the last few weeks in Russia? Russia was known by those who knew it best to have been always in fact democratic at heart, in all the vital habits of her thought, in all the intimate relationships of her people that spoke their natural instinct, their habitual attitude towards life. The autocracy that crowned the summit of her political structure, long as it had stood and terrible as was the reality of its power, was not in fact Russian in origin, character, or purpose; and now it has been shaken off and the great, generous Russian people have been added in all their naïve majesty and might to the forces that are fighting for freedom in the world, for justice, and for peace. Here is a fit partner for a League of Honor.

One of the things that has served to convince us that the Prussian autocracy was not and could never be our friend is that from the very outset of the present war it has filled our unsuspecting communities and even our offices of government with spies and set criminal intrigues everywhere afoot against our national unity of counsel, our peace within and without, our industries and our commerce. . . . That it means to stir up enemies against us at our very doors the intercepted note to the German Minister at Mexico City is eloquent evidence.

We are accepting this challenge of hostile purpose because we know that in such a Government, following such methods, we can never have a friend; and that in the presence of its organized power, always lying in wait to accomplish we know not what purpose, there can be no assured security for the democratic Governments of the world. We are now about to accept gage of battle with this natural foe to liberty and shall, if necessary, spend the whole force of the Nation to check and nullify its pretensions and its power. We are glad, now that we see the facts with no veil of false pretense about them, to fight thus for the ultimate peace of the world and for the liberation of its peoples, the German peoples included: for the rights of nations great and small and the privilege of men everywhere to choose their way of life and of obedience. The world must be made safe for democracy. Its peace must be planted upon the tested foundations of political liberty. We have no selfish ends to serve. We desire no conquest, no dominion. We seek no indemnities for ourselves, no material compensation for the sacrifices we shall freely make. We are but one of the champions of the rights of mankind. . . .

Just because we fight without rancor and without selfish object, seeking nothing for ourselves but what we shall wish to share with all free peoples, we shall, I feel confident, conduct our operations as belligerents without passion and ourselves observe with proud punctilio the principles of right and of fair play we profess to be fighting for. . . .

. . . We enter this war only where we are clearly forced into it because there are no other means of defending our rights. . . .

. . . We shall, happily, still have an opportunity to prove that friendship in our daily attitude and actions towards the millions of men and women of German birth and native sympathy who live amongst us and share our life, and we shall be proud to prove it towards all who are in fact loyal to their neighbors and to the Government in the hour of test. They are, most of them, as true and loyal Americans as if they had never known any other fealty or allegiance. They will be prompt to stand with us in rebuking and restraining the few who may be of a different mind and purpose. If there should be disloyalty, it will be dealt with with a firm hand of stern repression; but, if it lifts its head at all, it will lift it only here and there and without countenance except from a lawless and malignant few.

It is a distressing and oppressive duty, Gentlemen of the Congress, which I have performed in thus addressing you. There are, it may be, many months of fiery trial and sacrifice ahead of us. It is a fearful thing to lead this great peaceful people into war, into the most terrible and disastrous of all wars, civilization itself seeming to be in the balance. But the right is more precious than peace, and we shall fight for the things which we have always carried nearest our hearts,—for democracy, for the right of those who submit to authority to have a voice in their own Governments, for the rights and liberties of small nations, for a universal dominion of right by such a concert of free peoples as shall bring peace and safety to all nations and make the world itself at last free. To such a task we can dedicate our lives and our fortunes, everything that we are and everything that we have, with the pride of those who know that the day has come when America is privileged to spend her blood and her might for the principles that gave her birth and happiness and the peace which she has treasured. God helping her, she can do no other.

DOCUMENT 25.3
President Wilson's War Aims

The famous Fourteen Points address represented an effort by Wilson to appeal to liberals and radicals in Russia and the other Allied countries with a war aims program which would legitimate a continuation of the war against Imperial Germany. The message was successful in Western Europe, but in Russia it was rejected by the Bolsheviks, who went on to sign a separate peace with Germany at Brest-Litovsk shortly after.

We entered this war because violations of right had occurred which touched us to the quick and made the life of our own people impossible unless they were corrected and the world secured once for all against their recurrence. What we demand in this war, therefore, is nothing peculiar to ourselves. It is that the world be made fit and safe to live in; and particularly that it be made safe for every peace-loving nation which, like our own, wishes to live its own life, determine its own institutions, be assured of justice and fair dealing by the other peoples of the world as against force and selfish aggression. All the peoples of the world are in effect partners in this interest, and for our own part we see very clearly that unless justice be done to others it will not be done to us. The program of the world's peace, therefore, is our program; and that program, the only possible program, as we see it, is this:

I. Open covenants of peace, openly arrived at, after which there shall be no private international understandings of any kind but diplomacy shall proceed always frankly and in the public view.

II. Absolute freedom of navigation upon the seas, outside territorial waters, alike in peace

and in war, except as the seas may be closed in whole or in part by international action for the enforcement of international covenants.

III. The removal, so far as possible, of all economic barriers and the establishment of an equality of trade conditions among all the nations consenting to the peace and associating themselves for its maintenance.

IV. Adequate guarantees given and taken that national armaments will be reduced to the lowest point consistent with domestic safety.

V. A free, open-minded, and absolutely impartial adjustment of all colonial claims, based upon a strict observance of the principle that in determining all such questions of sovereignty the interests of the populations concerned must have equal weight with the equitable claims of the government whose title is to be determined.

VI. The evacuation of all Russian territory and such a settlement of all questions affecting Russia as will secure the best and freest coöperation of the other nations of the world in obtaining for her an unhampered and unembarrassed opportunity for the independent determination of her own political development and national policy and assure her of a sincere welcome into the society of free nations under institutions of her own choosing; and, more than a welcome, assistance also of every kind that she may need and may herself desire. The treatment accorded Russia by her sister nations in the months to come will be the acid test of their good will, of their comprehension of her needs as distinguished from their own interests, and of their intelligent and unselfish sympathy.

VII. Belgium, the whole world will agree, must be evacuated and restored, without any attempt to limit the sovereignty which she enjoys in common with all other free nations. No other single act will serve as this will serve to restore confidence among the nations in the laws which they have themselves set and determined for the government of their relations with one another. Without this healing act the whole structure and validity of international law is forever impaired.

VIII. All French territory should be freed and the invaded portions restored, and the wrong done to France by Prussia in 1871 in the matter of Alsace-Lorraine, which has unsettled the peace of the world for nearly fifty years, should be righted, in order that peace may once more be made secure in the interest of all.

IX. A readjustment of the frontiers of Italy should be effected along clearly recognizable lines of nationality.

X. The peoples of Austria-Hungary, whose place among the nations we wish to see safeguarded and assured, should be accorded the freest opportunity of autonomous development.

XI. Rumania, Serbia, and Montenegro should be evacuated; occupied territories restored; Serbia accorded free and secure access to the sea; and the relations of the several Balkan states to one another determined by friendly counsel along historically established lines of allegiance and nationality; and international guarantees of the political and economic independence and territorial integrity of the several Balkan states should be entered into.

XII. The Turkish portions of the present Ottoman Empire should be assured a secure sovereignty, but the other nationalities which are now under Turkish rule would be assured an undoubted security of life and an absolutely unmolested opportunity of autonomous development, and the Dardanelles should be permanently opened as a free passage to the ships and commerce of all nations under international guarantees.

XIII. An independent Polish state should be erected which should include the territories inhabited by indisputably Polish populations, which should be assured a free and secure access to the sea, and whose political and economic independence and territorial integrity should be guaranteed by international covenant.

XIV. A general association of nations must be formed under specific covenants for the purpose of affording mutual guarantees of political independence and territorial integrity to great and small states alike.

In regard to these essential rectifications of wrong and assertions of right we feel ourselves to be intimate partners of all the governments and peoples associated together against the Imperialists. We cannot be separated in interest or divided in purpose. We stand together until the end.

For such arrangements and covenants we are willing to fight and to continue to fight until they are achieved. . . .

DOCUMENT 25.4
The Problem of Bolshevism at the Paris Conference

At Paris the Wilson administration sought to check bolshevism and reintegrate Germany with a program of timely food relief. The following cablegram was sent in January 1919 to the chairman of the Appropriations Committee, House of Representatives.

I cannot too earnestly or solemnly urge upon the Congress the appropriation for which Mr. Hoover has asked for the administration of food relief. Food relief is now the key to the whole European situation and to the solutions of peace. Bolshevism is steadily advancing westward, is poisoning Germany. It cannot be stopped by force, but it can be stopped by food; and all the leaders with whom I am in conference agree that concerted action in this matter is of immediate and vital importance. The money will not be spent for food for Germany itself, because Germany can buy its food;

Source: Ray Stannard Baker and William E. Dodd, eds., *The Public Papers of Woodrow Wilson*, Vol. 5. *War and Peace* (New York: Harper & Bros., 1927), p. 389. Copyright 1926, 1954 by Edith Boling Wilson.

but it will be spent for financing the movement of food to our real friends in Poland and to the people of the liberated units of the Austro-Hungarian Empire and to our associates in the Balkans. I beg that you will present this matter with all possible urgency and force to the Congress. I do not see how we can find definite powers with whom to conclude peace unless this means of stemming the tide of anarchism be employed.

Woodrow Wilson

DOCUMENT 25.5
Wilson and the Blockade of Bolshevik Russia: 1919

The following statement of President Wilson makes clear that his opposition to the Bolshevik regime in Russia continued throughout the Paris Peace Conference. The president participated throughout 1919, albeit often ambivalently, in a variety of diplomatic, political, and military measures designed to contain and remove Lenin's government.

Reply of President Wilson to Inquiry of July 27, From the British, French, Italian and Japanese Representatives in the Council of Five, on the Question of a Proposed Blockade of Soviet Russia.

The President is not unmindful of the serious situation which exists in relation to neutral trade in the Baltic with the Russian ports controlled by the Bolsheviks. He has given careful consideration to the arguments advanced in the message transmitted at the request of Monsieur Clemenceau, and is not unmindful of their force in support of the proposed interruption of commerce with the ports mentioned. However, while he fully understands the reasons for em-

ploying war measures to prevent the importation of munitions and food supplies into the portion of Russia now in the hands of the Bolsheviks, he labours under the difficulty of being without constitutional right to prosecute an act of war such as a blockade affecting neutrals unless there has been a declaration of war by the Congress of the United States against the nation so blockaded.

The landing of troops at Archangel and Murmansk was done to protect the property and supplies of the American and Allied Governments until they could be removed. The sending of troops to Siberia was to keep open the railway for the protection of Americans engaged in its operation and to make safe from possible German and Austrian attack the retiring Czecho-Slovaks. The furnishing of supplies to the Russians in Siberia, while indicating a sympathy with the efforts to restore order and safety of life and property, cannot be construed as a belligerent act.

The President is convinced that if proper representations are made to the neutral countries during the war they can be induced to prohibit traffic in arms and munitions with the portions of Russia controlled by the Bolsheviks. The avowed hostility of the Bolsheviks to all Governments and the announced programme of international revolution make them as great a menace to the national safety of neutral countries as to Allied countries. For any Government to permit them to increase their power through commercial intercourse with its nationals would be to encourage a movement which is frankly directed against all Governments and would certainly invite the condemnation of all peoples desirous of restoring peace and social order.

The President cannot believe that any Government whose people might be in a position to carry on commerce with the Russian ports referred to would be so indifferent to the opinion of the civilised world as to permit it. The President therefore suggests that the so-called neutral Governments be approached by the Allied and

Source: *Foreign Relations, The Paris Peace Conference, 1919* (Washington, D.C.: U.S. Government Printing Office, 1946), vol. 7, pp. 644–45.

Associated Governments in joint note setting forth the facts of the case and the menace to such countries and to the world of any increase of the Bolshevik power, and requesting the neutral Governments to take immediate steps to prevent trade and commerce with Bolshevik Russia and to give assurance that the policy will be rigorously enforced in conjunction with other Governments which are equally menaced.

DOCUMENT 25.6
President Wilson Defends the Treaty and the League

In his speeches in defense of the League of Nations the president argued that the League would preserve the peace settlement of Versailles, help to contain the threat of revolution, and fulfill America's destiny of inspiring a liberal world order.

. . . After all the various angles at which you have heard the treaty held up, perhaps you would like to know what is in the treaty. I find it very difficult in reading some of the speeches that I have read to form any conception of that great document. It is a document unique in the history of the world for many reasons, and I think I cannot do you a better service, or the peace of the world a better service, than by pointing out to you just what this treaty contains and what it seeks to do.

In the first place, my fellow countrymen, it seeks to punish one of the greatest wrongs ever done in history, the wrong which Germany sought to do to the world and to civilization; and there ought to be no weak purpose with regard to the application of the punishment.

Source: Ray Stannard Baker and William E. Dodd, eds., *The Public Papers of Woodrow Wilson*, Vol. 6. *War and Peace* (New York: Harper & Bros., 1927), pp. 590–98. Copyright 1926, 1954 by Edith Boling Wilson.

She attempted an intolerable thing, and she must be made to pay for the attempt. The terms of the treaty are severe, but they are not unjust. I can testify that the men associated with me at the Peace Conference in Paris had it in their hearts to do justice and not wrong. But they knew, perhaps, with a more vivid sense of what had happened than we could possibly know on this side of the water, the many solemn covenants which Germany had disregarded, the long preparation she had made to overwhelm her neighbors, and the utter disregard which she had shown for human rights, for the rights of women, of children, of those who were helpless. They had seen their lands devastated by an enemy that devoted himself not only to the effort at victory, but to the effort at terror— seeking to terrify the people whom he fought. And I wish to testify that they exercised restraint in the terms of this treaty. They did not wish to overwhelm any great nation. They acknowledged that Germany was a great nation, and they had no purpose of overwhelming the German people, but they did think that it ought to be burned into the consciousness of men forever that no people ought to permit its government to do what the German Government did.

In the last analysis, my fellow countrymen, as we in America would be the first to claim, a people are responsible for the acts of their Government. If their Government purposes things that are wrong, they ought to take measures to see to it that that purpose is not executed. Germany was self-governed; her rulers had not concealed the purposes that they had in mind, but they had deceived their people as to the character of the methods they were going to use, and I believe from what I can learn that there is an awakened consciousness in Germany itself of the deep iniquity of the thing that was attempted. . . .

Look even into the severe terms of reparation—for there was no indemnity. No indemnity of any sort was claimed, merely reparation, merely paying for the destruction done, merely making good the losses so far as such losses could be made good which she had unjustly inflicted, not upon the governments, for the reparation is not to go to the governments, but upon the people whose rights she had trodden upon with absolute absence of everything that even resembled pity. There was no indemnity in this treaty, but there is reparation, and even in the terms of reparation a method is devised by which the reparation shall be adjusted to Germany's ability to pay it.

I am astonished at some of the statements I hear made about this treaty. The truth is that they are made by persons who have not read the treaty or who, if they have read it, have not comprehended its meaning. There is a method of adjustment in that treaty by which the reparation shall not be pressed beyond the point which Germany can pay, but which will be pressed to the utmost point that Germany can pay—which is just, which is righteous. It would have been intolerable if there had been anything else. For, my fellow citizens, this treaty is not meant merely to end this single war. It is meant as a notice to every government which in the future will attempt this thing that mankind will unite to inflict the same punishment. There is no national triumph sought to be recorded in this treaty. There is no glory sought for any particular nation. . . .

As I said, this treaty was not intended merely to end this war. It was intended to prevent any similar war. . . . That is what the League of Nations is for, to end this war justly, and then not merely to serve notice on governments which would contemplate the same things that Germany contemplated that they will do it at their peril, but also concerning the combination of power which will prove to them that they will do it at their peril. It is idle to say the world *will* combine against you, because it may not, but it is persuasive to say the world *is*

combined against you, and will remain combined against the things that Germany attempted. The League of Nations is the only thing that can prevent the recurrence of this dreadful catastrophe and redeem our promises.

The character of the League is based upon the experience of this very war. I did not meet a single public man who did not admit these things, that Germany would not have gone into this war if she had thought Great Britain was going into it, and that she most certainly would never have gone into this war if she dreamed America was going into it. And they all admitted that a notice beforehand that the greatest powers of the world would combine to prevent this sort of thing would prevent it absolutely. When gentlemen tell you, therefore, that the League of Nations is intended for some other purpose than this, merely reply this to them: If we do not do this thing, we have neglected the central covenant that we made to our people, and there will then be no statesmen of any country who can thereafter promise his people alleviation from the perils of war. The passions of this world are not dead. The rivalries of this world have not cooled. They have been rendered hotter than ever. The harness that is to unite nations is more necessary now than it ever was before, and unless there is this assurance of combined action before wrong is attempted, wrong will be attempted just so soon as the most ambitious nations can recover from the financial stress of this war.

Now, look what else is in the treaty. This treaty is unique in the history of mankind, because the center of it is the redemption of weak nations. There never was a congress of nations before that considered the rights of those who could not enforce their rights. There never was a congress of nations before that did not seek to effect some balance of power brought about by means of serving the strength and interest of the strongest powers concerned; whereas this treaty builds up nations that never could have won their freedom in any other way; builds them up by gift, by largess, not by obligations; builds them up because of the conviction of the men who wrote the treaty that the rights of people transcend the rights of governments, because of the conviction of the men who wrote that treaty that the fertile source of war is wrong. The Austro-Hungarian Empire, for example, was held together by military force and consisted of peoples who did not want to live together, who did not have the spirit of nationality as towards each other, who were constantly chafing at the bands that held them. . . . The old alliances, the old balances of power, were meant to see to it that no little nation asserted its right to the disturbance of the peace of Europe, and every time an assertion of rights was attempted they were suppressed by combined influence and force.

This treaty tears away all that: says these people have a right to live their own lives under the governments which they themselves choose to set up. That is the American principle, and I was glad to fight for it. When strategic claims were urged, it was matter of common counsel that such considerations were not in our thought. We were not now arranging for future wars. We were giving people what belonged to them. . . .

If there is no League of Nations, the military point of view will prevail in every instance, and peace will be brought into contempt, but if there is a league of nations, Italy need not fear the fact that the shores on the other side of the Adriatic tower above the lower and sandy shores on her side of the sea, because there will be no threatening guns there, and the nations of the world will have concerted, not merely to see that the Slavic peoples have their rights, but that the Italian people have their rights as well. I had rather have everybody on my side than be armed to the teeth. . . .

Some gentlemen have feared with regard to the League of Nations that we will be obliged to do things we do not want to do. If the treaty was wrong, that might be so, but if the treaty is right, we will wish to preserve right. I think I know the heart of this great people whom I, for the time being have the high honor to represent better than some other men that I hear talk. I have been bred, and am proud to have been bred, in the old revolutionary school which set this Government up, when it was set up as the friend of mankind, and I know if they do not that America has never lost that vision or that purpose. But I have not the slightest fear that arms will be necessary if the purpose is there. If I know that my adversary is armed and I am not, I do not press the controversy, and if any nation entertains selfish purposes set against the principles established in this treaty and is told by the rest of the world that it must withdraw its claims, it will not press them.

The heart of this treaty then, my fellow citizens, is not even that it punishes Germany. That is a temporary thing. It is that it rectifies the age-long wrongs which characterized the history of Europe. There were some of us who wished that the scope of the treaty would reach some other age-long wrongs. It was a big job, and I do not say that we wished that it were bigger, but there were other wrongs elsewhere than in Europe and of the same kind which no doubt ought to be righted, and some day will be righted, but which we could not draw into the treaty because we could deal only with the countries whom the war had engulfed and affected. But so far as the scope of our authority went, we rectified the wrongs which have been the fertile source of war in Europe. . . .

. . . Revolutions do not spring up overnight. Revolutions come from the long suppression of the human spirit. Revolutions come because men know that they have rights and that they are disregarded; and when we think of the future of the world in connection with this treaty we must remember that one of the chief efforts of those who made this treaty was to remove that anger from the heart of great peoples, great peoples who have always been suppressed, who had always been used, and who had always been the tools in the hands of governments, generally alien governments, not their own. The makers of the treaty knew that if these wrongs were not removed, there could be no peace in the world, because, after all, my fellow citizens, war comes from the seed of wrong and not from the seed of right. This treaty is an attempt to right the history of Euorpe, and, in my humble judgment, it is a measurable success. . . .

chapter

Rural-Urban Conflict in the 1920s

David M. Chalmers
University of Florida

The decade of the 1920s has held consider-able nostalgic appeal for later generations of Americans. Aided primarily by the motion pictures and the phonograph, seconded by misty memory, we have pictured the period as one of frenetic hedonism, based on booze, blues, and jazz; Sigmund Freud and Henry Ford; raccoon coats, rumrunners, and Runyon-esque gangsters. It was an era in which "the younger generation" made its bow as America's institutionalized number one problem and most emulated symbol in a society which small-town fundamentalism was never able to repress. This was the world of William Faulkner, Scott Fitzgerald, Ernest Hemingway, Ezra Pound, Hart Crane, and T. S. Eliot; of Al Capone, Babe Ruth, Theda Bara, and Rudy Vallee; of Warren Harding playing poker with the boys in the "little green house on K Street," and of Calvin Coolidge asleep in the White House. Many of the people who lived through the suc-ceeding decades of depression, world war, and cold war looked back at the twenties with con-siderable, though not always accurate, longing.

By the 1920s the United States was well on its way to becoming an urban society, and the value of industrial production had exceeded that of the farms for at least three decades. In 1900 the total national population reached seventy-six million, of which some 60 percent

were rural. By 1920, out of 106 million people, the nonurban portion had fallen to 48 percent, a growing part of which lived in rural hamlets and villages. This movement was to continue during the twenties at an increasing rate, and for the first time the actual number of people on the farms declined.

Of course, percentages only supply informa-tion and symbolize movement; they do not in themselves create discontent. Why had it taken until the 1920s for a reaction to rural decline to take place? After the hard times and turbulent agrarian protest of the 1870s, 1880s, and 1890s, the twentieth century had brought two decades of prosperity for the farmer, climaxing in the boom times of World War I. The Progressive Era was a period of great optimism, based upon a belief in human rationality and progress. Tra-ditional standards of truth, justice, patriotism, and morality seemed unchallenged. It was a period which the historian Henry F. May (*The End of American Innocence*) has described as "the time when people wanted to make a num-ber of sharp changes because they were so confident in the basic rightness of things as they were." America might be changing and the proportion of the rural population decreas-ing, but it was not initially apparent that the traditional, comforting American values were also on the decline. When these supports were clearly disappearing by the 1920s, the crisis of rural America took on psychological as well as economic dimensions.

With high wartime demand and prices, the farmer had expanded his production and his indebtedness. But the government withdrew its support from wheat and pork by the end of 1919. The following year, with a falling market—though not necessarily lower freight rates, interest, and taxes—agriculture went into a depression that continued until war broke out again in Europe at the end of the thirties.

Agriculture was not so sick, however, that it could not fight back. Its struggle was in part a rational attempt to increase farm income, which became focused on the McNary-Haugen bill to require the government to prop domestic prices by dumping agricultural surpluses abroad. This ran into conflict with the prevailing business orientation of the Republican party, which was willing to offer tax and tariff relief to industry and believed that the only solution for agriculture would be for farmers to reduce production and for economic law to reduce the number of farmers. A farm bloc in Congress, led by Republican progressives, got some tariff protection and farm credit, but Presidents Calvin Coolidge and Herbert Hoover vetoed the McNary-Haugen bill.

The farmer was not inclined, however, to blame all of his problems on mortgage costs and commodity prices. While some farm leaders, such as the Iowa spokesman *Wallace's Farmer,* shifted their concern from the primacy of agrarianism to the necessity for parity, there were others who had a profound feeling that society itself was being destroyed. Foreclosures and tenancy were increasing, as was the drift of the rural population, particularly the young, to the cities, drawn by the superior opportunities for money, mobility, and pleasure.

The values of the old-stock, traditional American society seemed to be increasingly overshadowed by the machine-centered, materialistic ones created by the racial and religious

pluralism of the cities. The farmer's response to this changing society often took the form of an attack upon it, rather than an attempt to find a place for agriculture within it. In a world in which President Coolidge could comment that the farmers never made any money anyway and in which the Democratic party had not yet assumed its role as a broad group-interest broker, "rum, race, and religion" were often more politically potent than economics. The presidential candidacy of Robert M. La Follette in 1924 did well in the western farm, mountain, and coastal states, but it represented a protest, hardly a program or a party. In the rural South, post-Populist frustration had long been focused upon the polyglot eastern cities.

But American society was too complex to be summed up only in terms of a simple rural-urban dichotomy. By 1920, approximately two out of every five persons classified as rural lived not on farms but in hamlets and small towns. These villages acted as the commercial intermediates between the farms and the cities, transmitting and producing goods, supplying services, and handling the farmer's transactions. Although a good share of their population was comprised of retired, tax-wary farmers, the conflict between farm and hamlet had reached back into the previous century. The division was most pronounced in the Middle West; but there was a wide-spread tendency for townspeople to look down on the farmer. He in turn sensed slight where he did not see it and considered the villager to be concerned primarily with the middleman's profit at his expense. The story is told of one small town that was forced to restore the old water trough and hitching post when the farmers took the removal as a personal insult and began motoring to neighboring villages to do their marketing. Arguments about bank interest rates, mortgages, and retail prices and credit were joined by disagreement over Sunday movies, sermons, and whether young John Thomas Scopes should have been allowed to teach Dayton, Tennessee, high school students that man "descended from a lower order of animals."

The small towns also had their economic problems. They, too, had over-expanded during the war, and now they suffered contraction and often banking failure. The great building boom of the twenties passed them by. Business property was deteriorating, and civic and social organizations were becoming less active. More and more, the rural community was being overshadowed by the city, which, while contributing the automobile service trade, drew the flivverized farmers and took over the role of supplier of nationally manufactured goods, replacing the blacksmith, butcher, and miller.

The townspeople saw the city as an anonymous, impersonal, dog-eat-dog society, ruled by corrupt politicians, immigrant bosses, labor leaders, and monopolists, all of whom lived off the hard-working countryfolk. The big cities embodied the opulent and immoral life of the very rich, and the secularism and agnostic atheism of the city churches and universities. The eastern metropolises were wet, Roman Catholic, immigrant, perhaps Bolshevik, probably un-American, and certainly not safe, either in their streets or in their influences. They were, in short, responsible for the problems that faced country life.

Many major cities, such as Cincinnati, Birmingham, Columbus, Indianapolis, Kansas City, Dallas, and Denver, and most of the smaller ones, were not greatly touched by the waves of immigrants from Southern and Eastern Europe who flooded into the country after the 1880s. Like Muncie, Indiana, which the sociologists Robert S. Lynd and Helen M. Lynd profiled in *Middletown: A Study in American Culture* [1929], such cities had been populated by old-stock Americans from the nearby farm lands. They had come to the city at a time when new industrial processes were successfully undercutting the formerly well-paid, prestigious craft-workers and shifting unchallenged civic leadership to the business community.

The Rotary and Kiwanis culture was rapidly becoming both lord and symbol of the small cities. So too was the pursuit of status in the form of conspicuous consumption which Sinclair Lewis presented so forcefully that the titles of his books *Main Street* and *Babbit* became an unflattering part of the American language. Common values joined Lewis's prototypic town of Gopher Prairie and Muncie's bustling, boosting 35,000 population; and perhaps most acutely in Muncie, the former deep sense of community was being lost in the newly dominant worlds of business and consumption. When a movement came along that could bring men together to seek aggressively the older community, it might well have great power. Such a force was the Ku Klux Klan during its brief life in the early and middle twenties.

The Ku Klux Klan, which had become a folk legend in the South as the savior of a downtrodden people during Reconstruction, was revived as a fraternal organization in 1915 by an ex-Methodist minister, "Colonel" William J. Simmons. Like many such orders, it was restricted to white, native-born Protestants, and Simmons expected it to have a mild success in southeastern United States. Its purposes were in-group gregariousness and moneymaking. It was not originally intended to be particularly anti-Negro or anti-anybody else. However, in the hands of skilled fraternal salesmen, operating in times still touched by wartime conformity, animosities, and restlessness, the Klan spread like a prairie fire up the Mississippi Valley, jumped the mountains to the West Coast, fanned out in the American hinterland, and pushed powerfully toward the North and East. The Klan was the great lodge of the American twenties, a parasite feeding upon the gregarious, xenophobic, small-town, old-stock American subculture.

While its main appeal was togetherness and excitement, its cause and its cohesiveness derived from nativism. The hundreds of thousands who flocked to the Klan had found their society changing and disturbing, and they sought a personified explanation. Who was at fault? Presidents Warren G. Harding and Calvin Coolidge were hardly active forces for change, nor was the Supreme Court, while Congress was safely Protestant and Masonic. It never occurred to the Klansmen to blame it all on structural steel, the dynamo, and the internal-combustion engine; the Klan's answer was conspiracy. It appealed to the uneasy feeling that the American way of life was under attack. The aggressor was identified as the unassimilable alien outsider, primarily the Southern and Eastern European immigrant, particularly the Roman Catholic, and then the Jew and the Negro. The highly fragmented American Protestant majority had a persecution complex out of which grew the Ku Klux Klan. The Klansman saw himself as a sentry on guard against alien subversion and the erosion of the old morality in the guise of the roadhouse and urban sin.

The Klan was more than just a smalltown organization; the cities, great and small, were being populated by the same native American stock as was to be found in the Ku Klux Klan, and these internal migrants brought their heartland values and their defensiveness with them.

The Klan marched, elected, and terrorized—literally—from Portland, Maine, to Portland, Oregon. It helped to elect at least sixteen senators and eleven governors, a number of them members of the hooded order, and reached its peak strength of about two million members in 1924. It was powerful in states such as Ohio, Indiana, Texas, Colorado, and Kansas, as well as Georgia and Alabama, and in cities such as Los Angeles, Indianapolis, Milwaukee, Detroit, Dallas, Denver, and Philadelphia. It was as prone to violence in California's San Joaquin Valley as in the North Carolina piedmont, although never to the extent of its night riding in Texas and Oklahoma.

Although the Klan sought to enforce its version of moral behavior, fought for prohibition and immigration restriction, and strove to keep

"the church in the wildwood" and "the little red schoolhouse" American, it had no constructive program. The Klan's underlying meaning lay not in its moral stance or its vigilantism, but in its attempt to explain and resist the changes that had taken place in the national society. Masking defensiveness in an aggressive form, the Klan became, during its period of power, as much a parody of the values it sought to support as any caustic epitaph ever written by H. L. Mencken.

Perhaps if the Klan had grown more slowly and had achieved better leadership, it might have endured as a fraternal order. However, continuous inner conflict over spoils and power, as well as the Klan's general violence and disruptiveness, lost it membership and community support; after 1925, it rapidly declined.

The high level of bitterness that marked the social conflicts of the 1920s was indicated by the degree which intellectuals proclaimed their loss of faith and interest in popular government and traditional values, and by the degree to which Yankee-Protestant rural and village America felt itself isolated, under attack, and—somehow—losing. This schism within the culture represented a national loss of security and direction in the face of great social change.

Many of the value drives of American life in the twentieth century seemed to converge on prohibition. Fundamentalist attack on "evil," southern uneasiness over the Negro, midwestern nativist distrust of the immigrant, the organizational fervor of the Women's Christian Temperance Union, and the political single-mindedness of the Anti-Saloon League combined with the opposition of middle-class social workers and progressives to the corrupting influence of the saloon and the liquor interests. The evangelical need to make men good and the progressive belief that law could be used to change the outer environment and thus reshape the inner one joined to drive alcohol from national life.

By the beginning of World War I, local

option or outright prohibition had swept the states. The national movement acted with the wartime need for foodstuffs and willingness to accept sacrifices to produce the Lever Act, halting the production of liquor during the emergency. The Eighteenth Amendment to the Constitution sought to make prohibition permanent. But what was begun as a noble experiment to redeem mankind soon became a defensive cause and symbol of the old village morality—bolstered by the Methodist, Episcopal, and Baptist churhes—against urban, immigrant citadels controlled by rum and Rome. As Andrew Sinclair pointed out in *Prohibition: The Era of Excess* (1962), prohibition left no room for temperance and appealed to the psychology of excess in both its supporters and its opponents. From the beach counties of New Jersey and the rural southern tier of New York State to the delta country of Illinois and the plains of Oklahoma, Klansmen rallied to the defense of a dry America. In 1924, for the first time, the Prohibition Party added planks on the Americanization of aliens and on the Bible to its platform. By the mid-twenties, prohibition had moved from the camp of optimistic, idealistic reform to that of defensive fundamentalism.

Although Klansmen often marched down church aisles while the choirs sang "Onward, Christian Soldiers," and listened with bowed heads while ministers intoned Romans 12:1 or sermonized about the evils of drink, the defense of Protestant fundamentals against the corrosive doctrines of modernism and Darwinism was the great issue that raged around many pulpits and schools. It was somewhat difficult to fuel general protest against modernism alone, for it did emphasize the transcendence of the ethical and moral nature of Jesus's ministry. Evolutionary doctrines, however, conflicted with the biblical story of creation and the uniqueness of man as the center of God's concern. Further, it offered both ape and Darwin as suitably graphic antagonists. The loss of confidence and sense of security that increas-

ingly afflicted rural and small-town America made many of its churches a defensive battlement for religion and morality. Leading *his* people for the last time against a corrupting urban East which had always rejected him, William Jennings Bryan devoted himself to defending the "Blood of the Lamb" against that of "the beast."

Although, in one form or another, Oklahoma, Florida, North Carolina, Texas, Louisiana, Missouri, and Arkansas also restricted the teaching of evolution, Tennessee's law of 1925 gained national attention. The state legislature, over the supine silence of the University of Tennessee, made it illegal to teach "any theory that denies the story of the divine creation of man as taught in the Bible, and to teach instead that man descended from a lower order of animals." Having discussed the situation over ice-cream sodas at the local drugstore in the small town of Dayton, a young high school teacher named John Thomas Scopes taught his class that "the earth was once a hot molten mass" which had cooled sufficiently for a "little germ of one-cell organism" to form, and that the organism "kept on evolving and from this was man."

The American Civil Liberties Union sent counsel, including the nation's most famous defense lawyer, Clarence Darrow, to defend Scopes, and William Jennings Bryan came up from Florida to help the prosecution. When the judge refused to let the defense use expert testimony to support the evolutionary hypothesis, Bryan permitted himself to be called to the stand to be cross-examined on the Bible. The high drama of a battle over the book of Genesis was exciting but inconclusive—and Bryan's death a few days after the trial deprived fundamentalism of its national champion. As with the declining membership of the Klan and the effect of prohibition, fundamentalism remained more a memorial pillar than a victorious arch to the one-time moral hegemony of old-stock, Yankee-Protestant America.

The frustration of rural and small-town America and the emergence of an urban society did not mean sudden political revolution or the emergence of a cosmopolitan cultural synthesis. The inflow of city dwellers, both from immigrant ships and from the farm, created conglomerates rather than a new politically conscious community. However, a crucial long-run political shift was under way. On the national scene it was appropriate that in Al Smith, New York City should produce the first truly big-city candidate for president. Smith was wet, Roman Catholic, only one generation away from his mother's Irish soil, and had come up through the Tammany machine from the Lower East Side's Fulton Fish Market. In defeating him in 1928, Iowa-born Herbert Hoover broke the hitherto solid South and carried all but six of the forty-eight states. Nevertheless, by the late 1920s the sons and daughters of the new immigration from southern and eastern Europe were reaching voting age. Across the nation, major cities which had earlier cast their vote for Harding and Coolidge were moving into the Democratic column, while Klansmen, fundamentalists, and prohibitionists helped to contribute to Republican successes in the North and Midwest.

For the business community, whether in Muncie or New York City, the clash and confusion of values did not dilute a high sense of optimism. Herbert Hoover, America's outstanding Secretary of Commerce, was pushing trade associations and writing that "American individualism" depended upon cooperation and upon the reduction of the great wastes of "over-reckless competition." The businessman's self-image was not one of conservatism, but of innovation, with technology and business leadership producing never-ending prosperity. On the whole, the social scientists, led by Charles A. Beard and Mary Beard, the economist Wesley C. Mitchell, the psychologist James B. Watson, and the educator John Dewey, agreed on the potential of enlightened social intelli-

gence. In their intensive study of Muncie, the Lynds maintained that tensions and other social problems developed because habit and institutions lagged unreasonably behind technology.

It was not the social scientists but the expressive intellectuals who sensed society's deeper fault lines in the 1920s. If rural, small-town America felt something slipping away, the artists, writers, and critics maintained that developments had not gone far enough. Intellectuals of the Progressive Era had believed in progress and morality, both natural and environmental, and had looked to and worked for the improvement of society. They had found in the people, as a mass, and in government, instruments which they trusted. The trauma of war, the peace that was not a peace, the prejudice of the masses, the misuse of government, and the materialism of America's business civilization led to a sense of alienation that Freud's teachings fostered and to which the cities gave refuge.

Intellectuals blamed their loss on the traditional establishment culture of America, which they denounced as stifling, repressive, and firmly intrenched in the puritanism of the American village. Ludwig Lewisohn spoke for many of the alienated when he asked: "What will you say to a man who believes in hell, or that the Pope in Rome wants to run the country or that the Jews caused the war? How would you argue with a Methodist minister from an Arkansas village, with a Kleagle of the Klan, with a 'this-is-a-white-man's-country' politician from central Georgia?" Seeking freedom in escape and exile, the intellectuals fled to Greenwich Village, or to the Left Bank, or into a world of art which was dedicated not to society but to private experience.

The old American belief in progress, the people, and the neighborliness of the small town once had been the strength and the refuge of American society; now the urbanites rejected it. Led by Sherwood Anderson in *Winesburg,*

Ohio (1919), Sinclair Lewis in *Main Street* (1920) and *Babbit* (1922), and H. L. Mencken in the *Smart Set* and the *American Mercury,* they flayed the idea that "the people" could save themselves or were worth saving. The most powerful army of creative artistic talent assembled since the days of Henry Thoreau and Herman Melville, chief among them being Ezra Pound and T. S. Eliot, Ernest Hemingway and William Faulkner, Scott Fitzgerald and Eugene O'Neill, E. E. Cummings and Hart Crane, found that their private paths led toward no American dream. Their alienation marked the passing of the old America. As Thomas Wolfe would show in his later description of the twenties, *You Can't Go Home Again* (1940), they had sensed that the dynamic forces and the home of America were no longer in the countryside.

Alongside of the defensiveness of rural and small-town America, the upward striving of the sons and daughters of the new immigration, the confident materialism of the business community, and disapproving jeremiads of the intellectuals, a new sociocultural force was making its presence known. The consumer culture was the crowning achievement of American industrial success. American productive efficiency and World War I made the United States the world's leading industrial and financial power. In the 1920s, that industrial system was increasingly geared to producing consumer goods for the expanding urban middle classes as well as for the wealthy. The electric light and indoor plumbing, automobiles, telephones, radios, electric stoves, refrigerators, washing machines, irons, vacuum cleaners, and the trip to the motion-picture show became family necessities. Consumer credit and installment buying functioned as a moving assembly line of consumption that made a proper companion to Henry Ford's moving assembly line of production.

The satirical suggestion of a contemporary novelist that at some future time "Oh, Ford!" might replace "Oh, God!" as a prime invoca-

tion of the deity offered a suggestion of the change in values that was taking place. The traditional Protestant producer ethic of hard work and thrift was slipping into a more secular world of leisure and consumer durables. The rising profession of advertising, speaking through the voice of Bruce Barton, turned consumption into a new form of idealism which he cannonized as "The American Way of Life." Growth and progress were one. American technology produced it, and by adopting the new lifestyle of consumption, the American middle classes were not only achieving self-fulfillment, but they were doing their part in creating "the highest standard of living in the world."

For those who had doubts about the moral values of materialism, Charles Lindbergh, the "Lone Eagle," who in 1927 flew nonstop across the Atlantic from New York to Paris, offered reassurance. In combining daring individual effort in attacking the new frontier of the sky with companionate mastery of the machine—WE, man and machine, was the title he picked for his book about the flight— Lindbergh united past and future. The message was that American future was good, and it made him the consummate hero of the times.

While Lindbergh's great feat could only happen once, Babe Ruth, the "King of Swat," could hit the ball over the fence or into the stands fifty times a season. A contemporary chronicler reported that more people knew who the football coach at Notre Dame was than could identify the American secretary of state. The heroes and role models of the twenties came from sports and the motion pictures. Although the marriage rate was rising and couples married at an earlier age, the modern lifestyle of middle-class urban America meant increased use of contraceptives, smaller families, and greater demands for both affection and commodities. Out of the enhanced emotional emphasis on the child and the longer period between adolescence and adult entrance into the work and family world, the "younger generation" emerged. While only the elite few could enjoy the pinnacle of college life, through the advertising, the movies, and the popular magazines, a much broader strata could enter or envy the new youth culture and its world of consumption and leisure.

However much moralists might question the emerging life style, from an economic point of view, the problem was that still not enough people were able to share it. America's technological revolution was dependent on mass consumption. As productivity and production increased, too few received the rewards. The failure of income distribution during the 1920s to create a sufficiently large market for what American industry produced created a dangerous imbalance. In the changing economy of modern America, it was not consumption values but underconsumption that threatened society.

SUGGESTED READINGS

Braeman, John et al., eds. *Change and Continuity in Twentieth-Century America: The 1920s.* Columbus: Ohio State University Press, 1968.

Burner, David. *The Politics of Provincialism: The Democratic Party in Transition, 1918–1932.* New York: Alfred A. Knopf, 1968.

Chalmers, David M. *Hooded Americanism: The History of the Ku Klux Klan.* 2d rev. ed. Durham, N.C.: Duke University Press, 1987.

Clark, Norman H. *Deliver Us from Evil: An Interpretation of American Prohibition.* New York: W. W. Norton, 1976.

Gatewood, Willard B., ed. *Controversy in the Twenties: Fundamentalism, Modernism, and Evolution.* Nashville: Vanderbilt University Press, 1968.

Kirschner, Don S. *City and Country: Rural Responses to Urbanization in the 1920s.* Westport, Conn.: Greenwood Press, 1970.

Leuchtenburg, William E. *The Perils of Prosperity, 1914–1942.* Chicago: University of Chicago Press, 1958.

Lynd, Robert S., and Helen M. *Middletown: A Study in American Culture.* New York: Harcourt Brace Jovanovich, 1929.

Perrett, Geoffrey. *American in the Twenties: A History.* New York: Simon & Schuster, 1982.

President's Research Committee on Social Trends. *Recent Social Trends in the United States.* New York: McGraw-Hill, 1933.

Susman, Warren I. *Culture as History: The Transformation of American Society in the Twentieth Century.* New York: Pantheon Books, 1984.

DOCUMENT 26.1
Immigration Restriction

With the passage of the National Origins Act of 1924, the United States made the restriction of immigration its national policy. People from most of Asia were excluded, and a quota system was set up which heavily favored northwestern Europe. A yearly limit of 164,000 persons of origin outside the Western Hemisphere was set. In the Senate debate over the act, a sense of belligerent insecurity underlay many of the arguments.

Mr. Shields. [Tenn.] Mr. President, the future immigration policy of the United States is challenging the most serious attention of the American people. They demand that this policy be changed from one of practically the open door to all peoples of the world to one of rigid restriction if not absolute prohibition of immigration. . . . The immigrants we are receiving to-day are of different character from those that came in the early history of our country, and the great numbers in which they are arriving is a cause of serious alarm and menaces the purity of the blood, the homogeneity, and the supremacy of the American people and the integrity and perpetuity of our representative form of government. . . .

The great majority of the present-day immigrants do not, like the old ones, distribute

Source: *Congressional Record,* April 16–28, 1924, pp. 6461–62, 6464–65, 6468, 6537, 6545.

themselves over the States, mingle with and become absorbed in the great body of American people, and build homes, cultivate lands, or, in other words, become permanent and loyal American citizens. They do not have the social characteristics of the original stock. They are not assimilable and do not seem to desire to be assimilated. They bring with them lower standards of living and labor conditions and strange customs and ideals of social justice and government. Civil and religious liberty do not attract them, but they come here to enjoy our prosperity and possess the country our forefathers redeemed from the wilderness and improved as none other in the world.

They largely congregate in cities and form communities of their several foreign nationalities; they speak their own languages and train their children to do so. . . .[M]ore than half of them remain unnaturalized and owe allegiance to foreign governments. . . . There are whole wards in New York and Chicago where the English language is seldom heard and no newspapers printed in it read. . . .

Mr. President, these undesirable immigrants are seriously endangering the peace and tranquility of our people and the supremacy of our laws and Government. . . . There are many who are intolerant of all restraint and all law and would introduce into this country the wildest doctrines of Bolshevism. We get the majority of the communists, the I.W.W.'s, the dynamiters, and the assassins of public officers from the ranks of the present-day immigrant. . . .

Mr. King. [Utah] Does not the Senator think . . . that the fact that the immigrant . . . rather isolated himself from the mass of the American people, resulted largely because of the exclusive manifestations of the native populations? . . . We assumed . . . a superiority over them; and the tendency of our manifestations was to make them herd together, to become gregarious, because they felt that we were drawing a line of cleavage between the American citi-

zen, the native born, and the immigrant. Does not the Senator think that much of the situation is due to the failure of the people of the United States to adopt a proper attitude toward the immigrant, to provide means of Americanization, and to prove legitimate and proper means more quickly to assimilate the immigrant into the social organism? . . .

Mr. Reed. [Mo.] . . . There has not been a race of men who have ever established themselves upon this earth but have assumed that they were God's chosen children. They have set up barriers against the stranger. In the savage days they imprisoned him or slaughtered him if he entered within their domains; and just in proportion as they adhered to that narrow policy they have circumscribed their own wellbeing and limited their own development; and just in proportion as nations have recognized the fact that they are only one of the great family of nations, just in proportion as they have generously opened their doors to the peoples of other countries, have nations grown into magnitude and power. . . .

Mr. Sheppard. [Texas] . . . As long as a stream of migrating peoples rushes over the gangways of the ships that bear them from other lands to this they produce a swirling, turbulent, disordered mass that is never permitted to reach an angle of racial, political, intellectual, or spiritual repose. While fertile lands in public or in private possession remained available on fairly easy terms and while the cities were still small the new accessions were distributed with a minimum of disturbance and maladjustment. With the disappearance, however, of the public-land frontier, the rise in price and the almost complete occupation of the habitable, cultivable, and readily obtainable areas until they are beyond the reach of the masses, who have only their labor to exchange, the extensive concentration of people in the factory districts and the cities, a condition has developed whereby the American standard of living . . . is being seriously imperiled, and whereby the discord and the turmoil of former years are rendered tenfold more dangerous and intense. . . .

Mr. Heflin. [Alabama] . . . Mr. President, down at Fort Mims, in my State . . . there was a fort in which the white people of that section dwelt . . . [T]here was a big gate in the wall around the fort, and when they closed that mighty gate to this walled-in place they were safe from the Indians. But they grew careless and indifferent, as some Americans have done on this question. One day . . . one of the girls living in the houses within this inclosure, looked down and saw the big gate open, and she said, "Who left that gate open?" They said, "That don't make any difference. There isn't an Indian in 50 miles of here." . . . Just then a little white boy . . . ran through the open gate and said, "I saw a man down by the river side with red paint on his face and feathers in his hair." They screamed with one voice, "Indians! Close the gates!" They started with a rush to the gate, but the Red Eagle, with his Creek warriors, had already entered. It was too late! Too late! . . . With the exception of two or three prisoners, they massacred the whole white population at Fort Mims.

I am appealing to the Senate of the United States to close the gates, close them now while we can. If we do not close them now, the time will come when we will be unable to close them at all. And in that sad day we will cry in vain, "Close the gates."

DOCUMENT 26.2
How the Ku Klux Klan Saw Things

In 1922 a coup d'état *in the Imperial Palace of the Ku Klux Klan, on Peachtree Street, in*

Source: Hiram Wesley Evans, "The Klan's Fight for Americanism," *North American Review*, March 1926, pp. 38–39.

Atlanta, Georgia, replaced "Colonel" William J. Simmons with a Dallas, Texas dentist named Hiram Wesley Evans. Although they had differed over the best way to develop the full financial possibilities of the Klan and over who was to enjoy the profits and the power, there was basic agreement about the menace that threatened America.

The Klan, therefore, has now come to speak for the great mass of Americans of the old pioneer stock. We believe that it does fairly and faithfully represent them, and our proof lies in their support. To understand the Klan, then, it is necessary to understand the character and present mind of the mass of old-stock Americans. The mass, it must be remembered, as distinguished from the intellectually mongrelized "Liberals."

These are, in the first place, a blend of various peoples of the so-called Nordic race, the race which, with all its faults, has given the world almost the whole of modern civilization. The Klan does not try to represent any people but these. . . .

In spite of it, however, these Nordic Americans for the last generation have found themselves increasingly uncomfortable, and finally deeply distressed. There appeared first confusion in thought and opinion, a groping and hesitancy about national affairs and the private life alike, in sharp contrast to the clear, straightforward purposes of our earlier years. There was futility in religion, too, which was in many ways even more distressing. Presently we began to find that we were dealing with strange ideas; policies that always sounded well, but somehow always made us still more uncomfortable.

Finally came the moral breakdown that has been going on for two decades. One by one all our traditional moral standards went by the boards, or were so disregarded that they ceased to be binding. The sacredness of our Sabbath, of our homes, of chastity, and finally even of our right to teach our own children in our own schools fundamental facts and truths were torn away from us. Those who maintained the old standards did so only in the face of constant ridicule.

Along with this went economic distress. The assurance for the future of our children dwindled. We found our great cities and the control of much of our industry and commerce taken over by strangers, who stacked the cards of success and prosperity against us. Shortly they came to dominate our government. The *bloc* system by which this was done is now familiar to all. Every kind of inhabitant except the Americans gathered in groups which operated as units in politics, under orders of corrupt, self-seeking and un-American leaders, who both by purchase and threat enforced their demands on politicians. Thus it came about that the interests of Americans were always the last to be considered by either national or city governments, and that the native Americans were constantly discriminated against, in business, in legislation and in administrative government.

So the Nordic American today is a stranger in large parts of the land his fathers gave him. . . .

DOCUMENT 26.3
H. L. Mencken on Prohibition

The most caustic critic of rural and small-town America was the outspoken Baltimore newspaperman, H. L. Mencken. His basic Nietzschean distrust of the people, or the "yokels," as he liked to call them, made his journal, the American Mercury, *required reading for the "in" set during the 1920s.*

The yokels hang on because old apportionments give them unfair advantages. The vote of a

Source: H. L. Mencken, *A Carnival of Buncombe,* ed. Malcolm Moos (Baltimore: The Johns Hopkins Press, 1956), pp. 160–61, 163.

malarious peasant on the lower Eastern Shore counts as much as the votes of twelve Baltimoreans. But that can't last. It is not only unjust and undemocratic; it is absurd. For the lowest city proletarian, even though he may be farm-bred, is at least superior to the yokel. He has had enterprise enough to escape from the cow and the plow, and he has enjoyed contact with relatively enlightened men. He knows a great deal more than the rustic, and his tastes are more civilized. In the long run he is bound to revolt against being governed from the dung-hill.

*   *   *   *   *

. . . Once the cities have liberated themselves from yokel rule, civilization will be free to develop in the United States. Today it is woefully hobbled by the ideas of peasants. We have many huge and grandiose villages, but, with the possible exception of New York and San Francisco, we have no cities. When an American, acquiring money, feels a yearning for civilized living, he has to go abroad. That is surely not a sound state of affairs. No one wants to civilize the peasant against his will, but it is plainly against reason to let him go on riding his betters.

DOCUMENT 26.4
William Jennings Bryan Defends the Faith

Throughout his political life, William Jennings Bryan combined a struggle for political success with belief in a Christian moral order. In his earlier career he fought against the attempts of corporate wealth to undo that order; and in the 1920s he came to believe that science and a secular urban society were undercutting

Source: William Jennings Bryan, *The Menace of Darwinism* (New York: Fleming H. Revell Co. 1922), pp. 15–17, 22–23, 49–51.

its religious foundations. In his last years he led the fundamentalist battle to protect biblical truths from being undermined in the schools by the doctrines and followers of Darwinism.

The hypothesis to which the name of Darwin has been given—the hypothesis that links man to the lower forms of life and makes him a lineal descendant of the brute—is obscuring God and weakening all the virtues that rest upon the religious tie between God and man. . . .

   . . . Man is infinitely more than science; science, as well as the Sabbath, was made for man. It must be remembered, also that all sciences are of equal importance. Tolstoy insists that the science of "How to Live" is more important than any other science, and is this not true? It is better to trust in the Rock of Ages, than to know the age of the rocks; it is better for one to know that he is close to the Heavenly Father, than to know how far the stars in the heavens are apart. And is it not just as important that the scientists who deal with matter should respect the scientists who deal with spiritual things, as that the latter should respect the former? If it be true, as Paul declares, that "the things that are seen are temporal" while "the things that are unseen are eternal," why should those who deal with temporal things think themselves superior to those who deal with the things that are eternal? Why should the Bible, which the centuries have not been able to shake, be discarded for scientific works that have to be revised and corrected every few years? The preference should be given to the Bible.

   . . . Darwinism is not science at all; it is guesses strung together. There is more science in the twenty-fourth verse of the first chapter of Genesis (And God said, let the earth bring forth the living creature after his kind, cattle and creeping things, and beast of the earth after his kind; and it was so.) than in all that Darwin wrote. . . .

   . . . At the University of Wisconsin (so a Methodist preacher told me) a teacher told his class that the Bible was a collection of myths. When I brought the matter to the attention of the President of the University, he criticized me but avoided all reference to the Professor. At Ann Arbor a professor argued with students against religion and asserted that no thinking man could believe in God or the Bible. At Columbia (I learned this from a Baptist preacher) a professor began his course in geology by telling his class to throw away all that they had learned in the Sunday school. There is a professor in Yale of whom it is said that no one leaves his class a believer in God. (This came from a young man who told me that his brother was being led away from the Christian faith by this professor.) A father (a Congressman) tells me that a daughter on her return from Wellesley told him that nobody believed in the Bible stories now. . . .

I submit three propositions for the consideration of the Christians of the nation:

First, preachers who break the bread of life to lay members should believe that man has in him the breath of the Almighty, as the Bible declares—not the blood of the brute, as the evolutionists affirm. He should also believe in the virgin birth of the Saviour.

Second, none but Christians in good standing and with spiritual conception of life should be allowed to teach in Christian schools. Church schools are worse than useless if they bring students under the influence of those who do not believe in the religion upon which the Church and church schools are built. Atheism and agnosticism are more dangerous when hidden under the cloak of religion than when they are exposed to view.

Third, the tax-payers should prevent the teaching in the public schools of atheism, agnosticism, Darwinism, or any other hypothesis that links man in blood relationship with the brutes. Christians build their own colleges in which to teach Christianity; let atheists and agnostics build their own schools in which to teach their doctrines—whether they call it atheism, agnosticism, or a scientific interpretation of the Bible. . . .

DOCUMENT 26.5
Cultural Lag

Middletown: A Study in American Culture *was a complete inventory and analysis of the American small city, here represented by Muncie, Indiana. Still regarded as a major milestone in American sociology, it presented the clash between the old and new in a changing society.*

. . . It is apparent that Middletown is carrying on certain . . . habitual pursuits in almost precisely the same manner as a generation ago, while in the performance of others its present methods bear little resemblance to the earlier ones. . . . Getting a living seemingly exhibits the most pervasive change, particularly in its technological and mechanical aspects; leisure time, again most markedly in material developments such as the automobile and motion picture, is almost as mobile; training the young in schools, community activities, and making a home would come third, fourth, and fifth in varying order, depending upon which traits are scrutinized; while, finally on the whole exhibiting least change, come the formal religious activities. . . .

    . . . Whether one is temperamentally well disposed towards social change or resistant to it, however, the fact remains that Middletown's life exhibits at almost every point either some change or some stress arising from failure to change. . . .

From *Middletown* by Robert S. Lynd and Helen Merrill Lynd, copyright, 1929, by Harcourt, Brace & World, Inc.; renewed, 1957, by Robert S. and Helen M. Lynd, pp. 497–502. Reprinted by permission of the publisher.

. . . New tools and inventions have been the most prolific breeders of change. They have entered Middletown's industrial life more rapidly than new business and management devices. Bathrooms and electricity have pervaded the homes of the city more rapidly than innovations in the personal adjustments between husband and wife or between parents and children. The automobile has changed the leisure-time life more drastically than have the literature courses taught the young, and tool-using vocational courses have appeared more rapidly in the school curriculum than changes in the arts courses. The development of the linotype and radio are changing the technique of winning political elections more than developments in the art of speech-making or in Middletown's methods of voting. The YMCA, built about a gymnasium, exhibits more change in Middletown's religious institutions than do the weekly sermons of its ministers or the deliberations of the Ministerial Association. By and large, a new tool or material device, the specific efficacy of which can be tested decisively and impersonally, is fairly certain to be fitted somehow into Middletown's accepted scheme of things, while opposed non-material factors, such as tradition and sentiment, slowly open up to make room for it. . . .

    . . . As Middletown has become reluctantly conscious from time to time of discrepancies in its institutional system it has frequently tended to avoid "doing something about" these "social problems" of "bad times," "the younger generation," "corrupt politics," "housing," "street traffic," and so on, by blaming the difficulty on the "nature of things" or upon the willfulness of individuals. When the "problem" has become so urgent that the community has felt compelled to seek and apply a "remedy," this remedy has tended to be a logical extension of old categories to the new situation, or an emotional defense of the earlier situation with a renewed insistence upon traditional verbal or other symbols, or a stricter enforcement or further elaboration of existing institutional devices: thus difficulties in the business world are met by a greater elaboration of financial devices and by an attempt to apply the familiar individual ethics to corporate activities, increase in crime by an elaboration of the police and court systems or the doubling of penalties, political corruption by harking back to the Constitution in all the schools, by nationwide oratorical contests, by getting more people out to vote, indifference to the church by the forming of more church organizations. . . .

DOCUMENT 26.6
The Small Town as "Dullness Made God"

Sinclair Lewis's novel about the unsuccessful efforts of a vivacious young wife, named Carol Kennicott, to bring vitality and culture to the mythical midwestern town of Gopher Prairie was taken up in the 1920s as the classic description of the philistine monotony of small-town America.

In reading popular stories and seeing plays, asserted Carol, she had found only two traditions of the American small town. The first tradition, repeated in scores of magazines every month, is that the American village remains the one sure abode of friendship, honesty, and clean sweet marriageable girls. Therefore all men who succeed in painting in Paris or in finance in New York at last become weary of smart women, return to their native towns, assert that cities are vicious, marry their childhood sweethearts and, presumably, joyously abide in those towns until death.

Source: Sinclair Lewis, *Main Street* (New York: Harcourt, Brace & Co., 1920), pp. 264–65. Copyright 1920 by Harcourt Brace Jovanovich, Inc.; copyright 1948, by Sinclair Lewis. Reprinted by permission of the publisher.

The other tradition is that the significant features of all villages are whiskers, iron dogs upon lawns, gold bricks, checkers, jars of gilded cattails, and shrewd comic old men who are known as "hicks" and who ejaculate "Waal I swan." This altogether admirable tradition rules the vaudeville stage, facetious illustrators, and syndicated newspaper humor, but out of actual life it passed forty years ago. Carol's small town thinks not in hoss-swapping but in cheap motor cars, telephones, ready-made clothes, silos, alfalfa, kodaks, phonographs, leather-upholstered Morris chairs, bridge-prizes, oil-stocks, motion-pictures, land-deals, unread sets of Mark Twain, and a chaste version of national politics.

With such a small-town life a Kennicott or a Champ Perry is content, but there are also hundreds of thousands, particularly women and young men, who are not at all content. The more intelligent young people (and the fortunate widows!) flee to the cities with agility and, despite the fictional tradition, resolutely stay there, seldom returning even for holidays. The most protesting patriots of the towns leave them in old age, if they can afford it, and go to live in California or in the cities.

The reason, Carol insisted, is not a whiskered rusticity. It is nothing so amusing!

It is an unimaginatively standardized background, a sluggishness of speech and manners, a rigid ruling of the spirit by the desire to appear respectable. It is contentment . . . the contentment of the quiet dead, who are scornful of the living for their restless walking. It is negation canonized as the one positive virtue. It is the prohibition of happiness. It is slavery self-sought and self-defended. It is dullness made God.

A savorless people, gulping tasteless food, and sitting afterward, coatless and thoughtless, in rocking-chairs prickly with inane decorations, listening to mechanical music, saying mechanical things about the excellence of Ford automobiles, and viewing themselves as the greatest race in the world.

DOCUMENT 26.7
The Shift from a Producer to a Consumer Culture

A leading historian of the twenties and thirties offers Bruce Barton, Henry Ford, and Babe Ruth as the heroes of the new world of consumption.

When Bruce Barton died at the age of 80 in 1967, it seemed almost inevitably and perfectly logical that at least one writer of his obituary should refer to his life story as "legendary in the best Horatio Alger sense." Among the most prominent men of his time, Barton had come out of a small Tennessee town to become one of the most widely read and respected authors of his day. He would serve in the Congress of the United States, run for the Senate, and even be considered as a possible presidential candidate. He was to found one of the most important advertising agencies and to shape the development of the advertising business— so crucial itself in shaping the new mass society of the period—in significant ways. . . . While Barton himself was known to millions of Americans through his writings and public service, his company could, in a special memorandum on the occasion of his death, point to the special meaning of his vast "contacts." "It meant contact with Presidents of the United States, with senators, with cabinet members, with leaders of industry. . . . Bruce could call anyone in the United States and time would be found for him." But perhaps most significant, Bar-

ton's life recalls Horatio Alger because, in a sense, he rewrote the American primer on success in a way that most effectively served the middle class of the 1920s. This revision provided a necessary kind of secular religion, a special vision of piety essential to the nation's transformation into a modern industrial mass society. His version of the success story helped ease the transition from an older, more producer-centered system with its traditional value structure to the newer, more consumer-centered system with its changed value structure. Barton's inspirational writings (and in a way this includes his brilliant advertising copy) found a way of bridging the gap between the demands of a Calvinistic producer ethic with its emphasis on hard work, self-denial, savings and the new, increasing demands of a hedonistic consumer ethic: spend, enjoy, use up . . .

Barton's original fame rested on his prolific and unsubtle contributions to inspirational literature. Some found his work sentimental, even cloying, but there seemed to be a ceaseless public demand for it. Many of these qualities appeared in his most famous advertising copy. What Bruce Barton possessed was an insight into human nature, especially into the character of the American middle class in a period of transformation. He had a special sensitivity to its fears and hopes, yearnings and ideals. Richard M. Huber rightly finds him a man "with a knack for retailing simple homilies"—very much like the poet Edgar Guest. It seemed both easy and natural when "this leading retailer of values poured most of his energies into retailing products . . ."

Barton's famous "Creed of an Advertising Man," first delivered as an address in 1927, is even more characteristic of his thinking and greatly contributed to an understanding of his 1920s vision of the importance of advertising in the social order. He writes:

> . . . I am in advertising because advertising
> is the power which keeps business out in the

Source: Warren I. Susman, "Piety, Profit, and Play: The 1920s," in *Men, Women, and Issues in American History,* eds. Howard H. Quint and Milton Cantor, vol. II, rev. ed., (Chicago: Dorsey Press), pp. 202–27.

open, which compels it to set up for itself public ideals of quality and service and to measure up to those ideals. Advertising is a creative force that has generated jobs, new ideas, has expanded our economy and has helped give us the highest standard of living in the world. Advertising is the spark plug on the cylinder of mass production, and essential to the continuance of the democratic process. Advertising sustains a system that has made us leaders of the free world: The American Way of Life. . . .

Advertising, then, was persuasion and persuasion could and would change the world; but advertising at the moment was doing its greatest and most necessary service in its special relationship to business—by publicizing products and urging consumers to buy them. (His method of dealing with Communism, stated later in life, is characteristic: ''Give every Russian a copy of the latest Sears-Roebuck Catalogue and the address of the nearest Sears-Roebuck outlet.'') The genius of Barton's own advertising copy was based on the assumption that the use of products advertised effectively contributed to growth and progress, sometimes of the nation but more often of the individual himself. The most successful ads would seek to employ the products of a business in the service of the sanctity or betterment of human life. Witness, for instance, one General Electric ad: ''Any woman who is doing any household task that a little electric motor can do is working for three cents an hour. Human life is too precious to be sold at the price of three cents an hour.''

. . . The ad shaped for each situation sought to provide everyone with a simple way to understand a rapidly standardizing and mechanizing way of life. In a world of increased complexities, mass technology, and fearful changes, such advertisements offered a chance to retain human dignity as well as individual meaning and development. Bruce Barton, the great mas-

ter of the uplift essay, without doubt had put uplift at the service of American business enterprise. . . .

Bruce Barton, it is clear, had been fascinated by ideas about salesmanship and religion many years before writing his 1925 best seller *The Man Nobody Knows*. He had often commented, in writing and conversation, what a great textbook the Bible could be for an advertising man. Barton's writings delighted in Biblical-like parables and even his advertising copy had a Biblical quality to its prose. But it was only in 1925, the year of the Scopes Trial and William Jennings Bryan's fundamentalist interpretation of the Old Testament, that the Republican business-oriented Barton finally provided his important and widely read interpretation of the New Testament, which especially emphasized the life of Jesus.

The initial task at hand was to develop a necessary new view of the personality of Jesus and the basic values that went with it. Barton took particular aim at the Sunday School image of Jesus: a weakling, a killjoy, a failure, a sissy, meek and full of grief. In its place there was a new Jesus: the physically strong carpenter, a healthy and vigorous outdoors man, a sociable companion, a strong and effective leader. ''A killjoy! He was the most popular dinner guest in Jerusalem! . . . A failure! He picked up twelve men from the bottom ranks of business and forged them into an organization that conquered the world.'' Barton insisted on Jesus' masculinity, suggesting his attractiveness to women, stressing his role as a father figure, even emphasizing the role of Jesus' own ''historical'' father, Joseph. Jesus emerges, as it were, a consumer himself, enjoying life and parties, turning water into wine. His methods are those of advertising; he is the founder of ''modern business'' and modern entrepreneurial tactics. Barton's understanding of what Jesus meant by his ''Father's business'' is the key to his own analysis. God seeks, Barton tells us, to develop perfect human beings, superior to circumstance, victorious over Fate. No single kind of human talent or effort can be spared if the experiment is to succeed. The race must be fed and clothed and housed and transported, as well as preached to, and taught and healed. Thus *all* business is his Father's business. All work is worship; all useful service prayer. And whoever works wholeheartedly at any worthy calling is a co-worker with the Almighty in the great enterprise which He has initiated but which he can never finish without the help of men.

The Man Nobody Knows first appeared in serial form in the *Woman's Home Companion* and then for several years in the late 1920s continued to ride high on the best-seller lists. Barton followed it in 1927 with *The Book Nobody Knows,* a study of the Bible. These works have never been without an audience since they were first published, but they remain peculiarly documents of the 1920s and in a sense the high points of Barton's career. . . .

Barton's salesman as hero replaced William Graham Sumner's savings bank depositor as hero for the conservative sons of American Puritan ministers—much as though one age of social order were in effect replacing another. At a time in which the values of a producer society dominated, Sumner, the Yale sociologist, could claim that the man who saved his money and practiced self-denial was the hero of civilization; in an age of increasing consumer orientation stressing sales and spending and joy rather than self-denial, Barton, the advertising man, glorified the salesman-businessman . . . By the time of Henry Ford's death in 1947, at least one of the crucial ideas in Bruce Barton's life and work—the proposition that business was service—was firmly fixed in American thought. Notwithstanding depression and World War, the idea of business success had also become sharply identified with the business of being American. Maybe Calvin Coolidge had said it crudely in the 1920s, but

the overwhelming majority of the public opinion makers in 1947 seemed to agree: the business of America *was* business. This identification was so complete that Ford himself as well as his achievements seemed to be, as *The New York Times* declared, the very "embodiment of America in an era of industrial revolution." Yet Ford's career had been made possible *because* of the American system itself; he was the product of our "free enterprise" way while also serving as the living symbol of its achievement and success. . . .

By 1893 the Duryea brothers successfully had demonstrated the first American gasoline automobile. Two years later, a meeting with Thomas A. Edison, perhaps Ford's only hero, encouraged him to continue work on his engine. By 1896 he had demonstrated his own first car; by 1899 the company asked him to choose between his hobby and his job. Ford made his decision: a full dedication of his future to the automobile. . . .

In 1907, against "sound" advice, Ford announced his mission and his dream:

> I will build a motor car for the great multitude. It will be large enough for the family but small enough for the individual to run and care for. It will be constructed of the best materials, by the best men to be hired, after the simplest designs that modern engineering can devise. But it will be so low in price that no man making a good salary will be unable to own one—and enjoy with his family the blessing of hours of pleasure in God's great open spaces.

From the vantage point of the time it was issued, this extraordinarily simple statement is breathtaking in its implications. It is, in fact, a prediction of a new social order, an introduction to the world that was to be in the 1920s. It had enormous significance for the individual, the family, the mass society—and perhaps even in a sense proposed a serious redefinition of each. It hinted at a new definition of work and of production. It projected the likelihood of a new lifestyle. It implied a new kind of possible egalitarianism unheard of in the world's history—and it did all of this not in the name of needs, basic requirements of life, but in terms of possible pleasure: here, indeed, was a consumer vision of the world.

The creation of the Model T—the Tin Lizzie, or the flivver, as "she" was also called—is the climax of the story, the final convergence of Ford and history. . . .

It resulted in the introduction of the famous moving assembly line, which involved an enormous financial commitment in terms of tools. The idea of continuous movement seemed simple enough, and it rested on two seemingly simple principles: (1) the work must be brought to the worker and not the worker to the work, and (2) the work must be brought waist high so no worker would have to stoop. Taking almost seven years to perfect, the system at Highland Park was an established fact by 1914, and the production revolution had been wrought. Men and machine, through the central conveyor belt, had been in effect merged into one gigantic machine. It made possible a dramatic reduction in the time required to produce a car. By 1920 one completed Model T rolled off the line every minute; by 1925 one every ten seconds. Production rose from 39,640 in 1911 to 740,770 in 1917. In 1920, every other car in the world was a Model T Ford. . . .

With production methods already radically altered by 1914, Ford announced yet another daring step. He proposed a new wage scheme, a kind of profit sharing (in advance of actual profits) in which the minimum for any class of work would be (under certain conditions) five dollars a day. At the same time, he reduced the working day from nine to eight hours. The key fact here was that in *no* sense was pay tied into productivity. There were conditions attached to the minimum-pay stipulation: certain minimum standards of conduct and behav-

ior as outlined by the company; that is, standards by which the company judged men to be "good workers." Ford, in effect, doubled the wages. . . .

And, as he was well aware, he had also made every workman a potential customer. . . .

By the 1920s, then, Ford and his new system were being widely hailed as the American System. The miracles he had wrought in production and consumption made his name synonymous with American success. . . . When George Herman Ruth, Jr., died in 1947, *The New York Times* devoted more than two of its large eight-column pages to him . . .

Ruth, Baseball's Great Star and Idol of Children, Had a Career Both Dramatic and Bizarre/World-Wide Fame Won on Diamond/Even in Lands Where Game is Unknown, Baseball's Star Player Was Admired. . . . Ruth Set Fifty-four Major League Records and Ten Additional Marks in American Circuit/Slugger Starred in 10 World Series/Ruth Set Major League Homer Mark on Total of 714—Hit Over 40 Eleven Seasons/Had Most Walks in 1923/All-Time Batting Great also Struck Out Most Times in Career Lasting 22 Years . . .

Baseball had been a successful professional activity since the 1870s, and by 1903 it had become sufficiently developed and well organized to create the beginnings of a mass audience and the source of significant careers for many young men. For Ruth—a man without learning, traditional skills, or alternate route—it offered a miraculous escape from the treadmill of poverty. Baseball could provide him with effective social mobility. Ruth was certainly neither the first nor the last of the children of fairly recent immigration and urban poverty to find their way to national status and success. Yet in many ways his career was among the most spectacular. One of St. Mary's brothers recommended Ruth to the owner of the Baltimore club, and he signed his first professional contract in 1914. That same year, his contract was sold for $2,900 to the Boston Red Sox, and with that organization he soon matured into a pitcher of rare ability.

While at Boston, Ruth also began to show remarkable prowess as a hitter. Baseball fans started to talk of his home runs, and by 1919 he was more often in the outfield than on the pitching mound. The following year was a turning point in both Ruth's career and in the game itself. The Yankees purchased his contract for $100,000 and also guaranteed the $350,000 mortgage on the financially shaky Red Sox stadium. It was a record sum—but the Babe delivered with a record number of home runs and enthusiastic fan response. The winter of 1920–1921, however, produced a scandal that rocked the entire structure of professional baseball. Gamblers had managed to buy the services of several members of the Chicago White Sox (subsequently labeled "Black Sox") to "throw" the 1919 World Series. The owners then reorganized baseball's business structure and appointed a stern federal judge, James Kenesaw Mountain Landis, as new high commissioner with unlimited power to assure the sanctity of the sport, though they still worried whether this reform would be enough, whether the fans would return. Many historians of the game attribute Ruth's brilliant performance during the following season as the most important factor in reviving spectator enthusiasm. Nine to ten million fans annually paid to see major league baseball in the 1920s. . . .

Whatever his achievements on the field, his growing contributions to the record books, the Babe also delighted millions of his countrymen by the sheer bigness of his affable personality and even by his awesome inability to curb his overwhelming appetites. Most Americans seemed to tolerate at least some of the indulgences of their big boy. No Ford or Barton, Ruth enjoyed spending money as well as earning it. An incorrigible gambler, and for large sums, he never seemed concerned about winning or losing. He loved expensive and fancy clothes. His interest in sex seemed limitless, and he frequented the better brothels even while in training or on tour with the ball club. His gluttony became equally legendary; he often overate and overdrank to the point of actual severe physical illness. Like so many celebrities in our modern mechanized age, Ruth's frequent illness, physical collapse, even hospitalization became almost routine. The Babe's most publicized collapse and hospitalization occurred during spring training in 1925, and the public apparently accepted the official explanation that his illness was the result of influenza and indigestion; the real cause, it appears, was a serious case of syphilis. A much concerned public watched intensely for reports of Ruth's condition. One well-known sportswriter called it "the stomach ache heard round the world."

Ruth was a heroic producer in the mechanized world of play. He was also an ideal hero for the world of consumption. Americans enjoyed the Babe's excess; they took comfort in the life of apparently enormous pleasures that Ruth enjoyed. Seldom if ever (even in this age of the rising popularity of Freudian thought) did they seem aware of what might exist behind this pattern of excess and illness. "Babe Ruth," Bill McGeehan said in 1925, "is our national exaggeration. . . . He has lightened the cares of the world and kept us from becoming overserious by his sheer exuberance."

Ruth found a way of making all of this pay; he made himself into a marketable product.

chapter

The New Deal

Dean Albertson
University of Massachusetts

"The story of the New Deal," according to historian Paul K. Conkin, "is a sad story, the ever recurring story of what might have been." In a similar vein Rexford Guy Tugwell, one of the New Deal's major architects, has written recently: "At some moments I thought Roosevelt saw how radical a reconstruction was called for; at others I guessed he would temporize. . . . I was right in this last. The New Deal was mild medicine. . . . [Roosevelt] could have emerged from the orthodox progressive chrysalis and led us into a new world. He chose rather rickety repairs for an old one."

Was the crisis of 1933 of such awesome proportion that the president of the United States could have done anything he wanted to do? How well did business leaders, government administrators, and the people, understand the changing nature of American capitalism during the era of the New Deal? In judging the New Deal, should we accept Roosevelt's statement that it ended prior to 1941, or should we regard the entire 12 years of Roosevelt's presidency as relevant to the assessment? Finally, to what extent do the social and economic problems of the 1970s have their roots in the accomplishments or failures of Roosevelt's New Deal administrations?

For many Americans of today's New Left, the New Deal was a total failure in that it preserved the market economy and paved the way for the coming of an alleged Pentagon "state-managed" economy.

For a larger number of Americans styled as liberals, New Deal reforms fortunately shored up an ailing capitalism and rescued democratic structures which were seriously threatened by fascism or communism or both.

For a minority of conservative older Americans, the New Deal's movement toward today's welfare capitalism and a semimanaged economy were nothing less than "creeping socialism." Accordingly, Roosevelt was a "traitor to his class."

For black Americans, who under New Deal relief programs were treated not unlike other poor people, the Roosevelt regime was an improvement over past administrations; yet, in retrospect, New Deal politics and policies had little effect in mitigating, let alone eliminating, racism in the United States.

President Herbert Hoover in his inaugural address on March 4, 1929, could observe with equanimity that "Through liberation from widespread poverty we have reached a higher degree of individual freedom than ever before. . . . In no nation are the fruits of accomplishment more secure." Less than eight months later, the great speculative bull market broke, and the U.S. economy spiraled down into the reaches of depression more pervasive and terrifying than had ever been known.

Hoover understood capitalism in all its parts. As secretary of commerce under Warren Harding and Calvin Coolidge, he had helped to build the system. And the system which he envisaged was a capitalism emergent from the rapacious days of laissez-faire, and governed—on behalf of business, labor, and "the people"—by a national administration which served as an impartial umpire. The whole conception depended upon all three groups coming together in a sense of a voluntarily self-governing "American community."

And what were the corporate interests building in the twenties? Even then the dim outlines of a conceptualized "monster machine" had appeared. Henry Ford's cars were rolling off the assembly line at a rate of well over two million a year, and as President Coolidge presciently noted, "The business of America was business." But people in Muncie, Indiana, were working harder than ever for diminishing satisfactions: male factory workers [in 1924] had a 1 in 424 chance of promotion; females earned a third less than males for comparable work; and only 15 percent of Muncie's families earned enough to pay an income tax. If Muncie's experience was typical, millions of Americans, ironically, were excluded from the benefits of the nation's vaunted consumption-oriented economy.

And there were other indications that American capitalism was less than healthy. Despite a rising national income [from $60.7 billion in 1922 to $87.2 billion in 1929], 26 million of the total 27.5 million American families earned less than $2,500 per year, which in 1929 was deemed necessary for a decent standard of living. As technological efficiency increased, production and profits rose. Between 1922 and 1929 managerial profit and dividends increased a hundredfold. During the same pe-

riod, as American Federation of Labor leadership sought to convince management of its true conservatism and devotion to capitalism, federation membership dropped from 5.1 million to 3.4 million. Thus was management able to keep down the wages of people who were magically expected to consume the goods which were produced in profusion. It was perfectly clear that technology had brought capitalism to its post-scarcity phase in America in the twenties and yet, in order to preserve capitalism itself, scarcity continued to be artificially maintained. It was no longer a matter of having to work in order to consume—it had become a matter of having to work for wages in order to buy goods at a price which yielded profits. Few Americans perceived an alternative.

Out of the glut of profits arose the speculative mania of the twenties. It began in real estate, spearheaded by ever-increasing lines of automobiles bound nightly for the suburbs over newly constructed macadam roads. Then it shifted to the stock market. During 1927 and into 1928 the market advanced—Radio Corporation of America from 85 to 420, Montgomery Ward from 117 to 440, DuPont from 310 to 525. By the beginning of 1929 a rising tide of prosperity, a New Era, bloomed for the thin stratum of upper middleclass families earning more than $2,500 per year. As the number of investment trusts increased, so did the activity of commercial banks in granting broker's loans. Buying stock on margin came to be a common gambit in fortune winning. One paid a small percentage of the stock price in cash, financing the remainder with a broker's loan at 12 percent interest. From 1927 to 1929, broker's loans rose from $3.4 billion to $8.5 billion, or roughly 8 percent of the gross national product value. Brokers' loans seemed at the time so comparatively risk-free that some corporations began to invest their surplus funds in them.

Meanwhile, the perils of a runaway market were known to Herbert Hoover. His choice, on assuming office, was to ease the market down in March 1929—or to let it plunge to its end. He could have publicly warned against further speculation. He could have asked for legislation curbing brokers' loans and margin buying. He could have suggested that the Federal Reserve System raise the rediscount rate. He did none of these things. And on "Black Thursday," October 24, 1929, nearly thirteen million stock shares were traded at prices ruinous to their former owners. Five days later, over sixteen million shares crossed the counter, and within a few weeks the devastation would be computed at a 40 percent decline in stock values. That elusive quality called "business confidence," so crucial to the proper functioning of a capitalistic economy, had been lost. Businesses cut inventories. Industry shelved expansion plans. American investment abroad was curtailed.

For the remaining three years of his administration, Herbert Hoover pleaded in vain for the shock of depression to fall on profits, not on wages. He begged his ideal "community" to look after its own—to solve nationwide depression locally and to disdain an enslaving federal bureaucracy. But Hoover's efforts more often than not consisted of government loans to big businesses and banks, leaving the president prey to Democratic party propaganda that he was a heartless, unfeeling leader. As if to confirm his aloofness from the suffering in July 1932, he loosed the army on several thousand veterans who had come to Washington demanding payment of a World War I bonus.

In the end, all was bootless. American capitalism sank to its knees under the crushing weight of nearly fifteen million unemployed.

Franklin Delano Roosevelt stood before thousands of applauding delegates to the Democratic National Convention in Chicago on July 2, 1932, to accept the presidential nomination, which he and his "brains trust" associates had with consummate political skill managed to wrest from the other contenders. When the

cheers and the last booming organ notes of "Happy Days Are Here Again" had stilled, the candidate seemed to serve notice of a break with the past. "Throughout the nation," he told them, "men and women, forgotten in the political philosophy of the government of the last years look to us here for guidance and for more equitable opportunity to share in the distribution of national wealth. . . ." And then: "I pledge you, I pledge myself, to a new deal for the American people. Let us all here assembled constitute ourselves prophets of a new order of competence and of courage. This is more than a political campaign; it is a call to arms. . . ."

Roosevelt then made an analysis of past American history, one which was to be the hallmark of New Deal rhetoric for a generation. The partnership of laissez-faire government and buccaneering capitalism may have been contributive to American industrial growth at a time when the nation was filling in its frontiers and creating the mightiest productive machinery on earth. But times had changed. The free land of the frontier was gone. The United States had entered World War I as a debtor nation and emerged as the largest international creditor. Infant industries had matured into complex, engulfing giants, unrestrained either by government or by moral self-regulation. Ownership of land, businesses, and factories (and the concomitant fruits of ownership—economic security, success, prestige, and the like) once were available on a small scale for many amidst national abundance. But by the 1930s, ownership was possible on a modest scale for only a few lucky winners. National and international cartels had replaced the family-owned factory. A managerial elite, hired by corporations on annual salaries to manage their affairs, had superseded the plant owner who had known his foreman and most of his workers by their first names.

With such changes as these, could democracy and individualism endure by nineteenth-century definitions? These values were thought to be the cornerstones of American greatness. But the old democracy and the old individualism were based on the competitive economics envisioned in Adam Smith's metaphysical "invisible hand" system, which saw society automatically propelling itself toward abundance by simply competing in accordance with the laws of the marketplace—laws that were far beyond the manipulation of mortal men. Clearly, an Industrial Revolution and a managerial revolution had occurred since Adam Smith revealed these "immutable" laws. Most Americans, to be sure, had been encouraged from grade school onward to glorify the virtue and necessity of competition. Could they continue to do so? Could capitalistic competition retain the guiding principle of business and industry when one-tenth of 1 percent of American corporations earned nearly half of the net income and owned over half of the assets of all corporations in the United States?

Thus came the New Deal in a period of profound, apathetic despair. But it was not the season for revolution: out of nearly forty million votes cast in 1932, the Socialists and Communists combined polled less than a million, and this in face of the fact that one quarter of the entire working force was jobless, their savings often wiped out. State funds for the relief of hunger and destitution were exhausted. Foreclosure and bankruptcy stalked the homes, farms, factories, and businesses of the nation. Iowa corn was being burned for fuel while poverty-stricken urbanites shivered in breadlines. Some people with an eye on the European scene, were talking about a "dictator"—by which they meant a Leader. "All we have to fear is fear itself," Roosevelt optimistically told them in his inaugural. "Something far more positive than acquiescence vests the President with the authority of a dictator," said newspaperwoman Anne O'Hare McCormick. "There is a country-wide dumping of responsibility on the Federal Government. If Mr. Roo-

sevelt goes on collecting mandates, one after another, until their sum is startling, it is because all the other powers . . . virtually abdicate in his favor. America today literally asks for orders." Yes, the president probably could have done anything he wanted to do!

But Roosevelt came to the presidency with no clear idea of what should be done. He hated the dole and believed in the morality of a balanced budget. With these dull tools, the tasks ahead were formidable. Clearly, business must be reinvigorated. The jobless must be sustained, then reemployed. The farmer must be raised from the threat of peasantry. Along with the measures for *recovery,* however, the institutions of the economy must be *reformed* so that the tragedy of depression might not again shake the foundations of democracy.

American democracy was said to follow the paths of free enterprise and individual initiative. Roosevelt saw it this way and never wavered. Despite occasional references to socialism by Tugwell and a few other advisers and cries of "bolshevism" from the hysterical right, a Marxian analysis, let alone a solution, of the American situation was never contemplated. That being so, how, then, could a free government wage war on national adversity without wrenching the entire political and economic machinery into such a high degree of centralization as to destroy both freedom and individualism? And what reforms could be carried out which hopefully would prevent depression from recurring and yet not alter the American system as to make it unpalatable to the majority vote required in an essentially conservative nation? In short, what could possibly be new about a New Deal that was locked into the capitalistic mode of production?

During the early years of the New Deal the question emphatically was not whether political democracy still prevailed in the nation. As recently as November 1932, after all, American democracy was sufficiently viable to throw Hoover and the Republicans out of office; presumably it might be used at a later date to visit similar retribution upon the Democrats. Rather, the issue concerned the relevance of political democracy to economic democracy. *If,* as New Dealers suggested, a worker was no longer free to choose his job and be reasonably sure of steady employment, *if* a farmer could be told on market day that his crop would bring less than the cost of growing it, *if* the small businessman had as his only alternatives ruinous competition or the sale of his plant to a chain operation, *if* the ordinary citizen had so little control over his destiny that one-third of a nation would be "ill-housed, ill-clad, ill-nourished," then of what practical value was the ballot? It was not government, said the New Dealers, which had taken economic liberty. It was the concentrated wealth and power of business and finance, and a fossilized belief in the inexorability of economic law.

To contemporaries the New Deal was incredibly confusing because of its many inconsistencies and the complexity of its proposals. The personality of President Roosevelt himself did little to alleviate the confusion. "There never was a prominent leader, who was more determined about his objectives, and never one who was more flexible about his means," said Tugwell of FDR. This very flexibility, this willingness on the part of Roosevelt and the rest of the New Dealers to "tinker with the works," contributed heavily to the unpatterned quality of the New Deal era.

Nonetheless, in retrospect, the goals of the Roosevelt "revolution" emerge with singular clarity—to preserve the dignity of the individual and his right to private property within the context of a capitalistic democratic society. Or, as Secretary of Agriculture Henry A. Wallace would round out the rhetoric, "the New Deal places human rights above property rights and aims to modify special privilege for the few to the extent that such modification will aid in providing economic security for the many." If in tone it made itself appear as a

break with past traditions, in content it was a direct line continuum with the progressivism of Theodore Roosevelt and Woodrow Wilson.

The immediate response of the New Deal to the problems it faced was a masterful discernment of the traditional American "middle" way. The new government set about following the only mandate given it by the citizenry— to do *something!* Closed banks were examined; nearly all were found to be solvent, and reopened. The gold content of the dollar was reduced and the nation moved to a semimanaged currency. White city boys who volunteered were packed off to the mountains in the dull green uniforms of the Civilian Conservation Corps, to hew undergrowth and plant trees. Mild beer and light wines were provided for a thirsty nation while the twenty-first Amendment to the Constitution made its way among the states. Salaries of government workers were slashed 15 percent across the board. Permissible stock margins were reduced. It was indeed a kaleidoscopic program. The principal themes of New Deal policy lay buried deep within the legislation.

The first major tenet of the early New Deal evoked anguished cries from the conservative right, since it embodied *planning.* Rooseveltian planning was basically experimentation, rather than the comprehensive planning of a socialist regime. For the prudent householder or the shrewd businessman *not* to plan ahead was considered the height of folly. But, according to the philosophy of conservative businessmen, planning by a government was the first step toward absolute regimentation. "If city planning has been worth while," asked Secretary of the Interior Harold L. Ickes, "why not plan nationally? Why not, for instance, plan so that the ample resources which we have, may be made to go around?" Gloomily, replied the deposed Hoover: "This direction must ultimately be reposed in government bureaus and they are comprised of human beings with dictatorial powers over us all." New Deal planning generally meant the formulation of interrelated national programs for rural and urban land use, for human and resource conservation, and for the overcoming of the depression. Contrary to Hoover's dire predictions, local individuals were usually consulted when it came to the implementation of national plans. In nearly all instances they approved the government's proposals; and they were asked to staff and assist in the administration of the resultant bureaucracy, as in the case of the world-renowned Tennessee Valley Authority (TVA).

A second precept of Roosevelt's administrations, deficit financing, caused even greater consternation. Congress gave the President authority to increase the national debt—to use the people's tax money for their benefit at a time when they desperately needed it. Roosevelt had promised to wage war on the depression, and, thus armed, the New Deal called forth what William James termed the "moral equivalents of war." It spent sums which were then thought to be enormous on work relief and public works. To Relief Administrator Harry Hopkins, cynics attributed the apocryphal quotation: "We will tax and tax, spend and spend, elect and elect." But from John Maynard Keynes, the brilliant British economist, came more cheering words: "You, Mr. President, having cast off such fetters [as regarding war to be the sole legitimate excuse for deficit financing], are free to engage in the interests of peace and prosperity the technique which has hitherto only been allowed to serve the purposes of war and destruction." New Deal budgets for the relief of human suffering between 1933 and 1940 totaled a little over $20 billion. In 1940, the public debt stood at nearly $43 billion. But, it is instructive to note, at the end of World War II, in 1945, the public debt had reached well over $258 billion. American priorities were roughly six times as destructive as constructive.

A third aspect of the early New Deal to provoke cynicism was its idealistic faith in co-operation. If rational, comprehensive planning, use of deficit financing, and invocation of "moral equivalents," could enlist a people to cooperate with its government to fight hunger and poverty, government might utilize the same instruments to achieve an "economic constitutional order." Initially, the Roosevelt administration decided not to attempt ineffectual trust-busting against the concentrated power of finance and industry. Neither would it attack the "economic royalists" head on by socializing major units of industry. The New Deal would *cooperate* with big business to bring about recovery from depression. The National Recovery Administration (NRA) defined the terms of that cooperation. Under NRA auspices, each segment of industry would draw up "codes of fair competition" which would set aside the old Sherman Act injunctions against restraint of trade. Competition of the Adam Smith sort was not obliterated. "It means only," said NRA Administrator Hugh S. Johnson, "that competition must keep its blows above the belt, and that there can be no competition at the expense of decent living." To the relief of profit-minded management, it also meant no real interference with capitalistic market economy.

Having asserted that government was to be the servant of its constituents, the New Deal was next faced with the promised redistribution of opportunity and wealth. Roosevelt approached this problem with a somewhat different conception of competition, one which existed among such groups as farmers, workers, and small businessmen. He professed to see his constituency as investors or voters or consumers. Such competition might produce the best chance for economic democracy. Wittingly or not, the New Deal program created, in the words of Reinhold Niebuhr, "the equilibrium of power which is the basis of justice in any society." Competition among large corporations has been rationalized in the earlier Progressive Era, while competition between labor and capital had been an uneven conflict between the financially impotent and the financially powerful. Now, under New Deal sponsorship, came Section 7(a) of the NRA guaranteeing labor's right to organize and to bargain collectively. Within two years, John L. Lewis, president of the United Mine Workers, would rip the old American Federation of Labor in half and lead his followers into the Committee for Industrial Organization. Ostensibly, the issue was craft unions versus industrial unions, but the split actually signaled the most aggressive unionizing effort the nation had ever witnessed. By 1940, after brutal strikes in steel, automobiles, rubber, and textiles, the AFL had doubled its membership, and the CIO was even larger than the AFL. Henceforth, it was hoped that the unions, as claimants for shares of the national wealth, might address either government or business on more equal terms.

If an equilibrium of power—involving farmers, workers, and businessmen—could endow society with a climate of economic justice, there still remained the average man's desire for economic security. Under terms of pre-World War I progressivism, such security could be had by climbing the ladder of advancement from hired hand to tenant farmer to landholder, or from worker to foreman to partner. The goal in either case was ownership. By the 1930s, it was apparent that the ladder to ownership had lost some of its rungs. Tenancy was increasing. Mobility upward from wages to salary was decreasing. Ownership of the nation's land, productive plants, and service enterprises had become concentrated in fewer and fewer hands. Recognizing that only an infinitesimal number of tenants or workers would ever achieve ownership, New Deal policies had the effect of bestowing upon the average American at least the *fruits of ownership*—security. Slum-clearance projects, low-interest home purchase loans, bank deposit insurance, and, above all, unemployment and old-age insurance provided an enlarged opportunity for the majority to en-joy some of the material well being of the opulent and to be freed from a measure of dependence upon the turn of economic fate. President Roosevelt, regarding the Social Security Act as the domestic capstone of his administration, took greater satisfaction from it than anything else he did. For this was the beginning of what since has come to be described as the "cradle-to-grave" security of the welfare state.

By the middle of Roosevelt's second term, times had changed, and so had the New Deal. From Europe came the threatening portents of World War II. America's unemployed had been largely absorbed by government work relief agencies. The NRA, poorly conceived, badly managed, and business dominated, had been swept from the scene in one of many laissez-faire decisions by the Supreme Court. Cooperation had failed. As conservatives in both parties gained strength, their demands for the end of a nationally planned economy grew more insistent. Early New Dealers of the planning-cooperation persuasion were dispatched on foreign missions—far from Washington. As their replacements entered the halls of government, the broad view of an interrelated economy, managed with high moral purpose in presumed accordance with the terms of human existence, gave way before "realistic" legalism and attempts to recover and regulate the classical competitive market.

Never was the New Deal alone able to defeat depression for those who endured its horror from 1929 to 1940. Never did Roosevelt gain suzerainty over the captains of finance and industry. The president, ever keen to achieve a balanced budget, put an end to deficit financing until a severe business recession in 1938 brought the government hastily back to "prime the pump." War appropriations, dwarfing the small sums allocated for the relief of human misery, soon restored economic good health to the nation.

Should the New Deal have carried America

into "democratic socialism?" Could it have done so? Some early New Dealers, such as Tugwell, would have replied affirmatively to both questions. But Tugwell's hopes were groundless. The average citizen, however much he may have suffered during the depression, was not inclined to consider fundamental political or economic changes. Moreover, he remained oblivious to the needs of black and poor Americans: John Dewey, indeed, had reason to be dismayed that so little had actually been done to change the root causes of human suffering. While applauding the progressive melioration that accompanied New Deal politics, he nonetheless lamented (in 1939) that his fellow countrymen still lived under scarcity capitalism and that the relationship between workers and the mode of production remained untouched. Dewey's observations were accurate. The New Deal was no radical revision of old values. Progressive to the core, it set out to save capitalism; and it did that.

SUGGESTED READINGS

Burns, James MacGregor. *Roosevelt: The Lion and the Fox*. New York: Harcourt Brace Jovanovich, 1956.

———. *Roosevelt: The Soldier of Freedom*. New York: Harcourt Brace Jovanovich, 1970.

Chambers, Clarke A. *The New Deal at Home and Abroad*. New York: Free Press, 1965.

Conkin, Paul K. *The New Deal*. New York: Thomas Y. Crowell, 1967.

Davis, Kenneth S. *F.D.R.: The New Deal Years, 1933–1937*. New York: Random House, 1986.

Freidel, Frank. *The New Deal*. Englewood Cliffs, N.J.: Prentice-Hall, 1964.

———. *Franklin D. Roosevelt*. 3 vols. Boston: Little, Brown, 1952–56.

Hamby, Alonzo L. *The New Deal*. New York: Weybright & Talley, 1969.

Leuchtenberg, William E. *Franklin D. Roosevelt and the New Deal 1932–1940*. New York: Harper & Row, 1963.

Lilienthal, David E. *TVA: Democracy on the March*. New York: Harper & Row, 1944.

Schlesinger, Arthur M. Jr. *The Coming of the New Deal*. Boston: Houghton Mifflin, 1959.

———. *The Politics of Upheaval*. Boston: Houghton Mifflin, 1960.

Sherwood, Robert E. *Roosevelt and Hopkins*. New York: Harper & Row, 1948.

Tugwell, Rexford O. *The Democratic Roosevelt*. Garden City, N.Y.: Doubleday Publishing, 1957.

Turkel, Studs. *Hard Times: An Oral History of the Great Depression*. New York: Pantheon Books, 1986.

Zinn, Howard. *New Deal Thought*. Indianapolis: Bobbs-Merrill, 1966.

DOCUMENT 27.1
We Shall Not Rest until That Minimum Is Achieved

Columbia University Professor of Economics Rexford G. Tugwell was forty-one years old when he became a member of Roosevelt's preelection "brain trust." Soon after the inauguration of the New Deal, he rose from assistant secretary of agriculture to undersecretary, to become one of the president's principal advisers. An outspoken protagonist of government planning and disciplined industry, he became a favored target of conservative opposition. Leaving Washington in 1937, Tugwell became successively governor of Puerto Rico and distinguished professor at the University of Chicago. The selections from speeches which he made during 1933 and 1934, given below, illustrate the directions his followers hoped the president would take during the early New Deal period.

There is no prearranged field of government which is set apart from the circumstances of

Source: Rexford G. Tugwell, *The Battle for Democracy* (New York: Columbia University Press, 1935), pp. 1–16, 78–96, and 256–67.

those who are governed. Relations here are always interdependent. As the circumstances of the people change, functions of government change. . . . It is a truism, too, to say that what is done by each of its divisions is affected by the whole orientation of the state. Like most truisms, this one contains a kernel of vital truth; it means, as respects ourselves, that executive, legislative, and judicial functions are not unalterably fixed, but are subject to revision. Government, or any part of it, is not in itself something; it is for something. It must do what we expect of it or it must be changed so that it will. . . .

Past circumstances produced needs (or supposed needs) which yielded theories in support of them. Toughest of those theories—so tough that, in the thinking of most men, it became an unalterable fact—was that which made competition a vital necessity, an end in itself, to be preserved at all costs. Competition was assumed to be an inherent part of democracy. Indeed competition and democracy came to be thought of as two aspects of one and the same value: a noncompetitive world was an undemocratic world.

Some two decades ago, it began to be apparent—or should have been—that competition and democracy were not Siamese twins, that they were separable, that in fact that separation had to be carried out if democracy were not to be stifled by competition. . . .

Competition, to depart from which was made unlawful, became a matter of legal compulsion. It meant compelled business confusion. Cooperative impulses, demanded by the current economic trend, were thwarted and repulsed. They expressed themselves only indirectly and unhealthily. What was sound and economically necessary was branded as wrong legally. . . .

. . . In this era of our economic existence, I believe it is manifest that a public interest well within the functions of government and well within the authority of government under our Constitution, commands the protection, the maintenance, the conservation, of our industrial faculties against the destructive forces of the unrestrained competition. And certainly the Constitution was never designed to impose upon one era the obsolete economic dogma which may have been glorified under it in an earlier one. For today and for tomorrow our problem is that of our national economic maintenance for the public welfare by governmental intervention—any theory of government, law or economics to the contrary notwithstanding. Hence the National Recovery Act and the Agricultural Adjustment Act of this administration. . . .

. . . To check and balance government to a point just short of inaction was the desideratum. The prevailing constitutional theory, and therefore the constitutional law, of course corresponded to this prevailing economic outlook.

At the center of this constitutional law was the conception of government as policeman. Government was to stop flagrant abuses, but not, in any circumstances, to do more. It was to be negative and arresting, not positive and stimulating. Its role was minor and peripheral. It was important in this one sense: It was to prevent interferences with the competitive system. Behind that system (so it was said and thoroughly believed) was an invisible hand which beneficently guided warring business men to the promotion of the general welfare.

The jig is up. The cat is out of the bag. There is no invisible hand. There never was. If the depression has not taught us that, we are incapable of education. Time was when the anarchy of the competitive struggle was not too costly. Today it is tragically wasteful. It leads to disaster. We must now supply a real and visible guiding hand to do the task which that mythical, nonexistent, invisible agency was supposed to perform, but never did.

Men are, by impulse, predominantly cooperative. They have their competitive impulses, to be sure; but these are normally subordinate. Laissez-faire exalted the competitive and maimed the cooperative impulses. It deluded men with the false notion that the sum of many petty struggles was aggregate cooperation. Men were taught to believe that they were, paradoxically, advancing cooperation when they were defying it. That was a viciously false paradox. Of that, today, most of us are convinced and, as a consequence, the cooperative impulse is asserting itself openly and forcibly, no longer content to achieve its ends obliquely and by stealth. We are openly and notoriously on the way to mutual endeavors.

And here is the importance of the rediscovery of the Constitution. We are turning our back on the policeman doctrine of government and recapturing the vision of a government equipped to fight and overcome the forces of economic disintegration. A strong government with an executive amply empowered by legislative delegation is the one way out of our dilemma, and on to the realization of our vast social and economic possibilities.

THE ECONOMICS OF THE RECOVERY PROGRAM

The general objective is clear and easily stated—to restore a workable exchangeability among the separate parts of our economic machine and to set it to functioning again; and beyond this to perfect arrangements which may prevent its future disorganization. This means that we must insure adequate income to the farmers, adequate wages to the workers, an adequate return to useful capital, and an adequate remuneration to management. What we want, really, is to provide the opportunity for every individual and every group to work and to be able to consume the product of others' work. This involves a creation of buying power which is coordinate with the creation of goods. We shall not rest nor be diverted to lesser things until that minimum is achieved. . . .

It is quite impossible to predict the shape of our newly invented economic institutions

may take in the future. That seems to me, in any case, unimportant. What is important is that we have undertaken a venture which is theoretically new in the sense that it calls for control rather than drift. In the years to come much ingenuity will be needed in the effort to isolate and strengthen the nerve centers of industrial civilization. We have yet to discover in determinate fashion what efforts are naturally those of common service, and so require a high degree of socialization, and what ones can safely be left to relatively free individual or group contrivance. We are turning away from the entrusting of crucial decisions, and the operation of institutions whose social consequences are their most characteristic feature, to individuals who are motivated by private interests. . . .

A new deal was absolutely inevitable. People will submit to grave privations and will even starve peaceably, if they realize that actual dearth exists, but no man and no race will starve in the presence of abundance.

*   *   *   *   *

The various recovery acts proceeded from a theory which . . . recognized the changes which had occurred in industrial society and it sought to secure the benefits of industry as it actually existed for the public good. It said, "Industry has developed out of the face-to-face stage; huge factories exist; central-office organizations control many even of these organizations, great as they are in themselves; financial controls are superimposed on this; scientific management has come to stay—therefore, the Government must legalize all these heretofore horrid developments so that it may shape them into social instruments. . . .

. . . Up to now much of the energy of business men has been dissipated in the overpraised conflicts of competition. Each was trying to beat the other fellow—to reach success by standing on the exhausted bodies of fallen competitors. And the success for which all this striving took place was usually defined as the right to exploit consumers by selling them goods of doubtful quality at prices which lowered the general standard of living. . . .

. . . We are fast approaching the time, therefore, when each industry will be able to devote its best energy to the fundamental purpose of industry—which is to produce goods rather than competition. . . .

This reconciliation of differences, however quickly it may come, or whatever contractual relationships it may establish among industries, is not, however, sufficient. For there always remains the essentially defenseless ultimate consumer. The Government may turn out to be his only refuge; and if this is so, the Government will have to assume more and more responsibility for pushing his case.

There are two broad ways in which industrial policy may be shaped from this point on to secure this objective. Industry may be required to define the quality of the goods it offers and to sell them at prices which are suitably low, so that when the transactions of a year, for instance, are totaled up it will be found that our energies and our producing plant have been used to the utmost and that the goods and services they yield have gone to consumers without increase of debt; or industry may be allowed to proceed with the policy of establishing high prices and maintaining them by limitation, and of selling goods whose qualities are mysterious to most consumers; and much of the resulting profits may be taken in taxes and returned to consumers as free goods by the Government— in the form of facilities for health and recreation, insurance against old age, sickness and unemployment, or in other ways. We shall have to accept one or the other of these policies because unless we do we shall sacrifice most of those objectives which we associate with what has been called the New Deal. The choice which lies before us is, therefore, a choice between a socially wise economic policy and the application of socialistic taxation. I prefer the former method.

One, certainly, of the distinguishing charac-

teristics of the present is the power of our industrial machine to produce goods. This power has astonished and frightened us. We have not known what to do about it. It required that we should either chain it up and prevent its free functioning or that we should reorganize our machinery of distribution so that consumers could take possession of the vast flow of goods. . . .

It is my belief that we shall prove unwilling to accept limitation in this sense as a permanent policy. This does not mean that we may not plan; it does not mean that we may not choose to use our resources in one way rather than another, limiting in some instances and expanding in others, so that all may run smoothly together as a considered and coordinated whole. . . .

I think it is perfectly obvious that we can have nothing new in the Government which does not correspond to a new need on the part of our people and of their economic institutions. The New Deal is a very definite attempt to evolve a new governmental-economic relationship in response to the needs and opportunities created by the past methods of operating our economy. To inhibit further growth of these new methods is, therefore, impossible and to attempt to deny their application is the ultimate folly of fossilized ways of thought. Using the traditional methods of a free people, we are going forward toward a realm of cooperative plenty the like of which the world has never seen. It will be no antiseptic utopia and no socialistic paradise, but a changing system in which free American human beings can live their changing lives. . . .

I have also stressed their experimental nature. That seems to me their most important characteristic, and that is something which is American if anything is. . . . There is no reason to think that year by year we shall not learn to better ourselves with the full use of energies and instruments which we have at our disposal. If this be Socialism, make the most of it!

DOCUMENT 27.2
Agriculture Cannot Survive in a Capitalistic Society as a Philanthropic Enterprise

Henry A. Wallace was Roosevelt's first secretary of agriculture, second vice president, and fourth secretary of commerce. In the selections presented here from his books, New Frontiers *and* Democracy Reborn, *he speaks out sharply on behalf of economic democracy for the farmer. In line with early New Deal thinking, Wallace calls for planning, cooperation, and obedience to the higher moral goals of democracy; contrary to the president's early policy of economic nationalism, Wallace already held definite views on the interrelatedness of the world's peoples and institutions. Seemingly beguiled here by a vision of the neighborly sharing of untrammeled production, the tough-minded secretary pursued farm parity by administering the Agricultural Adjustment acts as instruments of scarcity capitalism.*

AN AGRARIAN DRIVE TO CHANGE THE RULES

The experimental method of democracy may be slow, but it has the advantage of being sure. When you change people's minds you change the course of a nation.

Though abundance is at hand, we still live by old standards of denial. The situation is confusing. There are those who say that there cannot be a surplus so long as there is a single hungry Chinaman. Fundamentally and eventually this may be true; but these standpat sentimentalists who weep that farmers should practice controlled production do not suggest that clothing factories go on producing *ad infinitum*, regardless of effective demand for their mer-

chandise, until every naked Chinaman is clad. Nor do they feel that plow factories should abandon production control until every hungry Chinaman has a plow. We must play with the cards that are dealt. Agriculture cannot survive in a capitalistic society as a philanthropic enterprise. If the cry of those who bid our farmers think of all those hungry Chinamen, and plant more land, were heeded, it would mean that long before the last hungry Chinaman was taken care of, hundreds of thousands of American farm families would be destroyed.

The feeling that man should live by providing goods for his neighbors, not by withholding goods, goes very deep; and I believe that it is spreading. But the condition of greater balance and justice we now seek, in a capitalistic structure hastily mended, can certainly not be obtained by arranging that everybody work under the profit system except the farmer. The farmer's instinct has always been to be decent and unbusinesslike, to provide to the uttermost, never to deny. This instinct, obeyed by millions of scattered individuals in a society seeking profits and setting prices on a scarcity basis, took our farmers up the long hill to the poorhouse; and killed them as customers. Their death as consumers closed thousands of factories and helped to throw millions out of work. Now we are trying to give our farmers their rightful place in a more decent and balanced system, a system that will work democratically and make for neighborliness and a shared abundance. The people who raise the cry about the last hungry Chinaman are not really criticizing the farmers on the AAA, but the profit system, as we have inherited it from our past.

THE PURPOSES OF THE AAA

To organize agriculture, cooperatively, democratically, so that the surplus lands on which

Source: Henry A. Wallace, *New Frontiers* (New York: Reynal and Hitchcock, 1934), pp. 138–39. Reprinted by permission of Harcourt Brace Jovanovich.

Source: Henry A. Wallace, *Democracy Reborn,* ed. Russell Lord (New York: Reynal and Hitchcock, 1944), pp. 45–46. Reprinted by permission of Harcourt Brace Jovanovich.

men and women now are toiling, wasting their time, wearing out their lives to no good end, shall be taken out of production—that is a tremendous task. The adjustment we seek calls first of all for a mental adjustment, a willing reversal, of driving, pioneer opportunism and ungoverned *laissez faire*. The ungoverned push of rugged individualism perhaps had an economic justification in the days when we had all the West to surge upon and conquer; but this country has filled up now, and grown up. There are no more Indians to fight. No more land worth taking may be had for the grabbing. We must experience a change of mind and heart.

The frontiers that challenge us now are of the mind and spirit. We must blaze new trails in scientific accomplishment, in the peaceful arts and industries. Above all, we must blaze new trails in the direction of a controlled economy, common sense, and social decency. . . .

. . . This Act offers you promise of a balanced abundance, a shared prosperity, and a richer life. It will work, if you will make it yours, and make it work. I hope that you will come to see in this Act, as I do now, a Declaration of Interdependence, a recognition of our essential unity and of our absolute reliance upon one another.

DOCUMENT 27.3
A Great Plan Is Democracy's Answer

Born in 1899, David E. Lilienthal became director of the Tennessee Valley Authority in 1933, chairman of its board of directors in 1941. The following sections from his book, TVA: Democracy on the March, *make a strong case for public power, which has been part*

Source: David E. Lilienthal, *TVA: Democracy on the March* (New York: Harper & Bros., 1944), pp. 46, 75–76, 105–6, 125, 192–93, 195, 218, abridgment. Copyright, 1944 by David E. Lilienthal. Reprinted by permission of the publishers.

of the Democratic party creed since the age of Franklin D. Roosevelt. In describing government planning in the field of resource development, Lilienthal reveals his fundamental faith in democracy and his deeply felt sense of morality. The implication is clear: A democracy can plan without becoming dictatorial, and it can carry out its plans without enslaving its citizens.

A new chapter in American public policy was written when Congress in May of 1933 passed the law creating the TVA. For the first time since the trees fell before the settlers' ax, America set out to command nature not by defying her, as in that wasteful past, but by understanding and acting upon her first law—the oneness of men and natural resources, the unity that binds together land, streams, forests, minerals, farming, industry, mankind. . . .

People are the most important fact in resource development. Not only is the welfare and happiness of individuals its true purpose, but they are the means by which that development is accomplished; their genius, their energies and spirit are the instruments; it is not only "for the people" but "by the people." . . .

This hankering to be an *individual* is probably greater today than ever before. Huge factories, assembly lines, mysterious mechanisms, standardization—these underline the smallness of the individual, because they are so fatally impersonal. If the intensive development of resources, the central fact in the immediate future of the world, could be made personal to the life of most men; if they could see themselves, because it was true, as actual participants in that development in their own communities, on their own land, at their own jobs and businesses—there would be an opportunity for this kind of individual satisfaction, and there would be something to tie to. . . .

It is the unique strength of democratic methods that they provide a way of stimulating and releasing the individual resourcefulness and inventiveness, the pride of workmanship, the creative genius of human beings whatever their station or function. A world of science and great machines is still a world of men; our modern task is more difficult, but the opportunity for democratic methods is greater even than in the days of the ax and the hand loom. . . .

With the eyes of industry now upon this valley (as they are indeed upon many valleys the world over) planning a considerable industrial expansion here after the war, there is an opportunity to plan and to build so that our resources will endure, our natural beauty be spared despoliation. Here there is a chance to see to it that human well-being in city and town will not, through lack of ingenuity and foresight, be needlessly sacrificed. Shall we succeed? Is the only choice one between pastoral poverty and industrial slums? Can private industry utilize these resources, at a profit, and yet sustain their vigor and longevity? Can business and the common weal both be served? To be able to make an affirmative reply is a matter of the greatest moment.

In the Tennessee Valley the answers will turn to some extent upon how successful the TVA is in its efforts to weld a union of the public interest and the private interests of businessmen. We appear to be uncovering and developing in this valley principles and practices for effecting a jointure of public interests with private, by methods that are voluntary and noncoercive. Our actual experience is unpretentious as measured by the scope of the problem, but it is definitely encouraging and of not a little significance for industry and the people of the country generally. . . .

What the TVA, in specific ways, has sought to do can be simply stated: to accept an obligation to harmonize the private interest in earning a return from resources, with the dominant public interest in their unified and efficient development. The method—and this is the distinctive part of the experiment—is to bring to bear at

the grass roots the skills of public experts and administrators not for negative regulation but *to make affirmative action in the public interest both feasible and appealing to private industry.* By public interest I mean the interest of people—people as human beings—not ''the people'' in their institutional roles as wage earners or investors or voters or consumers. ''Underneath all, individuals,'' men and women and children. . . .

*   *   *   *   *

The TVA *is* a planning agency, the first of its kind in the United States. The great change going on in this valley is an authentic example of modern democratic planning; this was the expressed intent of Congress, by whose authority we act. . . .

. . . ''Unified development'' as I have described the idea in action is, in substance, the valley's synonym for ''planning. . . .''

Planning by businessmen, often under some other name, is recognized as necessary to the conduct of private enterprise. It has the virtue of a single and direct objective, one that can be currently measured, that is, the making of a profit. . . .

This is admittedly a grave defect of planning by the businessman. For his legitimate object, namely a profitable business, is not necessarily consistent with the object of society, that is, a prosperous and happy people. . . .

The idea of unified resource development is based upon the premise that by democratic planning the individual's interest, the interest of private undertakings, can increasingly be made one with the interest of all of us, i.e., the community interest. . . .

A great Plan, a moral and indeed a religious purpose, deep and fundamental, is democracy's answer both to our own home-grown would-be dictators and foreign antidemocracy alike. In the unified development of resources there is such a Great Plan: the Unity of Nature and Mankind. Under such a Plan in our valley we move forward. True, it is but a step at a time. But we assume responsibility not simply for the little advance we make each day, but for that vast and all-pervasive end and purpose of all our labors, the material well-being of all men and the opportunity for them to build for themselves spiritual strength.

Here is the life principle of democratic planning—an awakening in the whole people of a sense of this common moral purpose. Not one goal, but a direction. Not one plan, once and for all, but *the conscious selection by the people of successive plans.* . . .

We have a choice. There is the important fact. Men are not powerless; they have it in their hands to use the machine to augment the dignity of human existence. True, they may have so long denied themselves the use of that power to decide, which is theirs, may so long have meekly accepted the dictation of bosses of one stripe or another or the ministrations of benevolent nursemaids, that the muscles of democratic choice have atrophied. But that strength is always latent; history has shown how quickly it revives. How we shall *use* physical betterment—that decision is ours to make. We are not carried irresistibly by forces beyond our control, whether they are given some mystic terms or described as the "laws of economics." We are not inert objects on a wave of the future. . . .

DOCUMENT 27.4
Collectivism in Industry Compels Collectivism in Government

In his hard-hitting acceptance speech before the Democratic National Convention of 1936, Franklin D. Roosevelt began his attack on the

Source: Samuel I. Rosenman, ed., *The Public Papers and Addresses of Franklin D. Roosevelt*, 1938 vol., *The Continuing Struggle for Liberalism* (New York: Macmillan Co., 1941), pp. 305–20.

"economic royalists"—the "privileged princes of these new economic dynasties, thirsting for power, [reaching] out for control over Government itself." By 1938 the president had gleaned some startling statistics from the income tax rolls. In 1929, for instance, three-tenths of 1 percent of the American people received 78 percent of the stock dividends reported by individuals. In 1935–36, 47 percent of American families were living on less than $1,000 per year, while 1½ percent of American families were living on incomes totaling the combined income of the 47 percent. On April 29, 1938, Roosevelt sent his message to Congress on the concentration of economic power, proposing a program to "preserve private enterprise for profit." It is apparent from this message, selections from which are given below, that the earlier New Deal policy of cooperation with business had ended and that competition was to be restored to a government-regulated market. At the same time, it must also be realized that there had been no change whatever in the president's goals of individualism, private property, and democracy. The result of his message was the creation of the Temporary National Economic Committee, with Senator Joseph C. O'Mahoney as chairman. After three years of hearings, Senator O'Mahoney presented the committee's recommendations: that national corporations be chartered, that competition be maintained through effective enforcement of the antitrust laws, and that new business and small enterprise be given tax advantages. By the time the committee reported its findings, the United States was at war, and the whole matter was left to the searching scrutiny of future economists.

Unhappy events abroad have retaught us two simple truths about the liberty of a democratic people.

The first truth is that the liberty of a democracy is not safe if the people tolerate the growth of private power to a point where it becomes stronger than their democratic state itself. That, in its essence, is Fascism—ownership of Government by an individual, by a group, or by any other controlling private power.

The second truth is that the liberty of a democracy is not safe if its business system does not provide employment and produce and distribute goods in such a way as to sustain an acceptable standard of living.

Both lessons hit home.

Among us today a concentration of private power without equal in history is growing.

This concentration is seriously impairing the economic effectiveness of private enterprise as a way of providing employment for labor and capital and as a way of assuring a more equitable distribution of income and earnings among the people of the nation as a whole. . . .

We believe in a way of living in which political democracy and free private enterprise for profit should serve and protect each other— to ensure a maximum of human liberty not for a few but for all. . . .

That heavy hand of integrated financial and management control lies upon large and strategic areas of American industry. The small business man is unfortunately being driven into a less and less independent position in American life. You and I must admit that.

Private enterprise is ceasing to be free enterprise and is becoming a cluster of private collectivisms: masking itself as a system of free enterprise after the American model, it is in fact becoming a concealed cartel system after the European model. . . .

If you believe with me in private initiative, you must acknowledge the right of well-managed small business to expect to make reasonable profits. You must admit that the destruction of this opportunity follows concentration of control of any given industry into a small number of dominating corporations.

One of the primary causes of our present difficulties lies in the disappearance of price competition in many industrial fields, particu-

larly in basic manufacture where concentrated economic power is most evident—and where rigid prices and fluctuating payrolls are general.

Managed industrial prices mean fewer jobs. It is no accident that in industries, like cement and steel, where prices have remained firm in the face of a falling demand, payrolls have shrunk as much as 40 and 50 per cent in recent months. Nor is it mere chance that in most competitive industries where prices adjust themselves quickly to falling demand, payrolls and employment have been far better maintained. . . .

If private enterprise left to its own devices becomes half-regimented and half-competitive, half-slave and half-free, as it is today, it obviously cannot adjust itself to meet the needs and the demands of the country.

Most complaints for violations of the anti-trust laws are made by business men against other business men. Even the most monopolistic business man disapproves of all monopolies but his own. We may smile at this as being just an example of human nature, but we cannot laugh away the fact that the combined effect of the monopolistic controls which each business group imposes for its own benefit, inevitably destroys the buying power of a nation as a whole.

Competition, of course, like all other good things, can be carried to excess. Competition should not extend to fields where it has demonstrably bad social and economic consequences. The exploitation of child labor, the chiseling of workers' wages, the stretching of workers' hours, are not necessary, fair or proper methods of competition. I have consistently urged a federal wages and hours bill to take the minimum decencies of life for the working man and woman out of the field of competition. . . .

But generally over the field of industry and finance we must revive and strengthen competition if we wish to preserve and make workable our traditional system of free private enterprise.

The justification of private profit is private

risk. We cannot safely make America safe for the business man who does not want to take the burdens and risks of being a business man. . . .

A discerning magazine of business has editorially pointed out that big business collectivism in industry compels an ultimate collectivism in government.

The power of a few to manage the economic life of the nation must be diffused among the many or be transferred to the public and its democratically responsible government. If prices are to be managed and administered, if the nation's business is to be allotted by plan and not by competition, that power should not be vested in any private group or cartel, however benevolent its professions profess to be.

Those people, in and out of the halls of government, who encourage the growing restriction of competition either by active efforts or by passive resistance to sincere attempts to change the trend, are shouldering a terrific responsibility. Consciously, or unconsciously, they are working for centralized business and financial control. Consciously or unconsciously, they are therefore either working for control of the government itself by business and finance or the other alternative—a growing concentration of public power in the government to cope with such concentration of private power.

The enforcement of free competition is the least regulation business can expect.

The traditional approach to the problems I have discussed has been through the anti-trust laws. That approach we do not propose to abandon. On the contrary, although we must recognize the inadequacies of the existing laws, we seek to enforce them so that the public shall not be deprived of such protection as they afford. To enforce them properly requires thorough investigation not only to discover such violations as may exist but to avoid hit-and-miss prosecutions harmful to business and government alike. . . .

But the existing anti-trust laws are inadequate—most importantly because of new financial economic conditions with which they are powerless to cope. . . .

We have witnessed the merging-out of effective competition in many fields of enterprise. We have learned that the so-called competitive system works differently in an industry where there are many independent units, from the way it works in an industry where a few large producers dominate the market.

We have also learned that a realistic system of business regulation has to reach more than consciously immoral acts. The community is interested in economic results. It must be protected from economic as well as moral wrongs. We must find practical controls over blind economic forces as over blindly selfish men. . . .

To meet the situation I have described, there should be a thorough study of the concentration of economic power in American industry and the effect of that concentration upon the decline of competition. . . .

It is not intended as the beginning of any ill-considered ''trust-busting'' activity which lacks proper consideration for economic results. . . .

It is a program whose basic purpose is to stop the progress of collectivism in business and turn business back to the democratic competitive order.

It is a program whose basic thesis is not that the system of free private enterprise for profit has failed in this generation, but that it has not yet been tried. . . .

DOCUMENT 27.5
Old Problems Unsolved

Locked into the dogma of ''declining competition,'' ''trustbusting,'' and ''free private enterprise for profit,'' Roosevelt and

---

Source: John Dewey. ''The Economic Basis of the New Society,'' in *Intelligence in the Modern World* (New York: Random House, 1939), pp. 416–33. Reprinted with the permission of Joseph Ratner.

most New Deal thinkers were unable to contemplate the basic human relationship between workers and work. Writing in 1939, philosopher John Dewey reviewed the New Deal and concluded that as a force for fundamental change, it was little more than a slogan.

After the world depression of 1929, the earlier idea of reconstruction revived, not under that name but, in this country, under the slogan of the New Deal. It has become increasingly evident that the conditions which caused the World War remain in full force, intensified indeed by the growth of exacerbated Nationalism—which is the direction in which "internal social reorganization" has in fact mainly moved. Failure of the world communities to "meet and forestall" needed change with "sympathy and intelligence" has left us with the old problems unsolved and new ones added. . . .

How much progress has been made in the intervening years? How does the situation now stand? We have a recognition which did not exist before of social responsibility for the care of the unemployed whose resources are exhausted in consequence of unemployment. But at best, the method we employ is palliative: it comes after the event. The positive problem of instituting a social-economic order in which all those capable of productive work will do the work for which they are fitted remains practically untouched. . . .

In saying these things, I am expressing no sympathy for those who complain about the growing amount of money spent upon taking care of those thrown out of productive work and the consequent increase in taxation. Much less am I expressing sympathy with the reckless charges brought against the unemployed of loving idleness and wishing to live at the expense of society. Such complaints and charges are the product of refusal to look at the causes which produce the situation and of desire to find an alibi for their refusal to do anything to remove the causes—causes which are inherent in the existing social-economic regime. The problem of establishing social conditions which will make it possible for all who are capable to do socially productive work is not an easy one. I am not engaging in criticism because it has not been solved. I am pointing out that the problem is not even being thought much about, not to speak of being systematically faced. The reason for the great refusal is clear. To face it would involve the problem of remaking a profit system into a system conducted not just, as is sometimes said, in the interest of consumption, important as that is, but also in the interest of positive and enduring opportunity for productive and creative activity and all that signifies for the development of the potentialities of human nature.

What gain has been made in the matter of establishing conditions that give the mass of workers not only what is called "security" but also constructive interest in the work they do? What gain has been made in giving individuals, the great mass of individuals, an opportunity to find themselves and then to educate themselves for what they can best do in work which is socially useful and such as to give free play in development of themselves? The managers of industries here and there have learned that it pays to have conditions such that those who are employed know enough about what they are doing so as to take an interest in it. Educators here and there are awake to the need of discovering vocational and occupational abilities and to the need of readjusting the school system to build upon what is discovered. But the basic trouble is not the scantiness of efforts in these directions, serious as is their paucity. It is again that the whole existing industrial system tends to nullify in large measure the effects of these efforts even when they are made. . . .

If we take the question of production, what do we find? I pass by the basic fact that real production is completed only through distribution and consumption, so that mere improvement in the mechanical means of mass production may, and does, intensify the problem instead of solving it. I pass it over here because recurring crises and depressions, with the paradox of want amid plenty, has forced the fact upon the attention of every thoughtful person. The outcome is sufficient proof that the problem of production cannot be solved in isolation from distribution and consumption. I want here to call attention rather to the fact that the present method of dealing with the problem is *restriction* of productive capacity. For scarcity of materials and surplus of those who want to work is the ideal situation for profit on the part of those situated to take advantage of it. *Restriction of production* at the very time when *expansion* of production is most needed has long been the rule of *industrialists*. . . .

The ultimate problem of production is the production of human beings. To this end, the production of goods is intermediate and auxiliary. It is by this standard that the present system stands condemned. "Security" is a means, and although an indispensable social means, it is not the end. Machinery and technological improvement are means, but again are not the end. Discovery of individual needs and capacities is a means to the end, but only a means. The means have to be implemented by a social-economic system that establishes and uses the means for the production of free human beings associating with one another on terms of equality. Then and then only will these means be an integral part of the end, not frustrated and self-defeating, bringing new evils and generating new problems. . . .

A great tragedy of the present situation may turn out to be that those most conscious of present evils and of the need of thorough-going change in the social-economic system will trust to some shortcut way out, like the method of civil war and violence. Instead of relying upon the constant application of all socially available resources of knowledge and continuous inquiry they may rely upon the frozen intelligence of some past thinker, sect and party cult: frozen because arrested into a dogma.

That "intelligence," when frozen in dogmatic social philosphies, themselves the fruit of arrested philosophies of history, generates a vicious circle of blind oscillation is tragically exemplified in the present state of the world. What *claims* to be social planning is now found in Communist and Fascist countries. The *social* consequence is complete suppression of freedom of inquiry, communication and voluntary association, by means of a combination of personal violence, culminating in extirpation, and systematic partisan propaganda. The results are such that in the minds of many persons the very idea of social planning and of violation of the integrity of the individual are becoming intimately bound together. But an immense difference divides the *planned* society from a *continuously planning* society. The former requires fixed blueprints imposed from above and therefore involving reliance upon physical and psychological force to secure conformity to them. The latter means the release of intelligence through the widest form of coöperative give-and-take. The attempt to *plan* social organization and association without the freest possible play of intelligence contradicts the very idea in *social* planning. For the latter is an operative method of activity, not a predetermined set of final "truths."

chapter

President Roosevelt and American Foreign Policy

Robert H. Ferrell
Indiana University

Historical reputations have a way of going up and down, depending upon the judgment of individual generations, and it is fair to say that at the present time the reputation of President Franklin D. Roosevelt in the handling of American foreign relations may well be going down. The concern of Americans today is, of course, foreign affairs, and within that large category of public policy lie many problems, not least the problem of presidential leadership. The leadership of the Democratic Roosevelt in international affairs now appears to have been seriously, perhaps gravely flawed.

President Roosevelt's difficulties in foreign affairs were threefold. For one thing, he had very little preparation for dealing with problems of foreign policy. For a second, he often did not face up to issues in a simple, straightforward way. It may be that in the years just before American entrance into World War II the country was too divided for him to obtain support easily. Perhaps he found it awkward to be candid if such a course meant losing votes. For whatever reason he turned to subterfuge. A third inadequacy, which emerged during his later years in the presidency, was that he failed to make some decisions until it was almost too late. He listened to so many people arguing

intensely for their points of view, knew that a great many troubles would go away if ignored or given little attention, and was tempted to slough off decisions and trust to what Jefferson was wont to describe as "the chapter of accidents." Then, early in 1944, his health began to fail, another reason for putting matters off. During his last years in office he tended to watch issues; and only if absolutely necessary would he make a decision.

Roosevelt's prepresidential experience in foreign policy was in no sense noteworthy, indeed was slight, and this was part of his trouble once he reached the presidency. He had started in politics in New York State shortly after the turn of the century, in the Albany legislature, where he addressed local subjects, and had come onto the national scene in 1913 upon being named assistant secretary of the navy. This then number-two post in the Navy Department gave him a slight experience in foreign affairs prior to American entrance into World War I, mostly in regard to the Marine-supervised occupations of Veracruz in 1914, Haiti beginning in 1915, and the Dominican Republic in 1916 and thereafter. During American participation in World War I, in 1917–18, he busied himself with tasks of ship convoying, especially antisubmarine warfare. Any matters of higher foreign policy, so to speak, that came across his desk were not usually his to decide, but went to his chief, Secreatry of the Navy Josephus Daniels, who passed them to President Woodrow Wilson. Young Roosevelt, to be sure, was a Wilsonian and supported the League of Nations. As Democratic nominee for the vice presidency in 1920 he made speeches in favor of the League. He carelessly laced some of them with references to "running" Haiti and the Dominican Republic ("Why, I have been running Haiti and San Domingo for the past seven years"), and even claimed that he had written Haiti's constitution ("I wrote Haiti's constitution myself and, if I do say it, I think it is a pretty good constitution"). All this to the embarrassment of the party managers and perhaps President Wilson's secretary of state.

In the 1920s and early 1930s, during the Republican restoration, Roosevelt was on the sidelines, and for a while not even that—at the outset he was battling infantile paralysis, which suddenly afflicted him in 1921. To distract from illness his wife Eleanor persuaded him to enter a national contest for drawing up a plan of world peace, with a prize of $50,000 provided by the Philadelphia publisher Edward Bok; he did not receive the prize, but submitted a proposal advocating an International Conference, known as the Society of Nations, in place of the League of Nations. For the rest of the Republican era he watched the foreign policy measures of the day, the naval conferences at Washington (1921–22), Geneva (1927), London (1930), and the general disarmament conference that opened at Geneva in 1932. Whatever his thoughts about them he said little in public. Nor does he seem to have given much attention to the World Court issue or the Kellogg-Briand Pact to renounce and outlaw war. The former issue arose in the mid-1920s, but the U.S. Senate attached so many conditions to the court's protocol that

membership proved impossible. The Pact of Paris, the antiwar treaty of 1928, was nothing more than an international kiss, necessarily came to nothing, and Roosevelt rightfully gave it little attention. Like most Americans of the time he favored collection of the war debts owed by the former allies of 1917–18 and at the same time did not want the country to become directly involved in the collection of German reparations, from which these allies proposed to pay the United States. He fully shared the isolationist views of his countrymen, their belief that they had paid their debt to Lafayette.

During this period the "Soviet experiment," as it was known in the 1920s and early 1930s, did not inspire Roosevelt to much comment one way or the other. He observed it from afar. He had nothing to do with the initial setting of Russian policy during the Wilson administration. Within a year of the Bolshevik Revolution of November 1917, America introduced 14,000 troops into Murmansk and Vladivostok, but by 1920 the policy came down to nonrecognition and remained that throughout the decade. Roosevelt seems to have had no contact with the few Americans, members of the foreign service, who became close students of the Soviet Union, such individuals as the youthful George F. Kennan, Charles Bohlen, Elbridge Durbrow, and Loy Henderson, stationed by the State Department in Riga, capital of the independent Latvia, where they formed a "listening post" on things Russian, meanwhile seeking to learn the language and history of the peoples ruled by the Bolsheviks in Moscow. The department's Russian experts, thus trained and influenced, were presided over by the "chief" of its Russian department, Robert F. Kelley, a pronounced anti-Bolshevik. In the 1930s, Kelley was sent to Turkey and his department abolished, but the distaste for the Soviet Union—indeed suspicion of and hostility toward things Russian—that he had instilled in his young charges continued into the wartime and postwar years, a time when Russian experts had to deal with the central issue of American foreign policy, which was Soviet-American relations.

It is true that when Roosevelt became president in 1933 one of his first acts was to arrange the recognition of Soviet Russia, in the belief that diplomatic relations might help the largest country of the Old World understand the largest of the New. For the task, however, he chose as the first American ambassador the mercurial William C. Bullitt, a Philadelphia socialite and newspaperman. Bullitt wrote Roosevelt enthusiastically that he was teaching Red Army cavalrymen to play polo, having shipped equipment for them, and to give some regiments of the Moscow garrison a feeling for American life he provided them with baseball bats and gloves. By 1936 when he left the Soviet Union (transferred to an even more crucial embassy, that of Paris), Bullitt had discovered that a personal approach with the Russians gained nothing.

In the first four-year term of the Roosevelt administration the mistakes of foreign policy were mostly the errors of omission. They resulted from lack of wisdom. Few Americans, not least the president of the United States, understood that the serious problems of the era were not within the United States but abroad—were not with domestic economy but with foreign policy. It was the movement of international disorder, first appearing in the Japanese conquest of Manchuria in 1931–33, then in the attack by Italian troops upon Ethiopia in 1935, and then in the occupation of the Rhineland by German troops the following year, contrary to the Treaty of Versailles. The signal event of the era, an event that passed with little more than superficial comment by the people and government of the United States, was the accession to power of Adolf Hitler, who became chancellor of Germany in January 1933, a few weeks before Roosevelt became president of the United States.

The president, like his countrymen, was not alert to the danger. The best one can say for the dismal period 1933–37, when dictatorships in Germany, Japan, and Italy were beginning to consider a second World War, is that insofar as the United States was concerned, there was a policy as close to true isolation as any American government had practiced in the twentieth century, and perhaps even in the isolationist nineteenth century. President Roosevelt, in his first term, was simply inadequate as a leader in foreign affairs, whatever the successes of his domestic policy.

Leadership in foreign affairs during the first term, one should add, was not through the Department of State, for the president distrusted or at least found himself bored with the old Wilsonian Secretary of State Cordell Hull, whom he had taken into the cabinet as a gesture to southern conservatives of his party. The president preferred to work through the ambassadors and sought a spirit of camaraderie with them, encouraging personal letters to the White House that would bypass Department of State policy desks, not to mention the desk of Secretary Hull. And in this regard the present-day reader of the Roosevelt correspondence is struck by the "old boy network" nature of the exchanges and the impressionistic nature of the information. Ambassador Breckinridge ("Breck") Long in Rome informed the president of how straight the young fascists stood in their black-shirted uniforms, how impressive they were. In the increasingly dangerous 1930s, Roosevelt allowed such representation of American interests, although one must hasten to add that the nation's diplomats were probably no worse than in former times. The president corresponded lightly with his second-raters and chose to ignore the clear warnings of trouble advanced by the only historically minded ambassador in Europe, William E. Dodd, professor of American history at the University of Chicago, whom Roosevelt impulsively had accredited to the Nazi government in Berlin.

If the first term passed in epistolary exchanges, with little policy or concern, the second found the president forced to take a closer interest in foreign relations. By the time his second term came to an end in January 1941, he had proposed what was to become the Lend-Lease Act of March of that year, the single most important move in foreign affairs taken by the U.S. government prior to entrance into World War II.

It was the second term, and the opening months of the third in the spring and summer of 1941, in which President Roosevelt's leadership in foreign affairs appeared at its worst. Here it was not a matter of do-nothing, so much as doing a good deal by sleight of hand—a tactic unacceptable in the perspective of the present day that demands openness in presidential conduct. Already, in 1935, the first of a series of congressional measures proclaiming American neutrality in advance of any war anywhere, in Europe, Asia, or elsewhere, had shown the mood of the country. The president, unfortunately, did not display any leadership in heading off this legislation. The enactment of 1935 was continued in 1936, 1937, 1939, and 1941, in a series of laws that said far more about American foreign relations than should have been announced in advance. But during the 1937–41 period the more pressing problem— not theoretical, but actual—was the obviously worsening international scene: the Japanese invasion of China proper beginning in 1937, occupation of Austria in March 1938, Munich crisis over Czechoslovakia in September-October 1938, crisis over Danzig, which became ever more serious in the summer of 1939 and eventuated in the German attack on Poland on September 1 of that year, and the declaration of war on Germany by Britain and France a few days later. In the United States the first question was what the administration, which had managed to lead the nation to improve the economy although not lead the nation out of the depression (this did not happen until the country went to war in December 1941),

would do. The president at the outset was highly uncertain. When at long last he realized the threat to American interests both in Europe and in Asia, he chose a course, that was something less than candid, an oblique approach to aiding Britain against Germany and Japan.

At the beginning of his second term in 1937, Roosevelt had his hands full with the economic recession of that year. The president, however, was now looking to the increasingly aggressive moves in Europe and Asia (among other changes in the international climate, the Spanish Civil War had commenced in 1936 and was proceeding toward the defeat of the democratically elected if inept Loyalist government in 1939). He was concerned that the United States enter the balance of power in Europe and Asia in favor of democracy. In a famous speech in Chicago in October 1937, the year before the Munich crisis, he spoke of "quarantining" aggressors:

> The peace-loving nations must make a concerted effort in opposition to those violations of treaties and those ignorings of humane instincts which today are creating a state of international anarchy and instability from which there is no escape through mere isolation or neutrality. . . . When an epidemic of physical disease starts to spread, the community approves and joins in a quarantine of the patients in order to protect the health of the community against the spread of the disease. . . . War is a contagion, whether it be declared or undeclared.

Faced with uncertainty in the Department of State, and believing that he had raised more domestic opposition than was wise, Roosevelt backed away from this declaration. Sensitive to public opinion, he decided that he had failed to win approval, and wrote off the Chicago speech as a trial balloon that had come down. "It's a terrible thing," he told an associate, "to look over your shoulder when you are trying to lead—and to find no one there."

At the outset he did not go further than

words. It would be possible to list the increasingly belligerent speeches of President Roosevelt in 1938, 1939, and 1940 showing how, at least with words, he was castigating the aggressive rulers of Europe and Asia, and how he was trying to marshal the power of the United States to the support of such democratic nations as Britain and France. There was little rearmament, except passage of the Vinson Act in 1937, which promised to build the American navy up to the limit set by the naval disarmament conferences.

Perhaps words were all the president had to work with in the late 1930s, and yet one is not certain. It may be that to be critical of presidential speechmaking before and after the beginning of World War II in Europe is to ask of the president an impossible thing—to use the phrase of Woodrow Wilson prior to U.S. entry into World War I. The president faced an isolationist public. So sensitive were Americans to the possibility of war that they might well have voted Roosevelt out of office in the election of 1940 if the president had passed from words against the aggressors to proposals for rearmament. It is easy for students or professors in a later time to point out weaknesses of leadership, to note the artifices of leadership. It is easy to sacrifice leaders and statesmen on the altar of truth when it is their careers, not our own, that will go down. There is a theoretical quality in college and university studies: it is easy to send goats into the wilderness. Still, one has the feeling that the president moved too slowly, too obliquely.

The statement-making of the late 1930s turned into misrepresentation in 1940–41. After the defeat of France in June 1940, Roosevelt arranged for the British to receive munitions, and in September signed an executive agreement exchanging fifty World War I destroyers for leases of airfields and naval stations in British territories in the New World. Opponents claimed he was pushing the country into war. The Republican presidential candidate Wendell

Willkie in 1940 said that "if you elect me president I will never send an American boy to fight in any European war." The president then outdid his opponent. In Boston on October 30, he went all the way: "while I am talking to you, fathers and mothers, I give you one more assurance. I have said this before, but I shall say it again, and again and again. Your boys are not going to be sent into any foreign wars." Three days later in Buffalo he declared: "Your President says this country is not going to war." Willkie afterward explained his own promise as "a piece of campaign oratory." Roosevelt at the time pointed out to intimates that he, the president, had spoken only of "foreign wars" and not wars of national defense.

This trimming of public statements to fit the desire of the American people, whatever the realities of international affairs, appeared as a motif in President Roosevelt's behavior, once the third inaugural took place in January 1941. Confident that reelection had given him a mandate to extend aid to Britain in the war against Hitler, the president pushed through Congress the Lend-Lease Act of March 11, 1941, a record-breaking appropriation of $7 billion. It empowered the president to sell, transfer, lease, or lend munitions, weapons, airplanes, ships, food, and industrial materials to "the government of any country whose defense the President deems vital to the defense of the United States." This grant, denounced by isolationists as a blank check, was the most sweeping ever given a chief executive. It was virtually a declaration of war on the European Axis powers. The president announced it as a measure of national self-defense.

In the summer of 1941, Roosevelt's actions in foreign affairs diverged the farthest from truth in all the years of his presidency, March 1933 until his death on April 12, 1945. The president was attempting to obscure the principal problem raised by lend-lease, which was to get material to Britain after being manufactured and put aboard ship: if German submarines sank ships, there was not much point in Lend-Lease. The president knew the British navy was not strong enough to ensure the safety of lend-lease material, and engaged in a playful use of words in which he ordered the navy to convoy ships as far as Greenland and Iceland. He described convoys in the Atlantic as "patrols." When during a press conference a reporter asked the difference between a patrol and a convoy, he said it was the same difference as between a cow and a horse ("If one looks at a cow and calls it a horse that is all right with the President, but that does not make a cow a horse").

Probably the most singular of presidential statements before Pearl Harbor was the radio talk of September 11, 1941, after an action between the U.S. destroyer *Greer* and a German submarine. The *Greer* had trailed the submarine for three hours and twenty-eight minutes and broadcast its position to a British plane, which dropped four depth charges. Whereupon the Nazi vessel attacked the *Greer,* which answered with depth charges. According to the president's radio explanation

> [The *Greer*] was carrying American mail to Iceland. . . . She was then and there attacked by a submarine. . . . I tell you the blunt fact that the German submarine fired first upon this American destroyer without warning, and with deliberate design to sink her. . . . We have sought no shooting war with Hitler. We do not seek it now. But neither do we want peace so much that we are willing to pay for it by permitting him to attack our naval . . . ships while they are on legitimate business. . . . when you see a rattlesnake poised to strike, you do not wait until he has struck before you crush him. These Nazi submarines and raiders are the rattlesnakes of the Atlantic.

The president then announced to his radio audience that he had ordered the navy to begin convoys and to "shoot on sight."

In an article published after World War II the late historian Thomas A. Bailey contended

that the president had to "fool" the American people into war. The mood of the nation, Bailey wrote, was so euphoric that summer of 1941 that it was necessary to deceive the people for their own good.

One should add that the contention sometimes heard about President Roosevelt, during and after the war, that in the summer and autumn of 1941 he was engaged in an even larger piece of deception, fooling the American people into war by exposing the fleet at Pearl Harbor, thereby getting the country into World War II by the "back door" after the German government had refused to oblige by opening the Atlantic front door (i.e., Germany had failed to declare war despite hostilities in the Atlantic), has no truth, or at least no proof of such a plot has ever appeared. The government is too large a mechanism to allow such a plan, one sounding as if it came out of Renaissance Italy.

During the wartime years, from December 1941 to September 1945, Roosevelt was responsible for foreign policy for all except the last five months. Success graced his efforts. And yet in long retrospect one wonders if even in this period of activity the president might have been more effective.

Mobilization was far too slow, and reflected Roosevelt's glancing and sideways personality, inability to get things done in a direct way. In the first months the government's fumbling organization for war proved unable to focus on the problems. The president imposed one administrator upon another. He announced a "tsar" for mobilization, Donald Nelson. The latter did not long remain tsar. As a result the nation's heavy industry did not produce enough tanks, planes, guns and landing ships to permit the invasion of France before midsummer 1944. This delay contributed to the Holocaust—because the death camps got into full-scale operation in 1942 and 1943. To have shortened the war by even six months would have saved the lives of one million or two million Jews. The Jews of Hungary were driven to the gas chambers in May and June 1944, when the Western Allies were entering France.

In one wartime activity, the nuclear bomb program (the Manhattan Project), the tendency to delay lost a great opportunity. The Germans in 1938 had conducted the crucial nuclear experiment, the splitting of a uranium atom, and Roosevelt learned about it the next year when an intermediary brought a letter from Albert Einstein warning of the possibility of a bomb. The first appropriation, $6,000 for graphite for the emigre physicist Enrico Fermi, then working at Columbia University, was made on October 21, 1939. The Manhattan Project did not get under way until early 1942. Think what might have happened if the United States had gone all-out early in 1939!

Wartime leadership can be faulted on two more points. The first concerns signing of the grievous Civilian Exclusion Order No. 19, which dispatched 112,000 Japanese-Americans to concentration camps (delicately called "relocation centers") for the duration of the war. Not only were no disloyal deeds ever proven, this unfortunate executive order ignored constitutional guarantees. The second concerns Russian policy, the anti-Soviet heritage of the State Department. Distaste for the Soviet Union began in the Wilson administration, was established by the department's Russian experts in Riga, and confirmed by the department's Washington expert, Kelley. Roosevelt received this legacy of dislike and distrust. He had seen Russia's anti-Hitler policy of the 1930s overturned in an instant by the August 1939 Nazi-Soviet Pact. Perhaps he therefore refused to accept, at least in fullness of understanding, the cardinal fact of World War II, that the bulk of the German army in 1941–45 was engaged and eventually defeated by the Russian army. At the outset of hostilities in 1939–41 the Russians remained neutral, but when the blow came, the great German offensive that opened in June, 1941, they bore the brunt of World War II thereafter, with horrendous losses. The predictable result of their sacrifices

was a demand for buffer states to the west of European Russia. It was understandably a most serious demand. And yet President Roosevelt did not sense the Soviet geopolitical situation during World War II, and believed that when he met Joseph Stalin, first at Teheran in November–December 1943 and then for the second and last time at Yalta in early February 1945, he could persuade the Russian premier to allow a democratic form of government in all the East European countries and especially in Poland. Sweeping away this hope, Stalin refused to allow freedom for Eastern Europe. Most of the time at Yalta was devoted to discussion of Poland's boundaries and postwar government, and Roosevelt allowed the State Department to propose, and the Yalta conferees accepted, a Declaration of Liberated Europe that seemed to extend democratic rights and liberties. Despite these efforts, which may have been necessary if only to protect the administration's position with the many Americans of East European extraction, most of whom voted Democratic, the president did not sense the Soviet need for friendly regimes in Eastern Europe.

Thus, there can be criticism of Roosevelt's leadership before and during World War II. In the early and mid-1930s he failed to confront realities, although the reason perhaps was not his fault: the United States was isolationist, and policy in the 1920s and early 1930s was almost irrelevant to the major international issues in Europe and Asia. Understandably so. The country faced a grave economic situation, and during Roosevelt's first term, he concentrated on New Deal solutions to the Great Depression. When at last, in 1937–41, he began to deal with overseas reality, he did so largely in private and refused to share his understanding with the American people. Displaying a considerable lack of candor, he moved the nation toward confrontation. During the war itself, his actions were too slow to pursue the nuclear program expeditiously, too deliberate for Europe's Jews. Finally he failed to grasp the extent of Russia's contribution to victory over Hitlerism, and what that heroic effort meant in terms of Moscow's desire for buffer states in Eastern Europe.

The might-have-beens are perhaps not a productive area for the historian. One cannot change the past. The errors of history nonetheless take on a life of their own, live on into the present, and thereby affect the lives of Americans today.

SUGGESTED READINGS

Baker, Leonard. *Roosevelt and Pearl Harbor.* New York: Macmillan, 1970.

Buhite, Russell D. *Decisions at Yalta.* Wilmington, Del.: Scholarly Resources, 1986.

Bullitt, Orville H., ed. *For the President, Personal and Secret: Correspondence Between Franklin D. Roosevelt and William C. Bullitt.* Boston: Houghton Mifflin, 1972.

Burns, James MacGregor. *Roosevelt: The Lion and the Fox.* New York: Harcourt Brace Jovanovich, 1956.

————. *Roosevelt: The Soldier of Freedom, 1940–45.* New York: Harcourt Brace Jovanovich, 1970.

Dallek, Robert. *Franklin D. Roosevelt and American Foreign Policy: 1932–1945.* New York: Oxford University Press, 1979.

Daniels, Roger. *The Decision to Relocate the Japanese Americans.* Philadelphia: J. B. Lippincott, 1975.

Divine, Robert A. *The Illusion of Neutrality.* Chicago: University of Chicago Press, 1962.

————. *Roosevelt and World War II.* Baltimore: The Johns Hopkins Press, 1969.

Feingold, Henry L. *The Politics of Rescue: The Roosevelt Administration and the Holocaust, 1938–1945.* New Brunswick, N.J.: Rutgers University Press, 1970.

Herring, George C., Jr. *Aid to Russia, 1941–1946: Strategy, Diplomacy, the Origins of the Cold War.* New York: Columbia University Press, 1973.

Jonas, Manfred. *Isolationism in America.* Ithaca, N.Y.: Cornell University Press, 1966.

Kimball, Warren F., ed. *The Most Unsordid Act: Lend Lease, 1938–1941.* Baltimore: The Johns Hopkins Press, 1969.

————. *Churchill and Roosevelt: The Complete Correspondence.* 3 vols. Princeton, N.J.: Princeton University Press, 1984.

Nixon, Edgar B., ed. *Franklin D. Roosevelt and Foreign Affairs.* 3 vols. Cambridge, Mass.: Harvard University Press, 1969.

Offner, Arnold A. *American Appeasement.* Cambridge, Mass.: Harvard University Press, 1969.

————. "Appeasement and Aggression," in *Fifty Years Later: The New Deal Evaluated,* ed. Harvard Sitkoff. New York: Alfred A. Knopf, 1985.

Schewe, Donald B., ed. *Franklin D. Roosevelt and Foreign Affairs: January 1937–August 1939.* 17 vols. New York: Clearwater Publishing, 1979–83.

Waller, George M., ed. *Pearl Harbor: Roosevelt and the Coming of the War.* 3d ed. Lexington, Mass.: D. C. Heath, 1976.

Wilson, Theodore A. *The First Summit: Roosevelt and Churchill at Placentia Bay, 1941.* Boston: Houghton Mifflin, 1969.

Wiltz, John E. *From Isolation to War: 1931–1941.* New York: Thomas Y. Crowell, 1968.

Wohlstetter, Roberta. *Pearl Harbor: Warning and Decision.* Stanford, Calif.: Stanford University Press, 1962.

Wyman, David S. *Abandonment of the Jews.* New York: Pantheon Books, 1984.

DOCUMENT 28.1
Advice from Ambassador Bullitt

The first American ambassador to the Soviet Union had been a member of the delegation to the Paris Peace Conference of 1919, and at that time made a trip to Moscow as head of a small group to investigate the possibility

Source: Orville H. Bullitt, ed., *For the President, Personal and Secret: Correspondence between Franklin D. Roosevelt and William C. Bullitt* (Boston: Houghton Mifflin, 1972), pp. 61, 66–69, 73, 92–94.

of Bolshevik cooperation with the conference. The so-called Bullitt mission never had much of a chance. When its members returned to Paris and Bullitt reported that the new Russian regime was friendly to the West, President Wilson did not take him seriously, and Prime Minister David Lloyd George and Premier Georges Clemenceau dismissed his mission as amateurish. Bullitt resigned from the delegation, and in his testimony to the Senate Foreign Relations Committee gravely embarrassed Secretary Lansing by his indiscretions. An ebullient man, he attracted President Roosevelt. His subsequent letters to the president from Moscow were filled with a boyish charm.

On board steamship *Washington*
January 1, 1934

Personal and Confidential

My dear Mr. President:

. . . The first impression Stalin made was surprising. I had thought from his pictures that he was a very big man with a face of iron and a booming voice. On the contrary, he is rather short, the top of his head coming to about my eye level, and of ordinary physique, wiry rather than powerful. He was dressed in a common soldier's uniform, with boots, black trousers and a gray-green coat without marks or decorations of any kind. Before dinner he smoked a large underslung pipe, which he continued to hold in his left hand throughout dinner, putting it on the table only when he needed to use both knife and fork. His eyes are curious, giving the impression of a dark brown filmed with dark blue. They are small, intensely shrewd and continuously smiling. The impression of shrewd humor is increased by the fact that the "crow's feet" which run out from them do not branch up and down in the usual manner, but all curve upward in long crescents. His hand is rather small with short fingers, wiry rather than strong. His mustache covers his mouth so that it is difficult to see just what it is like, but when he laughs his lips curl in

a curiously canine manner. The only other notable feature about his face is the length of his nostrils. They are unusually long. With Lenin one felt at once that one was in the presence of a great man; with Stalin I felt I was talking to a wiry Gipsy with roots and emotions beyond my experience. . . .

After the tenth toast or so, I began to consider it discreet to take merely a sip rather than drain my glass, but [Foreign Commissar Maxim] Litvinov, who was next to me, told me that the gentleman who proposed the toast would be insulted if I did not drink to the bottom and that I must do so, whereupon I continued to drink bottoms-up. There were perhaps fifty toasts and I have never before so thanked God for the possession of a head impervious to any quantity of liquor. Everyone at the table got into the mood of a college fraternity banquet, and discretion was conspicuous by its absence. Litvinov whispered to me, "You told me that you wouldn't stay here if you were going to be treated as an outsider. Do you realize that everyone at this table has completely forgotten that anyone is here except the members of the inner gang?" That certainly seemed to be the case.

Stalin proposed my health several times and I did his once and we had considerable conversation. . . . Toward the end of the dinner Stalin rose and proposed the health and continued prosperity, happiness and triumph of the American Army, the American Navy, the President and the whole United States. In return, I proposed a toast "To the memory of Lenin and the continued success of the Soviet Union." . . .

After dinner we adjourned to an adjoining drawing room and Stalin seized Piatakov by the arm, marched him to the piano and sat him down on the stool and ordered him to play, whereupon Piatakov launched into a number of wild Russian dances, Stalin standing behind him and from time to time putting his arm around Piatakov's neck and squeezing him affectionately.

When Piatakov had finished playing, Stalin came over and sat down beside me and we talked for some time. He said he hoped that I would feel myself completely at home in the Soviet Union; that he and all the members of the Government had felt that I was a friend for so long, that they had such admiration for yourself and the things you were trying to do in America that they felt we could cooperate with the greatest intimacy. . . .

As I got up to leave, Stalin said to me, "I want you to understand that if you want to see me at any time, day or night, you have only to let me know and I will see you at once." This was a most extraordinary gesture on his part as he has hitherto refused to see any Ambassador at any time. . . . He seemed moved by a genuinely friendly emotion. Therefore, I thanked him and said that there was one thing that I should really like to have, that I could see in my mind's eye an American Embassy modelled on the home of the author of the Declaration of Independence on that particular bluff overlooking the Moscow River, and that I should be glad to know that that property might be given to the American Government as a site for an Embassy. Stalin replied, "You shall have it." Thereupon, I held out my hand to shake hands with Stalin and, to my amazement, Stalin took my head in his two hands and gave me a large kiss! I swallowed my astonishment, and, when he turned up his face for a return kiss, I delivered it. . . .

Yours devotedly,
William C. Bullitt

DOCUMENT 28.2
Advice from Ambassador Dodd

William E. Dodd was a distinguished historian of the American South and had taught many

Source: Edgar B. Nixon, ed., *Franklin D. Roosevelt and Foreign Affairs* (3 vols.: Cambridge, Mass.: The Belknap Press of Harvard University Press, 1969), vol. 2, pp. 180–81.

years at the University of Chicago. He was a Jeffersonian Republican in the antique sense of that designation, and his choice by President Roosevelt for the American embassy in Berlin seemed strange at the time and seems strange even in retrospect. Dodd's historical judgment proved a great help, however, even for Europe—for which area of the world, he was hardly expert. His dispatches from Berlin; his diary, which was published in later years; and his personal letters to the president all showed his perception. The dates of June 30 and July 25, 1934, referred to in the present letter, concern the so-called Blood Purge of many of Hitler's opponents and the attempted Nazi takeover of Austria by an internal coup. In the course of the latter affair Austrian Chancellor Engelbert Dollfuss was murdered.

Berlin, August 15, 1934

Dear Mr. President:

According to your suggestion of May 3rd when you gave me a few minutes of your time, I am summarizing the situation in Europe, with especial reference to Germany:

1. On October 17, I had a long interview with the Chancellor in the presence of the Foreign Minister. When I reminded them of your attitude about crossing borders in a military way, Hitler asserted most positively that he would not allow a German advance across the border even if border enemies had made trouble. I named the French, Austrian and Polish fronts, and he said war might be started by violent S.A. men contrary to his command. That would be the only way.

Now what has happened since? More men are trained, uniformed and armed (perhaps not heavy guns) than in 1914, at least a million and a half; and the funeral all the Ambassadors and Ministers attended at Tannenberg August 7 was one grand military display, contrary to von Hindenburg's known request. Every diplomat with whom I spoke regarded the whole thing as a challenge under cover. And we have plenty of evidence that up to 10 o'clock July

25 the Vienna *Putsch* against Austria was boasted of here and being put over the radio as a great German performance. Only when defeat became known was the tone changed and the radio speaker removed from his post, Habicht of Munich. So, I am sure war was just around the corner, 30,000 Austro-German Nazis waiting near Munich for the signal to march upon Vienna. These men had been maintained for a year on the Austrian border at the expense of the German people. So, it seems to me that war and not peace is the objective, and the Hitler enthusiasts think they can beat Italy and France in a month—nor is high-power aircraft wanting, the Wrights having sold them machines last April.

2. Last March, in another interview, the Chancellor almost swore to me, without witnesses, that he would never again allow German propaganda in the United States. On March 12 or 13, he issued an order that no man must be arrested and held in restraint more than 24 hours without a warrant. This was supposed to be in response to my representations about the harm done in the United States by violent treatment of the Jews here. I explained to you how, on the assumption that these promises would be kept, I managed to prevent a Hitler mock-trial in Chicago and otherwise persuaded American Jews to restrain themselves. But on the 12th of May I read excerpt on the boat from a speech of Goebbels which declared that "Jews were the syphilis of all European peoples." Of course this aroused all the animosities of the preceding winter, and I was put in the position of having been humbugged, as indeed I was. All the personal protests which I made late in May were without effect, except that the Foreign Office people expressed great sorrow.

I have reviewed these points because I think we can not depend on the promises of the highest authority when we have such facts before us. I am sorry to have to say this of a man who proclaims himself the savior of his country

and assumes on occasion the powers of President, the legislature and the supreme court. But you know all this side of the matter: June 30 and July 25!

3. One other point: Germany is ceasing as fast as possible the purchase of all raw stuffs from the United States, in some cases in direct violation of treaty obligations. She is mixing wood fibre in her cotton and woolen cloth, and is setting up plants for this purpose at great expense. Schacht acknowledges this today in conversation. He said: "We can not sell you anything but hairpins and knitting needles. How can we pay you anything?" He does not believe in the system, but he says it can not be stopped. . . .

William E. Dodd

DOCUMENT 28.3
Quarantining the Aggressors

The address at Chicago, October 5, 1937, has long been considered one of the president's first major efforts to awake the country to the danger to world peace presented by the aggressors in Europe and the Far East. Response to the measured condemnations of this speech was so adverse that the president quickly backed down.

PRESIDENT ROOSEVELT'S QUARANTINE SPEECH

. . . The political situation in the world, which of late has been growing progressively worse, is such as to cause grave concern and anxiety to all the peoples and nations who wish to live in peace and amity with their neighbors. . . .

There is a solidarity and interdependence about the modern world, both technically and

---

Source: *Peace and War: United States Foreign Policy, 1931–41* (Washington, D.C.: U.S. Government Printing Office, 1943), pp. 383–87.

morally, which makes it impossible for any nation completely to isolate itself from economic and political upheavals in the rest of the world, especially when such upheavals appear to be spreading and not declining. There can be no stability or peace either within nations or between nations except under laws and moral standards adhered to by all. International anarchy destroys every foundation for peace. It jeopardizes either the immediate or the future security of every nation, large or small. It is, therefore, a matter of vital interest and concern to the people of the United States that the sanctity of international treaties and the maintenance of international morality be restored. . . .

It seems to be unfortunately true that the epidemic of world lawlessness is spreading.

When an epidemic of physical disease starts to spread, the community approves and joins in a quarantine of the patients in order to protect the health of the community against the spread of the disease.

It is my determination to pursue a policy of peace and to adopt every practicable measure to avoid involvement in war. It ought to be inconceivable that in this modern era, and in the face of experience, any nation could be so foolish and ruthless as to run the risk of plunging the whole world into war by invading and violating in contravention of solemn treaties the territory of other nations that have done them no real harm and which are too weak to protect themselves adequately. Yet the peace of the world and the welfare and security of every nation is today being threatened by that very thing.

No nation which refuses to exercise forbearance and to respect the freedom and rights of others can long remain strong and retain the confidence and respect of other nations. No nation ever loses its dignity or good standing by conciliating its differences and by exercising great patience with and consideration for the rights of other nations.

War is a contagion, whether it be declared or undeclared. It can engulf states and peoples remote from the original scene of hostilities. We are determined to keep out of war, yet we cannot insure ourselves against the disastrous effects of war and the dangers of involvement. We are adopting such measures as will minimize our risk of involvement, but we cannot have complete protection in a world of disorder in which confidence and security have broken down.

If civilization is to survive the principles of the Prince of Peace must be restored. Shattered trust between nations must be revived.

Most important of all, the will for peace on the part of peace-loving nations must express itself to the end that nations that may be tempted to violate their agreements and the rights of others will desist from such a cause. There must be positive endeavors to preserve peace.

America hates war. America hopes for peace. Therefore, America actively engages in the search for peace.

DOCUMENT 28.4
The Einstein Letter to Roosevelt, August 2, 1939

The distinguished physicist Leo Szilard wrote the following letter, which Einstein signed. The economist Alexander Sachs delivered it to the president on October 11.

Sir:

Some recent work by E. Fermi and L. Szilard, which has been communicated to me in manuscript, leads me to expect that the element uranium may be turned into a new and important source of energy in the immediate future. Certain aspects of the situation seem to call

---

Source: Franklin D. Roosevelt Library, in Richard B. Morris, ed., *Significant Documents in United States History,* 2 vols. (New York: Van Nostrand, 1969), vol. 2, pp. 131–32.

for watchfulness and, if necessary, quick action on the part of the Administration. I believe, therefore, that it is my duty to bring to your attention the following facts and recommendations.

In the course of the last four months, it has been made probable—through the work of Joliot in France as well as Fermi and Szilard in America—that it may become possible to set up nuclear chain reactions in a large mass of uranium, by which vast amounts of power and large quantities of new radium-like elements would be generated. Now it appears almost certain that this could be achieved in the immediate future.

This new phenomenon would also lead to the construction of bombs, and it is conceivable—though much less certain—that extremely powerful bombs of a new type may be thus constructed. A single bomb of this type, carried by boat or exploded in a port, might very well destroy the whole port together with some of the surrounding territory. However, such bombs might very well prove to be too heavy for transportation by air.

The United States has only very poor ores of uranium in moderate quantities. There is some good ore in Canada and the former Czechoslovakia, while the most important source of uranium is the Belgian Congo.

In view of this situation you may think it desirable to have some permanent contact maintained between the Administration and the group of physicists working on chain reactions in America. One possible way of achieving this might be for you to entrust with this task a person who has your confidence and who could perhaps serve in an unofficial capacity. His task might comprise the following:

a. To approach Government Departments, keep them informed of the further developments, and put forward recommendations for Government action, giving particular attention to the problem of securing a supply of uranium ore for the United States.

b. To speed up the experimental work which is at present being carried on within the limits of the budgets of University laboratories, by providing funds, if such funds be required, through his contacts with private persons who are willing to make contributions for this cause, and perhaps also by obtaining the cooperation of industrial laboratories, which have the necessary equipment.

I understand that Germany has actually stopped the sale of uranium from the Czechoslovakian mines which she has taken over. That she should have taken such early action might perhaps be understood on the ground that the son of the German Under-Secretary of State, von Weizsacker, is attached to the Kaiser Wilhelm Institut in Berlin, where some of the American work on uranium is now being repeated.

Yours very truly,
A. Einstein

DOCUMENT 28.5
We Must Be the Great Arsenal of Democracy

Roosevelt's most effective means of rallying the American people behind his policies and programs was the radio fireside chat. The president, a masterful speaker, clearly enjoyed addressing the nation over the airwaves; he accompanied his words with gestures which in the days before television unfortunately could not be seen by the audience. The principal ideas expressed in this considerably reduced version of his fireside chat on national security, December 29, 1940, were to be repeated in a presidential address to Congress delivered eight days later.

My Friends:

This is not a fireside chat on war. It is a

Source: Samuel I. Rosenman, ed., *The Public Papers and Addresses of Franklin D. Roosevelt: War—and Aid to Democracies* (New York: Macmillan Co., 1941), pp. 633–44.

talk on national security; because the nub of the whole purpose of your President is to keep you now, and your children later, and your grandchildren much later, out of a last-ditch war for the preservation of American independence and all the things that American independence means to you and to me and to ours.

*   *   *   *   *

Never before since Jamestown and Plymouth Rock has our American civilization been in such danger as now.

For, on September 27, 1940, by an agreement signed in Berlin, three powerful nations, two in Europe and one in Asia, joined themselves together in the threat that if the United States of America interfered with or blocked the expansion program of these three nations—a program aimed at world control—they would unite in ultimate action against the United States.

The Nazi masters of Germany have made it clear that they intend not only to dominate all life and thought in their own country, but also to enslave the whole of Europe, and then to use the resources of Europe to dominate the rest of the world. . . .

*   *   *   *   *

Some of our people like to believe that wars in Europe and Asia are of no concern to us. But it is a matter of most vital concern to us that European and Asiatic warmakers should not gain control of the oceans which lead to this hemisphere.

One hundred and seventeen years ago the Monroe Doctrine was conceived by our Government as a measure of defense in the face of a threat against this hemisphere by an alliance in Continental Europe. Thereafter, we stood on guard in the Atlantic, with the British as neighbors. There was no treaty. There was no "unwritten agreement."

And yet, there was the feeling, proven correct by history, that we as neighbors could settle any disputes in peaceful fashion. The fact is that during the whole of this time the Western Hemisphere has remained free from aggression from Europe or from Asia.

Does anyone seriously believe that we need to fear attack anywhere in the Americas while a free Britain remains our most powerful naval neighbor in the Atlantic? Does anyone seriously believe, on the other hand, that we could rest easy if the Axis powers were our neighbors there?

If Great Britain goes down, the Axis powers will control the continents of Europe, Asia, Africa, Australasia, and the high seas—and they will be in a position to bring enormous military and naval resources against this hemisphere. It is no exaggeration to say that all of us, in all the Americas, would be living at the point of a gun—a gun loaded with explosive bullets, economic as well as military.

We should enter upon a new and terrible era in which the whole world, our hemisphere included, would be run by threats of brute force. To survive in such a world, we would have to convert ourselves permanently into a militaristic power on the basis of war economy.

*   *   *   *   *

Frankly and definitely there is danger ahead—danger against which we must prepare. But we well know that we cannot escape danger, or the fear of danger, by crawling into bed and pulling the covers over our heads.

Some nations of Europe were bound by solemn non-intervention pacts with Germany. Other nations were assured by Germany that they need *never* fear invasion. Non-intervention pact or not, the fact remains that they *were* attacked, overrun and thrown into the modern form of slavery at an hour's notice, or even without any notice at all. As an exiled leader of one of these nations said to me the other day—"The notice was a minus quantity. It was given to my Government two hours after German troops had poured into my country in a hundred places."

The fate of these nations tells us what it means to live at the point of a Nazi gun.

The Nazis have justified such actions by various pious frauds. One of these frauds is the claim that they are occupying a nation for the purpose of "restoring order." Another is that they are occupying or controlling a nation on the excuse that they are "protecting it" against the aggression of somebody else.

*   *   *   *   *

There are those who say that the Axis powers would never have any desire to attack the Western Hemisphere. That is the same dangerous form of wishful thinking which has destroyed the powers of resistance of so many conquered peoples. The plain facts are that the Nazis have proclaimed, time and again, that all other races are their inferiors and therefore subject to their orders. And most important of all, the vast resources and wealth of this American Hemisphere constitute the most tempting loot in all the round world.

Let us no longer blind ourselves to the undeniable fact that the evil forces which have crushed and undermined and corrupted so many others are already within our own gates. Your Government knows much about them and every day is ferreting them out. . . .

There are also American citizens, many of them in high places, who, unwittingly in most cases, are aiding and abetting the work of these agents. I do not charge these American citizens with being foreign agents. But I do charge them with doing exactly the kind of work that the dictators want done in the United States.

These people not only believe that we can save our own skins by shutting our eyes to the fate of other nations. Some of them go much further than that. They say that we can and should become the friends and even the partners of the Axis powers. Some of them even suggest that we should imitate the methods of the dictatorships. Americans never can and never will do that.

The experience of the past two years has proven beyond doubt that no nation can appease the Nazis. No man can tame a tiger into a kitten by stroking it. There can be no appeasement with ruthlessness. There can be no reasoning with an incendiary bomb. We know now that a nation can have peace with the Nazis only at the price of total surrender.

Even the people of Italy have been forced to become accomplices of the Nazis; but at this moment they do not know how soon they will be embraced to death by their allies.

The American appeasers ignore the warning to be found in the fate of Austria, Czechoslovakia, Poland, Norway, Belgium, the Netherlands, Denmark, and France. They tell you that the Axis powers are going to win anyway; that all this bloodshed in the world could be saved; that the United States might just as well throw its influence into the scale of a dictated peace, and get the best out of it that we can.

They call it a "negotiated peace." Nonsense! Is it a negotiated peace if a gang of outlaws surrounds your community and on threat of extermination makes you pay tribute to save your own skins?

Such a dictated peace would be no peace at all. It would be only another armistice, leading to the most gigantic armament race and the most devastating trade wars in all history. And in these contests the Americas would offer the only real resistance to the Axis powers.

With all their vaunted efficiency, with all their parade of pious purpose in this war, there are still in their background the concentration camp and the servants of God in chains.

The history of recent years proves that shootings and chains and concentration camps are not simply the transient tools but the very altars of modern dictatorships. They may talk of a "new order" in the world, but what they have in mind is only a revival of the oldest and the worst tyranny. In that there is no liberty, no religion, no hope.

The proposed "new order" is the very opposite of a United States of Europe or a United States of Asia. It is not a Government based upon the consent of the governed. It is not a union of ordinary, self-respecting men and women to protect themselves and their freedom and their dignity from oppression. It is an unholy alliance of power and pelf to dominate and enslave the human race.

The British people and their allies today are conducting an active war against this unholy alliance. Our own future security is greatly dependent on the outcome of that fight. Our ability to "keep out of war" is going to be affected by that outcome.

Thinking in terms of today and tomorrow, I make the direct statement to the American people that there is far less chance of the United States getting into war, if we do all we can now to support the nations defending themselves against attack by the Axis than if we acquiesce in their defeat, submit tamely to an Axis victory, and wait our turn to be the object of attack in another war later on.

If we are to be completely honest with ourselves, we must admit that there is risk in any course we may take. But I deeply believe that the great majority of our people agree that the course that I advocate involves the least risk now and the greatest hope for world peace in the future.

The people of Europe who are defending themselves do not ask us to do their fighting. They ask us for the implements of war, the planes, the tanks, the guns, the freighters which will enable them to fight for their liberty and for our security. Emphatically we must get these weapons to them in sufficient volume and quickly enough, so that we and our children will be saved the agony and suffering of war which others have had to endure.

Let not the defeatists tell us that it is too late. It will never be earlier. Tomorrow will be later than today.

Certain facts are self-evident.

In a military sense Great Britain and the British Empire are today the spearhead of resistance to world conquest. They are putting up a fight which will live forever in the story of human gallantry.

There is no demand for sending an American Expeditionary Force outside our own borders. There is no intention by any member of your Government to send such a force. You can, therefore, nail any talk about sending armies to Europe as deliberate untruth.

Our national policy is not directed toward war. Its sole purpose is to keep war away from our country and our people.

Democracy's fight against world conquest is being greatly aided, and must be more greatly aided, by the rearmament of the United States and by sending every ounce and every ton of munitions and supplies that we possibly spare to help the defenders who are in the front lines. It is not more unneutral for us to do that than it is for Sweden, Russia and other nations near Germany, to send steel and ore and oil and other war materials into Germany every day in the week.

We are planning our own defense with the utmost urgency; and in its vast scale we must integrate the war needs of Britain and the other free nations which are resisting aggression.

This is not a matter of sentiment or of controversial personal opinion. It is a matter of realistic, practical military policy, based on the advice of our military experts who are in close touch with existing warfare. These military and naval experts and the members of the Congress and the Administration have a single-minded purpose—the defense of the United States.

This nation is making a great effort to produce everything that is necessary in this emergency—and with all possible speed. This great effort requires great sacrifice.

I would ask no one to defend a democracy which in turn would not defend everyone in the nation against want and privation. The strength of this nation shall not be diluted by the failure of the Government to protect the economic well-being of its citizens.

* * * * *

We must be the great arsenal of democracy. For us this is an emergency as serious as war itself. We must apply ourselves to our task with the same resolution, the same sense of urgency, the same spirit of patriotism and sacrifice as we would show were we at war.

We have furnished the British great material support and we will furnish far more in the future.

There will be no "bottlenecks" in our determination to aid Great Britain. No dictator, no combination of dictators, will weaken that determination, by threats of how they will construe that determination.

The British have received invaluable military support from the heroic Greek army, and from the forces of all the governments in exile. Their strength is growing. It is the strength of men and women who value their freedom more highly than they value their lives.

I believe that the Axis powers are not going to win this war. I base that belief on the latest and best information.

We have no excuse for defeatism. We have every good reason for hope—hope for peace, hope for the defense of our civilization and for the building of a better civilization in the future.

I have the profound conviction that the American people are now determined to put forth a mightier effort than they have ever yet made to increase our production of all the implements of defense, to meet the threat to our democratic faith.

As President of the United States I call for that national effort. I call for it in the name of this nation which we love and honor and which we are privileged and proud to serve. I call upon our people with absolute confidence that our common cause will greatly succeed.

DOCUMENT 28.6
Roosevelt Speaks in Boston

President Roosevelt's speech of October 30 came shortly after Wendell L. Willkie, his Republican opponent in the 1940 election campaign, told a GOP rally in Baltimore: "If you elect him [Roosevelt] you may expect war in April, 1941." Roosevelt and his jittery advisers believed they had to reassure the mothers and fathers of America that their sons were not ticketed for slaughter on the battlefield. They were particularly anxious because of the location. Boston was marked by the Anglophobia of its citizens of Irish descent, and Massachusetts Democratic Senator David I. Walsh was a pronounced isolationist. Consequently, in his address the president catered to national fears and to local prejudices; he had sufficient political courage, however, to emphasize the necessity of extending further American aid to the British.

MR. MAYOR, MY FRIENDS OF NEW ENGLAND:

I've had a glorious day here in New England. And I don't need to tell you that I've been glad to come back to my old stamping ground in Boston. There's only one thing about this trip that I regret. I have to return to Washington tonight, without getting a chance to go into my two favorite States, Maine and Vermont.

This is the third inning. In New York City, two nights ago, I showed . . . how Republican leaders, with their votes and in their speeches, have been playing and still are playing politics with national defense.

Even during the past three years, when the dangers to all forms of democracy throughout

Source: *The New York Times*, October 31, 1940. Copyright by *The New York Times;* reprinted by permission.

the world have been obvious, the Republican team in the Congress has been acting only as a party team.

Time after time, Republican leadership refused to see that what this country needs is an all-American team. . . .

Our objective is to keep any potential attacker as far from our continental shores as we possibly can.

And you, here in New England, know well and visualize it, that within the past two months your government has acquired new naval and air bases in British territory in the Atlantic Ocean, extending all the way from Newfoundland on the north to that part of South America where the Atlantic Ocean begins to narrow, with Africa not far away. . . .

And while I am talking to you, fathers and mothers, I give you one more assurance.

I have said this before, but I shall say it again, and again and again. Your boys are not going to be sent into any foreign wars.

They are going into training to form a force so strong that, by its very existence, it will keep the threat of war far away from our shores. Yes, the purpose of our defense is defense. . . .

I have discussed the falsifications which Republican campaign orators have been making about the economic condition of the nation, the condition of labor and the condition of business.

They are even more ridiculous when they shed those old crocodile tears over the plight of the American farmer.

Now, if there is any one that a Republican candidate loves more than the laboring man in October and up to election day, it's the farmer.

And the very first one that he forgets after election day is the farmer. . . .

No, the American farmers will not be deceived by pictures of Old Guard candidates, patting cows and pitching hay in front of moving-picture cameras. . . .

Now, among the Republican leaders, among the Republican leaders who have voted against . . . practically every . . . farm bill for the United States is the present chairman of the Republican National Committee, that "peerless leader," that "farmers' friend"—Congressman Joe Martin of Massachusetts. . . .

I will have to let you in on a secret. It will come as a great surprise to you, and it's this:

I'm enjoying this campaign and I am really having a fine time. . . .

DOCUMENT 28.7
This Was Piracy

President Roosevelt's fireside chat of September 11, 1941, was an explanation and defense of his administration's policy of naval and air patrols in the Atlantic. The occasion for it was the sinking of an American destroyer by a German submarine a week earlier.

My Fellow-Americans:

The Navy Department of the United States has reported to me that on the morning of Sept. 4 the United States destroyer Greer, proceeding in full daylight toward Iceland, had reached a point southeast of Greenland. She was carrying American mail to Iceland. She was flying the American flag. Her identity as an American ship was unmistakable.

She was then and there attacked by a submarine. Germany admits that it was a German submarine. The submarine deliberately fired a torpedo at the Greer, followed later by another torpedo attack. In spite of what Hitler's propaganda bureau has invented, and in spite of what any American obstructionist organization may prefer to believe, I tell you the blunt fact that

Source: *The New York Times,* September 12, 1941. Copyright by *The New York Times;* reprinted by permission.

the German submarine fired first upon this American destroyer without warning, and with deliberate design to sink her.

Our destroyer, at the time, was in waters which the Government of the United States had declared to be waters of self-defense, surrounding outposts of American protection in the Atlantic. . . .

This was piracy, piracy legally and morally. It was not the first nor the last act of piracy which the Nazi government has committed against the American flag in this war, for attack has followed attack. . . .

In the face of all this we Americans are keeping our feet on the ground. Our type of democratic civilization has outgrown the thought of feeling compelled to fight some other nation by reason of any single piratical attack on one of our ships. We are not becoming hysterical or losing our sense of proportion. Therefore, what I am thinking and saying tonight does not relate to any isolated episode. . . .

To be ultimately successful in world mastery, Hitler knows that he must get control of the seas. He must first destroy the bridge of ships which we are building across the Atlantic and over which we shall continue to roll the implements of war to help destroy him, to destroy all his works in the end. He must wipe out our patrol on sea and in the air if he is to do it. He must silence the British Navy. . . .

This attack on the Greer was no localized military operation in the North Atlantic. This was no mere episode in a struggle between two nations. This was one determined step toward creating a permanent world system based on force, terror and on murder. . . .

Normal practices of diplomacy—note writing—are of no possible use in dealing with international outlaws who sink our ships and kill our citizens. . . .

We have sought no shooting war with Hitler. We do not seek it now. But neither do we want peace so much that we are willing to pay for it by permitting him to attack our naval and merchant ships while they are on legitimate business.

I assume that the German leaders are not deeply concerned tonight, or any other time, by what the real Americans or the American Government says or publishes about them. We cannot bring about the downfall of nazism by the use of long-range invective.

But when you see a rattlesnake poised to strike, you do not wait until he has struck before you crush him.

These Nazi submarines and raiders are the rattlesnakes of the Atlantic. They are a menace to the free pathways of the high seas. They are a challenge to our own sovereignty. They hammer at our most precious rights when they attack ships of the American flag—symbols of our independence, our freedom, our very life. . . .

Do not let us be hair-splitters. Let us not ask ourselves whether the Americans should begin to defend themselves after the first attack, or the fifth attack, or the tenth attack, or the twentieth attack.

The time for active defense is now.

Do not let us split hairs. Let us not say "We will only defend ourselves if the torpedo succeeds in getting home, or if the crew and the passengers are drowned.". . .

Upon our naval and air patrol—now operating in large numbers over a vast expanse of the Atlantic Ocean—falls the duty of maintaining the American policy of freedom of the seas—now. That means, very simply, very clearly, that our patrolling vessels and planes will protect all merchant ships—not only American ships but ships of any flag—engaged in commerce in our defensive waters. They will protect them from submarines; they will protect them from surface raiders.

This situation is not new. The second President of the United States, John Adams, ordered the United States Navy to clean out European privateers and European ships of war which were infesting the Caribbean and South American waters, destroying American commerce.

The third President of the United States, Thomas Jefferson, ordered the United States Navy to end the attacks being made upon American and other ships by the corsairs of the nations of North Africa.

My obligation as President is historic; it is clear; yes, it is inescapable.

It is no act of war on our part when we decide to protect the seas that are vital to American defense. The aggression is not ours. Ours is solely defense.

But let this warning be clear. From now on, if German or Italian vessels of war enter the waters the protection of which is necessary for American defense, they do so at their own peril. . . .

I have no illusions about the gravity of this step. I have not taken it hurriedly or lightly. It is the result of months and months of constant thought and anxiety and prayer. . . .

The American people have faced other grave crises in their history. . . . And with that inner strength that comes to a free people conscious of their duty, conscious of the righteousness of what they do, they will—with divine help and guidance—stand their ground against this latest assault upon their democracy, their sovereignty and their freedom.

DOCUMENT 28.8
Detention of Japanese-Americans

After Pearl Harbor the U.S. army commander on the West Coast, Lieutenant General John L. DeWitt, began to worry about the area's large population of Japanese-Americans. He created his own problem because "the very

<hr>

Source: U.S. Supreme Court, *Korematsu* v. *U.S.* (1944).

fact that no sabotage has taken place to date is a disturbing and confirming indication that such action will be taken." He envisioned 112,000 "potential enemies." The result was their transfer to detention camps inland where under armed guard and behind barbed wire aliens and citizens alike remained for the duration of the war. Endorsed by President Roosevelt and Congress, the issue came before the Supreme Court in 1944. Justice Hugo Black's majority opinion upheld the detention on the ground of military necessary. Three justices dissented.

KOREMATSU V. U.S.: THE MAJORITY OPINION

The petitioner, an American citizen of Japanese descent, was convicted in a federal district court for remaining in San Leandro, California, a "Military Area," contrary to Civil Exclusion Order No. 34, of the Commanding General of the Western Command, U.S. Army, which directed that after May 9, 1942, all persons of Japanese ancestry should be excluded from that area. . . .

It should be noted, to begin with, that all legal restrictions which curtail the civil rights of a single racial group are immediately suspect. That is not to say that all such restrictions are unconstitutional. It is to say that courts must subject them to the most rigid scrutiny. Pressing public necessity may sometimes justify the existence of such restrictions; racial antagonism never can.

. . . Regardless of the true nature of the assembly and relocation centers—and we deem it unjustifiable to call them concentration camps with all the ugly connotations that term implies—we are dealing specifically with nothing but an exclusion order. To cast this case into outlines of racial prejudice, without reference to the real military dangers which were presented, merely confuses the issue. Korematsu was not excluded from the Military Area because of hostility to him or his race. He *was* excluded because we are at war with the Japanese Empire, because the properly constituted military authorities feared an invasion of our West Coast . . . the military authorities considered that the need for action was great and time was short. We cannot—by availing ourselves of the calm perspective of hindsight—now say that at that time these actions were unjustified.

DISSENT BY JUSTICE FRANK MURPHY

This exclusion of ''all persons of Japanese ancestry, both alien and nonalien,'' from the Pacific Coast area on a plea of military necessity in the absence of martial law ought not to be approved. Such exclusion goes over ''the very brink of constitutional power'' and falls into the ugly abyss of racism. . . .

No adequate reason is given for the failure to treat these Japanese Americans on an individual basis by holding investigations and hearings to separate the loyal from the disloyal, as was done in the case of persons of German and Italian ancestry. . . .

Moreover, there was no adequate proof that the Federal Bureau of Investigation and the military and naval intelligence services did not have the espionage and sabotage situation well in hand during this long period. Nor is there any denial of the fact that not one person of Japanese ancestry was accused or convicted of espionage or sabotage after Pearl Harbor while they were still free. . . . It seems incredible that under these circumstances it would have been impossible to hold loyalty hearings for the mere 112,000 persons involved—or at least for the 70,000 American citizens—especially when a large part of this number represented children and elderly men and women. . . .

I dissent, therefore, from this legalization of racism. . . . All residents of this nation

are kin in some way by blood or culture to a foreign land. Yet they are primarily and necessarily a part of the new and distinct civilization of the United States. They must accordingly be treated at all times as the heirs of the American experiment and as entitled to all the rights and freedoms guaranteed by the Constitution.

DOCUMENT 28.9
Destruction of the Jews of Hungary

The following document offers mute testimony to the inability of the Roosevelt administration—or any government, short of invasion of German soil—to stop the Nazi policy of genocide. As World War II moved into its final year, 1944–45, Hitler began to notice how the satellite government of Admiral Nicholas Horthy in Hungary had allowed Jews to continue to live in that country. Early in 1944 he placed the entire Jewish community of Hungary, once the third largest in Europe, on his schedule for liquidation. On March 19, German troops took over Hungary, bringing with them the Sondereinsatzkommando, *or Special Command, under Adolf Eichmann. Horrified at the prospect, President Roosevelt issued a protest on March 24. Nonetheless the cattle cars began to roll toward Auschwitz; throughout the months of May and June approximately 12,000 Jews were deported daily. Rudolf Hoess, the Auschwitz commandant, rushed to Budapest to complain personally to Eichmann concerning the overburdening of the crematoria. Within a forty-six-day period somewhere between 400,000 and 437,000 Hungarian Jews were gassed.*

Source: *Foreign Relations of the United States: 1944*, vol. 1 (Washington, D.C.: U.S. Government Printing Office, 1966), pp. 1230–1231.

STATEMENT BY PRESIDENT ROOSEVELT

The United Nations are fighting to make a world in which tyranny and aggression can not exist; a world based upon freedom, equality and justice; a world in which all persons regardless of race, color or creed may live in peace, honor and dignity.

In the meantime in most of Europe . . . the systematic torture and murder of civilians—men, women and children— . . . continue unabated. . . .

In one of the blackest crimes of all history—begun by the Nazis in the day of peace and multiplied by them a hundred times in time of war—the wholesale systematic murder of the Jews of Europe goes on unabated every hour. As a result of the events of the last few days hundreds of thousands of Jews, who while living under persecution have at least found a haven from death in Hungary and the Balkans, are now threatened with annihilation as Hitler's forces descend more heavily upon these lands. That these innocent people, who have already survived a decade of Hitler's fury, should perish on the very eve of triumph over the barbarism which their persecution symbolizes, would be a major tragedy.

It is therefore fitting that we should again proclaim our determination that none who participate in these acts of savagery shall go unpunished. The United Nations have made it clear that they will pursue the guilty and deliver them up in order that justice be done. That warning applies not only to the leaders but also to their functionaries and subordinates in Germany and in the satellite countries. All who knowingly take part in the deportation of Jews to their death in Poland or Norwegians and French to their death in Germany are equally guilty with the executioner. All who share the guilt shall share the punishment.

Hitler is committing these crimes against humanity in the name of the German people. I ask every German and every man everywhere under Nazi domination to show the world by his action that in his heart he does not share these insane criminal desires. Let him hide these pursued victims, help them to get over their borders, and do what he can to save them from the Nazi hangman. I ask him also to keep watch, and to record the evidence that will one day be used to convict the guilty. . . .

As many as 100,000 individuals, Germans and other nationals, supervised the death camps where 6,000,000 Jews died, and defendants at the postwar trials at Nuremberg and elsewhere were only tokens for this huge complicity in the most dreadful deed of our century or any century. Eichmann lived quietly in Argentina until 1960 when Israeli agents spirited him to Jerusalem, where he underwent trial and execution two years later.

DOCUMENT 28.10
Report on the Yalta Conference

With but a few weeks to live—he died on April 12, 1945—President Roosevelt on March 1 addressed a joint session of Congress on his experiences at Yalta. Early the preceding year his health had begun to deteriorate. By the end of the summer in 1944 he was in poor physical condition, and when Senator Harry S. Truman lunched with him in August on the lawn behind the White House, Truman was shaken by Roosevelt's debility. The president had sought to pour cream in his coffee, and his hand shook so much he poured it all over the tablecloth. The Yalta Conference the following February was too much. FDR returned markedly tired. Contrary to his custom the president spoke to Congress while seated in the well of the House. To the assembled

---

Source: *Department of State Bulletin,* March 4, 1945.

lawmakers, he referred openly to his infirmity, which had seldom been discussed in the past. His address had a little of the old ring, of the happy warrior, but it was a poor effort, often disjointed, and his speech was slurred.

Mr. Vice President, Mr. Speaker, members of the Senate and of the House of Representatives:

It is good to be home.

It has been a long journey. I hope you will agree that it was a fruitful one.

Speaking in all frankness, the question of whether it is to be entirely fruitful or not lies to a great extent in your hands. For unless you here in the halls of the American Congress—with the support of the American people—concur in the decisions reached at Yalta, and give them your active support, the meeting will not have produced lasting results. . . .

I return from this trip—which took me as far as 7,000 miles from the White House—refreshed and inspired. The Roosevelts are not, as you may suspect, averse to travel. We thrive on it! . . .

There were two main purposes at the Crimean Conference. The first was to bring defeat to Germany with the greatest possible speed and with the smallest possible loss of Allied men. That purpose is now being carried out in great force. The German Army, and the German people, are feeling the ever-increasing might of our fighting men and of the Allied Armies. Every hour gives us added pride in the heroic advance of our troops over German soil toward a meeting with the gallant Red Army.

The second purpose was to continue to build the foundation for an international accord which would bring order and security after the chaos of war, and which would give some assurance of lasting peace among the nations of the world. . . .

It was Hitler's hope that we would not agree—that some slight crack might appear in the solid wall of Allied unity which would give him and his fellow gangsters one last hope of escaping their just doom. That is the objective for which his propaganda machine has been working for months.

But Hitler has failed.

Never before have the major Allies been more closely united—not only in their war aims but in their peace aims. . . .

DOCUMENT 28.11
Roosevelt's Failure to Ensure Democracy in Poland

The Yalta Conference undertook to form a postwar government in Poland that would include representatives of the Polish government-in-exile domiciled in London, and the so-called Lublin Committee, a group of Russian Communists of Polish extraction who had formed a provisional government in the Russian-occupied city of Lublin. Because the Russian army occupied Poland, FDR's position in negotiation was fundamentally weak. The Soviet government, to be sure, feared a postwar democratic government in Poland, which was likely to be anti-Soviet.

CABLE FROM ROOSEVELT TO STALIN, APRIL 1, 1945

I cannot conceal from you the concern with which I view the development of events of mutual interest since our fruitful meeting at Yalta. The decisions we reached there were good ones and have for the most part been welcomed with enthusiasm by the peoples of the world who saw in our ability to find a common basis of understanding the best pledge for a secure and peaceful world after this war.

Source: *Foreign Relations of the United States: 1945,* vol. 5 (Washington: U.S. Government Printing Office, 1967), pp. 194–196, 209–210.

Precisely because of the hopes and expectations that these decisions raised, their fulfillment is being followed with the closest attention. We have no right to let them be disappointed. So far there has been a discouraging lack of progress made in the carrying out, which the world expects, of the political decisions which we reached at the Conference particularly those relating to the Polish question. I am frankly puzzled as to why this should be and must tell you that I do not fully understand in many respects the apparent indifferent attitude of your Government. . . .

In the discussions that have taken place so far your Government appears to take the position that the new Polish Provisional Government of National Unity which we agreed should be formed should be little more than a continuation of the present Warsaw [Lublin Committee] Government. I cannot reconcile this either with our agreement or our discussions. While it is true that the Lublin Government is to be reorganized and its members play a prominent role it is to be done in such a fashion as to bring into being a new Government. This point is clearly brought out in several places in the text of the agreement. I must make it quite plain to you that any such solution which would result in a thinly disguised continuance of the present Warsaw regime would be unacceptable and would cause the people of the United States to regard the Yalta agreement as having failed. . . .

I wish I could convey to you how important it is for the successful development of our program of international collaboration that this Polish question be settled fairly and speedily. . . .

CABLE, FDR TO PRIME MINISTER CHURCHILL, APRIL 10

. . . We shall have to consider most carefully the implications of Stalin's attitude and what is to be our next step. I shall, of course, take no action of any kind, nor make any statement without consulting you, and I know you will do the same.

CABLE, FDR TO CHURCHILL, APRIL 11

I would minimize the general Soviet problem as much as possible because these problems, in one form or another, seem to arise every day and most of them straighten out. . . .

We must be firm, however, and our course thus far is correct.

[The president sent the last two cables from Warm Springs, Georgia, where he died on April 12.]

chapter 29

The Fifties

Blanche Wiesen Cook
Gerald Markowitz
John Jay College of Criminal Justice of the City University of New York

Long dismissed as "the age of the slob," the fifties continues to be largely ignored in major histories of the twentieth century. Senator J. William Fulbright described Eisenhower's administration as a period when Americans "could bask in the artificial sunlight" of "luxurious torpor," because the government "did not bother with serious things." Historian Eric Goldman wrote an essay called "Good-Bye to the 'Fifties—and Good Riddance." Goldman considered the fifties among "the dullest and dreariest in all our history. In 1963 a poll of seventy-five historians ranked Dwight David Eisenhower twenty-second in "presidential performance," behind Chester Alan Arthur—an indictment of the decade as well as the president.

Domestically and globally, however, the fifties was the height of America's golden years. The Yanks were still the world's heroes, liberators and candy-bearers. Everybody knew who the good guys were, although there were a few naughty boys and girls: James Dean, Marlon Brando, and Elvis Presley; Marilyn Monroe, and Jayne Mansfield. Dismissed as rebels without a cause, they inhabited blackboard jungles and gave an entire generation of youth an unprecedented flamboyance in costume and swagger. Blue jeans, leather jackets, and

"DAs," (duck-tail) hairstyles were sported by rebellious teenagers, both male and female, who now constituted an entirely new breed of American adolescent. "Little" Stevie Wonder, Hopalong Cassidy, the Lone Ranger, Howdy Doody, and Sal Mineo all contributed to the variety of costumes from then on both plausible and permissible.

All things American were eagerly imitated at home and abroad. Above all there was the cinema of America's greatest notables, ranging from Lauren Bacall and Humphry Bogart through Lana Turner and John Wayne, Judy Garland and Ronald Reagan. It was the era of *Bed Time for Bonzo*, *The Best Years of Our Lives* and *Seven Brides for Seven Brothers*. There were also occasional forays into 3-D, but that was a short-lived bust.

The fifties ushered in new styles and new sounds: Pearl Bailey and Liberace, Harry Belafonte and Perry Como, Rosemary Clooney and Eddie Fisher. This decade brought Jazz (Miles Davis, and Errol Garner's vastly popular "Concert by the Sea"); the country sounds of Hank Williams, Patti Page, and Pat Boone, joined by the blend that became "Rock-a-Billy," and the folk music revival led by the Weavers. But it was especially what New York disc jockey Alan Freed termed *rock and roll* that transformed America's and eventually the world's concept of music and the way young people moved. New names—such as Chuck Berry and Chubby Checkers, Bill Haley and the Comets were among the many who called on the young to "rock around the clock," and dance the bop and the slop—as well as the twist, the bunny hop, and the cha-cha-cha. The new jukeboxes and the new hangouts rivaled the surprises put on new cars: the weird tail fins decorating the convertibles that parked at the new drive-in movies.

Jackson Pollock (called in conventional circles, Jack the Dripper) and Lee Krasner popularized abstract expressionism which made New York dominant in the art world. A daring imaginative literature emerged—with such popular best-sellers as Grace Metalious' *Peyton Place,* Norman Mailer's *The Naked and the Dead,* James Jones's *From Here to Eternity,* J. D. Salinger's *The Catcher in the Rye* and *Frannie and Zooey,* Harper Lee's *To Kill a Mockingbird,* Herman Wouk's *The Caine Mutiny* and *Marjorie Morningstar;* with southern writers like Lillian Smith, Flannery O'Connor, and Carson McCullers; and with black writers, including James Baldwin, Ralph Ellison, and Rosa Guy.

A radical form of literary protest and a new community of Bohemians called "The Beats" also appeared. This black turtle-necked Bohemian circle began to express forbidden ideas and forbidden words. Although the decade was noted for its musical extravaganzas such as *West Side Story* and *The King and I,* new poets and playwrights like Denise Levertov, Adrienne Rich, Gwendolyn Brooks, Lorraine Hansberry, LeRoi Jones, Tennessee Williams, and Arthur Miller ushered in a new period of intensity and protest.

For some it was an era of comic books, bobby socks, bubble gum, and baseball cards. For others it was serious and marvelous. Everything seemed possible. After Sputnik, science education was given a boost, and bets were

taken about trips to the moon in our very own lifetime. While every community debated whether it would be unneighborly not to share one's fallout shelter, mothers began to organize to keep strontium 90 out of their children's milk and children worried about the future during take-cover drills under desks: was it really better to be dead than Red? Was that the only choice?

For all the comics and emphasis on consumerism and conformity, culturally and socially there were many important rebellions against "the organization man" fathers and all "the men in gray flannel suits." Usually attributed entirely to the sixties, the student movement, the civil rights movement (CORE, SCLC), the homosexual rights movement (the Mattachine Society, and the Daughters of Bilitis) as well as the contemporary peace movement (SANE, Women's Strike for Peace) all actually began during the forties or fifties. Indeed Rachel Carson's works *(The Sea Around Us* and *Silent Spring)* generated the contemporary ecology movement. Domestically, in many ways the fifties represented a tug-of-war—between convention and change, with television serving as the major battlefield. Until Elvis Presley made it to the "Ed Sullivan Show" in 1956, the agents of conformity had been winning hands down.

Television changed the landscape of the 1950s, and the nature of culture. It was an all-purpose medium, providing "wholesome" home entertainment as Edward R. Murrow analyzed the news with sincerity and the country watched Joseph McCarthy bellow point after point of order.

The medium embraced the message: postwar America was affluent, entertaining, and if not quite sexy, certainly cute. It opposed everything communist, radical, and un-American. There was no need for radical change since Americans had it all: the greatest economic boom in our national experience followed World War II. The desperation of the depression now seemed like ancient history. Between 1946 and 1959 the annual real income of U.S. wage earners increased by 25 percent. For the very first time, America's working people actually expected to have two days a week of leisure, and two weeks' paid vacation. Unionized workers won pensions, paid sick leaves, medical and hospitalization plans. The unemployment rate fell to a postwar low of 1.8 percent in October 1953. Fueling this great growth was consumer spending and the rapid expansion of the military-industrial complex. In fact the cold war made it all plausible and possible.

The rhetoric of the Red Menace moved Congress to vote for the permanent militarization of America, and introduced a military-fueled economy. While such fiscal conservatives as Secretary of the Treasury George Humphrey, and in the end Eisenhower as well, worried about the implications of an entrenched military-industrial complex, the American public was encouraged to enjoy thoughtlessly the consumer by-products of this heady moment. That the endless array of cars, washing machines, dryers, refrigerators, television sets, and record players would have been virtually impossible without the massive military spending that infused billions of dollars into the economy was never debated or even publicly discussed. Nevertheless, hindsight gives us the facts: in 1949 Congress appropriated $14 billion for the military. In 1953 Congress appropriated $50 billion for the military. Between 1953 and 1959 50 percent of Congress's budget went for defense spending.

The globalization of American influence and power which occurred during the 1950s was unprecedented in its costs and scope. Some called it neoimperialism, others called it postcolonialism. Whatever it was called, the rhetoric of freedom, liberation, and global democracy camouflaged the modern era of dirty tricks from disinformation to counterinsurgency. Eisenhower's demeanor as a bumbling, do-nothing president covered up the fact that he was in large part a covert president who routinely re-

sorted to national security/CIA operations that toppled democratically elected governments considered unfriendly to U.S. interests. In 1953 the United States overthrew the popular, elected, and nationalist Mossadegh government of Iran. The CIA chief in Iran, Kermit Roosevelt, dismissed Mossadegh as weak and thought his support limited to some religious mullahs and superstitious students and workers. In 1954 the United States overthrew the popular, elected, and democratic government of Jacobo Arbenz Guzmán, because he was inimical to the interests of the United Fruit Company, and appeared soft on communism. He was replaced by a series of U.S.-backed military dictators whose human rights abuses have been condemned for the past thirty years.

In March 1954 the U.S. National Security Council legitimized these activities with a new policy: NSC 5412 determined that "in the interests of world peace and U.S. national security, the overt foreign activities of the U.S. government should be supplemented by covert operations." The Central Intelligence Agency's mandate to conduct "espionage and counterespionage operations abroad" was now expanded. All covert operations were to be planned and executed so that

> . . . U.S. Government responsibility for them is not evident . . . and if uncovered the U.S. Government can plausibly disclaim any responsibility for them. Specifically, such operations shall include . . . propaganda, political action; economic warfare; preventive direct action, including sabotage, antisabotage, demolition; escape and evasion and evacuation measures; subversion against hostile states or groups including assistance to underground resistance movements, guerrillas and refugee liberation groups; support of indigenous and anticommunist elements . . . ; deceptive plans and operations. . . .

Most of these activities and policies remained secret, classified and unknown to most Americans for the next thirty years.

At home, the great symbol and the great

fact of post–World War II American prosperity was the emergence of single-family housing in the suburbs. The Servicemen's Readjustment Act of 1944 provided Veterans Administration (VA) mortgages similar to the Federal Housing Authority (FHA) mortgages of the 1930s. As a result, the sixteen million GIs who returned from World War II were guaranteed federal mortgages at whatever prices the builders set. Single-family housing starts went from 114,000 in 1944 to 1,692,000 in 1950.

During the 1950s suburbs grew ten times faster than central cities. Neat lawns on which no flowers or tomatoes were allowed to grow, now enveloped communities of houses all built according to formula and rigid form. No diversity was allowed, no creative gardening permitted. This homogeneity tended to be ethnic as well as stylistic. During the 1950s Alexander Levitt and his two sons built more than 140,000 units for middle-income wage earners in what was to remain white suburbia. As late as 1960, for example, not a single black resident lived in Long Island's Levittown.

Within each unit there was intended to be a television, washer-dryer, vacuum cleaner, and an all-purpose full-time housewife. Competitive rather than cooperative, each unit was expected to be self-contained and entirely dedicated to consumer spending. To "Make Room for Daddy," at home and in the workplace, the all-purpose suburban housewife was expected to work entirely at home and if somewhat isolated, she was nevertheless expected to be entirely contented.

The "privatization" of America was no accident. Although the realities of living enabled surburban women to find each other and create Tupperware® parties, join mah-jongg games, and found bridge and canasta clubs, these social circles remained profoundly apolitical. Technocrats and experts were expected to understand and make the big decisions. Community organizing for reform and social change were dismissed as relics of the 1930s, and were now condemned as un-American. Television

brought the mandate of the "vital center" of American politics, the attitudes and opinions of the bipartisan establishment, into every living room. Personal responsibility for public policy was discouraged.

The 1950s also involved a renewed celebration of rugged individualism. Ayn Rand and the heroes of her novels *The Fountainhead* and *Atlas Shrugged* contributed to a new conservatism that tilted the vital center to the right. Political and social discontent were increasingly regarded as personal and psychological disorders, subjects for Freudian therapy rather than political activity. At the scientific extreme were surgeons who prescribed frontal lobotomies for "hysterical" women, while at the vital center a host of scientists and technocrats increasingly mystified access to information. Discontent became a psychological and individual issue rather than a social or class issue.

This syndrome was increasingly propped up by a strident antiliberalism that manifested itself during the 1950s as McCarthyism. New Deal and Fair Deal Democrats were called "Commiecrats," and "phoney egg-sucking liberals" by Senator Joseph McCarthy whose name came to dominate the decade. Actually the anticommunist crusade began long before McCarthy's more publicized activities. Preceded by the Martin Dies's Special House Committee on Un-American Activities (HUAC) begun in 1938, the permanent committee was made famous in 1948 when young Congressman Richard Nixon decided that his career would most benefit from the kind of personal crusade against communists and Jews that helped him win a particularly ugly California election over New Dealer Helen Gahagan Douglas.

President Harry S Truman, himself the target of antiliberal attacks, was among the first anticommunist crusaders. In 1947 Truman's Executive Order 9835 introduced loyalty oaths and a monumental purge of federal government workers. Quickly copied by state and local governments, political orthodoxy became a requirement for employment for educators, entertainers, journalists, diplomats, and all public officials. Thousands of teachers were fired and such politically radical music groups as the Weavers were banned. Even their most popular nonpolitical song "Goodnight Irene" which was at the top of the hit parade and sold over a million records, was permanently removed from play over the airwaves of America.

Truman's loyalty program instituted an intellectual means test for American leadership or even civic participation. To ferret out the "disloyal," esteemed Americans were routinely asked:

> "Have you ever read Karl Marx?"
>
> "What do you think of Henry Wallace's third-party effort?"
>
> "Have you ever had Negroes in your home?"
>
> "There is a suspicion in the record that you are in sympathy with the underprivileged. Is this true?"
>
> "Did you ever write a letter to the Red Cross about segregation of blood?"
>
> "Have you ever read Thomas Paine? Upton Sinclair?"
>
> "When you were in X's home, did X's wife dress conventionally when she received her guests?"

Unionists and activists were particularly targeted. Shortly after World War II, several large strikes paralyzed major industrial centers. In 1946 the number of strikes and the number of workers involved surpassed all previous records. Communists and radicals had been elected to leadership positions of several major unions, including the United Electrical Workers, Mike Quill's Transport Workers Union, the National Maritime Workers, Harry Bridges's International Longshoremen's Association, and the Mine, Mill and Smelters Workers Union, and seemed generally to dominate the CIO (Congress of Industrial Organizations). By 1950 radicals had been systematically re-

moved from all leadership positions within the CIO; and those unions which refused to purge radicals were expelled from the CIO.

The Taft-Hartley Act of 1947 formalized conservative control of labor unions. The act required union officials to sign a "non-Communist affidavit." Any union that refused to comply could not be certified as a bargaining agent with the National Labor Relations Board, could not have a union shop clause in any contract, and could not appeal to the National Labor Relations Board for redress of grievances.

After World War II labor and radical parties won many elections in Italy, England, France, Greece, and Austria. Opposed to poverty and to a renewed anti-Russian crusade, the left and old New Deal coalition in the United States represented a threat to the emerging cold war consensus. The new military-industrial coalition, was dedicated to the American Century: The victory of U.S. industry and ideology worldwide. Radical political groups, such as Henry Wallace's 1948 Progressive party, which endorsed Soviet-American friendship, and the emergence of an anti-cold war peace movement, as well as other critical voices, represented a challenge to the success of the American Century.

To destroy this challenge a massive "anti-Communist" crusade, that ultimately splattered all left-liberal nonconformist thought, was unleashed. To maintain the pressure against radicalism, the HUAC and the Senate Internal Security Subcommittee went "into the field." From Milwaukee to Detroit to Pittsburgh to Baltimore to Hillsboro, North Carolina, to Los Angeles special investigators sniffed out and purged everyone from red to mauve. McCarthy's associate Roy Cohn described "the way to get results:" "Hold our hearings, get these people in public session, have them claim the Fifth Amendment, have the witnesses name them as Communists, have them fired." Although these activities did not destroy unionism absolutely, they permanently altered the relationship between labor and management. Labor militancy familiar to the 1930s, virtually disappeared. ''Sweetheart contracts'' to protect immediate bread-and-butter interests were negotiated, but at the expense of any future independent power for the union movement—both economically and politically.

Privatization and political orthodoxy were reenforced by several major political show trials. From the Smith Act indictments of July 28, 1948, which resulted in the longest criminal trial in U.S. history, to the indictment of career diplomat Alger Hiss in December 1948, to the execution of Ethel and Julius Rosenberg on June 19, 1953, to the harassment and degradation of atomic scientist J. Robert Oppenheimer, declared a security risk in June 1954, the 1950s bore witness to the politics of homogeneity and control.

On July 28, 1948 a federal grand jury in New York indicted twelve members of the national board of the U.S. Communist party. They were charged with violating the Alien Registration, or Smith Act, of 1940—the first peacetime sedition law in U.S. history since 1798. The law made it illegal to ''knowingly or willfully advocate, abet, advise, or teach the duty, necessity, desirability, or propriety of overthrowing or destroying any government in the United States by force or violence.'' It also prohibited participation in the writing or circulation of materials advocating such ideas and made membership in any group advocating such ideas illegal. The defendants were found guilty, and each received the maximum sentence of five years' imprisonment. Dozens of other Smith Act convictions followed.

In the summer of 1948 Alger Hiss, who had resigned from government service to become president of the Carnegie Endowment for International Peace, was named a Communist who passed secret documents by a self-confessed Communist spy, Whittaker Chambers, during HUAC's investigation of government espionage to expose the Demo-

crats' ''twenty years of treason.'' After Hiss denied the charges and sued Chambers for libel, Chambers led freshman Representative Richard Nixon and other members of HUAC to a pumpkin patch where the microfilmed documents were allegedly buried. With film cameras and radio crews at the ready, the pumpkin patch brigade unearthed the ''evidence.'' The statute of limitation on espionage having expired, Hiss could only be indicted for perjury. One trial ended in a hung jury; the second convicted him. Hiss was sentenced to five years in prison; and Richard Nixon who, as a member of HUAC, had led in questioning him, was catapulted into prominence. Nixon, among other committee members, repeatedly attacked the New Deal, and members of the liberal Democratic establishment were routinely condemned not only as ''bleeding heart pinkoes'' but as dupes of the Soviet Union, if not actually spies.

When Russia exploded its first atomic bomb in 1949, the FBI launched an extensive hunt to find who had ''stolen'' the U.S. atomic secret. Unlike Alger Hiss, the Rosenbergs were not prominent, affluent, or important. They were hard-working people who owned a small business in New York's Lower East Side. The Rosenbergs and their co-defendant, Morton Sobell, were rank-and-file Jewish communists, idealists inspired by the united front visions of the New Deal era. Ethel Rosenberg's brother David Greenglass, himself accused of stealing atomic secrets while a machinist at Los Alamos, New Mexico, where the first atomic bomb was assembled, charged the Rosenbergs with involvement in espionage. When the Rosenbergs denied their guilt and refused to consider any of the many deals offered to them while in prison, the government escalated its case and accused them of ''the crime of the century'': they personally gave atom bomb secrets to the Russians. As Judge Irving R. Kaufman sentenced the Rosenbergs to death in April 1951, he also found them personally responsible for every death and casualty in Korea. Eisenhower ignored all appeals for clemency from world leaders, including Pope Pius XII, and they were executed on June 19, 1953. Their execution served as a demonstration and a warning: unrepentant communists were traitors and spies, and might be executed.

J. Robert Oppenheimer, director of the Los Alamos atomic project and widely hailed as the "father of the atomic bomb," fell victim to the McCarthy spirit in 1954. Never accused of any misconduct, never charged with mishandling documents or sharing secrets, he was nevertheless demeaned and publicly humiliated for having communist sympathies and communist relatives. Actually, Oppenheimer's "crime" was his opposition to the development of thermonuclear weapons (the H-Bomb). His former colleagues, Edward Teller and Lewis Strauss, dedicated to the repeated testing of the "hydrogen" bomb despite serious health questions about radioactive "fallout," initiated his removal from government service. On June 29, 1954, the Atomic Energy Commission declared Oppenheimer a "security risk," removed him from government influence and blocked his access to government "secrets," including his own reports and papers.

In the midst of these show trials Congress passed several laws that were among the most repressive in U.S. history.

The Internal Security Act of 1950, passed over Truman's veto, established the Subversive Activities Control Board and prohibited any person to "combine, conspire or agree with any other persons which would substantially contribute to the establishment within the United States of a totalitarian dictatorship." "Communist-action" organizations were to register with the attorney general and to report names of officers, sources of funds, and membership lists. The law contained the most controversial "concentration camp" provision: In the event of war or insurrection, the president might declare "an internal security emer-

gency" and the attorney general could then detain all persons for whom there were "reasonable grounds" to believe they "probably will engage in, or probably will conspire with others to engage in, acts of espionage or sabotage." At its peak in 1955 the FBI's security index of people to be arrested under this provision included 26,000 individuals—including union organizers, journalists, lawyers, physicians, scientists, and teachers. Congress subsequently appropriated funds for the Department of Justice to establish six detention camps in Arizona, Florida, Pennsylvania, Oklahoma, and California. In 1952 Congress also passed the Immigration and Naturalization Act (the McCarran-Walter Act) which instituted second-class citizenship for the millions of naturalized Americans, who could now be and were deported by the score.

In addition to these infringements on freedom of speech, press, and assembly, the United States specifically limited its celebrated right to travel freely. In 1952 Truman's Secretary of State Dean Acheson declared that he would withhold passports from anyone there was "reason to believe" was in the Communist party, or who might be "going abroad to engage in activities which will advance the communist movement," or whose "conduct abroad is likely to be contrary to the best interest of the United States." As a result, passports were routinely withheld from those who wrote or spoke critically of U.S. policies, whether or not they were communist. Between May 1951 and May 1952, 300 Americans were denied the right to travel internationally. Ruth Shipley, then head of the passport office, reportedly boasted: "Nobody critical of U.S. foreign policy would leave the country." Succeeded by Frances Knight, whose policies were even more vigorous, passports were withheld from numerous citizens for the greatest variety of reasons, including Justice William O. Douglas (to go to China); Ring Lardner, Jr., a blacklisted Hollywood writer; Arthur Miller (prevented from traveling to Brussels to see a production of his anti-McCarthy play "The Crucible"); Otto Nathan, a German-Jewish refugee who was Einstein's best friend and adviser; and Paul Robeson, then the most famous black activist and performer, who was denied the right to travel between 1950 and 1958.

Perhaps the most insidious effort to limit and erase dissent and to achieve a one-note culture, was to be found in the annals of the Hollywood blacklist which remained in place for over a generation. HUAC invaded Hollywood twice, in 1947 and again in 1951. Never satisfied HUAC repeatedly returned to the subject of Hollywood subversion—in 1953, 1955, 1956, and 1958.

Dedicated to the elimination of all pro-New Deal producers, directors, screenwriters and stars, HUAC intended—by its weapons of publicity and exposure—to destroy their reputations, credibility, and very presence in American cultural life. Above all, HUAC was dedicated to ending Hollywood's love-affair with the U.S.-USSR Grand Alliance of World War II. A controlled, de-radicalized Hollywood taught America to love the Germans and hate the Russians almost as soon as World War II ended. Such films as *Mission to Moscow* (1943), *Song of Russia* (1943), and *Days of Glory* (1944) seemed to HUAC particularly un-American in their celebration of the wartime alliance, and the heroic Russian people— whose wartime casualty record of twenty million dead was now ignored or trivialized as Soviet propaganda. Everybody associated with such films became suspect. Innocence could only be proved by denouncing communism, communists, and everybody "soft" on the communist menace.

From 1947 on, Hollywood was divided between those who named names with enthusiasm, and those who refused to testify for reasons of self-protection, or reasons of principle. Wrapped in rigid legalese, HUAC eliminated all choices: one could take the Fifth Amend-

ment and be seen by all as an enemy of the state; or one could be a friendly witness, name names, and be given a hero's handshake which guaranteed continued access to work. Seventy-two friendly witnesses named over 300 film people who they considered past or present "communists" or "communist sympathizers." Screen Actors Guild president Ronald Reagan, George Murphey, Robert Montgomery, Robert Taylor, and Gary Cooper were among HUAC's most enthusiastic and "friendly" witnesses. They did more than denounce the communist influence on Hollywood. They invented a town honeycombed with stinging red bees. Gary Cooper, for example, testified that he had "turned down" many scripts "because I thought they were tinged with communistic ideas." But he could not remember any of them.

Those who refused to name names were held in contempt of Congress, imprisoned, and permanently blacklisted. Lives were destroyed. Many creative artists were never again employed; others moved to Europe or Mexico; and some changed their names. A small number were luckier and began working again during the 1960s. Alvah Bessie, Howard Da Silva, Dashiell Hammett, Lillian Hellman, Zero Mostel, Dorothy Parker, Anne Revere, Gale Sondergaard, and Dalton Trumbo were among the many whose lives and work were permanently affected. For a time some Hollywood notables organized to resist the outrages and established a Committee for the First Amendment, including John Huston, Lauren Bacall, Frank Sinatra, Groucho Marx, Humphrey Bogart, Judy Garland, and others. But they too were condemned for their efforts. Katharine Hepburn was told by Louis B. Mayer that there was so much opposition to her principled stand that he could not employ her again until she "became publicly acceptable." Humphrey Bogart was so harassed he quickly apologized for his "ill-advised" actions on behalf of the committee. John Huston explained: "Bogey owns a

54-foot yawl. When you own a 54-foot yawl, you've got to provide for her upkeep.''

Joseph McCarthy, the man who lent his name to this extravagant moment of American political conformity, called by Dalton Trumbo ''The Time of the Toad,'' was actually a latecomer on the scene. Television made McCarthy the media star of the anticommunist crusade. For years people referred to his February 7, 1950 Wheeling, West Virginia, antics and the way this gruff, never quite cleanly shaven, extravagantly crude senator brandished his briefcase: ''I have here in my hand the names of 205 members of the state department known to be communists and still employed.''

McCarthy's crusade against communists in government resulted in thousands of early retirements and hundreds of fired diplomats. But his activities soon backfired. After McCarthy's aides Roy Cohn and David Schein toured U.S. diplomatic posts in 1953, the mayor of Berlin told Adlai Stevenson that ''McCarthy had done more to hurt America abroad in eight months than Soviet propaganda did in eight years.'' In major European cities, the morale of the U.S. diplomatic corps was beyond depressed, it was destroyed. In Rome a foreign service officer was refused an assignment because he had ''kept company with Lillian Hellman in 1932.'' In Athens the flamboyant anticommunist Ambassador John Peurifoy, credited with beating back the Greek left (and later with the overthrow of the left-leaning Arbenz government in Guatemala), complained that McCarthy had insisted on his transfer to Latin America because he had refused to hand over certain secret and sensitive files. Committed to the removal of all ''queers,'' ''drunks,'' ''perverts,'' and assorted others who had kept the State Department both ''soft on communism'' and ''limp-wristed,'' McCarthy and his crowd aimed fast and wild. On April 8, 1954, A. A. Berle noted in his diary: ''Jane and Andrew Carey back from Ethiopia because, may God forgive us, the Security Service . . . de-

cided that Andy was a security risk because he had married Jane. The real reason was that they had invited Adlai Stevenson to dinner. . . . These are two conservative Republicans, who had behaved approximately like human beings. It makes you a bit sick.''

McCarthy's final play was his attack on the army as a hotbed of subversion. He had finally gone too far. Eisenhower had long resisted pressure to condemn McCarthy. To the dismay of many of his friends, Eisenhower had refused ''to get into the gutter with that guy.'' But now he took a stand. He refused to hand over military papers for the Army-McCarthy hearings. It was all over. Twenty million Americans bore witness to McCarthy's gratuitous announcement that Frederick Fisher, the legal assistant to the army's chief counsel, Joseph Welch, had once been a member of the National Lawyers' Guild, an organization of militant left-leaning lawyers, which had defended Communists. Finally McCarthy outdid himself. Hammering on and on, he lost the support of his own audience. No one would ever forget the mood of that moment when Welch said, ''Let us not assassinate this lad further, Senator. You have done enough. Have you no sense of decency, sir, at long last? Have you left no sense of decency?''

On November 11, 1954 the Senate voted 67 to 22 to condemn McCarthy for his abusive behavior. He had sullied the honor of the Senate and ''acted contrary to Senatorial traditions.''

McCarthy's crusade had been acceptable, even enjoyable, until it was done unto them. It had been a bipartisan massacre. When Eisenhower boasted that his administration had fired 1,456 federal workers within his first four months in office, and 2,200 shortly thereafter, the Democrats boasted that they had done even better when in office—and they had.

The year 1954 heralded a major shift in the history of the decade. On May 17, 1954 the U.S. Supreme Court decided unanimously in the case of *Brown* v. *Board of Education of Topeka, Kansas,* that school segregation was unconstitutional. Although the slow process of racial integration began shortly after World War II with Truman's executive order to integrate the armed forces, no integration orders were enforced until the Eisenhower administration. Partly because of the postwar climate worldwide, the rapid decolonization of the British and French empires in Africa and Asia, and America's assumption of influence and control in these regions, as well as the mandate of the cold war rivalry with the Soviet Union for popularity and primacy in these areas, the nation's race "etiquette" and assumptions about lynching and segregation came under new scrutiny.

Throughout the decade antilynch laws were introduced, only to be filibustered to death. But it became an increasing embarrassment to deny visiting diplomats and dignitaries from Africa the privilege of entering U.S. restaurants, hotels, and public places. Eisenhower integrated the nation's capital, and appointed Earl Warren chief justice of the Supreme Court. Although the president's own views on school integration were sluggish in the extreme (he once asked a dinner guest if he really wanted his sweet little granddaughter to sit next to "some big overgrown Negroes?"), he did send the troops to Little Rock to enforce the law, after a federal court ordered the integration of Central High School in 1957. In 1958 he integrated all Red Cross blood plasma by executive order. (During World War II and the Korean War U.S. blood plasma had been segregated white and Negro; Christian and Hebrew.)

Despite these dramatic beginnings, very little actually changed during the 1950s. Fewer than 5 percent of all schools in the South were integrated. De facto segregation prevailed everywhere: in housing, hospitals, public buildings, transportation facilities, restaurants, swimming pools, parks, and in the hearts and minds of most Americans. Unemployment rates for blacks remained two to three times above the white national average. In 1960 the black infant mortality rate was two-thirds higher than the white rate, while the black maternal death rate was six times higher. The South was still spending $5 to $7 for white education, for every $1 spent for black education. In Atlanta during the early 1950s there was not one kindergarten for blacks, not one community center, and only one park available to black citizens.

To retain white privilege, white citizen's councils and the Ku Klux Klan regrouped. Violent and repressive, with tacit law enforcement protection, the Klan rode virtually undisturbed for much of the decade. Indeed J. Edgar Hoover and the FBI blamed all "racial disturbances" on a massive communist conspiracy. As the KKK set about to preserve the nation's "racial integrity," in Alabama, for example, white and black integrationists were whipped and tortured and at least two men were emasculated. Riots, lynchings, the bombing of schools, churches, Jewish centers, and the burning of private homes all over the South followed the Court's decision. Violence and terror were used to extend the period of delay in integration that the Supreme Court actually encouraged. After all, instead of calling for immediate compliance with the law, the Court in *Brown* v. *Board of Education* had only requested that America's school districts "make a prompt and reasonable start toward full compliance."

"With all deliberate speed," a Little Rock, Arkansas, school board attempted a token nine-student integration plan in 1957. Unexpectedly, Governor Orville Faubus posted National Guardsmen outside Central High School "to preserve order." But the guardsmen turned the students away, blocked the doors, and did nothing while mobs attacked them. A fifteen-year-old student described her experience. Before she left home, she and her family had "a word of prayer." Then she was on her own: "They moved closer and closer. Somebody started yelling. 'Lynch her! Lynch her!' I tried to see a friendly face somewhere in the mob—someone who maybe would help. I looked into the face of an old woman, it seemed a kind face, but when I looked at her again, she spat on me. . . .''

Daisey Bates, president of the Arkansas NAACP, said that the students would not return "until they have the assurance of the president of the United States that they will be protected from the mob." Before Central High School reopened, Eisenhower declared that he would uphold the Constitution "by every legal means" at his command, ordered 1,000 members of the 101st Airborne Division into Little Rock, and federalized 10,000 Arkansas National Guardsmen. For the entire year the guardsmen protected the students from mobs who gathered daily outside the school while inside the students endured insults and outrages. Hot soup was poured on their heads and lighted cigarettes were dropped down their backs. But nine black teenagers integrated a white southern high school.

Elsewhere in the South school boards adopted "massive resistance" programs against integration. In Prince Edward County, Virginia, the entire public school system was simply closed. From 1959 to 1964 an entire educational generation was abandoned in order to keep out 1,700 black children. In New Orleans on November 14, 1960, U.S. deputy marshals, with the cooperation of the city police, escorted five first-grade black girls to two white schools. They were spat upon and their parents were stoned while white families boycotted the schools. By December the five girls attended almost-empty schools. In 1966, 75 percent of the school districts of the South were still segregated.

But during the 1950s new black leaders, and new organizations emerged that were to change forever the patterns of segregation and the expectations of Americans concerning human rights. The Supreme Court's 1954 decision

was the culmination of decades of legal action sponsored by the NAACP, founded in 1909, and the direct-action movement initiated by CORE in 1942. In 1950 Adam Clayton Powell's book *Marching Blacks* presaged the evolution of a new phase of the civil rights movement.

On December 1, 1955 Rosa Parks, refused to release her seat to a white man on a Montgomery, Alabama, bus. Rather than being a "tired old seamstress whose feet," as many historians have suggested, "simply hurt," she was an influential forty-two-year-old activist known and respected throughout Alabama. It was, then, no accident that she touched off a nonviolent revolution in the South. Rosa Parks had been secretary to E. D. Nixon when he was state chairman of the NAACP and had worked with A. Philip Randolph both in the Brotherhood of Sleeping Car Porters and in the 1940s March on Washington movement. When he was informed of Rosa Parks's arrest, he and Alabama's Women's Political Council were outraged. Plans to boycott Mongtomery's buses emerged out of the telephone calls between Nixon and the council. Three hundred eighty two days later the buses were integrated and Martin Luther King, Jr., and Ralph Abernathy became national figures.

Other new organizations emerged as the movement for racial justice grew. In January 1957 King, Abernathy, and Fred Shuttlesworth organized the Southern Christian Leadership Conference (SCLC) in Atlanta. Ella Baker, one of America's most vigorous political activists and a field secretary for the NAACP, became its first executive secretary. In 1960 she helped found the Student Nonviolent Coordinating Committee (SNCC). On February 1, 1960, in Greensboro, North Carolina, four black college freshmen sat-in at a whites-only Woolworth lunch counter and refused to move until they were served. Within six weeks black and white students were sitting-in all over the South. The campaign to integrate all tax-supported facilities produced: wade-ins at public beaches, read-ins at public libraries, kneel-ins at many churches, and walk-ins at public parks. By September 1961, 108 southern and border cities integrated their restaurants and finally black citizens entered the parks, libraries, and beaches for which they had always been taxed.

In 1957 the first Civil Rights Act since 1875 established a special division in the Department of Justice to protect the legal rights of black citizens. For the first time since Reconstruction, federal law enforcement officials were assigned to protect the right of black Americans to vote and to sit on juries. On May 6, 1960, Eisenhower signed another Civil Rights Act specifically designed to aid black voters to register. It provided criminal penalties for mob action intended to obstruct federal court orders and authorized federal judges to appoint voter registration referees. As a result of this act the NAACP, SCLC, SNCC, and CORE held major voter registration drives throughout the South. Everywhere they went they were met with mob violence. Not until Lyndon Baines Johnson's 1968 Civil Rights Act was the full authority of the federal government used to enforce civil rights.

As the 1950s ended millions of Americans joined the campaign for racial justice and international peace. Barbara Deming, then a civil rights and peace activist, described the first peace walk through the South in 1962. Hundreds of white Americans marched for peace from Nashville to Washington, D.C. but in the beginning were reluctant to integrate the march, agreeing with James Farmer—then head of CORE—who believed that it would tarnish the civil rights movement to mix the two issues. But blacks joined the white peace marchers in increasing numbers and the "causes were joined." That fact altered the perception black and white Americans had of the U.S. role in world affairs. Never again would it be possible to separate our nation's international posture from its domestic policies.

SUGGESTED READINGS

Belfrage, Cedric. *The American Inquisition, 1945– 1960.* Indianapolis: Bobbs-Merrill, 1973.

Bentley, Eric. *Thirty Years of Treason: Excerpts from Hearings before the House Committee on Un-American Activities, 1938–1968.* New York: Viking Press, 1971.

Biskind, Peter. *Seeing Is Believing: How Hollywood Taught Us to Stop Worrying and Love the '50's.* New York: Pantheon Books, 1983.

Caute, David. *The Great Fear: The Anti-Communist Purge under Truman and Eisenhower.* New York: Simon & Schuster, 1978.

Cook, Blanche Wiesen. *The Declassified Eisenhower: A Divided Legacy of Peace and Political Warfare.* New York: Penguin Books, 1984.

Donner, Frank J. *The Age of Surveillance.* New York: Alfred A. Knopf, 1980.

Foreman, James. *The Making of Black Revolutionaries.* New York: Macmillan, 1972.

Harper, Alan D. *The Politics of Loyalty: The White House and the Communist Issue, 1946–1952.* Westport, Conn.: Greenwood Press, 1969.

King, Martin Luther, Jr. *Stride toward Freedom.* New York: Harper & Row, 1958.

Kinoy, Arthur. *Rights on Trial: The Odyssey of a People's Lawyer.* Cambridge, Mass.: Harvard University Press, 1983.

Lattimore, Owen. *Ordeal by Slander.* New York: Bantam Books, 1950.

Meeropol, Robert and Michael. *We Are Your Sons: The Legacy of Ethel and Julius Rosenberg.* Urbana: University of Illinois Press, 1987.

Navasky, Victor. *Naming Names.* New York: Viking Press, 1980.

Potter, Senator Charles E. *Days of Shame.* New York: Coward, McCann, 1965.

Robeson, Paul. *Here I Stand.* Boston: Beacon, 1958.

Rovere, Richard H. *Senator Joe McCarthy.* Cleveland: World Publishing, 1959.

Smith, Lillian, *Our Faces Our Words.* New York: W. W. Norton, 1964.

Trumbo, Dalton. *The Time of the Toad.* New York: Harper & Row, 1972.

Zinn, Howard. *SNCC: The New Abolitionists*. Boston: Beacon Press, 1965.

DOCUMENT 29.1
NSC–68

President Harry S Truman received NSC-68 *on April 7, 1950. Top secret, and not declassified until 1975, it became the U.S. international relations blueprint for the cold war. It called for a major increase in defense spending, military aid, higher taxes, permanent combat readiness, an expanded nuclear arsenal, and permanent psychological, economic, and political warfare with the Soviet Union.*

*   *   *   *   *

The idea of freedom is the most contagious idea in history, more contagious than the idea of submission to authority. For the breath of freedom cannot be tolerated in a society which has come under the domination of an individual or group of individuals with a will to absolute power. Where the despot holds absolute power—the absolute power of the absolutely powerful will—all other wills must be subjugated in an act of willing submission, a degradation willed by the individual upon himself under the compulsion of a perverted faith. It is the first article of this faith that he finds and can only find the meaning of his existence in serving the ends of the system. The system becomes God, and submission to the will of God becomes submission to the will of the system. It is not enough to yield outwardly to the system—even Ghandian non-violence is not acceptable—for the spirit of resistance and the devotion to a higher authority might then remain, and the individual would not be wholly submissive.

Source: "NSC-68. A Report to the National Security Council," in *National War College Review*, 27 (May–June 1975), pp. 55–58.

The antipathy of slavery to freedom explains the iron curtain, the isolation, the autarchy of the society whose end is absolute power. The existence and persistence of the idea of freedom is a permanent and continuous threat to the foundation of the slave society; and it therefore regards as intolerable the long continued existence of freedom in the world. What is new, what makes the continuing crisis, is the polarization of power which now inescapably confronts the slave society with the free.

The assault on free institutions is world-wide now, and in the context of the present polarization of power a defeat of free institutions anywhere is a defeat everywhere. The shock we sustained in the destruction of Czechoslovakia was not in the measure of Czechoslovakia's material importance to us. In a material sense, her capabilities were already at Soviet disposal. But when the integrity of Czechoslovak institutions was destroyed, it was in the intangible scale of values that we registered a loss more damaging than the material loss we had already suffered.

Thus unwillingly our free society finds itself mortally challenged by the Soviet system. No other value system is so wholly irreconcilable with ours, so implacable in its purpose to destroy ours, so capable of turning to its own uses the most dangerous and divisive trends in our own society, no other so skillfully and powerfully evokes the elements of irrationality in human nature everywhere, and no other has the support of a great and growing center of military power.

The objectives of a free society are determined by its fundamental values and by the necessity for maintaining the material environment in which they flourish. Logically and in fact, therefore, the Kremlin's challenge to the United States is directed not only to our values but to our physical capacity to protect their environment. It is a challenge which encompasses both peace and war and our objectives in peace and war must take account of it.

1. Thus we must make ourselves strong, both in the way in which we affirm our values in the conduct of our national life, and in the development of our military and economic strength.

2. We must lead in building a successfully functioning political and economic system in the free world. It is only by practical affirmation, abroad as well as at home, of our essential values, that we can preserve our own integrity, in which lies the real frustration of the Kremlin design.

3. But beyond thus affirming our values our policy and actions must be such as to foster a fundamental change in the nature of the Soviet system, a change toward which the frustration of the design is the first and perhaps the most important step. Clearly it will not only be less costly but more effective if this change occurs to a maximum extent as a result of internal forces in Soviet society.

In a shrinking world, which now faces the threat of atomic warfare, it is not an adequate objective merely to seek to check the Kremlin design, for the absence of order among nations is becoming less and less tolerable. This fact imposes on us, in our own interests, the responsibility of world leadership. It demands that we make the attempt, and accept the risks inherent in it, to bring about order and justice by means consistent with the principles of freedom and democracy. We should limit our requirement of the Soviet Union to its participation with other nations on the basis of equality and respect for the rights of others. Subject to this requirement, we must with our allies and the former subject peoples seek to create a world society based on the principle of consent. Its framework cannot be inflexible. It will consist of many national communities of great and varying abilities and resources, and hence of

war potential. The seeds of conflicts will inevitably exist or will come into being. To acknowledge this is only to acknowledge the impossibility of a final solution. Not to acknowledge it can be fatally dangerous in a world in which there are no final solutions.

All these objectives of a free society are equally valid and necessary in peace and war. But every consideration of devotion to our fundamental values and to our national security demands that we seek to achieve them by the strategy of the cold war. It is only by developing the moral and material strength of the free world that the Soviet regime will become convinced of the falsity of its assumptions and that the pre-conditions for workable agreements can be created. By practically demonstrating the integrity and vitality of our system the free world widens the area of possible agreement and thus can hope gradually to bring about a Soviet acknowledgement of realities which in sum will eventually constitute a frustration of the Soviet design. Short of this, however, it might be possible to create a situation which will induce the Soviet Union to accommodate itself, with or without the conscious abandonment of its design, to coexistence on tolerable terms with the non-Soviet world. Such a development would be a triumph for the idea of freedom and democracy. It must be an immediate objective of United States policy.

There is no reason, in the event of war, for us to alter our over-all objectives. They do not include unconditional surrender, the subjugation of the Russian peoples or a Russia shorn of its economic potential. Such a course would irrevocably unite the Russian people behind the regime which enslaves them. Rather these objectives contemplate Soviet acceptance of the specific and limited conditions requisite to an international environment in which free institutions can flourish, and in which the Russian peoples will have a new chance to work out their own destiny. If we can make the Russian people our allies in this enterprise we will obviously have made our task easier and victory more certain.

The objectives outlined in NSC 20/4 (November 23, 1948) . . . are fully consistent with the objectives stated in this paper, and they remain valid. The growing intensity of the conflict which has been imposed upon us, however, requires the changes of emphasis and the additions that are apparent. Coupled with the probable fission bomb capability and possible thermonuclear bomb capability of the Soviet Union, the intensifying struggle requires us to face the fact that we can expect no lasting abatement of the crisis unless and until a change occurs in the nature of the Soviet system.

DOCUMENT 29.2
McCarthyism

Richard Rovere, for many years a staff writer for The New Yorker, *was among the first to analyze the life, career, and impact of Joseph McCarthy. For five years the United States seemed to be overwhelmed, and even intimidated, by a frank demagogue. Eleanor Roosevelt wrote that "McCarthy's methods, to me, look like Hitler's." In a similar vein Rovere wrote: "Like Hitler, McCarthy was a screamer, a political thug, a master of the mob, an exploiter of popular fears."*

In the following excerpt Rovere discusses the range of those whose politics or ambitions made McCarthy and McCarthyism possible.

*   *   *   *   *

Because McCarthyism had no real grit and substance as a doctrine and no organization, it is difficult to deal with as a movement. Adherence was of many different sorts. There were those who accepted McCarthy's leadership and would have been happy to see him President.

Source: Richard H. Rovere, *Senator Joe McCarthy* (Cleveland: World Publishing, 1960), pp. 20–23.

There were others who were indifferent to his person but receptive to what he had to say about the government. There were others still who put no particular stock in what he had to say and even believed it largely nonsense but felt that he was valuable anyway.

McCarthy drew into his following most of the zanies and zombies and compulsive haters who had followed earlier and lesser demagogues in the fascist and semifascist movements of the thirties and forties. At a typical McCarthy rally, there would be, seated in the front rows, thanks to early arrival, numbers of moon-struck souls wearing badges or carrying placards identifying them as Minute Women of the U.S.A., Sons of I Shall Return, members of the Alert Council for America, the Nationalist Action League, We the Mothers Mobilize, the Republoform, and so on. They knew all the words of "Nobody Loves Joe but the Pee-pul," and if this anthem was sung, their voices, generally on the shrill or reedy side, would be heard above the rest. But this was really the least part of it. McCarthy went far beyond the world of the daft and the frenzied—or, to put the matter another way, that world was greatly enlarged while he was about. Into it came large numbers of regular Republicans who had coolly decided that there was no longer any respectable way of unhorsing the Democrats and that only McCarthy's wild and conscienceless politics could do the job. He built, as Samuel Lubell pointed out in *Revolt of the Moderates,* a coalition of the aggrieved— of men and women not deranged but deeply affronted by various tendencies over the preceding two or three decades: toward internationalism, and, in particular, toward closer ties with the British; toward classlessness; toward the welfare state. There were Roman Catholics, particularly those of Irish descent, who saw in this aggressive Hibernian the flaming avenger of their own humiliations of the past and who could not believe that the criticism he provoked was based on anything but hatred of his Church and his name. To these and many others he was a symbol of rebellion. And beyond all this, he simply persuaded a number of people that he was speaking the essential truth; he sent up such vast and billowing clouds of smoke that many men and women who were not abnormally gullible became convinced that there must be a fire beneath it all.

In his following, there were many people who counted for quite a bit in American life— some because of wealth and power, some because of intelligence and political sophistication. He was an immediate hit among the Texas oilmen, many of whom were figures as bizarre and adventurous in the world of commerce and finance as he was in the world of politics. They liked his wildcatting style, and they liked him, and they hurried to contribute up to the legal limit to any campaign he approved, to shower him with Cadillacs and other baubles, and to compete for his presence at their parties, their hunts for white-winged doves, and other exotic entertainments favored by people whose income for a week may exceed that of many men for a lifetime. And there were intellectuals and intellectuals *manque* whose notions of *Realpolitik* had room for just such a man of action as McCarthy. Some of them, like James Burnham, John Chamberlain, Max Eastman, and William F. Buckley, Jr., were far from being fools. (Buckley, the editor of the *National Review,* linked the worlds of money and intellect; his father was in oil, and he was in writing, and in a book that makes an interesting souvenir of the period, *McCarthy and His Enemies,* which he wrote with L. Brent Bozell, he and his co-author made the breath-taking assertion that "McCarthyism . . . is a movement around which men of good will and stern morality can close ranks.") At any rate, the fools and the non-fools contributed mightily to his following, which *was* mighty, and there was a time when just about everyone who depended upon the favor of the people lived in fear of him because they believed that a hostile word from him would be a marching order to millions.

In January 1954, when the record was pretty well all in and the worst as well as the best was known, the researches of the Gallup Poll indicated that 50 per cent of the American people had a generally "favorable opinion" of him and felt that he was serving the country in useful ways. Twenty-one per cent drew a blank—"no opinion." The conscious, though not necessarily active, opposition—those with an "unfavorable opinion"—was 29 per cent. A "favorable opinion" did not make a man a McCarthyite, and millions were shortly to revise their view to his disadvantage. But an opposition of only 29 per cent is not much to count on, and it was small wonder that his contemporaries feared him. It was a melancholy time, and the Chief Justice of the United States was probably right when he said that if the Bill of Rights were put to a vote, it would lose.

DOCUMENT 29.3
Dalton Trumbo on Mind Control

Dalton Trumbo's pamphlet, The Time of the Toad, *was first published in 1949. Trumbo had been the highest-paid writer on MGM's payroll. The author of a prize-winning novel,* Johnny Got His Gun, *Trumbo's films included* Kitty Foyle *(1940) and* Thirty Seconds over Tokyo *(1944). One of the original Hollywood Ten, he was blacklisted after the HUAC hearings and sent to prison for contempt of Congress. Unable to get work under his own name until 1960, when he wrote the script for* Spartacus, *he nonetheless won an Oscar for the* The Brave One *in 1957, using the name Robert Rich. In this excerpt, Trumbo scorns the wide-ranging impact of the 1950s red scare on American culture and education.*

How goes Congressional censorship of motion pictures? It goes excellently. The Committee

Source: Dalton Trumbo, *The Time of the Toad* (New York: Harper & Row, 1949, 1972), pp. 48–55.

on Un-American Activities called for the discharge of ten men on political grounds. The motion picture monopoly promptly broke all existing contracts with the accused men and, in theory at least, banned them for life from the practice of their profession. Beyond the blacklisted ten there extends a vague and shadowy "gray list" composed of scores of men and women whose ideas and politics might possibly give offense to the committee. And beyond the gray list lies a wide and spreading area of general fear in which unconventional ideas or unpopular thoughts are carefully concealed by self-censorship.

The committee did not only tell the producers whom they might not employ: it also told them what kind of pictures they must make in the future. Throughout the hearings the committee demanded over and again why anti-Communist pictures were not being made and when they would be made.[1] The producers returned to their studios and immediately set about the production of the films for which the committee had called. *The Iron Curtain, I Married a Communist, The Red Menace, The Red Danube* and *Guilty of Treason*—all of them calculated to provoke hatred and incite to war—were made without reference to audience demand, possible profit, or normal entertainment value. They were produced as the direct result of Congressional command over the content of American motion pictures.

Even though it is customary in intellectual

circles to deplore motion pictures as an art, it would be a fatal mistake to underestimate them as an influence. They constitute perhaps the most important medium for the communication of ideas in the world today. The Committee on Un-American Activities recognizes them as such. The Circuit Court of Appeals recognizes them as such. The Legion of Decency and the National Association of Manufacturers and the American Legion and the National Chamber of Commerce recognize them as such. Unless intellectuals quickly come to the same conclusion and act as vigorously as their enemies, there is an excellent chance that the American motion picture monopoly, abasing itself as the German monopoly did, will succeed in its assigned task of preparing the minds of its audiences for the violence and brutality and perverted morality which is fascism.

How goes the encroachment of politics upon science? It goes very well. Scholarships have been restricted to the elite; the Congress has asserted its power over atomic decisions; the president has complained that the committee on Un-American Activities renders it difficult to find competent personnel; the Federation of Atomic Scientists has been all but silenced; the conspiracy between the military and the banks to surrender the incalculable riches of atomic energy into private hands progresses nicely.

Mr. De Voto declares:

There is a growing suspicion, which a lot of us would like aired, that the generals and admirals are demanding and being accorded the right to determine the political (and what others?) opinions of the scientists whose salaries they are paying. If they are not making that demand now, we can be quite sure they will be tomorrow.

Dr. Edward U. Condon, head of the United States Bureau of Standards, reveals that one of the charges made against him was that "you have been highly critical of the older ideas in

---

[1] "Under those circumstances, I would like to know whether or not Warner Brothers has made, or is making at the present time, any pictures pointing out the methods and the evils of totalitarian communism, as you so effectively have pointed out the evils of the totalitarian Nazis."—Mr. Richard Nixon to Mr. Jack Warner, HUAC Hollywood Hearings, October 20, 1947, p. 28.

"Under the circumstances, I think this committee is glad to hear that Warner Brothers is contemplating for the first time now making a motion picture in which they point out to the American people the dangers of totalitarian communism as well as fascism."—Mr. Richard Nixon to Mr. Jack Warner, Ibid., p. 29.

physics,'' and goes on to warn that "anti-intellectualism precedes the totalitarian pusch, and anti-intellectualism is on the upswing here.''

How goes the infliction of censorship upon art? It goes well. Representative George A. Dondero of Michigan has addressed Congress to the extent of ten columns in the Congressional Record on the subject of "Communism in the Heart of American Art—What to Do About It." Mr. Dondero was inflamed by a Gallery on Wheels—an art exhibit for the benefit of the men in veterans hospitals, to which twenty-eight artists had contributed their work.

The Congressman cited fifteen of the artists as Communists or sympathizers, and went into the political records of thirteen of them. Important among the charges he made was support of Mr. Henry A. Wallace's candidacy. Declaring that "the art of the Communist and the Marxist is the art of perversion," he denounced the contributors as ". . . radicals all . . . explaining their theories to an audience who could not get away from them. . . . They had a great opportunity not only to spread propaganda, but to engage in espionage." One important art gallery also came under Mr. Dondero's fire, which culminated in a demand for "a major investigation on the part of a competent governmental agency" and, while disavowing any intent of censorship, demanded "directional supervision" of art critics by their superiors.

Mr. Arthur Miller, art editor of the *Los Angeles Times* states that the Congressman's attacks "have resulted in the return of paintings by named artists to New York art dealers, the loss of a mural commission and the expulsion of at least one well-known artist, a National Academician, from a conservative artists' club." He also reports that "the reviews of one New York critic, respected by her colleagues, are reportedly being personally edited by her publisher. . . ."

Presumably the baiting of modern American art would not trouble President Truman, who ·

has participated in the sport himself; nor the State Department which, under Secretary Marshall, abjectly withdrew its traveling show of modern American artists at the first breath of "conservative" criticism and sold it as war surplus.

How goes the campaign against free inquiry in schools and universities? It goes extremely well. The roll call of professors purged during 1948: Dr. Clarence R. Athern, professor of philosophy and social ethics, Lycoming College; Professor Daniel D. Ashkenas, University of Miami; Professor James Barfoot, University of Georgia; Professor Lyman R. Bradley, head of the German department, New York University; Professor Joseph Butterworth, associate in English, University of Washington; Professor Leonard Cohen, Jr., University of Miami; Professor Charles G. Davis, University of Miami; Professor Ralph H. Gundlach, associate in psychology, University of Washington; Dr. Richard G. Morgan, Curator of the Ohio State Museum; Mr. Clyde Miller of Teachers College, Columbia University; Professor Luther K. McNair, Dean of Lyndon State Teachers College; Professor Herbert J. Phillips, assistant in philosophy, University of Washington; Dr. George Parker, professor of Bible and philosophy, Methodist Evansville College; Professor Ralph Spitzer, University of Oregon, Professor Don West of Oglethorpe.

Charges against these men ranged from stating under oath they were Communists and being in contempt of the Committee on Un-American Activities to supporting Mr. Wallace for the presidency and running for the governorship of Georgia.

But the formal leaders of American education have gone even farther toward restricting academic freedom. They have resolved to save their house from the arsonists of the Un-American Activities committee by setting fire to it themselves. In the recent report of the National Education Association and the American Association of School Administrators—a synopsis of which was overwhelmingly approved at the NEA convention—they have not only barred Communists from their faculties; they have thoughtfully handed down a plan for a complete renovation of the American mind.

The report was predicated upon the assumption that "the cold war will continue for many years" and therefore requires a "basic psychological reorientation for the American people as a whole." Admitting that "it is deeply patriotic to attempt to protect one's country and one's fellow citizens from the calamities of war" it nevertheless points out that "in the years just ahead it will not always be easy to teach such things as these in American schools." However "the schools of the United States will certainly be expected and required to continue their work in developing strong individual national loyalties" which inevitably will reveal "the need for healthy young people to wear uniforms and man machines. . . ." The report exhorts educators to work toward that time when education shall deserve to receive popular support "as an instrument of national policy."

Education, hitherto presumed to consist of free inquiry into the nature of truth, thus becomes merely an instrument of whatever policy the nation momentarily may pursue. That policy, determined outside the university and being on its own *ipse dixit* right, obviously cannot be subject to free inquiry. When policy has been made, inquiry ceases. National policy is truth, truth is national policy. It cannot be otherwise.

The report was signed by twenty leading educators, among them that politico-military pedagogue, General Dwight D. Eisenhower, and Dr. James B. Conant of Harvard, who immediately afterward found himself in a preposterous situation when the author of the Maryland Loyalty Bills—later declared unconstitutional—demanded that since Dr. Conant had pledged himself to bar Communists from the university in the future, he discharge those already employed. Dr. Conant replied with a resounding peroration against faculty witch hunts, but logic did not abide with him. He retired to the same corner into which Mr. Ernst knocked Mr. Schlesinger, there to receive unguents from the partial virgin who has made of that place her domain.

We have retreated almost the full distance from President Roosevelt's "No group and no government can properly prescribe precisely what should constitute the body of knowledge with which true education is concerned. The truth is found where men are free to pursue it" to William Jennings Bryan's "No teacher should be allowed on the faculty of any American University unless he is a Christian."

DOCUMENT 29.4
McCarthyism and Unionism

Arthur Kinoy had been one of the attorney's representing the United Electrical Worker's Union, one of the unions that refused to adhere to the Taft-Hartley anticommunist regulations. It remained a target for government investigators, who frequently worked in concert with General Electric and other major companies. In this excerpt from Kinoy's autobiography, Rights on Trial, *the author describes McCarthy's effort to intimidate the Union and its vigorous response.*

There was little time during the next months to think about the bitter, pointed words of Jerome Frank that Friday afternoon in New Haven, or to relive the frustrations and agonies of the futile last-minute attempt to hold off the deaths of Julius and Ethel Rosenberg. There was too much to do. It soon became clear that the victories we had just won in stemming the NLRB and grand jury attacks on the UE were

Source: Arthur Kinoy, *Rights on Trial. The Odyssey of a People's Lawyer* (Cambridge, Mass.: Harvard University Press, 1983), pp. 129–134.

only momentary. The destruction of this seemingly irrepressible group of militant trade unionists remained high on the agenda of those who were calling the shots in the escalation of the Cold War.

Late in the fall of 1953, we heard news from Massachusetts which boded no good for the union and, for us personally, raised warnings of a very busy winter. Back in 1950 at the General Electric plant in Lynn, the IUE, the rival union set up by Murray and the CIO, had succeeded, by a plurality of only several hundred votes in the ten thousand ballots cast by the workers, in ousting the UE as bargaining agent. Over the next three years a considerable amount of rethinking went on among the Lynn workers. Then in the middle of 1953, following the end of the open fighting in Korea, the company instituted a wholesale program of layoffs and speed-ups on the assembly line. At this point a large group of workers asked the UE to petition for a board election. The IUE used every legal trick in the book to hold off an election, but signed cards and testimony from workers in the plant were overwhelming evidence that the UE had tremendous support. The NLRB, frustrated by our injunction against its plans to bar the UE from all labor elections, on November 17 reluctantly agreed to a new election, to be held within thirty days. From what we were hearing from the organizers in Boston, the UE sentiment in the plant was growing fast.

Then the new attack hit. On the very same day that the NLRB released news of its agreement to a new election at the Lynn plant, Senator McCarthy announced that on the next day his Internal Security Committee planned to hold a closed hearing in Boston on security policies and alleged Communist infiltration at General Electric's Lynn and Everett plants. But the hearing the next morning was not closed; it was televised. During the hearing a self-styled "undercover agent for the FBI" informed the senator and the viewing public that he knew

at least thirty "Communist agents" at the Lynn plant. He conveniently named two workers who happened to be leading UE supporters in the forthcoming election. Less than an hour later, a representative of the company announced publicly that these two workers were being promptly suspended from employment. And less than a day later, twenty-eight other General Electric workers from plants throughout the country were suspended, as the result, McCarthy proudly announced to the press, of testimony given in secret session by the same undercover agent.

When a few days later this so-called undercover agent was exposed by the police chief of his home town, Fitchburg, Massachusetts, as an inveterate liar with a 34-year police record of arrests and convictions, even the local FBI office denied responsibility for him, claiming with some embarrassment that he was a "volunteer" witness and not an agent of theirs. But when this damaging bit of information came out, it received barely an inch of coverage in the local papers. McCarthy was riding high, at the height of his popularity and with massive public support.

At this point, Dave Scribner asked us to sit in on a discussion of the situation with the UE officers. Jim Matles, who was handling the Lynn campaign, brought us up to date. Something was changing. Cohn and McCarthy, by concentrating their attack on rank-and-file workers and local organizers this time, sidestepping what had been their previous emphasis on the national union officers, seemed to be preparing for some new move. Matles, Emspak, and Fitzgerald all stressed that it must be basically a company move. The firings came too quickly. As Fitzgerald said, looking at the list of the thirty suspended workers, if General Electric had singled out thirty of the most obstinate fighters against the speed-up that the company was pushing in the plants, they could not have done a better job. It was necessary for the union to begin quickly exposing the

McCarthy attacks as covers for a company move against the most effective union leaders in the plants. It was also necessary to make it dramatically and personally clear to the rank-and-file leadership—those subpoenaed and those waiting, a little scared, to be subpoenaed—that the UE national officers were right beside them in the fight.

How to do that? One of the officers half-longingly said, "Hell, if they had only subpoenaed *us* this time, we could really tell them off. They can't fire *us* from their plants." All at once everyone got excited. Why not call McCarthy and Cohn's bluff? Why not demand that they subpoena a UE officer? Why not? We had to find every possible way within the growing atmosphere of fear and terror to say loud and clear that this was no high-level government effort to eliminate a dangerous foreign conspiracy but rather a simple union-busting, company-directed move which working people in this country had experienced time and again.

A sensitive question then arose, as it often would for people's lawyers at vastly different moments of struggle. By demanding the right to appear before McCarthy in order to expose his underlying role as a company tool, were we in any way legitimizing his opposition? At that moment it seemed clear that there was no simple, one-dimensional answer which held true at all times under all circumstances. As one UE officer pointed out sharply, "It all depends on what we do there. Just let us get at him, and no one will think we are legitimizing anything." So once again it appeared that, for a people's lawyer, the key to testing the validity of a given approach was to recognize that what was sound and helpful at one moment might not be so useful at another moment. The test, as in our first experiences in Evansville, was still valid: how will it help to advance the fighting ability of the people?

Later that afternoon it was decided that Matles, being directly involved in the Lynn campaign, should be the one to take on McCar-

thy head on. After the meeting we gathered in Scribner's office and drafted a telegram to Cohn that must have bowled him over when he received it the next morning. It was probably the only time anyone had ever demanded receiving a subpoena from the McCarthy committee.

After waiting two days without an answer, Scribner decided to flush out Cohn. He used the one approach we knew Cohn and McCarthy could not take. Scribner called up Cohn and said simply, "Either give Matles a subpoena immediately, or we will call a press conference in Lynn and announce that you are scared to hear what Matles has to say." That did it. The next day the subpoena arrived at the office. Matles was to appear two days later, on November 25, in New York, not Lynn, and the hearing was to be a closed "executive session." Only one lawyer would be allowed to appear with the witness. As we did not want to give them any excuse to hold up the hearing, Scribner alone went with Matles to the hearing in the federal courtroom.

The report of the hearing made to us late that evening by Scribner was very exciting. The hearing, he told us, had been amazing. From the moment that Matles was called to testify, he had grabbed the initiative. The tone of the hearing was set by his first response to McCarthy. When McCarthy opened up his conventional political attack, Matles replied—as headlined in the next issue of the *UE News* two days later—"You're a liar, Senator." From then on, the proceeding was a debacle for Cohn and McCarthy, with Matles accusing McCarthy directly of playing General Electric's game and of giving the company "lawless and indecent aid."

At the end an incredible thing happened. McCarthy, who had been banging away with a gavel to stop Matles' testimony, jumped up, rushed down to where the witness sat, and stood glaring as Matles said right to his face, "You are doing a dirty thing, Senator, going to Lynn and Schenectady for the General Electric Company, terrorizing and browbeating decent working people. I tell you to stop it.''

McCarthy literally screamed at Matles, ''I want to set you straight on the purpose of this executive session. We've got a lot on you.'' To which Matles shot back, ''You've got nothing on me, not a damned thing. You've been trying to frame me on my non-Communist affidavits for three years, the pair of you, and you haven't done it. Let me ask you a question. Are you a spy for the General Electric Company? That question is as good coming from me to you as coming from you to me.''

At that point McCarthy blew up in a way he rarely ever had. He spun around and yelled at Cohn, ''Come on, we are wasting our time. Let's get the immigration authorities in here and get this man deported.'' And at that moment he revealed the real stimulus behind the long drawn-out denaturalization proceedings against Matles that would take place over the next four years.

The hearing ended abruptly on one last abrasive note, the full significance of which none of us could grasp at the time. Matles lashed back at Cohn and McCarthy with a question that was to contribute, six months later, to the Senate resolution of censure against McCarthy and to Cohn's firing as committee counsel. As Matles got up to leave, he turned to Cohn and put the question to him, ''What are you doing here, Cohn? I see you lost Schine. What about you?'' David Schine, another young ''special assistant'' to McCarthy, had just been drafted into the army, amid rumors that McCarthy had pulled every trick and brought every pressure to bear on the army high command to keep Schine from being drafted. Now the same stories were circulating about Cohn, who so far had managed to avoid the draft. Matles pressed his question, ''I put in my time in the armed services, Cohn. What are you doing here?''

This hit a raw nerve, and Cohn shot back,

''Do you want me to tell you?'' Then McCarthy, probably for the first time in his career as a Cold War investigator, found himself in the strange position of advising one of his own staff virtually to ''plead the Fifth,'' blurting out to Cohn, ''You don't have to answer that, Roy.''

This confrontation between Matles and Cohn and McCarthy became a powerful instrument in the protracted struggle over the next years. Time and again in the roughest days it helped to illustrate the counteroffensive that had to be developed if the Cold War strategy of big business was to be withstood. On the night of the hearing, the workers were given a blow-by-blow report on it at a large public meeting in Lynn. By the end of the year, few UE members did not know the story of the ''You're a liar, Senator'' confrontation. That showdown helped more than anything else to raise morale when fighting spirits were low. It drove home to all of us the critical need, in periods of long and frustrating struggle, of seeking out opportunities in the legal arena to provide sharp examples of courage and steadfastness to counterbalance the seeming invincibility of the establishment.

We needed such reminders in the months to come. On December 8, one day before the scheduled NLRB election at Lynn, General Electric dropped a bombshell which finally placed the Cohn-McCarthy moves during the entire preelection period in focus. The front pages of every plant newspaper trumpeted a new company policy, to go into effect immediately. The company announced that ''it would suspend employees who refused to testify under oath when questioned in public hearings conducted by competent government officials.'' This policy came to be known throughout General Electric plants as Policy No. 20.4, or the ''General Electric Fifth Amendment firing policy.'' Anyone named as a ''subversive'' before the McCarthy committee who failed to ''cooperate fully'' was to be fired by the company.

It was widely known that McCarthy had said repeatedly that all UE supporters were "subversives." The inference was inescapable. Anyone who became too closely identified with the UE was subversive. If they were subversive, the McCarthy committee would finger them. If they were fingered and did not play the company's game, they were fired.

Under a camouflage of pompous, patriotic reasons put forward by Ralph Cordiner, the General Electric president, this was the first unabashed public blacklist of union militants since the open shop days of the early 1930s. What no one knew at that time was that the whole approach—the committee subpoenaes, the fingering of UE militants, and the General Electric blacklisting—had been carefully worked out late in October at a secret meeting at the Mohawk Club in Schenectady between company representatives and McCarthy's aides Roy Cohn and George Anastos. This fact would not come out until over a year later during depositions made by company officers in the course of pressing our legal counterattack against Policy 20.4.

The company's blacklisting policy had an immediate effect on the Lynn election. The IUE retained representation rights at the plant by only a few hundred votes. This was a defeat for the UE, no question, but considering the general atmosphere of the times, it was a surprise that so many thousands of working people at the home plant of one of the largest and most powerful corporations had held out against the terror and hysteria and stood fast by the UE. Two or three days after the Lynn results, the UE officers urged that as part of a stand-and-fight policy against the wholesale layoffs and speed-ups taking place in major electrical plants throughout the country, we figure out some kind of legal attack against the Cordiner-Cohn-McCarthy scheme. They were looking for an approach that would cut through the phony patriotism of the company and expose the union-busting essence of the "cooperate with the committee or be fired" scheme.

DOCUMENT 29.5
"Separate but Equal" Has no Place

Since 1896, when the U.S. Supreme Court held in Plessy v. Ferguson *that "separate but equal" accommodations was the law of the land, a vicious system of segregation in all public and private aspects of American life prevailed. With this landmark decision of 1954, the Court unanimously decided that the nation's segregated educational system was unconstitutional, as well as cruel and unequal, and did not serve the best interests of the United States. Although the justices called for integration "with all deliberate speed," segregation, it might be observed, still exists across much of the country.*

Warren, C. J. These cases come to us from the States of Kansas, South Carolina, Virginia, and Delaware. They are premised on different facts and different local conditions, but a common legal question justifies their consideration together in this consolidated opinion.

In each of the cases, minors of the Negro race, through their legal representatives, seek the aid of the courts in obtaining admission to the public schools of their community on a nonsegregated basis. In each instance, they have been denied admission to schools attended by white children under laws requiring or permitting segregation according to race. This segregation was alleged to deprive the plaintiffs of the equal protection of the laws under the Fourteenth Amendment. In each of the cases other than the Delaware case, a three-judge

Source: *Brown* v. *Board of Education of Topeka*, 347 U.S. 483 (1954).

federal district court denied relief to the plaintiffs on the so-called "separate but equal" doctrine announced by this Court in *Plessy* v. *Ferguson,* 163 U.S. 537. Under that doctrine, equality of treatment is accorded when the races are provided substantially equal facilities, even though these facilities be separate. In the Delaware case, the Supreme Court of Delaware adhered to that doctrine, but ordered that the plaintiffs be admitted to the white schools because of their superiority to the Negro schools.

The plaintiffs contend that segregated public schools are not "equal" and cannot be made "equal," and that hence they are deprived of the equal protection of the laws. Because of the obvious importance of the question presented, the Court took jurisdiction. Argument was heard in the 1952 Term, and reargument was heard this Term on certain questions propounded by the Court.

Reargument was largely devoted to the circumstances surrounding the adoption of the Fourteenth Amendment in 1868. It covered exhaustively consideration of the Amendment in Congress, ratification by the states, then existing practices in racial segregation, and the views of proponents and opponents of the Amendment. This discussion and our own investigation convince us that, although these sources cast some light, it is not enough to resolve the problem with which we are faced. At best, they are inconclusive. The most avid proponents of the post-War Amendments undoubtedly intended them to remove all legal distinctions among "all persons born or naturalized in the United States." Their opponents, just as certainly, were antagonistic to both the letter and the spirit of the Amendments and wished them to have the most limited effect. What others in Congress and the state legislatures had in mind cannot be determined with any degree of certainty.

An additional reason for the inconclusive nature of the Amendment's history, with respect to segregated schools, is the status of public education at that time. In the South, the movement toward free common schools, supported by general taxation, had not yet taken hold. Education of white children was largely in the hands of private groups. Education of Negroes was almost nonexistent, and practically all of the race were illiterate. In fact, any education of Negroes was forbidden by law in some states. Today, in contrast, many Negroes have achieved outstanding success in the arts and sciences as well as in the business and professional world. It is true that public education had already advanced further in the North, but the effect of the Amendment on Northern States was generally ignored in the congressional debates. Even in the North, the conditions of public education did not approximate those existing today. The curriculum was usually rudimentary; ungraded schools were common in rural areas; the school term was but three months a year in many states; and compulsory school attendance was virtually unknown. As a consequence, it is not surprising that there should be so little in the history of the Fourteenth Amendment relating to its intended effect on public education.

In the first cases in this Court construing the Fourteenth Amendment, decided shortly after its adoption, the Court interpreted it as proscribing all state-imposed discriminations against the Negro race. The doctrine of "separate but equal" did not make its appearance in this Court until 1896 in the case of *Plessy* v. *Ferguson,* supra, involving not education but transportation. American courts have since labored with the doctrine for over half a century. In this Court, there have been six cases involving the "separate but equal" doctrine in the field of public education. In *Cumming* v. *Board of Education of Richmond County,* 175 U.S. 528, and *Gong Lum* v. *Rice,* 275 U.S. 78, the validity of the doctrine itself was not challenged. In more recent cases, all on the graduate school level, inequality was found in that specific benefits enjoyed by white students were denied to Negro students of the same educational qualifications. *State of Missouri ex rel. Gaines* v. *Canada,* 305 U.S. 337; *Sipuel* v. *Board of Regents of University of Oklahoma,* 332 U.S. 631; *Sweatt* v. *Painter,* 339 U.S. 629; *McLaurin* v. *Oklahoma State Regents,* 339 U.S. 637. In none of these cases was it necessary to reexamine the doctrine to grant relief to the Negro plaintiff. And in *Sweatt* v. *Painter,* supra, the Court expressly reserved decision on the question whether *Plessy* v. *Ferguson* should be held inapplicable to public education.

In the instant cases, that question is directly presented. Here, unlike *Sweatt* v. *Painter,* there are findings below that the Negro and white schools involved have been equalized, or are being equalized, with respect to buildings, curricula, qualifications and salaries of teachers, and other "tangible" factors. Our decision, therefore, cannot turn on merely a comparison of these tangible factors in the Negro and white schools involved in each of these cases. We must look instead to the effect of segregation itself on public education.

In approaching this problem, we cannot turn the clock back to 1868 when the Amendment was adopted, or even to 1896 when *Plessy* v. *Ferguson* was written. We must consider public education in the light of its full development and its present place in American life throughout the Nation. Only in this way can it be determined if segregation in public schools deprives these plaintiffs of the equal protection of the laws.

Today, education is perhaps the most important function of state and local governments. Compulsory school attendance laws and the great expenditures for education both demonstrate our recognition of the importance of education to our democratic society. It is required in the performance of our most basic public responsibilities, even service in the armed forces. It is the very foundation of good citizenship. Today it is a principal instrument in awakening the child to cultural values, in preparing him for later professional training, and in helping him to adjust normally to his environment. In these days, it is doubtful that any child may reasonably be expected to succeed in life if he is denied the opportunity of an education. Such an opportunity, where the state has undertaken to provide it, is a right which must be made available to all on equal terms.

We come then to the question presented: Does segregation of children in public schools solely on the basis of race, even though the physical facilities and other "tangible" factors may be equal, deprive the children of the minority group of equal educational opportunities? We believe that it does.

In *Sweatt* v. *Painter,* supra [339 U.S. 629, 70 S.Ct. 850], in finding that a segregated law school for Negroes could not provide them equal educational opportunities, this Court relied in large part on "those qualities which are incapable of objective measurement but which make for greatness in a law school." In *McLaurin* v. *Oklahoma State Regents,* supra [339 U.S. 637, 70 S.Ct. 853], the Court, in requiring that a Negro admitted to a white graduate school be treated like all other students, again resorted to intangible considerations: ". . . his ability to study, to engage in discussions and exchange views with other students, and, in general, to learn his profession." Such considerations apply with added force to children in grade and high schools. To separate them from others of similar age and qualifications solely because of their race generates a feeling of inferiority as to their status in the community that may affect their hearts and minds in a way unlikely ever to be undone. The effect of this separation on their educational opportunities was well stated by a finding in the Kansas case by a court which nevertheless felt compelled to rule against the Negro plaintiffs:

Segregation of white and colored children in public schools has a detrimental effect upon the colored children. The impact is greater when it has the sanction of the law; for the policy of separating the races is usually interpreted as denoting the inferiority of the Negro group. A sense of inferiority affects the motivation of a child to learn. Segregation with the sanction of law, therefore, has a tendency to retard the educational and mental development of Negro children and to deprive them of some of the benefits they would receive in a racially integrated school system.

Whatever may have been the extent of psychological knowledge at the time of *Plessy* v. *Ferguson,* this finding is amply supported by modern authority. Any language in *Plessy* v. *Ferguson* contrary to this finding is rejected.

We conclude that in the field of public education the doctrine of "separate but equal" has no place. Separate educational facilities are inherently unequal. Therefore, we hold that the plaintiffs and others similarly situated for whom the actions have been brought are, by reason of the segregation complained of, deprived of the equal protection of the laws guaranteed by the Fourteenth Amendment. This deposition makes unnecessary any discussion whether such segregation also violates the Due Process Clause of the Fourteenth Amendment.

Because these are class actions, because of the wide applicability of this decision, and because of the great variety of local conditions, the formulation of decrees in these cases presents problems of considerable complexity. On reargument, the consideration of appropriate relief was necessarily subordinated to the primary question—the constitutionality of segregation in public education. We have now announced that such segregation is a denial of the equal protection of the laws. In order that we may have the full assistance of the parties in formulating decrees, the cases will be restored to the docket, and the parties are requested to present further argument. . . . The

Attorney General of the United States is again invited to participate. The Attorneys General of the states requiring or permitting segregation in public education will also be permitted to appear as *amici curiae* upon request to do so by September 15, 1954, and submission of briefs by October 1, 1954.

It is so ordered.

DOCUMENT 29.6
Nonviolent Resistance

During the 1950s Martin Luther King, Jr., emerged as the leader of the contemporary civil rights movement. In the following section from Dr. King's memoir of the Montgomery bus boycott, Stride toward Freedom, *he explains the origins and essence of nonviolent resistance to segregation.*

. . . When I went to Montgomery as a pastor, I had not the slightest idea that I would later become involved in a crisis in which nonviolent resistance would be applicable. I neither started the protest nor suggested it. I simply responded to the call of the people for a spokesman. When the protest began, my mind, consciously or unconsciously, was driven back to the Sermon on the Mount, with its sublime teachings on love, and the Gandhian method of nonviolent resistance. As the days unfolded, I came to see the power of nonviolence more and more. Living through the actual experience of the protest, nonviolence became more than a method to which I gave intellectual assent; it became a commitment to a way of life. Many of the things that I had not cleared up intellectually concerning nonviolence were now solved in the sphere of practical action.

Source: Martin Luther King, Jr., *Stride toward Freedom: The Montgomery Story* (New York: Harper & Row, 1958), pp. 101–107.

Since the philosophy of nonviolence played such a positive role in the Montgomery Movement, it may be wise to turn to a brief discussion of some basic aspects of this philosophy.

First, it must be emphasized that nonviolent resistance is not a method for cowards; it does resist. If one uses this method because he is afraid or merely because he lacks the instruments of violence, he is not truly nonviolent. This is why Gandhi often said that if cowardice is the only alternative to violence, it is better to fight. He made this statement conscious of the fact that there is always another alternative: no individual or group need submit to any wrong, nor need they use violence to right the wrong; there is the way of nonviolence resistance. This is ultimately the way of the strong man. It is not a method of stagnant passivity. The phrase "passive resistance" often gives the false impression that this is a sort of "do-nothing method" in which the resister quietly and passively accepts evil. But nothing is further from the truth. For while the nonviolent resister is passive in the sense that he is not physically aggressive toward his opponent, his mind and emotions are always active, constantly seeking to persuade his opponent that he is wrong. The method is passive physically, but strongly active spiritually. It is not passive physically, but strongly active spiritually. It is not passive nonresistance to evil, it is active nonviolent resistance to evil.

A second basic fact that characterizes nonviolence is that it does not seek to defeat or humiliate the opponent, but to win his friendship and understanding. The nonviolent resister must often express his protest through noncoöperation or boycotts, but he realizes that these are not ends themselves, they are merely means to awaken a sense of moral shame in the opponent. The end is redemption and reconciliation. The aftermath of nonviolence is the creation of the beloved community, while the aftermath of violence is tragic bitterness.

A third characteristic of this method is that the attack is directed against forces of evil rather than against persons who happen to be doing the evil. It is evil that the nonviolent resister seeks to defeat, not the persons victimized by evil. If he is opposing racial injustice, the nonviolent resister has the vision to see that the basic tension is not between races. As I like to say to the people in Montgomery: "The tension in this city is not between white people and Negro people. The tension is, at bottom, between justice and injustice, between the forces of light and the forces of darkness. And if there is a victory, it will be a victory not merely for fifty thousand Negroes, but a victory for justice and the forces of light. We are out to defeat injustice and not white persons who may be unjust."

A fourth point that characterizes nonviolent resistance is a willingness to accept suffering without retaliation, to accept blows from the opponent without striking back. "Rivers of blood may have to flow before we gain our freedom, but it must be our blood," Gandhi said to his countrymen. The nonviolent resister is willing to accept violence if necessary, but never to inflict it. He does not seek to dodge jail. If going to jail is necessary, he enters it "as a bridegroom enters the bride's chamber."

One may well ask: "What is the nonviolent resister's justification for this ordeal to which he invites men, for this mass political application of the ancient doctrine of turning the other cheek?" The answer is found in the realization that unearned suffering is redemptive. Suffering, the nonviolent resister realizes, has tremendous educational and transforming possibilities. "Things of fundamental importance to people are not secured by reason alone, but have to be purchased with their suffering," said Gandhi. He continues: "Suffering is infinitely more powerful than the law of the jungle for converting the opponent and opening his ears which are otherwise shut to the voice of reason."

A fifth point concerning nonviolent resistance is that it avoids not only external physical violence but also internal violence of spirit. The nonviolent resister not only refuses to shoot his opponent but he also refuses to hate him. At the center of nonviolence stands the principle of love. The nonviolent resister would contend that in the struggle for human dignity, the oppressed people of the world must not succumb to the temptation of becoming bitter or indulging in hate campaigns. To retaliate in kind would do nothing but intensify the existence of hate in the universe. Along the way of life, someone must have sense enough and morality enough to cut off the chain of hate. This can only be done by projecting the ethic of love to the center of our lives.

In speaking of love at this point, we are not referring to some sentimental or affectionate emotion. It would be nonsense to urge men to love their oppressors in an affectionate sense. Love in this connection means understanding, redemptive good will. Here the Greek language comes to our aid. There are three words for love in the Greek New Testament. First, there is *eros*. In Platonic philosophy *eros* meant the yearning of the soul for the realm of the divine. It has come now to mean a sort of aesthetic or romantic love. Second, there is *philia* which means intimate affection between personal friends. *Philia* denotes a sort of reciprocal love; the person loves because he is loved. When we speak of loving those who oppose us, we refer to neither *eros* nor *philia;* we speak of a love which is expressed in the Greek word *agape*. *Agape* means understanding, redeeming good will for all men. It is an overflowing love which is purely spontaneous, unmotivated, groundless, and creative. It is not set in motion by any quality or function of its object. It is the love of God operating in the human heart.

Agape is disinterested love. It is a love in which the individual seeks not his own good, but the good of his neighbor (I Cor. 10:24). *Agape* does not begin by discriminating between worthy and unworthy people, or any

qualities people possess. It begins by loving others *for their sakes*. It is an entirely ''neighbor-regarding concern for others,'' which discovers the neighbor in every man it meets. Therefore, *agape* makes no distinction between friend and enemy; it is directed toward both. If one loves an individual merely on account of his friendliness, he loves him for the sake of the benefits to be gained from the friendship, rather than for the friend's own sake. Consequently, the best way to assure oneself that Love is disinterested is to have love for the enemy-neighbor from whom you can expect no good in return, but only hostility and persecution.

Another basic point about *agape* is that it springs from the *need* of the other person— his need for belonging to the best in the human family. The Samaritan who helped the Jew on the Jericho Road was ''good'' because he responded to the human need that he was presented with. God's love is eternal and fails not because man needs his love. St. Paul assures us that the loving act of redemption was done ''while we were yet sinners''—that is, at the point of our greatest need for love. Since the white man's personality is greatly distorted by segregation, and his soul is greatly scarred, he needs the love of the Negro. The Negro must love the white man, because the white man needs his love to remove his tensions, insecurities, and fears.

Agape is not a weak, passive love. It is love in action. *Agape* is love seeking to preserve and create community. It is insistence on community even when one seeks to break it. *Agape* is a willingness to sacrifice in the interest of mutuality. *Agape* is a willingness to go to any length to restore community. It doesn't stop at the first mile, but it goes the second mile to restore community. It is a willingness to forgive, not seven times, but seventy times seven to restore community. The cross is the eternal expression of the length to which God will go in order to restore broken community.

The resurrection is a symbol of God's triumph over all the forces that seek to block community. The Holy Spirit is the continuing community creating reality that moves through history. He who works against community is working against the whole of creation. Therefore, if I respond to hate with a reciprocal hate I do nothing but intensify the cleavage in broken community. I can only close the gap in broken community by meeting hate with love. If I meet hate with hate, I become depersonalized, because creation is so designed that my personality can only be fulfilled in the context of community. Booker T. Washington was right: "Let no man pull you so low as to make you hate him." When he pulls you that low he brings you to the point of working against community; he drags you to the point of defying creation, and thereby becoming depersonalized.

In the final analysis, *agape* means a recognition of the fact that all life is interrelated. All humanity is involved in a single process, and all men are brothers. To the degree that I harm my brother, no matter what he is doing to me, to that extent I am harming myself. For example, white men often refuse federal aid to education in order to avoid giving the Negro his rights; but because all men are brothers they cannot deny Negro children without harming their own. They end, all efforts to the contrary, by hurting themselves. Why is this? Because men are brothers. If you harm me, you harm yourself.

Love, *agape,* is the only cement that can hold this broken community together. When I am commanded to love, I am commanded to restore community, to resist injustice, and to meet the needs of my brothers.

A sixth basic fact about nonviolent resistance is that it is based on the conviction that the universe is on the side of justice. Consequently, the believer in nonviolence has deep faith in the future. This faith is another reason why the nonviolent resister can accept suffering without retaliation. For he knows that in his struggle for justice he has cosmic companionship. It is true that there are devout believers in nonviolence who find it difficult to believe in a personal God. But even these persons believe in the existence of some creative force that works for universal wholeness. Whether we call it an unconscious process, an impersonal Brahman, or a Personal Being of matchless power and infinite love, there is a creative force in this universe that works to bring the disconnected aspects of reality into a harmonious whole.

DOCUMENT 29.7
Toward Integration

In 1964 Lillian Smith collected the anonymous reminiscences of the new generation of civil rights activists. A white southern activist, she challenged the South's "race etiquette" in all of her work, notably in her novel Strange Fruit *(1944), her essays* Killers of the Dream *(1949),* The Journey *(1954), and* Now Is the Time *(1955), as well as* The South Today *a newspaper which she published from 1936 to 1945.*

To go back four years: that day, I'd been reading. *Franny and Zooey.* Everybody was reading it in our dorm. There were other books on Bill's shelf and mine, the usual things: Camus' *Sisyphus,* Dylan Thomas, Mailer, Sartre; I had just read *Borstal Boy.* We were English majors. I was trying out for an Ionesco play in French. All this is to suggest, I guess, that I didn't go in for the racial stuff, "sociological problems," our English prof called it. I hadn't even read Dick Wright. I just didn't like race talk.

My uncle kept his life raw with it. He was that kind, couldn't pass up a slight. Had to

_____
Source: Lillian Smith, *Our Faces, Our Words* (New York: W. W. Norton, 1964), pp. 23–37.

bleed. Active in NAACP. Always fighting the white man. Before I was born he was going after the Negro's rights. Once, I was about six or so, he said to me, "Tell me, do you know who you are?" I saw Mama look up, put her hand out to stop him, then as suddenly, she went back to stringing the beans for supper.

"I'm Jim," I said.

"Jim who?"

I told him.

"That's not important."

"Yes, it is," Mama said. "Jim is a person, he has a name, and he's going to make us proud of it, some day."

Uncle laughed. I thought it a mean laugh; maybe it was just an unhappy one. "Your mama don't want you to learn the facts of life," he said. "The most important fact for you, Jim, is that you are a Negro." He looked at Mama (she's his sister) as if to say, You can lie to him but not to me. "You're not a nigger—and don't you ever let anybody call you one. But you are a Negro. And the sooner you learn it the better. You're as good as anybody technically, but you are not, actually, until you get your rights as an American. White folks are not going to give them to you even though they belong to you. Remember: they stole 'em from you. Remember: folks don't like to return what they steal. You'll have to take 'em back. And to do it you'll have to work to get them; you can never let up, never for one minute let up."

Mama said, "Jim and I—we look at it another way. Jim's a human being, you're one, too (though you're not acting like one now)." She smiled. Uncle snorted. "Jim knows he's human—much like the other two and a half billion humans across the earth. He knows he's an individual and different from others; he knows it is good to be different and every human being has a right to be different. But color is a false difference; it is not important to Jim nor to me. It shouldn't be to anybody."

Uncle looked at me. Things were being said

I couldn't hear, I felt them whizzing between the two. Uncle's voice snagged on his words, "You believe all this, what your mother is saying?"

"Yes sir."

"Well, young man, what you going to do with all these fine notions?"

"He's going to grow up to be a real man, intelligent, decent, hardworking, who will leave a good mark on the world, I hope," said Mama.

"Ha!" said Uncle. "Just like that! Easy, too, huh?" My pup began chasing a chicken, I ran to help him. I didn't like Uncle's voice and I shied away from him after that day.

Mom works in the branch library, called the James Weldon Johnson Branch. (It is integrated, today, but it wasn't four years ago.) I used to go down every afternoon to read and look around. We had a lot of good juveniles at home, too; of course they were about white children, no little Negroes, but I accepted that. I guess I vaguely thought it strange not to put little Negroes in books, too—but it wasn't a hurting thought. Mom took me to the plays and concerts at the Negro college; I'd go sound to sleep but I liked going. I accepted my world; I didn't know any other; most children accept the world they're born into, even when it is a place where earthquakes play around.

After high school, I went to the college here at home. I lived in the dorm—and that day I am telling about, I was reading *Franny and Zooey,* and I was with it. I wasn't thinking, "I'm a Negro and all this is alien to me. It wasn't, it was real and human. A guy named Dan was talking to my roommate. I heard him say, "My mom was just getting over flu, see? And she'd been shopping all morning. She'd bought about fifty-five dollars' worth of stuff; she was matching a spool of thread when suddenly everything began to black out. She knew if she could sit down a few minutes and have a cup of coffee she'd be OK. But where in that store or anywhere else downtown could

she get it! She fainted. They had a time: somebody got her ammonia, somebody found a cot
for her, and somebody else brought her a cup
of coffee.''

Bill laughed. "One way to get it. It's not
funny, Dan. But there's a terrible irony—"

Dan nodded. "When it's your own mother
you don't think about irony.''

I closed the book. To hell with *Franny and
Zooey.* . . .

If Mom was tired and needed a cup of coffee
where could she get it downtown? Dammit to
hell, where could she get it? Jesus Christ! She
could buy out the store and still couldn't buy
one cup of coffee and sit down quietly and
drink it. You never thought about it before—
how about going to the john—did they let her
go to a restroom—

I saw Mom, suddenly. Right there, standing
in front of my whole life. Gray-eyed, gentle,
poised. Always so quietly poised. My God,
where did her serenity come from! She'd never
said a bitter word in her life against the whites,
not to me; and she wasn't a handkerchief-head,
either; talk about white folks giving you back
your ''dignity''—Mom's dignity couldn't have
been taken from her, it went down to the center
of her soul. I saw all this. I saw all she'd
tried to keep me from looking at, cesspools
and stinking ways, dirty alleys in streets and
minds—Mom all the time turning me toward
books, music, poetry, drama, ideas, science,
hoping, I guess, that I'd never catch on to
what it was really about. She couldn't stand
hate—I guess she didn't want me poisoned
by it.

''Dan,'' I said, ''let's make em open up
those places.''

''OK by me,'' said Dan.

That's the way the revolution started for
us. We were suddenly *there.* In it. We'd never
been a black boy, like Dick Wright down in
Mississippi. We'd never felt invisible, way
Ralph Ellison felt. We never felt we were Nothing; I was always sure I was Something. Well,

I admit it: we'd been mighty sheltered; our
race had never had it so good. I guess, as the
middle-class Negro in some of the upper-South
cities had it when I was growing up. I'd never
seen a Klansman in my life; had never seen a
race murder, never heard a mob on the loose.
I knew such things happened, read about them
but I guess I pushed them off. *They didn't
get on my mind.* I knew there were places I
couldn't go but having the college we were
able to enjoy many advantages even the whites
in our city didn't have. Somehow my pride
never got tangled up in it; oh, I knew I couldn't
enter certain places but I honestly believe I
didn't worry about this much more than the
average middle-class white southern kid wor-
ries who knows he can't join a millionaires'
club; I knew about Negro slums, Harlem, South
Side but thought about it in the same way most
white boys think about slums and bad housing
for whites. I was *sound asleep,* let me settle
for that. My mother was a lady to her fingertips;
I guess I pretended she was exactly like any
white lady with access to the same civilities
and courtesies.

Well—we were waking up. We dressed in
our Sunday clothes to look like the gentlemen
we made like we were, took our Bibles and
school books and started our sit-in. But before
we sat in, we did read up on what the others
had done in Greensboro and Tallahassee. We
knew we'd better get with this nonviolence
thing. We didn't have time to read Martin Buber
or Gandhi or Thoreau but we did take time
out to read Martin Luther King—all about redemption through suffering, ''absorbing'' the
cruelties of others . . . conciliation . . . compassion. I read it. Dan read it.

''My God,'' Dan said, ''what the hell is
redemption?''

I stared at him. There was nothing in *Franny
and Zooey* about redemption. Somebody said—
Bill, I think—''maybe we'd better read Camus'
The Fall.'' We decided we didn't have time.
We wouldn't say it but I think we felt we'd

better get going before we lost our nerve. "We'll get redeemed, later," Bill said solemnly, "we'd better go sit now." Dan was staring hard at me, it made me tremble, I felt things turning upsidedown. "Let's get going," I said. Voice sort of loud.

Well, we got going and sat in at Walgreen's. Don't know why we picked that one but we did. Maybe because we knew it was a chain store and might be more sensitive to pressures—but I don't know, we actually weren't doing much thinking. We walked to the counter, sat down, opened our books. Bill opened the Bible—and read it, too. I had my physics textbook; read one paragraph sixteen times without knowing what was in it. The white girl behind the counter, awfully young, turned pink then deathly white. She didn't say a word. Bill looked up, smiled, said quietly, "We'd like some coffee, please, and some doughnuts." She swallowed, swallowed again, shook her head. "I can't," she said. She wasn't mean. I felt sorry for her. "Please go away," she whispered, "they won't let me serve you." We sat there.

Pretty soon, two or three white kids came in, stared at us, one sat down next to me, hummed something, got up, walked out. We kept on reading. Some more came in; we didn't turn round to see but they were making a lot of noise. Then it happened: that cigarette; the goon stuck the burning thing into my back. Sit tight, don't move, take it; this is nonviolence, I told myself, you have to take it. A white guy came in, knocked the cigarette out of the other guy's hand; there was scuffling back of me; I didn't turn. A cop came in. Walgreen's closed the counter. We left.

That's how we started. Three weeks later, the lunch counter opened to everybody. By then, we were sitting in at Kress's. There were about twenty-five or more students helping us now, and more high-school kids than we needed; the high-school kids just poured into

the movement, completely unafraid, having a ball, but serious, too, deepdown.

We felt we had to hold meetings now to decide what to do, what not to do; we had to learn you can't lose your temper, you can't talk back, you can't hit back; you keep everything under control. Two of the college men couldn't make it; we told them to stay out of things until they could control their feelings; the high school kids were cool, and they listened. "You got to feel compassionate toward the whites," a worker from CORE told us; at our request he had come to train us. So we talked about compassion, forgiveness, talked about absorbing evil through our own suffering. "You'll find it works," the Core adviser told us; "if a white has any good in him, he'll respond to compassion and friendly talk; you got to remember that you can hate evil without hating the man who does the evil; it's like a doctor treating the evil of smallpox without hating the man who has it."

"Yeah," said one kid, "but you'd better fear that smallpox." Everybody laughed.

"Sure," said the teacher of nonviolence, "you've got to have sense; be wary, be shrewd, nobody was more shrewd than Gandhi, don't be reckless; but remember: negative nonviolence is not enough; it's got to be positive; you feel all the time that the other man, the one fighting you, can be redeemed; he's got to feel something good in you."

This was tough on most of us; we didn't want to be cowards; we felt it would do us a world of good to punch a white bully in the nose; we wondered if these goons possessed souls; maybe terror had to be met with terror; maybe those cops actually couldn't respond to love. We talked about this; but we knew, somewhere in us, that strategically a minority can't change things by violence, it would be suicide to try; and we began to see that while one goon may fail to respond to conciliation and friendly reason and this thing we called "love," hundreds of thousands of the public, white and Negro looking on, would begin to respond, begin to understand; and we dimly saw that when this happens change comes, real change. For this is the beginning of dialogue, of response of one human to another.

Well, back to the Kress business. Six girls were sitting in with us, very brave and gay. There was a lot of laughter and singing; maybe no movement in the world's history has ever been such a singing movement as this one. But things were getting tougher. A mean editorial appeared in the morning paper; the editor couldn't grasp the basic idea of truth and compassion in human relations; he honestly didn't believe we as Americans should protest the lack of our civil rights; he seemed to think we should just keep on as our grandfathers had done; but the editor was caught fast in the first decade of the century.

A week later, Kress's opened up. We moved on from Kress's to picketing the biggest department store in town. Somehow, I got in jail. That hurt Mom. *Her* son. They sent us there because we had "trespassed." I wanted to say, "Mom, I'm in jail so you can have a cup of coffee when you want one." I didn't say it. That cup of coffee had metamorphosed into everything Negroes lacked that was rightfully theirs as human beings. It looked like we'd have to open up the whole city, the whole region; then we'd have to go North and help them open up things there, too.

Now, here I am in Mississippi; working on a literacy program for the Negro sharecroppers in the Delta, getting them registered to vote; grassroots stuff. (Oh yes—somewhere along the way we stopped wearing our Sunday clothes. We wear jeans now.) We've collected thousands of books, trying to fix up centers where they can come and read. There're no real schools for the colored kids down here. Parents can't read or write, most of them. Money? That's funny. You don't sit in restaurants in a place like this. Where would they

get money to go to a restaurant? Where would they get clothes to wear? They don't have wants like that. They *need. Need everything.* This is zero. You begin here in the mud and dust at nothing and inch up. Got to. No other way. Whites are about as bad off as the Negroes. It is like the Indian villages, a Hindu visitor told us, only maybe worse; more fear, more pressure on the Negroes; hostile police. I didn't know all this existed, had no idea it could exist. In college, we didn't talk about these things, we read *Waiting for Godot.* What you reckon these kids here in the Delta are waiting for; I wish I knew. They're born and then they start waiting, waiting. Sometimes at night, you're riding along one of these bumpy rough roads through the fields, everything stretching away from you, sky tilted, stars spilling out of space, now and then a light way off, a thousand shadows where the shacks are. And you think, They're full of children, real honest-to-God children, and they're all waiting for something to happen here in our country, in the United States; and suddenly the waiting is a ghost choking me and I fight it, I shake it off whispering, Tomorrow I'll teach a kid to read: "This is a book; I want to know what is in it." One inch; one inch up.

DOCUMENT 29.8
The CIA and the Rosenbergs

Anti-Semitism was a major factor in the Rosenberg *case. The press emphasized that many rank-and-file communists and communist sympathizers were Jews, as well as the entire prosecuting staff, including Irving Saypol and Roy Cohn, and the trial judge Irving Kaufman. CIA Director Allan Dulles was very aware of this factor; and, in this declassified CIA*

Source: *Memorandum. Subject: The Rosenberg Case,* January 22, 1953.

document, he proposed a scheme that if successful would have great "psychological warfare" benefits.

MEMORANDUM

Subject: The Rosenberg Case

January 22, 1953

Proposal. A concerted effort to convince Julius and Ethel Rosenberg, convicted atom spies now under sentence of death, that the Soviet regime they serve is persecuting and ultimately bent on exterminating the Jews under its sovereignty. The action desired of the Rosenbergs is that they appeal to Jews in all countries to get out of the communist movement and seek to destroy it. In return, death sentence would be commuted.

Advantages. The importance of success in this venture can scarcely be overstated from a psychological warfare standpoint. The Communist Parties throughout the world have built up the Rosenbergs as heroes and as martyrs to "American anti-semitism." Their recantation would entail backfiring of this entire Soviet propaganda effort. It would be virtually impossible for world communism to ignore or successfully discredit the Rosenbergs. The couple is ideally situated to serve as leading instruments of a psychological warfare campaign designed to split world communism on the Jewish issue, to create disaffected groups within the membership of the Parties, to utilize these groups for further infiltration and for intelligence work. (Whether the defection of the Rosenbergs would yield significant information concerning other Soviet espionage groups is a matter for the FBI to appraise.)

Likelihood of Success. Apparently neither of the condemned has thus far wavered. An appraisal of the possibilities of their defection could be obtained from the FBI. The hypothesis suggested here is that the Soviet 'Doctors' accusations may have come as a great shock to them. Since they are Jews and have been placed in the role of victims to anti-semitism, it is believed that the new developments in Soviet policy vis-à-vis the Jews open new possibilities. It is also believed that people of the sort of the Rosenbergs can be swayed by duty where they can not be swayed by considerations of self-interest. They should not be asked to trade their principles for their lives—for one thing, such an appeal to cowardice would almost certainly fail. The argument should be rather that they are about to die for a system that has betrayed and is destroying their own people, that they have the moral obligation of influencing other Jews against communism. In short, they would be offered two things psychologically: (1) an opportunity to recant while preserving their self-respect and honor; (2) a new purpose in life.

The Ethical Issue. The purpose of the Government would be to gain a new instrument to make clear the sinister purposes of communism to its deluded followers and, incidentally, to save two lives. Certainly, neither purpose is immoral. The means, however, necessarily involves the coercion of prisoners for no discussions can be termed free if the upshot determines whether people live or die. If this coercive element makes the whole plan repugnant to our traditions of due process, then naturally it should not be undertaken. Presumably, the Attorney General should evaluate this. If the answer is favorable, consideration must be given to the consequences of failure to sway the Rosenbergs—the virtual certainty that the Communists will use the attempt for their propaganda. Therefore, it is proposed that the emissaries chosen be unofficial, without credentials from the Government of any sort and with no authority to commit it to any action.

Suggested Approach. The contact could be made by rabbis, representatives of Jewish organizations, former Communists. The last group would understand the mentality of the Rosenbergs far better than the others and would share with them common experiences and attitudes. However, the Rosenbergs would probably view them, not merely as enemies, but as traitors to the movement and this consideration seems to the writer to be decisive as far as the initial stage of conversations is concerned. Perhaps the ideal emissaries would be highly intelligent rabbis, representing reformed Judaism, with a radical background or sympathetic understanding of radicalism, and with psychiatric knowledge. Such men can be found. Here again, the viewpoint of the FBI would be of the greatest value.

(1) The emissaries do not need to be armed with a formal promise of clemency, for the Rosenbergs already understand that they can obtain commutation if they cooperate with the United States.

(2) Complete confidentiality in the discussions is imperative. The Rosenbergs may have strong doubts of the rightness of their course which they would wish to explore with sympathetic, intelligent and well-informed anti-Communists. However, since there are doubts and not certainties, they will wish to be able to die as martyrs if the doubts disappear after investigation. They would therefore fear that any talks they have with the emissaries might be used afterwards to destroy the propaganda value of their death for communism should they decide in the end upon death. Preservation of confidence as to the discussions should be pledged, subject to a similar confidence on the part of the Rosenbergs. The emissaries should be people of such unimpeachable moral stature that no suspicion of double dealing on their part could arise.

(3) Date of execution should be stayed until the emissaries ascertain whether or not the Rosenbergs are interested in entering into such protracted discussions. If they are not, the execution should proceed and the emissaries should preserve total silence.

(4) If the Rosenbergs desire to explore these matters, an execution stay of one to two months seems indicated. First, time is needed for a thorough discussion of all those phases of Soviet conduct which the condemned would have to weigh in their minds before reaching what is for them their biggest decision. This is not merely a matter of persecution of Jews, but of the basic character of the Soviet dictatorship. Second, the Rosenbergs should have time to read the most authoritative and convincing literature available on such matters as the U.S.S.R. slave labor camps. (It should be recalled that as Communist they were explicitly forbidden hertofore from either reading such books or having them in their possession.) Third, fruitful discussions can hardly be held if they occur, as it were, under the shadow of imminent execution.

(5) Should the operation succeed, generous commutation appears indicated—both to encourage others to defect and to utilize the Rosenbergs as figures in an effective international psychological warfare campaign against communism primarily on the Jewish issue.

DOCUMENT 29.9
SNCC

Students provided the impetus for the revitalization of the civil rights and peace movements throughout the United States. The following two documents from SNCC's founding convention capture the moral fervor of the movement and the integrity of the people active in it. James M. Lawson, Jr., a student at the Vanderbilt University School of Divinity,

Source: "Statement of Purpose," First General Conference of the Student Nonviolent Coordinating Committee, Raleigh, N.C., April 17, 1960.

was expelled in 1960 for his civil rights activities.

THE STUDENT NONVIOLENT COORDINATING COMMITTEE: "NONVIOLENCE IS THE FOUNDATION"

When the college student sit-in demonstrators of 1960 formed their Student Nonviolent Coordinating Committee (SNCC) it was to Martin Luther King and his philosophy that they at first looked. Later, for reasons of personality and tactics, SNCC and SCLC drifted apart. But the statement of purpose adopted at SNCC's founding convention, with its spirit of moral idealism and its emphasis on love and conscience, is a statement clearly based on the lofty principles expressed by Martin Luther King, Jr.

Statement of Purpose

We affirm the philosophical or religious ideal of nonviolence as the foundation of our purpose, the presupposition of our faith, and the manner of our action. Nonviolence as it grows from Judaic-Christian traditions seeks a social order of justice permeated by love. Integration of human endeavor represents the crucial first step towards such a society.

Through nonviolence, courage displaces fear; love transforms hate. Acceptance dissipates prejudice; hope ends despair. Peace dominates war; faith reconciles doubt. Mutual regard cancels enmity. Justice for all overthrows injustice. The redemptive community supersedes systems of gross social immorality.

Love is the central motif of nonviolence. Love is the force by which God binds man to Himself and man to man. Such love goes to the extreme; it remains loving and forgiving even in the midst of hostility. It matches the capacity of evil to inflict suffering with an even more enduring capacity to absorb evil, all the while persisting in love.

By appealing to conscience and standing on the moral nature of human existence, nonviolence nurtures the atmosphere in which reconciliation and justice become actual possibilities.

JAMES M. LAWSON, JR.: "WE ARE TRYING TO RAISE THE 'MORAL ISSUE'"

For the group that founded SNCC in 1960, James M. Lawson, Jr., was as much an inspiration as was Martin Luther King himself. Lawson, a student expelled from the Vanderbilt University Divinity School in Nashville, Tennessee, for civil rights activities, was largely responsible for the moral fervor, philosophical sophistication, and exemplary courage that made the Nashville group the most dynamic student movement between 1960 and 1962. In his address to SNCC's founding convention, Lawson publicly articulated the dissatisfaction many youths were feeling with the old-guard leaders, especially in the NAACP. Lawson is now pastor of a Methodist church in Memphis.

These are exciting moments in which to live.

Reflect how over the last few weeks, the "sit-in" movement has leaped from campus to campus, until today hardly any campus remains unaffected. At the beginning of this decade, the student generation was "silent," "uncommitted," or "beatnik." But after only four months, these analogies largely used by adults appear as hasty cliches which should not have been used in the first place. The rapidity and drive of the movement indicates that all the while American students were simply

Source: "Statement of Purpose" adopted at the first general conference of the Student Nonviolent Coordinating Committee, Raleigh, N.C., April 17, 1960. Printed with permission of SNCC.

Source: James M. Lawson, Jr., "From a Lunch-Counter Stool," address at SNCC conference, Raleigh, N.C., April 1960. Printed with permission of the author.

waiting in suspension; waiting for that cause, that ideal, that event, that "actualizing of their faith" which would catapult their right to speak powerfully to their nation and world.

The witness of enthusiastic, but mature young men and women, audacious enough to dare the intimidations and violence of racial injustice, a witness not to be matched by any social effort either in the history of the Negro or in the history of the nation, has caused this impact upon us. In his own time, God has brought this to pass.

But as so frequently happens, these are also enigmatic moments. Enigmatic, for like man in every age who cannot read the signs of the times, many of us are not able to see what appears before us, or hear what is spoken from lunch-counter stools, or understand what has been cried by jail cell bars.

Already the paralysis of talk, the disobedience of piety, the frustration of false ambition, and the insensitiveness of an affluent society yearn to diffuse the meaning and flatten the thrust of America's first major non-violent campaign.

One great university equates the movement to simply another student fad similar to a panty raid, or long black stockings. Many merchants zealously smothering their Negro customers with courtesy for normal services, anticipated an early end to the unprecedented binge. Certainly no southern white person and few Negroes expected the collegiates to face the hoses, jails, mobs and tear gas with such dignity, fearlessness, and non-violence. In fact, under any normal conditions, the mere threat of the law was sufficient to send the Negro scurrying into his ghetto. Even astute race reporters accentuate the protest element as the major factor.

Amid this welter of irrelevant and superficial reactions, the primary motifs of the movement, the essential message, the crucial issue raised are often completely missed. So the Christian student who has not yet given his support or mind to the movement might well want to know

what the issue is all about. Is it just a lot of nonsense over a hamburger? Or is it far more?

To begin, let us note what the issue is not. Many people of good-will, especially Methodists and Nashvillians, have considered my expulsion from Vanderbilt University and the self-righteousness of the press attack as the focus of attention. But nothing could be further from the truth. The expulsion, three months before the completion of the Bachelor of Divinity degree, drastically alters certain immediate personal plans. The press attack tended to make me a symbol of the movement. But such incidents illustrate an ancient way of escaping an existential moment. Call him "the son of the devil," or one of the "men who turn the world upside down," and there are always the gullible who will "swallow the camel."

Police partiality is not the issue. Nashville has been considered one of those "good" cities where racial violence has not been tolerated. Yet, on a Saturday in February, the mystique of yet another popular myth vanished. For only police permissiveness invited young white men to take over store after store in an effort to further intimidate or crush the "sit-in." Law enforcement agents accustomed to viewing crime, were able to mark well-dressed students waiting to make purchases, as loitering on the lunch-counter stools, but they were unable even to suspect and certainly not to see assault and battery. Thus potential customers, quietly asking for service, are disorderly, breaching the peace, inciting riots, while swaggering, vilifying, violent, defiant white young teenagers are law-abiding. The police of the nation have always reeked [wreaked] brutality upon minority groups. So our Nashville experience is nothing new, or even unexpected. We hold nothing against these hard-pressed officers. Such partiality, however, is symptomatic of the diagnosis only—an inevitable by-product—another means of avoiding the encounter. But the "sit-in" does not intend to make such partiality the issue.

Already many well-meaning and notable voices are seeking to define the problem in purely legal terms. But if the students wanted a legal case, they had only to initiate a suit. But not a single city began in this fashion. No one planned to be arrested or desired such. The legal battles which will be fought as a consequence of many arrests never once touch on the matter of eating where you normally shop, or on segregation *per se*.

The apparent misuse of local laws requires new legal definitions which can only be made in the courts, under the judgment of the Constitution of the United States. Old laws and ordinances originally written to hamper labor have been revived to stop or crush the sit-in; disorderly conduct codes which could be used against almost every conceivable peaceful demonstration; conspiracy to block trade charges. Obviously these have no relation to the Bill of Rights and are but gimmicks designed to impede civil liberty.

Let us admit readily that some of the major victories gained for social justice have come through the courts, especially the Supreme Court, while other branches of government were often neglecting their primary function to sustain the American experiment. The Negro has been a law-abiding citizen as he has struggled for justice against many unlawful elements.

But the major defeats have occurred when we have been unable to convince the nation to support or implement the Constitution, when a court decision is ignored or nullified by local and state action. A democratic structure of law remains democratic, remains lawful only as the people are continuously persuaded to be democratic. Law is always nullified by practice and disdain unless the minds and hearts of a people sustain law.

When elements of good-will called for law and order during the crisis in Little Rock, their pleas fell on deaf ears. In many sections of the country where law no longer sustains and enforces segregation, the segregation persists because it is etched upon the habits of mind and emotions of both Negro and white. Separate but equal in transportation has by the Supreme Court been judged as impossible and unconstitutional. Yet in many cities like Nashville the buses more or less remain segregated. Both Negro and white sustain the custom because their basic inner attitudes and fears remain unchanged. Eventually our society must abide by the Constitution and not permit any local law or custom to hinder freedom or justice. But such a society lives by more than law. In the same respect the sit-in movement is not trying to create a legal battle, but points to that which is more than law.

Finally, the issue is not integration. This is particularly true for the Christian oriented person. Certainly the students are asking in behalf of the entire Negro community and the nation that these eating counters become places of service for all persons. But it would be extremely short-sighted to assume that integration is the problem or the word of the "sit-in." To the extent to which the movement reflects deep Christian impulses, desegregation is a necessary next step. But it cannot be the end. If progress has not been at a genuine pace, it is often because the major groups seeking equal rights tactically made desegregation the end and not the means.

The Christian favors the breaking down of racial barriers because the redeemed community of which he is already a citizen recognizes no barriers dividing humanity. The Kingdom of God, as in heaven so on earth, is the distant goal of the Christian. That Kingdom is far more than the immediate need for integration.

Having tried to dispel the many smoke-screens spewed to camouflage the purpose and intent of the "sit-in," let me now try as carefully as possible to describe the message of our movement. There are two facets to that message.

In the first instance, we who are demonstrators are trying to raise what we call the "moral issue." That is, we are pointing to the viciousness of racial segregation and prejudice and calling it evil or sin. The matter is not legal, sociological or racial, it is moral and spiritual. Until America (South and North) honestly accepts the sinful nature of racism, this cancerous disease will continue to rape all of us.

For many years Negroes and white have pretended that all was well. "We have good race relations." A city like Nashville has acquired national fame about its progress in desegregation. Yet when the "sit-ins" began, the underlying hatred and sin burst to the surface. A police department with a good reputation for impartiality swiftly became the tool of the disease always there. A mayor, elected with overwhelming Negro support, made the decisions which permitted mob rule. If Nashville had "good race relations," why did such violence explode? The fact is that we were playing make-believe that we were good. All the while Negro and white by pretension, deliberate cooperation and conscious attitudes shared in such a deluded world.

The South and the entire nation are implicated in the same manner. True, there has been progress. For example, lynching has virtually disappeared (although there are many signs that even it might break forth again with unprecedented fury); but the real lynching continues unabated—the lynching of souls, persons (white and Negro) violating its victims absolutely, stripping them of human traits. This actual lynching goes on every day even while we make-believe that lynching is a phenomenon of the past. What's more, the masses of people, including most moderates of both "races," are glibly unaware of the lynching.

The non-violent movement would convict us all of sin. We assert, "Segregation (racial pride) is sin. God tolerates no breach of his judgment. We are an unhealthy people who contrive every escape from ourselves." Thus a simple act of neatly dressed, non-violent stu-

dents with purchases in their pockets, precipitated anger and frustration. Many "good" people (white and Negro) said, "This is not the way. We are already making adequate progress." Nonsense! No progress is adequate so long as any man, woman or child of any ethnic group is still a lynch victim.

That the non-violent effort has convicted us of sin, and thus appealed to consciences is attested by the new found unity and direction now established in Negro communities in places like Durham and Nashville. Witness further the many white people who say, "I never thought the problem was so serious. I feel so ashamed." Many of these people now support the movement.

In the second instance, the non-violent movement is asserting, "get moving. The pace of social change is too slow. At this rate it will be at least another generation before the major forms of segregation disappear. All of Africa will be free before the American Negro attains first-class citizenship. Most of us will be grandparents before we can live normal human lives."

The choice of the non-violent method, "the sit-in," symbolizes both judgment and promise. It is a judgment upon middle-class conventional, half-way efforts to deal with radical social evil. It is specifically a judgment upon contemporary civil rights attempts. As one high school student from Chattanooga exclaimed, "We started because we were tired of waiting for you adults to act."

The sum total of all our current efforts to end segregation is not enough to do so. After many court decisions, the deeper south we go, the more token integration (and that only in public schools) we achieve. *Crisis* magazine [published by the NAACP] becomes known as a "black bourgeois" club organ, rather than a forceful instrument for justice. Inter-racial agencies expect to end segregation with discussions and teas. Our best agency (the NAACP) accents fund-raising and court action rather than developing our greatest resource, a people no longer the victims of racial evil who can act in a disciplined manner to implement the constitution. The Negro church and minister function as in an earlier day and not as God's agents to redeem society.

But the sit-in is likewise a sign of promise: God's promise that if radically Christian methods are adopted the rate of change can be vastly increased. This is why non-violence dominates the movement's perspective. Under Christian non-violence, Negro students reject the hardship of disobedient passivity and fear, but embrace the hardship (violence and jail) of obedience. Such non-violence strips the segregationalist power structure of its major weapon: the manipulation of law or law-enforcement to keep the Negro in his place.

Furthermore, such an act attracts, strengthens and sensitizes the support of many white persons in the South and across the nation. (The numbers who openly identify themselves with the "sit-in" daily grow.)

Non-violence in the Negro's struggle gains a fresh maturity. And the Negro gains a new sense of his role in molding a redeemed society. The "word" from the lunch-counter stool demands a sharp re-assessment of our organized evil and a radical Christian obedience to transform that evil. Christian non-violence provides both that re-assessment and the faith of obedience. The extent to which the Negro joined by many others apprehends and incorporates non-violence determines the degree that the world will acknowledge fresh social insight from America.

DOCUMENT 29.10
Paul Robeson on Freedom

Paul Robeson, scholar, athlete, opera and film star, was the best-known American black

---

Source: Paul Robeson, *Here I Stand* (Boston: Beacon Press, 1958), pp. 38–42, 63–66.

citizen. When, after World War II, he vigorously opposed America's cold war policies, he was vilified in the press, denied concert hall appearances, banned from the media, and finally even prohibited from all travel, rendering him unable to earn a living. This excerpt from his autobiography, Here I Stand, *highlights his political philosophy and his successful fight to retain his passport.*

The Bible says "by their deeds shall ye know them," and the colored nations cannot go wrong by taking that ancient truth as their guide.

My views concerning the Soviet Union and my warm feelings of friendship for the peoples of that land, and the friendly sentiments which they have often expressed toward me, have been pictured as something quite sinister by Washington officials and other spokesmen for the dominant white group in our country. It has been alleged that I am part of some kind of "international conspiracy."

The truth is: *I am not and never have been involved in any international conspiracy or any other kind, and do not know anyone who is.* It should be plain to everybody—and especially to Negroes—that if the government officials had a shred of evidence to back up that charge, you can bet your last dollar that they would have tried their best to put me *under* their jail! But they have no such evidence, because that charge is a lie. By an arbitrary and, as I am insisting in the courts, *illegal* ruling they have refused me a passport. . . . [L]et me say that the denial of my passport is proof of nothing except the State Department's high-handed disregard of civil liberties.

In 1946, at a legislative hearing in California, I testified under oath that I was not a member of the Communist Party, but since then I have refused to give testimony or to sign affidavits as to that fact. There is no mystery involved in this refusal. As the witchhunt developed, it became clear that an important issue of Constitutional rights was involved in the making of such inquiries, and the film writers and directors who became known as the Hollywood Ten challenged the right of any inquisitors to violate the First Amendment's provisions of free speech and conscience. They lost their fight in the courts and were imprisoned, but since then the Supreme Court has made more liberal rulings in similar cases. The fundamental issue, however, is still not resolved, and I have made it a matter of principle, as many others have done, to refuse to comply with any demand of legislative committees or departmental officials that infringes upon the Constitutional rights of all Americans.

On many occasions I have publicly expressed my belief in the principles of scientific socialism, my deep conviction that for all mankind a socialist society represents an advance to a higher stage of life—that it is a form of society which is economically, socially, culturally, and ethically superior to a system based upon production for private profit. History shows that the processes of social change have nothing in common with silly notions about "plots" and "conspiracies." The development of human society—from tribalism to feudalism, to capitalism, to socialism—is brought about by the needs and aspirations of mankind for a better life. Today we see that hundreds of millions of people—a majority of the world's population—are living in socialist countries or are moving in a socialist direction, and that newly emancipated nations of Asia and Africa are seriously considering the question as to which economic system is the better for them to adopt. Some of their most outstanding leaders argue that the best road to their peoples' goals is through a socialist development and they point to the advances made by the Soviet Union, the People's Republic of China and other socialist countries as proof of their contention.

I do not intend to argue here for my political viewpoint, and, indeed, the large question as to which society is better for humanity is never settled by argument. The proof of the pudding is in the eating. Let the various social systems compete with each other under conditions of peaceful coexistence, and the people can decide for themselves. I do not insist that anyone else must agree with my judgment, and so I feel that no one is justified in insisting that I must conform to his beliefs. Isn't that fair? . . .

In the wide acquaintanceships that I have had over the years, I have never hesitated to associate with people who hold non-conformist or radical views, and this has been true since my earliest days in the American theatre where I first met people who challenged the traditional order of things. And so today, Benjamin J. Davis is a dear friend of mine and I have always been pleased to say so; and he has been for many years a leader of the Communist Party of this country. I have known Ben Davis for a long time: I admired him when, as a young lawyer in Atlanta, he bravely defended a framed-up Negro youth and eventually won the case; I admired him later when, as a City Councilman in New York, he championed the rights of our people; and I admired him when, during his imprisonment, he began a legal fight to break down the Jim Crow system in the Federal penitentiaries. How could I *not* feel friendly to a man like that?

I firmly believe that Ben Davis and his colleagues were unjustly convicted, as Justice Black and Justice Douglas insisted in their dissenting opinion; and I think that their dissent in that case will be upheld in the course of history, as was the lone dissent in 1896 of Justice Harlan in the *Plessy versus Ferguson* case which was reversed in 1954 by a unanimous Court decision that the infamous "separate but equal" doctrine was unconstitutional and that Jim Crow schools were therefore unlawful. Indeed, already in several other Smith Act cases convicted persons have been vindicated by higher court action. In one case that was appealed to a Federal court, Judge William H. Hastie's forthright stand for civil liberties and against the convictions was a minority opinion; but since then, as a result of other decisions by that court and the U.S. Supreme Court, the Smith Act victims have been completely vindicated.

The main charge against me has centered upon my remarks at the World Peace Conference held in Paris in 1949, and what I said on that occasion has been distorted and misquoted in such a way as to impugn my character as a loyal American citizen. I went to Paris from England where, the night before I left, I met with the Coordinating Committee of Colonial Peoples in London, together with Dr. Y. M. Dadoo, president of the South African Indian Congress. The facts about that meeting and what I said in Paris are contained in the testimony I gave before the House Committee on Un-American Activities (a more accurate term is "Un-American Committee"!) at a hearing to which I was summoned on June 12, 1956. (This was *seven years* after another person, who was not in Paris and who did not know what I said there, was called before that Committee to give his views on what I was supposed to have said!)

Referring to the London meeting and my remarks next day in Paris, I testified as follows:

> It was 2,000 students from various parts of the colonial world, from populations that would range from six to 700 million people, not just fifteen million. They asked me to address this [Paris] Conference and say in their name that they did not want war. That is what I said. There is no part of my speech in Paris which says that fifteen million Negroes would do anything. . . . But what is perfectly clear today is that 900 million other colored people have told you they will not [go to war with the Soviet Union]. Is that not so? Four hundred million in India and millions everywhere have told you precisely that the colored people are not going to die for anybody and they are going to die for their independence. We are dealing not with fifteen million colored people, we are dealing with hundreds of millions. . . . However, I did say, in passing, that it was unthinkable to me that any people would take up arms

in the name of an Eastland to go against anybody, and, gentlemen, I still say that. I thought it was healthy for Americans to consider whether or not Negroes should fight for people who kick them around.

> "What should happen, would be that this U.S. Government should go down to Mississippi and protect my people. That is what should happen.

Chairman Walter, co-author of the racist Walter-McCarran Immigration Act which I shall describe in a later chapter, did not like what I was saying and he started banging his gavel for me to stop. But I wasn't quite finished and I went on to say:

> I stand here struggling for the rights of my people to be full citizens in this country. They are not—in Mississippi. They are not—in Montgomery. That is why I am here today. . . . You want to shut up every colored person who wants to fight for the rights of his people!

Following that hearing, I was deeply moved and gratified by many comments in the Negro press which showed a sympathetic understanding of the position I took in Washington. Since not a line about Negro editorial opinion on this subject appeared in the white newspapers of this country, which never miss a chance to scandalize my name, and to quote any Negro who can be induced to do so. . . .

*   *   *   *   *

OUR RIGHT TO TRAVEL

My passport case is but one of several that have been brought into the Federal courts in recent years, challenging the power of the Passport Office of the State Department to decide that one or another applicant shall not be permitted to travel abroad. Whenever the Washington office-holders have decided in their own minds that such travel is "contrary to the best interests of the United States," passports have been denied. The Constitutional issues that are involved in these court cases, including my own, may soon be ruled upon by the Supreme Court; but it is not my intention here to discuss the legalistic aspects of this question. Nor is it my intention here to discuss the matter from the viewpoint of the personal wrongs I have suffered by being denied a passport. Suffice it to say that, while no one has charged that I have broken any law, I have been forced to suffer the loss of many thousands of dollars in fees offered to me as an artist in contracts that I have been unable to accept; and the legal expense of fighting my case for the past seven years has been considerable.

What concerns me here is the question of the right to travel in relation to the subject of Negro rights. The State Department will tell you that the fact that I am an advocate of Negro rights has nothing to do with the case, and to some people this might seem to be true since white persons as well as Negroes have been denied passports in this "cold-war" period. Nevertheless, there are facts—indisputable facts—which indicate that my concern for Negro rights is indeed at the heart of the case in which I am involved.

When my passport was revoked in 1950 (I had held one since 1922), I took the matter to court; and from the outset it was apparent that the Negro question was the crux of the matter. The State Department's brief, submitted to the Court of Appeals hearing in February, 1952, contained the following revealing statement in opposition to my claim of the right to travel:

> . . . Furthermore, even if the complaint had alleged, which it does not, that the passport was cancelled solely because of the applicant's recognized status as spokesman for large sections of Negro Americans, we submit that this would not amount to an abuse of discretion in view of appellant's frank admission that he has been for years extremely active politically in behalf of independence of the colonial people of Africa.

This attitude of the State Department should outrage every decent American, because the tradition of our country (which was itself born in a great revolution of colonies against alien rule) has always favored the concept that just government can exist only with the consent of the governed. For Negroes, the State Department's viewpoint must have even greater significance. When I, as a Negro American, can be restricted and charged with having acted against the "best interests of the United States" by working in behalf of African liberation, some very important questions arise: What are the best interests of *Negro* Americans in this matter? Can we oppose White Supremacy in South Carolina and not oppose that same vicious system in South Africa?

Yes, I have been active for African freedom for many years and I will never cease that activity no matter what the State Department or anybody else thinks about it. This is my right—as a Negro, as an American, as a man!

Not only do I deny that this activity makes me "un-American" but I say this: *Those who oppose independence for the colonial peoples of Africa are the real un-Americans!* No matter what any Washington officials may "decide," the verdict of history, which we are reading in the stormy events of our day, is unmistakably clear: Those forces which stand against the freedom of nations are not only wrong—they are doomed to utter defeat and dishonor! Our country is strong and mighty among the nations of the world, but America cannot survive if she insists upon bearing the burden of the crumbling system of Imperialism. The colonial peoples—the colored peoples of the world—are going to be free and equal no matter whose "best interests" are in the way.

But it simply is not true that the real interests of our country are opposed to colonial independence, and most Americans, white and Negro, are aware of that truth. Indeed, the fact that the men who direct our government feel it necessary to present their support of Imperialism in terms of defending the "Free World" is proof that the American people generally have a democratic outlook and believe in the independence of nations.

There are a great many Americans who are convinced that our Secretary of State, Mr. John Foster Dulles, has himself made many statements and has done many things which are contrary to the best interests of the United States (not to mention the virtually unanimous opinion held by the rest of the world on that subject). How, then, can such a man—who has been fittingly called "America's misguided missile" and whose "brink-of-war" policies have appalled mankind—arrogate to himself the power to pass judgment on another citizen and decide whether that person's travel is or is not in the "best interests of the United States"? As far as Negroes in particular are concerned, there is no white American, good or bad, high or low, who can arbitrarily rule on what is or is not in the best interests of the Negro people!

In presenting the State Department's position to a later Federal court hearing in my passport case, in 1955, U.S. Attorney Leo A. Rover said that Paul Robeson "during his concert tours abroad had repeatedly criticized the conditions of Negroes in the United States." I say: So what? I have criticized those conditions abroad as I have at home, and I shall continue to do so until those conditions are changed. What is the Negro traveler supposed to do— keep silent or lie about what is happening to his people back home? Not I! Furthermore, as long as other Americans are not required to be silent or false in reference to their interests, I shall insist that to impose such restrictions on Negroes is unjust, discriminatory and intolerable.

Our government may properly instruct its employees as to what they may or may not say when traveling abroad, but people who go abroad as private citizens are not servants of the State Department: on the contrary, the State Department is supposed to be the servant of the people. Hence, no job-holder in Washington has the legal or moral right to demand that any American traveler advocate the viewpoint of that official in order to get a passport. Patriotism—love of one's country and devotion to its people's interests—cannot be equated with the outlook of some Wall Street corporation lawyer who is appointed Secretary of State or with the views of some political office-seeker who is rewarded with the job of issuing passports. He who upholds the democratic principles of the Declaration of Independence and the Bill of Rights is no less a patriot when he does so abroad, and if such conduct is "embarrassing" to anyone at home—well, shame on him!

chapter 30

The United States and the Cold War

Richard J. Barnet
Institute for Policy Studies

The cold war is the story of two great powers, each with a set of expectations as to how the other should behave, which neither was willing to fulfill. For anyone concerned with historical understanding rather than propagandistic rhetoric the question "Who started the cold war?" has little meaning. A better way to put it is: How did the cold war happen? What has kept it going? It is impossible to understand the dynamics of this conflict without keeping in mind the stage on which the opening act was played, the smouldering world of 1945.

The United States emerged from World War II the most powerful nation in the history of the world. By almost any historical definition the United States was supreme. It alone possessed the secret of the atomic bomb, short-lived as that monopoly was to be. U.S. military forces, located on every inhabited continent, took permanent control of much of Japan's Pacific empire in the form of "strategic trusts." The war, which had brought all other participants close to economic ruin, victor and vanquished alike, had restored the American economy and left the United States in a position to manage the reconstruction of the world economy. The dollar was now the global currency. The United States was the No. 1 banker, creditor, and consumer of resources. The leader of what soon came to be known as the "Free

World," with 6 percent of the population of the earth, swiftly proceeded to burn, melt, or eat each year more than 50 percent of the earth's consumable resources to feel its expanding industrial base and affluent consumer economy.

The picture of the Soviet Union in 1945 could not provide more of a contrast. With more than 20 million of its people dead, its relatively primitive industrial facilities largely in ruins, and its territory wasted by four years of "scorched earth" war, the Soviet Union, having purchased survival at a terrible price, was still weak and vulnerable. True, it was unquestionably the No. 2 power on the planet, in part because of impressive military victories over Hitler, but principally because "victory" had spelled the end of the British and French empires that had long dominated European politics, along, of course, with the Italian, German, and Japanese empires. Soviet troops were in the middle of Europe, but the new Soviet empire was shaky indeed.

The United States entered the postwar era with a well-developed imperial creed. The United States, declared President Harry Truman in April 1945, should "take the lead in running the world in the way that the world ought to be run." From now on the twentieth century was, in Henry Luce's words, to be "The American Century." "It now becomes our time," Luce wrote in a widely circulated editorial in 1941, "to be the powerhouse from which the ideals spread throughout the world." Walter Lippmann warned in 1943 that America stood now at the center of Western civilization. It must assume the role of guarantor of the "Atlantic community" or face the prospect that Europe would fall under the pressure of an expanding Soviet Union and the "emerging peoples of Asia." Henry Wallace predicted that "the English-speaking peoples of the world will have to take the lead in underwriting world prosperity for a generation to come." Frank Knox, the secretary of the navy, declared that the United States and Britain, having crushed the Axis, should "police the seven seas." In the 1943 hearings on Lend-Lease, Republican Congressmen Karl Mundt and Charles Eaton found themselves in agreement with the old New Dealer Adolph Berle, that the United States must now seek world power "as a trustee for civilization." The basic tenet of the new imperial creed was anti-imperialism. The United States sought power not to perpetuate the "selfish" policies of the old colonial powers but to "organize the peace" and to "impose international law."

How was the Soviet Union to fit into the American Century? American attitudes toward the Soviet Union had evolved since the days of the 1917 Revolution when Woodrow Wilson sent an American expeditionary force to Russia to help, in Winston Churchill's famous phrase, strangle bolshevism in its cradle. When the military intervention failed the United States tried the same tactic of nonrecognition it would use thirty years later with respect to Communist China. It was not until 1933 that the Roosevelt administration finally entered into diplomatic relations with the Soviet Union. But suspicion and hostility toward the self-proclaimed revolutionary state remained. Even the wartime alliance, during which the Soviet Union held down the major force of the German armies for four years, did not dissipate the deep fear and antag-

onism toward Communist Russia felt in many quarters in the United States. All during the war much of the Catholic press maintained strong attacks on the godless Soviet state. Poles, Czechs, and other ethnic minorities kept alive the ancient fears and hatreds of the Great Russia they had brought with them from Eastern Europe. American intellectuals, some of them former communists, knew and cared about Stalin's conniving and murderous domestic policies; they saw him as the embodiment of evil and hence a world menace. The professional military like Admiral William Leahy, Franklin Roosevelt's and Truman's personal Chief of Staff, and the professional foreign service officers like Robert Murphy and, above all, the conservative bankers, lawyers, and businessmen—Forrestal, Clayton, McCloy, Lovett, Harriman, Acheson—who had been called in to manage to war, were always nervous about the Soviet Union, which they saw not as just another state but as the embodiment of Bolshevism. The very existence of a powerful socialist state, legitimated by its struggles against Hitler, professing an alternative model for achieving consumer affluence and social justice, posed a threat to an American Century of global free enterprise. Then, too, the peculiar Soviet diplomatic style, with its capricious treatment of Western diplomats and its hostile rhetoric, aroused suspicion among those who had worked most closely with the Soviet Union. (In studying the cold war, one should not underestimate the importance of personal encounters. General Lucius Clay, the U.S. commander in Berlin, once sent Washington into a war panic by sending a telegram suggesting that, while he couldn't say anything more definite, he just didn't like the way his Soviet opposite number was acting.) Yet the men who managed American foreign policy at the end of the war prided themselves above all in being "realists." They knew that they would have to deal with a Soviet Union which was the No. 2 power in the world.

At the end of World War II the United States

was uncertain as to how much power would have to be shared with the Soviet Union in the American Century. The Truman administration was prepared to recognize the Kremlin as the legitimate ruler of the prewar Soviet empire, but it was extremely reluctant to acquiesce in any further territorial expansion as a consequence of the Soviet victory. U.S.-Soviet relations, which had always been prickly even at the height of the wartime alliance, quickly became embittered over the issue of the control of Poland. At Yalta, Franklin D. Roosevelt had accepted a vague agreement about a "democratic" Poland which, as the hard-liner Admiral Leahy observed, was "so elastic that the Russians can stretch it all the way from Yalta to Washington without ever technically breaking it." Despite its cosmetic language, it is hard to read the Yalta agreements in their proper context of big power trading as anything other than a consignment of Poland to the Soviet sphere of influence. The Republicans would soon charge Roosevelt with "treason" for the "betrayal" of Poland, and the 1946 congressional elections showed conspicuous gains for Republican candidates in districts with large Polish and Eastern European populations. But in 1945, with the Red Army at the gates of Warsaw, the Americans had little bargaining power. "In this atmosphere of disturbance and collapse, atrocities and disarrangement," Assistant Secretary of War John J. McCloy reported to President Truman in April 1945, "we are going to have to work out a practical relationship with the Russians."

For the State Department in the spring of 1945 a "practical relationship" could be based on Soviet political domination of Poland, providing it did not result in "any interference with American property or trade in these sovereign countries." The old prewar *cordon sanitaire,* a string of Western-oriented, anti-Soviet regimes, was gone, but the United States still hoped to maintain "its own trading interests

and position" in Eastern Europe. The United States, then, did not intend to accord the Soviet Union the same exclusive hegemony in Eastern Europe that it had demanded for itself in Latin America ever since the Monroe Doctrine. The managers of the Truman administration saw nothing anomalous about insisting on the very rights for the No. 1 nation they would deny to the No. 2 nation. "I think that it's not asking too much," Secretary of War Stimson remarked in May 1945 in defense of this double standard, "to have our little region over here which has never bothered anybody."

The United States believed that the Soviet Union ought to behave in accordance with the new balance of power in the world and expected that the military superiority that the atomic bomb had brought it, together with America's economic might, would insure a properly "cooperative" Soviet policy. The United States would make the major decisions regarding the reconstruction of Japan and Germany, the role and character of the new world organization, the United Nations, and the management of the world economy. But Stalin lost no time in signalling his unwillingness to play the role assigned to him in the American Century.

Stalin emerged from World War II resolved to preserve the Soviet state in what he believed to be an even more hostile environment than the prewar world. Suspicious by nature, conscious that Hitler was only the latest of a wave of foreign invaders that had ravaged the Russian earth throughout its history, aware that a fundamentally anti-Soviet capitalist state had become the giant among nations, the Soviet dictator was obsessed with the question of national security. Hitler, the only man he had ever trusted, had betrayed him and almost cost him his empire. The generation of warfare Stalin had carried on against his own people in the form of purges, trials, deportations, and executions had left Soviet society weakened and the loyalty of its citizens in doubt. Much of the industrial plant for which Stalin had sacrificed a generation of peasants now lay in ruins.

At the same time the international prestige of the Soviet Union had never stood higher. A Soviet army was at the Elbe. Communist parties of Western Europe, which had played a heroic role in the resistance to the Nazis, emerged as the leading political forces in France and Italy. Unlike the Greek and Yugoslav parties, they were under the tight control of Moscow. The old vacillating regimes of prewar Europe, with their tired aristocrats, temporizing politicians, scheming clerics, and fascist collaborators, were discredited. Was it not possible that communism, personified by the heroic partisans of the antifascist struggle, was the true wave of the future?

Stalin's innate caution and his negative view of indigenous revolutionary movements kept him from exploiting these considerable political advantages. His eye was fixed on the borders of the Soviet Union. In Eastern Europe he moved with hesitation, despite his overwhelming military power over the area. Finland was allowed to maintain an independent, moderate noncommunist government at the price of declaring a "friendly" foreign policy toward the Soviet Union. In Austria a noncommunist government was set up under Red Army occupation. The Soviets held free elections in their zone in Austria in 1945 and suffered a resounding defeat. In Poland, Stalin moved ruthlessly to purge politicians of an independent bent, including many Communists, but, as former State Department planner Louis Halle has observed, he was genuinely reluctant to make Poland a satellite. A noncommunist Poland with a "friendly" foreign policy could have served as a buffer. A Communist Poland was a provocation to the West. Elsewhere in Eastern Europe Stalin exhibited the same pattern. In Romania, Foreign Minister Andrew Vishinsky suddenly descended in the midst of mounting chaos and demanded the premiership for Petru

Groza, a conservative who was willing to work closely with communists.

As late as November 8, 1946, the Communist daily *Scinteia* was wishing King Michael "a long life, good health, and a reign rich in democratic achievements." It was not until several months later that Romania became a People's Republic. Hungary's Communists did not obtain control until August 1947. In the same year a Communist dictatorship was finally imposed on Poland.

Just as the Truman administration expected a properly respectful Soviet Union not to stray far from its prewar borders and to acquiesce in the extension of American authority throughout the world, so Stalin expected that the Soviet Union, as a consequence of its great victory over Nazism, would be accorded a junior partnership in a global duopoly with the United States. Stalin, as State Department analysts at the time correctly saw it, wanted to carve up the world, but compared with the United States his appetites were modest. It was not that he was altruistic, self-effacing, or anti-imperialist. It was simply that his power was limited and that, perhaps as a result of his disastrous overconfidence in his dealings with Hitler, he consistently underestimated the power he had.

Stalin, according to Winston Churchill's account, "strictly and faithfully" kept to the agreement he made with the British not to aid the Greek Communists in their 1944 bid to take over the government. (Four years later when the United States under the Truman Doctrine had replaced Britain as the mainstay of the beleaguered Greek government, Stalin is said to have exclaimed to the Yugoslavs, "The uprising in Greece must be stopped, and as quickly as possible.") In accepting Churchill's mathematical descriptions of the Soviet and Western spheres of influence in Eastern Europe ("90 percent" Soviet influence in Romania, "80 percent" in Bulgaria, "50–50" in Yugoslavia) Stalin may well have assumed that these agreements, though the Roosevelt administration remained officially aloof from them, constituted a model for future relations, at once correct and cynical, among the strange allies of the victorious coalition.

There is much evidence for Marshall Tito's observation that Stalin moved to tighten his control over Eastern Europe in response to a series of American military and political moves, including the dispatch in early 1946 of a permanent U.S. flotilla to the Mediterranean. The United States could not have adopted a policy more calculated to induce Stalin to lay a heavy hand on Eastern Europe, including the takeover of Czechoslovakia in 1948. But that is not the whole story. Elsewhere at the periphery of his empire, Stalin sought to achieve some strategic improvements, to reclaim some former Russian territory as a tangible recompense for the sacrifices of the war, to get some new territorial concessions cheaply, all in the quest for a margin of security behind which he could reconstruct his shattered country. At the Teheran Conference in 1943 Churchill had looked with favor on the Soviets acquiring controlled access from the Black Sea to the Mediterranean through the Dardanelles, a traditional Russian objective. After the dispute over Poland had erupted, the British prime minister was less ready to make such a concession. Stalin began to put pressure on the Turkish government, demanding the return of the provinces of Khars and Ardahan, which had belonged to Imperial Russia between 1878 and 1918, and insisting upon Soviet naval bases on the Dardanelles and a revision of the Montreux Convention, which regulated the use of the Straits. The Soviets engaged in propaganda with Turkish minorities and ostentatiously deployed their military forces in Transcaucasia, near the Turkish border. The Turks sent repeated alarmist messages to Washington. In August 1946, Truman dispatched a stern note to Stalin and reinforced the U.S. Mediterranean fleet, remarking to his cabinet that "we might just as well find out now as in five or ten

years whether the Russians are bent on world conquest." Stalin quickly gave up his plans for the Dardanelles.

Crude and unjustified as it was, there was nothing in Stalin's move toward Turkey to suggest world conquest. This diplomatic thrust was an attempt by Stalin to take advantage of something he thought entitled to by virtue of his geographic position and his military power, and in this respect it was like his move toward Iran later the same year. Stalin directed the Communist-controlled Tudeh party to agitate for an autonomous provincial government in the Iranian province of Azerbaijan in an attempt to gain valuable oil concessions in the region. The United States dispatched another note which a State Department official at the time called "virtually an ultimatum," and Stalin backed down once more. The strong American reaction meant that there was to be no junior partnership for the USSR. The world had not only been divided, but divided into two very unequal "camps."

Wherever Stalin made his cautious moves to consolidate his hold over Eastern Europe or the abortive moves at the periphery of his empire, the Red Army was either on the scene or had been recently withdrawn. Beyond the reach of the Red Army Stalin followed his prewar policy of discouraging Communist revolutionary movements that could not be tightly controlled from Moscow or that could embarrass the Soviet Union in its diplomatic relations with other states. Stalin, who had advised Mao Tse-tung to accept Chiang's leadership in the 1920s and ordered the Spanish Communists in the 1930s to abandon their revolutionary goals, continued in the postwar period to pursue a frankly counterrevolutionary policy. The Soviet dictator believed, correctly as it turned out, that independent Communist revolutions did nothing to enhance the security of the Soviet state. Indeed, they posed a threat to Soviet interest. (Thus it is no accident, as the Soviets themselves like to say, that two of the three

Communist governments established by local revolutionaries independent of the Red Army—China and Albania—became enemies of the Soviet state, and a third, Yugoslavia, once also an enemy, is now at best a wary neighbor.)

Stalin, who had been right in minimizing the possibilities of revolution in the interwar period, now underestimated the revolutionary implications of the upheavals of World War II. He discouraged the French resistance and told the Communists who played a dominant role in it to line up behind General de Gaulle. Communist ministers in the early French cabinets were instructed to play a correct and cooperative role. He directed the Italian Communists, who were in a very strong position, to come to terms with the government of Marshal Badoglio. Tito, he demanded, must agree to the restoration of the Yugoslav monarchy. "The bourgeoisie is very strong," Stalin warned, "not only in Serbia but in China, Poland, Romania, France, Italy—everywhere." He was well aware that, at the moment of victory, the U.S. Army in Europe had orders to disarm the partisans in Italy and France and to take control of the factories and city governments that the Communists had seized.

The crucial questions for understanding this period have to do with the American response. Did the Truman administration understand what Stalin was up to? If Truman made the correct analysis, why did he adopt the policies he did? Assuming he made the wrong analysis, on the other hand, what was it about the triumphant, frightened America of 1946 that led it to see Stalin as the new Hitler?

Unfortunately, historical truth does not sort itself out quite so neatly. The fact is that the men of the Truman administration made a remarkably accurate estimate of Stalin's psychology and immediate intentions—and at the same time flew in the face of both in constructing American policies. An understanding of why that happened takes us beyond the history of international relations into the internal workings of the American government and American society.

Charles Bohlen, Dean Acheson, and other participants in the formation of the U.S. cold war policy now admit that they may have oversold the Soviet menace in 1946 and 1947. Following Senator Arthur Vandenberg's admonition of the time that they must "scare hell out of the American people," the managers of the Truman administration tried to enlist public support for a policy too subtle to be easily sold. There was, after four years of war, little sentiment in the United States for the jingoism of the American Century. The American people, suspicious of the "power politics" of Europe and eager to "bring the boys home," were not much attracted to the idea of taking over the "burdens" and "responsibilities" of the British and French empires. This was of course precisely the national security policy advanced by State Department and Pentagon planners beginning in 1943. For the planners themselves, the imperial model of national security needed no rationalization. The United States was merely stepping into an old role now left vacant by the upheavals of war. But for the public it did need rationalization. For a country that had had its first "red scare" in 1919, "Soviet Imperialism" was a perfect threat on which to build a new American empire.

That the men of the Truman administration had a less hysterical private view of Soviet intentions than their public statements indicated is suggested by the historical record and from such recent admissions as Dean Acheson's that they "may have exaggerated" the Soviet military threat. The Joint Chiefs of Staff testified repeatedly in Congress that there was no evidence that the Soviets intended to invade Western Europe, although the buildup of NATO was rooted in the opposite assumption. (Indeed, the Soviets, far more concerned about an invasion to the east, tore up the only rail tracks across Poland that fitted the odd Russian gauge.) State Department analysts such as El-dridge Durbrow were writing in 1944 that the Soviet Union would face economic collapse at the end of the war and would be in no shape to pose a military challenge to the United States.

More significant are the key documents that defined the official attitude toward Stalin's Russia and outlined the policy of containment. The most influential of these were the long dispatches which George Kennan, a senior foreign service officer stationed at the Moscow embassy, wrote to Washington in early 1946. These dispatches, which offered learned and elegant support for his own strong feelings of anticommunism, were promoted throughout the national security bureaucracy by James Forrestal, secretary of the navy, like a best-seller. They eventually found their way into a report which Clark Clifford, President Truman's counsel, prepared for him and which was to become the key statement in setting the tone and direction of cold war policy. The Clifford memorandum, drawing on Kennan's analysis, correctly emphasized Stalin's security fears: the Soviets feared "encirclement" by the capitalist states and believed that they would eventually initiate a war against the Soviet Union. Thus the Soviet Union must be prepared "for any eventuality" and must strengthen its military forces. Clifford argued that it was a "direct threat to American security" for the Soviets to prepare for a war with the leading capitalist nations which, according to the Soviets' own ideology, the capitalist nations would initiate. There was only one way to deal with such a threat:

> The language of military power is the only language which disciples of power politics understand. The United States must use that language in order that Soviet leaders will realize that our government is determined to uphold the interest of its citizens and the rights of small nations. Compromise and concessions are considered, by the Soviets, to be evidence of weakness and they are encouraged

by our "retreats" to make new and greater demands.

This was, of course, the policy of containment which with small modifications has been carried on to this day. The Soviet Union has been ringed with military bases, constantly challenged to keep up in an arms race in which the United States has had, until recently, overwhelmingly superior military power. The Clifford memorandum makes curious—and tragic—reading a generation later. Why Stalin, described as a paranoid leader who believes that dangerous enemies are about to encircle him, should "mellow," to use Kennan's term, by having his paranoid fantasies realized is never made clear. Of course the policy of "containment" had precisely the opposite effect. Stalin rearmed, launched a crash program to produce the atomic bomb, tightened his hold on Eastern Europe and half of Germany, blockaded Berlin in 1948, and, in the name of national security, resumed his permanent war against the Russian people.

Were the men of the Truman administration genuinely afraid of the Soviets, or was the "Soviet threat" just a pretext for the military policies necessary to establish the American Century? The answer, it seems to me, is that the Truman administration was dominated by a fear which, though often publicly exaggerated, was, nonetheless, as genuine as it was irrational.

Men like Averell Harriman, who dealt with the Soviets on a day-to-day basis as ambassador to Moscow, voiced the deepest alarm in the highest circles of government. "We might well have to face an ideological warfare just as vigorous and dangerous as fascism or Nazism," Harriman told Forrestal in the spring of 1945 while the war was still on. It was not Soviet military power but Communist ideology that was perceived as the great threat. In April 1945, Harriman warned that "half and maybe all of Europe might be communistic by the end of next winter." "No permanently safe international relations can be established," Secretary of War Stimson warned, "between two such fundamentally different national systems. With the best of efforts we cannot understand each other." As the war ended Harriman told the American commander in Berlin that "Hitler's greatest crime" was "opening the gates of East Europe to Asia." It was the difference in "ideology" that posed the great threat to American interests, and there would be no security until the Soviet Union reformed itself of its dangerous beliefs and stopped exporting them to the wretched, vulnerable masses of the earth.

Washington's view of Soviet ideology was heavily colored by its own ideology. The State Department's view of Stalinism bore little resemblance to what Stalin was preaching or practising. In France, Communist ministers joined the government and pursued a united-front strategy, under which they were the strongest force in the country, favoring a strong France with a formidable army and retention of the empire in Algeria as well as in Indochina. It was hardly the policy of international conspirators ready to serve their country up to the Russians. In Italy, too, the Communists sought to become a respectable, legitimate national party. (Only after the cold war had split Europe did the French and Italian Communist parties briefly attempt mass antigovernment strikes, a strategy which failed spectacularly.)

But the State Department, poring over the turgid literature of the Communist ideologues, professed to see a blueprint for world conquest. Jacques Duclos, leading French Communist, wrote an article in April 1945 in *Cahiers du Communisme* which the State Department took to be Moscow's "instructions" to the world communist movement for protracted conflict with the West. All the article said was that the Communist parties should not dissolve, as the American Communist party had done during the World War II, and that they should pursue a struggle for "national unity" while

fighting the "trusts." Like Stalin's "election speech" a few months later, this document was taken by highly placed Americans to be the "declaration of World War III."

Stalin, in Truman's eyes, had become the Hitler of today: "Unless Russia is faced with an iron fist and strong language, another war is in the making." The fear of the Soviet Union that pervaded the Truman administration was real enough, although it was based on virtually no objective evidence that the Soviet Union was going to commit "aggression" outside of the area of Eastern Europe which it had staked out as its minimum reward of victory. Years later defenders of the Truman administration's cold war policy point to allegedly threatening documents and speeches of the Soviets rather than actions to justify the early American cold war policy. (It was not until five years later, in 1950, with the North Korean invasion of South Korea that Stalin could be plausibly painted as a Hitler-like aggressor. That move, so uncharacteristic of the cautious Stalin, has been explained in Khrushchev's memoirs as a case of Stalin's entrapment by his obstreperous North Korean puppets. Whatever the case, Korea, which was correctly analyzed in the State Department as a local action, was publicly presented as evidence of a worldwide Communist military threat and was made the pretext for German rearmament, the strengthening of NATO, and the enormous rise in the U.S. military budget that has continued to this day.)

The fear of Stalinism grew out of the unwillingness of the United States to share power with a suspicious, treacherous Soviet dictator, and the awareness that the Soviet Union had the military and economic potential to compel her to share that power eventually. The American Century meant American supremacy. The United States had inherited the mantle of Britain as the peacemaker of the planet and, as the Truman Doctrine made clear, its writ ran throughout the globe. It was not America's destiny to share her new power with the old discredited empires like England and France, much less with a bloody dictatorship that espoused an alien, godless ideology. This then was the American dilemma: how to be supreme in the face of another power willing to acknowledge superiority but not supremacy. Some Americans thought the answer lay in preventive war. In 1950 the Secretary of the Navy Francis Matthews publicly suggested dropping some atom bombs on the Soviet Union. Though he was publicly reprimanded, many military men have publicly and privately endorsed the policy which Barry Goldwater once described as "lobbing one into the Kremlin's men's room." Lyndon Johnson and Melvin Laird, the former secretary of defense, were two of a long line of American statesmen who suggested the nuclear annihilation of the Soviet Union in a surprise attack in the event of unspecified "Soviet aggression" not necessarily involving a nuclear attack on the United States.

But that policy was not adopted. Instead, the United States asserted its supremacy by the policy of the double standard. Thus the United States established missiles within a few miles of the Soviet border in Turkey but was prepared to fight a nuclear war to compel the Soviets to remove their missiles from Cuba. American aircraft flew over the air space of the Soviet Union at a time when a Soviet attempt to duplicate that feat in American air space would have meant a major confrontation. The United States still asserts the right to maintain a permanent fleet in the Mediterranean, but a small Soviet fleet is a "threat." The United States began building military alliances in the Middle East in 1950, but Soviet penetration into the area in recent years is a menace to world peace. It has been easy to justify the double standard by using ideology. When the United States took over Britain's oil concessions in Iran, Roosevelt was thrilled at the chance to use Iran as an example of "what we could do by an unselfish American policy."

What is imperialism when done by other countries is development when done by the United States. By the same token the USSR now insists that its ships in the Mediterranean are a "peace" fleet while U.S. ships are a "war" fleet.

In recent years, as the Soviet Union has become more powerful, its leaders have relied less on bluster and invective. To use the State Department term, the *atmospherics* of U.S.-Soviet relations have improved. It is not because the Soviets have "mellowed," but because the Soviet Union is now powerful enough to compel the United States to accept something like the duopoly Stalin hoped for at the end of the war. Since the midfifties the Soviet Union has had the military capability to destroy American society no matter how many missiles or antimissiles the United States chooses to build. Thus, despite the militant rhetoric of John Foster Dulles, secretary of state under President Eisenhower, both sides accepted the existence of a standoff which has led slowly to a bizarre partnership of political convenience, accompanied by an intensified arms race. The Soviet Union had the power to counter America's intervention in Indochina which it lacked in Greece, Lebanon, Iran, Dominican Republic, and many other places where the United States used its military power to shore up subservient governments or to undermine governments deemed hostile to American interests. After a generation of cold war the Soviets are, indeed, "becoming more like us," as many commentators have observed, but this is hardly an encouraging development from the viewpoint of U.S. security. With far greater power at their disposal than Stalin ever had, with America's nuclear monopoly broken and its vaunted "superiority" rendered meaningless, Stalin's successors are far more adventurous in their foreign policy, notably in Cuba and the Middle East, than the old dictator ever dared to be. The Soviet Union is undoubtedly, despite continuing restrictions on human liberty, a pleasanter place in which to live than in Stalin's day, and with the split in the Communist world it is harder to believe in the ideological terrors of a monolithic ''world communism.'' But the Soviet Union is a far more formidable rival of the United States than it ever was in the Stalin era. There is little in the history of the last quarter century to suggest that ''containment'' has kept the peace or brought added security to the American people.

SUGGESTED READINGS

Acheson, Dean. *Present at the Creation: My Years in the State Department.* New York: W. W. Norton, 1969.

Alperovitz, Gar. *Cold War Essays.* New York: Anchor Books, 1970.

Barnet, Richard. *Intervention and Revolution: America's Confrontation with Insurgent Movements around the World.* New York: New American Library, 1968.

Bundy, McGeorge, and Stimson, Henry L. *On Active Service in Peace and War.* New York: Harper & Row, 1948.

Byrnes, James F. *Speaking Frankly.* New York: Harper & Row, 1947.

Forrestal, James J. *The Forrestal Diaries,* ed. Walter Millis. New York: Viking Press, 1951.

Halle, Louis J. *The Cold War as History.* New York: Harper & Row, 1967.

Kennan, George F. *Memoirs, 1925–1950.* Boston: Little, Brown, 1967.

Kolko, Gabriel. *The Politics of War: The World and United States Foreign Policy. 1943–1945.* New York: Random House, 1969.

LaFeber, Walter. *America, Russia, and the Cold War, 1945–66.* New York: John Wiley & Sons, 1967.

Lukacs, John A. *A New History of the Cold War,* 3d ed., expanded. New York: Anchor Books, 1966.

Williams, William Appleman. *The Tragedy of American Diplomacy.* New York: Dell Publishing Co., 1968.

DOCUMENT 30.1
The Soviet Union and American Power

In September of 1946, the Truman administration developed an analysis of the Soviet Union and a comprehensive view of the use of power in the American Century. These views were distilled in a memo by Clark Clifford, then counsel to President Truman.

It is perhaps the greatest paradox of the present day that the leaders of a nation, now stronger than it has ever been before, should embark on so aggressive a course because their nation is ''weak.'' And yet Stalin and his cohorts proclaim that ''monopoly capitalism'' threatens the world with war and that Russia must strengthen her defenses against the danger of foreign attacks. The U.S.S.R., according to Kremlin propaganda, is imperilled so long as it remains within a ''capitalistic encirclement.'' This idea is absurd when adopted by so vast a country with such great natural wealth, a population of almost 200 million and no powerful or aggressive neighbors. But the process of injecting this propaganda into the minds of the Soviet people goes on with increasing intensity.

The concept of danger from the outside is deeply rooted in the Russian people's haunting sense of insecurity inherited from their past. It is maintained by their present leaders as a justification for the oppressive nature of the Soviet police state. The thesis, that the capitalist world is conspiring to attack the Soviet Union, is

Source: Clark Clifford, in Arthur Krock, *Sixty Years on the Firing Line,* (New York: Funk & Wagnalls, 1968), Appendix.

not based on any objective analysis of the situation beyond Russia's borders. It has little to do, indeed, with conditions outside the Soviet Union, and it has arisen mainly from basic inner-Russian necessities which existed before the second World War and which exist today. . . .

The Soviet Government, in developing the theme of "encirclement," maintains continuous propaganda for domestic consumption regarding the dangerously aggressive intentions of American "atom diplomacy" and British imperialism, designed to arouse in the Soviet people fear and suspicion of all capitalistic nations.

Despite the fact that the Soviet Government believes in the incvitability of a conflict with the capitalist world and prepares for that conflict by building up its own strength and undermining that of other nations, its leaders want to postpone the conflict for many years. The western powers are still too strong, the U.S.S.R. is still too weak. Soviet officials must therefore not provoke, by their policies of expansion and aggression, too strong a reaction by other powers.

The Kremlin acknowledges no limit to the eventual power of the Soviet Union, but it is practical enough to be concerned with the actual position of the U.S.S.R. today. In any matter deemed essential to the security of the Soviet Union, Soviet leaders will prove adamant in their claims and demands. In other matters they will prove grasping and opportunistic, but flexible in proportion to the degree and nature of the resistance encountered.

Recognition of the need to postpone the "inevitable" conflict is in no sense a betrayal of the Communist faith. Marx and Lenin encouraged compromise and collaboration with non-communists for the accomplishment of ultimate communistic purposes. The U.S.S.R. has followed such a course in the past. In 1939 the Kremlin signed a non-aggression pact with Ger-

many and in 1941 a neutrality pact with Japan. Soviet leaders will continue to collaborate whenever it seems expedient, for time is needed to build up Soviet strength and weaken the opposition. Time is on the side of the Soviet Union, since population growth and economic development will, in the Soviet view, bring an increase in its relative strength. . . .

A direct threat to American security is implicit in Soviet foreign policy which is designed to prepare the Soviet Union for war with the leading capitalistic nations of the world. Soviet leaders recognize that the United States will be the Soviet Union's most powerful enemy if such a war as that predicted by Communist theory ever comes about and therefore the United States is the chief target of Soviet foreign and military policy.

A recent Soviet shift of emphasis from Great Britain to the United States as the principal "enemy" has been made known to the world by harsh and strident propaganda attacks upon the United States and upon American activities and interests around the globe. The United States, as seen by radio Moscow and the Soviet press, is the principal architect of the "capitalistic encirclement" which now "menaces the liberty and welfare of the great Soviet masses." These verbal assaults on the United States are designed to justify to the Russian people the expense and hardships of maintaining a powerful military establishment and to insure the support of the Russian people for the aggressive actions of the Soviet Government.

The most obvious Soviet threat to American security is the growing ability of the U.S.S.R. to wage an offensive war against the United States. This has not hitherto been possible, in the absence of Soviet long-range strategic air power and an almost total lack of sea power. Now, however, the U.S.S.R. is rapidly developing elements of her military strength which she hitherto lacked and which will give the

Soviet Union great offensive capabilities. Stalin has declared his intention of sparing no effort to build up the military strength of the Soviet Union. Development of atomic weapons, guided missiles, materials for biological warfare, a strategic air force, submarines of great cruising range, naval mines and mine craft, to name the most important, are extending the effective range of Soviet military power well into areas which the United States regards as vital to its security. . . .

Although the Soviet Union at the present moment is precluded from military aggression beyond the land mass of Eurasia, the acquisition of a strategic air force, naval forces and atomic bombs in quantity would give the U.S.S.R. the capability of striking anywhere on the globe. Ability to wage aggressive warfare in any area of the world is the ultimate goal of Soviet military policy.

* * * * *

The primary objective of United States policy toward the Soviet Union is to convince Soviet leaders that it is in their interest to participate in a system of world cooperation, that there are no fundamental causes for war between our two nations, and that the security and prosperity of the Soviet Union, and that of the rest of the world as well, is being jeopardized by the aggressive militaristic imperialism such as that in which the Soviet Union is now engaged.

However, these same leaders with whom we hope to achieve an understanding on the principles of international peace appear to believe that a war with the United States and the other leading capitalistic nations is inevitable. They are increasing their military power and the sphere of Soviet influence in preparation for the "inevitable" conflict, and they are trying to weaken and subvert their potential opponents by every means at their disposal. So long as these men adhere to these beliefs, it is highly

dangerous to conclude that hope of international peace lies only in "accord," "mutual understanding," or "solidarity" with the Soviet Union.

Adoption of such a policy would impel the United States to make sacrifices for the sake of Soviet-U.S. relations, which would only have the effect of raising Soviet hopes and increasing Soviet demands, and to ignore alternative lines of policy, which might be much more compatible with our own national and international interests.

The Soviet Government will never be easy to "get along with." The American people must accustom themselves to this thought, not as a cause for despair, but as a fact to be faced objectively and courageously. If we find it impossible to enlist Soviet cooperation in the solution of world problems, we should be prepared to join with the British and other Western countries in an attempt to build up a world of our own which will pursue its own objectives and will recognize the Soviet orbit as a distinct entity with which conflict is not predestined but with which we cannot pursue common aims.

As long as the Soviet Government maintains its present foreign policy, based upon the theory of an ultimate struggle between communism and capitalism, the United States must assume that the U.S.S.R. might fight at any time for the two-fold purpose of expanding the territory under communist control and weakening its potential capitalist opponents. The Soviet Union was able to flow into the political vacuum of the Balkans, Eastern Europe, the Near East, Manchuria and Korea because no other nation was both willing and able to prevent it. Soviet leaders were encouraged by easy success and they are now preparing to take over new areas in the same way. The Soviet Union, as Stalin euphemistically phrased it, is preparing "for any eventuality."

Unless the United States is willing to sacrifice its future security for the sake of ''accord'' with the U.S.S.R. now, this government must, as a first step toward world stabilization, seek to prevent additional Soviet aggression. The greater the area controlled by the Soviet Union, the greater the military requirements of this country will be. Our present military plans are based on the assumption that, for the next few years at least, Western Europe, the Middle East, China and Japan will remain outside the Soviet sphere. If the Soviet Union acquires control of one or more of these areas, the military forces required to hold in check those of the U.S.S.R. and prevent still further acquisitions will be substantially enlarged. That will also be true if any of the naval and air bases in the Atlantic and Pacific, upon which our present plans rest, are given up. This government should be prepared, while scrupulously avoiding any act which would be an excuse for the Soviets to begin a war, to resist vigorously and successfully any efforts of the U.S.S.R. to expand into areas vital to American security.

The language of military power is the only language which disciples of power politics understand. The United States must use that language in order that Soviet leaders will realize that our government is determined to uphold the interests of its citizens and the rights of small nations. Compromise and concessions are considered, by the Soviets, to be evidences of weakness and they are encouraged by our ''retreats'' to make new and greater demands. . . .

Whether it would actually be in this country's interest to employ atomic and biological weapons against the Soviet Union in the event of hostilities is a question which would require careful consideration in the light of the circumstances prevailing at the time. The decision would probably be influenced by a number of factors, such as the Soviet Union's capacity to employ similar weapons, which can not now be estimated. But the important point is that the United States must be prepared to wage atomic and biological warfare if necessary. The mere fact of preparedness may be the only powerful deterrent to Soviet aggressive action and in this sense the only sure guaranty of peace. . . .

In conclusion, as long as the Soviet Government adheres to its present policy, the United States should maintain military forces powerful enough to restrain the Soviet Union and to confine Soviet influences to its present area. All nations not now within the Soviet sphere should be given generous economic assistance and political support in their opposition to Soviet penetration. Economic aid may also be given to the Soviet Government and private trade with the U.S.S.R. permitted provided the results are beneficial to our interests and do not simply strengthen the Soviet program. We should continue to work for the cultural and intellectual understanding between the United States and the Soviet Union but that does not mean that, under the guise of an exchange program, communist subversion and infiltration in the United States will be tolerated. In order to carry out an effective policy toward the Soviet Union, the United States Government should coordinate its own activities, inform and instruct the American people about the Soviet Union, and enlist their support based upon knowledge and confidence. These actions by the United States are necessary before we shall ever be able to achieve understanding and accord with the Soviet Government on any terms other than its own.

Even though Soviet leaders profess to believe that the conflict between Capitalism and Communism is irreconcilable and must eventually be resolved by the triumph of the latter, it is our hope that they will change their minds and work out with us a fair and equitable settlement when they realize that we are too strong to be beaten and too determined to be frightened.

DOCUMENT 30.2
The Truman Doctrine

Perhaps the most crucial foreign policy statement of the postwar era was the following message of President Truman to Congress. In the speech many of the basic premises which have remained at the heart of U.S. policy for a generation are spelled out.

Mr. President, Mr. Speaker, Members of the Congress of the United States:

The gravity of the situation which confronts the world today necessitates my appearance before a joint session of the Congress.

The foreign policy and the national security of this country are involved.

One aspect of the present situation, which I wish to present to you at this time for your consideration and decision, concerns Greece and Turkey.

The United States has received from the Greek Government an urgent appeal for financial and economic assistance. Preliminary reports from the American Economic Mission now in Greece and reports from the American Ambassador in Greece corroborate the statement of the Greek Government that assistance is imperative if Greece is to survive as a free nation. . . .

Greece is not a rich country. Lack of sufficient natural resources has always forced the Greek people to work hard to make both ends meet. Since 1940 this industrious and peace-loving country has suffered invasion, four years of cruel enemy occupation, and bitter internal strife.

When forces of liberation entered Greece they found that the retreating Germans had destroyed virtually all the railways, roads, port facilities, communications, and merchant ma-

Source: Message of the President to Congress, March 12, 1947, in *Public Papers of the Presidents . . . Harry S. Truman . . . 1947.* (Washington, D.C.: Government Printing Office, 1963), pp. 176–80.

rine. More than a thousand villages had been burned. Eighty-five percent of the children were tubercular. Livestock, poultry, and draft animals had almost disappeared. Inflation had wiped out practically all savings.

As a result of these tragic conditions, a militant minority, exploiting human want and misery, was able to create political chaos which, until now, has made economic recovery impossible.

Greece is today without funds to finance the importation of those goods which are essential to bare subsistence. . . . The Greek Government has also asked for the assistance of experienced American administrators, economists, and technicians to insure that the financial and other aid given to Greece shall be used effectively in creating a stable and self-sustaining economy and in improving its public administration.

The very existence of the Greek state is today threatened by the terrorist activities of several thousand armed men, led by Communists, who defy the Government's authority at a number of points, particularly along the northern boundaries. A commission appointed by the United Nations Security Council is at present investigating disturbed conditions in northern Greece and alleged border violations along the frontier between Greece on the one hand and Albania, Bulgaria, and Yugoslavia on the other.

Meanwhile, the Greek Government is unable to cope with the situation. The Greek Army is small and poorly equipped. It needs supplies and equipment if it is to restore authority to the Government throughout Greek territory.

Greece must have assistance if it is to become a self-supporting and self-respecting democracy.

The United States must supply that assistance. We have already extended to Greece certain types of relief and economic aid, but these are inadequate.

There is no other country to which democratic Greece can turn.

No other nation is willing and able to provide the necessary support for a democratic Greek Government.

The British Government, which has been helping Greece can give no further financial or economic aid after March 31. Great Britain finds itself under the necessity of reducing or liquidating its commitments in several parts of the world, including Greece.

* * * * *

Greece's neighbor, Turkey, also deserves our attention.

The future of Turkey as an independent and economically sound state is clearly no less important to the freedom-loving peoples of the world than the future of Greece. The circumstances in which Turkey finds itself today are considerably different from those of Greece. Turkey has been spared the disasters that have beset Greece. And during the war the United States and Great Britain furnished Turkey with material aid.

Nevertheless, Turkey now needs our support.

Since the war Turkey has sought additional financial assistance from Great Britain and the United States for the purpose of effecting that modernization necessary for the maintenance of its national integrity.

That integrity is essential to the preservation of order in the Middle East.

The British Government has informed us that owing to its own difficulties, it can no longer extend financial or economic aid to Turkey.

As in the case of Greece, if Turkey is to have the assistance it needs, the United States must supply it. We are the only country able to provide that help.

I am fully aware of the broad implications involved if the United States extends assistance to Greece and Turkey, and I shall discuss these implications with you at this time.

One of the primary objectives of the foreign policy of the United States is the creation of conditions in which we and other nations will be able to work out a way of life free from coercion. This was a fundamental issue in the war with Germany and Japan. Our victory was won over countries which sought to impose their will, and their way of life, upon other nations.

To insure the peaceful development of nations, free from coercion, the United States has taken a leading part in establishing the United Nations. The United Nations is designed to make possible lasting freedom and independence for all its members. We shall not realize our objectives, however, unless we are willing to help free peoples to maintain their free institutions and their national integrity against aggressive movements that seek to impose upon them totalitarian regimes. This is no more than a frank recognition that totalitarian regimes imposed upon free peoples, by direct or indirect aggression, undermine the foundations of international peace and hence the security of the United States.

The peoples of a number of countries of the world have recently had totalitarian regimes forced upon them against their will. The Government of the United States has made frequent protests against coercion and intimidation, in violation of the Yalta agreement, in Poland, Rumania, and Bulgaria. I must also state that in a number of other countries there have been similar developments.

* * * * *

The world is not static, and the *status quo* is not sacred. But we cannot allow changes in the *status quo* in violation of the Charter of the United Nations by such methods as coercion, or by such subterfuges as political infiltration. In helping free and independent nations to maintain their freedom, the United States will be giving effect to the principles of the Charter of the United Nations.

It is necessary only to glance at a map to realize that the survival and integrity of the Greek nation are of grave importance in a much wider situation. If Greece should fall under the control of an armed minority, the effect upon its neighbor, Turkey, would be immediate and serious. Confusion and disorder might well spread throughout the entire Middle East.

Moreover, the disappearance of Greece as an independent state would have a profound effect upon those countries in Europe whose peoples are struggling against the great difficulties to maintain their freedoms and their independence while they repair the damages of war.

It would be an unspeakable tragedy if these countries, which have struggled so long against overwhelming odds, should lose that victory for which they sacrificed so much. Collapse of free institutions and loss of independence would be disastrous not only for them but for the world. Discouragement and possibly failure would quickly be the lot of neighboring peoples striving to maintain their freedom and independence.

Should we fail to aid Greece and Turkey in this fateful hour, the effect will be far-reaching to the West as well as to the East.

We must take immediate and resolute action.

I therefore ask the Congress to provide authority for assistance to Greece and Turkey in the amount of $400,000,000 for the period ending June 30, 1948. In requesting these funds, I have taken into consideration the maximum amount of relief assistance which would be furnished to Greece out of the $350,000,000 which I recently requested that the Congress authorize for the prevention of starvation and suffering in countries devastated by the war.

In addition to funds, I ask the Congress to authorize the detail of American civilian and military personnel to Greece and Turkey, at the request of those countries, to assist in the tasks of reconstruction, and for the purpose of supervising the use of such financial and material assistance as may be furnished. I recommend that authority also be provided for the instruction and training of selected Greek and Turkish personnel.

DOCUMENT 30.3
Soviet Policy in Eastern Europe

The Soviet Union reacted to the diplomacy of the Truman administration by tightening its grip on Eastern Europe. In a speech on the 30th anniversary of the Revolution of November 7, 1917, V. M. Molotov, foreign minister of the USSR, explained Soviet policy.

The Soviet Union has invariably carried out, and is carrying out, the policy of peace and international collaboration. Such are the relations of the Soviet Union with all the countries which evince a desire to collaborate.

The policy outlined by Comrade Stalin is opposed at present by another policy, based on quite different principles. Here we can talk first and foremost of the foreign policy of the United States, as well as that of Great Britain. Possibly there exists in the United States a program of economic development of the country for some period ahead. However, the press has not yet announced anything about this, although press conferences take place there quite frequently. On the other hand, much noise is being spread about various American projects, connected now with the Truman Doctrine, now with the Marshall plan.

Reading of all these American plans for aid to Europe, aid to China, and so on, one might think that the domestic problems of the United

Source: *The New York Times*, November 7, 1947, p. 3.

States have long ago been solved, and that now it is only a question of America's putting the affairs of other states in order, dictating its policy to them and even the composition of their governments.

In reality, matters are not like that. If the ruling circles of the U.S.A. had no cause for anxiety concerning domestic affairs especially in connection with an approaching economic crisis, there would not be such a superfluity of economic projects of U.S.A. expansion, which in their turn are based on the aggressive military-political plans of American imperialism.

Now they no longer hide the fact that the United States of America, not infrequently together with Great Britain, is acquiring ever new naval and air bases in all parts of the globe, and even adapts whole states for such like aims, especially if closely situated to the Soviet Union.

Who does not complain about the pressure of American imperialism in that respect? Even if the governments of certain big states of Europe, Asia and America preserve a kind of solid silence in regard to this matter, it is clear that certain small states are faced by an absolutely intolerable position. Denmark, for instance, cannot achieve the restoration of her national sovereignty over Greenland, which the Americans do not want to leave after the end of the war. Egypt legitimately demands the withdrawal of British troops from her territory. Britain refuses to do that, and America supports the British imperialists in these matters also.

It is, however, clear that the creation of military bases in various parts of the world is not designed for defense purposes, but as a preparation for aggression. It is also clear that if, up to now, the combined British-American General Staff, created during the second World War, has been maintained, this is not being done for peace-loving purposes, but for the purpose of intimidating with the possibility of new aggression.

It would be a good thing for all this to be known to the American people, for under the so-called Western freedom of the press, when almost all newspapers and radio stations are in the hands of small cliques, the aggressive cliques of the capitalists and their servitors, it is difficult for the people to know the real truth.

It is interesting that in expansionist circles of the U.S.A. a new, peculiar sort of illusion is widespread—while having no faith in their internal strength—faith is placed in the secret of the atom bomb, although this secret has long ceased to exist.

Evidently the imperialists need this faith in the atom bomb which, as is known, is not a means of defense but a weapon of aggression. . . .

It is well known that the industry of the United States of America in the period between the two world wars has grown, although its development proceeded extremely unevenly and twice fell considerably below the level of 1913. For all that, during the second World War American industry grew rapidly, became inflated and began to yield enormous profits to the capitalists and state revenues, which American state monopoly capitalism is putting into circulation and applying to exert pressure everywhere in Europe and China, in Greece and Turkey, in South America and in the Middle East.

Certainly there are not a few who like to make use of a war situation. . . .

Today the ruling circles of the U.S.A. and Great Britain head one international grouping, which has as its aim the consolidation of capitalism and the achievement of the dominations of these countries over other peoples. These countries are headed by imperialist and anti-democratic forces in international affairs, with the active participation of certain Socialist leaders in several European states. . . .

As a result of post-war Anglo-American policy the British and American zones of occupation of Germany were united into a jointly administered bizonal territory—which has been given the name of "Bizonia" in the press— so that an Anglo-American policy could be unilaterally carried out there independently of the Control Council, in which representatives of all four occupying powers participate.

Our representatives in Germany are today virtually concerned only with the Soviet zone. A situation has arisen which cannot but produce alarm among the German people also, since, as the result of the Anglo-American policy, there exists the joint zone and other zones, but there is no Germany, no single German state.

The Soviet Union considers it necessary that the decisions of the Yalta and Potsdam conferences on the German question, decisions which provided for the restoration of Germany as a single, democratic state, should be put into effect. Moreover, in the Soviet Union it is entirely understood that the joint zone is not Germany and that the German people has a right to the existence of its own state which, it goes without saying, must be a democratic state and must not create the threat of new aggression for other peace-loving states.

At the present time there exists the Anglo-American plan—by giving some aims to calm the population of the Anglo-American zone of Germany—for basing themselves here on the former capitalists who were recently the Hitlerite support, and for utilizing with their aid the joint zone with its Ruhr industrial basin as a threat against those countries which do not display slavish submissiveness with regard to the Anglo-American plans for domination in Europe.

But these adventurists' plans, based on Germany, will lead to nothing good and it goes without saying, will be rejected by democratic Europe.

From the example of the German question, one can see how widely present day Anglo-American principles diverge from the principles of the Soviet state, how Anglo-American principles are steeped in open imperialism, while the Soviet stands firmly on democratic positions.

The Soviet Union, in common with other democratic states, stands for peace and international collaboration on democratic principles. Under present conditions, this demands the uniting of all forces of the anti-imperialist and democratic camp in Europe and beyond the boundaries of Europe, so that an insurmountable barrier shall be created against imperialism, which is becoming more active, and against its new policy of aggression.

The rallying of democratic forces and courageous struggle against imperialism in its new plans for war adventures will unite the peoples into a powerful army, the equal of which cannot be possessed by imperialism, which denies the democratic rights of the people, infringing on the sovereignty of the nations and basing its plans on threats and adventures.

Uneasiness and alarm are growing in the imperialist ranks, since everybody sees that the ground is shaking under the feet of imperialism, while the forces of democracy and socialism are daily growing and consolidating.

What can the policy of imperialism offer people? Nothing but strengthening of oppression, the rebirth of the vestiges of hated fascism and imperialistic adventures.

It is necessary to open the peoples' eyes and to unite all the democratic and anti-imperialistic forces in order to foil any plans for the economic enslavement of nations and any new adventures on the part of the imperialists.

The historic experience of the Soviet Union has confirmed the justice of the great Lenin's words on the invincibility of the people which took power into their hands. Lenin said: "One can never conquer a people where the majority of workers and peasants have realized, sensed and seen that they are upholding their own sovereign power, the power of the working people, the victory of whose cause, if upheld, will secure for them and their children the possibility of enjoying all the benefits of culture, all the achievements of human labor.''

The task of our time is to unite all the anti-imperialistic and democratic forces of the nations into one mighty camp, welded together by the unity of their vital interests against the imperialist and anti-democratic camp and its policy of enslavement of the peoples and new adventures.

A sober attitude to the matter shows simultaneously that in our time new imperialistic adventures constitute a dangerous game with destinies of capitalism.

DOCUMENT 30.4
Henry Wallace Opposes American Policy

Although the cold war policy of the Truman administration won a broad consensus of support, there were a number of dissenters, including columnist Walter Lippmann and leading Republican Senator Robert A. Taft. The most prominent contemporary critic of cold war policy was Henry A. Wallace, who in 1948 ran for the presidency on a third-party ticket largely because of the issues raised in the article which follows.

How do American actions since V-J Day appear to other nations? I mean by actions the concrete things like $13 billion of the War and Navy Departments, the Bikini tests of the atomic bomb and continued production of bombs, the plan to arm Latin America with our weapons, production of B-29's and planned production of B-36's, and the effort to secure air bases spread over half the globe from which the other half of the globe can be bombed. I cannot but feel that these actions must make it look

Source: Henry A. Wallace, ''The Path to Peace with Russia,'' *The New Republic* (September 30, 1946), vol. 115, pp. 401–6. Reprinted by permission of *The New Republic*.

to the rest of the world as if we were only paying lip-service to peace at the conference table. These facts rather make it appear either (1) that we are preparing ourselves to win the war which we regard as inevitable or (2) that we are trying to build up a predominance of force to intimidate the rest of mankind. How would it look to us if Russia had the atomic bomb and we did not, if Russia had 10,000-mile bombers and air bases within a thousand miles of our coast lines and we did not?

Some of the military men and self-styled ''realists'' are saying: ''What's wrong with trying to build up a predominance of force? The only way to preserve peace is for this country to be so well armed that no one will dare attack us. We know that America will never start a war.''

The flaw in this policy is simply that it will not work. In a world of atomic bombs and other revolutionary new weapons, such as radioactive poison gases and biological warfare, a peace maintained by a predominance of force is no longer possible.

Why is this so? The reasons are clear:

First. Atomic warfare is cheap and easy compared with old-fashioned war. Within a very few years several countries can have atomic bombs and other atomic weapons. Compared with the cost of large armies and the manufacture of old-fashioned weapons, atomic bombs cost very little and require only a relatively small part of a nation's production plant and labor force.

Second. So far as winning a war is concerned, having more bombs—even many more bombs—than the other fellow is no longer a decisive advantage. If another nation had enough bombs to eliminate all of our principal cities and our heavy industry, it wouldn't help us very much if we had ten times as many bombs as we needed to do the same to them.

Third. The most important, the very fact that several nations have atomic bombs will inevitably result in a neurotic, fear-ridden, itching-trigger psychology in all the peoples of the world, and because of our wealth and vulnerability we would be among the most seriously affected. Atomic war will not require vast and time-consuming preparations, the mobilization of large armies, the conversion of a large proportion of a country's industrial plants to the manufacture of weapons. In a world armed with atomic weapons, some incident will lead to the use of those weapons.

There is a school of military thinking which recognizes these facts, recognizes that when several nations have atomic bombs, a war which will destroy modern civilization will result and that no nation or combination of nations can win such a war. This school of thought therefore advocates a "preventive war," an attack on Russia now, before Russia has atomic bombs. This scheme is not only immoral but stupid. If we should attempt to destroy all the principal Russian cities and her heavy industry, we might well succeed. But the immediate countermeasure which such an attack would call forth is the prompt occupation of all continental Europe by the Red Army. Would we be prepared to destroy the cities of all Europe in trying to finish what we had started? This idea is so contrary to all the basic instincts and principles of the American people that any such action would be possible only under a dictatorship at home.

Thus the "predominance of force" idea and the notion of a "defensive attack" are both unworkable. The only solution is the one which you have so wisely advanced and which forms the basis of the Moscow statement on atomic energy. That solution consists of mutual trust and confidence among nations, atomic disarmament and an effective system of enforcing that disarmament.

*   *   *   *   *

We should ascertain from a fresh point of view what Russia believes to be essential to her own security as a prerequisite to the writing of the peace and to coöperation in the construction of a world order. We should be prepared to judge her requirements against the background of what we ourselves and the British have insisted upon as essential to our respective security. We should be prepared, even at the expense of risking epithets of appeasement, to agree to reasonable Russian guarantees of security. . . .

American products, especially machines of all kinds, are well established in the Soviet Union. For example, American equipment, practices and methods are standard in coal mining, iron and steel, oil and non-ferrous metals.

Nor would this trade be one-sided. Although the Soviet Union has been an excellent credit risk in the past, eventually the goods and services exported from this country must be paid for by the Russians by exports to us and to other countries. Russian products which are either definitely needed or which are non-competitive in this country are various non-ferrous metal ores, furs, linen products, lumber products, vegetable drugs, paper and pulp and native handicrafts. . . .

Many of the problems relating to the countries bordering on Russia could more readily be solved once an atmosphere of mutual trust and confidence is established and some form of economic arrangements is worked out with Russia. These problems also might be helped by discussions of an economic nature. Russian economic penetration of the Danube area, for example, might be countered by concrete proposals for economic collaboration in the development of the resources of this area, rather than by insisting that the Russians should cease their unilateral penetration and offering no solution to the present economic chaos there.

This proposal admittedly calls for a shift in some of our thinking about international matters. It is imperative that we make this shift. We have little time to lose. Our post-war actions have not yet been adjusted to the lessons to be gained from experience of Allied coöperation during the war and the facts of the atomic age.

It is certainly desirable that, as far as possible, we achieve unity on the home front with respect to our international relations; but unity on the basis of buiding up conflict abroad would prove to be not only unsound but disastrous. I think there is some reason to fear that in our earnest efforts to achieve bipartisan unity in this country we may have given way too much to isolationism masquerading as tough realism in international affairs.

DOCUMENT 30.5
A Warning from the Chamber of Commerce

The government was not alone in devoting energies to public education on foreign policy issues. In a pamphlet, entitled Communist Infiltration in the United States, *the Chamber of Commerce of the United States raised the issue of the connection between domestic subversion and foreign policy.*

COMMUNISM AN ORGANIZED MOVEMENT

Communism is an organized and even fanatical world movement. Its ideology holds that the opposition between it and private capitalism is complete and unalterable. As a result, it holds that capitalism must die in the throes of bloody revolution. Such a movement cannot be appeased by improvements in the standard of living of the people in capitalist nations. It is dangerous to make any contrary assumption. Marx said that capitalism is essentially exploitive, that it must oppress the workers, and hence that it must be overthrown by force. Communists believe this with blind fanaticism and privately preach violent revolution. The successful working of free enterprise may make it difficult for Communism to gain recruits, but it will

Source: Report of the Committee on Socialism and Communism, Copyright, Chamber of Commerce of the United States, *Communist Infiltration in the United States* (Washington, D.C., 1946), pp. 7–11; 16–24.

not dampen the faith of the confirmed Communist. Nor would it prevent the triumph of Communism here through conquest by a foreign power, aided by our domestic Fifth Column, namely, the infiltration of Communists and their sympathizers in government, the armed forces, labor, and other important spheres of American life. . . .

THE COMINTERN

As the instrument of the crusade to crush private capitalism, the Communist International has been organized. The aims of this world movement, called the Comintern, are to organize and stimulate Communist movements in all the nations of the world. Its openly professed objectives are to foster revolution in all capitalist lands. While technically distinct from the Soviet Government, it is in fact an agency of that State. Its headquarters are in Moscow and its leaders are the most powerful men in the Communist hierarchy.

The Comintern was ostensibly dissolved in 1943 as a gesture of cooperation between the Soviet Union and its allies. A detailed study of the *Report of the Royal Commission,* issued in June, 1946, in connection with the Canadian espionage trials casts grave doubt upon the reality of the dissolution. On the contrary, there is documented and irrefutable evidence that the Comintern organized major espionage rings among its allies throughout the war.

SOVIET EXPANSIONISM

In addition to the ideology of Communism, many persons see in the Comintern a tool of a new form of old-fashioned power politics. Indeed, the Trotsky branch of Communism maintains that the Stalinists have deserted Marx and are merely seeking personal power on a world scale. Whatever be the merits of this theory, it is a fact that the Soviet Union has expanded its territories tremendously as a result of the war. It currently controls Eastern and much of Central Europe, the Balkans (except

Greece), Manchuria, Northern Korea and North China. It is pressing towards Turkey and the Near East, in order to control the Mediterranean and the Persian Gulf.

The Soviet Union has openly announced plans for the greatest army, navy, air force, and military scientific arm in the world. It is questionable whether its own industrial potential could maintain such a force, although the new five-year plans are directed towards such a goal. But Soviet technology has been strengthened through the use of German and Czech workers and technology. Currently, the Soviet Union is putting pressure upon Sweden to orient its economy towards the East. Many analysts feel that the Molotov plan for a unified Germany would bring all German technology within the Soviet sphere. If the skill of the West can be wedded to the unlimited human and natural resources of the East, within twenty years the Soviet Union might be more powerful militarily than any combination of nations arrayed against her.

Against this background of Soviet hostility towards the capitalist world, gigantic military preparations, and an unabashed expansionist policy, the role of the Comintern seems ominous. It is revealed as a Fifth Column preparing the way for internal Communist revolution, when feasible, or for conquest from without by imperial Communism. It is at once an agency for espionage and revolutionary agitation. Such were the clear findings of the Canadian Commissioners, who reported that domestic Communists admitted a loyalty to the Soviet Union higher than that to their own country.

* * * * *

WHAT COMMUNISM MEANS TO AMERICA

The system just described in general terms is by no means remote from American life. On the contrary, it affects us in many important ways. Among these the first in order of importance may well be the domain of international affairs. One has but to accept the surface, not the worst, interpretation of recent Soviet moves, and one is left with profound feelings of disquiet.

The Soviet Union has proclaimed its intention to become the greatest military power on earth. It has already stretched beyond its borders to absorb nearly half of Europe and some of the richest parts of Asia. Parties under its control are active in the other half of Europe, with reasonable chances of extending Soviet influence to the Atlantic. Finally, the Comintern is meddling in most of the rest of the world, with special attention to Latin America, the orient, colonial countries, and the Arab world. Its theme is one of unremitting hostility toward the English-speaking world.

When this activity is compared with that of the Axis during the late Thirties, the points of similarity are greater than the points of difference. Those who then perceived the drift before others and cried out, as did Winston Churchill, were called warmongers. The same treatment is given today to those who observe the well-publicized facts summarized above. Yet we would be remiss in duty towards our country if we ignored them. We know that the Soviet people themselves want peace and good will towards other nations. But in the too familiar pattern, their leaders feed them warlike propaganda instead of peace, and military preparations instead of a higher standard of living. Observers of these facts tend to discount Stalin's peace line of September, 1946, as being a mere tactical move. The axiom that actions speak louder than words must be invoked once again against world Communism.

* * * * *

COMMUNISTS AND THE LABOR MOVEMENT

Communists have striven successfully to infiltrate the American labor movement. Organized labor, when captured, is to them a source of funds, a propaganda outlet, a means for stirring discent, and, if necessary, a weapon of sabotage. Controlled unions contribute heavily to the various Party fronts and causes. They in turn serve as fronts for diverse propaganda schemes. They can picket consulates and government offices with practiced skill. When conditions warrant, strikes can be provoked so as to create the atmosphere of unrest in which Communism thrives. And, finally, if Comintern policy so dictates, they can actually sabotage essential production. Thus, the 1945 shipping strike "to bring back the soldiers" (American, not Russian) was an example of political sabotage.

In general, American Communists have been more successful in seizing power in the Congress of Industrial Organizations than in the American Federation of Labor. In the latter organization, they have some strength in New York and Los Angeles, and scattered control elsewhere. They have achieved real footholds in the painters union, in the hotel and restaurant unions, and in the film and stage unions. They are seeking, with some success, to infiltrate some of the independent railroad unions and the International Association of Machinists. But their stronghold is the Congress of Industrial Organizations. . . .

PRESENT TREND IN THE LABOR MOVEMENT

The situation today is fluid, since Communist control is being occasionally challenged with success. On the other hand, Communists in turn make new gains periodically. At the time of this writing, two excellent surveys have been made of radicalism in labor. The correctness of these studies is attested privately by non-Communist labor leaders.

In general, the studies found that Communists had control of about one-third of the voting strength of the C.I.O. Executive Board. Their die-hard opponents controlled about one-fifth. Among the remainder, there were enough fellow-travelers to bring Communist strength to a majority in complex and obscure issues, such as foreign policy. On domestic issues the lines have been sharply drawn, with non-Communists having the balance of power.

HOW COMMUNISTS CONTROL LABOR

While communists initially seized power through organizing unions, they maintain or lose control largely in terms of their strength in the locals of these unions. To understand their control over labor, it is vitally necessary to realize how they gain control over the various locals. If they must start from scratch in a given situation, they usually send a few key organizers to work in a plant to join a union. These men show skill in speaking and fighting for workers' "rights," and soon obtain a minor office. At the same time, they cultivate ambitious opportunists and disgruntled minorities.

When they are ready to seize control, they usually make impossible demands upon the existing union officers and circulate slanderous rumors about them. Then they form an election slate consisting of opportunists with some following, representatives of racial and national minorities, and pleasant but weak characters who will be dependent upon them for advice. In large plants, where personal knowledge of the union officers is slight, the rumor campaigns and the aggressive program put out by the Communists are usually sufficient to install their slate in office in whole or in part.

Once Communists have gained power in a local, they often try to expel or discredit any potential opposition. They prolong meetings so that the membership will not attend. This permits their minority to vote funds, pass resolutions, and adopt action programs. By such tactics they often perpetuate power indefinitely. If in the beginning the Communists control the international union, they can often assume and maintain power from the very beginning of a new local. . . .

COMMUNISM AND GOVERNMENT

Both truth and much nonsense have been written about Communist penetration into government. There were those who visualized all New Dealers as starry-eyed radicals. Some labeled any program which changed the established order of things as Communist. This loose use of terms has caused considerable mischief. The result has been that at times the Communists could take credit for widely popular reform measures. Indiscriminate denunciation threatened to make Communism quite respectable. This was unfortunate, since it covered up a real and dangerous penetration of government.

Communist penetration of government since 1933 stems primarily from one phenomenon: the broadmindedness of the average liberal both in government and on the outside. The period characterized as the New Deal was humanitarian and reformist in its aims. As a result, there flocked to Washington large numbers of self-styled liberals, bent on reforming the Nation's economic system and curing social ills as seen by them. Bold experimentation became the order of the day. Our capitalist system was alleged to be so feeble that only daring and even recklessness could save the day.

In such an atmosphere, practically any philosophy was tolerated, provided only that it promised some modification of capitalist free enterprise. No political system was too extreme for the liberal to treat with sympathy, save only Fascism, which Communist propaganda had cleverly distorted into a ''tool of reactionary big business.'' It was only natural that under these conditions, a considerable portion of Communists attained civil service status. Some reached positions of authority. Once they had power, they behaved in a most illiberal manner. They were careful to appoint only like-minded individuals to officers under their control, and they schemed relentlessly to drive their opponents from government service. They achieved a considerable measure of success.

DOCUMENT 30.6
The Cuban Missile Crisis

The high water mark of the U.S.-Soviet confrontation was the Cuban Missile Crisis of October 1962. In this television speech to the American people, President Kennedy gives his reasons for the quarantine of Cuba and the threat of military action.

Good Evening, My Fellow Citizens.

This Government, as promised, has maintained the closest surveillance of the Soviet military build-up on the Island of Cuba. Within the past week, unmistakable evidence had established the fact that a series of offensive missile sites is now in preparation on that imprisoned island. The purpose of these bases can be none other than to provide a nuclear strike capability against the Western Hemisphere.

Upon receiving the first preliminary hard information of this nature last Tuesday morning at 9 A.M., I directed that our surveillance be stepped up. And having now confirmed and completed our evaluation of the evidence and our decision of a course of action, this Government feels obliged to report this new crisis to you in fullest detail.

The characteristics of these new missile sites indicate two distinct types of installations. Several of them include medium-range ballistic missiles, capable of carrying a nuclear warhead for a distance of more than 1,000 nautical miles. Each of these missiles, in short, is capable of striking Washington, D.C., the Panama Canal, Cape Canaveral, Mexico City, or any other city in the southeastern part of the United States, in Central America or in the Caribbean area.

Additional sites not yet completed appear to be designed for intermediate range ballistic

President Kennedy's radio-television address, October 22, 1962. *Bulletin*, The Department of State (November 12, 1962) vol. 47, pp. 715–20.

missiles—capable of travelling more than twice as far—and thus capable of striking most of the major cities in the Western Hemisphere, ranging as far north as Hudson's Bay, Canada, and as far south as Lima, Peru. In addition, jet bombers, capable of carrying nuclear weapons, are now being uncrated and assembled in Cuba, while the necessary air bases are being prepared.

This urgent transformation of Cuba into an important strategic base—by the presence of these large, long-range and clearly offensive weapons of sudden mass destruction—constitutes an explicit threat to the peace and security of all the Americas, in flagrant and deliberate defiance of the Rio Pact of 1947, the traditions of this Nation and Hemisphere, the Joint Resolution of the 87th Congress, the Charter of the United Nations, and my own public warnings to the Soviets on September 4 and 13. This action also contradicts the repeated assurances of Soviet spokesmen, both publicly and privately delivered, that the arms build-up in Cuba would retain its original defensive character, and that the Soviet Union had no need or desire to station strategic missiles on the territory of any other nation.

The size of this undertaking makes clear that it had been planned for some months. Yet only last month, after I had made clear the distinction between any introduction of ground-to-ground missiles and the existence of defensive anti-aircraft missiles, the Soviet Government publicly stated on September 11 that, and I quote, "the armaments and military equipment sent to Cuba are designed exclusively for defensive purposes," and there is, and I quote the Soviet Government, "no need for the Soviet Union to shift weapons . . . for a retaliatory blow to any other country, for instance Cuba," and that, and I quote the Soviet Government, "the Soviet Union has so powerful rockets to carry these nuclear warheads that there is no need to search for sites for them beyond the boundaries of the Soviet Union." That statement was false.

Only last Thursday, as evidence of this rapid offensive build-up was already in my hand, Soviet Foreign Minister Gromyko told me in my office that he was instructed to make it clear once again, as he said his Government had already done, that Soviet assistance to Cuba, and I quote "pursued solely the purpose of contributing to the defence capabilities of Cuba," that, and I quote him, "training by Soviet specialists of Cuban nationals in handling defensive armaments was by no means offensive," and that "If it were otherwise," Mr. Gromyko went on, "the Soviet Government would never become involved in rendering such assistance." That statement also was false.

Neither the United States of America nor the world community of nations can tolerate deliberate deception and offensive threats on the part of any nation, large or small. We no longer live in a world where only the actual firing of weapons represents a sufficient challenge to a nation's security to constitute maximum peril. Nuclear weapons are so destructive, and ballistic missiles are so swift, that any substantially increased possibility of their use or any sudden change in their deployment may well be regarded as a definite threat to peace.

For many years, both the Soviet Union and the United States—recognizing this fact—have deployed strategic nuclear weapons with great care, never upsetting the precarious status quo which ensured that these weapons would not be used in the absence of some vital challenge. Our own strategic missiles have never been transferred to the territory of any other nation under a cloak of secrecy and deception. And our history—unlike that of the Soviets since we ended World War II—demonstrates that we have no desire to dominate or conquer any other nation or impose our system upon its people. Nevertheless, American citizens have become adjusted to living daily on the bulls eye of Soviet missiles located inside the U.S.S.R. or in submarines. In that sense, missiles in Cuba add to an already clear and present danger—although, it should be noted, the nations of Latin America have never previously been subjected to a potential nuclear threat.

But this secret, swift, extraordinary build-up of Communist missiles—in an area well-known to have a special and historical relationship to the United States and the nations of the Western Hemisphere, in violation of Soviet assurances, and in defiance of American and hemispheric policy—this sudden, clandestine decision to station strategic weapons for the first time outside of Soviet soil—is a deliberately provocative and unjustified change in the status quo which cannot be accepted by this country and if our courage and our commitments are ever to be trusted again by either friend or foe.

The 1930's taught us a clear lesson: aggressive conduct, if allowed to go unchecked and unchallenged, ultimately leads to war. This Nation is opposed to war. We are also true to our word. Our unswerving objective, therefore, must be to prevent the use of these missiles against this or any other country, and to secure their withdrawal or elimination from the Western Hemisphere.

Our policy has been one of patience and restraint, as befits a peaceful and powerful nation, which leads a world-wide alliance. We have been determined not to be diverted from our central concerns by mere irritants and fanatics. But now further action is required—and it is under way—and these actions may only be the beginning. We will not prematurely or unnecessarily risk the course of world-wide nuclear war in which even the fruits of victory would be ashes in our mouth—but neither will we shrink from that risk at any time it must be faced.

Acting, therefore, in the defense of our own security and of the entire Western Hemisphere, and under the authority entrusted to me by the Constitution as endorsed by the Resolution of the Congress, I have directed that the following initial steps be taken immediately:

First: To halt this offensive build-up, a strict quarantine on all offensive military equipment under shipment to Cuba is being initiated. All ships of any kind bound for Cuba, from whatever nation or port, will, if found to contain cargoes of offensive weapons, be turned back. This quarantine will be extended, if needed, to other types of cargo and carriers. We are not at this time, however, denying the necessities of life as the Soviets attempted to do in their Berlin Blockade of 1948.

Second: I have directed the continued and increased close surveillance of Cuba and its military build-up. The Foreign Ministers of the OAS, in their communique of October 6, rejected secrecy on such matters in this hemisphere. Should these offensive military preparations continue, thus increasing the threat to the hemisphere, further action will be justified. I have directed the Armed Forces to prepare for any eventualities—and I trust that, in the interest of both the Cuban people and the Soviet technicians at the sites, the hazards to all concerned of continuing this threat will be recognized.

Third: It shall be the policy of this nation to regard any nuclear missile launched from Cuba against any nation in the Western Hemisphere as an attack by the Soviet Union on the United States, requiring a full retaliatory response upon the Soviet Union.

Fourth: As a necessary military precaution, I have reinforced our Base at Guantanamo, evacuated to-day the dependents of our personnel there and ordered additional military units on a stand-by on an emergency basis.

Fifth: We are calling tonight for an immediate meeting of the Organization of Consultation under the Organization of American States, to consider this threat to hemispheric security and to invoke Articles 6 and 8 of the Rio Treaty in support of all necessary action. The United Nations charter allows for regional security arrangements—and the nations of this hemisphere decided long ago against the military presence of outside powers. Our other allies around the world have also been alerted.

Sixth: Under the Charter of the United Nations, we are asking tonight that an emergency meeting of the Security Council be convoked without delay to take action against this latest Soviet threat to world peace. Our Resolution will call for the prompt dismantling and withdrawal of all offensive weapons in Cuba, under the supervision of U.N. observers, before the quarantine can be lifted.

Seventh and Finally: I call upon Chairman Khrushchev to halt and eliminate this clandestine, reckless and provocative threat to world peace and to stable relations between our two Nations. I call upon him further to abandon this course of world domination, and to join in an historic effort to end the perilous arms race and to transform the history of man. He has an opportunity now to move the world back from the abyss of destruction—by returning to his Government's own words that it had no need to station missiles outside its own territory, and withdrawing these weapons from Cuba—by refraining from any action which will widen or deepen the present crisis—and then by participating in a search for peaceful and permanent solutions.

This Nation is prepared to present its case against this Soviet threat to peace, and our own proposals for a peaceful world, at any time and in any forum—in the OAS, in the United Nations, or in any other meeting that could be useful—without limiting our freedom of action. We have in the past made strenuous efforts to limit the spread of nuclear weapons. We have proposed the elimination of all arms and military bases in a fair and effective disarmament treaty. We are prepared to discuss new proposals for the removal of tensions on both sides—including the possibilities of a genuinely independent Cuba, free to determine its own destiny. We have no wish to war with the Soviet Union—for we are a peaceful people who desire to live in peace with all other peoples.

But it is difficult to settle or even discuss these problems in an atmosphere of intimidation. That is why this latest Soviet threat—or any other threat which is made either independently or in response to our actions this week—must and will be met with determination. Any hostile move anywhere in the world against the safety and freedom of peoples to whom we are committed—including in particular the brave people of West Berlin—will be met by whatever action is needed.

Finally, I want to say a few words to the captive people of Cuba, to whom this speech is being directly carried by special radio facilities. I speak to you as a friend, as one who knows of your deep attachment to your Fatherland, as one who shares your aspirations for liberty and justice for all. And I have watched, and the American people have watched, with deep sorrow how your nationalist revolution was betrayed—and how your Fatherland fell under foreign domination. Now your leaders are no longer Cuban leaders inspired by Cuban ideals. They are puppets and agents of an international conspiracy which has turned Cuba against your friends and neighbors in the Americas—and turned it into the first Latin American Country to become a target for nuclear war—the first Latin American Country to have these weapons on its soil.

These new weapons are not in your interest. They contribute nothing to your peace and well-being. They can only undermine it. But this country has no wish to cause you to suffer or to impose any system upon you. We know that your lives and land are being used as pawns by those who deny you freedom.

Many times in the past, the Cuban people have risen to throw out tyrants who destroyed their liberty. And I have no doubt that most Cubans today look forward to the time when they will be truly free—free from foreign domination, free to choose their own leaders, free to select their own system, free to own their own land, free to speak and write and worship without fear or degradation. And then shall Cuba be welcomed back to the society of free nations and to the associations of this hemisphere.

My fellow citizens: Let no one doubt that this is a difficult and dangerous effort on which we have set out. No one can foresee precisely what course it will take or what costs or casualties will be incurred. Many months of sacrifice and self-discipline lie ahead—months in which both our patience, and our will, will be tested—months in which many threats and denunciations will keep us aware of our dangers. But the greatest danger of all would be to do nothing.

The path we have chosen for the present is full of hazards, as all paths are—but it is the one most consistent with our character and courage as a Nation and our commitments around the world. The cost of freedom is always high—but Americans have always paid it. And one path we shall never choose, and that is the path of surrender or submission.

Our goal is not the victory of might but the vindication of right—not peace at the expense of freedom, but both peace and freedom, here in this hemisphere, and, we hope, around the world. God willing, that goal will be achieved.

Thank you and good night.

chapter

The Military–Industrial Complex, 1946–1987

Peter d'A. Jones
University of Illinois, Chicago

On January 20, 1961, the then oldest president in U.S. history handed over the White House to his successor, the youngest. Just three days before, in an unusual farewell address, President Dwight D. Eisenhower had warned the incoming Kennedy administration and the country in general of two "threats" which faced Americans. The first was in the system: the growth of what Eisenhower called the "military-industrial complex." The second was complementary: the danger of public policy falling "captive" to the dictates of an emerging "scientific-technological elite."

Though unexpected by many Americans, Eisenhower's farewell warning was no recent lesson to the president himself. Even as a general, Eisenhower had expressed suspicion of the power of the military in civilian life. He had battled the military over defense appropriations throughout his two terms. For Ike the warning was "the most challenging message I could leave with the people of this country."

The retiring president had beaten Adlai Stevenson in the election of 1952. Genuinely hesitant at first to enter politics at all, by the time of his electoral victory General Eisenhower had certain very clear and firm intentions in mind. The uppermost was what he called,

repeatedly, "fiscal responsibility." But the federal budget continued to grow over the years and was made to balance (and that very narrowly) in only three out of Ike's eight budgets: 1956, 1957, and 1960. The deficit of 1959 was the largest in thirteen years.

The truth is that if the federal establishment was large in 1952, it was larger still in 1961 (and larger still again in 1986). If the government was "meddling" in the economy in 1952, it was still further involved eight years later, in spite of the president's attempts to increase the scope of the private sector in such areas as public utilities and atomic power. Not even an avowedly conservative two-term Republican administration could check the incursion of the federal government in any serious or lasting way. In fact, the economy of the 1960s needed a new name. "Capitalism," at least without some heavily qualifying adjective, was clearly a misnomer. Certain structural economic and social changes had taken place and were ongoing. The rhetoric of the politicians, whether conservatives or neo-Keynesian reformers, had not caught up with changed realities.

The economy of the 1980s needed a new name even more, with President Ronald Reagan's old-fashioned, "supply-side" economics, which dated back to the nineteenth century.

President Eisenhower's own phrase, "the military-industrial complex," was close to the mark in identifying some of the recent changes in American capitalism, especially since he added the even deeper insight—the associated danger of the "scientific-technological elite." The farewell speech was written by Ike's adviser, the political scientist Dr. Malcolm Moos (president of the University of Minnesota after 1967), who was inspired by the flood of armaments sales publicity that crossed his desk. Ike agreed with Dr. Moos's adverse reaction to such publicity. But at the heart of the president's anxiety was the massive growth of federal power since the New Deal and World War II, increasingly tied after the Korean conflict to the fact that an ever-larger sector of the national economy was engaged in work on federal defense contracts. Such contracts were in turn dependent only upon the military's own estimate of its needs, as filtered very imperfectly through the administration and Congress. In the 1950s and 1960s Congress was reluctant to cut, or even to scrutinize, military appropriations.

An early critic to bring the problem to public attention was the late C. Wright Mills, a brilliant sociologist at Columbia University (of which Eisenhower was president from 1948 to 1953). In *The Power Elite* (1956), Mills popularized the notion that there existed an American "power structure." Mills portrayed the personnel in the higher echelons of several walks of life in the United States—millionaires, military chiefs, politicians, executives, "celebrities"—and the mass society which created them and made their prestige and power possible. He found extensive overlap of personnel among elites. Two of his chapters, "The Warlords" and "The Military Ascendancy," set the tone for future criticism and debate about the military-industrial complex. Two years later, in *The Causes of World War III* (1958), Mills spoke of America's "permanent war

economy," and claimed that many people in the power elite understood clearly that national prosperity was tied to the war economy. Thus, "peace scares" caused panics on Wall Street, and federal spokesmen justified bigger and better bombs as a cure for unemployment. Mills regarded the connection between prosperity and war contracts as the chief reason the elite was willing to accept what he called "the military metaphysic." This would hence be a major cause of World War III. President Eisenhower, of course, was unlikely to take the argument this far. But he did share Mills's deep concern that civilian control of the military was now at stake in American society.

In 1961 this concern was reiterated in a much stronger fashion in an influential special issue of the *Nation* written by the journalist Fred J. Cook, entitled *Juggernaut: The Warfare State.* Cook took a conspiratorial view of events, and talked of a "master design" to merge the military with big business and impose government "from the top." Cook and other writers made Americans aware of the process by which, over the 1950s, the defense budget had risen to about half of all federal expenditures and to about 10 percent of the gross national product, and had left taxpayers with a military bill of about $50 billion a year. Writing seventeen years later in a second article, also in the *Nation,* Cook noted with astonishment that Congress had just voted to the military $116.3 billion (1978). Apparently the Vietnam War, with all its human tragedy, did not make a great deal of difference to federal lawmakers.

The military-industrial complex grew even more rapidly in power and influence during the next decade under Presidents John F. Kennedy and Lyndon B. Johnson, once Ike's relatively restraining hand was gone and war had broken out in Vietnam. At its center lay the massive Department of Defense (DOD). By 1968 the office of secretary of defense had largely overshadowed others under the White House—including the State Department that

John Foster Dulles had built up in the 1950s. After commandeering 8 to 10 percent of the nation's total output for twenty years or so, the DOD came to regard such a slice of the national income as its own by right. Ironically, a fashionable economic theory of the 1960s that claimed that a nation could achieve an industrial revolution by creatively reinvesting 10 percent of its gross national product each year was developed by White House adviser Walt W. Rostow, possibly the most famous "hawk" in Washington. If true, Rostow's theory is a good measure of what the United States lost over the years through defense spending.

As early as 1952, DOD had investments estimated at four times the book value of all manufacturing corporations in the United States—about $200 billion. It came to own about thirty million or more acres of the national soil. It became America's largest buyer, spender, employer of labor and contractor. It wielded enormous monopoly-buying power which could force suppliers to do the bidding of the customer—over large areas of the economy. The DOD could outbid any rival, public or private, that tried to compete with it for skilled labor, scientific and technical manpower, raw materials, and production facilities. After all, it had a certain income each year, guaranteed by Congress and the public.

By the 1960s the DOD was controlling an internal empire of about 20,000 prime contracting corporations and perhaps 100,000 subcontracting firms, with all their managers, accountants, office staff, scientists and technicians, production workers, and stockholders. Small wonder that the official AFL-CIO union leadership consistently supported defense spending and escalations of the Vietnam War at each annual convention; that cities, states, and regions became dependent on federal war contracts and constantly pushed their congressmen to do something for them; that four key committees chaired by conservative southerners, the House and Senate armed services and appropri-

ations committees could affect by their political decisions the entire economy of whole regions of the United States; that some Americans, like C. Wright Mills and President Eisenhower, began to fear what might happen "if peace broke out."

By 1967 the U.S. Labor Department estimated that almost eight million workers owed their livings directly to war contracts—over 10 percent of the entire labor force. Multiplied by a modest family factor of three, this made about 23 million Americans dependent on the military-industrial complex; but these were only those *directly* affected. Hubert H. Humphrey, while still a senator in 1964, began to ask questions about the power not only of the DOD, but also of the large firms taking the contracts. "The continued concentration of economic power and loss of the government's decision-making power over aspects of defense policy are trends that should worry us," he said. Who in fact had the greatest influence on defense and military policy? The importance of the *economic* aspects of defense decisions was openly admitted in official documents, perhaps most openly when Humphrey himself was vice president. The president's *Economic Report* of 1967 for example, made clear that "the expansion of defense spending contributed to a significant change in the climate of public opinion. The Vietnam buildup assured American businessmen that no economic reverse would occur in the near future." And not only the business community was softened in its attitude toward the administration and the war, for ". . . Defense investment and social security liberalisation in combination speeded the growth of disposable income. Consumer spending responded strongly . . ." Clearly, by the late 1960s it was difficult to discover who in the United States was *not* affected by the military-industrial complex: its influence had proliferated throughout the economy, to universities, to labor unions, to American consumers in general, and even abroad to "satellite" military-industrial complexes maintained by friendly foreign powers with American help. Military spending abroad, in fact, created a chronic oversupply of U.S. dollars in Europe, threatened American balance of payments very seriously, and brought ignominious pressure on the dollar, as happened in 1971.

It is easy to be moralistic or "conspiratorial" in describing the rise of the military-industrial complex. Under what historical conditions did the complex arise? Why did the American people allow it to grow and support it? Juan Bosch, former president of the Dominican Republic, regards "Pentagonism," as he called it, as a new substitute for old-fashioned imperialism; it grew up, he claimed, because the United States had no restraining institutions to stop it growing. The United States, said Bosch, was a helpless mass society trying to live by an obsolete individualistic value structure. More specifically, the complex grew out of World War II. There was interpenetration of business corporations, the military, and the government earlier in American history—for instance, during World War I—but no permanent "complex" survived that war. Indeed, the American 1920s and 1930s saw a classic revulsion against war and armaments and sensationalist attacks on war contract profiteers and munitions salesmen as "merchants of death." Politicians like Senator Gerald P. Nye of North Dakota built careers on such issues. World War II was the real turning point. First, President Roosevelt dealt directly with the Joint Chiefs of Staff in running the war, going over the heads of his cabinet secretaries. Major war decisions were made essentially by Roosevelt himself, aided by the Joint Chiefs and Harry Hopkins. The secretaries of war and the navy often did not hear about such decisions until after they were made. Military chiefs attended diplomatic conferences, helped Roosevelt negotiate with the Allies, and cloaked everything with heavy security. Meanwhile Congress, spurred by the attack on Pearl Harbor, gave Roosevelt and the

military a free hand financially. The Manhattan Project, which built the atomic bombs used against Japan, despite its great size and complexity as an operation, went on entirely unknown to Harry S Truman—either as chairman of the committee to investigate war production, or later, as vice president of the United States. He had been president some days before he finally learned the details of the bomb.

This project alone (and there were others) brought the universities, the government, the military, and private industry together in a "complex" which would not conveniently evaporate once the war was over. Demands of the Allies for unconditional surrender of both Germany and Japan, their insistence on total military victory, and their occupation of the enemy territories for some years after the war all gave great presitge, power, and experience to military leaders and kept the complex going. A man like General Douglas MacArthur was supreme in his theater of war and remained supreme in Japan afterwards.

Harry Truman did nothing to reverse Roosevelt's policy of heavy dependence on military chiefs in diplomatic policymaking. They accompanied him to Potsdam, and as his cold war policy of containment of communism developed, Truman reorganized the defense structure of the nation. He was the essential creator of the system under which Americans lived for forty years thereafter. In 1947 his National Security Act and other measures established the National Security Council, the National Security Resources Board, the Central Intelligence Agency, and the unified Department of Defense. It was now *hard to draw the lines among diplomacy, military policy, academic life, business, and government.* The "external" constraints or "threats" were, of course, the apparent menace of Soviet Russia in Europe and the spread of communism in Asia. Here, 1949 was the crucial year, with the revelation of a Soviet atomic bomb and the victory of the Red forces in China. A security mania built up rapidly in the nation, with purges of government officials; oaths of loyalty imposed on schoolteachers, trade unionists, and, others; and official investigations launched by Truman himself. While the president tried to pursue a policy of Fair Deal reforms at home coupled with strong anticommunism abroad, lobbying groups were emerging to support a growing military-industrial complex, groups that only needed the Korean War to push the complex toward self-sustaining growth.

As early as 1944 the business executive Charles E. Wilson advocated a "permanent war economy" (the source of C. Wright Mill's phrase). Wilson asked every major war contractor to appoint a senior executive with experience in the defense establishment and the reserve rank of colonel or above. One of the most sinister and collusive aspects of the complex of the later 1950s and 1960s was indeed the open hiring of military retirees by defense corporations. The step from military procurement officer to adviser of a firm, or even chairman of the board, was easy and logical, in view of the early age set for military retirement.

Senator William Proxmire's hearings of 1969 revealed that the top 100 contractors employed over 2,000 officers of the rank of colonel or above (navy captain)—including former admirals and generals. The biggest defense company, Lockheed, used 210 former officers. (In 1971 Lockheed, in dire financial difficulties, had to be bailed out by the federal government with public funds.) Another company, Litton, which already employed a general and a former assistant defense secretary, more than doubled its defense business just before hiring yet another assistant secretary in 1969. As General MacArthur foresaw in December 1954: ". . . the Armed Forces of a nation and its industrial power have become one and inseparable. The integration of the leadership of one into the leadership of the other is not only logical but inescapable." Writers have tried to pinpoint the emergence of the military-indus-

trial complex with one single incident—such as Eisenhower's own memorandum of 1946 urging continued collaboration among the military, scholars, and business; or *NSC 68*, a defense paper submitted to the White House in 1950, urging a defense buildup *before* the Korean War broke out—but it is clear that the industry-military relationship is one of natural symbiosis arising out of a historical matrix of events and conditions.

Each vested interest soon developed lobbying groups. The National Security Industrial Association, created by Navy Secretary James Forrestal, in 1944 grouped together defense companies that hoped to keep in close touch with the armed services after the war. Other lobbies included the American Ordnance Association, the Aerospace Industries Association, and the three armed services groups—the Navy League, the Air Force Association, and the Association of the U.S. Army. Veterans groups, parts of the mass media, chambers of commerce, house publications of contracting corporations, all helped. The Pentagon itself, with its over 6,000 public relations experts, spent vast sums of public money on hard-sell campaigns for particular viewpoints or weapons systems and to influence public policy. Total publicity spending of the military, according to the Proxmire investigation, came to over $47 million a year in the later sixties—including "public information services" of the branches, films, television shows, pamphlets, tours, speeches, seminars, and "legislative liaison" with congressmen.

Should the military in a democratic society be in a position to use public money to influence policy? When General A. D. Starbird, project manager of the Sentinel-Safeguard ABM system, launched a massive propaganda campaign for the system and his seventeen-page directive was published by a sharp journalist, the American public began to wonder what was going on. But the Senate committee that checked on the "Starbird Memorandum" in 1969 was far more interested in uncovering evidence of waste, cost overruns, inefficiency, and high profits in defense contracting than in the overall question: Who was in charge of national priorities? President Eisenhower's warning of 1961 was still largely unheeded.

"Everybody with any sense knows that we are finally going to a garrison state," he said angrily in March 1959. The president came to fear that too many generals had "all sorts of ideas," and his final press conference condemned the publicity of arms manufacturers. Such propaganda, said Ike, produced "almost an insidious penetration of our own minds that the only thing this country is engaged in is weaponry and missiles."

Eisenhower's restraint was made possible partly by a reduction of general-purpose forces and partly by greater dependence for defense (at least against any supposed attack from Russia) on nuclear "deterrence" and the use of strategic nuclear weapons. The 1950s saw the budding of a strange blossom on the tree of scholarship: defense studies, "thinking about the unthinkable"—usually in rich "think tanks," private research organizations heavily subsidized by the Department of Defense. The best known of the war gamesmen, Herman Kahn, had pretensions to being scientific. He helped to popularize a new vocabulary of "deterrence"—not of "defense," since that was acknowledged to be impossible in the nuclear age. Minimum deterrence, counterforce strategy, preemptive strike, escalation, credible first-strike capability—such pseudo-scientific phrases encouraged Americans to believe they could hold "value-free" debates on the atomic holocaust. Although Kahn's methodology has since been exposed, he and others gave the benediction of "science" to the workings of the military-industrial complex.

John F. Kennedy disliked Eisenhower's nuclear policy and tried to bring more "options," into the defense strategy. During the 1960 presidential campaign he accused Ike of causing a "missile gap" (later disavowed); Kennedy sought a policy of "flexible response." This cost money. He immediately increased defense spending in 1961—both on general-purpose and on strategic forces. As late as 1962 Ike was still complaining about defense costs, but meanwhile the "McNamara revolution" was taking place in the Defense Department.

Kennedy had appointed as defense secretary a management genius, a man of fortitude and toughness, Robert McNamara, who was determined to reestablish civilian control over defense planning and spending. He proposed to do this by applying the latest industrial management techniques to his department—the PPB system (Planning, Programming, and Budgeting) to allow rational forward planning and use of systems analysis and operations research; and cost-benefit tools. McNamara's whole aim was to make the choices as well as the relative costs of the choices clear to those who had to make the decisions on defense policy.

McNamara's later years in the DOD were dogged by the escalating, never-ending Vietnam War. Overall defense spending rose. The military-industrial complex thrived. It seemed as if all that McNamara's genius and dedication had achieved was to make the complex more *efficient*. Did greater efficiency produce greater civilian control over the military? Hardly. For many Americans the complex seemed even bigger and more out of control than ever. McNamara won most of his own battles with the military and the corporate contractors—over the TFX plane, the F—111, and over the M—16 rifle—though whether his winning views were in the end the correct ones has remained in doubt. He lost a struggle to cut National Guard and army reserve strength and to merge the two. He did manage, if not to cut, at least to maintain defense spending at an even level down to 1965—before large Vietnam expenditures changed the picture. The United States received more in both conventional and nuclear capability for its defense outlays of 1965 than for roughly similar size outlays in 1960. Yet, most of McNamara's savings were in general-purpose forces—controverisal base closings, for example. He never managed to control the huge prime contracts and cost overruns on advanced weapons systems.

Finally McNamara became associated in the public mind with the ABM system, which could lead only to the magnification of the military-industrial complex for years ahead. For some time he stubbornly opposed deploying the anti-ballistic missile system: he found it too expensive, unreliable, and inferior in deterrence effect to strong offensive forces. However, electoral politics building up toward the presidential year of 1968 probably brought him around to favor the so-called thin ABM system as protection against the Chinese rather than against the Russian "threat." He was attacked bitterly by military spokesmen who wanted a "thick" ABM system and still feared sudden attack from Soviet Russia as well as China. Other sectors regarded his move over to the ABM as a clear victory for the military-industrial complex. Under the new Republican administration after the election of 1968, many of the civilian controllers and "whiz kids" that McNamara had brought into the Defense Department were released, and the Joint Chiefs appeared in the ascendant once more as advisers on policy matters.

Behind the huge defense buildup of the Kennedy and Johnson years lay a deeply held popular belief that America was so rich it could afford both "guns and butter." The nation could *afford* to spend 10 percent of GNP on defense. As the chairman of the House Armed Services Committee said in 1967 about the "thin" and "thick" ABM systems: "We are an affluent nation. . . . We are now right at $750 billion GNP; and responsible people tell us it is headed for a trillion. So we can afford it. Why not have the two of them, and keep the Soviets off balance . . . ?" Kennedy,

Johnson, and their aides all believed in this idea. But by about 1968 a newer realization was creeping in. First, the Vietnam War was costing far more than anyone ever intended—more than Korea; it was already America's second costliest war and would not seem to end. Second, the decline and depletion of the nonmilitary sector, pointed out years before by writers like John Kenneth Galbraith, was now even more evident, with rotting cities, decayed public transportation, private and public education on the edge of bankruptcy, and racial conflicts and crime mounting, and millions of Americans officially admitted as being poverty stricken.

So around 1968 the press and the American public rediscovered the military-industrial complex, and floods of articles and books appeared to denounce it in great detail. For the first time since the Korean War the military sector was really under fire at home; Congress began investigating cost overruns and paying more attention to its public duties in scanning appropriations. A new presidency and a new secretary of defense also attracted attention to the complex. As Vietnam War news got worse and antiwar opposition at home became more strident, even members of armed services committees began to ask whether it was worth it. For a variety of reasons, American public opinion had previously allowed the military-industrial complex to blossom like a deadly plant. Was the attitude of the public about to change, after a quarter of a century? Not very likely.

The 1972 Nixon budget proposed cutting defense costs to about one third of federal spending, though this was still an enormous sum of $77 billion. The question of when the Vietnam War could end was still open. In Seattle, a great aerospace city, a huge placard asked bitterly in 1971: "Will the Last Person To Leave Seattle Please Turn Out The Lights?"

While the nation still had to prove to itself and to the world that peace pays better than war and that its economic prosperity was not entirely dependent on defense contracts, the military-industrial complex itself was not about to give up on further expansion. To think of this would not be in the nature of large management enterprises.

President Gerald Ford—who took over in 1974 after Nixon's resignation, because of the unprecedented Watergate scandal—made no attempt to cut the military budget or to reduce the military-industrial complex. To the contrary. His Democratic successor, President Jimmy Carter of Georgia, spoke of defense cuts in his campaign; but his first and only administration would be dogged by the specter of unemployment and stagflation. By 1978 Carter already seemed to be waffling on such controversial weapons as the cruise missile and the expensive B-1 manned bomber. But *detente* between the Soviet Union and the United States actually ended with the Russian invasion of Afghanistan in December 1979 and the new "Carter doctrine" of containing Soviet expansionism.

With Republican President Ronald Reagan electoral victory in 1980, cold war rhetoric was revived. Reagan spoke of the Soviet Union as an "evil empire" and more than matched John Foster Dulles in his moral harangues. Regarding Carter as "spineless," he talked about the "window of vulnerability" in nuclear and conventional arms that had appeared between the Soviets and the United States. The "window of vulnerability" scare helped Reagan, much as other scares helped past presidents, providing a rationale for inflating the defense budget, especially for building the MX missile.

Once in office the president proposed a five-year $1.5 *trillion* increase in defense spending. Congress whittled down his military shopping list, but overall defense spending leapt: it was $210 billion in 1983 and $231 billion in 1984. Then he sought to go beyond "strategic sufficiency" to outright American supremacy. His

"freeze" and "no-first-strike" resolutions were devious, seeming to deflect U.S. policy from its true course. A new "generation" of weapons were to be placed in the American arsenal: MX missiles with ten warheads each; Trident submarines; B-1 bombers; advanced F-16 and F-18 fighters; precision-guided battle weapons; intermediate-range nuclear missiles, like the ground-launched Cruise and Pershing 2; and the M-1 tank. In 1986 the cost of all this hardware was $302.5 billion.

Furthermore, Reagan (in concert with NATO), and over some domestic and overseas opposition, deployed intermediate-range nuclear missiles in Western Europe in 1983, and in 1984 he disclosed his Star Wars concept—a space-based antimissile defense, to destroy incoming nuclear weapons before they struck home—the "Strategic Defense Initiative." The cold war had finally reached Space, though most scientists agree that creation of an impermeable shield is virtually impossible. *Star Wars* was a new occasion for the press and public to rediscover the military-industrial complex and this time the coverage was international.

Like Ike with his budget deficits, Reagan was plagued by his own deficits. "Fiscal responsibility" was out-of-the-window in his budgets: his first administration had enlarged the federal debt by $650 billion, an amount almost equivalent to the *total* deficit from Franklin Roosevelt to Jimmy Carter. David Stockman, as head of the Office of Management and Budget for Reagan until 1985, found it almost impossible to cut defense spending. Stockman had final say over the budget requests of all agencies, except the Defense Department. Thus the appetite of the military-industrial complex remained voracious, though the term was inadequately named from the outset. It was a "military-industrial-academic-*governmental* complex" in which the federal executive held the whip hand.

SUGGESTED READINGS

Adams, Gordon. *The Iron Triangle*. Washington, D.C.: Council on Economic Priorities, 1981.

Barnet, Richard J. *The Economy of Death*. New York: Atheneum Publishers, 1969.

Bosch, Juan, *Pentagonism: A Substitute for Imperialism*. New York: Grove Press, 1968.

Cerf, Christopher, and Beard, Henry. *The Pentagon Catalog*. New York: Workman Publishing, 1986.

Cook, Fred J. *Juggernaut: The Warfare State*. New York: Macmillan, 1962.

Eisenhower, Dwight D. *The White House Years*, vols. 1 and 2. Garden City, N.Y.: Doubleday Publishing, 1963, 1965.

Enke, Stephen, ed. *Defense Management*. Englewood Cliffs, N.J.: Prentice-Hall, 1967.

Galbraith, John Kenneth. *The New Industrial State*. Boston: Houghton Mifflin, 1967.

Green, Philip. *Deadly Logic: The Theory of Nuclear Deterrence*. New York: Schocken Books, 1968.

Hughes, Emmet J. *The Ordeal of Power*. New York: Atheneum Publishers, 1963.

Jones, Peter d'A. *The USA: A History of Its People and Society*. vol 2. Chicago: Dorsey Press, 1976.

Lapp, Ralph. *The Weapons Culture*. Baltimore: Penguin Books, 1969.

Melman, Seymour. *Pentagon Capitalism* New York: McGraw-Hill, 1970.

————. *The Permanent War Economy*. New York: Simon & Schuster, 1974.

Mills, C. Wright. *The Power Elite*. New York: Oxford University Press, 1956.

Proxmire, William. *Report from the Wasteland*. New York: Praeger Publishers, 1970.

Report from Iron Mountain: On the Possibility and Desirability of Peace. New York: Delta Books, 1967.

Stockman, David A. *The Triumph of Politics: How the Reagan Revolution Failed*. New York: Harper & Row, 1986.

Stone, I. F. *The Haunted Fifties*. New York: Vintage Books, 1963.

Thompson, E. P. *Star Wars*. New York: Pantheon Books, 1985.

DOCUMENT 31.1
Origins of the Military-Industrial Complex

The military-industrial complex arose out of a tangled matrix of historical forces and circumstances during World War II; it was kept alive by the cold war and thrived mightily after the Korean conflict. Among early suggestions that the postwar world would have to see a continued close cooperation among research scientists, the military, and industry was a memorandum sent out by General Dwight D. Eisenhower in 1946 as Chief of Staff.

Memorandum for Directors and Chiefs of War Department General and Special Staff Divisions and Bureaus and the Commanding Generals of the Major Commands:
Subject: *Scientific and Technological Resources as Military Assets.*

The recent conflict has demonstrated more convincingly than ever before the strength our nation can best derive from the integration of all of our national resources in time of war. It is of the utmost importance that the lessons of this experience be not forgotten in the peacetime planning and training of the Army. The future security of the nation demands that all those civilian resources which by conversion or redirection constitute our main support in time of emergency be associated closely with the activities of the Army in time of peace.

The lessons of the last war are clear. The military effort required for victory threw upon the Army an unprecedented range of responsibilities, many of which were effectively discharged only through the invaluable assistance

Source: The original memorandum signed by Eisenhower may be seen in the Henry L. Stimson Papers. By permission of Yale University Library.

supplied by our cumulative resources in the natural and social sciences and the talents and experience furnished by management and labor. The armed forces could not have won the war alone. Scientists and business men contributed techniques and weapons which enabled us to outwit and overwhelm the enemy. Their understanding of the Army's needs made possible the highest degree of cooperation. This pattern of integration must be translated into a peacetime counterpart which will not merely familiarize the Army with the progress made in science and industry, but draw into our planning for national security all the civilian resources which can contribute to the defense of the country.

Success in this enterprise depends to a large degree on the cooperation which the nation as a whole is willing to contribute. However, the Army as one of the main agencies responsible for the defense of the nation has the duty to take the initiative in promoting closer relation between civilian and military interests. It must establish definite policies and administrative leadership which will make possible even greater contributions from science, technology, and management than during the last war.

In order to ensure the full use of our national resources in case of emergency, the following general policies will be put into effect:

1. *The Army must have civilian assistance in military planning as well as for the production of weapons.* Effective long-range military planning can be done only in the light of predicted developments in science and technology. . . .

More often than not we can find much of the talent we need for comprehensive planning in industry or universities. . . . A most effective procedure is the letting of contracts for aid in planning. The use of such a procedure will greatly enhance the validity of our planning as well as ensure sounder strategic equipment programs.

2. *Scientists and industrialists must be given the greatest possible freedom to carry out their research.* The fullest utilization by the Army of the civilian resources of the nation cannot be procured merely by prescribing the military characteristics and requirements of certain types of equipment. Scientists and industrialists are more likely to make new and unsuspected contributions to the development of the Army if detailed directions are held to a minimum. The solicitation of assistance under these conditions would not only make available to the army talents and experience otherwise beyond our reach, but also establish mutual confidence between ourselves and civilians. It would familiarize them with our fundamental problems and strengthen greatly the foundation upon which our national security depends.

3. *The possibility of utilizing some of our industrial and technological resources as organic parts of our military structure in time of emergency should be carefully examined.* The degree of cooperation with science and industry achieved during the recent war should by no means be considered the ultimate. There appears little reason for duplicating within the Army an outside organization which by its experience is better qualified than we are to carry out some of our tasks. The advantages to our nation in economy and to the Army in efficiency are compelling reasons for this procedure.

4. *Within the Army we must separate responsibility for research and development from the functions of procurement, purchase, storage and distribution.* Our experience during the war and the experience of industry in time of peace indicate the need for such a policy. The inevitable gap between the scientist or technologist and the user can be bridged, as during the last war, by field experimentation with equipment still in the developmental stage. For example, restricted-visibility operations with the aid of radar, such as blind bombing and control of tactical air, were made possible largely by bringing together technologists who

knew the potentialities of the equipment and field commanders familiar with combat conditions and needs. Future cooperation of this type requires that research and development groups have authority to procure experimental items for similar tests.

5. *Officers of all arms and services must become fully aware of the advantages which the Army can derive from the close integration of civilian talent with military plans and developments.* This end cannot be achieved merely by sending officers to universities for professional training. It is true that the Army's need for officers well trained in the natural and social sciences requires a thorough program of advanced study for selected military personnel, but in addition we must supply inducements which will encourage these men in the continued practical application of scientific and technological thought to military problems. A premium must be placed on professional attainments in the natural and social sciences as well as other branches of military science. . . .

In the interest of cultivating to the utmost the integration of civilian and military resources and of securing the most effective unified direction of our research and development activities, this responsibility is being consolidated in a separate section on the highest War Department level. The Director of this section will be directly supported by one or more civilians, thus ensuring full confidence of both the military and the civilian in this undertaking. By the rotation of civilian specialists in this capacity we should have the benefit of broad guidance and should be able to furnish science and industry with a firsthand understanding of our problems and objectives. By developing the general policies outlined above under the leadership of the Director of Research and Development the Army will demonstrate the value it places upon science and technology and further the integration of civilian and military resources.

General Eisenhower
April 27, 1946

DOCUMENT 31.2
War Games: The Rowen Report

Part of the military-industrial complex was the war games industry: groups of defense theorists, sometimes with backgrounds in physics and mathematics—rarely humanists— who advised the policymakers. A report to the Joint Economic Committee of Congress by Henry Rowen (later president of RAND) on the national security needs of the 1960s helped set the tone for that whole decade. Here he summarized many of the arguments fashionable at that time, suggested that the United States could afford high defense spending, and considered the possibility of our initiating a tactical nuclear first-strike.

A significant proportion of U.S. economic resources are devoted to national security. At the present time, we allocate to this crucial national objective over one-half of all Federal expenditures and just under 10 percent of our gross national product. In return for these expenditures we do not receive security in any absolute sense, for that goal is clearly unattainable in the nuclear age. On the contrary, our defense objectives are multiple, they interact and partially conflict, they exist in an environment of great strategic, technological, and political uncertainty. . . .

Our large economy makes it possible for us to support our Military Establishment with a much smaller proportion of our total output than in the Soviet Union whose considerably smaller economy supports a military establishment comparable to ours. This enables us to greatly expand our defense effort if we choose. . . .

However, even large increases in defense

Source: Joint Economic Committee, *Study of Employment, Growth and Price Levels,* Study Paper No. 18: "National Security and the American Economy in the 1960's" (Washington, D.C.: U.S. Government Printing Office, 1960).

spending would not have drastic consequences for our way of life. We could manage moderate increases in defense without any reduction of our present levels of consumption and investment. Even large increases might be possible without any reduction in the private sector of the economy. This, in fact, was done during the Korean war. The direct effects on the economy were reduced unemployment, and leisure, and some price and wage inflation. Inflation could be avoided by offsetting moderate tax increases to limit demand in the private sector of the economy. . . .

The principal objective of U.S. military policy has come to be the deterrence of nuclear attack on the United States. We *must* attain it. But attaining it means having the ability to receive a well-designed and well-executed surprise nuclear attack and to strike back effectively. The advantage a nuclear-armed aggressor possesses in a surprise attack is formidable. . . . Each delivered enemy bomb could do great damage, especially given our low level of civil defense preparation, and a large attack might destroy most of our population and economy. However, there are important possibilities for limiting damage. . . . With an expanded program aimed at limiting nuclear damage, and with luck, much of our population and economy might survive a general war. . . .

THE WORLD ANNIHILATION VIEW

. . . Many distinguished people regard a general thermonuclear war as risking all mankind. They hold that nuclear war cannot be a rational instrument of policy. . . . It appears that such a war would lead to a shortening of life, an increased incidence of genetic defects and of leukemia and bone cancer throughout the world. Serious as these effects are, these worldwide radiation effects would probably come to less than that from natural background radiation. Moreover, there is little evidence that the nuclear powers are planning to procure weapon systems that will lead to greater world-

wide fallout damage in the future. The opposite may be true. Without depreciating the awful consequences of a large nuclear war, especially for the participants, it would be dangerous to assume that an aggressor would be deterred from launching a war by worldwide radiation effects. . . .

The Mutual Suicide View. Much more serious would be the effect of a general nuclear war on the participants. Possible attacks, equivalent to several thousand megatons of TNT delivered on the United States, could kill over half of our population. Moreover, our entire population is at risk. This fact, along with the expectations that Soviet civil society is similarly exposed, leads to the view that a general war would inevitably mean the destruction of both sides.

Belief that nuclear war inevitably would result in mutual suicide results in an almost exclusive focus on deterrence-only policies; that is, policies intended to prevent war, not to mitigate its consequences if it were to come nonetheless. . . . A nuclear war might be blind destruction, but on the other hand it might not. At best, it would offer a risky prospect. Nevertheless, although well-chosen defense policies can reduce the likelihood of war, it seems doubtful they can reduce its likelihood to zero. These considerations argue for something more than complete dependence on nuclear deterrence. . . .

Extended Deterrence. Much of the burden of the defense of Europe in the 1950's has rested on the threat of a U.S. attack against the Soviet Union even in the face of nonnuclear aggression. The extended deterrence doctrine recognizes that the threat of U.S. initiation of general nuclear war has been and is an important bulwark of our defense abroad and seeks to make it more credible. . . .

Massive Retaliation. This doctrine applies the threat of general nuclear war, or the threat of actions which make a big war substantially more likely, to the defense of much of the free world. However, if our threat of general war retains some validity in the defense of so vital an area as Europe, it loses much for other parts of the world. And the expected shifts in the military power balance in the 1960's will diminish the validity of this doctrine throughout. In sum, it appears that a greater concentration on direct defense of all overseas areas will be needed. . . .

Dependence on Tactical Nuclear Forces. A policy of defending overseas areas by using small nuclear weapons on the battlefield would interpose a level of defense between the use of nonnuclear weapons and all-out nuclear war. They would give us graduated deterrence. However, the Russians have these weapons, too; a tactical nuclear war would be two-sided. One consequence is that such an exchange might result in great civilian damage in the area fought over. Another is that although any war between the United States and the Communist bloc carries the grave risk of exploding into all-out war, a nuclear war would seem substantially more likely to do so than a nonnuclear one. Even so, we cannot dispense with a tactical nuclear capability; in some circumstances we might elect to initiate this type of war. . . .

DOCUMENT 31.3
President Eisenhower's Warning

President Eisenhower's farewell address to the nation on January 18, 1961, surprised and shocked many Americans, and gave greater credibility to the fears of earlier critics of defense policies.

My fellow Americans, three days from now, after half a century in the service of our country, I shall lay down the responsibilities of office

---

Source: *Congressional Record,* February 16, 1961, pp. 2210–11.

as, in traditional and solemn ceremony, the authority of the Presidency is vested in my successor.

This evening I come to you with a message of leavetaking and farewell, and to share a few final thoughts with you, my countrymen. . . .

We now stand ten years past the midpoint of a century that has witnessed four major wars among great nations. Three of these involved our own country. Despite these holocausts America is today the strongest, the most influential and most productive nation in the world. Understandably proud of this preeminence, we yet realize that America's leadership and prestige depend, not merely upon our unmatched material progress, riches, and military strength, but on how we use our power in the interests of world peace and human betterment.

Throughout America's adventure in free government our basic purposes have been to keep the peace; to foster progress in human achievement, and to enhance liberty, dignity, and integrity among people and among nations. To strive for less would be unworthy of a free and religious people. Any future traceable to arrogance, or our lack of comprehension or readiness to sacrifice would inflict upon us grievous hurt both at home and abroad.

Progress toward these noble goals is persistently threatened by the conflict now engulfing the world. It commands our whole attention, absorbs our very beings. We face a hostile ideology—global in scope, atheistic in character, ruthless in purpose, and insidious in method. Unhappily, the danger it poses promises to be of indefinite duration. To meet it successfully, there is called for, not so much the emotional and transitory sacrifices of crisis, but rather those which enable us to carry forward steadily, surely, and without complaint the burdens of a prolonged and complex struggle—with liberty the stake. . . .

Crises there will continue to be. In meeting them, whether foreign or domestic, great or small, there is a recurring temptation to feel costly action could become the miraculous solution to all current difficulties. A huge increase in newer elements of our defense; development of unrealistic programs to cure every ill in agriculture; a dramatic expansion in basic and applied research—these many other possibilities, each possibly promising in itself, may be suggested as the only way to the road we wish to travel.

But each proposal must be weighed in the light of a broader consideration: The need to maintain balance in and among national programs—balance between the private and the public economy, balance between cost and hoped-for advantage—balance between the clearly necessary and the comfortably desirable; balance between our essential requirements as a nation and the duties imposed by the Nation upon the individual; balance between actions of the moment and the national welfare of the future. Good judgement seeks balance and progress; lack of it eventually finds imbalance and frustration.

The record of many decades stands as proof that our people and their Government have, in the main, understood these truths and have responded to them well, in the face of stress and threat. But threats, new in kind or degree, constantly arise. I mention two only.

A vital element in keeping the peace is our military establishment. Our arms must be mighty, ready for instant action, so that no potential aggressor may be tempted to risk his own destruction.

Our military organization today bears little relation to that known by any of my predecessors in peacetime, or indeed by the fighting men of World War II or Korea.

Until the latest of our world conflicts, the United States had no armaments industry. American makers of plowshares could, with time and as required, make swords as well. But now we can no longer risk emergency improvision of national defense; we have been compelled to create a permanent armaments industry of vast proportions.

Added to this, 3½ million men and women are directly engaged in the defense establishment. We annually spend on military security more than the net income of all U.S. corporations.

This conjunction of an immense military establishment and a large arms industry is new in the American experience. The total influence—economic, political, even spiritual—is felt in every city, every statehouse, every office of the Federal Government.

We recognize the imperative need for this development. Yet we must not fail to comprehend its grave implications. Our toil, resources, and livelihood are all involved; so is the very structure of our society.

In the councils of government, we must guard against the acquisition of unwarranted influence, whether sought or unsought, by the military-industrial complex. [Italics added.] The potential for the disastrous rise of misplaced power exists and will persist.

We must never let the weight of this combination endanger our liberties or democratic processes. We should take nothing for granted. Only an alert and knowledgeable citizenry can compel the proper meshing of the huge industrial and military machinery of defense without peaceful methods and goals, so that security and liberty may prosper together.

Akin to, and largely responsible for the sweeping changes in our industrial-military posture, has been the technological revolution during recent decades.

In this revolution, research has become central; it also becomes more formalized, complex, and costly. A steadily increasing share is conducted for, by, or at the direction of, the Federal Government.

Today, the solitary inventor, tinkering in his shop, has been overshadowed by task forces of scientists in laboratories and testing fields. In the same fashion, the free university, historically the fountainhead of free ideas and scientific discovery, has experienced a revolution in the conduct of research.

Partly because of the huge costs involved, a Government contract becomes virtually a substitute for intellectual curiosity. For every old blackboard there are now hundreds of new electronic computers.

The prospect of domination of the Nation's scholars by Federal employment, project allocations, and the power of money is ever present—and is gravely to be regarded.

Yet, in holding scientific research and discovery in respect, as we should, we must also be alert to the equal and opposite danger that *public policy could itself become the captive of a scientific-technological elite.* [Italics added.]

It is the task of statesmanship to mold, to balance, and to integrate these and other forces, new, and old, within the principles of our democratic system—ever aiming toward the supreme goals of our free society.

Another factor in maintaining balance involves the element of time. As we peer into society's future, we—you and I, and our Government—must avoid the impulse to live only for today, plundering, for our own ease and convenience, the previous resources of tomorrow.

We cannot mortgage the material assets of our grandchildren without risking the loss also of their political and spiritual heritage. We want democracy to survive for all generations to come, not to become the insolvent phantom of tomorrow. . . .

Disarmament with mutual honor and confidence, is a continuing imperative. Together we must learn how to compose differences, not with arms, but with intellect and decent purpose. Because this need is so sharp and apparent I confess that I lay down my official responsibilities in this field with a definite sense of disappointment.

As one who has witnessed the horror and lingering sadness of war—as one who knows that another war could utterly destroy this civilization which has been so slowly and painfully built over thousands of years—I wish I could say tonight that a lasting peace is in sight.

Happily, I can say that war has been avoided. Steady progress toward our ultimate goal has been made. But, so much remains to be done. As a private citizen, I shall never cease to do what little I can to help the world advance along that road. . . .

DOCUMENT 31.4
Guns and Butter: The U.S. Reply to the United Nations

Behind much of the American public's acceptance of the existence of the military-industrial complex lay the notion that the United States was so rich it could afford a policy of both ''guns and butter''—high defense spending and continued economic growth. This idea was badly shaken by the coming of recession with inflation in the later 1960s. But in December 1961, ''guns and butter'' dominated American thought, as was revealed in this confident reply to the UN Secretary-General on the possible impact of disarmament for the U.S. economy.

1. The current national defense effort of the United State takes about one-tenth of our gross national product and employs somewhat less than that portion of our employed labor force. This allocation of human and material resources must be seen against the background of the vast and costly changes which have been taking place in the technology of arms, and of the tremendous enlargement, geographically and otherwise, in the security requirements of the United States as the leading power in the free world. As a component of total economic demand, defense expenditures are not of such magnitude that the economy is vitally dependent on them. In fact, the American economy

Source: U.S. Arms Control and Disarmament Agency: *The Economic and Social Consequences of Disarmament* (Washington, D.C., June 1964).

proved itself after World War II to be very resilient to a considerably greater and more rapid reduction in defense expenditure than would be involved under any disarmament program starting at the present level of armaments.

2. The currently recognized needs of Americans individually and collectively are so extensive that, if translated into economic demand, they would more than offset the loss of demand resulting from an agreed disarmament program. The factors required to effect this translation of civilian needs into economic demand are well understood. Moreover, there are increasingly refined tools available with which to observe, analyze, and influence the development of the economy. Advance planning and sensible policies at all levels of government will be essential to the maintenance of overall economic activity in the face of the progressive elimination of defense demand.

3. Unquestionably, any program of disarmament will in the short and intermediate run give rise to problems of adjustment in all factors of production. However, these adjustment problems—of varying intensity depending on the timing, phasing, and duration of any agreed disarmament program—are not novel to the American economy; quite apart from previous successful adjustments to major changes in defense expenditures, the economy is constantly undergoing adjustment in a wide range of industries as a result of changes in technology and economic demand. Concerted effort on the part of government at all levels and of business and labor, to bring to bear numerous available instruments and, if necessary, to create additional ones, can reduce to a minimum any hardship and waste in the adjustment process under a program for general and complete disarmament.

4. The United States has long recognized that general and complete disarmament would present opportunities for enlarged assistance to less developed countries and has sponsored United Nations resolutions in this sense. However, the United States has not waited for disar-

mament; it has extended foreign economic aid over the past 20 years on a scale unequaled by any other country. . . . When and as disarmament is achieved, the American people can be expected to face imaginatively the added challenges and opportunities which this development would hold for the welfare of mankind.

5. In the area of international economic relations the elimination, as a result of disarmament, of U.S. Government defense-related expenditures abroad, and of defense-related imports of raw materials and other commodities, would have a corrective effect on the U.S. balance-of-payments deficit. There would probably be a noticeably adverse effect in only a few countries; these effects could be overcome with increased external economic assistance and growth and diversification in the respective economies. The elimination of military-oriented production and trade controls under disarmament would permit more international trade to flow on the basis of comparative advantage.

DOCUMENT 31.5
Military Procurement Policies: A Community of Interests

Senator William Proxmire of Wisconsin, long a major legislative investigator of the military-industrial complex, has been looking into "pyramiding profits and costs in the missile procurement program" since 1964. In the selection below, Senator Proxmire suggests the close correspondence of business and military interests.

. . . Recently I asked the Department of Defense for a list of certain high ranking retired military officers employed by the 100 companies who had the largest volume of military

Source: *Congressional Record,* March 24, 1969, pp. S3072–S3078.

prime contracts. I did this in connection with the hearings of the Subcommittee on Economy in Government of the Joint Economic Committee.

In fiscal year 1968 these 100 companies held 67.4 percent of the $38.8 billion of prime military contracts, or $26.2 billion.

The Defense Department has now supplied to me the list of high ranking military officers who work for these 100 companies. They include the subsidiaries. In one case, that of the 35th ranking contractor, four firms were involved in a joint venture.

I asked only for the names of those retired military officers of the rank of Army, Air Force, Marine Corps colonel or Navy captain and above. Excluded are all officers below those ranks. I asked for only retired regular officers and not reserve officers, although in a very few cases the reserve officers may be included.

TOP 100 COMPANIES EMPLOY OVER 2,000 RETIRED OFFICERS

The facts are that as of February, 1969, some 2,072 retired military officers of the rank of colonel or Navy captain and above were employed by the 100 contractors who reported. This is an average of almost 22 per firm. I shall ask to have printed in the *Record* as exhibit A of my statement a list of the 100 companies, ranked according to the dollar volume of their prime military contracts, and the number of high ranking retired officers they employ.

TEN COMPANIES EMPLOY OVER 1,000

The 10 companies with the largest number on their payrolls employed 1,065 retired officers. This is an average of 106 per firm. These 10 companies employed over half the total number of high ranking former officers employed by all the top 100 defense contractors. These com-

panies, listed according to the number of retired officers employed by them, are given in Table 1.

TABLE 1. Ten military prime contractors employing largest number of high ranking retired military officers, and value of their fiscal year 1968 contracts

Company and rank by number of high-ranking retired officers employed	Number employed Feb. 1, 1969	Net dollar value of defense contracts, fiscal year 1968 (in millions)
1. Lockheed Aircraft Corp	210	$1,870
2. Boeing Co.	169	762
3. McDonnell Douglas Corp.	141	1,101
4. General Dynamics	113	2,239
5. North American Rockwell Corp.	104	669
6. General Electric Co.	89	1,489
7. Ling-Temco-Vought, Inc.	69	758
8. Westinghouse Electric Corp.	59	251
9. TRW, Inc.	56	127
10. Hughes Aircraft Co.	55	286
Total	1,065	$9,522

KEY ABM CONTRACTORS EMPLOY 22 PERCENT OF TOTAL

Among the major defense contractors involved in producing the key components of the antiballistic-missile system—ABM—nine of them employ 465 retired officers. This is an average of 51 each.

In 1968 they held contracts valued at $5.78 billion and, of course, will receive many billions more if the ABM system is deployed.

These companies and the number of retired officers they employ are given in Table 2.

TABLE 2. Major prime contractors involved in ABM system and number of high ranking retired military officers employed by them

1. McConnell Douglas	141
2. General Electric	89
3. Hughes Aircraft	55
4. Martin Marietta	40
5. Raytheon	37
6. Sperry Rand	36
7. RCA	35
8. AVCO	23
9. A.T.&T	9
Total	465

COMPARISON OF 1969 WITH 1959

. . . In 1959, the total number employed was only 721–88 of 100 companies reporting—or an average of slightly more than eight per company.

In 1969 the 100 largest defense contractors—95 of the 100 companies reporting—employed 2,072 former high military officers, or an average of almost 22 per company.

In 1959 the 10 companies with the highest number of former officers employed 372 of them.

In 1969 the top 10 had 1,065, or about three times as many.

Some 43 companies which reported were on both the 1959 and 1969 list of the top 100 largest contractors. There were several more who were on the list in both years but failed to report in one or the other year. But we can compare the 43 companies. These 43 companies employed 588 high ranking former officers in 1959. In 1969 these same companies employed 1,642 retired high ranking retired officers.

In each case where a comparison can be made, namely, in the total number of former high ranking officers employed by the top 100 contractors, the top 10 contractors employing the largest number, and the number employed by firms reporting in both 1959 and 1969, the number employed has tripled. It has increased threefold.

Roughly three times the number of retired high ranking military officers are employed by the top 100 companies in 1969 as compared with 1959.

What is the significance of this situation? What does it mean and what are some of its implications?

First of all, it bears out the statement I made on March 10 when I spoke on the "blank check" for the military, that the warning by former President Eisenhower against the danger of "unwarranted influence, whether sought or unsought, by the military-industrial complex," is not just some future danger.

That danger is here. . . .

Second, I do not claim nor even suggest that any conspiracy exists between the military and the 100 largest defense contractors. I do not believe in the conspiracy theory of history. I charge no general wrongdoing on *the part of either group*. . . .

COMMUNITY OF INTEREST

But what can be said, and should properly be said, is that there is a continuing community of interest between the military, on the one hand, and these industries on the other.

What we have here is almost a classic example of how the military-industrial complex works.

It is not a question of wrongdoing. It is a question of what can be called the "old boy network" or the "old school tie."

This is a most dangerous and shocking situation. It indicates the increasing influence of the big contractors with the military and the military with the big contractors. It shows an intensification of the problem and the growing community of interest which exists between the two. It makes it imperative that new weapon systems receive the most critical review and that defense contracts be examined in microscopic detail. . . .

Third, this matter is particularly dangerous in a situation where only 11.5 percent of military contracts are awarded on a formally advertised competitive bid basis. It lends itself to major abuse when almost 90 percent of all military contracts are negotiated, and where a very high proportion of them are negotiated with only one, or one or two, contractors.

Former high-ranking military officers have an entree to the Pentagon that others do not have. I am not charging that is necessarily wrong. I am saying that it is true.

Former high-ranking officers have personal friendships with those still at the Pentagon which most people do not have. Again, I charge no specific wrongdoing. But it is a fact.

In some cases former officers may even negotiate contracts with their former fellow officers. Or they may be involved in developing plans and specifications, making proposals, drawing up blueprints, or taking part in the planning process or proposing prospective weapon systems. And they may be doing this in cooperation with their former fellow officers with whom they served with and by whom, in some cases, even promoted. . . .

In addition, there is the subtle or unconscious temptation to the officer still on active duty. After all, he can see that over 2,000 of his fellow officers work for the big companies. How hard a bargain does he drive with them when he is 1 or 2 years away from retirement? . . .

When the bulk of the budget goes for military purposes; when 100 companies get 67 percent of the defense contract dollars; when cost overruns are routine and prime military weapon system contracts normally exceed their estimates by 100 to 200 percent; when these contracts are let by negotiation and not by competitive bidding; and when the top contractors have over 2,000 retired highranking military officers on their payrolls; there are very real questions as to how critically these matters are reviewed and how well the public interest is served.

DOCUMENT 31.6
The Language of Threat

The idea that the United States was somehow beleaguered, threatened from without and within by Communist conspiracies, produced the "Fortress America" psychology of the 1950s. Like the guns and butter argument, it helped underpin the hold of the military-industrial complex on the economy and society. Yet, despite the changes in national style from the late 1960s on, we can see in Defense Secretary Melvin Laird's report for fiscal year 1971 a continued reliance on the language of "threat." Notice also, toward the end of this reading, that Secretary Laird criticizes McNamara's overcentralisation of the Defense Department.

THE THREAT TO NATIONAL SECURITY

The first requirement we faced upon assuming office was to reappraise the spectrum of threats that exist in the world today. These threats dictate to a large degree how we should implement our basic policies in conjunction with our allies. As I noted earlier, changes in the strategic threat that might result from successful arms limitation talks could have a major impact on the direction we take in our future strategic programs. Similarly the emergence of additional nuclear-capable nations such as Communist China influences our force planning. . . .

Source: Department of Defense, *Statement of Secretary to House Subcommittee on Defense Appropriations, Fiscal Year 1971* (Washington, D.C.: U.S. Government Printing Office, 1970).

Permit me to highlight the four major aspects of the military threat which we have had to consider and which we must constantly review.

1. The Strategic Nuclear Threat

The Soviet strategic nuclear threat is impressive and it is growing. We now estimate the number of SS-9 Intercontinental Ballistic Missiles (ICBMs) deployed or under construction to be over 275, rather than 230 as I reported publicly less than a year ago. The number of SS-11 ICBMs has also increased significantly. The Soviets continue to test improvements in offensive weapons, including SS-9 multiple re-entry vehicles and modified SS-11 payloads. Production of nuclearpowered ballistic missile submarines has continued above previously projected rates at two Soviet shipyards.

Communist China has continued to test nuclear weapons in the megaton range and could test its first ICBM within the next year. However, the earliest estimated date that they could have an operational ICBM capability now appears to be 1973, or about one year later than last year's projection. It appears more likely that such a capability will be achieved by the mid-1970s. A force of 10 to 25 ICBMs might be operational some two to three years later.

2. The General Purpose Forces Threat

The general purpose forces threat also remains strong. In the most critical theater, that facing the NATO Central Region, the Warsaw Pact could, in a relatively short time, assemble a force of about 1.3 million men and associated combat equipment. In Asia, Communist China and North Korea continue to maintain substantial armed forces.

The major Soviet naval threat continues to be from the torpedo and cruise-missile firing submarine force. By mid-1971, the Soviets should have about 300 submarines, including 65 with nuclear power. These forces could pose a considerable threat to our deployed naval forces and to the merchant shipping essential to the support of our European and Asian allies. Additionally, Soviet Naval Air Force bombers equipped with cruise missiles could pose a threat to our naval forces operating within range of the Soviet Union.

It is clear that the Soviet Union is embarked on an ambitious program to achieve a global military capability. . . .

3. The Technological Threat

In the long term, one of the most serious threats confronting the United States is the large and growing military research and development effort of the Soviet Union.

The implications of this Soviet effort for our future security cannot be clearly foreseen at this time. Because the Soviet Union is a closed society, they can conduct their military research and development programs behind a thick veil of secrecy, making it very difficult for us to assess their progress in a timely manner. However, we have seen evidence of this technology in the new systems they are deploying, including the FOXBAT interceptor aircraft, nuclear-powered ballistic missile and attack submarines, and other impressive weapons. . . .

4. The Insurgency Threat

One of the most effective techniques used by Communist nations has been insurgency supported by external assistance. As the President noted in proclaiming the Nixon Doctrine on November 3rd, we intend to assist our friends and allies in coping with such threats, largely through military and economic assistance when requested and as appropriate, while looking to the nation directly threatened to assume the primary responsibility for providing the manpower for its defense. . . .

THE CHALLENGE AT HOME

In addition to the military threats posed from outside our borders, we faced significant challenges within our borders.

At home, there was a growing mood of self-doubt. Our youth and other segments of our population were becoming increasingly frustrated over the war in Vietnam which was pushing defense expenditures higher and higher, while our casualties were second only to those we suffered in World War II. Despite the rising costs in human and material resources, hope for success seemed dim. As we assumed office in January 1969, no clear end was in sight, either in Southeast Asia or at the conference table in Paris.

Partly as a result of the Vietnam war, high prices and growing taxes were threatening the living standards of the pensioned and the salaried. There was a clear need and a growing demand to put our Government's fiscal affairs back in order. The Federal Budget needed to be balanced to start bringing serious inflation under control. Most importantly, our national priorities had to be reordered.

Moreover, our society was troubled by divisions which too often alienated the races and divided the generations.

As we assumed office in this environment, the Department of Defense was also confronted with frustration and disillusionment. Blame for mediocre results of some past policies and programs fell largely on the shoulders of the military. . . .

In addition, there were administrative problems with the Department of Defense.

I inherited a system designed for highly centralized decisionmaking. Over-centralization of decisionmaking in so large an organization as the Department of Defense leads to a kind of paralysis. Many decisions are not made at all, or, if they are made, lack full coordination and commitment by those who must implement the decisions. The traffic from lower to higher echelons may be inhibited; relevant and essential inputs for the decisionmaker can be lost. In addition, there seemed to be insufficient participation by other agencies with important responsibilities for national security.

I was also disturbed that although long-range plans existed, they did not always reflect realistic planning within foreseeable resources. . . .

DOCUMENT 31.7
Cost Overruns and Failure of Equipment

Senator William Proxmire in the 1980s took the lead in investigating the doings of the military-industrial complex, as he did in the 1960s. Two examples of his scrutiny were the M-1 tank (in 1981) and the C-5A cargo plane (in 1983).

Both excerpts are from the opening statements by Proxmire who was chairing the committee.

THE M-1 TANK (1981)

Senator Proxmire. The subcommittee will come to order.

Gentlemen, we are very happy to have you here. This is a pretty grim problem that faces us, and I think it is just typical of the problems that our defense effort has and I am looking forward eagerly to having your analysis of it and your recommendation as to what we can do about it. The M-1 tank problem falls into three categories: Cost overruns; disappointing

Source: Joint Economic Committee, *The M-1 Tank and NATO Readiness,* Subcommittee on International Trade, Finance and Security Economics. 97th Congress, First Session, July 21 and 22, 1981. (Washington, D.C.)

Joint Economic Committee, *C-5A and Air Force Defense Profits Policy,* Subcommittee on International Trade. Finance and Security Economics. 98th Congress, First Session, November 1, 1983. (Washington, D.C.)

test results in the areas of reliability and maintainability; and future effects on readiness. The M-1 program follows two earlier Army efforts to build a new main battle tank in the late sixties and early seventies. Both were canceled because of cost and performance problems.

In 1974 it was estimated that 3,323 M-1 tanks would cost $3 billion, or $900,000 each. The current estimate is that 7,058 M-1 tanks will cost $19 billion, or $2.5 million each. And there is reason to believe that the costs will go considerably higher, to perhaps as much as $3 million before we're through. Adjusting for the increase in quantities, there is presently a cost overrun of about $5 billion.

Now, the Army obviously, needs a new tank and every study of our NATO forces that I've seen demonstrates the need to improve the level of readiness. It is precisely these needs that cause concern about the M-1. Will the Army's new tank actually increase or lower the readiness of our forces, and will the astronomical costs of this program represent a prudent investment in military preparedness or a drain on the economy and the Federal budget?

More important than the cost overruns, and I mean more important than the cost overruns, although all of us are very concerned about that—I certainly am; they are appalling. But more important than the cost overruns are the disappointing results of the M-1 tests that have been reported by the General Accounting Office.

The third and latest series of M-1 tests were started last year and completed at the end of May of this year. Today I understand you gentlemen will present your analysis of the results of the tests. The facts about the latest tests are critical for several reasons. The Army will decide in December whether to increase the production rate from 30 to 60 tanks per month. More than $2 billion has already been budgeted to be spent on the M-1 in fiscal year 1982. That amount will undoubtedly go much higher as the program proceeds.

Is the tank ready to go into full production? Is it ready to be sent to Europe? The Army has had big difficulties with building a new tank. It has made a serious blunder in sending a new tank to Europe in the recent past. It is not generally known that the A-2 version of M-60 is still in the process of being recalled because of problems with the tank. I understand that 543 of these tanks have been brought back from Europe and are still being brought back because they turned out to be useless. According to my staff, these useless tanks cost about $675 million in 1981 dollars.

THE C-5A CARGO PLANE (1983)

Senator Proxmire. The meeting will come to order.

The Joint Economic Committee's interest in government contracting and defense procurement dates back to the 1950's when, under the leadership of Senator Paul Douglas, who was then chairman of the committee, hearings were held to look into the wasteful spending practices associated with these activities. Senator Douglas' path-breaking investigations led to his conviction that the goal of economy in government could not be attained until economic principles are applied to government contracting.

The Joint Economic Committee has continued the work begun by Senator Douglas through numerous hearings concerning specific procurements, as well as inquiries into the effects of defense spending and procurement policies on the economy and the defense industrial base. Indeed, it was understood at the time of the abolition of the Joint Defense Production Committee that the Joint Economic Committee would continue its efforts and expand them so as to assist the banking committees in their monitoring of the Defense Production Act.

Today's hearing is another in a series of inquiries into the Air Force C-5A cargo plane program held under the auspices of the Joint

Economic Committee. Our first hearings into this program were conducted in 1968, when the huge cost overrun on the C-5A was uncovered.

The present series began in 1976 with a review of the role of the C-5A. When the full dimensions of the problem of the defective wings became known, we turned our attention to this new facet of perhaps the most disastrous weapons procurement in modern history.

The Air Force originally planned to buy 120—that is 120—C-5A's at a cost of $3.4 billion. That allowed for inflation. Or $23 million each. Due to cost overruns in the production of the aircraft by Lockheed, the quantity was reduced to 81 planes and the cost of producing them increased to $5 billion, or $62 million each. In other words, there was an increase from $23 million to $62 million per copy. The failure of the wings is adding another $1.5 billion to the overall cost, bringing the total unit cost to about $82 million for each C-5A, nearly three times the original estimate.

In 1980, I asked the GAO to do a study of the C-5A wing cracking problem and the Air Force program for making the repairs. In its report, issued March 22, 1982, GAO found that the wing problem occurred because Lockheed had deviated from the original contract specifications, but that it was not financially liable because the contract had been converted from fixed price to cost plus in the course of a bailout of the company arranged by former Deputy Secretary of Defense David Packard.

One of the questions I raised in my request to GAO was reserved for more time-consuming analysis. This question asked whether Lockheed was entitled to make a profit on the wing repair contract. GAO has now completed its study of this question and its report forms the basis for this hearing.

The GAO report presents Congress with one of the most ridiculous situations I have seen as a U.S. Senator, and I have been in this body for more than 26 years. On the one hand, GAO concludes that Lockheed was legally obli-

gated to do much or most of the wing repairs without a profit and that the Air Force was incorrect in failing to recognize this obligation. The Air Force proceeded to award contracts to Lockheed with profits totaling about $150 million.

On the other hand, GAO concludes that there is no legal basis to avoid paying the profits. In other words, the taxpayer, who was required to pay the cost of correcting the contractor's mistake because of a bailout agreement engineered by the Pentagon, is now being required to pay the same contractor a profit for correcting that contractor's mistake of a faulty Air Force legal decision.

So I think the question must be asked whether this suggests that if a contractor wants to increase his profits, one of the best ways is to build defective equipment. The more defects he has to correct, the more money he makes.

We used to argue that there was a disincentive for cutting costs because the higher the cost, the greater the profit. But now, we are in a new area where the bigger the mistake, the higher the profit.

The Air Force seems to be rewarding failure.

DOCUMENT 31.8
The Pentagon Catalog

In 1984 and 1985 a scandal was caused by the revelation that the Defense Department had been overcharged for certain items in its budget by the defense industries. It was at a time when the general public were dismayed by Reagan's cuts in social services, education, and threatened cuts in social security. The Pentagon Catalog is a spoof, based on real prices of items.

Source: C. Cerf and H. Beard. *The Pentagon Catalog.* New York: Workman Publishing, 1986.

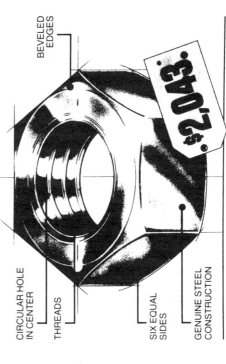

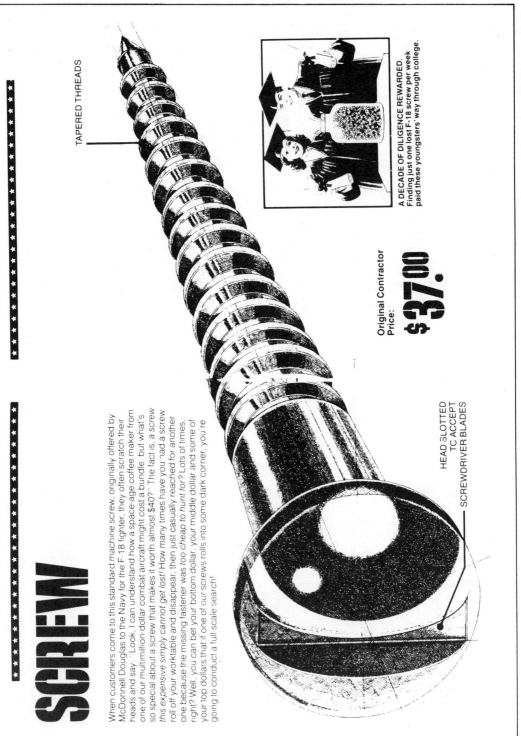

SCREW

When customers come to this standard machine screw, originally offered by McDonnell Douglas to the Navy for the F-18 fighter, they often scratch their heads and say: "Look, I can understand how a space-age coffee maker from one of our multimillion-dollar combat aircraft might cost a bundle, but what's so special about a screw that makes it worth almost $40?" The fact is, *a screw this expensive simply cannot get lost!* How many times have you had a screw roll off your worktable and disappear, then just casually reached for another one because the missing fastener was *too cheap to hunt for?* Lots of times, right? Well, you can bet your bottom dollar, your middle dollar and some of your top dollars that if one of *our* screws rolls into some dark corner, you're going to conduct a full-scale search!

TAPERED THREADS

HEAD SLOTTED
TC ACCEPT
SCREWDRIVER BLADES

Original Contractor
Price:

$37.⁰⁰

A DECADE OF DILIGENCE REWARDED.
Finding just one lost F-18 screw per week paid these youngsters' way through college.

Sources: Defense Budget Project; U.S. Senate, Committee on Governmental Affairs, staff investigation, Center for Defense Information, Washington, D.C.: Transcript of Appearance by A. Ernest Fitzgerald and Senator Charles Grassloy on the *Donahue Show* (*Donahue* Transcript #08214), 1984.

"TOILET SEAT"

"It gives new meaning to the word 'throne.'"
—Senator William S. Cohen

Could your present toilet seats withstand the incessant rolling and jolting of a barrage of powerful earthquakes? If an acid cloud escaped from a neighboring factory and polluted the atmosphere of your home, would your present seats emerge corrosion-free? If you or a member of your family were unexpectedly called upon to detach your toilet seats and carry them around for a long period of time, would the seats be light enough to permit you to do so in comfort and safety? Tough questions, we'll admit. But it's about time somebody asked them. Luckily for you, we at Pentagon Products are asking them now. And, if you answered "no" to any or all of them, then . . . *have we got the product for you!* It's Toilet Cover Assembly No. 941673.101, from the Lockheed-California Company, a corporation whose principal products — fighter planes and bombers — are built to survive an all-out enemy assault. What mere toilet seat fabricator can make that claim?

Of course, Toilet Cover Assembly No. 941673.101 won't fit on a standard-size toilet — that's one of the reasons for its higher cost. But once you cast your eyes on this plastic-and-fiberglass beauty, you won't think twice about remodeling your plumbing to accommodate it. After all, when you-know-what is on the line, you owe it to yourself not to settle for anything less than a "royal flush."

Original Contractor Price:

$640.09

Contractor Part Number: 941673.101

SENATE SEAT. Senator William V. Roth proudly displays one of our Toilet Cover Assemblies.

UNUSUALLY LARGE SEATING AREA FOR EXTRA COMFORT

DESIGNED TO WITHSTAND THE SHOCK OF THOUSANDS OF AIRCRAFT LANDINGS

RIVETS HOLD SEAT FIRMLY IN PLACE

NO ANNOYING SEAMS

PRECISION CRAFTED OF LIGHTWEIGHT, CORROSIVE-RESISTANT, THERMO-FORMED POLYCARBONATE MATERIAL

Sources: New York *Times*, February 2 and June 2, 1985; Washington *Post*, February 5, February 6 and April 20, 1985.

chapter 32

Blacks in Twentieth-Century America

John Bracey
University of Massachusetts

At the onset of the twentieth century, W. E. B. Du Bois, one of the nation's leading scholars, proclaimed that:

> The problem of the twentieth century is the problem of the color-line,—the relation of the darker to the lighter races of men in Asia and Africa, in America and the islands of the sea.

Booker T. Washington, founder of Tuskegee Institute and the unofficial leader of the Afro-American community, called more optimistically for a "New Negro for the New Century." Both were attempting to come to grips with the inescapable reality that these were extremely harsh times for black Americans. The 1896 U.S. Supreme Court decision in the case of *Plessy* v. *Ferguson* provided the ultimate legal sanction for the doctrine of "separate but equal." This ruling left intact, and encouraged the passage of additional laws, the massive web of antiblack legislation more popularly known as "Jim Crow." By 1910 virtually every southern state had laws that effectively deprived Negroes of the vote, established separate school systems from kindergarten through college, mandated separate facilities in all areas of public accommodation, and forbade intermarriage between whites and Negroes. Numerous local statutes and ordinances proscribed the actions

of Negroes in every area of daily life from the use of drinking fountains, attending movie houses, participating in cultural and athletic events, to use of public libraries. The "etiquette" of Jim Crow further limited the scope of black behavior in such matters as the sharing of sidewalks with whites, how one would be addressed as an individual, quality of service at stores, and the general range of acceptable attitudes toward whites. An outpouring of "scholarly" and "scientific" studies rationalized this triumph of white supremacy. Back of all these statutes, studies, and customs stood the legal force of state, federal, and local police, and the illegal force of the lynch mob. Black populations were relegated to the status of social and political powerlessness.

Black Americans, three quarters of whom lived in rural settings and did agricultural work, were at what historian Rayford Logan described as the "nadir" of their sojourn in the United States. A minority population with insufficient resources to leave the United States, and no place to go during the height of western colonial expansion, one can easily understand the plight of those who gave in to the pressure and turned to drugs, alcohol, or to acts of synchophancy and betrayal, or to acts of crime, violence, and destruction directed against their fellow sufferers.

However, the majority of black Americans, by all indications, held on to their belief that life could and would get better, and devoted their efforts to making that belief real. In addition to racism, the external processes of industrialization, urbanization, expansion of capitalism, and war worked to define the social parameters within which blacks as individuals and as a group had to live and make decisions. The internal processes involved the pursuit of two strategies on the individual and on the group levels. The first strategy—dictated by minority status—was the seeking out, encouraging and taking advantage of divisions within the white population. Regardless of whether the ultimate goal was integration or some form of separatism, support from, or at least neutrality on the part of large numbers of whites was an essential ingredient for success. The second strategy was to build institutions and organizations based primarily on racial loyalty and solidarity in order to survive, and to maintain as much control as possible, again regardless of the ultimate goal.

Within the black community there is a premium placed on individualism and individual achievements, always in tension with the necessity or desirability of presenting as unified a front as possible to the larger society. There is more than a little irony in being forced to organize oneself as a Negro in order to be treated as an individual, in organizing separately in order to integrate and in appealing to whites for support for separate "autonomous" institutions.

Within the confines of the Jim Crow South and the developing ghettoes of the North, blacks built institutions—such as churches, cultural organizations, fraternal orders, businesses, and schools—that enabled them to withstand the sharper blows of racist oppression. At the same time they continued to build these institutions and support such activities that promote greater access to the resources of the larger society.

The continued growth of industrial capitalism accompanied by the growth of cities began to pull large numbers of blacks from rural to urban areas in the North and within the South prior to World War I. Economic depression in southern agriculture and such harsher aspects of Jim Crow as rapes, beatings, and lynchings provided the "push" factors. The National Association for the Advancement of Colored People (NAACP) formed in 1909 and the National Urban League in 1911, both had headquarters in New York City. The NAACP was founded by a group of white and black liberals and socialists to advocate the full range of solutions to problems posed by Jim Crow: the right to vote, equal education opportunity, right to fair trial, right to sit on juries, antilynching legislation, equal service on railroads and other public vehicles, equal access to public accommodations and services, and equal employment opportunity. Their strategies included litigation, legislative lobbying and open-ended public discussion, of and condemnation of all acts of racial oppression and expressions of white supremacy.

The National League on Urban Conditions among Negroes (the National Urban League) had heavy involvement on the part of white philanthropists and industrialists in carrying forward the two-pronged program of helping blacks get access to jobs in industry and in helping them to make the adjustment to city life. World War I was a further stimulus to the mass migration of blacks from the southern rural areas into the urban areas of the Northeast, Midwest, and Pacific Coast, transforming a predominantly peasant population to one that included a substantial number of industrial workers and city dwellers. The mixture of blacks and whites together in large numbers set the tone for life in the city during the period during and following World War I. A new black assertiveness developed with the strength that comes from sheer numbers. Blacks, grouped together from all areas of the South, now saw their group potential. Liberated from the rigid restrictions of a Jim Crow existence and the South, and many of the men back from participating in armed combat against whites in Europe, blacks were not as easily intimidated. The end of the war was marked by a number of race riots generally provoked by white distaste for the actions of black veterans or by fear of blacks moving into previously all-white neighborhoods.

The postwar era saw the rise of the black nationalist sentiments that had been building in black America since the 1880s. When Marcus Garvey came to the United States in 1916, he found a receptive audience among the new urban migrants, returning veterans, and West Indian immigrants. Garvey's was the one organization that did not demand that black people curb their exuberance and newfound expression of joy in being black. Neither the NAACP nor the Urban League met this need of the black masses. Garvey's Universal Negro Improvement Association was such a successful organization among urban blacks that it forced even the new assimilationist black middle classes to take an interest in the life of the masses of black people and thereby helped to generate the Harlem renaissance.

Urban political machines, especially in Kansas City, Chicago, Cleveland, and New York, made relatively successful strenuous efforts to involve blacks in the political process. Blacks, however, still voting for the party of Abraham Lincoln and Frederick Douglass, gave their support to the Republicans while the white immigrant groups were drawn into the Democratic party.

The depression in the 1930s had serious consequences for the political and economic development of black America. The gains made in black employment and in the establishment of black businesses during the 1920s were largely wiped out. During the depression the unemployment rate of urban blacks was more than double that of urban whites; while rural blacks were pushed off the plantations by own-ers who no longer needed their labor and who had financial support from the New Deal agricultural programs. The resultant migration served to swell the ranks of the urban unemployed. Two movements originating from outside black America made inroads among blacks. The Communist party, because of its policy favoring interracial organizing both in its own ranks and in the new industrial unions that it was instrumental in organizing, attracted some blacks. The other was the Democratic machines that controlled the dispensation of federal funds for New Deal urban programs. Throughout the 1930s, blacks began to leave the Republican party and to vote for FDR under the slogan, ''Let Jesus lead you and Roosevelt feed you.'' By the end of World War II, the black vote was safely in the Democratic column. New black leaders such as Arthur Mitchell and William Dawson of Chicago as well as Adam Clayton Powell, Jr., of New York were evidence of this new black political strength.

Movements from within the black community proceeded along a number of lines. In the mid 1930s the NAACP under the leadership of Charles Houston initiated its plan to legally attack Jim Crow laws starting with educational institutions. Du Bois thought that the economic effects of the depression were not being given adequate consideration. When the organization rejected his views that blacks ought to take advantage of the group strengths provided by a segregated existence in order to survive, he was forced to resign. Beginning in the mid-1930s the NAACP became increasingly concerned about the plight of black workers.

The black community also initiated two distinct job movements during the depression. One, the ''Don't buy where you can't work'' movement used tactics such as picket lines, boycotts, and selective intimidation to secure jobs for black workers located within the black community itself. The second was a movement to get secretarial and clerical jobs for black high school and college graduates in stores and businesses also located within the black community. This concern for jobs culminated in the March on Washington Movement headed by A. Philip Randolph. Organized to put pressure on the federal government to get blacks a fair share of the jobs in the growing wartime industries, Randolph threatened to bring more than 100,000 jobless blacks to Washington in the summer of 1941. The march never took place, but FDR issued an executive order banning job discrimination in government and defense industries and setting up the Fair Employment Practices Committee (FEPC).

Many blacks, some of whom were former members of the Garvey movement, joined the numerous religious groups that combined concern with the soul with concrete efforts to secure food, shelter, and work for their members. Father Divine, Elder Micheaux, and Daddy Grace were the most prominent leaders of the many sects that sprang up.

World War II, like World War I, encouraged deep and lasting transformations of black America. Blacks gained employment in wartime industries, and when the war was over, held on to enough jobs to increase the numbers and power of the black middle classes. The demands for fair treatment that have typically accompanied black participation in the nation's wars were intensified during and after World War II because of the anti-Fascist rhetoric of the United States and its allies. Blacks adopted the double V slogan for victory against fascism abroad and against racism at home. The war and its immediate aftermath were marked by violent conflicts between white and black workers over jobs, housing, and social services as even more blacks left the rural South to move to the North and West to work. There were large-scale riots in Detroit, Philadelphia, and other northern and western cities.

After 1945 several factors combined to initiate and sustain the black efforts to gain full equality that have been a major characteristic of post–World War II American life. The most important external factors were the gradual shift in white opinion toward a more liberal view of blacks, the increasing awareness of the contradiction of practicing racism at home after fighting a costly war against fascism abroad, the effect of the national liberation movements in Asia and Africa, and the onset of a cold war in which the Russians capitalized on American shortcomings in the area of race relations. The most significant ingredients were the heightened initiatives taken by blacks themselves. The years of the late 1940s and early 1950s were those in which the NAACP fought and won the legal battles for equal rights that laid the foundation for the mass demonstrations and nonviolent direct action that came later.

In 1954 the U.S. Supreme Court in *Brown* v. *Board of Education* declared school segregation unconstitutional. In addition to reversing the Court's 1896 *Plessy* v. *Ferguson* decision supporting the separate-but-equal doctrine, the *Brown* decision was significant because of the Court's use of social and psychological data demonstrating that segregation was damaging to the personality of black young people. Through the use of nonviolent, direct action techniques segments of the black community, with substantial support from whites, began the efforts to make real the quality promised by the growing body of U.S. Supreme Court decisions and the Civil Rights Acts of 1957 and 1960. Since the early 1940s the interracial Congress of Racial Equality (CORE) had been engaging in sit-ins to challenge discrimination in public accommodations in northern and border states. In 1947 members of CORE made the first "freedom ride," called a Journey of Reconciliation, into the upper South. Rosa Parks, and other now forgotten local leaders, sparked the Montgomery, Alabama, bus boycott of 1955–56, which projected Martin Luther King, Jr., into national prominence. Following the successful boycott that forced the integration of Montgomery's public buses in 1957, King founded the Southern Christian Leadership Conference (SCLC), which carried out voter registration and nonviolent direct action campaigns.

The "Negro Revolt" began in earnest on February 1, 1960, in Greensboro, North Carolina. Four black students from North Carolina Agricultural and Technical College refused to leave a Woolworth lunch counter until they were served. Sit-ins, kneel-ins, wade-ins, stand-ins all became common phenomena throughout the South as blacks moved to achieve equality in public accommodations. In April 1960 representatives of student groups on the campuses of southern black colleges met in Raleigh, North Carolina, and formed the Student Nonviolent Coordinating Committee (SNCC).

CORE's 1961 freedom ride challenged bus segregation in the Deep South, filled Mississippi jails with demonstrators, and secured an Interstate Commerce Commission (ICC) ruling requiring integration of all interstate buses and terminal facilities. In November 1961 SNCC went to Albany, Georgia, to assist a local youth movement that was testing the new ruling, thus precipitating a series of dramatic demonstrations with SCLC rushing to give its support.

The Albany demonstrations were significant as part of the series of major nonviolent direct action campaigns, whose high points included the Birmingham demonstrations, the March on Washington of 1963, and the March from Selma to Montgomery in 1965. Taken together, these protests helped galvanize Congress into passing the Civil Rights Act of 1964 and the Voting Rights Act of 1965. The 1964 act forbade discrimination in public accommodations and employment. The attorney general could institute suits and deny federal funds to local agencies that practiced discrimination. The Voting Rights Act eliminated all qualifying tests for registration that inhibited the right to vote on the basis of race or color.

In the ghettos of the North, with legal and political equality long written into law, the civil rights movement found more difficult and complex issues, such as de facto school segregation,

trade union and housing discrimination, and institutional racism. Nonviolence and integration were not popular concepts among many urban blacks, especially those who were as much in sympathy with the Black Muslims and Malcolm X as with Martin Luther King.

The Nation of Islam was a black nationalist group founded in the early 1930s by Elijah Muhammed. It remained small and relatively unknown until the late 1950s, when the brilliant and charismatic minister, Malcolm X, brought the Black Muslims into national prominence. Malcolm's ideas and assumptions were the antithesis of Reverend King's. King was a Christian, Malcolm a Muslim; King viewed blacks as Americans, Malcolm viewed the blacks as a colony and part of the Third World; King believed in Christian love and nonviolence, Malcolm in using whatever methods were necessary to achieve liberation; King believed in integration, Malcolm in separation. Both were assassinated before they reached the age of forty.

The complexity of the issues involved in combating institutionalized racism in the North soon become apparent. Chicago provides an example. After several summers of nonviolent demonstrations, two school boycotts, and a riot had made little headway in achieving an open city for blacks, the Coordinating Council of Community Organizations (CCCO) invited King to Chicago to see if his tactics could work in the urban North. Most observers viewed the campaign as a failure.

The mid-1960s witnessed a series of ghetto rebellions beginning in Harlem in 1964, followed by much more massive eruptions in Watts in 1965, in Detroit and Newark in 1967, and culminating with nationwide outbreaks in April 1968, after King was assassinated. In July 1967 President Johnson set up a National Advisory Commission on Civil Disorders, chaired by Governor Otto Kerner of Illinois, to investigate the recent riots. The report placed the blame on the racism of white America: "White society is deeply implicated in the ghetto. White institutions created it, white institutions maintained it, and white society condones it.'' The report also recommended constructive social changes that by and large have been ignored. However, in most large cities, recommendations for more effective techniques of riot control have been implemented.

The largely ineffective attempts to ameliorate the conditions of blacks encouraged the formation of more militant groups, such as the Black Panther party founded in 1966 in California by Huey Newton and Bobby Seale. The Black Panthers were the most prominent of several groups that developed among black youth with the decline of nonviolent direct action civil rights organizations and the rise of black power. Their tough-sounding rhetoric and provocative actions invited repression by federal and local authorities. Police raids on Panther headquarters across the nation and the tendency to view black young men primarily as a police problem paved the way for the continued neglect of the real social problems that made the Panthers possible in the first place.

The first fifteen years following the *Brown* decision witnessed dramatic black protest and activism. Yet changes in the patterns of American race relations have not brought true racial equality and have left the life of the bulk of the lower-class blacks virtually unchanged or in some ways much worse. Under the Nixon administration the optimism of the 1960s gave way to talk of the end of the Second Reconstruction.

During the years of the Nixon administration, colleges and universities began the move away from open enrollment and the encouragement of high-risk students, toward the older "acceptable" standards for admission. Black students did not receive the financial and tutorial support necessary to complete a four-year program. Many black students were shunted off into community colleges with no hope of going further. The Nixon cutback on student loans further limited the opportunities for blacks to gain entrance to colleges.

At the community level, resistance to integration has expressed itself as opposition to busing and support of the neighborhood school concept. At the same time, neither local school systems nor the state and federal governments were willing to provide the funds necessary to ensure an adequate education for black children in the schools where they predominate.

In the area of equal employment opportunity, Nixon courted the traditionally antiblack elements in organized labor, such as the building trades unions, appointing one of them secretary of labor in his second administration. The Philadelphia plan, the Chicago plan, and their counterparts in other cities, which were designed to at least attempt to increase the number of blacks at all levels in the trade union movement, have met with little success.

Rising crime rates, drug addiction, and youth gang activity make life in the urban ghetto even more difficult. The 1970s saw the legacies of the oppression of the past 100 years still weighing heavily and the promises of the 1960s largely unfulfilled.

The decade of activism following the *Brown* decision which witnessed the destruction of legal segregation was accompanied throughout by white resistance. The shift from what whites saw as a strategy to achieve individual civil rights (integration) to one that was designed to empower blacks as a group (black power) gave some whites the opportunity to abandon the struggle for racial justice and others a model for organizing white ethnic groups in opposition to black interests. White southerners and white ethnics ouside the South were key elements in the election of Richard Nixon in 1968 and 1972, and Ronald Reagan in 1980 and 1984. Jimmy Carter won a narrow victory in the presidential race in 1976 with the support of blacks. The election and reelection by wide margins of presidents openly hostile to the further advancement of blacks has prevented the continuation of a strong federal stance in favor of racial justice. The widespread belief among whites that blacks have achieved legal equality and are entitled to no further support, combined with a new racism that sees blacks as criminals, drug users, and welfare cheats have prevented the continuation of serious efforts to address the economic and social conditions of lower-class blacks.

Further complicating the situation has been the rise of a white women's movement based on expanded economic opportunities and backed by the Civil Rights Act of 1964 which outlawed discrimination based on sex as well as race. White women and men have taken advantage of open enrollment and student aid policies originally designed to increase the number of nonwhite minorities. White females have benefited also from affirmative action policies that allow white males to satisfy antidiscrimination guidelines by hiring white females instead of nonwhites. It is not surprising that white females gave Ronald Reagan a majority of their votes in 1980 and 1984.

Job competition from nonwhite immigrants from Asia, Latin America, the Middle East, and the Caribbean has eroded the economic position of those blacks at the lowest strata of the working class.

Unable to make substantial headway in the private sector and the professions, including higher education, blacks have used their vote to attempt to make gains in the political arena. One of the few causes for optimism has been the slow, but still impressive, increase in the number of black elected officials at the local, county, state, and national levels. Analogous to the situation at the turn of the century when politics and social policies were fought out in the educational arena, today the focal point is electoral politics. A greater proportion of black elected officials are ministers and educators than are found among whites. Among the ministers are the mayor of Atlanta (Andrew Young), the head of the House Budget Committee (William Gray), the delegate from the District of Columbia (Walter Fauntroy), and the

first serious candidate for a presidential nomination (Jesse Jackson).

The congressional Black Caucus throughout the years of the Reagan presidency proposed an alternative to the budgets of the major parties: for example, limiting weapons expenditures and emphasizing such human concerns as medical care, education, job training, and revitalization of urban areas. These budgets seldom are taken seriously. The congressional Black Caucus has been much more successful in achieving sanctions against South Africa.

The outlook for the future is guardedly optimistic. The major problems remaining include the deterioration of physical settings and social institutions such as schools in the older urban centers, an unemployment rate always twice that for whites, drug and alcohol abuse and related crimes, high rate of teenage pregnancies, the increasing number of households headed by females near or below the poverty level. The formation of new groups of black professionals and civil servants to attempt to address those problems, the potential for disruption and the strength of the black vote have prevented the situation from deteriorating completely. Black Americans discovered how to survive slavery; they will figure out a way to survive and move forward in the late twentieth century.

SUGGESTED READINGS

Aptheker, Herbert, ed. *Against Racism: Unpublished Essays, Papers, Addresses, 1887–1961, W.E.B. Du Bois.* Amherst: University of Massachusetts Press, 1985.

Bracey, John, et al., eds. *Black Nationalism in America.* Indianapolis: Bobbs-Merrill, 1970.

Drake, St. Clair, and Horace Cayton, *Black Metropolis: A Study of Negro Life in a Northern City.* New York: Harcourt Brace Jovanovich, 1945.

Du Bois, W. E. B. *Dusk of Dawn: An Essay toward an Autobiography of a Race Concept.* New York: Harcourt Brace Jovanovich, 1940.

Giddings, Paula. *When and Where I Enter: The Impact of Black Women on Race and Sex in America.* New York: William Morrow, 1984.

Harris, William H. *The Harder We Run: Black Workers since the Civil War.* New York: Oxford University Press, 1982.

Jones, Jacqueline. *Labor of Love, Labor of Sorrow: Black Women, Work and the Family from Slavery to the Present.* New York: Basic Books, 1985.

Kluger, Richard. *Simple Justice: The History of Brown vs Board of Education.* New York: Alfred A. Knopf, 1976.

Lewis, David L. *King: A Critical Biography.* 2d ed. Urbana: University of Illinois Press, 1978.

Meier, August, and John Hope Franklin, eds., *Black Leaders of the Twentieth Century.* Urbana: University of Illinois Press, 1982.

Meier, August, et al., eds. *Black Protest Thought in the Twentieth Century.* Indianapolis: Bobbs-Merrill, 1971.

Rosengarten, Theodore, ed. *All God's Dangers: The Life of Nate Shaw.* New York: Alfred A. Knopf, 1975.

Walton, Hanes. *Invisible Politics: Black Political Behavior.* Albany: State University of New York Press, 1985.

X, Malcolm. *The Autobiography of Malcolm X.* New York: Grove Press, 1965.

DOCUMENT 32.1
Lift Ev'ry Voice and Sing

"Lift Ev'ry Voice and Sing" was written in 1900 by James Weldon Johnson (1871–1938), a poet, novelist, and politician, and his brother J. Rosamond Johnson (1873–1954), a songwriter and entertainer. By the 1920s the song had earned the designation as the "Negro National Anthem" that it has enjoyed ever

since. "Lift Ev'ry Voice and Sing" expresses the stubborn optimism and deep faith in the ultimate achievement of social justice that have informed the lives and struggles of Afro-Americans in the twentieth century.

Lift ev'ry voice and sing,
Till earth and heaven ring,
Ring with the harmonies of liberty;
Let our rejoicing rise,
High as the list'ning skies,
Let it resound loud as the rolling sea.
Sing a song full of the faith that the dark past has taught us,
Sing a song full of hope that the present has brought us,
Facing the rising sun,
Of our new day begun,
Let us march on till victory is won.

Stony the road we trod,
Bitter the chast'ning rod,
Felt in the days when hope unborn had died;
Yet with a steady beat,
Have not our weary feet
Come to the place for which our fathers sighed?
We have come over a way that with tears has been watered,
We have come, treading our path thro' the blood of the slaughtered,
Out from the gloomy past,
Till now we stand at last
Where the white gleam of our bright star is cast.

God of our weary years,
God of our silent tears,
Thou who has brought us thus far on our way,
Thou who has by Thy might
Let us into the light,
Keep us forever in the path, we pray;
Lest our feet stray from the places, our God, where we met Thee,
Lest, our hearts drunk with the wine of the world, we forget Thee;
Shadowed beneath Thy hand,

Source: James Weldon Johnson and J. Rosamond Johnson, *Lift Ev'ry Voice and Sing.* (New York: Edward B. Marks Music Corporation, 1900).

May we forever stand,
True to our God, True to our native land.

DOCUMENT 32.2
The Negro in Chicago

This selection from the first major study of a race riot, that in Chicago the summer of 1919, delineates the wide array of groups and organizations American Negroes formed in order to survive in a segregated environment, and to pressure the larger society for change. The combination of institutional development and pressure to expand the range of opportunities again is based on a blend of pragmatism and group solidarity and optimism.

In 1900 the most congested area of Negro residence, called the "Black Belt," was district thirty-one blocks long and four blocks wide, extending from Harrison Street on the north to Thirty-ninth Street on the south, between Wabash and Wentworth avenues. Although other colonies had been started in other parts of the city, notably the West Side, at least 50 percent of the 1900 Negro population of 30,150 lived in this area. As this main area of Negro residence grew, the proportion of Negroes to the total Negro population living in it increased until in 1920 it contained 90 percent of the Negroes of the city.

II. THE ORGANIZATION OF THE NEGRO COMMUNITY

In the discussion of race contacts attention is called to the peculiar conditions which compel Negroes of the city to develop many of their own institutions and agencies. Partly from ne-

cessity and partly from choice, they have established their own churches, business enterprises, amusement places, and newspapers. Living and associating for the most part together, meeting in the same centers for face-to-face relations, trusting to their own physicians, lawyers, and ministers, a compact community with its own fairly definite interests and sentiments has grown up.

The institutions within the Negro community that have been developed to aid it in maintaining itself and promoting its own welfare, are of four general types: (1) commercial and industrial enterprises; (2) organizations for social intercourse; (3) religious organizations; (4) agencies for civic and social betterment.

1. Commercial and Industrial Enterprises

Commercial and industrial establishments conducted by Negroes are listed by Ford S. Black in his yearly *Blue Book,* which serves as a directory of Negro activities. They increased from 1,200 in 1919 to 1,500 in 1920. . . .

2. Organizations For Social Intercourse

Various organizations for social intercourse and mutual helpfulness have developed in the Negro community. Some are local lodges or branches of national organizations, and others are purely local and independent. Some are simply for social intercourse, and others have in addition benefit features, professional interests, etc. Frequent reference is made in the family histories given in this report to these various organizations.

Fraternal Organizations. Fraternal organizations are an old institution among Negroes. In the South they rank next in importance to the church; in the North they have considerable prestige. Membership is large and interest is strong. . . .

Source: The Chicago Commission on Race Relations, *The Negro in Chicago: A Study of Race Relations and a Race Riot.* Chicago: University of Chicago Press, 1922. Courtesy of University of Chicago Press.

3. Religious Organizations

Negro Churches. The church is one of the first and probably one of the strongest institutions among Negroes. The importance of churches in the Negro community lies not only in their large membership and religious influence, but in their provision of a medium of social control for great numbers of Chicago Negroes, and in their great value in promoting the adjustment of newcomers.

In the South the churches are the principal centers for face-to-face relations. They serve as a medium for the exchange of ideas, making and maintaining friendships, community co-operation, collective striving, group competition, as well as for the dissemination of information, assistance and advice on practical problems, and the upholding of religious ideals. The pastors know the members personally, and the church exercises a definite control over individual behavior.

The church is often the only Negro social institution with an unhampered opportunity for development. In most southern cities, Negroes have no Y.M.C.A., public playground, welfare organizations, public library, gymnasium, orderly dance halls, public parks, or theaters. The church in a large degree takes the place of these and fills a vacancy created by the lack of the public facilities ordinarily found in white communities. In many instances it determines the social standing of the individual Negro. No one can escape the opprobrium attached to the term "sinner" if he is not a member of the church, however successful otherwise.

The minister is the recognized leader of the Negroes, and often their legal adviser and school teacher. He is responsible for the social good behavior of his people. No movement can get the support of the people unless it has his sanction.

In the North the function of both Negro church and pastor is different. Negroes can find other places than the church for their leisure time; numerous urban and civic organizations with trained workers look after their interests, probably better than the church. In the Y.M.C.A. they find religion related to the development of their bodies and minds. In northern cities enterprises and movements thrive without the good-will or sanction of the clergy, and even against their protest.

The field wholly occupied in the South by the church is shared in the North by the labor union, the social club, lectures, and political and other organizations. Some of the northern churches, realizing this, have established employment agencies and other activities of a more social nature in response to this new demand. . . .

In a very few cases, Negroes are found to be members of white churches, but the Negro churches have an entirely Negro membership with Negro pastors.

"Store-Front" Churches. The "store-front" church membership is merely a small group which, for one reason or another, has sought to worship independently of any connection with the larger churches. The establishment of such a church may be the result of a withdrawal of part of the membership of a larger church. They secure a pastor or select a leader from their own number and continue their worship in a place where their notions are not in conflict with other influences. Most frequently a minister formerly in the South has come with or followed his migrant members and has reestablished his church in Chicago. Or again a group with religious beliefs and ceremonies not in accord with those of established churches may establish a church of its own. The groups are usually so small and the members so poor as to make the purchase of a building impossible. The custom has been to engage a small store and put chairs in it. Hence the name "store-front" church.

4. Social and Civic Agencies

Social agencies in the Negro communities are an expressin of group effort to adjust itself to the larger community. Within the Negro community there are two types, those especially for Negroes and those which are branches of the agencies of the larger community but located conveniently for use by Negroes.

Agencies Especially For Negroes

Chicago Urban League. This organization is one of the thirty-two branches of the National Urban League whose headquarters are in New York City. It was established in Chicago in 1917 during the period of heaviest migration of Negroes to the city. The numerous problems consequent upon this influx guided the development of the League's activities. Its executive board and officers are whites and Negroes of high standing and influence in both the white and Negro groups, and it is supported by voluntary subscriptions. Within four years this organization has taken the leading place among all the social agencies working especially among Negroes. It has a well-trained staff of twelve paid workers, and its work is carried out along the lines accepted in modern social work. The League has organized its activities as follows: Administration Department, Industrial Department, Research and Records Department, Children's Department, settlement work. . . .

Wabash Avenue Y.M.C.A. This organizatio nis a branch of the local Young Men's Christian Association, but because of its location and the peculiar social problems of its membership and vicinity, it has become one of the strongest agencies of the community. Its work is among boys and young men, many of whom are industrial workers in various plants. Community work is vigorously promoted. In 1920 an enthusiastic group of 1,137 boys was enlisted in a neighborhood clean-up campaign,

and 100 community gardens were put in operation. Moving pictures and community singing were provided during the summer months. . . .

In addition to the foregoing work this institution has promoted efficiency and industrial clubs among Negro workers in industrial plants, three glee clubs, noonday recreational programs, and nine baseball teams.

Chicago Branch of the National Association for the Advancement of Colored People. This organization aims to carry out the general policies of the National Association as far as they apply to Chicago. The national purpose is to combat injustice against Negroes, stamp out race discriminations, prevent lynchings, burnings, and torturings of Negroes, and, when they do occur, to demand the prosecution of those responsible, to assure to every citizen of color the common rights of an American citizen, and secure for colored children equal opportunity in public-school education.

In Chicago, the principal efforts of this organization have been in the line of securing justice for Negroes in the courts and opposing race discriminations in public accommodations. Its most active period followed the riots of 1919. With a number of competent attorneys, white and Negro, it gave legal support to Negro riot victims and followed through the courts the cases of many Negroes accused of participation in rioting. . . .

DOCUMENT 32.3
Negro Literature for Negro Pupils

Alice Dunbar-Nelson (1875–1935)—poet, journalist, educator, politician—makes an

Source: Alice Dunbar-Nelson, "Negro Literature for Negro Pupils," *Southern Workman*, LI (February 1922), pp. 59–63. Courtesy of Hampton University Archives.

argument for an education geared to the specific needs of Negro students. Her concern here is how best to organize an oppressed minority to make an impact on the society as a whole.

The ancient Greeks, wishing to impress upon their children the greatness of Hellas, made the schoolboys memorize Homer, particularly those passages dealing with wars and conquests. The Romans saturated their youth with Roman literature, history, and law. The Hebrew children of all ages are versed, grounded, and crammed with the Mosaic and Rabbinical law. The Chinese child learns volumes of Confucius. The French child recites La Fontaine, even before he can read. Spain drives home the epic of the Cid to the youth of her land— and so on, through all history, ancient and modern; each land, each nation, impresses most painstakingly upon the rising generation the fact that it possesses a history and a literature, and that it must live up to the traditions of its history, and make that literature a part of its life.

The reason for this is obvious. If a people are to be proud and self-respecting they must believe in themselves. Destroy a man's belief in his own powers, and you destroy his usefulness—render him a worthless object, helpless and hopeless. Tell a people over and over again that they have done nothing, can do nothing, set a limitation for their achievement; impress upon them that all they have or can hope to have is the product of the minds of other peoples; force them to believe that they are pensioners on the mental bounty of another race,— and they will lose what little faith they may have had in themselves, and become stultified non-producers. Any parent or teacher knows how disastrous is the result of telling a child how splendidly some other child has done, and asking why he does not go and do likewise. The one so adjured usually does the exact opposite, in a bitterness of resentment and gloom,

it being one of the vagaries of human nature to act contrariwise.

All this is by way of reminding ourselves that for two generations we have given brown and black children a blonde ideal of beauty to worship, a milk-white literature to assimilate, and a pearly Paradise to anticipate, in which their dark faces would be hopelessly out of place. That there has not been a complete and absolute stultification of the efforts of the race toward self-expression is due only to the fact that we are a people of peculiar resiliency and combativeness. The effect of this kind of teaching is shown in the facts that the beautiful brown dolls, which resemble their tiny playmothers, still have some difficulty in making their way into the homes of our people; that some older religionists still fondly hope that at death, and before St. Peter admits them into Paradise, they will be washed physically white; that Negro business enterprises are still regarded with a doubtful eye; and that Negro literature is frequently mentioned in whispers as a dubious quantity.

There is a manifest remedy for this condition, a remedy which the teachers of the race are applying gradually, wherever the need has been brought to their attention. We must begin everywhere to instill race pride into our pupils; not by dull statistics, nor yet by tedious iterations that we are a great people, and "if you do not believe it, look at this table of figures, or at the life of so-and-so." Idle boasting of past achievements always leaves a suspicion in the mind of the listener that the braggart is not sure of his ground and is bolstering up his opinion of himself. But we will give the children the poems and stories and folk lore and songs of their own people. We do not teach literature; we are taught by literature. The subtlest, most delicate, and lasting impression of childhood are those gained by the chance poem, the eagerly absorbed fable, the lesson in the reader, the story told in the Sunday-school lesson. The fairy prince and the delectable princess have their charm, as opening up a vista into an enchanted land, but the poem that touches closely the heart of a child, and belongs to it because of its very nearness to his own life, is the bit of literature that lifts him above the dull brown earth and makes him akin to all that is truly great in the universe.

*   *   *   *   *

Every teacher in a colored school is a missionary. More than the mere instilling of so much knowledge in the heads of the pupils must he or she teach many other things, character through pride of race being one of the greatest. For the youth who is proud of his race and will endeavor to live up to its traditions, and will hesitate to do mean things lest they sully the escutcheon. As we have said before, the sentiment of pride and honor fostered in the Negro youth will fire his ambition, his desire to accomplish, even as others of his race have done before him. It is only the exceptional case, the overmastering genius who is thrilled with the desire to conquer because no other has done so. The ordinary one—and there are so many more of him than there are of any other kind—needs encouragement from the deeds of others.

But statistics mean nothing to children; they are colorless things, savoring too much of tables in arithmetic to be deeply intriguing. The child mind must have concrete examples, for it is essentially poetic and deals in images. It is not enough to say that black men fought in the Revolutionary War to the extent of so many in so many regiments. But there are a number of well-told, crisply narrated stories of Crispus Attucks, and even some narrative poems celebrate the first blood shed in the Revolutionary War. It is not enough to say that black slaves, from Massachusetts to Maryland, stood by the Nation when red-coated Tories overran the land. Dunbar's spirited ballad of "Black Samson of Brandywine" will fix the idea in the youthful mind, even as "Paul Revere's Ride" has fixed the date of the battle of Concord and Lexington in the minds of generations of young Americans, white and black, from Maine to California.

It is well for Negro children to know that the delightful fables of Æsop are the satires of a black slave, and that the author of the incomparable "Three Musketeers," which rejoices the swashbuckling instincts of the adolescent, was of Negro descent. There are exquisite little nature lyrics, particularly snow scenes, by Pushkin (obtainable in translation) as perfect in their picturization, in a way, as those of Bryant, or that of Lowell's "First Snowfall"; and it would make the young chests swell with pride to know that these are the work of one of the greatest of Russian poets—an acknowledged Negro.

Apart from these exotic instances, the children might well be taught the folk tales of the race, as rich in content and moral lesson as can be found in any folk tales, from Æsop and Reynard the Fox to Uncle Remus. There is a mine of suggestion in Alphonso Stafford's "African Folk Stories." That classic, "The Seedling," by Dunbar, has delighted the little folks of a generation, with its botanical lesson encouched in delicate verse, and the inevitable moral admonition, which all children secretly love, at the end.

By the side of Maggie Tulliver we may place Zora, of "The Quest of the Silver Fleece (DuBois)"; against Spartacus and his address to the gladiators, is Dessalines and his defiant reminiscences; thrilling rescue stories might be matched by the rescue of the lad in Durham's "Diane"; or by the round-up scene from "The Love of Landry" (Dunbar), to give the proper Western flavor to the boy or girl in love with the Bill Hart type. In company with "The Charge of the Light Brigade" is the "Second Louisiana," and the "Finish of Patsy Barnes" (Dunbar), for those who love the small boy who overcomes obstacles for the sake of the mother ill at home. Thanksgiving is commemorated by Braithwaite as delightfully as ever Stevenson "gave thanks for many things" not to mention "Christmas," by Dunbar, or similar poems by those others who have followed in his tread.

And the winged words of Booker Washington and Frederick Douglass! The biographies of those who have accomplished great things in the face of heavy odds! Romances of lives as thrilling as the romances which have grown up around Lincoln and Daniel Boone! The girl, Phyllis, and the lad, Paul! How much finer for the Negro boy and girl to know of these lives, and of the work they did; to read the burning, living words that are the work of their own blood and kin; to feel that the lowly ones of the cabins in the country, or the tenements and alleys in the city, may yet give to the world some gift, albeit small, that will inspire and ennoble countless dark-faced children struggling up towards the light.

Assuredly we will teach our boys and girls, not only their own history and literature, but works by their own authors. We will, ourselves, first achieve a sense of pride in our own productions, with a fine sense of literary values which will not allow us to confuse trivialities and trash with literature. We will learn to judge a thing as good, because of its intrinsic value and not because it is a Negro's! We will be as quick to throw away valueless stuff written by a black man or woman, as if it were written by a white man or woman. In other words we will recognize but one absolute standard, and we will preserve for our children all that approximates that standard, and teach them to reverence the good that is in their own because it is good.

And by so doing, we shall impress most deeply upon the young people of our race, by our own literature, that most valuable of all lessons:—

Be proud, my race, in mind and soul:
Thy name is writ on glory's scroll
   In characters of fire;
High, midst the clouds of Fame's bright sky,
Thy banner's blazoned folds now fly,
   And Truth shall lift them higher.

DOCUMENT 32.4
From Self-Pity to Self-Respect

This excerpt from a pamphlet written by Martin Luther King, Jr., in 1956 is one of his first published statements explaining his philosophy of nonviolent resistance.

OUR STRUGGLE

The segregation of Negroes, with its inevitable discrimination, has thrived on elements of inferiority present in the masses of both white and Negro people. Through forced separation from our African culture, through slavery, poverty, and deprivation, many black men lost self-respect.

In their relations with Negroes, white people discovered that they had rejected the very center of their own ethical professions. They could not face the triumph of their lesser instincts and simultaneously have peace within. And so, to gain it, they rationalized—insisting that the unfortunate Negro, being less than human, deserved and even enjoyed second class status.

They argued that his inferior social, economic and political position was good for him. He was incapable of advancing beyond a fixed position and would therefore be happier if encouraged not to attempt the impossible. He is subjugated by a superior people with an advanced way of life. The "master race" will

---

Source: Martin Luther King, Jr., *Our Struggle: The Story of Montgomery* (New York: Congress of Racial Equality, 1956).

be able to civilize him to a limited degree, if only he will be true to his inferior nature and stay in his place.

White men soon came to forget that the Southern social culture and all its institutions had been organized to perpetuate this rationalization. They observed a caste system and quickly were conditioned to believe that its social results, which they had created, actually reflected the Negro's innate and true nature.

In time many Negroes lost faith in themselves and came to believe that perhaps they really were what they had been told they were— something less than men. So long as they were prepared to accept this role, racial peace could be maintained. It was an uneasy peace in which the Negro was forced to accept patiently injustice, insult, injury and exploitation.

Gradually the Negro masses in the South began to re-evaluate themselves—a process that was to change the nature of the Negro community and doom the social patterns of the South. We discovered that we had never really smothered our self-respect and that we could not be at one with ourselves without asserting it. From this point on, the South's terrible peace was rapidly undermined by the Negro's new and courageous thinking and his ever-increasing readiness to organize and to act. Conflict and violence were coming to the surface as the white South desperately clung to its old patterns. The extreme tension in race relations in the South today is explained in part by the revolutionary change in the Negro's evaluation of himself and of his destiny and by his determination to struggle for justice. *We Negroes have replaced self-pity with self-respect and self-depreciation with dignity.*

When Mrs. Rosa Parks, the quiet seamstress whose arrest precipitated the non-violent protest in Montgomery, was asked why she had refused to move to the rear of a bus, she said: "It was a matter of dignity; I could not have faced myself and my people if I had moved."

Many of the Negroes who joined the protest did not expect it to succeed. When asked why, they usually gave one of three answers: "I didn't expect Negroes to stick to it," or, "I never thought we Negroes had the nerve," or, "I thought the pressure from the white folks would kill it before it got started."

In other words, our non-violent protest in Montgomery is important because it is demonstrating to the Negro, North and South, that many of the stereotypes he has held about himself and other Negroes are not valid. Montgomery has broken the spell and is ushering in concrete manifestations of the thinking and action of the new Negro.

We now know that:

We can stick together. In Montgomery, 42,000 of us have refused to ride the city's segregated buses since December 5. Some walk as many as fourteen miles a day.

Our leaders do not have to sell out. Many of us have been indicted, arrested, and "mugged." Every Monday and Thursday night we stand before the Negro population at the prayer meetings and repeat: "It is an honor to face jail for a just cause."

Threats and violence do not necessarily intimidate those who are sufficiently aroused and non-violent. The bombing of two of our homes has made us more resolute. When a handbill was circulated at a White Citizens Council meeting stating that Negroes should be "abolished" by "guns, bows and arrows, sling shots and knives," we responded with even greater determination.

Our church is becoming militant. Twenty-four ministers were arrested in Montgomery. Each has said publicly that he stands prepared to be arrested again. Even upper-class Negroes who reject the "come to Jesus" gospel are now convinced that the church has no alternative but to provide the non-violent dynamics for social change in the midst of conflict. The $30,000 used for the car pool, which transports over 20,000 Negro workers, school children and housewives, has been raised in the churches. The churches have become the dispatch centers where the people gather to wait for rides.

We believe in ourselves. In Montgomery we walk in a new way. We hold our heads in a new way. Even the Negro reporters who converged on Montgomery have a new attitude. One tired reporter, asked at a luncheon in Birmingham to say a few words about Montgomery, stood up, thought for a moment, and uttered one sentence: "Montgomery has made me proud to be a Negro."

Economics is part of our struggle. We are aware that Montgomery's white businessmen have tried to "talk sense" to the bus company and the city commissioners. We have observed that small Negro shops are thriving as Negroes find it incovenient to walk downtown to the white stores. We have been getting more polite treatment in the white shops since the protest began. We have a new respect for the proper use of our dollar.

We have discovered a new and powerful weapon—non-violent resistance. Although law is an important factor in bringing about social change, there are certain conditions in which the very effort to adhere to new legal decisions creates tension and provokes violence. We had hoped to see demonstrated a method that would enable us to continue our struggle while coping with the violence it aroused. Now we see the answer: face violence if necessary, but refuse to return violence. If we respect those who oppose us, they may achieve a new understanding of the human relations involved.

We now know that the Southern Negro has come of age, politically and morally. Montgomery has demonstrated that we will not run from the struggle, and will support the battle for equality. The attitude of many young Negroes a few years ago was reflected in the common expression, "I'd rather be a lamp post in Harlem than Governor of Alabama." Now the idea expressed in our churches, schools,

pool rooms, restaurants and homes is: "Brother, stay here and fight non-violently. 'Cause if you don't let them make you mad, you can win." The official slogan of the Montgomery Improvement Association is "Justice without Violence."

DOCUMENT 32.5
The Chicago Freedom Movement

This "program" is just one of numerous examples of how the philosophy of nonviolent resistance was adapted to the situation of urban ghettos outside of the South. Note the shift to an emphasis on the need for political and social power.

The Chicago Freedom Movement is a coalition of forces for the purpose of wiping out slums, ghettoes and racism. Its core is formed by the unity of the Southern Christian Leadership Conference (S.C.L.C.) and the Coordinating Council of Community Organizations (C.C.C.O.). S.C.L.C., operating under the leadership of Dr. Martin Luther King, Jr., was invited to Chicago by C.C.C.O. because of its dynamic work in the South. C.C.C.O. is a coalition of thirty-six (36) Chicago civil-rights and Negro community organizations. Cooperating with the Chicago Freedom Movement are a number of religious organizations, social agencies, neighborhood groups and individuals of good will.

Many groups in the Chicago region share with Negroes common problems of slum housing, welfare dependency, inferior education, police brutality, and color discrimination. Puerto Rican and Mexican Chicagoans are becoming increasingly vocal about these problems, and the Freedom Movement is seeking ways to join in a united effort with its Latin American brothers. Therefore, the Freedom

---

Source: "Program of the Chicago Freedom Movement," July 1966. Mimeographed, no imprint (1966).

Movement is making many proposals that provide for the improvement and upgrading of conditions of Latin Americans, other non-whites and some white minorities.

The Freedom Movement proposals and demands are designed to set the broad guidelines for a just and open city in which all men can live with dignity. Three interrelated goals set forth the direction to such a society:

1. To bring about equality of opportunity and of results.
2. To open up the major areas of metropolitan life of housing, employment, and education.
3. To provide power for the powerless.

Many will affirm these goals and wish that they could be achieved. But very little will happen unless Negroes, Latin Americans, other oppressed minorities and their white friends join hands and organize to bring about change—for power does not yield to pleading.

The Freedom Movement will achieve its goals through the organization of a non-violent movement which provides the power to participate in the decisions which now subjugates rather than elevates, which suppresses man's humanity rather than expresses it.

In order to generate the necessary power the movement will:

1. Organize a series of direct actions which will make the injustices so clear that the whole community will respond to the need to change.
2. Organize people in every sector of the ghettoes—in neighborhoods, in schools, in welfare unions, in public housing, in hospitals, to give the strength of numbers to the demands for change.
3. Strengthen the institutions which contribute to the goals of a just and open society and withdraw support from those institutions—banks, businesses, newspapers and professions—which drain the resources of the ghetto communities without contributing in return.

4. Demand representation of the organizations of the ghetto community (Chicago Freedom Movement) on decision-making bodies at every level of government, industry, labor, and church, affecting the lives of people in the ghetto.
5. Promote political education and participation so that the needs and aspirations of Negroes and other oppressed minorities are fully represented.

The Chicago Freedom Movement and its constituent organizations use many means to bring about change. Community organization, education, research, job development, legal redress and political education are all weapons in the arsenal of the Movement. But, its most distinctive and creative tool is that of non-violent direct action.

DOCUMENT 32.6
Statement by Stokely Carmichael

Stokely Carmichael (1941–   ) then chairman of the Student Nonviolent Coordinating Committee (SNCC), offers one of many attempts to define black power. *SNCC's use of the term in the summer of 1966 brought it to national and international prominence.*

The goal of our (SNCC's) programme is indeed "black power." What does this mean? It means, for example, that in Lowndes County if a Negro is elected tax assessor, he will be able to collect and channel funds for the building of better roads and schools—things which determine the quality of daily life. If elected

Source: The Radical Education Project, *Black Power SNCC Speaks for Itself: A Collection of Interviews and Statements* (Ann Arbor: The Radical Education Project, n.d.).

sheriff, he can end police brutality. It means, ultimately, the freeing of colonies—which is what the ghettos of this country, North and South, really are. If, for example, the Negroes of Watts had organized their political power, Los Angeles Police Chief Parker might not remain in office today.

SNCC will therefore be working for freedom through the acquisition of economic and political power on the local level. We will encourage black people to use their majority where it exists, as other Americans use theirs, to exercise control of local government. Such power bases can then work to change statewide or nationwide patterns of oppression through negotiation—from strength, rather than weakness. Negroes cannot form alliances with the white community until they have that strength, and until there are white groups with which Negroes *can* coalesce.

As we work toward organizing black power, we intend also to help build a base of poor whites—not moderates but militants—with whom poor Negroes may eventually combine their strength. This is the form of coalition we can accept.

We have also found that the power of black people as a group force cannot be developed as long as they are fearful and believe, consciously or unconsciously, that they are inferior. We must change the attitude expressed by a Wilcox County, Ala., Negro who voted for the white sheriff on May 3, saying, "We aren't ready to have a coloured sheriff. The white folks wouldn't have liked that a bit."

We are therefore encouraging the developing of 'black consciousness': pride in black history, culture, institutions, as other ethnic groups have developed cultural awareness and pride. In the light of all this, it should be clear why we believe black organizers can organize best in the black community. It should also be remembered that what attracted Southern students to SNCC in the first place was that nowhere else in the society could they participate in some-

thing with social significance not dominated by whites. The phrase 'something of our own' represents a feeling which brings with it commitment, energy, creativity.

None of our thinking about black power is basically new to SNCC. Nor has "pro-black" ever meant "anti-white"—unless whites choose to make it so.

The heart of our present programme, in short, is our belief that the key to basic change is power and it must be the power of group strength—as every oppressed people in history has learned. The Black Belt of America, which extends from the Southern U.S. to Brazil, has been the home of an absolutely powerless black mass for nearly two centuries. In Africa today, millions remain powerless because they are black and because they are property-less. Black people in this country must use their weight, their majority power where it exists, to voice the needs of black people wherever they are. We understand that Lowndes County cannot be free independently of black people everywhere, for the struggle is one of a people.

DOCUMENT 32.7
We Still Have a Dream: The Rainbow Coalition's New Direction for America

The Reverend Jesse L. Jackson's (1941–   ) run for the Democratic nomination for U.S. president in 1984 and the issues set forth in his speech to the National Conference of Black Mayors indicate both how far Black Americans have come, and how much farther Afro-Americans and the nation have to go.

. . . Sometimes we do not really know what we can do or what we have done because others

Source: Reverend Jesse L. Jackson, "Speech before the National Conference of Black Mayors," Hartford, Connecticut, April 19, 1985.

are so busy telling us what we can't do. We won 85 percent of the black votes cast last year in the Democratic primaries but that was only 60 percent of our 3.5 million votes. Twenty-one percent of our vote was white, 10 percent was Hispanic, and that last 9 percent was Asian-Americans, Native Americans, and Arab-Americans, who we proved had a right to participate in the political process like everyone else. We have begun to move the party and the country towards jobs, peace and justice in a new and fundamental way.

What do I mean by that? I mean that when we started the experts told us that we would be lucky to win 100 delegates, 150 tops. Well we ended up with 465 delegates at the convention in San Francisco, and if we had received our fair share of delegates in proportion to the popular vote which we won, a new study concludes that we were robbed of 400 delegates. Mondale admits that he won fairly with unfair rules. In a system where the delegate votes were proportioned fairly, Mondale would have been 400 short, Hart would have remained basically the same, 300 short, and the Rainbow would have had the determining votes. That is why this conference should go on record giving its unequivocal support to the Fairness Commission.

The Rainbow experiment worked—and continues to grow.

A new direction is what the Rainbow campaign stood for last year, and it is what the Rainbow coalition stands for this year. We stand by our dream to redirect the nation to new and humane priorities. That was our agenda yesterday. It is our agenda today.

Last week *The New York Times* showed a picture of Reagan, Bush, Schlesinger, Kirkpatrick, and Brzenski lobbying together for aid to the contras. Top Democrats and Republicans one party: two names. This entity has no meaning to Progressives. Kennedy code word: "New Center"; Hart code word "New Patriotism"; Kirk code word "Anti-Caucus" (which applies to blacks only so far); Gov. Babbitt's code word "Anti-Caucus-Caucus." These code words are reactionary symbols and signals that have no meaning for the dispossessed of our nation. The Rainbow code word must be "Humane Priorities." That is a signal that we care for everybody and that there is room for everybody in the distribution of goods and services in this nation.

In brief, the Rainbow was born last year.— As it matures in its next phase, our priorities surely appeal to black mayors and mayors who care for all of the American people everywhere.

Let me share with you now the Rainbow program for the future. It is an agenda [in] which black mayors need to play a key leadership role.

1. The Rainbow Campaign '84 will become the Rainbow Organization '85. We shall focus on expanding the 61 districts we won; increasing voter registration; and establishing a Rainbow *PAC* to help finance critical campaigns and significant mayors like Mayor Milner, Mayor Washington, Mayor Hatcher, and former Mayor Stokes, who have had to run without Democratic party support.

2. South African Divestment. We are calling upon all mayors to seek ordinances in their cities which will prohibit the use of pension funds or any public funds to corporations that do business with South Africa. We say that everyone who was opposed to the Third Reich in '45 must be opposed to the Fourth Reich in '85. We must measure human rights by one yardstick.

3. The New Economic Justice Coalition. We are calling for a partnership between farmers, governors and urban mayors to bring the producers and the consumers together. I have just concluded an agreement between Governor Rudy Perpich of Minnesota and Mayor Donald Frazier of Minneapolis, that will bring together the people who need the food and the people who grow it. We need to expand this coalition throughout the country. The hungry need the farmers—and the farmers need the hungry.

4. Nuclear Free Zones. We must choose the human race over the nuclear race. None of our planning for the future, no hopes for our children can be realized if there is a nuclear holocaust. Therefore, we urge all black mayors to make their cities the safest places in America by declaring them nuclear free zones. . . . The money needed in the cities is going into weapons designed to destroy the human race.

5. Development Zones. We must rebuild our cities. We must create development zones in which there's a partnership between the workers, the community and the public and private sectors. The key is an economic magnet with investment incentives not just tax incentives. An equal partnership characterized by parity. Banks must be encouraged by government money and insurance policies to make low interest and interest-free loans. We must plan the remodeling of our cities and create job training for community residents so they can participate in the rebuilding and reach out to our colleges to attract our young people to contribute their skills in the redevelopment of our cities.

6. African Hunger Holocaust. The problem of hunger in Africa cannot be solved solely by the money it requires, as do most problems. We urge the mayors to adopt an Ethiopian village as a sister city project. We need to arrange to send some of our citizens over to Africa to see for themselves what is going on and help Africa get back on its feet.

7. Voting Rights Enforcement and the Elimination of Voting Dilution Schemes. Voter registration in the absence of voting rights enforcement is a sham. Ten years after the Voting Rights Act in the 10 states from Virginia to Texas where 53 percent of the nation's black

population resides, there is exactly one black congressman out of 115. Are we to believe that it is because we have bad breath? The fact is that gerrymandering, annexation, at-large elections and other schemes render our vote, and also that of our Hispanic brothers and sisters, only marginally effective. An absolute key to political empowerment, therefore, is having the Voting Rights Act enforced, having district lines drawn in fair and equitable ways so that our votes count and our voices are heard. We lost the MX missile vote by the margin of disenfranchised blacks in the South.

8. Affirmative Action. Based on the Memphis Supreme Court decision the Reagan Justice Department is trying to turn back the cloak on race realtions by overturning affirmative action plans in 56 cities, counties and states. This national policy must be challenged and defeated.

9. Human Rights Must Be the Litmus Test of American Foreign Policy. African, Asian and Middle East Policy is key to our future as a nation—because these continents constitutes three fourths of the human race.

10. Spiritual Regeneration. The level of dope and alcohol abuse among our youth in schools and in the military is a threat to our social development and national security. Therefore, spiritual regeneration based on moral authority must be a key part of our political agenda because the character of our people will determine our ability to change the course of our nation and our world toward justice and peace.

We have the character and the capacity if we manifest the *will* to lead the Democratic party and this democratic republic to heights hitherto unknown—keep the faith and let nothing/nobody break your spirit!

chapter

The War in Vietnam

Lawrence S. Wittner
State University of New York, Albany

In the spring of 1975 when the United States lost the war in Vietnam, it highlighted some curious ironies. A small, impoverished peasant society had frustrated the world's mightiest military-industrial power. A thirty-years' war to crush Vietnamese communism ended with remarkably little support from the American people. And strangest of all (although rarely commented upon), the successful Vietnamese revolutionaries and the U.S. government had once cooperated closely.

During World War II, when the Japanese invaders of Indochina enjoyed the close cooperation of French colonial officials, Americans gravitated naturally toward support of the region's only effective resistance movement, the Viet Minh. Formed by Vietnamese revolutionaries, the Viet Minh emerged in wartime under the leadership of a remarkable Vietnamese nationalist named Ho Chi Minh—sailor, waiter, poet, and veteran Communist. In the summer of 1945, the first contingent from America's wartime intelligence agency, the Office of Strategic Services (OSS), arrived in Vietnam, and was greatly impressed by the rebel underground's courage, selflessness, and popularity. Considering Ho a "true patriot" and a valuable part of the war effort, the Americans arranged for shipments of arms to the Viet Minh, helped to train Ho's troops, and relayed his appeals

for independence to the Free French. By August, the Viet Minh had wrested all of Vietnam from Japanese control, prompting massive victory celebrations throughout the country. "The reception was fantastic," an OSS officer reported. "The people seemed to genuinely love Ho." Ho, in turn, seemed to admire equally his American patrons. For a new crop of French officials, arriving to reimpose their colonial authority, the situation appeared ominous. Charles de Gaulle's representative warned: "We are faced with a joint maneuver . . . to oust the French from Indochina."

But American-Vietnamese relations soon deteriorated. Although President Franklin Roosevelt had told his advisers that Indochina "should never be simply handed back to the French to be milked by their imperialists," American policy shifted under his successor, Harry Truman. Only a week after Japan's surrender, Truman assured de Gaulle that the United States would not interfere with any French reconquest of Indochina. Indeed, Truman found not only the ships and uniforms for a 70,000-man French expeditionary force, but agreed to sell the French $160 million in war equipment. Thus, despite Ho's continued appeals for American assistance, the U.S. government ultimately threw in its lot with the French.

The reversal of American policy toward Indochina reflected not only the differing perspectives of Roosevelt and Truman, but the overall shift in foreign policy from World War to cold war. With communism increasingly perceived as the great enemy of the nation's ambitions in the world, American policymakers viewed the prospect of a Viet Minh success with apprehension. Their anxiety was heightened after Mao Tse-tung's triumph in China. A National Security Council memorandum of February 1950 contended that the United States should take "all practical measures . . . to prevent further communist expansion in Southeast Asia." Several months later, American policymakers agreed upon a program of direct military and economic aid to the French war effort in Indochina. Thanks to these decisions, the United States was soon funding 80 percent of the war's costs.

By 1954, the French were on the verge of defeat. That spring, with the Viet Minh closing in on a major French force at Dien Bien Phu, Paris placed a frantic call to Washington for help. In response, Secretary of State John Foster Dulles, Vice President Richard Nixon, and the Joint Chiefs of Staff pressed for American intervention. But President Dwight Eisenhower rejected their proposals; he was impressed by the caution of congressional leaders, the unwillingness of American allies to participate, and the stubborn insistence of the French upon their imperial prerogatives. As a result, the French war in Vietnam collapsed, and in June an Indochina Peace Conference convened at Geneva.

The 1954 Geneva conference reached a settlement which most delegates could agree on, albeit with reservations. But it was completely unacceptable to the United States. Granting independence to Vietnam, Laos, and Cambodia, the agreement provided that Vietnam would be temporarily divided at the 17th parallel to allow for French withdrawal and national elections. Significantly, it noted that this division was "provisional" and did not constitute

"a political or territorial boundary." Pending reunification, neither zone was to make foreign military alliances or allow foreign military bases upon its soil. Reviewing the Geneva accords, the National Security Council termed them a "disaster" that "completed a major forward stride of Communism which may lead to the loss of Southeast Asia." Consequently, the U.S. government refused to sign the accords and, indeed, moved quickly to subvert them. On August 20, President Eisenhower approved a program to support the premier of France's South Vietnamese puppet state, Ngo Dinh Diem (installed in June at Dulle's behest), while "encouraging" Diem to broaden his regime and strengthen his armed forces.

With American backing, Diem consolidated a personal dictatorship in South Vietnam, incarcerating as many as 100,000 suspected opponents in concentration camps. Meanwhile, American advisers organized Diem's police, armed forces, educational system, and government administration. By 1958, the United States had assumed virtually the entire cost of South Vietnam's government. Secretary of Defense Robert McNamara later observed that "only the U.S. after 1954 held the South together . . . and enabled Diem to refuse to go through with the . . . nationwide 'free' elections." Many in Vietnam, of course, were not pleased with this turn of events. Sporadic uprisings, often non-Communist, took place in the south, although the North Vietnamese, still seeking the implementation of the Geneva accords, withheld their approval. Finally, however, in December 1960, Hanoi sent its blessings to the insurgents, who organized themselves into the National Liberation Front (NLF).

When John F. Kennedy entered the White House in 1961, the NLF was making considerable progress, drawing upon thousands of South Vietnamese and smaller numbers of southerners returning from the north. With his top advisers urging an expanded military commitment,

Kennedy acted in May, secretly ordering hundreds of Green Berets and military advisers to South Vietnam, a buildup of Saigon's armed forces, "sabotage and light harassment" of North Vietnam, and planning for the dispatch of large numbers of American combat forces. As of October 1963, Kennedy had sent 16,732 American military personnel to South Vietnam. Described as "advisers," they were in reality piloting helicopters on combat support operations, superintending population removal programs, flying aircraft on surveillance and reconnaissance missions, and directing military action against North Vietnam. In September 1963, the president was asked on television if he had any doubts about the "domino theory," popularized by his predecessor. "No, I believe it," he remarked. "If South Vietnam went, it . . . would give the impression that the wave of the future in Southeast Asia was China and the Communists. So I believe it."

The Vietnamese, however, remained stubbornly independent. Despite the impressive "kill ratios" and "body counts" cited by American military authorities, Diem's opponents grew bolder. In the spring and summer of 1963, South Vietnam's secret police—directed by Diem's brother-in-law and trained and financed by the American Central Intelligence Agency—clashed repeatedly with thousands of demonstrating Buddhists, many of them priests, monks, and nuns. Some immolated themselves in protest. Meanwhile, a group of South Vietnamese generals sought U.S. authorization for a coup. Embarrassed by Diem's police state tactics and frightened by the disintegration of South Vietnam, the Kennedy administration gave its approval. In November, the generals made their move, overturning the government and, unexpectedly, killing Diem as well.

Kennedy himself was assassinated shortly thereafter, but the sudden deaths of the two "free world" leaders did little to alter the interventionist course of American foreign policy.

When Ambassador Henry Cabot Lodge, Jr., met with the new president, Lyndon Johnson, shortly after Kennedy's death, Johnson assured him: "I am not going to lose South Vietnam." Other Kennedy carryovers agreed. "It is on this spot that we have to break the liberation war," Walt Rostow insisted. "If we don't break it here we shall have to face it again in Thailand, Venezuela, elsewhere. Vietnam is a clear testing ground for our policy in the world." Starting in early 1964, the administration increased the level of covert operations against North Vietnam while planning to obtain a congressional resolution that would sanction further U.S. military escalation. Yet obtaining a legislative blank check was a tricky business near election time, particularly with Johnson campaigning as a "peace candidate," pledged not to use American troops in the war or to bomb North Vietnam. The administration's opportunity, however, came in early August 1964, when two American destroyers off the Gulf of Tonkin claimed to have been fired upon by North Vietnamese torpedo boats. Although there seemed little logic or evidence for such an attack, the president seized upon the incident to push through Congress the support resolution he had been carrying in his pocket for weeks. Thereafter, as Johnson swept to a landslide victory over Barry Goldwater, government officials made secret plans for extending the war.

In early 1965, as the American public waited expectantly for the "Great Society" to unfold, the administration launched its program of military escalation. The United States Air Force began three years of steadily heightening bombing raids over North Vietnam. At the same time, the president dramatically increased the bombing of the south, designating vast areas as "free fire zones" in which Americans were authorized to kill anything that moved. While the bombing had little strategic value, American policymakers insisted it would "break the will" of the Vietnamese insurgents. More crucial to the success of American power was the dispatch of large numbers of combat troops. By 1968, there were 535,000 American soldiers in Vietnam, engaging in vast "search and destroy" operations. In the countryside, U.S. officials experimented with a new village "pacification" program, combining the assassination of thousands of suspect individuals with plans for material improvements in the lives of the peasants. Few villages, of course, could withstand the fierce hail of American bombs, napalm, white phosphorous, and antipersonnel weapons. Nevertheless, Washington's policymakers took heart at the depopulation of the countryside, since it deprived the insurgents of their traditional rural support while forcing millions of refugees into those small areas under Saigon's control.

Johnson's escalation of the conflict in 1965 made it clear that rather than merely "aiding" and "advising" the Saigon government, the United States was fighting a war; and, moreover, a war which a growing minority of Americans considered unjust, immoral, unconstitutional, or merely senseless. Almost immediately, antiwar speeches, sit-ins and picketing erupted across the country. On college campuses, massive "teach-ins" provided the first effective forum for critics of the war, galvanizing students and faculty into an active force for peace. Naturally, draft call-ups gave young people a particularly immediate relationship to the conflict, and many responded by burning their draft cards, refusing induction, or holding sit-ins at Selective Service centers. From the cotton fields of the South to the black ghettos of the North, civil rights activists condemned a war policy which they believed would doom the chances for social justice at home. Violent upheavals convulsed the nation's ghettos, expressing the growing despair of the black community. At the same time, thousands of Americans took part in peace demonstrations, which grew rapidly in size and intensity. In April 1965, Students for a Democratic Society (SDS) sponsored the largest antiwar gathering in Washington's history, drawing 20,000 people. By 1967, mammoth peace demonstrations occurred all across the country; in New York City alone, 125,000 demonstrators surged through a driving rain.

President Johnson fared somewhat better in Congress, but here, too, his support steadily eroded. Senators Wayne Morse and Ernest Gruening had been the only congressional opponents of the Gulf of Tonkin resolution; but after the inception of the air war in early 1965, other senators crossed over into the ranks of the "doves": George McGovern, Frank Church, Eugene McCarthy, Gaylord Nelson, Stephen Young, Mike Mansfield, Vance Hartke, Robert Kennedy, and a handful of others. Most came from the Democratic party's northern liberal wing; the most prominent exception and perhaps the most powerful congressional critic of the war was J. William Fulbright of Arkansas, chairman of the Senate Foreign Relations Committee. Unlike the antiwar forces gathering strength across the nation, congressional doves avoided sharp attacks upon the war, preferring instead to question the efficacy of the bombing or to call for efforts to begin negotiations. Nevertheless, their dissent, coupled with the emergence of antiwar sentiment in the general populace, provided serious evidence that Johnson's much-prized political "consensus" was dissolving.

Yet the president could mobilize powerful forces in his behalf. Industry, the military, and the mass media usually gave the war unflinching support, as did most Republican and southern Democratic legislators. Moving rightward throughout the cold war era, many labor leaders enthusiastically endorsed Johnson's escalation of the war, and condemned peace demonstrators for encouraging "the enemy." Moreover, the administration leaned heavily upon the clandestine arm of government. Responding to Johnson's pressure, the CIA launched Operation Chaos, a massive espionage effort within the United States that entailed opening mail, burglarizing homes, soliciting information from college administrators or local police, wiretapping individuals, spying on dissenters, and infiltrating peace and civil rights groups. Under its Cointelpro program, the Federal Bureau of Investigation worked to disrupt and destroy dissident organizations. It broke up meetings, employed agent provocateurs, distributed false or scurrilous information, encouraged racial discord, dispatched fraudulent letters, convinced institutions to fire dissidents or to deny groups meeting places, and occasionally roughed up demonstrators. Eventually, CIA operations produced an index of 300,000 Americans, while FBI files bulged with information on more than a million. In addition, the Internal Revenue Service, the National Security Agency, and Military Intelligence engaged in political activities. By the fall of 1968, more Army counterintelligence agents were spying on protestors in the United States than were employed in any other operation throughout the world, including the Indochina War.

Despite the Johnson administration's commitment to contain insurgency abroad and at home, affairs were getting out of hand. In Vietnam, American military might wreaked unprecedented havoc and destruction, but did not seem capable of winning the war. At the end of January 1968, the National Liberation Front forces launched the momentous Tet offensive, capturing much of the countryside and even large cities, such as Hue, which they held for almost a month. In Saigon, the fighting reached the U.S. embassy. Declaring that the United States had "never been in a better relative position," General William Westmoreland promptly demanded—and was denied—another 206,000 American troops. And almost simultaneously, Johnson lost control of his party. In the fall of 1967, Senator Eugene McCarthy had begun a seemingly hopeless "peace campaign" to contest the president's renomination. Yet by early 1968, riding a crest of antiwar sentiment and drawing upon the ef-

forts of thousands of college students, the McCarthy bandwagon moved into high gear. That March, he stunned political experts by delivering a devastating setback to the president in the New Hampshire primary. Shortly thereafter, he scored a resounding victory over the president in Wisconsin. With Johnson's political weakness exposed, Robert Kennedy also entered the political fray. The administration's Vietnam policy was "bankrupt," Kennedy told cheering crowds. "At the end of it all there will be only more Americans killed" and "more thousands of Vietnamese slaughtered." On the night of March 31, Johnson appeared on television to announce a cutback in the bombing of North Vietnam and his own withdrawal from the presidential race.

Although the peace movement demonstrated the unpopularity of "Johnson's War," it lacked, as yet, the cohesion and breadth of commitment necessary to put an end to the conflict. Like all social movements, the antiwar struggle was waged by a dedicated minority, who needed allies within the broader, less-committed society. In 1968, college students were clearly in the vanguard, bolstered by clergy, intellectuals, civil rights leaders, and assorted radicals and reformers. Beyond their ranks, the movement's fervor noticeably diminished. Concerned primarily with their own struggle for social and political advancement, many black Americans remained relatively indifferent to the war. Indeed, a large proportion of American combat troops in Vietnam was black—a fact which did not escape the more critical appraisals of SNCC, CORE, and SCLC. Blue-collar workers played even less of a role in opposition to the war, although, interestingly, polls found them considerably less hawkish than often assumed. Trumpeted by the mass media, the much-vaunted "youth rebellion" was largely confined to college students. And even within student ranks—which, in general, tended to be dovish—opinions varied widely. At some of the nation's most prestigious colleges and universities, where antiwar sentiment flourished, demonstrators blocked military recruiting, drove Dow Chemical (manufacturer of napalm) and other war-tainted firms off the campus, and challenged numerous ROTC programs. At other educational institutions, however, the peace movement made more modest headway. Turning this heterogeneous constituency into a winning political coalition proved a difficult task, particularly because the unorthodox style of some elements (for example, students and blacks) offended the sensibilities of others, particularly blue-collar workers.

Moreover, the reins of power remained firmly in the hands of the warmakers. Johnson's speech of March 31 was not, in reality, a move toward peace. Instead, he hoped to pacify domestic critics and, thereby, gain time to continue the war. Also Vice President Hubert Humphrey took the field as Johnson's political surrogate. Although Humphrey did not win a single primary, his political fortunes were enhanced by the division—more personal than political—between the McCarthy and Kennedy forces. And when Kennedy finally surged to the fore after the party's California primary, an assassin's bullet suddenly ended his life and transformed the political race. Rallying the support of the party machines, the South, and the labor unions, Humphrey steamrollered through to a 1968 Democratic convention victory in Chicago.

Of course, by this time his victory was a hollow one. Thousands of embittered protesters had thronged the streets and the Chicago convention hall. Affirming his loyalty to the president's policies, Humphrey offered the disaffected nothing and endorsed the bloody repression dispensed by Mayor Richard Daley's Chicago police. Quite understandably, the spectacle of protesters, delegates and anyone else within range being savagely beaten by police, sharpened the polarization within the Democratic party and the nation. In big city ghettos, angry black militants preached urban guerrilla warfare. On college campuses, student radicals seized administration buildings, proclaiming their liberation by "the revolution." Other Americans, frightened by the growing dissension, flocked to the authoritarian call of Alabama Governor George Wallace. With the nation torn apart by the Vietnam War and its consequences, the real victor in 1968 was the Republican nominee, Richard Nixon, who promised disgruntled voters both "law and order" and a "secret plan" to end the war.

In reality, Nixon had no plan to end the war—only a program designed to confuse or defeat its critics. Balancing his hawkish foreign policy goals with his dovish political needs, the new president announced a policy of "Vietnamization": slow troop withdrawals accompanied by escalated bombing raids, a strengthened South Vietnamese army, and enhanced military weaponry. By the end of his first year in office, Nixon had withdrawn about 10 percent of the American combat troops from Vietnam. On the other hand, he had also expanded U.S. military operations in neighboring Laos and Cambodia—operations that necessitated falsified reports and a national news blackout in an effort to keep them hidden from everyone but the "enemy." In April 1970, Nixon grew bolder, going on television to announce that he had ordered American combat troops and bombers into previously neutral Cambodia. "We will not be humiliated. We will not be defeated," he declared. "If the United States acts like a pitiful helpless giant, the forces of totalitarianism and anarchy" would soon threaten everywhere. In early 1971, American bombers and helicopters accompanied South Vietnamese forces in their invasion of Laos. This action, too, explained the secretary of defense, had "shortened" the war.

Somehow, though, the war continued—always at new levels of ferocity. Frustrated in its efforts to achieve a military victory, the American government resumed the bombing of North Vietnam in December 1971, carried out record-level B-52 strikes throughout Indochina the following month, and suspended the peace talks in Paris in March 1972. That spring, the North Vietnamese and the NLF launched a major offensive, and in response the Nixon administration mobilized the largest naval and aerial armada since World War II. It intensified the bombing of North and South Vietnam (including Hanoi and Haiphong), mined all of North Vietnam's harbors, and destroyed the rail links between North Vietnam and China. In Saigon, South Vietnam's latest dictator, General Nguyen Van Thieu, vowed to "kill the Communists to the last man." And, indeed, thanks to American support, South Vietnam maintained the fourth largest army, the third largest navy, and the sixth largest air force in the world, as well as an estimated 200,000 political prisoners in jails and torture cages. By the end of 1972, American warplanes had dropped on Indochina more than three times the tonnage of bombs that had been used in World War II, inflicting widespread suffering and devastation. According to a Senate study, there were 1.5 million civilian casualties in North and South Vietnam alone. Large stretches of Indochina had been rendered uninhabitable.

The Nixon administration's continuation of the war contributed to the profound sense of alienation and social crisis that had gripped the United States since the late 1960s. Polls found public support for government, business, and traditional American institutions plummeting. By contrast, crime, violence, and drug addiction dramatically increased. "Pigs" became a term describing police, government officials, or simply those in power. Although ghetto upheavals largely ceased in the 1970s, race relations in the United States steadily deteriorated. Revolting against the traditional Western faith in science, competition, and material progress, millions of the young turned toward a counterculture that promised love, sensory fulfillment, and community. Others, less willing to make a total break with American life, introduced new and discordant elements into

it: floppy blue jeans, shaggy hair, deafening music, and an earthy, direct, sometimes scatological, language. Inspired not only by the black struggle but by the growing breakdown of traditional mores, homosexuals, Indians, Chicanos, and other minorites demanded their rights and called for destruction of the old order. Women also found their voice and, in growing numbers, asserted their claim to equality and justice. America's widespread malaise was nowhere more evident than in the sudden turn to modes of escape: mysticism, witchcraft, drugs, exotic psychotherapies, and religious revivals.

Caught up in this wave of popular revolt, the peace movement acquired an overwhelming momentum. Antiwar forces turned out an estimated two million Americans for nationwide demonstrations in the fall of 1969. More than 80 members of Congress endorsed them. Meanwhile, draft resistance mounted steadily, with widespread refusal of induction and destruction of draft records. Within the armed forces, dissident newspapers and organizations flourished, while desertions soared. American combat soldiers donned peace symbols, took part in antiwar protests, sat down on the battlefield, and, sometimes, killed ("fragged") their officers. Although the increasing alienation of SDS, SNCC, and CORE rendered them politically impotent, Nixon's invasion of Cambodia unleashed a national upheaval. Students seized control of universities, demonstrators fought police and national guardsmen, and even federal employees staged public demonstrations against the administration. When, at Kent State University in Ohio and at Jackson State University in Mississippi, law enforcement officials opened fire on protesting students, killing six and wounding twenty-one, the nation neared chaos. Like a prehistoric monster awakened from its long sleep, Congress lumbered ponderously toward legislating what the polls showed that the vast majority of Americans demanded: disengagement from the war. By 1972, antiwar forces and their reformist allies were strong enough to win control of the Democratic party. Nominating South Dakota Senator George McGovern, a vigorous opponent of the war, on the first ballot, they adopted the most ambitous platform for peace and social justice in modern times.

Faced with unprecedented opposition, the Nixon administration fought back with a ferocity unprecedented in American history. The president publicly berated his opponents as a "band of violent thugs" and appealed for support to "the great silent majority" of Americans. Attacking the "misfits," "anarchists," "Communists," and "ideological eunuchs" of the peace movement, Vice President Spiro Agnew contended that it was time "to sweep that kind of garbage out of our society." Although such rhetorical blasts failed to generate much enthusiasm for the war, they did serve to intimidate the television networks, to instigate "hard-hat" attacks upon student demonstrators, and to indicate the administration's policy toward its critics. Shortly after taking office, Nixon and his White House staff had ordered government intelligence agencies to step up their assaults on political dissidents. As a result, virtually the entire range of citizens' action groups and American institutions became the objects of government espionage or subversion: the civil rights movement; student groups; civil liberties organizations; the women's liberation movement; colleges and universities; church groups; underground newspapers; critical mayors, legislators, and newspeople; the environmental movement; magazines and publishers; and particularly the antiwar movement. Indeed, by 1972, government intelligence agencies, spearheaded by the FBI, had a significant portion of the delegates to the Democratic National Convention under surveillance, and had targeted many of their organizations for disruption. Moreover, as the Watergate scandal later revealed, the White House maintained its own secret corps of spies, saboteurs, con men, extortionists, forgers, burglars, and muggers, who were ordered to undermine political opponents, manufacture the appearance of public support for the president, and interfere with the 1972 elections.

With the approach of the 1972 elections, in which Nixon made his ludicrous emergence as a "peace candidate," the administration turned to manufacturing the politically expedient illusion of an Indochina settlement. Several days before voters went to the polls, Secretary of State Henry Kissinger announced that peace was "at hand." In reality, a face-saving but inherently unstable agreement had been reached. Responding to the economic and diplomatic allures of detente, Russia and China pressed North Vietnam to cooperate with Nixon. At the same time, Washington promised the Vietnamese Communists—either in secret negotiations or in the Paris accords, which were signed in January 1973—that, in return for stopping the fighting, they could look foward to the withdrawal of the last American troops, the end of American bombing raids, the retention of their own forces in South Vietnam, billions of dollars in postwar U.S. reconstruction aid, and political instrumentalities to determine South Vietnam's future (for example, elections and the release of political prisoners). Naturally, the Thieu government in Saigon mustered little enthusiasm for this arrangement; but it was eventually mollified by massive military aid, assurances that the United States would not press for implementation of the political provisions, and, most significantly, a pledge of renewed American military intervention in the event of further military difficulties. Thus, in spite of the nonintervention guarantee of the Paris accords, Nixon privately assured Thieu that, even if he defied them, the Saigon regime would be protected by the military might of the United States. The reality behind the illusion, then, was that the South Vietnamese government remained Washington's artifact.

The whole facade soon became evident. Nixon's political strength, so crucial to the Thieu regime's survival, rapidly dissolved with the unremitting exposure of the Watergate affair, one small element in the administration's overall abuse of power. Maneuvering desperately, Nixon failed to head off the storm of popular protest which ultimately forced him to resign in disgrace. Meanwhile, the war flared up again in Vietnam. Ignoring the Paris agreement, the Saigon government had initiated military action to retake rebel territory. For a time, the Communist forces had accepted the Paris accords and had called for implementation of their political provisions. In early 1975, however, with much Communist territory captured or under seige and no political action or economic aid in sight, the North Vietnamese launched a limited offensive to restore their political strongholds in the south. Despite Saigon's military advantage, including total control of the air, South Vietnamese troops fled in a rout, surrendering almost two thirds of the country without a fight. Along the way, they terrorized refugee-clogged cities and abandoned a billion dollars worth of American military equipment. Nixon's chosen successor, Gerald Ford, implored Congress to rescue the floundering Thieu government with still another dose of military assistance; but this time the legislators stood firm. And little wonder! Polls revealed that only 28 percent of Americans supported the president's request for additional military aid. As the Saigon regime crumpled, U.S. officials sought the safety of American aircraft carriers waiting offshore, abandoning Vietnam to their one-time friends of thirty years before.

The U.S. venture in Vietnam had barely collapsed before President Ford told Americans that they should quickly forget it. "The lessons of the past in Vietnam," he said, "have already been learned . . . and we should have our focus on the future." But the future was linked to the past, including a war that had killed or maimed millions of Vietnamese, resulted in more than a quarter million U.S. casualties (including 55,000 dead), cost taxpayers perhaps $200 billion, and seriously eroded the

fabric of American society. Consequently, for many Americans, a crucial lesson of the war was to avoid military intervention in other nations. This conclusion, however, conflicted with the desires of Washington policymakers. Secretary of Defense James Schlesinger warned that the United States would not show the same "restraint" in Korea. Ford and Kissinger vigorously championed military intervention in Angola. In keeping with their extraordinary efforts to repress domestic critics, many government officials seemed to believe that the real lesson of the war was the necessity of circumscribing the power of the American people. "Every time . . . the enemy was beginning to hurt," lamented General Westmoreland, "the political situation and emotions of certain segments of the American people forced the politicians to pull back." Because "the American people are impatient," explained former Secretary of State Dean Rusk, American policymakers would have to act "quickly" and perhaps "lower the nuclear threshold." Rusk thought it might "be necessary to have censorship" in future conflicts while General Maxwell Taylor argued that presidents would "be well-advised . . . to silence future critics of war by executive order." In general, then, Americans agreed that democracy and imperial war were incompatible. What they differed over was which they preferred.

SUGGESTED READINGS

Chomsky, Noam. *American Power and the New Mandarins.* New York: Random House, 1967.

———. *At War with Asia.* New York: Random House, 1970.

Ellsberg, Daniel. *Papers on the War.* New York: Simon & Schuster, 1972.

———. *Hell in a Very Small Place.* Philadelphia: J. P. Lippincott, 1966.

Fall, Bernard. *The Two Viet-Nams: A Political and Military Analysis.* New York: Praeger Publishers, 1963.

Ferber, Michael, and Lynd, Staughton. *The Resistance,* Boston: Beacon Press, 1971.

FitzGerald, Frances. *Fire in the Lake: The Vietnamese and the Americans in Vietnam,* Boston: Little, Brown, 1972.

Halberstam, David, *The Best and the Brightest.* New York: Random House, 1972.

Herring, George C. *America's Longest War: The United States and Vietnam, 1950–1975.* New York: John Wiley & Sons, 1979.

Kahin, George M., and Lewis, John W. *The United States in Vietnam.* New York: Dial Press, 1967.

Kendrick, Alexander. *The Wound Within: America in the Vietnam Years, 1945–1974.* Boston: Little Brown, 1974.

Lacouture, Jean. *Vietnam: Between Two Truces.* New York: Random House, 1966.

———.*Ho Chi Minh: A Political Biography.* New York: Random House, 1968.

The Pentagon Papers: The Senator Gravel Edition. 5 vols. Boston: Beacon Press, 1972.

Schell, Jonathan. *The Time of Illusion.* New York: Alfred A. Knopf, 1976.

Taylor, Telford. *Nuremberg and Vietnam: An American Tragedy.* Chicago: Quadrangle Books, 1970.

Williams, William A. et al. *America in Vietnam: A Documentary History.* Garden City, NY: Doubleday Publishing, 1985.

DOCUMENT 33.1
The Secret Planning of the War

The following materials are drawn from The Pentagon Papers, *a secret Defense Department study of the Vietnam War, revealed to Americans by Daniel Ellsberg. The National Security Council report of 1950 illustrates the early U.S. commitment to assuring the defeat of the Viet Minh. "Action for South Vietnam," the later draft of a paper first prepared in the*

Source: *The Pentagon Papers: The Senator Gravel Edition* (5 vols. Boston: Beacon Press, (1972), vol. 1, pp. 361–62; vol. 3, pp. 398–601, 687–91.

fall of 1964 by Assistant Secretary of Defense John McNaughton, reflects the counter-revolutionary hopes of U.S. policymakers as well as their plans, during Johnson's "peace campaign," to escalate the war to North Vietnam. Much the same thinking is contained in a memorandum to Johnson by White House Assistant for National Security McGeorge Bundy in early 1965.

REPORT BY THE NATIONAL SECURITY COUNCIL ON THE POSITION OF THE UNITED STATES WITH RESPECT TO INDOCHINA

(February 27, 1950)

The Problem

1. To undertake a determination of all practicable United States measures to protect its security in Indochina and to prevent the expansion of communist aggression in that area.

Analysis

2. It is recognized that the threat of communist aggression against Indochina is only one phase of anticipated communist plans to seize all of Southeast Asia. It is understood that Burma is weak internally and could be invaded without strong opposition or even that the Government of Burma could be subverted. However, Indochina is the area most immediately threatened. It is also the only area adjacent to communist China which contains a large European army, which along with native troops is now in armed conflict with the forces of communist aggression. A decision to contain communist expansion at the border of Indochina must be considered as a part of a wider study to prevent communist aggression into other parts of Southeast Asia.

3. A large segment of the Indochinese

nationalist movement was seized in 1945 by Ho Chi Minh, a Vietnamese who under various aliases has served as a communist agent for thirty years. He has attracted non-communist as well as communist elements to his support. In 1946, he attempted, but failed to secure French agreement to his recognition as the head of a government of Vietnam. Since then he has directed a guerrilla army in raids against French installations and lines of communication. French forces which have been attempting to restore law and order found themselves pitted against a determined adversary who manufactures effective arms locally, who receives supplies of arms from outside sources, who maintained no capital or permanent headquarters and who was, and is able, to disrupt and harass almost any area within Vietnam. . . .

*   *   *   *   *

Conclusions

10. It is important to United States security interests that all practicable measures be taken to prevent further communist expansion in Southeast Asia. Indochina is a key area of Southeast Asia and is under immediate threat.

11. The neighboring countries of Thailand and Burma could be expected to fall under Communist domination if Indochina were controlled by a Communist-dominated government. The balance of Southeast Asia would then be in grave hazard.

12. Accordingly, the Departments of State and Defense should prepare as a matter of priority a program of all practicable measures designed to protect United States security interests in Indochina.

JOHN T. MCNAUGHTON
ACTION FOR SOUTH VIETNAM

(November 6, 1964)

1. U.S. aims:
    a. To protect US reputation as a counter-subversion guarantor.
    b. To avoid domino effect especially in Southeast Asia.
    c. To keep South Vietnamese territory from Red hands.
    d. To emerge from crisis without unacceptable taint from methods.

2. Present situation: The situation in South Vietnam is deteriorating. Unless new actions are taken, the new government will probably be unstable and ineffectual, and the VC [Vietcong] will probably continue to extend their hold over the population and territory. It can be expected that, soon (six months? two years?), *(a)* government officials at all levels will adjust their behavior to an eventual VC take-over, *(b)* defections of significant military forces will take place, *(c)* whole integrated regions of the country will be totally denied to the GVN, *(d)* neutral and/or leftwing elements will enter the government, *(e)* a popular front regime will emerge which will invite the United States out, and *(f)* fundamental concessions to the VC and accommodations to the DRV will put South Vietnam behind the Curtain. . . .

4. Inside South Vietnam: Progress inside SVN is important, but it is unlikely despite our best ideas and efforts. . . .

5. Action against DRV: Action against North Vietnam is to some extent a substitute for strengthening the government in South Vietnam. That is, a less active VC (on orders from DRV [Government of North Vietnam]) can be matched by a less efficient GVN [Government of South Vietnam]. We therefore should consider squeezing North Vietnam.

6. Options open to us: We have three options open to us (all envision reprisals in the DRV for DRV/VC ''spectaculars'' against GVN as well as U.S. assets in South Vietnam). . . .

*   *   *   *   *

9. Information actions. The start of military actions against the DRV will have to be accompanied by a convincing world-wide public information program. (The information problem will be easier if the first U.S. action against the DRV is related in time and kind to a DRV or VC outrage or "spectacular," preferably against SVN as well as U.S. assets.)

McGEORGE BUNDY
A POLICY OF SUSTAINED REPRISAL

(February 7, 1965)

We believe that the best available way of increasing our chance of success in Vietnam is the development and execution of a policy of *sustained reprisal* against North Vietnam—a policy in which air and naval action against the North is justified by and related to the whole Viet Cong campaign of violence and terror in the South. . . .

. . . We emphasize that our primary target in advocating a reprisal policy is the improvement of the situation in *South* Vietnam. Action against the North is usually urged as a means of affecting the will of Hanoi to direct and support the VC. We consider this an important but longer-range purpose. The immediate and critical targets are in the South—in the minds of the South Vietnamese and in the minds of the Viet Cong cadres. . . .

. . . We have the whip hand in reprisals as we do not in other fields. . . .

. . . We cannot assert that a policy of sustained reprisal will succeed in changing the course of the contest in Vietnam. It may fail. . . . [But] a reprisal policy—to the extent that it demonstrates U.S. willingness to employ this new norm in counter-insurgency—will set a higher price for the future upon all adventures of guerrilla warfare, and it should therefore

somewhat increase our ability to deter such adventures. . . .

. . . A program of sustained reprisal, with its direct link to Hanoi's continuing aggressive actions in the South, will not involve us in nearly the level of international recrimination which would be precipitated by a go-North program which was not so connected. For this reason the International pressures for negotiation should be quite manageable.

DOCUMENT 33.2
Johnson's Public Defense of the War (July 28, 1965)

Angered by the growing popular opposition to the conflict, the president used every possible occasion to defend his policies and call for public support. This statement is drawn from his press conference of July 28, 1965. Interestingly, it departs rather dramatically from the sentiments expressed in the then-secret Pentagon Papers.

. . . Three times in my lifetime, in two world wars and in Korea, Americans have gone to far lands to fight for freedom. We have learned at a terrible and brutal cost that retreat does not bring safety and weakness does not bring peace.

It is this lesson that has brought us to Viet-Nam. This is a different kind of war. There are no marching armies or solemn declarations. Some citizens of South Viet-Nam, at times with understandable grievances, have joined in the attack on their own government.

But we must not let this mask the central fact that this is really war. It is guided by North Viet-Nam, and it is spurred by Communist China. Its goal is to conquer the South,

Source: *Department of State Bulletin,* vol. 53 (August 16, 1965), p. 262.

to defeat American power, and to extend the Asiatic dominion of communism.

There are great stakes in the balance.

Most of the non-Communist nations of Asia cannot, by themselves and alone, resist the growing might and the grasping ambition of Asian Communism.

Our power, therefore, is a very vital shield. If we are driven from the field in Viet-Nam, then no nation can ever again have the same confidence in American promise or in American protection.

In each land the forces of independence would be considerably weakened and an Asia so threatened by Communist domination would certainly imperil the security of the United States itself.

We did not choose to be the guardians at the gate, but there is no one else.

Nor would surrender in Viet-Nam bring peace, because we learned from Hitler at Munich that success only feeds the appetite of aggression. The battle would be renewed in one country and then another country, bringing with it perhaps even larger and crueler conflict, as we have learned from the lessons of history.

Moreover, we are in Viet-Nam to fulfill one of the most solemn pledges of the American nation. Three Presidents—President Eisenhower, President Kennedy, and your present President—over 11 years have committed themselves and have promised to help defend this small and valiant nation.

Strengthened by that promise, the people of South Viet-Nam have fought for many long years. Thousands of them have died. Thousands more have been crippled and scarred by war. We just cannot now dishonor our word, or abandon our commitment, or leave those who believed us and who trusted us to the terror and repression and murder that would follow.

This, then, my fellow Americans, is why we are in Viet-Nam.

DOCUMENT 33.3
The Face of War

The brave rhetoric masked a sordid reality. Fighting an elusive enemy that enjoyed widespread popular support, American military forces in Indochina regularly employed fragmentation bombs, napalm, and chemical weapons against the civilian population, and often resorted to indiscriminate killing and torture. The following personal accounts are drawn from the report of the International Commission of Enquiry Into United States Crimes in Indochina, which heard testimony in Oslo, Norway, during June 1971.

Dang Kim Phung (a woman from Gia Dinh province, South Vietnam). The American GIs and the puppet troops are very savage. . . . Two of my uncles were killed. One was shot dead, and one was decapitated. . . . One of my aunts was killed by a shell splinter. One of my little brothers was killed by toxic chemicals. I myself was three times the victim of U.S. atrocities. . . .

. . . It was on the 24th of June, 1968. . . . A reconnaissance plane whirled over and over my region. It fired a rocket. My friends and I immediately took refuge in an underground shelter. Then three low-flying helicopters went over. They dropped barrels of toxic chemicals. . . . Smoke began to enter the shelter, and we were stifling. . . . We tried to get out . . . but then we started coughing and spitting blood. Our skins became quickly covered with blisters. A few days later I felt very tired. Even a week later I lost my appetite and had diarrhea no matter what I ate. Now these evil effects are still being felt by me. My sight is

Frank Browning and Dorothy Forman, eds., *The Wasted Nations: Report of the International Commission of Enquiry into United States Crimes in Indochina* (New York: Harper & Row, 1972), pp. 148–56, 165–75.

blurred, and I have many digestive difficulties. . . .

Now I shall tell you about the U.S. artillery shelling of my commune. On October 10, 1968, at about 7 P.M., when we were having our dinner, shells began to fall on my village. . . . When you hear this sound of the ultrarapid battery shell, it falls immediately upon you. At that moment I had no time to take refuge, I was on my hammock, and so a bomb splinter went into my left leg. I was brought to the infirmary of the district. I was hospitalized for 20 days. Despite treatment the splinter is still in my leg. . . .

On the 16th of February, 1969, which was the twelfth of the lunar calendar—almost two weeks after the new year Tet festival, we were enjoying the festival at that time. At about 7 A.M. a reconnaissance plane circled over and over my village and fired a rocket. Then three jet planes went over. These three bombers fired exploding bombs in a large area, at high velocity for a long time—steel pellet bombs. When the bombing was almost over I went out of the shelter and I saw that everything was destroyed and the trees were torn down. Then three more jet planes came over and began to bomb. There were incendiary bombs. One of these bombs fell directly on my house. One of these incendiary products stuck to my trousers. And to my face. Then I stripped off my clothes and took refuge. Then I fainted. I knew nothing.

More than a week later I recovered consciousness and found myself in the district hospital. For the first month after that I could see nothing. My eyes were covered with liquids. I could not open my mouth. Three months later I could eat some rice, but the rice had to be mixed with water, with a soup. I feel much pain in my wounds, and they stank. I have been often sent to the emergency hospital, the first aid hospital. Five and six months later, still my wounds could not be healed, and we had to patch up the wound with a piece

of skin. At present I am not able to do anything, and when it is cold, I feel severe pains in my hands and particularly at the ends of my fingers, and I feel also much pain in my wounds. When it is hot, I have a burning feeling in my skin, and I get a headache. I cannot drop for a long time my two arms. The days I spent in the hospital were the saddest and the most dramatic days of my life because I was a young and sound girl, and . . . I became an invalid and wounded for life.

Le Van Tan (a 14-year old boy from Quang Nam province, South Vietnam). In the strategic hamlet where I lived was my sister, my three little sisters, and my little brother living there with me.

I remember that it was in April 1965, at midnight that American artillery from An Hoa began pounding my village. I was sleeping with my mother, my two little sisters, and my little brother on the same bed.

My mother awoke and sat up and a shell entered her chest and killed her. [Le Van Tan begins to cry, and for a time cannot speak any further.]

A few days later American troops came up to my village. . . .

These troops burned down houses everywhere, and they beat the people who refused to be brought away.

I myself, with my sisters and brother, was also brought away with other people to be exposed to the sun. Afterwards my grandmother and I were herded into the strategic hamlet of Xe Mioc. There were many people, but they gave nothing to us, and we had to sleep on the ground.

We remained there from 1965 to 1967 in the strategic hamlet. There were three walls of barbed wire. They nominated the chief of the hamlet, with the assistant chief of the hamlet, to control the entrance. . . .

In my village we go out to the field very early in the morning, at four or at five o'clock in the morning, but in the strategic hamlet they only allow us to go out into the field at eight o'clock. At five o'clock we have to come back. If we are late in coming back, we are beaten because they suspect those ones of being enemy agents—connections for the communists.

For instance, Mr. Tu, Mr. Coc, and Mr. Cang were savagely beaten. Mr. Coc had his leg broken because he came late.

In this strategic hamlet people are usually hungry. There is not enough food, and so they easily fall ill. We are living huddled together and most of the women and children and aged women all ill and are afflicted with diseases. My own grandfather was dead and my little brother died from cholera and a number of other little children like my little brother also died.

Each family must have a card of control. If a member of the family is absent or if there is someone strange in the family, then they shoot or arrest and kill the people in that family. . . .

Aged people guarded the hamlet in the nighttime. Women stood sentry in the daytime. If there was an explosion, people were beaten, arrested or shot to death. . . .

In 1968, during one month, they shut the gate of the strategic hamlet for one month. The inmates protested and struggled to go out and to return to their native places. Among those who tried to run to the gate and to go out was myself and my little sister. They threw grenades and shot at random at the crowd. My little sister was shot dead and also my grandfather on my mother's side. I escaped and I fled. When I returned again to the strategic hamlet, I saw that my little sister was killed and that many other people were killed and many wounded. Blood was shed in profusion. There were many corpses. . . .

In June 1968, they dropped bombs on my strategic hamlet. Many people were killed. Some of them disappeared but, due to the stink-

ing of the corpses, it was discovered that those people had been buried by the explosion of the bombs.

In June 1970, there was an explosion near my house. The chief of the strategic hamlet began to beat the people and arrested two people and me. We were handcuffed and brought to Duc Duc. They arrested three of us and detained us separately and began to torture us for 12 days.

They began to interrogate me. I said that I know nothing. On the 18th of June they brought me to the jail of Hoi An with my eyes covered by a handkerchief.

They detained me in the Hoi An jail for 50 days, during which time they continued to interrogate me. I said that I knew nothing. There I was savagely tortured. . . .

When I went back to the strategic hamlet, I was very sick—very weak. I could not work. There was only my sister who worked for us. With the assistance of the neighbors I could survive.

In October 1970, there was a big flood in the strategic hamlet. Many houses were destroyed in the flood, and they were afraid that the people of the hamlet would escape to their native places, so they rounded everyone up, and they herded them into the hills, and they pounded the hills where people might take refuge, and many persons were drowned by the flood and also killed in the hills by the artillery fire. Many corpses were floating on the river and also buffalo, cows, and oxen. . . .

People now say that this flood was due to the spraying of toxic chemicals in the jungles. . . . The destruction of the forests, the woods, caused a water overflow, and this flood was part of that overflow.

In January 1971 when I was out farming, I availed myself of the opportunity to flee with some friends to a liberated area. The people of the liberated area cared for me.

Now there remain my big sister and my two little sisters in the strategic hamlet.

Danny Notley (a 23-year-old U.S. soldier from the Americal Division). During training there were constant references made to the Vietnamese people as gooks, dinks, slopeheads. . . . We were subjected to this type of language day in and day out until it became more or less common to us. . . . I had a drill sergeant. One time I asked him what it was like in Vietnam, and he said: "It's like hunting rabbits and squirrels." . . .

After having been in my unit for approximately two months, we were sent on an operation into the Song My River Valley. . . .

I was walking about fourth or fifth back in the column of about eight to ten men, a squad patrol. Being new, and being somewhat naive, not having seen any combat yet, I still had the mistaken idea that war was just like I had seen it in all the John Wayne and Audie Murphy movies—that we were going to make contact with the enemy and that there was going to be a fight. As we approached the village, I actually expected to see armed hostile forces . . . and [instead] . . . there were a number of women and children standing on the near side of the village to us.

As we walked into the village, the people who were walking in front of me, without saying a word . . . just started shooting people. I estimated that there were approximately ten women and children. . . . These people were all killed.

At this time I was somewhat in a state of shock; I was very upset. I couldn't understand what I was seeing. . . .

The strange thing of it was that the men who were doing the shooting hadn't had to say a word to anyone. It was as if they had done this a hundred times before. . . . They had been brutalized so badly that they did not realize the reality of what they were doing, and I was so upset that I couldn't understand what was going on.

After having killed the first group of people, we moved . . . on into the village, where there

was a second group. . . . Why these people didn't run I don't know, but they didn't. They were just standing there like the first group. I guess because they really couldn't believe what was happening either.

At this time my squad leader, a sergeant E-5, ordered me to fire. I had a canister round, which is a shotgun round for the M-79, an antipersonnel round. There is a great amount of debate among soldiers themselves as to whether this round is meant to kill people or just to maim. . . . My squad leader ordered me to fire. He said: "It's about time that you tried out one of those canister rounds," as if he was curious to see what it would do.

I was so upset, and I was so scared that I complied with his order. I was afraid not to comply with his order. . . .

I fired my weapon. Whether or not I hit anyone or killed anyone I will never know because immediately after firing the rest of the people opened up with their M-16s. . . .

After that, after I had realized what I had done, I refused to take part in it anymore. I just stood there and watched. They found another group of people.

They killed this other group of people, and after that we left the village. . . .

I believe that at the time we called in a body count of 13 North Vietnamese. Who determined this number I do not know. . . . It is interesting to note that in the official press release out of Saigon this body count had been inflated to 21. Obviously there were more people killed than that, but . . . somewhere along the line they added eight more bodies to make it look good. . . .

Myself, I felt this was very wrong, somebody is going to go to jail, there is going to be an investigation, and, as I said, I guess at the time I was somewhat naive. . . .

People have asked me why I didn't report this when I was in Vietnam. The fact is that it is beaten into your heads when you are in basic training and in the army, that there is

such a thing called the chain of command.
. . . Everyone in my chain of command already knew about this incident, and since they didn't do anything about it, and since a great amount of emphasis among GIs—the rank and file GI in Vietnam—is survival, don't make trouble, stay out of trouble so you can go home, I didn't feel that there was anything I could do. My squad leader knew about it; he participated in it. My platoon leader knew about it; he participated in it. My battalion commander knew about it. . . . I really felt that I didn't have any means of recourse. It was also so emotionally upsetting for me to have seen and participated in something like this that I completely suppressed this in my mind; I did not admit to myself what had happened. But the reality of what I saw there . . . *is* the war in Indochina.

DOCUMENT 33.4
Martin Luther King, Jr., "Beyond Vietnam"

Martin Luther King, Jr., was not only a champion of social justice but an eloquent opponent of the Vietnam War. He delivered this address at Riverside Church, New York City, on April 4, 1967.

. . . I come to this platform tonight to make a passionate plea to my beloved nation. . . .

. . . There is . . . a very obvious and almost facile connection between the war in Vietnam and the struggle I, and others, have been waging in America. A few years ago there was a shining moment in that struggle. It seemed as if there was a real promise of hope for the poor—both black and white—through

Source: Joanne Grant, ed., *Black Protest: History, Documents, and Analyses* (Greenwich, Conn.: Fawcett Publications, 1968), pp. 418–25.

the poverty program. There were experiments, hopes, new beginnings. Then came the build-up in Vietnam and I watched the program broken and eviscerated as if it were some idle political plaything of a society gone mad on war, and I knew America would never invest the necessary funds or energies in rehabilitation of its poor so long as adventures like Vietnam continued to draw men and skills and money like some demoniacal destructive suction tube. So I was increasingly compelled to see the war as an enemy of the poor. . . .

. . . It was [also] sending their sons and their brothers and their husbands to fight and to die in extraordinarily high proportions. . . . We have been repeatedly faced with the cruel irony of watching Negro and white boys on TV screens as they kill and die together for a nation that has been unable to seat them together in the same schools. So we watch them in brutal solidarity burning the huts of a poor village but we realize that they would never live on the same block in Detroit. I could not be silent in the face of such cruel manipulation of the poor.

My third reason moves to an even deeper level of awareness, for it grows out of my experience in the ghettos of the North over the last three summers. As I have walked among the desperate, rejected and angry young men I have told them that Molotov cocktails and rifles would not solve their problems. . . . But they asked—and rightly so—what about Vietnam? . . . Their questions hit home, and I knew that I could never again raise my voice against the violence of the oppressed in the ghettos without having first spoken clearly to the greatest purveyor of violence in the world today—my own government. . . .

Now, it should be incandescently clear that no one who has any concern for the integrity and life of America today can ignore the present war. If America's soul becomes totally poisoned, part of the autopsy must read "Vietnam.'' It can never be saved so long as it destroys the deepest hopes of men the world over. . . .

As I ponder the madness of Vietnam and search within myself for ways to understand and respond in compassion my mind goes constantly to the people of that peninsula. I speak now not of the soldiers on each side, not of the junta in Saigon, but simply of the people who have been living under the curse of war for almost three continuous decades now. I think of them too because it is clear to me that there will be no meaningful solution there until some attempt is made to know them and hear their broken cries.

They must see Americans as strange liberators. The Vietnamese people proclaimed their own independence in 1945. . . . We refused to recognize them. Instead, we decided to support France in its reconquest of her former colony. . . .

After the French were defeated it looked as if independence and land reform would come again through the Geneva agreements. But instead there came the United States, determined that Ho should not unify the temporarily divided nation. . . .

The only change came from America as we increased our troop commitments in support of governments which were singularly corrupt, inept and without popular support. All the while the people read our leaflets and received regular promises of peace and democracy—and land reform. Now they languish under our bombs and consider us—not their fellow Vietnamese—the real enemy. They move sadly and apathetically as we herd them off the land of their fathers into concentration camps where minimal social needs are rarely met. They know they must move or be destroyed by our bombs. So they go—primarily women and children and the aged.

They watch as we poison their water, as we kill a million acres of their crops. They must weep as the bulldozers roar through their areas preparing to destroy the precious trees. They wander into the hospitals, with at least 20 casualties from American firepower for one Vietcong-inflicted injury. They wander into the towns and see thousands of the children, homeless, without clothes, running in packs on the streets like animals. They see the children degraded by our soldiers as they beg for food. They see the children selling their sisters to our soldiers, soliciting for their mothers. . . .

Perhaps the more difficult but no less necessary task is to speak for those who have been designated as our enemies. What of the National Liberation Front—that strangely anonymous group we call VC or Communists? . . . What do they think of our condoning the violence which led to their own taking up of arms? How can they believe in our integrity when now we speak of ''aggression from the North'' as if there were nothing more essential to the war? . . . Surely we must see that the men we supported pressed them to their violence. Surely we must see that our own computerized plans of destruction simply dwarf their greatest acts.

. . . They ask how we can speak of free elections when the Saigon press is censored and controlled by the military junta. And they are surely right to wonder what kind of new government we plan to help form without them—the only party in real touch with the peasants. They question our political goals and they deny the reality of a peace settlement from which they will be excluded. Their questions are frighteningly relevant. Is our nation planning to build on political myth again and then shore it up with the power of new violence?

. . . If we are mature, we may learn and grow and profit from the wisdom of the brothers who are called the opposition.

So, too, with Hanoi. In the North, where our bombs now pummel the land, and our mines endanger the waterways, we are met by a deep but understandable mistrust. . . . In Hanoi are the men who led the nation to independence . . . and were betrayed by the weakness of Paris and the willfulness of the colonial armies. It was they who led a second struggle against French domination at tremendous costs, and then were persuaded to give up the land they controlled between the 13th and 17th parallel as a temporary measure at Geneva. After 1954 . . . they realized they had been betrayed again. . . .

. . . I am as deeply concerned about our own troops there as anything else. . . . We are adding cynicism to the process of death, for they must know after a short period there that none of the things we claim to be fighting for are really involved. Before long they must know that their government has sent them into a struggle among Vietnamese, and the more sophisticated surely realize that we are on the side of the wealthy and the secure while we create a hell for the poor.

Somehow this madness must cease. We must stop now. I speak as a child of God and brother to the suffering poor of Vietnam. I speak for those whose land is being laid waste, whose homes are being destroyed, whose culture is being subverted. I speak for the poor of America who are paying the double price of smashed hopes at home and death and corruption in Vietnam. I speak as a citizen of the world, for the world stands aghast at the path we have taken. I speak as an American to the leaders of my own nation. The great initiative in this war is ours. The initiative to stop it must be ours. . . .

The world demands a maturity of America that we may not be able to achieve. It demands that we admit that we have been wrong from the beginning of our adventure in Vietnam, that we have been detrimental to the life of the Vietnamese people. . . .

. . . These are the times for real choices and not false ones. We are at the moment when our lives must be placed on the line if our nation is to survive its own folly. Every man of humane convictions must decide on the protest that best suits his convictions, but we must all protest.

DOCUMENT 33.5
COINTELPRO: The FBI's Covert Action Programs against American Citizens

Stung by criticism of their actions and determined to persevere in the war effort, American policymakers increasingly resorted to political repression. In the 1970s, when Congress began to investigate the freewheeling activities of U.S. intelligence agencies, it uncovered a massive campaign of federal espionage and disruption designed to stifle political dissent, particularly of the antiwar variety. This selection, drawn from the "Church Committee Report," examines one such enterprise undertaken by the FBI. Although the FBI claimed to have terminated COINTELPRO in 1971, the committee found evidence that the program was continuing. Thus far, Congress has failed to pass any legislation to reform or curb the abuses of U.S. intelligence agencies.

COINTELPRO is the FBI acronym for a series of covert action programs directed against domestic groups. In these programs, the Bureau went beyond the collection of intelligence to secret action designed to "disrupt" and "neutralize" target groups and individuals. . . .

Many of the techniques used would be intolerable in a democratic society even if all of the targets had been involved in violent activity, but COINTELPRO went far beyond that. The

Source: *Final Report of the Select Committee to Study Governmental Operations With Respect to Intelligence Activities* (Washington, D.C.: U.S. Government Printing Office, 1976), vol. 3, pp. 3–77.

unexpressed major premise of the programs was that a law enforcement agency has the duty to do whatever is necessary to combat perceived threats to the existing social and political order. . . .

Under the COINTELPRO programs, the arsenal of techniques used against foreign espionage agents was transferred to domestic enemies. . . . In the course of COINTELPRO's 15-year history, a number of individual actions may have violated specific criminal statutes; a number of individual actions involved risk of serious bodily injury or death to the targets (at least four assaults were reported as "results"); and a number of actions, while not illegal or dangerous, can only be described as "abhorrent in a free society." . . .

The Bureau approved 2,370 . . . actions. . . .

. . . The lack of any Bureau definition of "New Left" resulted in targeting almost every anti-war group. . . .

. . . Certainly, COINTELPRO took in a staggering range of targets. . . . The choice of individuals and organizations to be neutralized and disrupted ranged from the violent elements of the Black Panther Party to Martin Luther King, Jr., . . . and . . . the supporters of peaceful social change, including the Southern Christian Leadership Conference and the Inter-University Committee for Debate on Foreign Policy. . . .

The clearest example of actions directly aimed at the exercise of constitutional rights are those targeting speakers, teachers, writers or publications, and meetings or peaceful demonstrations. Approximately 18 percent of all approved COINTELPRO proposals fell into these categories.

The cases include attempts (sometimes successful) to get university and high school teachers fired; to prevent targets from speaking on campus; to stop chapters of target groups from being formed; to prevent the distribution of books, newspapers, or periodicals; to disrupt news conferences; to disrupt peaceful demonstrations, including . . . most of the large anti-war marches; and to deny facilities for meetings. . . .

A. EFFORTS TO PREVENT SPEAKING

An illustrative example of attacks on speaking concerns the plans of a dissident stockholders' group to protest a large corporation's war production at the annual stockholders meeting. The field office was authorized to furnish information about the group's plans (obtained from paid informants in the group) to a confidential source in the company's management. The Bureau's purpose was not only to "circumvent efforts to disrupt the corporate meeting," but also to prevent any attempt to "obtain publicity or embarrass" corporate officials.

In another case, anonymous telephone calls were made to the editorial desks of three newspapers in a Midwestern city, advising them that a lecture to be given on a university campus was actually being sponsored by a Communist-front organization. . . . One of the newspapers contacted the director of the university's conference center. He in turn discussed the meeting with the president of the university who decided to cancel the meeting. The sponsoring organization, supported by the ACLU [American Civil Liberties Union], took the case to court, and won a ruling tht the university could not bar the speaker. (Bureau headquarters then ordered the field office to furnish information on the judge.) . . .

B. EFFORTS TO PREVENT TEACHING

. . . In one case, a high school teacher was targeted for inviting two poets to attend a class at his school. The poets were noted for their efforts in the draft resistance movement. This invitation led to an investigation by the local police, which in turn provoked sharp criticism from the ACLU. The field office was authorized to send anonymous letters to two local newspapers, to the city Board of Education, and to the high school administration, suggesting that the ACLU should not criticize the police for probing into high school activities, "but should rather have focused attention on [the teacher] who has been a convicted draft dodger." The letter continued, "[the teacher] is the assault on academic freedom and not the local police." The purpose of the letter, according to Bureau documents, was "to highlight [the teacher's] antidraft activities at the local high school" and to "discourage any efforts" he may make there. . . .

In another case, a university professor who was "an active participant in New Left demonstrations" had publicly surrendered his draft card and had been arrested twice (but not convicted) in antiwar demonstrations. The Bureau decided that the professor should be "removed from his position" at the university. The field office was authorized to contact a "confidential source" at a foundation which contributed substantial funds to the university, and "discreetly suggest that the [foundation] may desire to call to the attention of the University administration questions concerning the advisability of [the professor's] continuing his position there." The foundation official was told by the university that the professor's contract would not be renewed, but in fact the professor did continue to teach. The following academic year, therefore, the field office was authorized to furnish additional information to the foundation official on the professor's arrest and conviction (with a suspended sentence) in another demonstration. . . .

In a third instance, the Bureau attempted to "discredit and neutralize" a university professor on the Inter-University Committee for Debate on Foreign Policy, in which he was active. The field office was authorized to send a fictitious-name letter to influential state political figures, the mass media, university administrators, and the Board of Regents, accusing

the professor and "his protesting cohorts" of "giving aid and comfort to the enemy," and wondering "if the strategy is to bleed the United States white by prolonging the war in Vietnam and pave the way for a takeover by Russia." No results were reported.

*   *   *   *   *

IV. COINTELPRO TECHNIQUES

A. Propaganda

The Bureau's COINTELPRO propaganda efforts stem from the same basic premise as the attacks on speaking, teaching, writing and meeting: propaganda works. Certain ideas are dangerous, and if their expression cannot be prevented, they should be countered with Bureau-approved views. Three basic techniques were used: (1) mailing reprints of newspaper and magazine articles to group members or potential supporters intended to convince them of the error of their ways; (2) writing articles for or furnishing information to "friendly" news media sources to "expose" target groups; and (3) writing, printing, and disseminating pamphlets and fliers without identifying the Bureau as the source. . . .

"Friendly" Media. Much of the Bureau's propaganda efforts involved giving information or articles to "friendly" media sources who could be relied upon not to reveal the Bureau's interests. . . . Field offices also had "confidential sources" (unpaid Bureau informants) in the media, and were able to ensure their cooperation.

The Bureau's use of the news media took two different forms: placing unfavorable articles and documentaries about target groups, and leaking derogatory information intended to discredit individuals. . . .

The Bureau also planted derogatory articles about the Poor People's Campaign, the Institute for Policy Studies, the Southern Students Organizing Committee, the National Mobilization Committee, and a host of other organizations it believed needed to be seen in their "true light."

Bureau-Authored Pamphlets and Fliers. The Bureau occasionally drafted, printed, and distributed its own propaganda. These pieces were usually intended to ridicule their targets, rather than offer "straight" propaganda on the issue. . . .

B. Efforts to Promote Enmity and Factionalism within Groups or between Groups

Approximately 28 percent of the Bureau's COINTELPRO efforts were designed to weaken groups by setting members against each other, or to separate groups which might otherwise be allies, and convert them into mutual enemies. The techniques used included anonymous mailings . . . to group members criticizing a leader or an allied group; using informants to raise controversial issues; forming a "notional"—a Bureau-run splinter group—to draw away membership from the target organization; encouraging hostility up to and including gang warfare between rival groups; and the "snitch jacket."

Encouraging Violence between Rival Groups. The Bureau's attempts to capitalize on active hostility between target groups carried with them the risk of serious physical injury to the targets. . . .

Anonymous Mailings. The Bureau's use of anonymous mailings to promote factionalism range from the relatively bland mailing of reprints or fliers criticizing a group's leaders for living ostentatiously or being ineffective speakers, to reporting a chapter's infractions to the group's headquarters intended to cause censure or disciplinary action.

Critical letters were also sent to one group purporting to be from another, or from a member of the group registering a protest over a proposed alliance. . . .

Labeling Targets as Informants. The "snitch jacket" technique—neutralizing a target by labeling him a "snitch" or informant, so that he would no longer be trusted—was used in all COINTELPROs. The methods utilized ranged from having an authentic informant start a rumor about the target member, to anonymous letters or phone calls, to faked informants' reports. . . .

D. Disseminating Derogatory Information to Family, Friends, and Associates

Although this technique was used in relatively few cases it accounts for some of the most distressing of all COINTELPRO actions. Personal life information, some of which was gathered expressly to be used in the programs, was then disseminated, either directly to the target's family through an anonymous letter or telephone call, or indirectly, by giving the information to the media. . . .

E. Contacts with Employers

The Bureau often tried to get targets fired, with some success. If the target was a teacher, the intent was usually to deprive him of a forum and to remove what the Bureau believed to be the added prestige given a political cause by educators. In other employer contacts, the purpose was to eliminate a source of funds for the individual or (if the target was a donor) the group, or to have the employer apply pressure on the target to stop his activities. . . .

. . . Targets include an employee of the Urban League, who was fired because the Bureau contacted a confidential source in a foundation which funded the League; a lawyer known for his representation of "subversives," whose nonmovement client received an anonymous letter advising it not to employ a "well-known Communist Party apologist"; and a television commentator who was transferred after his station and superiors received an anonymous protest letter. The commentator, who had a weekly religious program, had expressed admiration for a black nationalist leader and criticized the United States's defense policy. . . .

F. Use and Abuse of Government Processes

Selective Law Enforcement. . . . A typical example of the attempted use of local authorities to disrupt targeted activities is the Bureau's attempt to have a Democratic Party fund raiser raided by the state Alcoholic Beverage Control Commission. . . .

Interference with Judicial Process. . . . Justice is supposed to be blind. Nevertheless, when a target appeared before a judge, a jury, or a probation board, he sometimes carried an unknown burden; the Bureau had gotten there first.

. . . A university student who was a leader of the Afro American Action Committee had been arrested in a demonstration at the university. The Bureau sent an anonymous letter to the county prosecutor intended to discredit her. . . . Another anonymous letter containing the same information was mailed to a local radio announcer. . . .

Candidates and Political Appointees. The Bureau apparently did not trust the American people to make the proper choices in the voting booth. Candidates who, in the Bureau's opinion, should not be elected were therefore targeted. . . .

. . . A Midwest lawyer whose firm represented "subversives" (defendants in the Smith Act trials) ran for City Council. The lawyer had been active in the civil rights movement in the South, and the John Birch Society in

his city had recently mailed a book called "It's Very Simple—The True Story of Civil Rights" to various ministers, priests, and rabbis. The Bureau received a copy of the mailing list from a source in the Birch Society and sent an anonymous follow-up letter to the book's recipients noting the pages on which the candidate had been mentioned and calling their attention to the "Communist background" of this "charlatan." The Bureau also sent a fictitious-name letter to a television station on which the candidate was to appear, enclosing a series of informative questions it believed should be asked. The candidate was defeated. He subsequently ran (successfully, as it happened) for a judgeship. . . .

G. Exposing "Communist Infiltration" of Groups

This technique was used in approximately 4 percent of all approved proposals. The most common method involved anonymously notifying the group (civil rights organization, PTA,. Boy Scouts, etc.) that one or more of its members was a "Communist," so that it could take whatever action it deemed appropriate. Occasionally, however, the group itself was the COINTELPRO target. In those cases, the information went to the media, and the intent was to link the group to the Communist Party.

For example, one target was a Western professor who was the immediate past president of a local peace center, "a coalition of anti-Vietnam and antidraft groups." He had resigned to become chairman of the state's McCarthy campaign organization, but it was anticipated that he would return to the peace center after the election. According to the documents, the professor's wife had been a Communist Party member in the early 1950s. This information was furnished to a newspaper editor who had written an editorial branding the SDS and various black power groups as "professional revolutionists." The information was intended to "expose these people at this time when they are receiving considerable publicity to not only educate the public to their character, but disrupt the members" of the peace organization.

DOCUMENT 33.6
Resistance

In May 1968, a group of Catholic activists staged a daylight raid on the draft board in Catonsville, Maryland, destroying hundreds of draft files with home-brewed napalm before the eyes of startled onlookers. That October, they were tried in Baltimore federal court and sentenced to stiff prison terms. One of the pieces of evidence introduced at the trial was this "meditation," written by Father Daniel Berrigan shortly before the action.

Some ten or twelve of us (the number is still
    uncertain)
will if all goes well (ill?) take our religious
    bodies
during this week
to a draft center in or near Baltimore
There we shall   of purpose and
    forethought
remove the 1-A files   sprinkle them in the
    public street
with home-made napalm   and set them afire
For which act we shall beyond doubt
be placed behind bars for some portion of
    our natural lives
in consequence of our inability
to live and die content in the plagued city
to say "peace peace" when there is no
    peace
to keep the poor poor
the thirsty and hungry thirsty and hungry
Our apologies   good friends

Source: Daniel Berrigan, *The Trial of the Catonsville Nine* (Boston: Beacon Press, 1970), pp. 93–95.

for the fracture of good order   the burning
    of paper
instead of children   the angering of the
    orderlies
in the front parlor of the charnel house
We could not   so help us God   do
    otherwise
For we are sick at heart   our hearts
give us no rest for thinking of the Land of
    Burning Children. . . .
And so we stretch out our hands
to our brothers throughout the world
We who are priests to our fellow priests
All of us who act against the law
turn to the poor of the world   to the
    Vietnamese
to the victims   to the soldiers who kill and
    die
for the wrong reasons for no reason at all
because they were so ordered by the
    authorities
of that public order which is in effect
a massive institutionalized disorder
We say: killing is disorder
life and gentleness and community and
    unselfishness
is the only order we recognize
For the sake of that order
we risk our liberty   our good name
The time is past when good men may be
    silent
when obedience
can segregate men from public risk
when the poor can die without defense
How many indeed must die
before our voices are heard
how many must be tortured dislocated
starved maddened?
How long must the world's resources
be raped in the service of legalized murder?
When at what point will you say no to this
    war?
We have chosen to say
with the gift of our liberty
if necessary our lives:

the violence stops here
the death stops here
the suppression of the truth stops here
this war stops here
Redeem the times!
The times are inexpressibly evil
Christians pay conscious   indeed religious
    tribute
to Caesar and Mars
by the approval of overkill tactics   by
    brinksmanship
by nuclear liturgies   by racism   by
    support of genocide. . . .
They pay lip service to Christ
and military service to the powers of death

And yet   and yet   the times are
    inexhaustibly good
solaced by the courage and hope of many
The truth rules   Christ is not forsaken
In a time of death some men
the resisters   those who work hardily for
    social change
those who preach and embrace the truth
such men overcome death. . . .
We think of such men
in the world   in our nation   in the
    churches
and the stone in our breast is dissolved
we take heart once more.

New Women: From the 1920s to the Present

Nancy Woloch
Columbia University

American women entered the 1920s with high expectations. Elated by the ratification of woman suffrage in 1920, many anticipated the power to enact social reforms, to raise the tone of political life, and in one suffragist's words, "to play a part in the making of the world." Although the vote did not fulfill all the goals of its advocates, winning it marked a turning point in women's history. Within the next half century, women's roles were transformed by new options, ideals, and aspirations, and above all, by the changing circumstances of modern life.

The decade of the 1920s was a launchpad for modern roles, one of them political. For the first time, women ran for public office, both parties welcomed women into their national committees, and politicians competed for the "women's vote." In 1921, Congress passed the Sheppard-Towner Act, the first federally funded health care plan, which provided maternal and childcare clinics in many states. By mid-decade, however, the "women's vote" had failed to materialize. Since women did not vote as a bloc, legislators lost interest in catering to them. While former suffragists analyzed what had gone wrong, new tensions split the prewar women's movement. In 1923 the

National Woman's party, a small group of suffrage veterans, proposed an Equal Rights Amendment (ERA) that would erase sex as a legal classification. The proposal never made headway in Congress, or even reached the floor of the House. But it antagonized reform-minded feminists, such as those in the Women's Trade Union League and in the Women's Bureau of the U.S. Department of Labor, which was formed in 1919 to safeguard the interests of women in industry. An ERA, claimed its opponents, would invalidate protective laws that limited the exploitation of women workers. Once united behind suffrage, feminists now debated a new issue: Was it preferable to be considered "equal" or "special"? Would legal equality jeopardize working women? Did ERA supporters run the risk, as historian Mary Beard charged, of "forsaking humanism in the quest for feminism?"

Internal disputes aside, the prewar women's movement faced new obstacles: a more conservative political climate and a shrinking constituency. Significantly women's organizations remained active throughout the 1920s, but feminist energies veered off in many directions. Some former suffragists joined the new League of Women Voters, a training ground for civic

417

affairs; others turned to party politics, the revived peace movement, the southern women's interracial movement, or Margaret Sanger's birth control campaign. Still others shifted their attention from public causes to private channels. "I have traded my sense of exhilarating defiance . . . for an avenue of unimpeded self-expression," a former suffragist declared.

One new direction was vocation, career, and the goal of "economic independence." During the 1920s, middle-class women surged into new jobs in white-collar work, the business world, and the professions. The modern woman, said *Nation* editor Freda Kirchwey, was "out in the world and in competition with men." She also hoped to merge marriage with career, as did one in five professional women in 1920, one in four in 1930, and more thereafter. Discarding the spirit of cooperation, the new young woman professed "no loyalty to women en masse," journalist Dorothy Bromley observed. "Self-conscious" rather than "sex-conscious," she prized her "freedom as an individual." The youngest women proved most immune to the feminist call; indeed, they were "likely to be bored" whenever feminism was mentioned, social scientist Lorine Pruette noted. Preoccupied with their personal liberation—from tradition, inhibition, and old-fashioned restraints—young women sought "individualism" and "equality" in their private lives. The flamboyant flapper symbolized their change in style. "Breezy, slangy, informal in manner," as a contemporary observer described her, the prewar flapper had been an upper-middle-class phenomena. But during the twenties her exhibitionism, competitiveness, and aura of defiance—her "manners and morals"—sifted downward through the larger ranks of the middle class.

The exuberant thrust of the 1920s was short lived. Once the Great Depression struck, a search for security replaced the quest for individualism and squelched many expectations of the postwar decade. As job opportunities vanished, women's hopes of "economic independence" fell, career aspirations dwindled, and feminist zeal went into eclipse. Most women faced the depression at home, where new trends emerged. During the 1930s, the marriage rate dropped, desertion increased, and the birthrate, which had been declining steadily, plunged another 13 percent. Still, hard times enhanced the significance of women's traditional roles. When male "breadwinners" lost their jobs and family income fell, housewives filled the breach by "making do"—with meatless recipes, hand-me-down clothes, a revival of home industry, and household businesses. Sociologists who studied the families of the unemployed reported that men "cut adrift from their usual routines" succumbed to helplessness. But "the women's world remained largely intact and . . . became if anything more absorbing." "I think hard times is harder on a man," one housewife recalled.

The depression affected women's role in the work force as well. When unemployment rose, government, the labor movement, and public opinion polls urged an end to the hiring of married women, who, it was thought, deprived male providers of jobs. Women fought the prevailing mood by opposing the Economy Act of 1933, which in effect fired wives of federal employees from government posts. Similarly, they protested other inequities such as those National Recovery Act (NRA) codes that provided lower wages for women than for men doing the same work and the exclusion of many women workers from the benefits of New Deal legislation such as the Social Security Act. Black women voiced their complaints independently; over half lost their jobs, and they were rarely accepted in government work-relief programs. But hard times brought some surprises in the labor market. Despite denunciations of working wives, women overall were less likely to lose their jobs than men: heavy industry was hit harder than the service sector, in which most women worked and which recovered faster. For the same reason, women entered the labor force with more ease than men. During the 1930s the number of working women rose 25 percent and the number of working wives shot upward by an astounding 50 percent.

Women of the 1930s also achieved new visibility in public life. During the first Roosevelt administration, women with backgrounds in suffrage and social welfare gained appointments to high-level governments jobs. Labor Secretary Frances Perkins, a former social worker who had served as FDR's industrial commissioner in New York State, became the first woman cabinet member; Ellen Woodward, a Mississippi suffragist, headed women's work-relief programs under CWA and WPA; Mary W. Dewson, another veteran of social welfare, led the women's division of the Democratic party. Women's contributions to the New Deal were personified by Eleanor Roosevelt, who capitalized on a decade of experience in feminist organizations to reach unprecedented prominence in public life. Tireless campaigner, political strategist, presidential adviser, syndicated columnist, and radio personality, the First Lady publicized women's activities and crusaded for her favorite causes, whether the federal homestead program, an antilynching law, or work relief camps for women. In her depression advice tract, *It's Up to the Women* (1933), Eleanor Roosevelt told her readers to assert themselves both as ''inspirations of the home'' and as activists in civic affairs.

Urged to leave the work force in the 1930s, women were exhorted to enter it during World War II. As the manpower supply shrank, federal agencies such as the War Manpower Commission and the Office of War Information began luring women into war jobs. During the war, about six million women joined the labor force. The number of women workers increased by over half, and the proportion of women who worked leapt from 27 to 37 percent. Defense industries experienced the biggest influx. Moving into well-paid work in airplane plants,

shipyards, steel mills, and ammunition factories, women ran cranes and lathes, repaired engines, cut sheet metal, and made instrument panels. In auto production, one out of four workers was female. Geographical mobility increased as women migrated to defense production centers, and occupational mobility increased as well. Despite continued racial discrimination, many black women moved out of domestic work into better-paid jobs in the service sector or defense production. Perhaps the most important wartime change was in the makeup of the female labor force: three out of four new women workers were married, an omen of developments to come.

But the impact of the wartime ''emergency'' did not alter long-held convictions about woman's ''place.'' The public accepted women's labor in defense industry as a temporary expedient, acceptable only ''for the duration.'' Government propaganda promoted women's war work by emphasizing traditional roles (''her man is out there''). Women exerted little influence on public policy, even in the labor field. Although the Women's Bureau diligently issued directives on the fair treatment of new workers, employers had no obligation to follow them. Child care facilities never caught up with need. Indeed, public opinion linked the working mother with other wartime hazards, such as family breakups, rising divorces, child neglect, juvenile delinquency, and teenage immorality. War, in short, did not necessarily boost the cause of sexual equality. On the contrary, the scarcity of men increased their value, just as wartime disruptions fueled desires for ''normalcy.'' One OWI correspondent conveyed a popular view in 1943 when he expressed a desire ''to get these women back where they belong, amid the environment of home life.''

At the war's end, plans to demobilize women workers and make room for returning veterans took effect swiftly. When defense plants closed or converted to civilian production, some four million women lost their jobs; in the auto industry by the spring of 1946, only 8 percent of workers were women. Caught in a double bind, the Women's Bureau claimed that women did not want "to get ahead at the expense of veterans," although they hoped to retain "some, if not all of the gains" of the war years. The major gain, high wages, quickly vanished. A wartime campaign for "equal pay for equal work" floundered in 1946, when Congress defeated an equal pay bill. But once at work, many women were loath to leave. The end of the war did not halt the long-term expansion of the female labor force, as the decades ahead would prove.

Postwar America was as much a "new era" as the 1920s—an era of massive economic growth. The gross national product soared, median family income doubled, upward mobility beckoned, and middle-class membership mushroomed. Suburban development, fostered by low-interest mortgages and federal funding for highway construction, offered new opportunities for young families, and birthrates reversed their downward trend. The postwar baby boom peaked in 1957, when a woman could expect an average of 3.76 children. Growing families and suburban life meant a commitment to car pools, child rearing, and "togetherness" as promoted in *McCalls* (1954). Increased buying power, meanwhile, gave women unprecedented roles in the economy. During the postwar decade, the market was flooded with new or once-scarce consumer goods from cars and televisions to home appliances and frozen foods. Consumer credit rose fivefold, promotion budgets doubled, and marketing research targeted the homemaker—the family's chief purchasing agent. Many women welcomed the vocation of homemaker and consumer. To those who had grown up during the depression and war periods, the prospect of stability and affluence held great appeal. Advertisers bolstered their domestic roles, as did psychologists, educators, and other experts. Bemoaning

the working mother, the press exalted the homemaker. "No job is more exacting, more necessary, or more rewarding than that of housewife and mother," journalist Agnes Meyer proclaimed in a 1950 article that set the tone for the decade ahead.

But postwar economic expansion had another impact, too: employers needed workers and middle-class families needed second incomes. Women's role in the work force continued to increase. By the end of the 1950s, twice as many women were at work as in 1940, and during the 1960s, two out of three new workers were women. Postwar women did not surge into heavy industry, as they had during the war, but into more traditional female work— clerical, service, and sales jobs, and school-teaching—all expanding areas. Likely to be married, middle-aged, and middle-class, the new woman worker justified her role with a traditional rationale: her wages helped her family to maintain a middle-class lifestyle. The postwar decades were nonetheless a time of contradictions. While pollsters reported that "no woman is happier than a housewife," the Women's Bureau exhorted employers to take advantage of "woman power."

The contradictions of women's lives in postwar America emerged in the report of President Kennedy's Commission on the Status of Women, an advisory group formed in 1961 to compensate for the administration's paucity of high-level women appointees. The commission's report (1963) reflected the concerns of women workers, who now comprised one third of the labor force. Although dismissing demands for an ERA, the report catalogued legal inequities. It also urged day-care programs, paid maternity leaves, state equal pay laws (a federal law was passed in 1963), and women's appointments to political positions. The contradictions in women's lives drew far more public attention in Betty Friedan's 1963 best-seller, *The Feminine Mystique,* an indictment of the "housewife-heroine" of the 1950s. After

World War II, Friedan charged, women had been told that "they could desire no greater destiny than to glory in their own femininity." This dogma bound them to the home, while depriving them of purposeful activity, individualism, and a sense of identity.

Betty Friedan did not call explicitly for radical change or a feminist crusade; the *Feminine Mystique* was no summons to arms. Directed at educated, middle-class women, it urged them to find individual solutions, not collective ones. But Friedan's message was fortuitously timed, for the civil rights movement of the early 1960s created a climate of protest that directly promoted a feminist revival. Attracting extensive media attention, the movement spurred egalitarian arguments, urged remedial legislation, and set a precedent for ending discrimination.

Such lessons were not lost on future feminists. After Title 7 of the Civil Rights Act of 1964 prohibited sex discrimination as well as race discrimination in employment, women contended that the Equal Employment Opportunity Commission (EEOC) ignored sex discrimination complaints. Their grievances led to the formation of the National Organization for Women (NOW; 1966), which declared itself "a civil rights movement for women." A traditional pressure group, NOW demanded "a truly equal partnership of the sexes, as part of the worldwide revolution of human rights." Within a year, a more radical wing of feminist protest erupted among younger women in the civil rights movement and New Left. In the context of campaigns against racial injustice and establishment power, they had experienced not only an expansion of self-esteem but a new awareness of sexual inequity. Some concluded that "assumptions of male superiority" were as "crippling" as racism. Demanding a transformation of gender roles and social institutions, the radicals called for "women's liberation."

By the start of the 1970s, the new feminism had exploded into a ferment of action. NOW's membership surged, the spirit of "women's lib" spread, and women's protest groups formed in colleges, offices, labor unions, and professions. Many groups adopted the radicals' innovative technique of "consciousness-raising," in which, explained activist Susan Brownmiller, "women's experience at the hands of men was analyzed as a *political* phenomena." Conflict developed between the two wings of the movement. Younger radicals felt that NOW, with its agenda of legislative change, was "hopelessly bourgeois." NOW looked on the radicals as wild-eyed extremists with muddled goals. "Equal employment is the gut issue," said Betty Friedan, NOW's first president. Attitudes toward men were also at variance. Many radicals attacked "man" as the oppressor, while NOW, urging a "partnership of the sexes," claimed that ending sex discrimination would benefit men and women alike. Nonetheless, despite feuds between feminist factions, the core of a common platform emerged. The new feminists demanded equal employment opportunity, day-care facilities, liberalization of state abortion laws, and an end to "sexism"—which, explained activist Robin Morgan, meant "the definition of and discrimination against half the human species by the other half."

Like earlier feminist crusades, the new feminism was primarily a movement of white, middle-class, educated women. Alienated by liberationist rhetoric, working-class women felt that feminists devalued and demeaned what most women did. Black women, who found racism more oppressive than sexism, were similarly skeptical. As black lawyer Pauli Murray claimed, they were judged "disloyal to racial interests, if they insisted on women rights." But despite its middle-class constituency, the new feminism was also distinctive. Unlike the woman suffrage campaign, it was diffuse in structure and purpose. "It's not a movement, it's a state of mind," one proponent declared. New feminists also rejected the traditional female power base, the home. While earlier generations of feminists had campaigned to extend the values of the home, their successors seemed anxious to get out of it. Finally, compared to the fifty-year suffrage struggle, the new movement achieved immediate results. Capitalizing on the civil rights precedent, feminists swiftly elicited a barrage of concessions from the federal government—from Congress, the courts, and the executive branch.

In 1972, Congress adopted an Equal Rights Amendment, prohibiting abridgement of rights "on account of sex" by the United States or by any state. Legislators also passed many other equity measures, such as equal credit opportunities, child care deductions for working parents, and equal benefits for married women in federal service. In two 1973 decisions, *Roe* v. *Wade,* and *Doe* v. *Bolton,* the U.S. Supreme Court declared that state laws restricting abortion were unconstitutional on the grounds that they invaded the right of privacy. In other decisions, the federal courts rejected protective laws, prohibited sex-labeling of jobs, and ensured equal pay for equal work. The executive played a role, too. In 1967 President Johnson extended an executive order prohibiting race discrimination in federal jobs to include sex discrimination and by 1970 the Labor Department was issuing guidelines to federal contractors to ensure "affirmative action." The only major feminist defeat occurred in 1972 when President Nixon rejected a comprehensive child care act to fund day-care facilities, on the grounds that the bill would weaken the family.

The push toward equity emerged in many other areas, from opinion polls to professional goals. In the early 1970s, a majority of citizens surveyed declared themselves in favor of efforts to "change women's status." Throughout the decade, the number of women candidates for public office increased, especially at the state and local level. By the end of the 1970s, most formerly all-male colleges, including the national service academies, admitted women. Now a majority of the college population,

women entered professional schools and prestigious professions in record numbers. The most important revolution of the 1970s was in fact a vocational one, a revolution in part abetted by feminism but more accurately converging with it.

During the 1970s and 1980s, women entered the work force at unprecedented rates, accelerating a trend that had been building up since World War II. In some cases, they moved into jobs once held mainly by men, such as bartenders or insurance adjusters. In even larger numbers, they moved into "new jobs," for as analyst Andrew Hacker points out, the transition to a technological economy and changes in the nature of work made women especially desirable employees. By 1980 over half of women were wage earners, compared to 35 percent in 1950. Simultaneously, the makeup of the female labor force changed. Discarding the role of "housewife-heroine" with alarming speed, married women rushed into the job market; the proportion of wives who worked leapt from 15 percent in 1940 to 30 percent in 1960 to over 50 percent in 1980. By 1985, when women were 45 percent of the work force, almost 70 percent of mothers of school-age children earned wages outside the home, as did half of all mothers of infants under one. No longer was paid employment relegated to poor women, young women, or single women. The middle-class homemaker had become a wage earner and the working mother was the norm.

Women's roles in the family—and families themselves—changed as rapidly as the female labor force. Again, the rise of feminism coincided with other major developments. One was a decline in family size, for the birthrate had been dropping steadily since 1957. In 1980 a woman might expect to have 1.86 children—compared to 3.6 in 1960, just after the baby boom peaked. Simultaneously, family life became less stable. Divorce rates soared from the sixties onward. By 1980, half of the marriages could be expected to end in divorce, compared to one in six in 1920. Meanwhile, during the 1970s, when feminism was at its peak, the numbers of families headed by women doubled, as did the numbers of women living alone.

Only the fortunate few, therefore, could expect to be the beneficiaries of prospering "two-career" families; the less fortunate might anticipate downward mobility. By the start of the 1980s, two thirds of the long-term poor were women and children and two out of three female-headed families received welfare. The rapid "feminization of poverty" resulted in part from escalating separation and divorce, which left women with diminished incomes and child care expenses. Another cause was a rapid rise in illegitimacy. During the 1970s, the number of families headed by unwed mothers increased over 400 percent. The increase was most drastic in the black community. By the mid-1980s, 75 percent of all black babies were born to unwed mothers and almost 60 percent of black families with children were headed by women, compared to 35 percent in 1970. Some analysts attributed the new trend to a steady drop in black male employment. The post-World War II economy that produced a black middle class, explained Eleanor Holmes Norton, former chairman of the EEOC in the Carter administration, had "destroyed the family structure of the black working class."

By the 1980s, the new feminism had long survived the era of reform in which it erupted. But the legislative momentum that prevailed a decade earlier had faded. Although the impact of the women's movement led to some unique "firsts"—the appointment of Sandra Day O'Connor to the U.S. Supreme Court in 1981 and the nomination of Geraldine Ferraro for the vice presidency in 1984—many aspects of the feminist agenda proved controversial. In June 1982, after a prolonged campaign, the ERA narrowly failed to win the approval of the requisite thirty-six states, despite the exten-

sion of the deadline for ratification. "Right-to-Life" advocates challenged the U.S. Supreme Court's legitimization of abortion by calling for a constitutional amendment to prohibit it. Controversy arose over affirmative action plans as well as over a campaign for "comparable worth" in employment, which meant equal pay for women and men doing different but comparable jobs. A "gender gap" in voting patterns seemed to reflect women's unequal economic circumstances more than feminist sensibilities. And several issues, such as a nationwide antipornography campaign, pitted feminists against each other.

The conflicts of the 1980s illustrated the extent to which "women's issues" had become public issues. They also indicated that disagreement over the nature—or desirability—of sexual equality was likely to provoke continued debate. Since the 1960s, feminism had changed laws and policies, institutions, and attitudes. But concurrent changes in women's lives, from the rise of the married worker to the feminization of poverty, raised yet new questions about women's roles in society—and the impact of those roles on others. Had the feminine mystique of the 1950s been replaced by a feminist mystique that made similarly unrealistic demands on its adherents? Could full-time wage earning be easily reconciled with traditional family roles? How would women's increased work force participation affect men, marriage, children, social relations, and the job market? Did older homemakers and working-class women profit from feminist gains to the same extent as well-educated, middle-class women? If women had made unparalleled progress toward equal status, why were more women than ever living in poverty, heading families alone, or depending on public support? Could full equality between men and women be assured, what costs and consequences, social and economic, would be attached? Recent women's history suggests that rapid shifts in values and behavior entail new risks and liabilities as well as options and benefits. It also confirms that any change in women's roles, sudden or incremental, will have wide repercussions on society at large.

SUGGESTED READINGS

Chafe, William H. *The American Woman: Her Changing Social, Economic, and Political Role, 1920–1970*. New York: Oxford University Press, 1972.

Cott, Nancy F. *The Grounding of Modern Feminism*. New Haven and London: Yale University Press, 1987.

Ehrenreich, Barbara. *The Hearts of Men: American Dreams and the Flight from Commitment*. New York: Doubleday Publishing, 1983.

Evans, Sara. *Personal Politics: The Roots of Women's Liberation in the Civil Rights Movement and the New Left*. New York: Alfred A. Knopf, 1979.

Fass, Paula S. *The Damned and the Beautiful: American Youth in the 1920s*. New York: Oxford University Press, 1977.

Filene, Peter G. *Him/Her/Self: Sex Roles in Modern America*. 2d ed. Baltimore: The Johns Hopkins University Press, 1986.

Hartmann, Susan M. *The Home Front and Beyond: American Women in the 1940s*. Boston: Twayne Publishers, 1982.

Jones, Jacqueline. *Labor of Love, Labor of Sorrow: Black Women, Work, and the Family from Slavery to the Present*. New York: Basic Books, 1985.

Kessler-Harris, Alice. *Out to Work: A History of Wage-Earning Women in America*. New York: Oxford University Press, 1982.

Rothman, Sheila M. *Woman's Proper Place: A History or Changing Ideals and Practices, 1870 to the Present*. New York: Basic Books, 1978.

Showalter, Elaine, ed. *These Modern Women: Autobiographical Essays from the 1920s*. Old Westbury, N.Y.: The Feminist Press, 1978.

Ware, Susan. *Holding Their Own: American Women in the 1930s*. Boston: Twayne Publishers, 1982.

Yates, Gayle Graham. *What Women Want: The Ideas of the Movement*. Cambridge, Mass.: Harvard University Press, 1973.

DOCUMENT 34.1
Depression Families

When depression struck in the 1930s, many sociologists investigated the ramifications of unemployment on family life. How were domestic roles affected when traditional "breadwinners" lost their jobs, when family income suddenly dwindled or vanished, and when wives were transformed into wage earners? In the following excerpts from a study of unemployed men, Barnard Professor Mirra Komarovsky examined the depression's impact on marital relations.

Profound, indeed, must be the importance of the role of the provider for the man's self-esteem to cause him to say, "I would rather starve than let my wife work." Or, "I would rather turn on the gas and put an end to the whole family than let my wife support me."

One man said that the worst thing about unemployment was having to go on relief. The next worst thing was having his wife work, as she had for a few months. To be supported by her, even for a short time, made him very unhappy. In fact, he is sure they would have drifted apart if she had continued longer. He would have left her. The whole thing was wrong. She was not the same; he was not the same. It was awful to have to ask her for tobacco, or to have to tell the landlady, "My wife will come, and I will pay you," or to be expected to have the dinner ready when she came home, or to have her too tired to talk to him at dinner. When he works and comes home tired, she is waiting for him and they have a nice talk together. But the other way it was quite different. At one time both of them

Source: Mirra Komarovsky, *The Unemployed Man and His Family* (New York: The Dryden Press, 1940), pp. 76–77, 130–133.

worked. That was better. Then the one who got home first cooked the meal. But even that was all wrong.

It is interesting to see that in this particular family the wife is devoted to the husband and has attempted to make her employment as painless as possible for her husband. She tells this story:

When she first told her husband that she would look for work, he disapproved of it. She went right ahead. She could tell that every evening he was anxious until she told him that the search for work during the day had been fruitless. He could hardly conceal his pleasure. One day she did find a job in a department store. His first reaction was to tell her that in times of depression it is easier for a woman to find a job than it is for a man. She knew that he was unhappy and sulky, and tried to think of some way of reconciling him to her work. At the end of the first week she asked him to come to the store and meet some of the people she worked with, and also to help her carry the pay envelope home. He said he wouldn't come, but at closing time she found him waiting for her. After a while she noticed that he hated to have her pay the rent. She decided to let him pay the rent. Her sudden sickness made her discontinue working. She doesn't think he would have become reconciled to it had she continued for a long time.

* * * * *

The question arises as to how far the events of the depression changed the sex life of the couple. In many cases the interviewers found it difficult to approach the respondents on their sex life. Women were more able to question wives on this point and men were more successful with husbands. Individuals differed very much in their ability to talk about their sex experiences.

The main question as to whether there has been any change at all during the depression in sex relations is answered affirmatively by most people. For 38 of the 59 cases information on sex was adequate. Of the 38, there were 16 that showed no change, while in 22 cases sex relations decreased in frequency and in 4 of the 22 cases relations ceased altogether. No increases in frequency were noted, save in one case, in which the comment was made, ''I think you want one another more when you're having hard luck than when everything is all right.'' It is safe then to say that sex life decreased, if it was affected at all.

In each case the respondent was asked for his or her reason for the change. Of the 22 families in which there was a decline, 8 claim that this came about for some reason not connected with the depression, such as ill health and the aging of the couple. But the remainder, 14, gave some cause directly connected with the depression: fear of pregnancy was mentioned by 11 people, 2 said that relations were decreased because the wife lost respect for the husband because of the depression, and one claimed that ''general anxiety'' caused the decline. . . .

Fear of pregnancy seems to be a specter haunting many of these families. Eleven of them gave this as the reason for the decline in sex relations. These people apparently felt that merely by decreasing frequency of relations they avoided the danger of having children. Many of them felt that families on relief had no right to have more children. . . .

Decline in sex relations may also be due to the loss of respect and affection for the unemployed husband. In some cases the failure of the husband affected the wife's response to him as a lover. This apparently was the situation in the Garland family:

Mrs. Garland said that her husband seemed a bigger man to her when he was employed and was making good money. Of course his unemployment had changed her attitude towards him. ''When a man cannot provide for the family and makes you worry so, you lose your love for him. A husband has to have four qualifications—first, second, and third he should be able to support the family, and fourth he should have personality.'' Her husband doesn't fulfill any of these qualifications. If she had the money she would probably get a divorce. Mrs. Garland said she did enjoy sex relations prior to unemployment, but does not now. She herself does not understand the reason for the change.

DOCUMENT 34.2
"When You Hire Women"

As female employment rose during World War II, the Women's Bureau of the Department of Labor issued a stream of reports on women workers as well as directives to the companies that hired them. The following recommendations to employers, published in 1944, suggested tactics to help women adjust to jobs in heavy industry, such as training programs, counseling services, and equal opportunity for promotion. Sharing the public's concern about working mothers, the Women's Bureau also urged that applicants with young children be questioned about their provisions for child care.

Today women—hundreds of thousands of them—are at work in war industries. Unafraid of the hard, tedious, and dangerous jobs, they are working in shipyards, in aircraft and instrument factories, in arsenals and steel mills. World War II, with its great influx of women into jobs previously marked "men only," presents both management and labor with many new and puzzling problems. Employers may benefit by reading of the successful experience of others in employing women.

First. Sell the idea of women workers to present employee staff—the foremen and men workers.

A shipyard called its foremen together, the labor stringency was discussed, and the foremen themselves decided it was advisable to employ women. They in turn sold the idea to the men in their respective departments. Though this yard had been strictly a male domain, the men have been exceptionally cooperative. Another shipyard distributed to every foreman mimeographed material which contained the statement, "Half the people in the world are women—your mother, wife, sister, daughter. The women who are coming into the plant are just like them."

Second. Survey jobs to decide which are most suitable for women.

In an excellent job analysis in a gun plant, the following procedure was followed. Women were asked to lift repeatedly weights of varying amounts while in a sitting and standing position. It was found that fatigue was noticeable at the point where 18 to 21 pounds was lifted from 20 to 25 times an hour. Eighteen pounds was set as the limit for women where direct lifting was done repeatedly.

Third. Make adaptation of jobs to fit smaller frames and lesser muscular strength of women.

A drill manufacturer installed a conveyer system, electric button controls instead of levers and wheels, platforms to bring about better relation of arm to machine-bed.

A steel-castings foundry eliminated much heavy lifting by reducing the size of shovels, dumping carts, and sand-buggies, and installing chain hoists.

An engine-parts manufacturer broke down operations so that light work could be segregated from heavy work.

Fourth. Provide service facilities in the plant to accommodate anticipated number of women.

Washrooms and locker rooms, toilets, and rest-rooms should be planned for.

A shipbuilding company has provided excellent rest rooms for women. They are clean, have leather chairs and lounges, tables where lunches may be eaten. The washrooms are also clean, well lighted, ventilated.

Source: *When You Hire Women,* Women's Bureau, Department of Labor, Special Bulletin No. 14 (Washington, D.C.: U.S. Government Printing Office, 1944).

Fifth. Appoint a woman personnel director to organize and head a woman-counselor system.

A large ammunition plant, with thousands of women employees, put into practice an effective counseling system, with a director, assistant director, area supervisors, and consultants.

In one aircraft plant the assistance given by women counselors to new women employees includes loans for lodging, food, and transportation until receipt of the first pay check.

In some plants counselors have given the shopping problem their immediate attention, as women employees reported this a reason for absenteeism. In one instance, they called upon grocery stores in nearby towns, as a result of which the stores take turns staying open evenings.

Sixth. Select women carefully and for specific jobs.

Determine what requirements the job makes of the employee. What is demanded in terms of height, long reach, strength, steady nerves? Does it call for alertness, judgement, manipulative ability, speed?

Manual dexterity and intelligence tests may be given applicants, but they are used only as an aid to personnel selection.

Family responsibilities of women should be taken into consideration.

The interviewers should know what home duties the woman has, and if possible place her on the most appropriate shift. Employment of mothers of children under 14 is strongly opposed by authorities. If they must work, their placement on the day shift is recommended. Mothers should be questioned closely as to whether adequate provision for the care of young children has been made. Harassed mothers make poor workers.

Seventh. Develop a program for the induction and training of women.

Many women employees have never been inside a factory before; they may be frightened and disturbed by machines and noise.

A shipyard has its newly employed women spend the first day learning company policy and procedure. They are given talks on safety and hygiene. Foremen have asked that this policy be adopted for men also, as they say that women start in to work better than the men.

Eighth. Establish good working conditions, effective in reducing turn-over, improving morale, and recruiting new women workers.

The maximum eight-hour day and forty-eight-hour week, with one day of rest in seven, has been advocated jointly by eight government agencies.

Where possible, women should be provided with chairs, built on posture lines and adjustable to both the worker and the job.

Ninth. Supervise women workers intelligently.

Foremen and leadmen may need special training if they are not experienced in supervising women.

The following paragraphs are taken from general instructions on supervision of women, issued by the Office of the Assistant Secretary of the Navy:

Proceed slowly for about the first two weeks. After they lose their fear of the machines, and after they become accustomed to the noise and vibration, they may be quicker than men in their work.

Help women who have never worked in industry build confidence in themselves. Help them feel that they can do the job successfully, that they need not feel ''dumb.''

In your effort to be kind, don't do a woman's work for her or she will become bored.

A foreman should be tactful, wise, and understanding in his treatment of women workers. He should be able to soothe ruffled feelings as well as to administer first aid. Women are inquisitive and willing to learn. For a competent and tactful foreman, they will be loyal and conscientious.

Tenth. Give women equal opportunity with men.

When women make good on their jobs, they should be given a chance to be upgraded and an opportunity to transfer.

Training on the job and supplementary training should be followed by actual promotion when a woman has demonstrated her capacity for an advancement in both jobs and wages. Develop foreladies.

Equal opportunity with men means that wage rates throughout the plant should be based on a straight job analysis.

The National Foremen's Institute says, "You can't induct a woman into war work and tell her she's going to fill the shoes of a man who has been called to arms, and then pay her only 80 percent of his wages, without stigmatizing her instantly with the idea that she really isn't as good as the man whose job she took over."

Eleventh. Encourage women to make suggestions.

Women's inventiveness and ingenuity may develop shortcuts.

DOCUMENT 34.3
Defending the Homemaker

The influx of women into the work force during the war generated fears about the alleged consequences of female employment, such as neglected children, family disintegration, and community collapse. Sharing such fears, journalist Agnes Meyer, the wife of a wealthy financier and mother of five, charged that materialism and selfishness were leading women from domestic life to the workplace. In a 1950 speech at Howard University, later published in the Atlantic, *she urged women to return to their most important roles, mothers and homemakers.*

Instead of apologizing for being a "mere housewife," as so many do, women should make society realize that upon the housewife now falls the combined tasks of economist, nutrition expert, sociologist, psychiatrist, and educator.

Source: Agnes E. Meyer, "Women Aren't Men," *Atlantic* 186 (August 1950), pp. 33–36.

Then society would confer upon the housewife the honor, recognition, and status it deserves. Today, however, the duties of the homemaker have become so depreciated that many women feel impelled to work outside the home in order to retain the respect of the community. It is one thing if women work to help support the family. It is quite another thing—it is a destructive influence—if society forces women into the labor market in order that they may respect themselves and gain the respect of others.

Women must boldly announce that no job is more rewarding than that of housewife and mother. Then they will be free to become once more the moral force of society through the stabilization of the home. . . . But they can only do this if they will accept the fact that their functions as women arc very different from those of men. What modern woman has to recapture is the wisdom that just being a woman is her central task and greatest honor. It is a task that challenges her whole character, intelligence, and imagination.

If we look at the social scene about us we find very hopeful indications that women, especially the young married women, have begun to realize these fundamental truths. . . . On the other hand it is no less true that there have never been so many women who are dissatisfied with being women and therefore with being wives and mothers. There have never been so many women who are unnecessarily torn between marriage and a career. There have never been so many mothers who neglect their children because they find some trivial job more interesting. I know this from wide contact with neglected children. The most pathetic are those who come from well-to-do homes. The poor child whose mother has to work has some inner security because he knows in his little heart that his mother is sacrificing herself for his well-being. But the neglected child from a well-to-do home, who realizes instinctively that his mother prefers her job to him, often hates her with a passionate intensity. These are the children who frequently get into the worst difficulties because they are the most deeply hurt and resentful.

What ails these women who consciously or unconsciously reject their children? Surface influences of a competitive, materialistic world have obscured the importance of women's role as the repository of continuity and of purposeful living derived from their biological and social functions. Our technological civilization has atrophied their emotions, and nothing is more horrible than a woman whose instinctive reactions have been destroyed. They are far more egotistical than men, more fiercely aggressive, more insensitive, not only to the beauty but to the decency of life. They have become masculine without even knowing it. . . .

I am not trying to drive all women back into the home. The married woman who is rebellious about family life does her children more harm by staying home in such a frame of mind than by leaving them to some kindly relative or sending them to boarding school. It is the frame of mind of such women that is wrong, that must be understood and changed. For these women are equally disastrous as an influence in their working environment. God protect us from the efficient, go-getter businesswoman whose feminine instincts have been completely sterilized. Wherever women are functioning, whether in the home or in a job, they must remember that their chief function as woman is a capacity for warm, understanding, and charitable relationships. Women are throwing their greatest natural gift out the window when they cease to function as experts in cooperative living.

It is distressing, therefore, to hear the oft-repeated that woman must be a personality first and a woman only secondarily. This cliché revives in a new form the dualistic conflict between nature and spirit, body and mind, the conscious and the unconscious, which weakens all personality, whether male or female, but is especially disastrous to woman at a time when an arid and strictly academic education has already dangerously widened the gap be-

tween her emotional and intellectual capacities. Are women people? Only to the extent that they fuse their inherited and acquired characteristics into a dynamic, harmoniously functioning unity which alone is worthy of being called personality.

DOCUMENT 34.4
Consciousness-Raising

A proliferation of women's groups committed to feminist goals caught the attention of the press and the public in the late 1960s. In an article on the origins of "women's liberation," writer Susan Brownmiller, an activist in the feminist revival, explained the technique of "consciousness-raising" used by diverse women's discussion groups.

There is a small group of women that gathers at my house or at the home of one or another of our 15 members each Sunday evening. Our ages range from the early twenties to the late forties. As it happens, all of us work for a living, some at jobs we truly like. Some of us are married, with families, and some are not. Some of us knew each other before we joined the group and some did not. Once we are settled on the sofa and the hard-backed chairs brought in from the kitchen, and the late-comers have poured their own coffee and arranged themselves as best they can on the floor, we begin our meeting. Each week we explore another aspect of what we consider to be our fundamental oppression in a male-controlled society. . . .

Two years ago the 50 or so women in New York City who had taken to calling themselves the women's liberation movement met on Thursday evenings at a borrowed office on East 11th Street. The official title of the group was the New York Radical Women. There was

Source: Susan Brownmiller, "Sisterhood Is Powerful": A Member of the Women's Liberation Movement Explains What It's All About," *The New York Times Magazine* (March 15, 1970), pp. 27ff.

some justification at the time for thinking grandly in national terms, for similar groups of women were beginning to form in Chicago, Boston, San Francisco, and New York. New York Radical Women came by its name quite simply: the women were young radicals, mostly under the age of 25, and they came out of the civil rights and/or peace movements, for which many of them had been full-time workers. A few years earlier, many of them might have been found on the campuses of Vassar, Radcliffe, Wellesley, and the larger coed universities, a past they worked hard to deny. What brought them together to a woman-only discussion and action group was a sense of abuse suffered at the hands of the very protest movements that had spawned them. As "movement women," they were tired of doing the typing and fixing the food while "movement men" did the writing and leading. Most were living with or married to movement men who, they believed, were treating them as convenient sex objects or as somewhat lesser beings. . . .

In short, "the movement" was reenforcing, not eliminating, their deepest insecurities and feelings of worthlessness as women—feelings which quite possibly had brought them into radical protest politics top begin with. So, in a small way, they had begun to rebel. They had decided to meet regularly—without their men—to talk about their common experience. . . .

In Marxist canons, "the woman question" is one of the many manifestations of a sick, capitalist society which "the revolution" is supposed to finish off smartly. Some of the women who devoted their Thursday evenings to New York Radical Women believed they were merely dusting off and streamlining an orthodox, ideological issue. Feminism was bad politics and a dirty word since it excluded the larger picture.

But others in the group, like Anne Koedt and Shuli Firestone, an intense and talkative young activist, had begun to see things from a different, heretical perspective. Woman's oppressor was Man, they argued, and not a specific economic system. After all, they pointed out, male supremacy was still flourishing in the Soviet Union, Cuba and China, where power was still lodged in a male bureaucracy. . . . The heretics tentatively put forward the idea that feminism must be a separate movement of its own.

New York Radical Women's split in perspective—was the ultimate oppressor Man or Capitalism?—occupied endless hours of debate at the Thursday evening meetings. Two warring factions emerged, dubbing each other "the feminists" and "the politicos." But other things were happening as well. For one thing, new women were coming in droves to the Thursday evening talkfest, and a growing feeling of sisterhood was permeating the room. Meetings began awkwardly and shyly, with no recognized chairman and no discernible agenda. Often the suggestion, "Let's sit closer together, sisters," helped break the ice. But once the evening's initial awkwardness had passed, volubility was never a problem. "We had so much to say," an early member recalled, "and most of us had never said it to another woman before."

Soon *how* to say it became an important question. Young women like Carol Hanisch, a titian-haired recruit to the civil rights movement from a farm in Iowa, and her friend Kathy Amatniek, a Radcliffe graduate and working film editor, had spent over a year in Mississippi working with SCNC. There they had been impressed with the Southern-revival-style mass meetings at which blacks got up and "testified" about their own experience with "the Man." Might the technique also work for women? And wasn't it the same sort of thing that Mao Tse-tung had advocated to raise political consciousness in Chinese villages? . . .

The personal testimony method encouraged *all* women who came to the meeting to speak their thoughts. The technique of "going around the room" in turn brought responses from many who had never opened their mouths at male-dominated meetings and were experiencing the same difficulty in a room full of articulate members of their own sex. Specific questions such as, "If you've thought of having a baby, do you want a girl or a boy?" touched off accounts of what it meant to be a girl-child—the second choice in a society that prizes boys. An examination of "What happens to your relationship when your man earns more money than you, and what happens when *you* earn more money than him?" brought a flood of anecdotes about the male ego and money. "We all told similar stories," relates a member of the group. "We discovered that, to a man, they all felt challenged if we were the breadwinners. It meant that we were no longer dependent. We had somehow robbed them of their 'rightful' role."

"We began to see our 'feminization' as a two-level process," says Anne Koedt. "On one level, a woman is brought up to believe that she is a girl and that it is her biological destiny. She isn't supposed to want to achieve anything. If, by some chance, she manages to escape the psychological damage, she finds that the structure is prohibitive. Even though she wants to achieve, she finds she is discouraged at every turn and she still can't become President."

Few topics, the women found, were unfruitful. . . .

"Consciousness-raising," in which a woman's personal experience at the hands of men was analyzed as a *political* phenomena, soon became a keystone of the women's liberation movement.

DOCUMENT 34.5
Women versus Men in the Work Force

Of twenty-four million new workers in the 1970s, almost fourteen million were women.

Source: "Women vs. Men in the Work Force," *The New York Times Magazine,* December 9, 1984, pp. 124ff.

Political scientist Andrew Hacker, an analyst of contemporary trends, examines the causes of rising female employment in recent years and some of its implications for women and men.

The road signs have been changed—no longer "Men at Work" but "People Working." Every occupation reported by the Census Bureau, up to and including stevedores and boilermakers, lists women as well as men. Forty-four percent of all employed Americans are women. What's more, the percentage continues to rise, which poses a sobering question: Are the gains being made by women in the workplace coming at the expense of men?

On the face of it, the answer is clear. Unless total employment in the nation expands more rapidly than it has, some substantial number of men are going to continue to lose out in the job race to women. But the process by which the change is taking place is complex, and the explanation goes beyond the political and legal pressures that are part of women's campaign for equal rights.

There have been changes in the character of work that have encouraged the hiring of women. In the insurance industry, for example, the positions of adjusters and examiners were once held largely by men, who went out and inspected dented fenders. Today, the work consists mainly of sitting at a computer terminal, entering insurance claims. Women now hold 65 percent of these jobs, up from 27 percent in 1970. In general, women are filling the new, lower-paying jobs in offices and in the service industry.

Some jobs that were once all-male preserves changed with the introduction of modern equipment. That happened in the meatpacking industry, where automatic machines for moving sides of beef have eased the need for so much heaving and hoisting. Since 1970, the proportion of packinghouse butchers who are women has increased by more than one-third.

In some cases, changes in society's perception of what represents "men's work" are involved. During the last decade, for example, the number of bartenders in the nation rose by about 130,000. However, 100,000 of these new openings were filled by women.

Among the most vivid cases of displacement are those in the upper reaches of the workplace. The proportion of women among graduate students has been increasing dramatically, providing stiff competition for young men who, a generation earlier, might have been all but certain of executive or professional careers. Between 1960 and 1983, the male proportion among lawyers has declined from 98 to 85 percent. Over the same period of time, the percentage of men in advertising fell from 86 to 52 percent; in banking and financial management, from 91 to 61 percent.

In fact, over the last several decades, the proportion of men who hold any kind of job has been declining. Among adult men, only 78 percent now belong to the labor force, compared with 86 percent in 1960. . . .

Where have the new jobs for women come from? As it happens, while white women were arriving at new insights about what they wanted to do with their lives, the economy was undergoing basic changes. Great gains were being made in productivity, largely because machines were replacing workers in the manufacturing sector. . . . The jobs that have disappeared in . . . heavy-duty industries were held mainly by men. And the new jobs that have come along are being taken mainly by women.

While cutting blue-collar employment, few companies have reduced their overall workforce. Instead they have devised new office positions, especially to cope with the so-called "information explosion." Companies have also moved more strongly into the service sector, producing new jobs in fields from fast-food outlets to computer-consulting firms. . . .

It was not that the new positions had a specific gender written on them. Despite recent changes stimulated by the women's movement, women in our society still tend to differ from men in upbringing and outlook, and some of their attributes have a tangible value in the current job market.

Many of the new occupations, for example, call for a relatively high degree of literacy, in both language and numbers. This is the case, not only with office work, but also across a range of responsibilities from taking airline reservations to monitoring hospital intensive care units.

At almost every level, the call is for more literate employees. And, for the first time in our history, women are clearly emerging as better educated than men. . . .

Why worry? For years, men have monopolized the world of careers. Now, with fairer job competition, we are discovering that men cannot depend on their gender for preferment. We must accept the consequences of our commitment to equal opportunity. Yet it would be foolhardy not to estimate the effects of the change and prepare for them.

As it happens, we already have had some glimpses of what can occur when women advance at a faster pace than men. Consider the experience of black Americans. Studies show that black women who finish high school have a fair chance of success in the employment market. For black men in search of work, racial discrimination is a major barrier, but experts such as Alvin Poussaint of the Harvard Medical School also stress a lack of education. . . . Black males have a higher drop-out rate, compared with black females, and are less likely to enter college. Among black youth, only 85 males finish high school for every 100 females. And among blacks currently in college, there are only 71 men for every 100 women.

Similar patterns prevail with employment. While white women now fill 48 percent of all professional positions—from engineering to nursing—held by white Americans, black women account for 66 percent of all black professionals. Black women make up 57 percent of black accountants and auditors, as against a 37 percent share for white women among whites. Among college teachers, the respective ratios for white and black women are 36 and 50 percent; among lawyers, they are 13 and 31 percent.

The husband's inability to earn enough to make him the family's principal source of support is, most authorities believe, one of the major causes of the high rate of marital break-ups in the black community. Among white Americans aged 25 to 65, a total of 73 percent have resident husbands, whereas the comparable figure among black women is 44 percent.

Historic differences in the treatment of blacks and whites make comparisons difficult; even so, there may be some warning signs here for at least a segment of the white population. We may see more white men joining this country's underclass. One ominous sign: the proportion of young white males who drop out of high school has grown by 26 percent during the past decade. They may find themselves continuously unemployed. And they may find their marriages troubled. In fact, the divorce rate among white couples has been rising faster than among blacks. . . .

The United States has made great progress toward ending barriers based on sex. In the years ahead, more women will be attaining what they want: to be considered full human beings, sharing the rights and opportunities—and paychecks—previously reserved for men. About a dozen years ago, Gloria Steinem remarked that "If women's lib wins, perhaps we all win." At the time, few of us thought much about that "perhaps," perhaps because we wanted to believe there could be prizes for everyone. But now men are learning that women have always known: that when one gender makes gains, it can require a loss for the other.

This country has always encouraged competition in the economic sphere, but never envisaged it would make rivals of the sexes. At this point, it seems clear that the greatest adjustments will have to be made by men. But women will also have to face the prospect of living with men they have outpaced.

chapter

American Political History: 1960–1987

William H. Chafe
Duke University

W hen John F. Kennedy was inaugurated president in January 1961, it seemed to many Americans, literally, that a new generation had taken over the politics of the country. His lean frame silhouetted against the Capitol dome, the vibrant young leader challenged his fellow citizens to "Ask not what your country can do for you, but what you can do for your country." The torch had been passed to a new generation, Kennedy said, "born in this century, tempered by war and a hard and bitter peace," ready now to explore a series of new frontiers, "to pay any price, and bear any burden" in this, a time of maximum peril for freedom around the globe. To anyone hearing his words, or seeing the ritual, the day's events augured a time of new beginnings, of dynamic leadership in achieving social reform at home, and of reclaiming national strength abroad.

As with most folklore, substantial truth resides in this collective memory of John Kennedy's beginnings as president. Change was in the air, symbolized by a president who played touch football and bounced his young daughter on his knee. From his pledge to send a man to the moon "this decade" to his proposal that young Americans become ambassadors to the world through the Peace Corps, the new president conveyed, at least through his style and words, a commitment to innovation.

Good reason exists, as well, to see the years from Kennedy to Reagan as a distinctive epoch in recent history, each person representing a "book-end" for an era. During the quarter century from the early sixties to the late eighties, most of the trends in American society that grew out of World War II came to a head. More social change occurred during the sixties and seventies than in any comparable period of American history. At the height of that change, forces of insurgent protest challenged the very foundations of American social and cultural institutions. When those insurgent forces came into conflict with defenders of the status quo in 1968, the whole of post–World War II history was changed. A new conservatism triumphed in the country, and many of the advances of the sixties came under attack. The ascendancy of Ronald Reagan to the White House in 1980 gave popularizers on the right a personal symbol, just as evocative and charismatic, as Kennedy had been twenty years earlier. Political leadership thus became a barometer of what had and had not happened in America. If in reality, Kennedy was more a part of the politics of the fifties than of the sixties when he took office, and Reagan ended up being more a pragmatist than an ideological purist, there is still poetic justice in seeing these figures—whom we have made larger than life—

as personifying the shifts that occurred during a remarkable period of history.

THE KENNEDY-JOHNSON YEARS

Notwithstanding Kennedy's subsequent reputation as a symbol of the social activism of the 1960s, it is important to recognize that he began as a relative conservative on domestic affairs, a person who moved into a more activist posture only when compelled to by the civil rights movement. Like so many politicians of the center in the fifties, Kennedy believed strongly in the basic soundness of America's social and economic system. Most of the country's problems, he declared, were "*technical* problems, . . . administrative problems. They . . . do not lend themselves to the great sort of 'passionate movements' which have stirred this country so often in the past." For the young Democratic candidate, the central issue domestically was simply the need "to do better," to get the economy moving again. If one could just "fine-tune" the economic system, the growth in gross national product (GNP) would take care of such social problems as poverty. "A rising tide," Kennedy was fond of saying, "lifts all boats." In Kennedy's view, there were no serious domestic ills that warranted dramatic change.

Nor was Kennedy significantly different from his predecessors on foreign policy, except perhaps in the shrillness of his rhetoric and the intensity of his exhortations to man the watchtowers of freedom. Although at various times in the past (especially with regard to Algeria's fight against colonialism and the importance of acknowledging nationalism in Southeast Asia), he had departed from the simplistic Cold War insistence that anyone not for us was against us, Kennedy more than compensated for his deviations by urging Americans to take the offensive against the Soviets. "Our responsibility," he told Congress, "is to be the chief defender of freedom." It was time, he said, "to move outside the home for-

tress, and . . . challenge the enemy in fields of our own choosing."

Consistent with these views, Kennedy made the battle against communism the centerpiece of his first two years in office, each month absorbed in a new crisis—the Bay of Pigs in April; Laos in May; a summit with Khruschev in June; the Berlin Wall in July; and building atomic shelters and calling up the reserves in August. "As the sun rose over the farthermost shores of Cathay and began its slow process across the heavens," one journalist wrote, "it was [always] one minute to midnight somewhere, and something would happen; a government would fall, there would be a significant outbreak of violence [and] all over Washington, men would rise early to answer the bidding to crisis and to greatness. . . ."

Domestic affairs attracted far less attention. Kennedy sent a typical Democratic shopping list to Congress in 1961 and 1962—higher minimum wages, increased social security benefits, a Manpower Retraining Act, and a proposal to create a Department of Urban Affairs. But most of his energies in the domestic arena went toward seeking faster economic growth and calibrating price and wage increases to productivity. When the steel industry threatened to disrupt that strategy with sudden price increases in 1962, Kennedy flew into action, mobilizing administration forces to persuade "big steel" to roll back its price hike. But nowhere else did JFK show such passion. Tariff reform was his primary domestic goal for 1962. Notwithstanding Kennedy's rhetorical commitments to civil rights during the 1960 campaign, he gave little but lip service to legislative action on this, America's number one domestic shame. It even took him twenty-two months to sign an executive order to make federally financed housing available on a nondiscriminatory basis, an action he had pointed to in 1960 as an example of how the president could provide leadership on moral issues "with the simple stroke of a pen." For most of the first two years of Kennedy's term, then, there seems little basis for seeing the president as a leader of activism or reform. Rather, as columnist Joseph Kraft said, his motto seemed to be, "no enemies to the right."

What changed all of that, and eventually gave credibility to Kennedy's image as a reformer, was the collective force of countless black Americans *insisting* that America live up to its professed belief in equality and justice for all people. The movement had been making that demand for years, of course, from the black veterans who returned from Normandy to seek the right to vote, to the school children in Little Rock, the bus patrons in Montgomery, and the four young freshmen in Greensboro who asked for a cup of coffee at Woolworth's. But now the movement intensified, in the Delta counties of Alabama and Mississippi; in Albany, Georgia; in St. Augustine, Florida. When Birmingham exploded during the spring of 1963, the entire nation became involved, millions watching as TV newscasts each night showed the brutalization of black women and children by police dogs and fire hoses.

Initially, the Kennedy administration tried its traditional approach of behind-the-scenes compromise. But this time it would not work. Fulfilling their own sense of mission, Police Commissioner Bull Conor and his allies refused to go along, resorting to outrageous violence to disrupt any chance of progress. When, subsequently, Alabama's Governor George Wallace threw down the gauntlet of interposition, threatening to block the desegregation of the University of Alabama with his own body, it became clear that *this* civil rights crisis would not fade into the background.

In response John Kennedy finally made a personal and substantive commitment to civil rights legislation. Identifying for the first time with the movement itself, Kennedy told the nation in a televised address that civil rights was "above all a moral issue, . . . as old as the Scriptures . . . and as clear as the Constitu-

tion." Who among us, he asked, "would be content to have the color of his skin changed and stand in [the Negro's] place? Who among us would then be content with the counsels of patience and delay?" Proposing a broad range of reforms, from equal access to public accommodations, to abolition of economic discrimination based on race, Kennedy devoted his own resources and those of his administration to securing support for racial equality.

Significantly, Kennedy's departure on civil rights occurred the same week as his decision to initiate a war on poverty. His action highlighted the inextricable connection between racial and economic inequality, underlining the disproportionate incidence among blacks of low incomes, high infant mortality, and unemployment. The number of blacks who were poor helped to persuade Kennedy that a fight on the issue of racial justice alone was not enough, and that the struggle to abolish poverty was equally significant—and a fight that could not be won simply by having a "rising tide lift all boats."

Finally that same month, Kennedy launched a bold new initiative in foreign policy, in the process thoroughly repudiating much of his previous Cold Warrior rhetoric. In the aftermath of confronting directly the horror of nuclear annihilation during the Cuban Missile Crisis of October 1962, Kennedy appears to have reassessed his approach to international conflict. It was time, he declared in a speech at American University, for both the United States and the Soviet Union to reexamine their premises. No system of government, he declared, was totally evil, or good. Negotiation and reconciliation offered the only true hope for peace, because in the end, "our most basic common link is that we all inhabit this small planet. We all breathe the same air. We all cherish our children's future and we are all mortal." Two months later, Russia and the United States signed a treaty banning atomic weapons testing in the atmosphere.

Three actions on civil rights, poverty, and peace were initiated; three signs that a new presidency was in the offing. Three reasons why, in retrospect, we have seen the Kennedy years as the start of an era of reform. If John F. Kennedy had begun his presidency with only a stylistic commitment to innovation, he had finally, by the summer of 1963, commenced the process of turning style into substance. Despite the legacy of the Vietnamese war which he had done so much to expand, Kennedy appeared by the fall of 1963 to have embarked decisively on a new path, one whose promise, at least in hindsight, seems to have been full of possibility for peace and justice.

It became Lyndon Johnson's responsibility to secure, then expand, the agenda of reform that Kennedy had initiated before his assassination in November 1963. A brilliant politician, Johnson had built his entire career around his extraordinary capacity to forge consensus out of conflict, and to transcend the parochialism of regional and partisan passions by speaking for "all the people." Describing his political identity in 1958, Johnson said:

> I am a free man, a U.S. Senator and a Democrat, in that order. I am also a liberal, a conservative . . . a businessman, a consumer . . . and I am all these things in no fixed order . . . At the heart of my own beliefs is a rebellion against this very process of classifying, labeling, and filing Americans under headings.

As Senate Majority Leader during the 1950s, Johnson had raised the practice of cajoling and manipulating his colleagues to the level of a fine art. Although his term as vice president had afforded far fewer opportunities for displaying his talents, Johnson entered the crisis of the assassination perhaps better qualified than any person in the nation to create a coalition of support for a domestic agenda that would outstrip even the New Deal in its scope and ambition.

With unerring intuition, Johnson began by identifying himself with Kennedy's vision. "Everything I had ever learned in the history books," he later recalled, "taught me that martyrs have to die for causes. John Kennedy had died. . . . I had to take the dead man's program and turn it into a martyr's cause. That way Kennedy would live on forever, and so would I." A native southerner, LBJ made his first mission the enactment of Kennedy's civil rights measure. "We have talked long enough in this country about equal rights," he told Congress. "It is time now to write the next chapter— and to write it in the books of law." In similar fashion, the new president rallied congressional support for Kennedy's tax cut, and with consummate skill, made the "war on poverty" a centerpiece of his 1964 State of the Union message.

But Johnson wanted much more than simply to be the instrument for fulfilling Kennedy's legacy. His lifelong goal had been to emulate, then ultimately surpass, the legislative record achieved by his political "father," Franklin Roosevelt. Hence, he sought his own program and vision, defining it to a University of Michigan audience in the spring of 1964 as the creation of "The Great Society." America had attained wealth, Johnson declared, and was committed to eliminating racial injustice and economic squalor. Now, he said, the challenge was to build a civilization where the quality of life would match the quantity of material goods, and where "the city of man serves not only the needs of the body . . . but the desire for beauty and hunger for community." In effect, Johnson proposed an America where no one was ill-clothed or ill-fed, where everyone enjoyed dignity and justice, and where the life of music and art was accessible to all.

To a remarkable extent, Johnson succeeded in enacting his Great Society program. Aided by a record-shattering victory over Barry Goldwater in 1964 ("did I do better than FDR in '36?" Johnson asked), the president shifted into high gear, determined to maximize his political clout while the voters' mandate was still fresh in the legislators' minds. The array of new laws was dazzling—medicare, federal aid to education, mass transit, rent subsidies, Headstart, a teacher's corps, mental health, environmental safety, model cities, and a revolutionary new voting rights bill guaranteeing black Americans the ballot. As one journalist said, "Johnson asketh and the Congress giveth."

But even as Johnson scaled the heights of success, his cherished consensus was crumbling beneath him. The most obvious source of erosion was the president's tragic insistence on deepening America's commitment to the war in Vietnam. Inexperienced in foreign policy, unsure of what Kennedy would have done, and traumatized by the fear that appearing "soft" on communism would endanger his domestic program, Johnson embraced the war, quickly becoming entrapped by a vicious cycle of escalation, defeat, and then greater escalation. If Kennedy had expanded the commitment of American troops to Vietnam from 800 to 15,000, Johnson would follow his predecessor's example, refusing to back down in the face of possible defeat. Because he feared the reaction of Congress and the voters if he told the truth, Johnson lied about the extent of his military buildup, dissembled when critics called him to task, and eventually became a prisoner of his own fortress in the White House, unable to overcome or dissuade the growing army of critics who, by 1967 and 1968, insisted that the war was stupid and immoral, and that the president must be replaced.

Even before these events, domestic critics had become increasingly disenchanted with the pace of change and the apparent desire of "the Establishment" to *control* the demands of insurgent forces. Many civil rights workers, for example, concluded that the administration would cooperate with reform only if it dictated the terms. When Mississippi activists went to

the 1964 Democratic Convention armed with compelling evidence that they deserved to be seated as delegates rather than white supremacists (who were already committed to Barry Goldwater), Johnson and his allies offered only a token compromise, primarily because of their desire to remain in charge. All too often, it seemed, white liberals failed to deliver on promises. Moreover, growing numbers of black activists had become convinced that integration into the existing "system" was a false objective, and that capitalism itself had to change before racism could be abolished.

Significantly, other social activists went through a similar process. By the end of the Johnson administration, supporters of the anti-poverty crusade, the women's movement, and the student movement—all offshoots of the civil rights struggle—had traversed the same ground from reform to radicalism, calling into question the most basic values and institutions of American middle-class society. With the war in Vietnam providing a rallying point for all dissidents, the stage was set for a decisive confrontation between those seeking radical change, and those rushing to defend the status quo.

The presidential campaign of 1968 served as the occasion for acting out the confrontation. Those who still hoped that change could occur *within* the system embraced the candidacies of Eugene McCarthy or Robert F. Kennedy, both of whom pledged an immediate end to the war in Vietnam as well as far-reaching domestic reform. On the other side, Alabama's Governor George Wallace and former vice president Richard Nixon offered support for those fed up with activism. "If any demonstrator ever lays down in front of my car," Wallace told one audience, "it will be the last car he will ever lay down in front of." Nixon, in turn, promised to speak out on behalf of "the forgotten Americans, the non-shouters, the non-demonstrators . . . those who do not break the law, . . . who love this country [and] cry out . . . 'that is enough, let's get some new leadership'.'' Rarely had political rhetoric so accurately reflected the profound passions dividing the country.

In the end, it was the roller-coaster emotional traumas of 1968 that determined, as much as anything, the outcome. In January, the Vietcong's TET offensive exploded the administration's contention that the war was being won, helping in the process to fuel an anti-Johnson vote that gave Eugene McCarthy victory in the nation's first presidential primary. Then came the announcement of Robert Kennedy's candidacy, followed quickly by the stunning revelation that Johnson would not be a candidate for reelection. But that was all prelude. In April, Martin Luther King, Jr., was assassinated just as he was mobilizing Poor People for a massive new march on Washington. In response, riots broke out in nearly every major city, suggesting the depth of anger among black Americans about their treatment in white America. Then, just six weeks later, Robert Kennedy was gunned down in Los Angeles. The two people who most personified the quest for substantive political change were now gone. When the Democrats gathered in Chicago, they nominated Hubert Humphrey, Johnson's vice president, as their candidate. But outside, riots raged in the streets as police clubbed young demonstrators come to make one last plea for peace. The frenzy and turmoil were exhausting. Perhaps the only surprising thing about Richard Nixon's victory in November was the thin margin by which he won. The confrontation was over. A new conservative ascendancy had begun.

NIXON, FORD AND CARTER

Richard Nixon was as complicated—and private—a personality as ever occupied the White House. Raised in relative poverty, he set out to achieve the American Dream. From all external indications, he succeeded, moving from a distinguished law school, through a fine service record as a naval officer, into a political career that began in Congress and culminated in winning the presidency. But beneath the surface there were indications of a more troubled spirit. Nixon broke into a dean's office in law school to steal an exam, and resorted to smearing his political opponents as ''commie sympathizers'' in order to win election.

The same contradictions crept into his presidency. When Nixon took the ''long view,'' he frequently was capable of strategic brilliance, especially in his foreign policy initiatives opening relations with China and inaugurating detente with the Soviet Union. At times, Nixon seemed to make decisions based on his sense of how they would look a century later to a discerning historian. But at other times he was obsessed with present advantage, showing himself petty, venal, vindictive, and at times paranoid. Side by side with his ''opening'' toward China came his secret bombing of Cambodia and his apparent desire to convince North Vietnam that he was a ''madman'' capable of unleashing atomic weapons in order to win the war. Even his closest advisers were never sure of which Nixon was in charge— the wise and detached visionary, or the insecure and petulant powerseeker.

Not surprisingly, the same dualism characterized Nixon's domestic policies. Initially, Nixon presented himself as a disciple of consensus, pledging to ''bring the American people together [and] . . . to be open to men and women of both parties.'' Persuaded by Daniel Patrick Moynihan that he could be an American Disraeli (the conservative as reformer), Nixon endorsed improvement of the welfare system, protection of the environment, and enhancement of consumer rights. But at the same time, he practiced the politics of polarization, lambasting busing, seeking to block court-ordered desegregation of the schools, and demanding the appointment of U.S. Supreme Court justices who would defend law and order (code words for ending ''permissiveness''). With Vice

President Spiro Agnew as point man, Nixon and his allies sought to paint liberalism as a northeast conspiracy bent on destroying traditional American strength and virtue. While Agnew denounced the "sniveling, handwringing power structure" and the "ideological eunuchs" who endorsed antiwar protests, the president himself lashed out at the "terrorists of the far left," urging the Silent Majority to "stand up and be counted against the appeasement of the rock-throwers and obscenity shouters in America."

In the end, it was this second political strategy that dominated the Nixon years. Convinced by his advisers that he could forge a permanent Republican majority by appealing to the conservativism of the Old South and the New Sunbelt (Florida, Arizona, New Mexico, and California), Nixon eventually jettisoned his brief role as Disraeli. Instead, he allied himself with forces of traditionalism on race, portrayed the northeast media as deviant and alien, and set out to use regional pride and cultural nationalism as vehicles for solidifying his power. Had he simply followed that line to its logical conclusion, Nixon might well have become one of the most politically successful presidents of the twentieth century. But then the venal side of Nixon took over, turning a shrewd and subtle strategy into a perverse, vindictive determination to *eliminate* all enemies. At that moment, the Nixon presidency began to self-destruct.

The Watergate scandal had its inception the first time that Nixon sought to use extralegal means to cover up his secret bombing of Cambodia, launder campaign funds, or spy upon political foes. By the time burglars entered the Democratic party offices at the Watergate hotel in June of 1972, so many *other* "dirty tricks" had already been perpetrated that a complete cover-up was the only way to prevent disclosure of how completely corruption had permeated the administration. Once a single source started to talk, in turn, the whole scheme began to

unravel. As Majority Leader Tip O'Neill told one colleague in January 1973: "All my years tell me what's happening. They did so many bad things during that campaign that there is no way to keep it from coming out. . . . The time is going to come when impeachment is going to hit this Congress."

By the spring of 1973, O'Neill's observation seemed prophetic. First came the revelations of Watergate burglar James McCord's ties to high officials in the administration, then the disclosures of White House counsel John Dean about the use of the CIA and FBI in the cover-up, and finally the startling announcement that a tape-recording system in the White House had left a permanent record of all this. No matter how many times Nixon insisted, "I am not a crook," or attempted to deflect investigations by firing Special Prosecutors, the nation now knew there was a source that could, definitively, prove or disprove the president's guilt. When finally that source was made public, Nixon had no choice except to resign. Addressing the American people the next day, the new president Gerald Ford observed, "Our long national nightmare is over."

If the nightmare was over, however, confusion and national self-doubt remained. The crisis of the Nixon presidency coincided with a series of setbacks to the nation as a whole. From the beginnings of the postwar era, American pre-eminence in the world had been premised on a booming economy with seemingly unlimited potential for growth, as well as total dominance in the military/foreign-policy arena. Now, both those underpinnings came under question. The Arab oil embargo of 1973 shattered America's illusion of complete control over its own energy and economic resources. As gas lines lengthened and prices soared, the American people felt the first chastening effects of being dependent on someone else's mineral wealth. In the meantime, inflation skyrocketed, largely as a result of the failure of both the Johnson and Nixon administrations to devise sensible tax policies to pay for the Vietnam War. America's final defeat in that war, in turn, smashed the smug assumption that the United States could always dictate its will to other powers because of military superiority. In short, there was abundant reason for Americans to feel threatened even without Watergate. When confidence in the country's political leadership was dealt a devastating blow as well, the justification for uncertainty was overwhelming.

Despite his initial success in calming the American people, Gerald Ford failed to provide the long-range strength and vitality needed to restore national pride. In a classic self-inflicted political wound, Ford frittered away his own credibility as a politician by pardoning Richard Nixon for any and all crimes that he had committed—this while most of Nixon's key aides were serving jail terms or awaiting trial. Ford's own response to the country's economic crisis hurt his popularity further, as he vetoed bills for federal aid to education and health care, drove interest rates to new highs, and offered little but more sacrifice as a way out of the economic doldrums. Although Ford achieved some notable foreign policy triumphs, including a new arms control agreement with the Russians, he clearly had not turned the country around. As one Democrat said in anticipation of the 1976 election, "we could run an aardvark this year and win."

Jimmy Carter, of course, was no aardvark. One of a new generation of "progressive" southern governors, he came from the right part of the country to challenge the Republican party's new electoral base, boasted of being businesslike and efficient in controlling government spending, and above all, preached, with moralistic intensity, the importance of restoring truth, integrity, and decency to government. Carter had the intuitive genius to understand the value of running "against Washington" at a time when "Washington" symbolized corruption and confusion. Furthermore, he did so

as a "born-again" Christian who prayed daily, confessed his sinfulness, and offered the reassuring message that the American people deserved a government "as good, as competent, as moral, and as filled with love" as they were. From Plains, Georgia, with a simplicity and an appeal that no national Democrat could hope to match, Jimmy Carter seemed the ideal candidate for a country seeking to cleanse its national soul.

But Carter too became a victim, initially of his own political naiveté, then ultimately of national and international developments he could not control. The first problem Carter faced was his inability to function effectively within the ground rules of the Washington "system" he had so shrewdly attacked during his campaign. What had been a virtue in October, however, became a liability in January. Arguably, Carter was one of the smartest men to occupy the White House in the twentieth century. Intrigued by detail, a quick learner, and intellectually sophisticated, he believed that the president should be a wise steward who examined complicated questions, devised wise solutions, and then presented them for enactment. He did not believe in political bargaining or cutting last minute deals over bourbon and branch water. But Washington did not work that way. Congress did not appreciate being excluded from the process of policy formulation, and resented being offered "answers" from on-high, as though Carter were a Platonic philosopher king. Thus Carter got off on the wrong foot with the "pols" in Washington, and despite some good ideas, especially on energy, never succeeded in supplying effective political leadership that would win support for a new agenda of programs to solve the country's economic and social problems.

Carter's larger dilemma, though, was that events kept outpacing his capacity to exercise control. Initially it was interest rates and a new energy shortage, then the paralyzing Iranian hostage crisis. In effect, when the Ayatollah

Khomeini sanctioned the captivity of more than fifty Americans for over 400 days, he confirmed in the most galling and embarrassing manner possible the new sense of dependency and helplessness that had overtaken the American people with the energy crisis and the fall of Vietnam. Carter dealt intelligently with the Iranian imbroglio. He understood the limits that had been placed on the nation and recognized all the dangers that reckless action would precipitate. But as he became obsessed with solving the crisis, his presidency became inextricably tied to its symbolism. If the crisis bespoke the nation's impotence, Carter became the personification of the country's shame. Thus, his good intentions and fine rhetoric notwithstanding, Carter became part of the problem of political bewilderment and uncertainty, and his presidency one more victim of the nation's malaise over its lost sense of direction and efficacy. It was a situation made to order for a Hollywood Hero, and there in the wings stood Ronald Reagan, ready to rescue America and help his fellow citizens once more to "stand tall."

RONALD REAGAN AND THE TRIUMPH OF CONSERVATISM

The essential genius of Ronald Reagan was his ability to tell the American people exactly what they wanted to hear, then to act on his words, usually in convincing fashion. Although he came from a Democratic household and had himself been head of a liberal union, Reagan switched both party and philosophy in the 1960s. A popular TV host and conservative propagandist, Reagan traveled the country exhorting audiences to get government off their backs, support laissez-faire economic policies, and roll back the forces of communism. His ability to function effectively in office was proven during the eight years he served as California's governor, though observers noted that in a crunch, Reagan often sacrificed his ideological conservatism for a pragmatic solution.

Now, running for the presidency against Jimmy Carter, he seemed to offer the answers that insecure and troubled Americans wanted: they *were* strong, freedom could triumph over communist tyranny, the United States would regain military and economic dominance in the world.

To a remarkable extent, Reagan proved able to follow through on his promises, partly due to simple good luck, partly because of extraordinary political skill. Entering the White House with a huge public mandate, Reagan wasted no time in proposing a massive legislative program, asking Congress to cut welfare programs, slash taxes, increase military spending by $1.5 trillion over five years, and deregulate the economy. Although his economic proposals made little sense (how could you balance the budget if you were *cutting* taxes and *raising* military expenditures), Reagan blithely dismissed his critics and successfully mobilized his allies. By the end of his first two years, he had secured the passage of virtually his entire legislative program. Although unemployment remained high, inflation was now under control, and by 1983, prosperity had returned—just in time for the 1984 election.

In foreign policy as well, Reagan proved enormously popular. With the hostages released on the day of his inauguration, the president began with a clean slate—a slate he soon filled with rhetorical denunciations of the Soviet "evil empire" and vigorous assertions of American determination to assert its will wherever and whenever it chose. Acting as though detente were a synonym for original sin, Reagan challenged the Soviets in Africa, the Middle East, and Latin America. He sent 10,000 paratroopers into Grenada, allegedly to prevent a communist regime from taking over, ordered the CIA to mine the harbors of Nicaragua (in clear violation of international law), and sent U.S. Marines into wartorn Lebanon, at least in part to counter Soviet-backed Syrian forces. Ironically, even when his actions led to disaster, as when 274 Marines were killed by a truck bomb in Beirut, the president escaped blame. He was a "teflon" president, journalists noted. Nothing bad that happened ever "stuck" to him, while all the good things seemed directly a result of his actions.

By the end of his first term, Ronald Reagan appeared a total success as president. He had brought America back, restored national pride, reversed the growth of Great Society/New Frontier programs, and in the process, solidified a conservative Republic constituency in the South and Sunbelt that fulfilled Richard Nixon's fondest dreams. A vigorous New Right saw Reagan as the champion of their opposition to abortion, the Equal Rights Amendment (ERA), and school busing, while "yuppies," that new generation of upwardly mobile professionals, saw the president as guarantor of their economic freedom. By the time of the election, Reagan had so succeeded in identifying himself with a revitalized sense of national confidence that an attack on his candidacy was like an attack on America itself. Not surprisingly, Walter Mondale, the Democratic candidate, won only one state and the District of Columbia in the final vote tally. What Nixon had begun but not finished due to Watergate, Reagan had now brought close to reality.

By the end of his term, of course, Reagan too had succumbed to the self-destructive forces seemingly endemic to the "imperial presidency." The "teflon" appeared to wear off as the public learned that the man who pledged never to negotiate with terrorists had in fact sent millions of dollars in arms to Iran to ransom American hostages, and that an administration supposedly devoted to law and order was honeycombed by officials under indictment for violating the law. During the Iran-Contra hearings of 1987, Americans even learned that some White House officials planned to create a "secret" intelligence operation to function, outside the law, as an instrument of *their particular definition of the national interest*. When the stock market crash of October 19, 1987,

exposed the vulnerability of Reaganomics and uncontrolled deficit spending, many began to question the whole approach of the Reagan presidency. Still, it would be a mistake to underestimate the legacy of the Reagan years, especially the institutionalization of conservative policies at home or the resurgence of nationalism and military bravado associated with his foreign policy.

CONCLUSION

In many ways, Ronald Reagan's presidency seemed to round out and complete an era. During the administration of John F. Kennedy the United States had enjoyed a measure of power and prosperity unprecedented in postwar history. A new sense of excitement and possibility spread across the land. Part of that sense of possibility centered on the hope, so long deferred, that racial justice and social equality might finally be achieved. Over the next few years, that hope fueled the process of social change. The pressure for reform forced John Kennedy to pursue in action the promise of leadership that had previously existed only in words. That same pressure for reform eventually generated a critique of American society that led to demands for radical change in the values and institutions of the entire social system. When those demands entered the electoral process in 1968, the contest for the presidency became, in effect, a referendum on whether the American people wished to call a halt to further social reform.

With Ronald Reagan's election, the ascendancy of conservatism that began in 1968 reached its zenith. Once again, America enjoyed a powerful sense of national pride, often accompanied by a belligerent pose toward the outside world. Traditional values had a new champion, at least in theory. And if a very untraditional national deficit threatened to undermine much that had been preserved or gained, that was for another generation to contend with. Ronald Reagan himself, like John F. Kennedy a quarter century earlier, stood as an almost larger than life figure—at least until the scandals of "Irangate"—symbolizing a political viewpoint and perhaps completing a political era.

What would come next remained unclear. Obviously, the imperial presidency was still a subject of intense debate. So too was the danger of exceeding the limits of law and political responsibility that resided in a White House that assumed absolute power to decide what was right. If Americans held Ronald Reagan responsible for violating the public trust on arms sales to Iran and blamed his economic policies for the stock market crash of 1987, then perhaps the conservative consensus of the 1970s and 80s would crumble, just as the liberal consensus was shattered in the late 1960s.

How the Democrats would respond, in turn, was equally unpredictable. By all indications, they too had learned much about excess during the seventies and eighties. Once identified as the party of the counterculture and insurgency, Democrats in the mid-1980s seemed intent on remolding their image, holding on to their commitment to social justice and compassion, but concerned also with embracing traditional values of law and order, family, and patriotism. When New York's Governor Mario Cuomo addressed the 1984 Democratic Convention, he articulated this new synthesis, boasting of his own immigrant roots, celebrating the American Dream, but also reinforcing the responsibilities that all Americans have to each other, "as a large family," to keep and protect each others' health and welfare.

With Ronald Reagan's departure from the White House, a political era had come to an end. It is hard to imagine another as full of tension, passion, or struggle. But that is what each generation has said until its successor has made its own history. In light of the challenges of famine, environmental destruction, racial and economic inequality, and the threat of nuclear annihilation that await those who will assume power in the twenty-first century, only a fool would predict that the struggles of the next generation will be any less exciting, or passionate, than those of the past quarter century.

SUGGESTED READINGS

Chafe, William H. *The Unfinished Journey: America since World War II*. New York: Oxford University Press, 1986.

Hamby, Alonzo. *Liberalism and Its Challengers*. New York: Oxford University Press, 1985.

Hodgson, Godfrey. *America in Our Time: From World War II to Nixon—What Happened and Why*. Garden City, N.Y.: Doubleday Publishing, 1976.

Kearns, Doris. *Lyndon Johnson and the American Dream*. New York: Harper & Row, 1976.

Leuchtenburg, William E. *A Troubled Feast*. Boston: Little, Brown, 1983.

Reich, Robert. *The Next American Frontier*. New York: Times Books, 1983.

Schell, Jonathan. *A Time of Illusion*. New York: Random House, 1976.

Sitkoff, Harvard. *The Struggle for Black Equality*. New York: Hill & Wang, 1983.

Wittner, Lawrence. *Cold War America: From Hiroshima to Watergate*. New York: Holt, Rinehart and Winston, 1983.

DOCUMENT 35.1
John F. Kennedy's Radio and Television Report to the American People on Civil Rights, June 11, 1963

Through much of his administration, John F. Kennedy operated within a framework of

Source: From *Public Papers of the Presidents of the United States: John F. Kennedy 1963*. (Washington, D.C.: 1964), pp. 468–471.

*continuity with past foreign and domestic
policies. Notwithstanding his rhetorical calls
for innovation and boldness, the president
acted as though there were no social problems
at home requiring decisive action. On
international issues, meanwhile, he was the
quintessential cold warrior. Both these stances
were consistent with the politics of the fifties.
Now, in June of 1963, Kennedy suddenly
changed course. Prodded by civil rights
demonstrations, he committed his
administration to a far-reaching program of
reforms in race relations; and chastened by
the perilous brush with nuclear annihilation
during the Cuban missile crisis of the previous
October, he urged a thorough reassessment
of cold war attitudes. In effect, these two
speeches represented a marked departure for
the Kennedy presidency, a sign of what might
have come had Kennedy not been assassinated
in November 1963.*

Good evening, my fellow citizens:

This afternoon, following a series of threats
and defiant statements, the presence of Alabama National Guardsmen was required on the
University of Alabama to carry out the final
and unequivocal order of the United States District Court of the Northern District of Alabama.
That order called for the admission of two
clearly qualified young Alabama residents who
happened to have been born Negro.

That they were admitted peacefully on the
campus is due in good measure to the conduct
of the students of the University of Alabama,
who met their responsibilities in a constructive
way.

I hope that every American, regardless of
where he lives, will stop and examine his conscience about this and other related incidents.
This Nation was founded by men of many nations and backgrounds. It was founded on the
principle that all men are created equal, and
that the rights of every man are diminished
when the rights of one man are threatened.

Today we are committed to a worldwide
struggle to promote and protect the rights of
all who wish to be free. And when Americans
are sent to Viet-Nam or West Berlin, we do
not ask for whites only. It ought to be possible,
therefore, for American students of any color
to attend any public institution they select without having to be backed up by troops.

It ought to be possible for American consumers of any color to receive equal service in
places of public accommodation, such as hotels
and restaurants and theaters and retail stores,
without being forced to resort to demonstrations
in the street, and it ought to be possible for
American citizens of any color to register and
to vote in a free election without interference
or fear of reprisal.

It ought to be possible, in short, for every
American to enjoy the privileges of being
American without regard to his race or his
color. In short, every American ought to have
the right to be treated as he would wish to be
treated, as one would wish his children to be
treated. But this is not the case.

The Negro baby born in America today,
regardless of the section of the Nation in which
he is born, has about one-half as much chance
of completing a high school as a white baby
born in the same place on the same day, one-
third as much chance of completing college,
one-third as much chance of becoming a professional man, twice as much chance of becoming
unemployed, about one-seventh as much
chance of earning $10,000 a year, a life expec-
tancy which is 7 years shorter, and the prospects
of earning only half as much.

This is not a sectional issue. Difficulties over
segregation and discrimination exist in every
city, in every State of the Union, producing
in many cities a rising tide of discontent that
threatens the public safety. Nor is this a partisan
issue. In a time of domestic crisis men of good
will and generosity should be able to unite
regardless of party or politics. This is not even
a legal or legislative issue alone. It is better

to settle these matters in the courts than on the streets, and new laws are needed at every level, but law alone cannot make men see right.

We are confronted primarily with a moral issue. It is as old as the scriptures and is as clear as the American Constitution.

The heart of the question is whether all Americans are to be afforded equal rights and equal opportunities, whether we are going to treat our fellow Americans as we want to be treated. If an American, because his skin is dark, cannot eat lunch in a restaurant open to the public, if he cannot send his children to the best public school available, if he cannot vote for the public officials who represent him, if, in short, he cannot enjoy the full and free life which all of us want, then who among us would be content to have the color of his skin changed and stand in his place? Who among us would then be content with the counsels of patience and delay?

One hundred years of delay have passed since President Lincoln freed the slaves, yet their heirs, their grandsons, are not fully free. They are not yet freed from the bonds of injustice. They are not yet freed from social and economic oppression. And this Nation, for all its hopes and all its boasts, will not be fully free until all its citizens are free.

We preach freedom around the world, and we mean it, and we cherish our freedom here at home, but are we to say to the world, and much more importantly, to each other that this is a land of the free except for the Negroes; that we have no second-class citizens except Negroes; that we have no class or cast system, no ghettoes, no master race except with respect to Negroes?

Now the time has come for this Nation to fulfill its promise. The events in Birmingham and elsewhere have so increased the cries for equality that no city or State or legislative body can prudently choose to ignore them.

The fires of frustration and discord are burning in every city, North and South, where legal remedies are not at hand. Redress is sought

in the streets, in demonstrations, parades, and protests which create tensions and threaten violence and threaten lives.

We face, therefore, a moral crisis as a country and as a people. It cannot be met by repressive police action. It cannot be left to increased demonstrations in the streets. It cannot be quieted by token moves or talk. It is a time to act in the Congress, in your State and local legislative body and, above all, in all of our daily lives.

It is not enough to pin the blame on others, to say this is a problem of one section of the country or another, or deplore the fact that we face. A great change is at hand, and our task, our obligation, is to make that revolution, that change, peaceful and constructive for all.

Those who do nothing are inviting shame as well as violence. Those who act boldly are recognizing right as well as reality.

Next week I shall ask the Congress of the United States to act, to make a commitment it has not fully made in this century to the proposition that race has no place in American life or law. The Federal judiciary has upheld that proposition in a series of forthright cases. The executive branch has adopted that proposition in the conduct of its affairs, including the employment of Federal personnel, the use of Federal facilities, and the sale of federally financed housing.

But there are other necessary measures which only the Congress can provide, and they must be provided at this session. The old code of equity law under which we live commands for every wrong a remedy, but in too many communities, in too many parts of the country, wrongs are inflicted on Negro citizens and there are no remedies at law. Unless the Congress acts, their only remedy is in the street.

I am, therefore, asking the Congress to enact legislation giving all Americans the right to be served in facilities which are open to the public—hotels, restaurants, theaters, retail stores, and similar establishments.

This seems to me to be an elementary right.

Its denial is an arbitrary indignity that no American in 1963 should have to endure, but many do.

I have recently met with scores of business leaders urging them to take voluntary action to end this discrimination and I have been encouraged by their response, and in the last 2 weeks over 75 cities have seen progress made in desegregating these kinds of facilities. But many are unwilling to act alone, and for this reason, nationwide legislation is needed if we are to move this problem from the streets to the courts.

I am also asking Congress to authorize the Federal Government to participate more fully in lawsuits designed to end segregation in public education. We have succeeded in persuading many districts to desegregate voluntarily. Dozens have admitted Negroes without violence. Today a Negro is attending a State-supported institution in every one of our 50 States, but the pace is very slow.

Too many Negro children entering segregated grade schools at the time of the Supreme Court's decision 9 years ago will enter segregated high schools this fall, having suffered a loss which can never be restored. The lack of an adequate education denies the Negro a chance to get a decent job.

The orderly implementation of the Supreme Court decision, therefore, cannot be left solely to those who may not have the economic resources to carry the legal action or who may be subject to harassment.

Other features will be also requested, including greater protection for the right to vote. But legislation, I repeat, cannot solve this problem alone. It must be solved in the homes of every American in every community across our country.

In this respect, I want to pay tribute to those citizens North and South who have been working in their communities to make life better for all. They are acting not out of a sense of legal duty but out of a sense of human decency.

Like our soldiers and sailors in all parts of the world they are meeting freedom's challenge on the firing line, and I salute them for their honor and their courage.

My fellow Americans, this is a problem which faces us all—in every city of the North as well as the South. Today there are Negroes unemployed, two or three times as many compared to whites, inadequate in education, moving into the large cities, unable to find work, young people particularly out of work without hope, denied equal rights, denied the opportunity to eat at a restaurant or lunch counter or go to a movie theater, denied the right to a decent education, denied almost today the right to attend a State university even though qualified. It seems to me that these are matters which concern us all, not merely Presidents or Congressmen or Governors, but every citizen of the United States.

This is one country. It has become one country because all of us and all the people who came here had an equal chance to develop their talents.

We cannot say to 10 percent of the population that you can't have that right; that your children can't have the chance to develop whatever talents they have; that the only way that they are going to get their rights is to go into the streets and demonstrate. I think we owe them and we owe ourselves a better country than that.

Therefore, I am asking for your help in making it easier for us to move ahead and to provide the kind of equality of treatment which we would want ourselves; to give a chance for every child to be educated to the limit of his talents.

As I have said before, not every child has an equal talent or an equal ability or an equal motivation, but they should have the equal right to develop their talent and their ability and their motivation, to make something of themselves.

We have a right to expect that the Negro community will be responsible, will uphold the law, but they have a right to expect that the law will be fair, that the Constitution will be color blind, as Justice Harlan said at the turn of the century.

This is what we are talking about and this is a matter which concerns this country and what it stands for, and in meeting it I ask the support of all our citizens.

Thank you very much.

DOCUMENT 35.2
John F. Kennedy's Commencement Address at American University in Washington, June 10, 1963

President Anderson, members of the faculty, board of trustees, distinguished guests, my old colleague, Senator Bob Byrd, who has earned his degree through many years of attending night law school, while I am earning mine in the next 30 minutes, ladies and gentlemen:

It is with great pride that I participate in this ceremony of the American University, sponsored by the Methodist Church, founded by Bishop John Fletcher Hurst, and first opened by President Woodrow Wilson in 1914. This is a young and growing university, but it has already fulfilled Bishop Hurst's enlightened hope for the study of history and public affairs in a city devoted to the making of history and to the conduct of the public's business. By sponsoring this institution of higher learning for all who wish to learn, whatever their color or their creed, the Methodists of this area and the Nation deserve the Nation's thanks, and I commend all those who are today graduating.

Professor Woodrow Wilson once said that every man sent out from a university should be a man of his nation as well as a man of his time, and I am confident that the men and

Source: From *Public Papers of the Presidents: John F. Kennedy 1963*. (Washington, D.C.: 1964), pp. 459–464.

women who carry the honor of graduating from this institution will continue to give from their lives, from their talents, a high measure of public service and public support.

"There are few earthly things more beautiful than a university," wrote John Masefield, in his tribute to English universities—and his words are equally true today. He did not refer to spires and towers, to campus greens and ivied walls. He admired the splendid beauty of the university, he said, because it was "a place where those who hate ignorance may strive to know, where those who perceive truth may strive to make others see."

I have, therefore, chosen this time and this place to discuss a topic on which ignorance too often abounds and the truth is too rarely perceived—yet it is the most important topic on earth: world peace.

What kind of peace do I mean? What kind of peace do we seek? Not a Pax Americana enforced on the world by American weapons of war. Not the peace of the grave or the security of the slave. I am talking about genuine peace, the kind of peace that makes life on earth worth living, the kind that enables men and nations to grow and to hope and to build a better life for their children—not merely peace for Americans but peace for all men and women—not merely peace in our time but peace for all time.

I speak of peace because of the new face of war. Total war makes no sense in an age when great powers can maintain large and relatively invulnerable nuclear forces and refuse to surrender without resort to those forces. It makes no sense in an age when a single nuclear weapon contains almost ten times the explosive force delivered by all of the allied air forces in the Second World War. It makes no sense in an age when the deadly poisons produced by a nuclear exchange would be carried by wind and water and soil and seed to the far corners of the globe and to generations yet unborn.

Today the expenditure of billions of dollars

every year on weapons acquired for the purpose of making sure we never need to use them is essential to keeping the peace. But surely the acquisition of such idle stockpiles—which can only destroy and never create—is not the only, much less the most efficient, means of assuring peace.

I speak of peace, therefore, as the necessary rational end of rational men. I realize that the pursuit of peace is not as dramatic as the pursuit of war—and frequently the words of the pursuer fall on deaf ears. But we have no more urgent task.

Some say that it is useless to speak of world peace or world law or world disarmament— and that it will be useless until the leaders of the Soviet Union adopt a more enlightened attitude. I hope they do. I believe we can help them do it. But I also believe that we must reexamine our own attitude—as individuals and as a Nation—for our attitude is as essential as theirs. And every graduate of this school, every thoughtful citizen who despairs of war and wishes to bring peace, should begin by looking inward—by examining his own attitude toward the possibilities of peace, toward the Soviet Union, toward the course of the cold war and toward freedom and peace here at home.

First: Let us examine our attitude toward peace itself. Too many of us think it is impossible. Too many think it unreal. But that is a dangerous, defeatist belief. It leads to the conclusion that war is inevitable—that mankind is doomed—that we are gripped by forces we cannot control.

We need not accept that view. Our problems are manmade—therefore, they can be solved by man. And man can be as big as he wants. No problem of human destiny is beyond human beings. Man's reason and spirit have often solved the seemingly unsolvable—and we believe they can do it again.

I am not referring to the absolute, infinite concept of universal peace and good will of which some fantasies and fanatics dream. I do not deny the value of hopes and dreams but we merely invite discouragement and incredulity by making that our only and immediate goal.

Let us focus instead on a more practical, more attainable peace—based not on a sudden revolution in human nature but on a gradual evolution in human institutions—on a series of concrete actions and effective agreements which are in the interest of all concerned. There is no single, simple key to this peace—no grand or magic formula to be adopted by one or two powers. Genuine peace must be the product of many nations, the sum of many acts. It must be dynamic, not static, changing to meet the challenge of each new generation. For peace is a process—a way of solving problems.

With such a peace, there will still be quarrels and conflicting interests, as there are within families and nations. World peace, like community peace, does not require that each man love his neighbor—it requires only that they live together in mutual tolerance, submitting their disputes to a just and peaceful settlement. And history teaches us that enmities between nations, as between individuals, do not last forever. However fixed our likes and dislikes may seem, the tide of time and events will often bring surprising changes in the relations between nations and neighbors.

So let us persevere. Peace need not be impracticable, and war need not be inevitable. By defining our goal more clearly, by making it seem more manageable and less remote, we can help all peoples to see it, to draw hope from it, and to move irresistibly toward it.

Second: Let us reexamine our attitude toward the Soviet Union. It is discouraging to think that their leaders may actually believe what their propagandists write. It is discouraging to read a recent authoritative Soviet text on *Military Strategy* and find, on page after page, wholly baseless and incredible claims— such as the allegation that ''American imperialist circles are preparing to unleash different types of wars . . . that there is a very real threat of a preventive war being unleashed by American imperialists against the Soviet Union . . . [and that] the political aims of the American imperialists are to enslave economically and politically the European and other capitalist countries . . . [and] to achieve world domination . . . by means of aggressive wars.''

Truly, as it was written long ago: ''The wicked flee when no man pursueth.'' Yet it is sad to read these Soviet statements—to realize the extent of the gulf between us. But it is also a warning—a warning to the American people not to fall into the same trap as the Soviets, not to see only a distorted and desperate view of the other side, not to see conflict as inevitable, accommodation as impossible, and communication as nothing more than an exchange of threats.

No government or social system is so evil that its people must be considered as lacking in virtue. As Americans, we find communism profoundly repugnant as a negation of personal freedom and dignity. But we can still hail the Russian people for their many achievements—in science and space, in economic and industrial growth, in culture and in acts of courage.

Among the many traits the peoples of our two countries have in common, none is stronger than our mutual abhorrence of war. Almost unique, among the major world powers, we have never been at war with each other. And no nation in the history of battle ever suffered more than the Soviet Union suffered in the course of the Second World War. At least 20 million lost their lives. Countless millions of homes and farms were burned or sacked. A third of the nation's territory, including nearly two thirds of its industrial base, was turned into a wasteland—a loss equivalent to the devastation of this country east of Chicago.

Today, should total war ever break out again—no matter how—our two countries would become the primary targets. It is an ironic but accurate fact that the two strongest powers are the two in the most danger of devastation. All we have built, all we have worked for, would be destroyed in the first 24 hours. And even in the cold war, which brings burdens and dangers to so many countries, including this Nation's closest allies—our two countries bear the heaviest burdens. For we are both devoting massive sums of money to weapons that could be better devoted to combating ignorance, poverty, and disease. We are both caught up in a vicious and dangerous cycle in which suspicion on one side breeds suspicion on the other, and new weapons beget counterweapons.

In short, both the United States and its allies, and the Soviet Union and its allies, have a mutually deep interest in a just and genuine peace and in halting the arms race. Agreements to this end are in the interests of the Soviet Union as well as ours—and even the most hostile nations can be relied upon to accept and keep those treaty obligations, and only those treaty obligations, which are in their own interest.

So, let us not be blind to our differences—but let us also direct attention to our common interests and to the means by which those differences can be resolved. And if we cannot end now our differences, at least we can help make the world safe for diversity. For, in the final analysis, our most basic common link is that we all inhabit this small planet. We all breathe the same air. We all cherish our children's future. And we are all mortal.

Third: Let us reexamine our attitude toward the cold war, remembering that we are not engaged in a debate, seeking to pile up debating points. We are not here distributing blame or pointing the finger of judgment. We must deal with the world as it is, and not as it might have been had the history of the last 18 years been different.

We must, therefore, persevere in the search for peace in the hope that constructive changes within the Communist bloc might bring within reach solutions which now seem beyond us. We must conduct our affairs in such a way that it becomes in the Communists' interest to agree on a genuine peace. Above all, while defending our own vital interests, nuclear powers must avert those confrontations which bring an adversary to a choice of either a humiliating retreat or a nuclear war. To adopt that kind of course in the nuclear age would be evidence only of the bankruptcy of our policy—or of a collective death-wish for the world.

To secure these ends, America's weapons are nonprovocative, carefully controlled, designed to deter, and capable of selective use. Our military forces are committed to peace and disciplined in self-restraint. Our diplomats are instructed to avoid unnecessary irritants and purely rhetorical hostility.

For we can seek a relaxation of tensions without relaxing our guard. And, for our part, we do not need to use threats to prove that we are resolute. We do not need to jam foreign broadcasts out of fear our faith will be eroded. We are unwilling to impose our system on any unwilling people—but we are willing and able to engage in peaceful competition with any people on earth.

Meanwhile, we seek to strengthen the United Nations, to help solve its financial problems, to make it a more effective instrument for peace, to develop it into a genuine world security system—a system capable of resolving disputes on the basis of law, of insuring the security of the large and the small, and of creating conditions under which arms can finally be abolished.

At the same time we seek to keep peace inside the non-Communist world, where many nations, all of them our friends, are divided over issues which weaken Western unity, which invite Communist intervention or which threaten to erupt into war. Our efforts in West New Guinea, in the Congo, in the Middle East, and in the Indian subcontinent, have been persistent and patient despite criticism from both

sides. We have also tried to set an example for others—by seeking to adjust small but significant differences with our own closest neighbors in Mexico and in Canada.

Speaking of other nations, I wish to make one point clear. We are bound to many nations by alliances. Those alliances exist because our concern and theirs substantially overlap. Our commitment to defend Western Europe and West Berlin, for example, stands undiminished because of the identity of our vital interests. The United States will make no deal with the Soviet Union at the expense of other nations and other peoples, not merely because they are our partners, but also because their interests and ours converge.

Our interests converge, however, not only in defending the frontiers of freedom, but in pursuing the paths of peace. It is our hope—and the purpose of allied policies—to convince the Soviet Union that she, too, should let each nation choose its own future, so long as that choice does not interfere with the choices of others. The Communist drive to impose their political and economic system on others is the primary cause of world tension today. For there can be no doubt that, if all nations could refrain from interfering in the self-determination of others, the peace would be much more assured.

This will require a new effort to achieve world law—a new context for world discussions. It will require increased understanding between the Soviets and ourselves. And increased understanding will require increased contact and communication. One step in this direction is the proposed arrangement for a direct line between Moscow and Washington, to avoid on each side the dangerous delays, misunderstandings, and misreadings of the other's actions which might occur at a time of crisis.

We have also been talking in Geneva about other first-step measures of arms control, designed to limit the intensity of the arms race and to reduce the risks of accidental war. Our primary long-range interest in Geneva, however, is general and complete disarmament—designed to take place by stages, permitting parallel political developments to build the new institutions of peace which would take the place of arms. The pursuit of disarmament has been an effort of this Government since the 1920's. It has been urgently sought by the past three administrations. And however dim the prospects may be today, we intend to continue this effort—to continue it in order that all countries, including our own, can better grasp what the problems and possibilities of disarmament are.

The one major area of these negotiations where the end is in sight, yet where a fresh start is badly needed, is in a treaty to outlaw nuclear tests. The conclusion of such a treaty, so near and yet so far, would check the spiraling arms race in one of its most dangerous areas. It would place the nuclear powers in a position to deal more effectively with one of the greatest hazards which man faces in 1963, the further spread of nuclear arms. It would increase our security—it would decrease the prospects of war. Surely this goal is sufficiently important to require our steady pursuit, yielding neither to the temptation to give up the whole effort nor the temptation to give up our insistence on vital and responsible safeguards.

I am taking this opportunity, therefore, to announce two important decisions in this regard.

First: Chairman Khrushchev, Prime Minister Macmillan, and I have agreed that highlevel discussions will shortly begin in Moscow looking toward early agreement on a comprehensive test ban treaty. Our hopes must be tempered with the caution of history—but with our hopes go the hopes of all mankind.

Second: To make clear our good faith and solemn convictions on the matter, I now declare that the United States does not propose to conduct nuclear tests in the atmosphere so long as other states do not do so. We will not be the first to resume. Such a declaration is no substitute for a formal binding treaty, but I hope it will help us achieve one. Nor would such a treaty be a substitute for disarmament, but I hope it will help us achieve it.

Finally, my fellow Americans, let us examine our attitude toward peace and freedom here at home. The quality and spirit of our own society must justify and support our efforts abroad. We must show it in the dedication of our own lives—as many of you who are graduating today will have a unique opportunity to do, by serving without pay in the Peace Corps abroad or in the proposed National Service Corps here at home.

But wherever we are, we must all, in our daily lives, live up to the age-old faith that peace and freedom walk together. In too many of our cities today, the peace is not secure because freedom is incomplete.

It is the responsibility of the executive branch at all levels of government—local, State, and National—to provide and protect that freedom for all of our citizens by all means within their authority. It is the responsibility of the legislative branch at all levels, wherever that authority is not now adequate, to make it adequate. And it is the responsibility of all citizens in all sections of this country to respect the rights of all others and to respect the law of the land.

All this is not unrelated to world peace. "When a man's ways please the Lord," the Scriptures tell us, "he maketh even his enemies to be at peace with him." And is not peace, in the last analysis, basically a matter of human rights—the right to live out our lives without fear of devastation—the right to breathe air as nature provided it—the right of future generations to a healthy existence?

While we proceed to safeguard our national interests, let us also safeguard human interests. And the elimination of war and arms is clearly in the interest of both. No treaty, however much it may be to the advantage of all, however tightly it may be worded, can provide absolute security against the risks of deception and evasion. But it can—if it is sufficiently effective in its enforcement and if it is sufficiently in the interests of its signers—offer far more security and far fewer risks than an unabated, uncontrolled, unpredictable arms race.

The United States, as the world knows, will never start a war. We do not want a war. We do not now expect a war. This generation of Americans has already had enough—more than enough—of war and hate and oppression. We shall be prepared if others wish it. We shall be alert to try to stop it. But we shall also do our part to build a world of peace where the weak are safe and the strong are just. We are not helpless before that task or hopeless of its success. Confident and unafraid, we labor on—not toward a strategy of annihilation but toward a strategy of peace.

The President spoke at the John M. Reeves Athletic Field on the campus of American University after being awarded an honorary degree of doctor of laws. In his opening words he referred to Hurst R. Anderson, president of the university, and Robert C. Byrd, U.S. Senator from West Virginia.

DOCUMENT 35.3
The Great Society

When Lyndon Johnson became president after John F. Kennedy's assassination, he sought to do two things simultaneously: first, to carry forward the mission of his martyred predecessor, and second, to use that record as a basis for establishing his own mark on history, a distinctive "Johnson" imprint that would make his years in office even more memorable than those that had gone before with the New Deal and the New Frontier. In the speech excerpted below, Johnson defined

Source: From *Public Papers of the Presidents of the United States: Lyndon B. Johnson 1963–64.* (Washington, D.C., 1965), pp. 704–7.

that imprint. His administration, he told a University of Michigan audience, would work for a Great Society, one that would not only abolish poverty, but also achieve a "quality of civilization" higher than that of any previous era. It was a dream Johnson was uniquely positioned to make real, but one that, tragically, he helped to subvert because of his commitment to the Vietnam War.

. . . For a century we labored to settle and to subdue a continent. For half a century we called upon unbounded invention and untiring industry to create an order of plenty for all of our people.

The challenge of the next half century is whether we have the wisdom to use that wealth to enrich and elevate our national life, and to advance the quality of our American civilization.

Your imagination, your initiative, and your indignation will determine whether we build a society where progress is the servant of our needs, or a society where old values and new visions are buried under unbridled growth. For in your time we have the opportunity to move not only toward the rich society and the powerful society, but upward to the Great Society.

The Great Society rests on abundance and liberty for all. It demands an end to poverty and racial injustice, to which we are totally committed in our time. But that is just the beginning.

The Great Society is a place where every child can find knowledge to enrich his mind and to enlarge his talents. It is a place where leisure is a welcome chance to build and reflect, not a feared cause of boredom and restlessness. It is a place where the city of man serves not only the needs of the body and the demands of commerce but the desire for beauty and the hunger for community.

It is a place where man can renew contact with nature. It is a place which honors creation for its own sake and for what it adds to the understanding of the race. It is a place where men are more concerned with the quality of their goals than the quantity of their goods.

But most of all, the Great Society is not a safe harbor, a resting place, a final objective, a finished work. It is a challenge constantly renewed, beckoning us toward a destiny where the meaning of our lives matches the marvelous products of our labor.

Aristotle said: "Men come together in cities in order to live, but they remain together in order to live the good life." It is harder and harder to live the good life in American cities today.

The catalogue of ills is long: there is the decay of the centers and the despoiling of the suburbs. There is not enough housing for our people or transportation for our traffic. Open land is vanishing and old landmarks are violated.

Worst of all expansion is eroding the precious and time-honored values of community with neighbors and communion with nature. The loss of these values breeds loneliness and boredom and indifference.

Our society will never be great until our cities are great. Today the frontier of imagination and innovation is inside those cities and not beyond their borders.

A second place where we begin to build the Great Society is in our countryside. We have always prided ourselves on being not only America the strong and America the free, but America the beautiful. Today that beauty is in danger. The water we drink, the food we eat, the very air that we breathe, are threatened with pollution. Our parks are overcrowded, our seashores over-burdened. Green fields and dense forests are disappearing.

A third place to build the Great Society is in the classrooms of America. There your children's lives will be shaped. Our society will not be great until every young mind is set free to scan the farthest reaches of thought and imagination. We are still far from that goal.

In many places, classrooms are overcrowded and curricula are outdated. Most of our qualified teachers are underpaid, and many of our paid teachers are unqualified. So we must give every child a place to sit and a teacher to learn from. Poverty must not be a bar to learning, and learning must offer an escape from poverty.

But more classrooms and more teachers are not enough. We must seek an educational system which grows in excellence as it grows in size. This means better training for our teachers. It means preparing youth to enjoy their hours of leisure as well as their hours of labor. It means exploring new techniques of teaching, to find new ways to stimulate the love of learning and the capacity for creation.

For better or for worse, your generation has been appointed by history to deal with those problems and to lead America toward a new age. You have the chance never before afforded to any people in any age. You can help build a society where the demands of morality, and the needs of the spirit, can be realized in the life of the nation.

So, will you join in the battle to give every citizen the full equality which God enjoins and the law requires, whatever his belief, or race, or the color of his skin?

Will you join in the battle to give every citizen an escape from the crushing weight of poverty?

Will you join in the battle to make it possible for all nations to live in enduring peace—as neighbors and not as mortal enemies?

Will you join in the battle to build the Great Society, to prove that our material progress is only the foundation on which we will build a richer life of mind and spirit?

There are those timid souls who say this battle cannot be won; that we are condemned to a soulless wealth. I do not agree. We have the power to shape the civilization that we want. But we need your will, your labor, your hearts, if we are to build that kind of society.

So let us from this moment begin our work so that in the future men will look back and say: It was then, after a long and weary way, that man turned the exploits of his genius to the full enrichment of his life.

DOCUMENT 35.4
Richard Nixon's Oath of Office and Second Inaugural Address, January 20, 1973

Richard Nixon was as well prepared for the presidency as any politician in American history. As congressman, senator, and then vice president, he had participated in many of the decisive moments of the postwar era. Finally winning election to the White House in 1968, he now had the opportunity to redefine the foreign and domestic contours of that era. Ironically, Nixon chose to do so in a manner that contradicted much of his previous political history. Once known as a "liberal" Republican on civil rights and domestic economic issues, he now pursued a policy of polarization at home, using "social isues" of busing and welfare to mobilize a conservative constituency angry at blacks and poor people. Simultaneously, Nixon reversed his long-standing record as a cold warrior and pioneered detente with the USSR and China. The following speech, Nixon's Second Inaugural, brings together these two themes, highlighting the new paths Nixon had chosen to make his mark on history.

I, RICHARD NIXON, do solemnly swear that I will faithfully execute the Office of President of the United States, and will to the best of my ability, preserve, protect and defend the Constitution of the United States, so help me God.

Source: From *Public Papers of the Presidents: Richard Nixon 1973.* (Washington, D.C.: 1974), pp. 12–15.

Mr. Vice President, Mr. Speaker, Mr. Chief Justice, Senator Cook, Mrs. Eisenhower, and my fellow citizens of this great and good country we share together:

When we met here four years ago, America was bleak in spirit, depressed by the prospect of seemingly endless war abroad and of destructive conflict at home.

As we meet here today, we stand on the threshold of a new era of peace in the world.

The central question before us is: How shall we use that peace?

Let us resolve that this era we are about to enter will not be what other postwar periods have so often been: a time of retreat and isolation that leads to stagnation at home and invites new danger abroad.

Let us resolve that this will be what it can become: a time of great responsibilities greatly borne, in which we renew the spirit and the promise of America as we enter our third century as a nation.

This past year saw far-reaching results from our new policies for peace. By continuing to revitalize our traditional friendships, and by our missions to Peking and to Moscow, we were able to establish the base for a new and more durable pattern of relationships among the nations of the world. Because of America's bold initiatives, 1972 will be long remembered as the year of the greatest progress since the end of World War II toward a lasting peace in the world.

The peace we seek in the world is not the flimsy peace which is merely an interlude between wars, but a peace which can endure for generations to come.

It is important that we understand both the necessity and the limitations of America's role in maintaining that peace.

Unless we in America work to preserve the peace, there will be no peace.

Unless we in America work to preserve freedom, there will be no freedom.

But let us clearly understand the new nature

of America's role, as a result of the new policies we have adopted over these past 4 years.

We shall respect our treaty commitments.

We shall support vigorously the principle that no country has the right to impose its will or rule on another by force.

We shall continue, in this era of negotiation, to work for the limitation of nuclear arms and to reduce the danger of confrontation between the great powers.

We shall do our share in defending peace and freedom in the world. But we shall expect others to do their share.

The time has passed when America will make every other nation's conflict our own, or make every other nation's future our responsibility, or presume to tell the people of other nations how to manage their own affairs.

Just as we respect the right of each nation to determine its own future, we also recognize the responsibility of each nation to secure its own future.

Just as America's role is indispensable in preserving the world's peace, so is each nation's role indispensable in preserving its own peace.

Together with the rest of the world, let us resolve to move forward from the beginnings we have made. Let us continue to bring down the walls of hostility which have divided the world for too long, and to build in their place bridges of understanding—so that despite profound differences between systems of government, the people of the world can be friends.

Let us build a structure of peace in the world in which the weak are as safe as the strong, in which each respects the right of the other to live by a different system, in which those who would influence others will do so by the strength of their ideas and not by the force of their arms.

Let us accept that high responsibility not as a burden, but gladly—gladly because the chance to build such a peace is the noblest endeavor in which a nation can engage; gladly also because only if we act greatly in meeting our responsibilities abroad will we remain a great nation, and only if we remain a great nation will we act greatly in meeting our challenges at home.

We have the chance today to do more than ever before in our history to make life better in America—to ensure better education, better health, better housing, better transportation, a cleaner environment—to restore respect for law, to make our communities more livable—and to ensure the God-given right of every American to full and equal opportunity.

Because the range of our needs is so great, because the reach of our opportunities is so great, let us be bold in our determination to meet those needs in new ways.

Just as building a structure of peace abroad has required turning away from old policies that have failed, so building a new era of progress at home requires turning away from old policies that have failed.

Abroad, the shift from old policies to new has not been a retreat from our responsibilities, but a better way to peace.

And at home, the shift from old policies to new will not be a retreat from our responsibilities, but a better way to progress.

Abroad and at home, the key to those new responsibilities lies in the placing and the division of responsibility. We have lived too long with the consequences of attempting to gather all power and responsibility in Washington.

Abroad and at home, the time has come to turn away from the condescending policies of paternalism—of "Washington knows best."

A person can be expected to act responsibly only if he has responsibility. This is human nature. So let us encourage individuals at home and nations abroad to do more for themselves, to decide more for themselves. Let us locate responsibility in more places. And let us measure what we will do for others by what they will do for themselves.

That is why today I offer no promise of a purely governmental solution for every problem. We have lived too long with that false promise. In trusting too much in government, we have asked of it more than it can deliver. This leads only to inflated expectations, to reduced individual effort, and to a disappointment and frustration that erode confidence both in what government can do and in what people can do.

Government must learn to take less from people so that people can do more for themselves.

Let us remember that America was built not by government, but by people; not by welfare, but by work; not by shirking responsibility, but by seeking responsibility.

In our own lives, let each of us ask—not just what will government do for me, but what can I do for myself?

In the challenges we face together, let each of us ask—not just how can government help, but how can I help?

Your National Government has a great and vital role to play. And I pledge to you that where this Government should act, we will act boldly and we will lead boldly. But just as important is the role that each and every one of us must play, as an individual and as a member of his own community.

From this day forward, let each of us make a solemn commitment in his own heart: to bear his responsibility, to do his part, to live his ideals—so that together we can see the dawn of a new age of progress for America, and together, as we celebrate our 200th anniversary as a nation, we can do so proud in the fulfillment of our promise to ourselves and to the world.

As America's longest and most difficult war comes to an end, let us again learn to debate our differences with civility and decency. And let each of us reach out for that one precious quality government cannot provide—a new level of respect for the rights and feelings of one another, a new level of respect for the individual human dignity which is the cherished birthright of every American.

Above all else, the time has come for us to renew our faith in ourselves and in America.

In recent years, that faith has been challenged.

Our children have been taught to be ashamed of their country, ashamed of their parents, ashamed of America's record at home and its role in the world.

At every turn we have been beset by those who find everything wrong with America and little that is right. But I am confident that this will not be the judgment of history on these remarkable times in which we are privileged to live.

America's record in this century has been unparalleled in the world's history for its responsibility, for its generosity, for its creativity, and for its progress.

Let us be proud that our system has produced and provided more freedom and more abundance, more widely shared, than any system in the history of the world.

Let us be proud that in each of the four wars in which we have been engaged in this century, including the one we are now bringing to an end, we have fought not for our selfish advantage, but to help others resist aggression.

And let us be proud that by our bold, new initiatives, by our steadfastness for peace with honor, we have made a breakthrough toward creating in the world what the world has not known before—a structure of peace that can last, not merely for our time, but for generations to come.

We are embarking here today on an era that presents challenges as great as those any nation, or any generation, has ever faced.

We shall answer to God, to history, and to our conscience for the way in which we use these years.

As I stand in this place, so hallowed by history, I think of others who have stood here before me. I think of the dreams they had for America and I think of how each recognized that he needed help far beyond himself in order to make those dreams come true.

Today I ask your prayers that in the years ahead I may have God's help in making decisions that are right for America, and I pray for your help so that together we may be worthy of our challenge.

Let us pledge together to make these next 4 years the best 4 years in America's history, so that on its 200th birthday America will be as young and as vital as when it began, and as bright a beacon of hope for all the world.

Let us go forward from here confident in hope, strong in our faith in one another, sustained by our faith in God who created us, and striving always to serve His purpose.

DOCUMENT 35.5
America's Crisis of Confidence

Very early in his campaign for the presidency, Jimmy Carter developed a new and successful mode of relating to the American people. Speaking partly as a moralist, partly as a preacher, he communicated a sense of caring deeply about the underlying values of the American people. When Carter encountered obstacles in persuading Congress to support his legislative objectives, he returned to his campaign style of communication, seeking to reach over the heads of Congress to speak directly to the American people about his concerns. In the speech that follows, Carter traces America's problems to an underlying "crisis of confidence," a disease of the soul. The speech reveals both Carter's strength and his weakness. He successfully identifies a feeling of uncertainty in the body politic. But he fails to provide politically pragmatic answers that will effectively answer the problem.

This is a special night for me. Exactly three years ago on July 15, 1976, I accepted the nomination of my party to run for President

Source: From *Public Papers of the Presidents: Jimmy Carter, 1979*. (Washington, D.C.: 1980), pp. 1235–1241.

of the United States. I promised to you a President who is not isolated from the people, who feels your pain and shares your dreams and who draws his strength and his wisdom from you.

During the past three years, I've spoken to you on many occasions about national concerns: the energy crisis, reorganizing the Government, our nation's economy and issues of war, and especially peace. But over those years the subjects of the speeches, the talks and the press conferences have become increasingly narrow, focused more and more on what the isolated world of Washington thinks is important.

Ten days ago I had plans to speak to you again about a very important subject—energy. For the fifth time I would have described the urgency of the problem and laid out a series of legislative recommendations to the Congress, but as I was preparing to speak I began to ask myself the same question that I now know has been troubling many of you: Why have we not been able to get together as a nation to resolve our serious energy problem?

It's clear that the true problems of our nation are much deeper—deeper than gasoline lines or energy shortages. Deeper, even, than inflation or recession. And I realize more than ever that as President I need your help, so I decided to reach out and to listen to the voices of America. I invited to Camp David people from almost every segment of our society: business and labor; teachers and preachers; governors, mayors and private citizens.

And then I left Camp David to listen to other Americans. Men and women like you. It has been an extraordinary 10 days and I want to share with you what I heard.

ADVICE FROM THE PEOPLE

First of all, I got a lot of personal advice. Let me quote a few of the typical comments that I wrote down.

This from a Southern Governor: ''Mr. President, you're not leading this nation, you're just managing the Government.''

''You don't see the people enough anymore.''

''Some of your Cabinet members don't seem loyal. There's not enough discipline among your disciples.''

Many people talked about themselves and about the condition of our nation. This from a young woman in Pennsylvania: ''I feel so far from government. I feel like ordinary people are excluded from political power.'' And this from a young Chicano: ''Some of us have suffered from recession all our lives. Some people have wasted energy but others haven't had anything to waste.'' And this from a religious leader: ''No material shortage can touch the important things like God's love for us or our love for one another.''

* * * * *

Several of our discussions were on energy, and I have a notebook full of comments and advice. I'll read just a few.

''We can't go on consuming 40 percent more energy than we produce. When we import oil, we are also importing inflation plus unemployment. We've got to use what we have. The Middle East has only 5 percent of the world's energy, but the United States has 24 percent.''

And this is one of the most vivid statements: ''Our neck is stretched over the fence and OPEC has the knife.''

* * * * *

These 10 days confirmed my belief in the decency and the strength and the wisdom of the American people, but it also bore out some of my long-standing concerns about our nation's underlying problems. I know, of course, being President, that Government actions and legislation can be very important.

That's why I've worked hard to put my campaign promises into law, and I have to admit with just mixed success. But after listening to the American people I have been reminded again that all the legislatures in the world can't fix what's wrong with America.

A FUNDAMENTAL THREAT

So I want to speak to you tonight about a subject even more serious than energy or inflation. I want to talk to you right now about a fundamental threat to American democracy.

I do not mean our political and civil liberties. They will endure. And I do not refer to the outward strength of America—the nation that is at peace tonight everywhere in the world with unmatched economic power and military might. The threat is nearly invisible in ordinary ways. It is a crisis of confidence. It is a crisis that strikes at the very heart and soul and spirit of our national will.

We can see this crisis in the growing doubt about the meaning of our own lives and in the loss of a unity of purpose for our nation.

The erosion of our confidence in the future is threatening to destroy the social and the political fabric of America. The confidence that we have always had as a people is not simply some romantic dream or a proverb in a dusty book that we read just on the Fourth of July. It is the idea which founded our nation and which has guided our development as a people. Confidence in the future has supported everything else—public institutions and private enterprise, our own families and the very Constitution of the United States. Confidence has defined our course and has served as a link between generations.

We've always believed in something called progress. We've always had a faith that the days of our children would be better than our own.

CLOSING THE DOOR ON OUR PAST

Our people are losing that faith. Not only in Government itself, but in their ability as citizens to serve as the ultimate rulers and shapers of our democracy. As a people, we know our past and we are proud of it. Our progress has been part of the living history of America, even the world. We always believed that we were part of a great movement of humanity itself called democracy, involved in the search for freedom. And that belief has always strengthened us in our purpose. But just as we are losing our confidence in the future, we are also beginning to close the door on our past.

In a nation that was proud of hard work, strong families, closeknit communities and our faith in God, too many of us now tend to worship self-indulgence and consumption. Human identity is no longer defined by what one does but by what one owns.

But we've discovered that owning things and consuming things does not satisfy our longing for meaning.

We have learned that piling up material goods cannot fill the emptiness of lives which have no confidence or purpose. The symptoms of this crisis of the American spirit are all around us. For the first time in the history of our country a majority of our people believe that the next five years will be worse than that past five years. Two-thirds of our people do not even vote. The productivity of American workers is actually dropping and the willingness of Americans to save for the future has fallen below that of all other people in the Western world.

As you know there is a growing disrespect for Government and for churches and for schools, the news media and other institutions. This is not a message of happiness or reassurance but it is the truth. And it is a warning. These changes did not happen overnight. They've come upon us gradually over the last generation. Years that were filled with shocks and tragedy.

We were sure that ours was a nation of the ballot, not of the bullet, until the murders of John Kennedy and Robert Kennedy and Mar-

tin Luther King, Jr. We were taught that our armies were always invincible and our causes were always just only to suffer the agony of Vietnam. We respected the Presidency as a place of honor until the shock of Watergate. We remember when the phrase "sound as a dollar" was an expression of absolute dependability until 10 years of inflation began to shrink our dollar and our savings. We believed that our nation's resources were limitless until 1973, when we had to face a growing dependence on foreign oil.

These wounds are still very deep. They have never been healed.

ISOLATION OF GOVERNMENT

Looking for a way out of this crisis, our people have turned to the Federal Government and found it isolated from the mainstream of our nation's life. Washington, D.C., has become an island. The gap between our citizens and our Government has never been so wide. The people are looking for honest answers, not easy answers, clear leadership, not false claims and evasiveness and politics as usual. What you see too often in Washington and elsewhere around the country is a system of government that seems incapable of action.

You see a Congress twisted and pulled in every direction by hundreds of well-financed and powerful special interests. You see every extreme position defended to the last vote, almost to the last breath, by one unyielding group or another.

Often you see paralysis and stagnation and drift. You don't like it.

And neither do I.

What can we do? First of all, we must face the truth and then we can change our course. We simply must have faith in each other. Faith in our ability to govern ourselves and faith in the future of this nation. Restoring that faith and that confidence to America is now the most important task we face.

It is a true challenge of this generation of

Americans. One of the visitors to Camp David last week put it this way: We've got to stop crying and start sweating; stop talking and start walking; stop cursing and start praying. The strength we need will not come from the White House but from every house in America.

We know the strength of America. We are strong. We can regain our unity. We can regain our confidence. We are the heirs of generations who survived threats much more powerful and awesome than those that challenge us now.

TURNING POINT IN HISTORY

Our fathers and mothers were strong men and women who shaped the new society during the Great Depression, who fought world wars and who carved out a new charter of peace for the world. We ourselves are the same Americans who just 10 years ago put a man on the moon. We are the generation that dedicated our society to the pursuit of human rights and equality.

And we are the generation that will win the war on the energy problem, and in that process rebuild the unity and confidence of America. We are at a turning point in our history. There are two paths to choose. One is the path I've warned about tonight—the path that leads to fragmentation and self-interest. Down that road lies a mistaken idea of freedom.

* * * * *

All the traditions of our past, all the lessons of our heritage, all the promises of our future point to another path: the path of common purpose and the restoration of American values. That path leads to true freedom for our nation and ourselves. We can take the first steps down that path as we begin to solve our energy problem. Energy will be the immediate test of our ability to unite this nation.

* * * * *

You know we can do it. We have the natural resources. We have more oil in our shale alone

than several Saudi Arabias. We have more coal than any nation on earth. We have the world's highest level of technology. We have the most skilled work force, with innovative genius.

And I firmly believe we have the national will to win this war.

* * * * *

DOCUMENT 35.6
"The Second American Revolution"

If Franklin Roosevelt initiated the modern era of politics with his New Deal, Ronald Reagan sought to bring that era to an end with "supply-side" economics, huge tax cuts, and Draconian slashes in the social welfare system FDR had begun. The irony was that Reagan had started his political life as an admirer of FDR, and throughout his presidency, cited FDR as a model of presidential leadership. He even outdid FDR in the role that the creator of the "fireside chat" had seemed to make his own— that of the "great communicator." In this speech Reagan charts his vision of the new American revolution that he hoped to bring to America, one where government would lessen its role in people's lives and old-fashioned values would be revitalized.

Mr. Speaker, Mr. President, distinguished members of the Congress, honored guests and fellow citizens. I come before you to report on the state of our union. And I am pleased to report that, after four years of united effort, the American people have brought forth a nation renewed—stronger, freer and more secure than before.

Four years ago, we began to change—forever, I hope—our assumptions about government and its place in our lives. Out of that

Source: From *Weekly Compilation of Presidential Documents*, Vol. 21, 1–11 (1985), pp. 67–70.

change has come great and robust growth—in our confidence, our economy and our role in the world. . . .

Four years ago, we said we would invigorate our economy by giving people greater freedom and incentives to take risks, and letting them keep more of what they earned.

We did what we promised, and a great industrial giant is reborn. Tonight we can take pride in 25 straight months of economic growth, the strongest in 34 years: a three-year inflation average of 3.9 percent the lowest in 17 years; and 7.3 million new jobs in two years, with more of our citizens working than ever before. . . .

We have begun well. But it's only a beginning. We are not here to congratulate ourselves on what we have done, but to challenge ourselves to finish what has not yet been done.

We are here to speak for millions in our inner cities who long for real jobs, safe neighborhoods and schools that truly teach. We are here to speak for the American farmer, the entrepreneur and every worker in industries fighting to modernize and compete. And, yes, we are here to stand, and proudly so, for all who struggle to break free from totalitarianism; for all who know in their hearts that freedom is the one true path to peace and human happiness. . . .

We honor the giants of our history not by going back, but forward to the dreams their vision foresaw. My fellow citizens, this nation is poised for greatness. The time has come to proceed toward a great new challenge—a Second American Revolution of hope and opportunity; a revolution carrying us to new heights of progress by pushing back frontiers of knowledge and space; a revolution of spirit that taps the soul of America, enabling us to summon greater strength than we have ever known; and, a revolution that carries beyond our shores the golden promise of human freedom in a world at peace.

Let us begin by challenging conventional wisdom: There are no constraints on the human mind, no walls around the human spirit, no barriers to our progress except those we ourselves erect. Already, pushing down tax rates has freed our economy to vault forward to record growth.

In Europe, they call it "the American Miracle." Day by day, we are shattering accepted notions of what is possible. . . .

We stand on the threshold of a great ability to produce more, do more, be more. Our economy is not getting older and weaker, it's getting younger and stronger; it doesn't need rest and supervision, it needs new challenge, greater freedom. And that word—freedom—is the key to the Second American Revolution we mean to bring about.

Let us move together with an historic reform of tax simplification for fairness and growth. Last year, I asked then-Treasury Secretary Regan to develop a plan to simplify the tax code, so all taxpayers would be treated more fairly, and personal tax rates could come further down.

We have cut tax rates by almost 25 percent, yet the tax system remains unfair and limits our potential for growth. Exclusions and exemptions cause similar incomes to be taxed at different levels. Low-income families face steep tax barriers that make hard lives even harder. The Treasury Department has produced an excellent reform plan whose principles will guide the final proposal we will ask you to enact.

One thing that tax reform will not be is a tax increase in disguise. We will not jeopardize the mortgage interest deduction families need. We will reduce personal tax rates as low as possible by removing many tax preferences. We will propose a top rate of no more than 35 percent, and possibly lower. And we will propose reducing corporate rates while maintaining incentives for capital formation. . . .

Tax simplification will be a giant step toward unleashing the tremendous pent-up power of our economy. But a Second American Revolution must carry the promise of opportunity for all. It is time to liberate the spirit of enterprise in the most distressed areas of our country.

This government will meet its responsibility to help those in need. But policies that increase dependency, break up families and destroy self-respect are not progressive, they are reactionary. Despite our strides in civil rights, blacks, Hispanics and all minorities will not have full and equal power until they have full economic powers. . . .

Let us resolve that we will stop spreading dependency and start spreading opportunity; that we will stop spreading bondage and start spreading freedom.

There are some who say that growth initiatives must await final action on deficit reductions. The best way to reduce deficits is through economic growth. More business will be started, more investments made, more jobs created and more people will be on payrolls paying taxes. The best way to reduce government spending is to reduce the need for spending by increasing prosperity. . . .

To move steadily toward a balanced budget we must also lighten government's claim on our total economy. We will not do this by raising taxes. We must make sure that our economy grows faster than growth in spending by federal government. In our fiscal year 1986 budget, overall government program spending will be frozen at the current level; it must not be one dime higher than fiscal year 1985. And three points are key:

First, the social safety net for the elderly, needy, disabled and unemployed will be left intact. Growth of our major health care programs, Medicare and Medicaid, will be slowed, but protections for the elderly and needy will be preserved.

Second, we must not relax our efforts to restore military strength just as we near our goal of a fully equipped, trained and ready professional corps. National security is government's first responsibility, so, in past years, defense spending took about half the federal budget. Today it takes less than a third.

We have already reduced our planned defense expenditures by nearly $100 billion over the past four years, and reduced projected spending again this year. You know, we only have a military industrial complex until a time of danger. Then it becomes the arsenal of democracy. Spending for defense is investing in things that are priceless: peace and freedom.

Third, we must reduce or eliminate costly government subsidies. For example, deregulation of the airline industry has led to cheaper airfares, but on Amtrak taxpayers pay about $35 per passenger every time an Amtrak train leaves the station. It's time we ended this huge federal subsidy.

Our farm program costs have quadrupled in recent years. Yet I know from visiting farmers, many in great financial distress, that we need an orderly transition to a market-oriented farm economy. We can help farmers best, not by expanding federal payments, but by making fundamental reforms, keeping interest rates heading down and knocking down foreign trade barriers to American farm exports. . . .

In the long run, we must protect the taxpayers from government. And I ask again that you pass, as 32 states have now called for, an amendment mandating the federal government spend no more than it takes in. And I ask for the authority used responsibly by 43 governors to veto individual items in appropriations bills. . . .

Nearly 50 years of government living beyond its means has brought us to a time of reckoning. Ours is but a moment in history. But one moment of courage, idealism and bipartisan unity can change American history forever. . . .

Every dollar the federal government does not take from us, every decision it does not make for us, will make our economy stronger, our lives more abundant, our future more free. . . .

There is another great heritage to speak of this evening. Of all the changes that have swept America the past four years, none brings greater promise than our rediscovery of the value of faith, freedom, family, work and neighborhood.

We see signs of renewal in increased attendance in places of worship: renewed optimism and faith in our future; love of country rediscovered by our young who are leading the way. We have rediscovered that work is good in and of itself; that it ennobles us to create and contribute no matter how seemingly humble our jobs. We have seen a powerful new current from an old and honorable tradition—American generosity. . . .

I thank the Congress for passing equal access legislation giving religious groups the same right to use classrooms after school that other groups enjoy. But no citizen need tremble, nor the world shudder, if a child stands in a classroom and breathes a prayer. We ask you again—give children back a right they had for a century-and-a-half or more in this country.

The question of abortion grips our nation. Abortion is either the taking of human life, or it isn't; and if it is—and medical technology is increasingly showing it is—it must be stopped. . . .

Of all the changes in the past 20 years, none has more threatened our sense of national well-being than the explosion of violent crime. One does not have to have been attacked to be a victim. The woman who must run to her car after shopping at night is a victim; the couple draping their door with locks and chains are

victims; as is the tired, decent cleaning woman who can't ride a subway home without being afraid.

We do not seek to violate rights of defendants, but shouldn't we feel more compassion for victims of crime than for those who commit crime? For the first time in 20 years, the crime index has fallen two years in a row; we've convicted over 7,400 drug offenders, and put them, as well as leaders of organized crime, behind bars in record numbers.

But we must do more. I urge the House to follow the Senate and enact proposals permitting use of all reliable evidence that police officers acquire in good faith. These proposals would also reform the *habeas corpus* laws and allow, in keeping with the will of the overwhelming majority of Americans, the use of the death penalty where necessary.

There can be no economic revival in ghettos when the most violent among us are allowed to roam free. It is time we restored domestic tranquility. And we mean to do just that. . . .

Tonight I have spoken of great plans and great dreams. They are dreams we can make come true. Two hundred years of American history should have taught us that nothing is impossible. . . . Anything is possible in America if we have the faith, the will and the heart.

History is asking us, once again, to be a force for good in the world. Let us begin—in unity, with justice and love.

Thank you and God bless you.

chapter

American Social History: 1960–1987

Maurice Isserman
Smith College

At first glance, the history of the United States from the 1960s through the mid-1980s reveals only a bewildering and seemingly inexplicable series of political, social, and cultural changes, from the "rebellious" 1960s to the self-indulgent "me decade" of the 1970s to the "new patriotism" and "family values" of the 1980s. A major problem confronting students of contemporary American history is the fact that, considered separately, each of the three decades from the 1960s through the 1980s has a coherence that, considered as a whole, they seem to lack. Were Americans simply being frivolous in those years, incessantly seeking after new leaders and sensations, a nation of moody faddists who could swing from a Lyndon Johnson to a Richard Nixon or from a Jimmy Carter to a Ronald Reagan as casually as they abandoned "MASH" for "Rambo" or scotch and sodas for "designer water"? But if we put aside the habit of thinking of the recent past in terms of convenient stereotypes neatly divided by decade, then the history of the United States in these years reveals a pattern otherwise obscured from view.

For many Americans John F. Kennedy's inaugural in January 1961 seemed to hold the promise of opening a new era of unlimited opportunities—for individuals and for the nation. In his presidential campaign Kennedy had promised to "get America moving again," and his inspirational inaugural address touched a responsive chord even among some who had not voted for him the previous November. "Let the word go forth from this time and place, to friend and foe alike," Kennedy declared in ringing tones, "that the torch has been passed to a new generation of Americans, born in this century, tempered by war, disciplined by a hard and bitter peace." The key phrase in that passage was "new generation." Kennedy *was* the first president born in the twentieth century, and his taking of the oath of office seemed to proclaim the collective achievement of a generation of Americans whose youthful memories were shaped by the shared adversity of the depression and World War II. Standing beside Dwight Eisenhower, the balding, grandfatherly man he was replacing in the White House, Kennedy exuded youthful vigor and potential. The promise of Kennedy's "New Frontier" was a paradoxical one: America *as a nation* would be poised to meet any challenge that it set for itself or that was set by its enemies—but at the same time Americans *as individuals* could truly begin to enjoy the prosperous society they had uneasily inhabited since the end of World War II. Kennedy's well-publicized fondness for Ian Fleming's spy novels was a fitting symbol of the new age: Fleming's protagonist, the suave and deadly James Bond, was "licensed to kill" but he was also a conspicuous consumer of fine wines, well-made clothes, and beautiful women.

In the 1950s Americans enjoyed a level of material abundance unprecedented in history. A flood of new consumer goods, including televisions, electric clothes dryers, automatic garbage disposals, and long-playing records poured onto the market, while another recent innovation known as the credit card made it easier than ever for consumers to make impulsive purchases. But the rampant consumerism of the decade carried with it an undertone of anxiety, informed by memories of the depression, and reinforced by the three sharp if temporary economic recessions the nation suffered during the Eisenhower presidency. Marketing strategists complained about the lingering traces of an earlier, thriftier ethos that undermined the effectiveness of advertising. As one motivational researcher explained to a business audience:

> We are . . . confronted with the problem of permitting the average American to feel moral . . . even when he is spending, even when he is not saving, even when he is taking two vacations a year and buying a second or third car. One of the basic problems of prosperity, then is to demonstrate that the hedonistic approach to his life is a moral, not an immoral one.

In *Hard Times,* Studs Terkel's oral history of the Great Depression, a union organizer who had been a child in the 1930s recalled his feelings of shame when his father was thrown out of work: "Sure things were tough, but why should I be the kid who had to put a piece of cardboard into the sole of my shoe to go to school?" Such memories left a lasting impact on the depression generation. As the same man told Terkel: "I now have twenty times more shirts than I need, because all during that time, shirts were something I never had." Consumer

spending patterns were complicated by these lasting feelings of insecurity. Spending was often rationalized as something parents undertook for the benefit of their children: "We did it for the kids," served as an all-purpose justification for new televisions, backyard swimming pools, and basement "rec rooms." Advertisers had a much less complicated task in selling to the new "youth market": the children of the postwar "baby boom" got to enjoy the new consumer cornucopia without guilt. From the Davy Crockett fad of the early 1950s to the Beatles craze of the early 1960s, advertisers perfected their pitch and helped shape a distinctive generational consciousness among the nation's young consumers. Their task was made all the easier by social and economic trends which extended the preadult phase of life; a college education became the norm rather than a privilege, as the B.A. became necessary certification for nonblue-collar employment. "Youth communities" sprang up on the outskirts of college campuses, often in the cheap and decaying housing available on the edge of black ghettoes. There, freed from adult supervision and not yet facing the responsibilities of job and mortgages, young people began to experiment with new manners, mores, sexual behavior, and, in some instances, illegal pharmaceutical substances.

In the early 1960s the U.S. economy enjoyed the combined benefits of a favorable trade balance, cheap and abundant energy sources, a New Frontier-initiated boom in defense spending, and a sizable tax cut. The level of unemployment dropped steadily while inflationary pressures only slowly began to mount. As the "go-go" gross national product (GNP) expanded from one year to the next, the parents of baby boomers at last began to relax, imagining that a permanent condition of prosperity had been achieved. The more secure middle-class Americans felt about their own circumstances, the more willing they were to acknowledge the existence of poverty in their midst, and to consider steps to alleviate the plight of the poor (particularly since they were assured by the nation's leaders that this could be done through a relatively painless process of extending to all Americans the opportunity to partake of an ever-expanding economic pie). Renewed concern for the nation's poor also reflected the growing influence of the civil rights movement, and the lessening of cold war tensions. While the civil rights movement was mainly concerned with securing blacks the constitutional rights already possessed by white Americans, the moral authority this cause enjoyed in the early 1960s made many Americans sympathetic to the argument that blacks should not only have right to sit at the nation's lunch counters, but also should be given the wherewithal to afford more hamburgers. And when Kennedy and Khrushchev drew back from the nuclear precipice of the Cuban missile crisis the nation heaved a collective sigh of relief—which made it possible to tolerate greater questioning of both the international and domestic status quo than had been the case at the height of the cold war. Kennedy's inspirational "torch-passing" rhetoric could lead in different directions: to a celebration of Green Berets counterinsurgency efforts in South Vietnam, but also—though this was far from Kennedy's initial intention—to a legitimation of the adoption of new social and political values by young Americans.

"Come mothers and fathers/Throughout the land," Bob Dylan implored in his nasal twang in "The Times They Are A-Changin'" in 1963, "And don't criticize/What you can't understand/Your sons and your daughters/Are beyond your command/Your old road is rapidly agin'." Increasingly, youthful political activists on the nation's campuses believed that they had been endowed with a special mission to redeem the nation from injustice and error. Kennedy's assassination in November 1963 marked a turning point: although Lyndon Johnson was more consistently concerned with domestic reform than his predecessor, he was unable to inspire the same trust and identification among the young. By 1965 campus activists, who collectively came to be known as the "New Left," had broken with the liberal assumptions of Kennedy's New Frontier and Johnson's Great Society, and with those who embraced them. These liberals of the older generation were now scorned as uncertain allies in the civil rights struggle, and as the chief instigators of the war in Vietnam. The main radical group on campus, Students for a Democratic Society (SDS), grew spectacularly after 1965. It offered a vision of a cultural as well as a political alternative, keeping pace in its politics with the increasingly assertive mood of cultural defiance that prevailed among young people. By 1965 Bob Dylan's lyrics had lost the gentle edge of "The Times They Are A-Changing," and demonstrated a contemptuous dismissal of the older generation: ". . . something is happening here/But you don't know what it is/Do you, Mister Jones?", Dylan sneered in "Ballad of a Thin Man." As the war in Vietnam escalated, and as white police and black rioters fought a mini-civil war in the ghettoes in a series of "long hot summers," the New Left's early dream of redeeming America was replaced by the belief that the nation was being justifiably punished for its sins. The campus antiwar movement reached its height during the national student strike in May 1970, a strike provoked by the American invasion of Cambodia and the killing of four students at Kent State University by Ohio National Guardsmen. A Harris poll taken that spring reported that 76 percent of college students agreed with the statement that "basic changes in the system" were necessary, while 44 percent agreed with the statement that social progress required "radical pressures from outside the system." SDS had already abandoned the slogan "End the War," and promised instead to "Bring the War Home."

Despite some superficial similarities in

rhetoric, the beliefs of the New Left differed dramatically from those of earlier generations on the Left. Young activists took affluence for granted and despised its corrupting influence, unlike the Socialists and Communists of the 1930s who denounced capitalism for its inability to provide the minimum decencies of life to the poor. The great revolutionary drama of the New York theater in the 1930s had been Clifford Odets's *Waiting for Lefty,* which ended with the "workers" in the cast and the audience joining together in chanting "Strike, strike, strike!" Perhaps the closest equivalent to Odets's work in the 1960s was the enormously popular play by Peter Brooks, *Marat/Sade,* which suggested that conventional politics, even conventional revolutionary politics, was exhausted as a force for change. The final scene in *Marat/Sade* provoked the same kind of audience empathy as the climax of *Waiting for Lefty,* but this time the identification was not with striking workers but with rioting lunatics in an insane asylum, who sang "We want our revolution . . . NOW!" Earlier generations of radicals had derided capitalism as an anarchic, irrational system; the new radicals scorned the system because it was *too* rational, based on a soul-destroying set of technological and bureaucratic imperatives that stifled individual expression. Pop social critics, like Yale professor Charles Reich, took this critique and gave it an apolitical twist in his best-selling book *The Greening of America:* young Americans, he argued, were proving that through an act of personal will they could transcend the limits of the existing culture:

> The plan, the program, the grand strategy, is this: resist the State, when you must; avoid it, when you can; but listen to music, dance, seek out nature, laugh, be happy, be beautiful, help others whenever you can . . . love and cherish each other, love and cherish yourselves, stay together.

New Left activists might have preferred Mao's little red book to Reich's little green

book, but their own actions increasingly reflected personal rather than political agendas. Jim Mellen, one of the founders of Weathermen, the faction that captured the leadership of SDS in 1969, reflected in later years on the appeal of violent politics to student radicals at the end of the 1960s:

> When we started saying . . . that the violent revolution is here and now, it enthralled a lot of people . . . One of the things that enthralled them was the opportunity to go out and do something existential, like James Dean. The political effectiveness of an act was less important than the demonstration of one's own character.

The quest for personal fulfillment became the center of radical politics in the late 1960s and proved the most enduring legacy left after the collapse of the organized New Left in the early 1970s.

Within a few years of the 1970 student strike the New Left had virtually disappeared. Conservative political analysts, Richard Scammon and Ben Wattenberg, argued in their 1970 book *The Real Majority* that the "new politics" of the 1960s had never really reflected the sentiments of the American heartland. The average American voter, they argued, was "unyoung, unpoor, and unblack." Their composite portrait of the "Middle Voter" turned out to be a:

> forty-seven-year-old housewife from the outskirts of Dayton, Ohio, whose husband is a machinist. . . . To know that the lady in Dayton is afraid to walk the streets alone at night, to know that she has a mixed view about blacks and civil rights because before moving to the suburbs she lived in a neighborhood that became all black, to know that her brother-in-law is a policeman, to know that she does not have the money to move if her new neighborhood deteriorates . . . to know all this is the beginning of contemporary political wisdom.

But conservatives were mistaken when they imagined that Richard Nixon's electoral victories in 1968 and 1972 betokened a return to the pre-1960s status quo. The New Left had proved a dismal failure in its self-proclaimed role as *political* vanguard. Nevertheless as a *cultural* vanguard, it wielded enormous and growing influence—though, ironically, its true influence would not be felt until after it had ceased its organizational existence. Throughout the years when the ''great silent majority'' supposedly spoke through the Nixon administration, the cultural revolution unleashed by the New Left stealthily undermined the generational ramparts that had seemed so impenetrable during the preceding decade. Attitudes toward sex, gender roles, family, work, and achievement that had been new and daring in Berkeley and Madison in the early 1960s became commonplace in Topeka and Dayton in the course of the 1970s. The chances were that by the mid-1970s Scammon and Wattenberg's archetypal Dayton housewife had taken a job in the local supermarket, enrolled in a dance or exercise class at the Y, and was only waiting for her last child to finish high school so that she could divorce her husband. The fact that she had voted for Richard Nixon in 1968 and 1972 may have been the ''beginning of contemporary political wisdom,'' but it was a thoroughly inadequate guide to social and cultural trends in the 1970s.

In what pollster Daniel Yankelovich called a ''case history of 'cultural diffusion' '' the baby boomers converted their parents to a new ethic of self-fulfillment. The ingrained self-denying ethos of the Depression generation eroded in the 1960s. Older Americans may have resented the cultural freedoms assumed or demanded by the younger generation; they also envied them. The trend toward more relaxed standards of sexual behavior, and changing attitudes toward the meaning of family, work, and leisure had roots extending back well into the nineteenth century. But it was the historical role of the New Left, and more generally the youth ''counterculture'' of the 1960s, to proclaim these new attitudes openly and unashamedly. And with the ''chilling'' of the New Left in the aftermath of the Kent State deaths, many Americans who had been appalled by the political aspects of the 1960s youth revolt now availed themselves of its cultural fruits. Statistics reveal some of the magnitude of this change. By 1975 the ''traditional'' family (two parents, two or more children, with the father the sole breadwinner) accounted for only 13.5 percent of married households. Three quarters of all married women worked outside the home, as did one half of all married women with school-age children. The divorce rate doubled in the 1960s and 1970s, as did the number of female-headed households. Single-person households emerged in the 1980s Census as the fastest growing category of living arrangement, outnumbering the ''typical'' family household for the first time. The birthrate dropped below replacement rate: in the 1950s the average American woman gave birth to three or four children; by the end of the 1970s the average dropped to below two births per woman. Although social behavior usually changes more quickly than cultural attitudes, the new rules swiftly won acceptance. As the number of unmarried couples living together doubled between 1960 and the late 1970s, polls revealed that the percentage of Americans who condemned premarital sex dropped from 85 percent in 1967 to 37 percent in 1979. By the end of the 1970s 75 percent of Americans agreed that it was morally acceptable to be single and have children—though the fact that many of those who chose to do so were teenagers who could support themselves and their children only by relying on public assistance would in time stir some second thoughts.

Bearing these social and cultural changes in mind provides a new perspective from which to consider the meaning of Nixon's electoral triumphs. What Nixon offered to the electorate in 1968 was the promise of the early 1960s without the turmoil of the later 1960s. The "new Nixon" who took office in 1969 had pledged himself to ending the Vietnam War and winding down the Cold War. (He proved more sincere and effective in accomplishing the latter than the former task.) He was a born-again Keynesian who left the main structure of the New Deal and the Great Society intact. (In fact, government spending on "entitlement" programs greatly increased during Nixon's first term in office.) A truly conservative political revival would have summoned Americans to a regimen of discipline and self-sacrifice, but Nixon's version of "law and order" was designed instead to give Americans a secure setting in which they could indulge themselves in the new ethic of self-fulfillment.

Though outwardly committed to an indulgent and benevolent politics, Nixon's fiercely partisan and punitive instincts finally tripped him up. As a result of the Watergate scandal, and a decade of deceptions and disappointments in Vietnam, Americans grew disillusioned with politics. The percentage of the public who agreed with the statement that they could "trust the government in Washington to do what's right" declined from 56 percent in 1958 to 29 percent in 1978. Jimmy Carter, a one-term Georgia governor with little experience in national politics, was the first beneficiary of this anti-Washington mood. The theme of his successful 1976 presidential campaign was summed up in the title of his book *Why Not the Best?*. Carter promised the voters honesty and competence, rather than a specific set of proposals or a political philosophy.

Disillusioned with public life, tired of foreign and domestic crusades, Americans turned all the more eagerly to the satisfactions of their private lives. But the economic underpinnings of the new cultural values were dropping away at just the moment that self-fulfillment had replaced self-denial as the dominant ethic. What some observers labeled a "Revolution of Falling Expectations" took place in the course of the 1970s. As the go-go years of 1960s prosper-

ity gave way to inflation, recession, and unemployment, gloom replaced confidence. The percentage of Americans agreeing with the statement "hard work always pays off" dropped from 58 percent to 43 percent between 1969 and 1976. By 1980 *Fortune* magazine reported that "most people nowadays aspire to little more than holding on to what they've already got, and many become downright despondent when they contemplate the world their children will inherit."

The economic hard times of the 1970s stemmed from various sources, foreign and domestic. Lyndon Johnson's reluctance to raise taxes to pay for an increasingly unpopular war in Vietnam set off the start of an inflationary spiral later accelerated by the OPEC oil embargo of 1973. The inflation rate for the 1970s averaged 8.1 percent, climbing to double digits in the last years of the Carter administration. Real wages, which had risen steadily from the end of World War II until 1972 began a nose dive in that year, with average spendable weekly earnings for a family of four dropping almost 10 percent from then until 1980. As a result the level of per capita income of Americans dropped from first in the world to seventh in the course of the early 1970s. The United States could no longer claim to be number one in the living standards of its people—or in the competitiveness of its industry. International competition finally caught up with overconfident American manufacturers. The United States saw its first trade deficit in the twentieth century in 1971, one that grew steadily throughout the next decade and a half. West Germany and Japan, having rebuilt their war-shattered economies with the most modern technologies and forms of labor and management organization available, proved particularly fierce competitors. By 1981 the Japanese alone controlled 23 percent of the U.S. automobile market, 25 percent of the television market, and 50 percent of the radio and recording equipment market. Though business leaders often blamed American workers for having created this situation through demands for high wages, the declining competitiveness of American industry had much more to do with a shift in investment strategy on the part of American corporations, part of a major change in the structure of the U.S. economy. Increasingly the corporations that had risen to dominant roles in the American economy via manufacturing were seeking new sources of income far removed from their original economic base. By 1982, for example, the United States Steel Corporation's stake in the steel industry represented less than 40 percent of its total assets. Steel corporations found it more profitable to invest in energy companies, real estate, shopping malls, and a host of other nonmanufacturing enterprises, than to reinvest their still considerable profits in new factories and machinery. This trend grew so flagrant that by the late 1970s even the business press was alarmed. In 1977 *Business Week* criticized the steel industry's habit of treating its old factories "as cash boxes for corporate growth in other areas." Symbolic of the shift in the structure of the U.S. economy from manufacturing to service was the fact that by the end of the 1970s McDonald's hamburger chain employed more workers than U.S. Steel. Between 1960 and 1980 the percentage of nonfarm employees in manufacturing dropped from 30 to just over 22 percent while those employed in service industries climbed from 13.6 to 19.5 percent. When manufacturing corporations did choose to reinvest their profits in production, the investments they made were designed to eliminate rather than to create jobs, substituting robots for human labor, or unskilled for skilled labor. Many firms shifted the base of their operations from the traditional industrial heartland of the Northeast and upper Midwest to the Sunbelt states of the Deep South and the Southwest, in pursuit of a nonunion labor force willing to work for lower than prevailing wages, and communities willing to offer industry substantial tax benefits. Between 1967 and 1976 the

Northeast and Midwest lost 1.5 million manufacturing jobs—900,000 shifted to the Sunbelt, while the remainder were either eliminated or sent abroad, to such places as Mexico, Taiwan, and South Korea. All of these changes led to growing rates of unemployment, and a declining rate of unionization among American workers.

It was Jimmy Carter's misfortune to enter the White House just as these unhappy economic trends made their full force felt. There was little that any president could have done, at least in the short run, to remedy the economic downturn of the 1970s. But Carter made things much worse for himself politically by choosing to respond to the crisis by sounding the conservative themes of disciplined self-sacrifice that Richard Nixon had had the good sense to avoid in his own time in office. In the famous "malaise speech" of 1979 Carter delivered a jeremiad summoning Americans to reject "self-indulgence and consumption"—and in doing so, only succeeded in identifying himself as the cause and symbol of economic hard times.[*] Ronald Reagan, who capped his debate with Carter in 1980 with the brilliant peroration, "Are you better off than you were four years ago? Is it easier for you to go and buy things in the stores than it was four years ago? . . ." took full advantage of Carter's misstep.

The "Reagan revolution" of the early 1980s represented a peculiar and unstable coalition of traditional and "New Right" conservatives who were reacting against the self-fulfillment ethic and all it implied (abortion, gay rights, the "decline of the family," and so on), and paradoxically a much larger group of voters who turned against Carter because they felt that their opportunities to indulge themselves in the new lifestyles, values, and aspirations were being threatened by the downturn in the economy. The fact that the onset of hard times

---

[*] See Document 35.5, Jimmy Carter, "America's Crisis of Confidence."

coincided with the post-Vietnam, post-Water-gate disillusionment with the government seemed to set up a conflict between individual pursuit of self-fulfillment on the one side and government bureaucrats and their clients (blacks, welfare mothers, labor unions, etc.) on the other. Reagan made substantial inroads into the traditional blue-collar strongholds of Democratic voters by identifying "big government" as the source of economic distress. Inflation pushed workers into higher tax brackets while decreasing their purchasing power. If the general increase in prices was beyond any-one's control, tax rates were not. Reagan's message was all the more potent because he was able to link together reactions to economic distress with the sense many people had that America was being pushed around in the world. The United States was still smarting from the national humiliation in Vietnam when the econ-omy began to falter. As far as most Americans could remember or were concerned, things started to go seriously awry in the economy with the OPEC oil embargo. A favorite image employed by newspaper cartoonists during the 1973 and 1979 oil embargos portrayed Ameri-can consumers being held up at the gas pump by arrogant and rapacious Arab sheiks. When the U.S. embassy in Teheran was seized by followers of the Ayatollah Khomeini in Novem-ber 1979, and the leadoff story on the television news every night for a year was one of "Amer-ica held hostage," it seemed to many as if the nation's domestic and foreign problems were all of a piece. The Republicans portrayed Carter and the Democrats as equally incapable of resisting raids on the federal treasury by "welfare cheats" at home and raids on Ameri-can installations by political and religious fanat-ics abroad. A mixture of domestic frustration and international humiliation proved the ideal setting for Reagan's message and presidential ambitions.

Americans followed a long and winding path from Kennedy's "New Frontier" to the "Reagan revolution." Viewed against a back-drop of changing social patterns and cultural beliefs, the political choices they made along the way seem less fickle and more understand-able. Led by the young and followed by the middle-aged, Americans, in the 1960s and 1970s, discarded the ethic of self-denial. In turning "left" or "right" in their politics in those years Americans were consistently disap-pointed in their search for leaders who would prove able to provide a setting in which a genu-ine and lasting self-fulfillment could become possible.

SUGGESTED READINGS

Bellah, Robert N., et al. *Habits of the Heart, Individ-ualism and Commitment in American Life.* Berke-ley, Calif.: University of California Press, 1985.

Carroll, Peter N. *It Seemed Like Nothing Happened: The Tragedy and Promise of America in the 1970s.* New York: Holt, Rinehart & Winston, 1982.

Clecak, Peter. *America's Quest for the Ideal Self, Dissent and Fulfillment in the 60s and 70s.* New York: Oxford University Press, 1983.

Matusow, Allen J. *The Unraveling of America: A History of Liberalism in the 1960s.* New York: Harper & Row, 1984.

O,Neill, William L. *Coming Apart, An Informal History of America in the 1960's.* New York: Quadrangle Books, 1971.

Phillips, Kevin P. *Post-Conservative America: Peo-ple, Politics, and Ideology in a Time of Crises.* New York: Random House, 1982.

Sale, Kirkpatrick. *SDS.* New York: Random House, 1973.

DOCUMENT 36.1
Two Dylan Songs

Bob Dylan's music both reflected and helped shape the outlook of the younger generation in the 1960s. Dylan began his career as a "protest singer" in the mold of Woody Guthrie and Pete Seeger, but by mid-decade had developed a surrealistic and electrically amplified style all his own. "The Times They Are A-Changin' " (1963) and "Ballad of a Thin Man" (1965) capture this transition.

"THE TIMES THEY ARE A-CHANGIN' "

Come gather 'round people
Wherever you roam
And admit that the waters
Around you have grown
And accept it that soon
You'll be drenched to the bone.
If your time to you
Is worth savin'
Then you better start swimmin'
Or you'll sink like a stone
For the times they are a-changin'.

Come writers and critics
Who prophesize with your pen
And keep your eyes wide
The chance won't come again
And don't speak too soon
For the wheel's still in spin
And there's no tellin' who
That it's namin'.
For the loser now
Will be later to win
For the times they are a-changin'.

Come senators, congressmen
Please heed the call
Don't stand in the doorway
Don't block up the hall
For he that gets hurt
Will be he who has stalled
There's a battle outside
And it is ragin'.
It'll soon shake your windows
And rattle your walls
For the times they are a-changin'.

Come mothers and fathers
Throughout the land
And don't criticize

What you can't understand
Your sons and your daughters
Are beyond your command
Your old road is
Rapidly agin'.
Please get out of the new one
If you can't lend your hand
For the times they are a-changin'.

The line it is drawn
The curse it is cast
The slow one now
Will later be fast
As the present now
Will later be past
The order is
Rapidly fadin'.
And the first one now
Will later be last
For the times they are a-changin'.

"BALLAD OF A THIN MAN"

You walk into the room
With your pencil in your hand
You see somebody naked
And you say, "Who is that man?"
You try so hard
But you don't understand
Just what you'll say
When you get home

Because something is happening here
But you don't know what it is
Do you, Mister Jones?

You raise up your head
And you ask, "Is this where it is?"
And somebody points to you and says
"It's his"
And you say, "What's mine?"
And somebody else says, "Where what is?"
And you say, "Oh my God
Am I here all alone?"

Because something is happening here
But you don't know what it is
Do you, Mister Jones?

You hand in your ticket
And you go watch the geek
Who immediately walks up to you
When he hears you speak
And says, "How does it feel
To be such a freak?"
And you say, "Impossible"
As he hands you a bone

Because something is happening here
But you don't know what it is
Do you, Mister Jones?

You have many contacts
Among the lumberjacks
To get you facts
When someone attacks your imagination
But nobody has any respect
Anyway they already expect you
To just give a check
To tax-deductible charity organizations

You've been with the professors
And they've all liked your looks
With great lawyers you have
Discussed lepers and crooks
You've been through all of
F. Scott Fitzgerald's books
You're very well read
It's well known

Because something is happening here
But you don't know what it is
Do you, Mister Jones?

Well, the sword swallower, he comes up to
  you
And then he kneels
He crosses himself
And then he clicks his high heels
And without further notice
He asks you how it feels
And he says, "Here is your throat back
Thanks for the loan"

Because something is happening here
But you don't know what it is
Do you, Mister Jones?

Now you see this one-eyed midget
Shouting the word "NOW"
And you say, "For what reason?"
And he says, "How?"
And you say, "What does this mean?"
And he screams back, "You're a cow
Give me some milk
Or else go home"

Because something is happening here
But you don't know what it is
Do you, Mister Jones?

Well, you walk into the room
Like a camel and then you frown
You put your eyes in your pocket
And your nose on the ground
There ought to be a law
Against you comin' around
You should be made
To wear earphones

Because something is happening here
But you don't know what it is
Do you, Mister Jones?

DOCUMENT 36.2
"Elvis Told Us To Let Go!" (Jerry Rubin excerpt)

Jerry Rubin, an antiwar activist, founder of the Yippies, and defendant in the Chicago 8 conspiracy trial, scorned the conventional political tactics favored by earlier generations of radical activists. Instead, he sought to capture the media's attention through outrageous pranks, costumes, and rhetoric. In this excerpt from his 1970 book "Do It!", he reflected on the cultural history of the past two decades.

Source: Jerry Rubin, *Do It!* (New York: Simon & Schuster, 1970), pp. 17–20; 106–108; 132–133; 209–215. Copyright © 1970 by the Social Education Foundation. Reprinted by permission of Simon & Schuster, a Division of Gulf & Western Corporation.

ELVIS PRESLEY KILLED IKE EISENHOWER

The New Left sprang, a predestined pissed-off child, from Elvis' gyrating pelvis.

> tell ya somethin' brother
> found a new place to dwell
> down on the end of Lonely Street
> it's Heartbreak Hotel.

On the surface the world of the 1950's was all Eisenhower calm. A cover story of "I Like Ike" father-figure contentment.

Under the surface, silent people railed at the chains upon their souls. A latent drama of repression and discontent.

Amerika was trapped by her contradictions.

Dad looked at his house and car and manicured lawn, and he was proud. All of his material possessions justified his life.

He tried to teach his kids: he told us not to do anything that would lead us from the path of Success.

> **work** don't play
> **study** don't loaf
> **obey** don't ask questions
> **fit in** don't stand out
> **be sober** don't take drugs
> **make money** don't make waves

We were conditioned in self-denial:

We were taught that fucking was bad because it was immoral. Also in those pre-pill days a knocked-up chick stood in the way of Respectability and Success.

We were warned that masturbation caused insanity and pimples.

And we were confused. We didn't dig why we needed to work toward owning bigger houses? bigger cars? bigger manicured lawns?

We went crazy. We couldn't hold it back any more.

Elvis Presley ripped off Ike Eisenhower by turning our uptight young awakening bodies around. Hard animal rock energy beat/surged hot through us, the driving rhythm arousing repressed passions.

Music to free the spirit.

Music to bring us *together*.

Buddy Holly, the Coasters, Bo Diddley, Chuck Berry, the Everly Brothers, Jerry Lee Lewis, Fats Domino, Little Richard, Ray Charles, Bill Haley and the Comets, Fabian, Bobby Darin, Frankie Avalon; they all gave us the life/beat and set us free.

Elvis told us to *let go!*

>   *let go!*
>   *let go!*
>   *let go!*
>   *let go!*
>   *let go!*
>   *let go!*
>   *let go!*
>   *let go!*
>   *let go!*
>   *let go!*
>   *let go!*
> *let go!*

Affluent culture, by producing a car and car radio for every middle-class home, gave Elvis a base for recruiting.

While a car radio in the front seat rocked with "Turn Me Loose," young kids in the back seat were breaking loose. Many a night was spent on dark and lonely roads, balling to hard rock beat.

The back seat produced the sexual revolution, and the car radio was the medium for subversion.

Desperate parents used permission to drive the car as a power play in the home: "If you don't obey, you can't have the car Saturday night."

It was a cruel weapon, attacking our gonads and our means of getting together.

The back seat became the first battleground in the war between the generations.

Rock 'n' roll marked the beginning of the revolution.

DOCUMENT 36.3
Politics Turns to Therapy

Cultural historian Christopher Lasch, looking back on the New Left after its collapse, thought there was a connection between the concerns of the self-styled revolutionaries like Jerry Rubin and the "culture of narcissism" that he felt had come to dominate American life in the 1970s.

FROM POLITICS TO SELF-EXAMINATION

Having displaced religion as the organizing framework of American culture, the therapeutic outlook threatens to displace politics as well, the last refuge of ideology. Bureaucracy transforms collective grievances into personal problems amenable to therapeutic intervention; in clarifying this process, this trivialization of political conflict, the new left of the sixties made one of its most important contributions to political understanding. In the seventies, however, many former radicals have themselves embraced the therapeutic sensibility. Rennie Davis leaves radical politics to follow the teenage guru, Maharaj Ji. Abbie Hoffman, former leader of the Yuppies, decides that it is more important to get his own head together than to move multitudes. His onetime associate, Jerry Rubin, having reached the dreaded age of thirty and having found himself face to face with his private fears and anxieties, moves from

Source: Christopher Lasch, *The Culture of Narcissism, American Life in an Age of Diminishing Expectations* (New York: W. W. Norton & Co. 1978), pp. 13–16.

New York to San Francisco, where he shops voraciously—on an apparently inexhaustible income—in the spiritual supermarkets of the West Coast. "In five years," Rubin says, "from 1971 to 1975, I directly experienced est, gestalt therapy, bioenergetics, rolfing, massage, jogging, health foods, tai chi, Esalen, hypnotism, modern dance, meditation, Silva Mind Control, Arica, acupuncture, sex therapy, Reichian therapy, and More House—a smorgasbord course in New Consciousness."

In his coyly titled memoir, *Growing (Up) at Thirty-seven*, Rubin testifies to the salutary effects of this therapeutic regimen. After years of neglecting his body, he gave himself "permission to be healthy" and quickly lost thirty pounds. Health foods, jogging, yoga, sauna baths, chiropractors, and acupuncturists have made him feel, at thirty-seven, "like twenty-five." Spiritual progress proved equally gratifying and painless. He shed his protective armor, his sexism, his "addiction to love," and learned "to love myself enough so that I do not need another to make me happy." He came to understand that his revolutionary politics concealed a "puritan conditioning," which occasionally made him uneasy about his celebrity and its material rewards. No strenuous psychic exertions seem to have been required to convince Rubin that "it's O.K. to enjoy the rewards of life that money brings."

He learned to put sex "in its proper place" and to enjoy it without investing it with "symbolic" meaning. Under the influence of a succession of psychic healers, he raged against his parents and the righteous, punitive "judge" within himself, eventually learning to "forgive" his parents and his superego. He cut his hair, shaved his beard, and "liked what I saw." Now "I entered rooms and no one knew who I was, because I didn't fit their image of me. I was thirty-five but I looked twenty-three."

Rubin sees his "journey into myself" as part of the "consciousness movement" of the seventies. Yet this "massive self-examination" has produced few indications of self-understanding, personal or collective. Self-awareness remains mired in liberationist clichés. Rubin discusses the "female in me," the need for a more tolerant view of homosexuality, and the need to "make peace" with his parents, as if these commonplaces represented hard-won insights into the human condition. As a skillful manipulator of the common coin, a self-confessed "media freak" and propagandist, he assumes that all ideas, character traits, and cultural patterns derive from propaganda and "conditioning." Apologizing for his heterosexuality, he writes, "Men do not turn me on, because I was propagandized as a child to think that homosexuality is sick." In therapy, he attempted to reverse "the negative programming of childhood." By convincing himself that a collective deconditioning will provide the basis for social and political change, he has tried to build a rickety bridge between his political activities in the sixties and his current preoccupation with his own body and "feelings." Like many ex-radicals, he has succeeded only in exchanging current therapeutic slogans for the political slogans he used to mouth with equal disregard of their content.

Rubin claims that the "inner revolution of the seventies" grew out of an awareness that the radicalism of the sixties had failed to address itself to the quality of personal life or to cultural questions, in the mistaken belief that questions of "personal growth," in his words, could wait "until after the revolution." This accusation contains a certain amount of truth. The left has too often served as a refuge from the terrors of the inner life. Another ex-radical, Paul Zweig, has said that he became a communist in the late fifties because communism "released him . . . from the failed rooms and broken vases of a merely private life." As long as political movements exercise a fatal attraction for those who seek to drown the sense of personal failure in collective action—as if collec-

tive action somehow precluded rigorous attention to the quality of personal life—political movements will have little to say about the personal dimension of social crisis.

Yet the new left (unlike the old left) did begin to address this issue, in the brief period of its flowering in the mid-sixties. In those years, there was a growing recognition—by no means confined to those associated with the new left—that personal crisis on the scale it has now assumed represents a political issue in its own right, and that a thoroughgoing analysis of modern society and politics has to explain among other things why personal growth and development have become so hard to accomplish; why the fear of growing up and aging haunts our society; why personal relations have become so brittle and precarious; and why the "inner life" no longer offers any refuge from the danger around us. The emergence in the sixties of a new literary form, combining cultural criticism, political reportage, and reminiscence, represented an attempt to explore these issues—to illuminate the intersection of personal life and politics, history and private experience. Books like Norman Mailer's *Armies of the Night*, by disposing of the convention of journalistic objectivity, often penetrated more deeply into events than accounts written by allegedly impartial observers. The fiction of the period, in which the writer made no effort to conceal his presence or point of view, demonstrated how the act of writing could become a subject for fiction in its own right. Cultural criticism took on a personal and autobiographical character, which at its worst degenerated into self-display but at its best showed that the attempt to understand culture has to include analysis of the way it shapes the critic's own consciousness. Political upheavals injected themselves into every discussion and made it impossible to ignore the connections between culture and politics. By undermining the illusion of culture as a separate and autonomous development uninfluenced by the distri-

bution of wealth and power, the political upheaval of the sixties also tended to undermine
the distinction between high culture and popular
culture and to make popular culture an object
of serious discussion.

DOCUMENT 36.4
Our Bodies, Ourselves

Our Bodies, Ourselves *was first published in
1969 by a group of young radical feminists
who called themselves the Boston Women's
Health Book Collective. The book sought to
free women from dependence upon the
traditional (male-dominated) medical
profession, by providing an alternative source
of information about women's physical and
mental health, reproduction, birth control,
sexuality, and relationships. Initially published
by a small radical press in Boston, the book
was soon reprinted by a major publisher, and
brought out in two revised editions over the
next decade. The book's continued popularity
is suggestive of the way that the values espoused
by a militant minority in the 1960s came to
penetrate the surrounding culture in the
1970s.*

KNOWING WHEN TO LEAVE

Many of us struggle along for years in relationships that are not rewarding or affirming, wanting to make them better but not succeeding,
and not yet convinced that we would be better
off if we left. We may come again and again
to the brink of leaving, and then back off.
This is not because things are not quite "bad
enough"; even women whose men are violent
toward them[1] or are alcoholics or drug abusers
or have incapacitating emotional problems of-

Source: *The New Our Bodies, Ourselves* (New York:
Simon & Schuster, 1984), pp. 139–140.

[1] See Chapter 8, "Violence Against Women," for a
fuller discussion of domestic abuse.

ten find themselves staying or struggling with
whether or not to leave, or how to leave. What
holds us back? We may, even with all the
problems, still love our partner and be reluctant
to lose him; we may feel loyal to him and
perhaps not want to hurt him. Perhaps we think
that breaking our commitment is a great personal failure, that we will be harshly judged
by friends and family. We may try to stay
together "for the good of the children" or may
dread the prospect of being alone. And there
is often the very real fear that we will not be
able to support ourselves, and perhaps our children, financially. Yet many women do ultimately decide that they want to end their relationships.

> *At first Phil seemed to revel in my accom-
plishments, my growing self-confidence. But
I also grew more able to challenge him where
he didn't want to be challenged. I have wanted
more from him: more involvement with the
children, more sharing of paid jobs and
housework. I want him to value my strength
as I have come to value myself more. His
response has been to have a string of affairs,
all with women who are much younger than
I am and, as you might guess, totally unde-
manding, unthreatening, willing to accept him
precisely as he is.*

> *My relationship with Greg ended when I
said that it was no longer working for us
and that nothing we were doing was making
it any better. He was not a person with whom
I could fully engage. We never really learned
to fight well together . . . not just having
arguments but learning to compromise well.
I felt turned off sexually, attracted to others,
and the pleasure of being with him was gone.
I would come home and not want to tell him
what was exciting that day. . . . I preferred
to tell other people who seemed more "simpa-
tico." What was hardest about the divorce
was that the family part of our relationship
was good. . . . It was painful to let go of
the father of my kids. It was scary to give
my own needs so much weight.*

The man I was living with began to under-cut everything I did—to devalue my work, to be jealous of my friends and my small successes. When I got bogged down in a project, rather than encouraging me he would point out how the project was probably ill-conceived and not of much use anyway. The longer things went on, the more of my good creative energy went into trying to make the relationship work, and the less energy I had for my work and the rest of my life.

When I was first thinking about getting out of my marriage, I would think, Well, I get a lot of satisfaction out of being a parent and I'm very close to my kids. I get a lot of satisfaction from my friendships and I have a really good work situation. My relationship isn't so good, but maybe you just can't have everything. My husband had some serious problems, so I felt I couldn't blame him or just leave him. I never stopped to consider what it was doing to me to be spending years of my life with someone who was giving me so little. After a while I built up so much resentment that I just wasn't able to treat him in a loving way. And I began to be afraid that I would lose my capacity to love someone. I knew that I had a potential for loving that wasn't getting expressed. Yet it was a leap to assume that getting out of our marriage meant that I would have a good relationship again.

If you wind up just accommodating your partner to prevent fights rather than having some hope that it's worth sitting down and trying to work things out; if your relationship is based on evasiveness, deception and with-holding; if it is characterized by stagnation and a lack of room for change and growth; or if it just doesn't seem that your life is better in the relationship than it would be out of it, then it is time to consider ending it. You don't need to do this in isolation. There are good books on the subject. . . . Turning to friends, particularly ones who are willing to talk openly about their divorces or hard times with their partners,

can be an excellent source of support and insight. Individual or group therapy can help, as can support groups. Much as we know it is important to work very hard to build a relationship, it is also important to leave before we are damaged by it.

Though it may seem to be contradictory to advocate paying attention to our relationships and at the same time trying to be a separate person and seek other friendships, these multiple aspects of our lives can and do enrich rather than detract from one another. They also provide a balance which stimulates our growth and promotes our joy and well-being—our capacity for independence along with our capacity for intimacy.

We have been married for thirteen years. . . . Daniel is not my best friend. We are quite different in many ways, have different friends, interests and so on. There are ways in which I'm not even as intimate with him as I am with some of my women friends. But ever since I met him, I have not felt the excru-ciating loneliness which was the core of my life for twenty-six years. Being with him, knowing that we are partners in life, has per-mitted me to grow from an extremely unhappy, lonely person with little self-esteem and a lot of self-hatred into a happy, fulfilled and self-loving woman. My identity is not derived from him, but being with him has enabled me to create a major transformation in myself.

DOCUMENT 36.5
Reagan Obituary for John Wayne

In 1979 Ronald Reagan was gearing up for his successful 1980 campaign for the presidency. He took the occasion of John Wayne's death to sound some of the patriotic

Source: Ronald Reagan, "Unforgettable John Wayne," *Reader's Digest,* October 1979, pp. 115–119.

themes that would serve him so well in 1980 and 1984.

We called him Duke, and he was every bit the giant off screen he was on. Everything about him—his stature, his style, his convictions—conveyed enduring strength, and no one who observed his struggle in those final days could doubt that strength was real. Yet there was more. To my wife, Nancy, "Duke Wayne was the most gentle, tender person I ever knew."

In 1960, as president of the Screen Actors' Guild, I was deeply embroiled in a bitter labor dispute between the Guild and the motion-picture industry. When we called a strike, the film industry unleashed a series of stinging personal attacks against me—criticism my wife was finding difficult to take.

At 7:30 one morning the phone rang and Nancy heard Duke's booming voice: "I've been readin' what these damn columnists are saying about Ron. He can take care of himself, but I've been worrying about how all this is affecting you." Virtually every morning until the strike was settled several weeks later, he phoned her. When a mass meeting was called to discuss settlement terms, he left a dinner party so that he could escort Nancy and sit at her side. It was, she said, like being next to a force bigger than life.

Countless others were also touched by his strength. Although it would take the critics 40 years to recognize what he was, the movie-going public knew all along. In this country and around the world, he was the most popular box-office star of all time. For an incredible 25 years he was rated at or around the top in box-office appeal. His films grossed $700 million—a record no performer in Hollywood has come close to matching. Yet John Wayne was more than an actor; he was a force around which films were made. As Elizabeth Taylor Warner stated last May when testifying in favor of the special gold medal Congress struck for him: "He gave the whole world the image of what an American should be."

STAGECOACH TO STARDOM

He was born Marion Michael Morrison in Winterset, Iowa. When Marion was six, the family moved to California. There he picked up the nickname Duke—after his Airedale. He rose at 4 A.M. to deliver newspapers, and after school and football practice he made deliveries for local stores. He was an A student, president of the Latin Society, head of his senior class and an all-state guard on a championship football team.

Duke had hoped to attend the U.S. Naval Academy and was named as an alternate selection to Annapolis, but the first choice took the appointment. Instead, he accepted a full scholarship to play football at the University of Southern California. There coach Howard Jones, who often found summer jobs in the movie industry for his players, got Duke work in the summer of 1926 as an assistant prop man on the set of a movie directed by John Ford.

One day, Ford, a notorious taskmaster with a rough-and-ready sense of humor, spotted the tall U.S.C. guard on his set and asked Duke to bend over and demonstrate his football stance. With a deft kick, Ford knocked Duke's arms from beneath his body and the young athlete fell on his face. Picking himself up, Duke said in that voice which even then commanded attention, "Let's try that once again." This time Duke sent Ford flying. Ford erupted in laughter, and the two began a personal and professional friendship which would last a lifetime.

From his job in props, Duke worked his way into roles on the screen. During the Depression he played in grade-B westerns until John Ford finally convinced United Artists to give him the role of the Ringo Kid in his classic film *Stagecoach*. John Wayne was on the road to stardom. He quickly established his versatility in a variety of major roles: a young seaman in Eugene O'Neill's *The Long Voyage Home,* a tragic captain in *Reap the Wild Wind,* a rodeo rider in the comedy *A Lady Takes a Chance.*

When war broke out, Duke tried to enlist but was rejected because of an old football injury to his shoulder, his age (34), and his status as a married father of four. He flew to Washington to plead that he be allowed to join the Navy but was turned down. So he poured himself into the war effort by making inspirational war films—among them *The Fighting Seabees, Back to Bataan* and *They Were Expendable.* To those back home and others around the world he became a symbol of the determined American fighting man.

Duke could not be kept from the front lines. In 1944 he spent three months touring forward positions in the Pacific theater. Appropriately, it was a wartime film, *Sands of Iwo Jima,* which turned him into a superstar. Years after the war, when Emperor Hirohito of Japan visited the United States, he sought out John Wayne, paying tribute to the one who represented our nation's success in combat.

As one of the true innovators of the film industry, Duke tossed aside the model of the white-suited cowboy/good guy, creating instead a tougher, deeper-dimensioned western hero. He discovered Monument Valley, the film setting in the Arizona-Utah desert where a host of movie classics were filmed. He perfected the choreographic techniques and stuntman tricks which brought realism to screen fighting. At the same time he decried pornography, and blood and gore in films. "That's not sex and violence," he would say. "It's filth and bad taste."

"I SURE AS HELL DID!"

In the 1940s, Duke was one of the few stars with the courage to expose the determined bid by a band of communists to take control of the film industry. Through a series of violent strikes and systematic blacklisting, these people were at times dangerously close to reaching their goal. With theatrical employes' union leader Roy Brewer, playwright Morrie Ryskind and others, he formed the Motion Picture Alliance for the Preservation of American Ideals to challenge this insidious campaign. Subsequent Congressional investigations in 1947 clearly proved both the communist plot and the importance of what Duke and his friends did.

In that period, during my first term as president of the Actors' Guild, I was confronted with an attempt by many of these same leftists to assume leadership of the union. At a mass meeting I watched rather helplessly as they filibustered, waiting for our majority to leave so they could gain control. Somewhere in the crowd I heard a call for adjournment, and I seized on this as a means to end the attempted takeover. But the other side demanded I identify the one who moved for adjournment.

I looked over the audience, realizing that there were few willing to be publicly identified as opponents of the far left. Then I saw Duke and said, "Why I believe John Wayne made the motion." I heard his strong voice reply, "I sure as hell did!" The meeting—and the radicals' campaign—was over.

Later, when such personalities as actor Larry Parks came forward to admit their Communist Party backgrounds, there were those who wanted to see them punished. Not Duke. "It takes courage to admit you're wrong," he said, and he publicly battled attempts to ostracize those who had come clean.

Duke also had the last word over those who warned that his battle against communism in Hollywood would ruin his career. Many times he would proudly boast, "I was 32nd in the box-office polls when I accepted the presidency of the Alliance. When I left office eight years later, somehow the folks who buy tickets had made me number one."

Duke went to Vietnam in the early days of the war. He scorned VIP treatment, insisting that he visit the troops in the field. Once he even had his helicopter land in the midst of a battle. When he returned, he vowed to make a film about the heroism of Special Forces soldiers.

The public jammed theaters to see the resulting film, *The Green Berets*. The critics, however, delivered some of the harshest reviews ever given a motion picture. The *New Yorker* bitterly condemned the man who made the film. The New York *Times* called it "unspeakable . . . rotten . . . stupid." Yet Duke was undaunted. "That little clique back there in the East has taken great personal satisfaction reviewing my politics instead of my pictures," he often said. "But one day those doctrinaire liberals will wake up to find the pendulum has swung the other way."

FOUL-WEATHER FRIEND

I never once saw Duke display hatred toward those who scorned him. Oh, he could use some pretty salty language, but he would not tolerate pettiness and hate. He was human, all right: he drank enough whiskey to float a PT boat, though he never drank on the job. His work habits were legendary in Hollywood—he was virtually always the first to arrive on the set and the last to leave.

His torturous schedule plus the great personal pleasure he derived from hunting and deep-sea fishing or drinking and card playing with his friends may have cost him a couple of marriages; but you had only to see his seven children and 21 grandchildren to realize that Duke found time to be a good father. He often said, "I have tried to live my life so that my family would love me and my friends respect me. The others can do whatever the hell they please."

To him, a handshake was a binding contract. When he was in the hospital for the last time and sold his yacht, *The Wild Goose,* for an amount far below its market value, he learned the engines needed minor repairs. He ordered those engines overhauled at a cost to him of $40,000 because he had told the new owner the boat was in good shape.

Duke's generosity and loyalty stood out in a city rarely known for either. When a friend needed work, that person went on his payroll. When a friend needed help, Duke's wallet was open. He also was loyal to his fans. One writer tells of the night he and Duke were in Dallas for the première of *Chisum*. Returning late to his hotel, Duke found a message from a woman who said her little girl lay critically ill in a local hospital. The woman wrote, "It would mean so much to her if you could pay her just a brief visit." At 3 o'clock in the morning he took off for the hospital where he visited the astonished child—and every other patient on the hospital floor who happened to be awake.

I saw his loyalty in action many times. I remember that when Duke and Jimmy Stewart were on their way to my second inauguration as governor of California they encountered a crowd of demonstrators under the banner of the Vietcong flag. Jimmy had just lost a son in Vietnam. Duke excused himself for a moment and walked into the crowd. In a moment there was no Vietcong flag.

FINAL CURTAIN

Like any good John Wayne film, Duke's career had a gratifying ending. In the 1970s a new era of critics began to recognize the unique quality of his acting. The turning point had been the film *True Grit*. When the Academy gave him an Oscar for best actor of 1969, many said it was based on the accomplishments of his entire career. Others said it was Hollywood's way of admitting that it had been wrong to deny him Academy Awards for a host of previous films. There is truth, I think, to both these views.

Yet who can forget the climax of the film? The grizzled old marshal confronts the four outlaws and calls out: "I mean to kill you or see you hanged at Judge Parker's convenience. Which will it be?"

"Bold talk for a one-eyed fat man," their leader sneers.

Then Duke cries, "Fill your hand, you son-ofabitch!" and, reins in his teeth, charges at them firing with both guns. Four villains did not live to menace another day.

"Foolishness?" wrote Chicago *Sun-Times* columnist Mike Royko, describing the thrill this scene gave him. "Maybe. But I hope we never become so programmed that nobody has the damn-the-risk spirit."

Fifteen years ago when Duke lost a lung in his first bout with cancer, studio press agents tried to conceal the nature of his illness. When Duke discovered this, he went before the public and showed us that a man can fight this dread disease. He went on to raise millions of dollars for private cancer research. Typically, he snorted: "We've got too much at stake to give government a monopoly in the fight against cancer."

Earlier this year, when doctors told Duke there was no hope, he urged them to use his body for experimental medical research, to further the search for a cure. He refused painkillers so he could be alert as he spent his last days with his children. When he died on June 11, a Tokyo newspaper ran the headline, "Mr. America passes on."

"There's right and there's wrong," Duke said in *The Alamo*. "You gotta do one or the other. You do the one and you're living. You do the other and you may be walking around · but in reality you're dead."

Duke Wayne symbolized just this, the force of the American will to do what is right in the world. He could have left no greater legacy.

DOCUMENT 36.6
"Patriotism And Its Symbols"

Not all Americans were swept up in the "new conservatism" of the 1980s. Ralph Nader, who rose to prominence in the 1960s by criticizing

Source: Ralph Nader, "Patriotism and Its Symbols," *Washington Post*, July 6, 1986.

the safety record of Detroit's auto manufacturers, inspired a generation of consumer advocates and environmental activists who continued their educational and lobbying efforts throughout the 1970s and 1980s. In this article, Nader cast a skeptical eye on the public relations extravaganza that surrounded the unveiling of the newly refurbished Statue of Liberty in 1986.

Around the dinner table in the New England town where I grew up, our parents would observe at just the proper time in our political discussions that loving our country meant working hard to make it more lovable. The flag, they would add, could take care of itself.

This advice did not keep their children from rushing down to the annual July Fourth parade on Main Street or arguing over the desirability of America the Beautiful versus the Star Spangled Banner as our national anthem. Commemoration of the nation's Independence Day was fun, and it made us feel good.

It wasn't long before my mother and father found an opportunity to restate their message. They did not adopt the defensive patriotism of many immigrants who were sensitive lest their foreign accents and customs seem to cast doubt on their love of the USA.

"When I sailed past the Statue of Liberty in 1912," my father once said to us, "I took it seriously." He and my mother wanted to exercise—not massage—their new freedoms on behalf of greater justice and a better democracy. They were all too alert to the fate of nations and peoples who wallow in collective praise at the expense of exercising their rights against the abuses of power and the blockage of opportunity.

The 1940s were easy for patriotism. Against the backdrop of World War II, who wasn't a patriot? The '50s were the Eisenhower years, when patriotic feeling elected a wartime commander who, unlike men in that office who never served in the military, rarely flaunted their patriotism. The '60s were a reaction to the smugness and conformity of the prior 15 years. The challengers accused the self-styled super-patriots of using the flag as a bandana or fig leaf to hide shame, injustice and aggression, particularly against minorities at home and the Vietnamese abroad.

For different reasons, Nixon's Watergate and Jimmy Carter delayed the inevitable backlash—and return to patriotism—until the fallout from the Iranian hostage crisis spilled over into the waiting hands of Ronald Reagan.

In the '80s, patriotism and its symbols increasingly have become media extravaganzas for commercial and political exploitation. Such shows and speeches, disassociated as they are from contemporary deeds and national missions, have become refuges for holders of power who seek to define and control the nation's patriotic sentiments.

The profitable hoopla surrounding the Statute of Liberty is more than show business. Organizing millions of school children to collect quarters and dollars to refurbish the statue was done in a style akin to the monument idolatry of far less democratic regimes abroad. How many of these children learned anything about civil liberties and civil rights in our country during this drive? The promoters were not sympathetic to such linkage.

The challenge is to find activities in our own daily lives that give meaning to our patriotic slogans, and that allow us to define our love for our country through civic achievement. Patriotism is a powerful idea, and one that should be defined by citizens, not by their rulers alone. For me, the meaning of patriotism lies in working to make America more lovable.

The corporatization of our nation's patriotic symbols did not start with this year's Statue of Liberty celebration. George Washington's birthday has for decades been overwhelmingly a time for sales. Early elementary-school teachers have told me that when they raise a picture of President Washington in class for identification, their pupils reply: "He's the car sales-

man," "He sells stereos." Who has not seen, ad nauseum, the transformation by television and print advertising of Lincoln, Franklin, Jefferson, and Einstein—into pitchmen asking us to buy furniture, appliances, insurance and bank services? An executive for an insurance company named after Lincoln wrote me once, after I sent him a query about commercialization, saying he believed his company was enhancing Lincoln's reputation.

The mercantile sheen is overpowering the historical memory of America's leaders, especially among the younger generations who grew up in a television age. When was the last time a Lincoln's or Washington's Birthday was an occasion for celebrating what these men and their times accomplished?

Our national political leaders, much like the corporations, view the sentiments and symbols of the patria as grist in the selling of themselves during and between elections.

Consider Ronald Reagan, an artful master of patriotic ceremonies and rhetoric. Hardly missing an occasion, whether in a sports arena or on a former battlefield, he tells us how much he loves America. With a disarming flattery that only a former actor could perfect, he performs his "Miller Time" politics. But shouldn't his oratorical fervor be measured by actual behavior and accomplishments? Or, as semanticists have warned might happen, have the words themselves become the deeds?

To me, loving America should mean energetic efforts to apply existing laws to advance the cleanliness and safety of the water, the air, the soil and the food supply. Loving America should mean maintaining its public investment in highways, soil-erosion control, forests and estuaries. Loving America is furthering the public trust of its public lands, its public airwaves and its public election processes. Loving America is avoiding economic policies that have pushed our country into the No. 1 debtor nation in the world, the biggest trade and budget deficits in the world, a chronically high unemployment and poverty rate and a slow rate of economic growth.

Loving America means loving little Americans in need of nutrition and health care. It means loving poor and disabled Americans with a responsive government. It means loans to students and training assists to unemployed youngsters. It means law and order against the powerful who prey upon the powerless. It means a refusal to undermine civil rights, civil liberties, the right of privacy, and the freedom of information. It could also mean a national drive on illiteracy and its immense human and economic costs.

How does President Reagan measure up to these standards of patriotism? Not well, to put it charitably.

But what about his greatest patriotic pride—the re-arming of America. True, we are in an even greater state of Mutually Assured Destruction capability. There are plans for more and bigger missiles. There is also more fraud, abuse, waste and corruption inherent in a vastly larger military budget. There is also an appallingly weak conventional military capability.

But how difficult it is to question these national problems when the media and the public are daunted by a president waving a huge American flag against the Evil Empire. Manipulative patriotism is a feedstock for Reagan, which allows him to rise above accountability for his own policies.

There are good reasons to reject phony commercial and political expressions of patriotism. The former debases a great asset for any organized society. The latter misuses that asset as a mechanism of submission and control—or, as recent history of other countries has demonstrated, as a method for collective madness and destruction.

The patriotic dazzle surrounding controversial issues also can short-circuit deliberate thinking and the protection of dissent. To be sure, there will always be struggles over the symbols of patriotism. But we should strive nonetheless, to discern a kind of patriotism that is not an abstraction steeped in nostalgia, but a real, living monument that can be judged by the standard of "liberty and justice for all."

Finally, if "consent of the governed" is to have any meaning, the abstract ideal of country has to be separated from those who rule it; otherwise the corporate and political governments cannot be evaluated by citizens. And it is the citizenry who must provide the nourishment for a many-splendored patriotism that is open to all people to perfect in their neighborhoods, communities, states and nation.

Let one example illustrate this point: Much of our drinking water is contaminated with heavy metals, organic chemicals and other carriers of silent violence to the health of millions of people. Since 1974, a Safe Drinking Water Act has been available to presidents for making that water safer.

In five and a half years, despite a duty and knowledge to act, President Reagan has not issued a single contaminant-control standard under that law. By a bipartisan vote of 94 to 0, the Senate recently sent him legislation with deadlines for issuing some major regulations dealing with drinking-water hazards. He signed the bill with reluctance.

Unless citizens can turn a national mission for clean drinking water into a patriotic endeavor, Reagan is not likely to become enthusiastic. So latent is his sense of patriotism regarding drinking-water cleanup that it is likely to be quickened only if it could be proved conclusively that the cause of America's contaminated drinking water is an international communist conspiracy.

A patriotism that has been narrowed for use by government and corporations asks only for servile nods or a burst of applause from its subjects. A new and broader patriotism requires a thinking assent from its citizens. In today's era of proliferating atomic weapons, if patriotism is to have any "manifest destiny," it is in building a world where all humankind is our bond in peace.

Index

ABOUT THE AUTHORS

Howard Quint did his undergraduate work at Yale University, earning his M.A. degree at Stanford University and his Ph.D. at Johns Hopkins University. He taught at the University of South Carolina, Johns Hopkins University, the University of Wisconsin, and the University of New Mexico. From 1959, he was Professor of History and Chairman of the Department of History at the University of Massachusetts in Amherst. He was a visiting Fulbright Lecturer at the University of Mexico and the University of Bologna. He is the author of *The Forging of American Socialism* and *Profile in Black and White* and editor/coauthor of *The Talkative President* and *Men, Women and Issues*. He died on June 23, 1981.

Milton Cantor received his B.A. from Brooklyn College, his M.A. from the University of Pennsylvania, and his Ph.D. from Columbia University, all in history. He has taught at Columbia University, Brooklyn College, Rutgers University, New School for Social Research, Michigan State University, and Williams College. He has served as Managing Editor of *Labor History* and as Advisory Editor of *The Massachusetts Review*. He is the author of *Max Eastman* and *The Divided Left: American Radicalism in the 20th Century*. He has been editor and coeditor of *Men, Women and Issues, Black Labor in America, Hamilton, Documents of American History, Biographical Dictionary of American Labor Leaders, Pocket History of the United States*, and others. He is presently Professor of History at the University of Massachusetts in Amherst.

Dean Albertson is a Professor of History at the University of Massachusetts in Amherst. He received his undergraduate education at the University of California in Berkeley, and in 1955 earned his Ph.D. at Columbia University. He has also taught at the University of California in Berkeley, at New York University, and at Brooklyn College. He and Allan Nevins founded the first Oral History Project at Columbia University in 1948. He is the author of *Roosevelt's Farmer: Claude R. Wickard in the New Deal*, and editor of *Eisenhower as President, American History Visually, The Study of American History*, and *Rebels or Revolutionaries: Student Movements of the 1960s*.

A NOTE ON THE TYPE

The text of this book was set in 10/12 Times Roman, a film version of the face designed by Stanley Morison, which was first used by *The Times* (of London) in 1932. Part of Morison's special intent for Times Roman was to create a face that was editorially neutral. It is an especially compact, attractive, and legible typeface, which has come to be seen as the "most important type design of the twentieth century."

Composed by Arcata Graphics/Kingsport

Printed and bound by Arcata Graphics/Kingsport